COVID-19 AND THE SUSTAINABLE DEVELOPMENT GOALS

COVID-19 AND THE SUSTAINABLE DEVELOPMENT GOALS

Edited by

MOHAMMAD HADI DEHGHANI

Department of Environmental Health Engineering, School of Public Health, Tehran University of Medical Sciences (TUMS), Tehran, Iran

Institute for Environmental Research, Center for Solid Waste Research, Tehran University of Medical Sciences, Tehran, Iran

RAMA RAO KARRI

Faculty of Engineering, Universiti Teknologi Brunei, Bandar Seri Begawan, Brunei Darussalam

SHARMILI ROY

School of Medicine, Division of Oncology, Stanford University, Stanford, CA, United States

ELSEVIER

Elsevier
Radarweg 29, PO Box 211, 1000 AE Amsterdam, Netherlands
The Boulevard, Langford Lane, Kidlington, Oxford OX5 1GB, United Kingdom
50 Hampshire Street, 5th Floor, Cambridge, MA 02139, United States

ISBN: 978-0-323-91307-2

For information on all Elsevier publications
visit our website at https://www.elsevier.com/books-and-journals

Publisher: Joseph P. Hayton
Acquisitions Editor: Kathryn Eryilmaz
Editorial Project Manager: Czarina Osuyos
Production Project Manager: Maria Bernard
Cover Designer: Vicky Pearson

Typeset by STRAIVE, India

Dedication

In the name of God, the Most Gracious, the Most Merciful.

I am thankful to God Almighty that I succeeded in writing this book with the help of my colleagues.

I dedicate this book to my parents, my brothers, and my sister who are always praying for me. I especially appreciate my lovely wife and children (Amir Parsa and Yasamin) who contribute to my progress and success with their patience and forbearance.

I dedicate this book to the defenders and martyrs of healthcare in the Islamic Republic of Iran. I also dedicate this book to healthcare professionals around the world who are at the forefront of the fight against COVID-19.

Prof. Dr. Mohammad Hadi Dehghani

I dedicate this book to the memory of my beloved father Karri Sri Ramulu.

I specially want to dedicate this book to the inspiring women (Mother-Karri Kannathalli; Wife-Soni; Colleague-Dr. Malai Zeiti; Inspirators-HE Nahida Rahman Shumona, Bangladesh Ambassador & HE Homeira Rigi Zirouki, Republic of Iran Ambassador).

I also dedicate this book to healthcare professionals around the world who are at the forefront of the fight against COVID-19.

Finally, thank my lovely children Yajna and Jay, and in-laws L.V. Rao and Prameela, without their support and understanding, this book and my research achievements would not have been possible.

Dr. Rama Rao Karri

I dedicate this book to my father Mr. Pranab Jyoti Roy and my mother Mrs. Kalyani Roy. Without their continuous support and motivation, it would not have been possible for me to achieve my best.

I also thank my husband Mr. Vivek Majumdar. Without his support, inspiration, and continuous motivation, this book and my research achievements would not have been possible.

Lastly, I want to thank my PhD supervisor Dr. Minhaz Uddin Ahmed for his proper guidance and supervision, without which my research achievements would not have been feasible.

Dr. Sharmili Roy

Contents

Contributors

Abdulelah M. Aldhahir
Respiratory Care Department, Faculty of Applied Medical Sciences, Jazan University, Jazan, Saudi Arabia

Hamoud Alenezi
Process Systems Engineering Centre (PROSPECT), Faculty of Chemical and Energy Engineering, Universiti Teknologi Malaysia, Johor Bahru, Johor, Malaysia

Saeed M. Alghamdi
National Heart and Lung Institute, Imperial College London, London, United Kingdom; Faculty of Applied Medical Sciences, Umm Al-Qura University, Makkah, Saudi Arabia

Ahmad S. Almamary
National Heart and Lung Institute, Imperial College London, London, United Kingdom; Respiratory Therapy Department, King Saud Bin Abdulaziz University for Health Sciences, Ahsa, Saudi Arabia

Jaber S. Alqahtani
Department of Respiratory Care, Prince Sultan Military College of Health Sciences, Dammam, Saudi Arabia

Malik Althobiani
Department of Respiratory Therapy, King Abdulaziz University, Jeddah, Saudi Arabia

Salar Bakhtiyari
Department of Clinical Biochemistry, Ilam University of Medical Sciences, Ilam, Iran

Dhanya Balachandran
CSIR-National Environmental Engineering Research Institute (CSIR-NEERI), Nagpur, Maharashtra, India

Hemant Bherwani
CSIR-National Environmental Engineering Research Institute (CSIR-NEERI), Nagpur, Maharashtra; Academy of Scientific and Industrial Research (AcSIR), Ghaziabad, Uttar Pradesh, India

J. Brema
Karunya Institute of Technology and Sciences, Coimbatore, Tamil Nadu, India

Chetna Chauhan
School of Management, Universidad de Los Andes, Bogotá, Colombia

Alaka Das
CSIR-National Environmental Engineering Research Institute (CSIR-NEERI), Nagpur, Maharashtra, India

Monalisha Ghosh Dastidar
Research School of Engineering, College of Engineering and Computer Science, Australian National University, Canberra, ACT, Australia

Kithma De Silva
Department of Food, Plant and Environmental Sciences, Faculty of Agricultural, Dalhousie University, Halifax, NS, Canada

Chee-Yuen Gan
Analytical Biochemistry Research Centre, Inkubator Inovasi Universiti (I2U), Sains USM, Universiti Sains Malaysia, Penang, Malaysia

Sneha Gautam
Karunya Institute of Technology and Sciences, Coimbatore, Tamil Nadu, India

Hajar Haghighi
Department of Health Management, Policy & Economics, School of Public Health, Tehran University of Medical Sciences (TUMS), Tehran, Iran

Lara Hamdanieh
Department of Health in Emergencies and Disasters, School of Public Health, Tehran University of Medical Sciences, Tehran, Iran

Malai Zeiti Binti Sheikh Abdul Hamid
Centre for Communication, Teaching & Learning (CCTL); Wellness Research Thrust, Universiti Teknologi Brunei, Bandar Seri Begawan, Brunei Darussalam

Samuel Jacob
Department of Biotechnology, School of Bioengineering, College of Engineering and Technology, Faculty of Engineering and Technology, SRM Institute of Science and Technology, Kattankulathur, Tamil Nadu, India

Mohsen Jalilian
Health and Environment Research Center, Ilam University of Medical Sciences, Ilam, Iran

Hojatollah Kakaei
Health and Environment Research Center; Department of Occupational Health Engineering, School of Health, Ilam University of Medical Sciences, Ilam, Iran

Gholam Ali Karegar
Faculty of physical education and sports sciences, Allameh Tabataba'i University, Tehran, Iran

Rama Rao Karri
Wellness Research Thrust; Petroleum and Chemical Engineering, Faculty of Engineering, Universiti Teknologi Brunei, Bandar Seri Begawan, Brunei Darussalam

Yajnasri Karri
Jerudong International School, Bandar Seri Begawan, Brunei Darussalam

Sara Keshkar
Faculty of physical education and sports sciences, Allameh Tabataba'i University, Tehran, Iran

Agatha Sylvia Khalko
Department of Botany, Marwari College, Ranchi University, Ranchi, Jharkhand, India

Saleh Komies
Faculty of Engineering, Department of Electrical and Electronic Engineering, Imperial College London, London, United Kingdom

G. Pavan Kumar
Operations Management, IIM Lucknow, Lucknow, Uttar Pradesh, India

Rakesh Kumar
Academy of Scientific and Industrial Research (AcSIR), Ghaziabad, Uttar Pradesh; Council of Scientific and Industrial Research (CSIR), Anusandhan Bhawan, New Delhi, India

Syazana Abdullah Lim
Food Science and Technology, School of Applied Sciences and Mathematics, Universiti Teknologi Brunei, Mukim Gadong A, Brunei Darussalam

Navonil Mal
Department of Botany, University of Calcutta, Kolkata, West Bengal, India

Amin Mirzaei
Health and Environment Research Center, Ilam University of Medical Sciences, Ilam, Iran

Shirsendu Nandi
Quantitative Techniques and Operations Management Area, FORE School of Management, New Delhi, India

Abdallah Y. Naser
Department of Applied Pharmaceutical Sciences and Clinical Pharmacy, Faculty of Pharmacy, Isra University, Amman, Jordan

Simin Nasseri
Department of Environmental Health Engineering, School of Public Health, Tehran University of Medical Sciences, Tehran, Iran

Chimurkar Navinya
Interdisciplinary Program in Climate Studies, Indian Institute of Technology Bombay, Mumbai, Maharashtra, India

Louis Anto Nirmal
Department of Biotechnology, School of Bioengineering, College of Engineering and Technology, Faculty of Engineering and Technology, SRM Institute of Science and Technology, Kattankulathur, Tamil Nadu, India

Heshmatollah Nourmoradi
Health and Environment Research Center, Ilam University of Medical Sciences, Ilam, Iran

Modupeola Elizabeth Olalere
School of Computer Science, Universiti Sains Malaysia, Gelugor, Malaysia

Olusegun Abayomi Olalere
Analytical Biochemistry Research Centre, Inkubator Inovasi Universiti (I2U), Sains USM, Universiti Sains Malaysia, Penang, Malaysia

Abbas Ostadtaghizadeh
Department of Health in Emergencies and Disasters, School of Public Health, Tehran University of Medical Sciences, Tehran, Iran

Harish C. Phuleria
Interdisciplinary Program in Climate Studies; Environmental Science and Engineering Department, Indian Institute of Technology Bombay, Mumbai, Maharashtra, India

Veena Raj
Faculty of Integrated Technologies, Universiti Brunei Darussalam, Gadong, Brunei Darussalam

Rajiv Chandra Rajak
Department of Botany, Marwari College, Ranchi University, Ranchi, Jharkhand, India

Azam Raoofi
Department of Health Management, Policy & Economics, School of Public Health; Health Equity Research Centre (HERC), Tehran University of Medical Sciences (TUMS), Tehran, Iran

Sharmili Roy
Division of Oncology, School of medicine, Stanford University, Palo Alto, CA, United States

Venkataramanaiah Saddikuti
Operations Management, IIM Lucknow, Lucknow, Uttar Pradesh, India

Gour Gopal Satpati
Department of Botany, Bangabasi Evening College, University of Calcutta, Kolkata, West Bengal, India

Vivek Sharma
Department of Chemical Engineering, Indian Institute of Technology Bombay, Mumbai, Maharashtra, India

Knawang Chhunji Sherpa
Microbial Processes and Technology Division, CSIR-National Institute for Interdisciplinary Science and Technology (NIIST), Thiruvananthapuram, Kerala, India

Rohit Sindhwani
Operations Management, IMT Ghaziabad, Ghaziabad, Uttar Pradesh, India

Dharmaveer Singh
Symbiosis Institute of Geoinformatics, Symbiosis International (Deemed University), Pune, India

Sarada Sutradhar
School of Pharmaceutical and Population Health Informatics, Dehradun Institute of Technology, Dehradun, Uttarakhand, India

Lim Suzylily
General Studies Division, Politeknik Brunei, Bandar Seri Begawan, Brunei Darussalam

Amirhossein Takian
Department of Health Management, Policy & Economics; Department of Global Health & Public Policy, School of Public Health; Health Equity Research Centre (HERC), Tehran University of Medical Sciences (TUMS), Tehran, Iran

Ebru Topcu
Department of Economics, Nevsehir Haci Bektas Veli University, Nevsehir, Turkey

Suman Yadav
Environmental Science and Engineering Department, Indian Institute of Technology Bombay, Mumbai, Maharashtra, India

About the editors

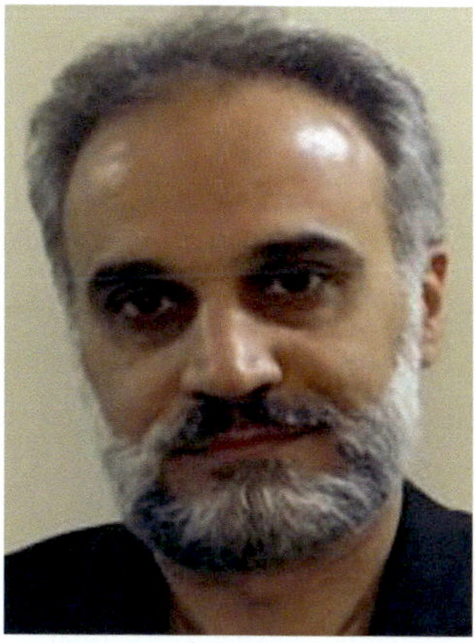

Prof. Dr. Mohammad Hadi Dehghani is a Full Professor in the Department of Environmental Health Engineering, School of Public Health, Tehran University of Medical Sciences (TUMS), Tehran, Islamic Republic of Iran. His scientific research interests are focused on environmental science. He is the author of various research studies published in national and international journals and conference proceedings and the head of several research projects at TUMS. He has authored 12 books and more than 200 full papers published in peer-reviewed journals. He is an editorial board member, guest editor, and reviewer for many national and international journals and is a member of several international science committees around the world. He is supervisor and advisor for many PhD and MSc theses at TUMS. He is currently also a member of the Iranian Association of Environmental Health (IAEH) and the Institute for Environmental Research (IER) at TUMS. He is coeditor for five edited books currently being published by Elsevier: (1) *Soft Computing Techniques in Solid Waste and Wastewater Management*, (2) *Environmental and Health Management of Novel Coronavirus Disease (COVID-19)*, (3) *Pesticides Remediation Technologies from Water and Wastewater*, (4) *Sustainable Materials for Sensing and Remediation of Noxious Pollutants*, (5) *Industrial Wastewater Treatment Using Emerging Technologies for Sustainability*.

Dr. Rama Rao Karri is a Senior Assistant Professor in the Faculty of Engineering, Universiti Teknologi Brunei, Brunei Darussalam. He has a PhD from Indian Institute of Technology (IIT) Delhi and a master's degree in Chemical Engineering from IIT Kanpur. He has worked as a postdoctoral research fellow at NUS, Singapore, for about 6 years and has over 17 years of working experience in academics, industry, and research. He has experience of working in multidisciplinary fields with expertise in various evolutionary optimization techniques and process modeling. He has published 150+ research articles in reputed journals, book chapters and conference proceedings with a combined Impact factor of 479.2 and has an h-index of 24 (Scopus - citations: 2100+) and 26 (Google Scholar -citations: 2500+). Among 75 journal publications, 60 articles published are Q1 and high IF journals. He is an editorial board member in 10 renowned journals and peer-review member for more than 93 reputed journals and peer reviewed more than 410 articles. Also, he handled 112 articles as an editor.

He also has the distinction of being listed in the top 2% of the world's most influential scientists in the area of environmental sciences and chemical for Year 2021. The List of the Top 2% Scientists in the World compiled and published by Stanford University is based on their international scientific publications, number of scientific citations for research, and participation in the review and editing of scientific research. He is also a recipient of Publons Peer Reviewer Award as top 1% of global peer reviewers for Environment & Ecology and Crossfield categories for the year 2019. He is also delegating as advisory board member for many international conferences. He held a position as Editor-in-Chief (2019-2021) in *International Journal of Chemoinformatics and Chemical Engineering*, IGI Global, USA. He is also Associate editor in *Scientific Reports*, Nature Group (IF:4.996) & *International Journal of Energy and Water Resources* (IJEWR), Springer Inc. He is also a Managing Guest editor for Spl. Issues: 1) "Magnetic nano composites and emerging applications", in *Journal of Environmental Chemical Engineering* (IF: 7.968), 2) "Novel CoronaVirus (COVID-19) in Environmental Engineering Perspective", in *Journal of Environmental Science and Pollution Research* (IF: 5.19), Springer. 3) "Nanocomposites for the Sustainable Environment", in *Applied Sciences Journal* (IF: 2.679), MDPI. He along with his mentor, Prof. Venkateswarlu has authored an Elsevier book, "*Optimal state estimation for process monitoring, diagnosis and control*". He is also co-editor and managing editor for 8 Elsevier, 1 Springer and 1 CRC edited books. Elsevier: 1) *Sustainable Nanotechnology for Environmental Remediation*, 2) *Soft computing techniques in solid waste and wastewater management*, 3) *Green technologies for the defluoridation of water*, 4) *Environmental and health management of novel coronavirus disease (COVID-19)*, 5) *Pesticides remediation technologies from water and wastewater: Health effects and environmental remediation*, 6) *Hybrid Nanomaterials for Sustainable Applications*, 7) *Sustainable materials for sensing and remediation of noxious pollutants*. 8) *Water Treatment using Engineered Carbon Nanotubes* - Springer: 1) *Industrial wastewater treatment using emerging technologies for sustainability*. CRC: 1) *Recent Trends in Advanced Oxidation Processes (AOPs) for micro-pollutant removal.*

Dr. Sharmili Roy is currently pursuing her second postdoctoral research in Oncology/Medical Research in the Division of Oncology, School of Medicine, Stanford University, Palo Alto, CA, United States. She earned her PhD from Universiti of Brunei Darussalam, Brunei, under the supervision of Prof. Minhaz Uddin Ahmed. Prior to joining Stanford University, she worked for her first postdoctoral training at the Indian Institute of Technology (IIT) Guwahati, India, as a National Post Doctorate Fellowship (NPDF) holder funded by SERB, Government of India. Her current research is focused on the development of next generation sequencing (NGS) technology with various clinical samples, especially with many types of cancer DNA samples, molecular diagnostics of cancer, and DNA digital data storage process. She gained expertized on point of care biosensors technology development based on loop-mediated isothermal amplification (LAMP) during her PhD tenure. She has published several high impact factor research papers in journals such as *Biosensors and Bioelectronics*, *Analytical Methods*, *ACS Sensors*, *Food Control*, *Food Chemistry*, *Electroanalysis*, in addition she has three USA patents and ten book chapters. She is also co edited two books published by Springer and Elsevier 1) *Diagnostic Strategies for COVID-19 and other Coronaviruses* 2) *Environmental and Health Management of Novel Coronavirus Diseases (COVID-19).*

Foreword

This book emphasizes the impacts of the COVID-19 pandemic on the sustainable development goals (SDGs), including the environment, public and mental health, political and economic aspects, arts, culture and tourism, energy, water and soil, and climate change. It also presents the challenges, opportunities, and future perspectives arising from this pandemic. Therefore, the book provides updated knowledge and the latest information about the global effects of COVID-19 on SDGs. The lack of improved conceptual books was visibly felt during the COVID-19 pandemic. This was the driving force for the editors to put together this edited book on COVID-19 and SDGs. Therefore, I recommend reading this valuable book to all students, professionals, and managers who work in the field of COVID-19 and SDGs.

Alireza Mesdaghinia[a,b]
[a]Emeritus Professor of Environmental Health, Tehran University of Medical Sciences, Tehran, Iran
[b]Iranian Association of Environmental Health, Tehran, Iran

Acknowledgments

I thank my coeditors without whose support and cooperation this book would not have been possible. I also thank my colleagues in the Department of Environmental Health Engineering for their valuable support. I also thank all the authors who contributed chapters presenting their valuable research.

Prof. Dr. Mohammad Hadi Dehghani

I thank Prof. Zohrah, Vice Chancellor, Universiti Teknologi Brunei, and the higher management for their support. I also thank my coeditors without whose support and cooperation this book would not have been possible. I also thank all the authors who contributed chapters presenting their valuable research.

Dr. Rama Rao Karri

I thank Stanford University for the encouragement and providing the necessary facilities for the completion of this work. I also thank my coeditors without whose support and cooperation this book would not have been possible. I appreciate all the authors who contributed chapters with utmost dedication and effort to complete this book.

Dr. Sharmili Roy

Introduction

The severe acute respiratory syndrome coronavirus 2 (SARS-CoV-2) is a potential pandemic-causing zoonotic virus that belongs to the Coronaviridae family. The ongoing global pandemic caused by SARS-CoV-2 is a health crisis of global concern. The COVID-19 pandemic has become a major global health threat due to the increasing number of cases and associated mortality. The contagious nature and the enhanced transmission rate of the virus are the primary causes for the rapid spread of the disease globally. The human-to-human transmission of the virus primarily occurs through direct or indirect contact with infected respiratory droplets. Such contact is established either by inhalation or by direct contact with a contaminated surface or infected body fluid such as saliva and urine. The ability of the virus to remain active in the suspension of infected respiratory droplets over a long period of time and to be carried over long distances makes this pathogen airborne.

Epidemiological information has reinforced the evidence on COVID-19 transmission from one individual to another through direct or indirect contact (contaminated surfaces and objects) and close contact with infected people by respiratory secretions. The COVID-19 pandemic is spreading daily, and the world is trying to control its increasing impact on both human health and the environment. Implementing containment protocols and a rapid infection control response are of prime importance to contain and mitigate the risk of virus transmission. To reduce unsafe conditions and avoid dissemination, environmental scientists, among others, are trying to identify the environmental variables that may affect the propagation of COVID-19.

Studies have shown that COVID-19 has negative and positive impacts on the environment. COVID-19 has improved air quality all over the world. It has led to reduction in air pollutants, greenhouse gas emissions, and water and noise pollution, which in turn have led to the improvement of ecological conditions all over the world. However, COVID-19 has also had negative impacts. It has resulted in an increase in municipal and medical waste generation, including disposal of masks, gloves, and disinfectants, and reduction of recycling.

This book discusses how the coronavirus pandemic has influenced the sustainable development goals (SDGs) and affected their implementation.

This is the main driving force for writing this book. Therefore, an effort has been made to present the global impacts of COVID-19 on hunger and the food crisis, good health and well-being, quality of education, science and technology, access to affordable and clean energy, poverty, decent work, economic growth and world trade, clean water, life below water and life on land, climate changes, psychological problems, social factors, political factors, cultural factors and tourism industry, sports industry, human rights, and disaster risk management. This book also presents the source of origination; mechanism of human COVID-19; and risk factors, challenges, opportunities, and future perspectives arising from this pandemic.

Due to the lack of conceptual books was published during this pandemic, this book caters broadly to students and academics who are working in the fields of environmental health science (water and wastewater, air quality and climate changes, waste), sustainable development (SDGs), virology, health policy, and public health. It will also be useful to researchers, professionals, policymakers, students, and academicians who are working in fields such as toxicology, socioeconomical research, energy and transportation, culture and art, education, tourism industry, sports industry, and psychology. Although a few books on coronaviruses have been published recently, until now there has been no book published that focuses exclusively on COVID-19 and SDGs.

Mohammad Hadi Dehghani[a,b]
[a]Department of Environmental Health Engineering, School of Public Health, Tehran University of Medical Sciences, Tehran, Iran
[b]Institute for Environmental Research, Center for Solid Waste Research, Tehran University of Medical Sciences, Tehran, Iran

Rama Rao Karri
Petroleum and Chemical Engineering, Faculty of Engineering, Universiti Teknologi Brunei (UTB), Bandar Seri Begawan, Brunei Darussalam

Sharmili Roy
Division of Oncology, School of Medicine, Stanford University, Palo Alto, CA, United States

PART ONE

COVID-19 effects on sustainable global goals (SDG's)

CHAPTER ONE

Effect of COVID-19 on food security, hunger, and food crisis

Hojatollah Kakaei[a,b], Heshmatollah Nourmoradi[a], Salar Bakhtiyari[c], Mohsen Jalilian[a], and Amin Mirzaei[a]

[a]Health and Environment Research Center, Ilam University of Medical Sciences, Ilam, Iran
[b]Department of Occupational Health Engineering, School of Health, Ilam University of Medical Sciences, Ilam, Iran
[c]Department of Clinical Biochemistry, Ilam University of Medical Sciences, Ilam, Iran

1. Introduction

COVID-19 outbreak has brought hunger to millions of people around the world.[1] Various strategies such as physical distance, school closures, trade restrictions, and countries' lockdown to control the pandemic have increased the nutritional challenges around the world, especially in low- and middle-income countries (LMICs) with the highest populations.[2,3] These restrictions have likely disrupted agricultural production and concerned millions of people about access to adequate food. Various experts in this field believe that this hunger crisis is global. The sudden loss of productivity and income, falling oil prices, low tourism revenue, problems such as climate change, and other factors are all related to the outbreak of COVID-19.[1] A recent FAO report (2019) found that 820 million people have been suffering from starvation worldwide. The Global Report on Food Crisis (FSIN, 2020) also showed that approximately 135 million people in 55 countries are affected by acute food insecurity, of which 73 million are in 36 countries in Africa.[4] The United Nations reported that COVID-19 is likely to increase poverty and food insecurity on a global scale. Therefore achieving the goals of sustainable development is considered a top priority. Other international organizations such as the Food and Agriculture Organization of the United Nations (FAO) and the International Food Policy Research Institute (IFPRI) have also supported this concept.[5] People's health and nutrition in food crises are at greater risk due to their inability to access healthcare and their inability to reimburse their expenses.[4]

COVID-19 and the Sustainable Development Goals
https://doi.org/10.1016/B978-0-323-91307-2.00005-5

2. Food insecurity

Food insecurity is one of the factors contributing to the increase in food poverty and malnutrition in middle and low standard of living communities, which during epidemics such as COVID-19 can affect the nutritional conditions of a large population of the world.

Food insecurity is defined as the persistent concern about access to sufficient and affordable food at all times.[1] Food insecurity causes stress in people. One of the most important reasons for people's stress is where and how to get enough food due to unemployment and low income during the COVID-19 epidemic.[6] Poverty, low-income family health, poor livelihoods and household management strategies can lead to food insecurity. The severity and classification of food insecurity depend on family members' perceptions of food and food budgets. Consequences and threats of food insecurity hurt mental, social, and psychological-emotional status. Food insecurity can be mild, moderate, or severe. The classification depends on the severity of the uncertainty, anxiety about access to food, unbalanced diet, and changes in diet quality (Fig. 1).[5]

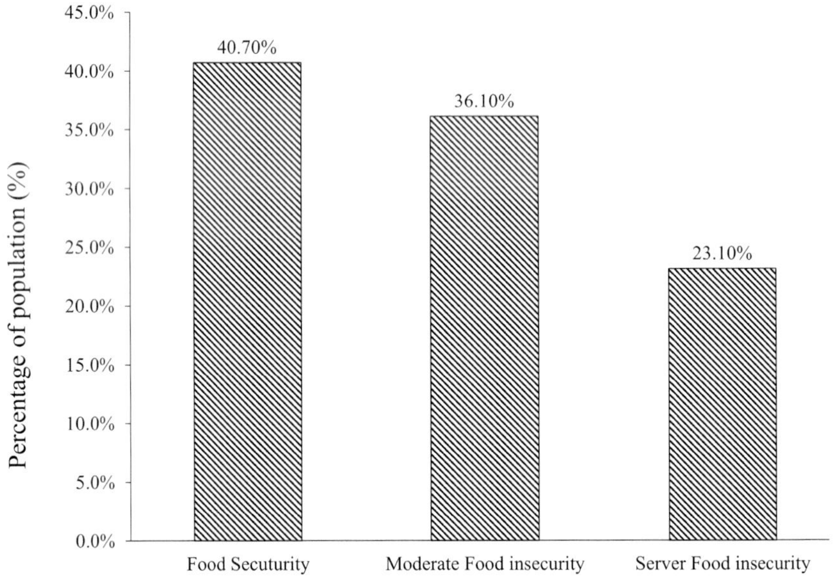

Fig. 1 Food insecurity among the population in Jordan during the quarantine.[5]

The FAO defines food security as "the right of all persons to have adequate physical, economical and safe access to meet their nutritional needs at all times, as well as to choose their food preferences for an active and healthy life." Food is specifically mentioned, as a part of the right to a standard of living (adequacy of food to protect the health of the individual and family), in Article 25 of the Universal Declaration of Human Rights.[7–9] The right to food has been discussed in several international conferences since 1948. In the Rome Declaration on Global Food Security (1996), all countries except Australia and the United States agreed that food is a fundamental human right.[9,10]

Some important factors of food insecurity can include conflict, poverty, climate change, economic downturn, and ecosystem disruption. Therefore the ability of a country to create food security depends on the available resources, policies, cultural and natural capacity of the country, and the extent of practical use of these resources.[11] According to the United Nations, food insecurity has now increased from 23.3% in 2014 to 26.4% in 2018. Before COVID-19 in September 2019, about 821 million people (more than 10% of the world's population) suffered from hunger.[12] The report on the use of the Food Bank in the UK shows that about three million people received food packages between 2018 and 2019, compared to approximately 41,000 in 2009 and 2010.[13] However, at the height of the COVID-19 crisis, there was a further gap in food demand and rising food prices.[14]

In the United States, household food insecurity increased from 11% in 2018 to 38% in March 2020. In April 2020, 35% of households with children aged 18 years old and under were food insecure. Households with food insecurity may be less likely to follow social distancing recommendations during the COVID-19 epidemic for access to food resources. Because these people have less flexibility in their jobs, they are inevitably at greater risk due to reduced incomes and, consequently, reduced access to food.[15] The Food and Agriculture Organization of the United Nations (FAO) believes that food insecurity can be investigated in four dimensions: availability, access, quality, and stability. Despite the few instances of food access disruption and instability due to transportation disruption or temporary hoarding, the main effects of COVID-19 on people's food security are related to physical access.[16–19] The FAO reports that the COVID-19 outbreak has affected agriculture and food security in two important ways: food supply and demand. For this reason, food security is exposed to serious risks during the COVID-19 crisis.[20]

3. COVID-19 and food access

The food chain is a network that connects the agricultural system to the consumer fork. This food chain includes the processes of production, packaging, distribution, and storage of food. At the beginning of the COVID-19 pandemic, social quarantine by governments caused people to flock to food products sales centers, leading to shortages of some food products in many countries.[20] Behavioral patterns of people with food insecurity can change through the food supply.[21,22] Weak monitoring systems, job losses, and limited transportation systems are key factors that hinder the national food supply and demand.[23] Demand is related to the ability of consumers to buy certain goods or services in any given period. Purchasing power and income also have a large impact on demand (Fig. 2).[20]

As a result, food prices (for example, wheat and rice) have risen and continue to rise. Hence, global food security warnings have been issued due to food shortages, rising food prices, or loss of income due to the high rate of unemployment.[1] The COVID-19 pandemic has boosted demand for online food delivery. For example, during COVID-19, a 20 to 30% increase in restaurant food delivery was observed online in Taiwan.[3] In China, online food demand was increased during COVID-19 due to quarantine conditions but did not lead to food shortages.[20] COVID-19 directly and strongly affects food access. These effects are felt through a disruption of food access, shifts in consumer demand for cheaper foods with low nutritional value, and instability in food prices.[24] Access to food during COVID-19 is very poor in many countries. In the United States, of the approximately 520 food retailers, about 88% of them present no fresh and unprocessed food. Only 12% provide enough fresh food to support a healthy diet.[25]

COVID-19 primarily threatens access to food through the loss of income to buy food. The poorest households spend about 70% of their income on food and have limited access to financial markets; therefore, their food security is particularly vulnerable to income shocks. The International Monetary Fund (IMF) has forecasted a 5% decline in the world economy during 2020.[26] This report shows that the global recession is much deeper than the global financial crisis of 2008–09. These economic consequences will reduce trade, sales of oil and other commodities, international travel, and transportation restrictions in the early countries of the epidemic (China, Europe, and the United States) and low- and middle-income countries. In developing countries, the economic costs include COVID-19

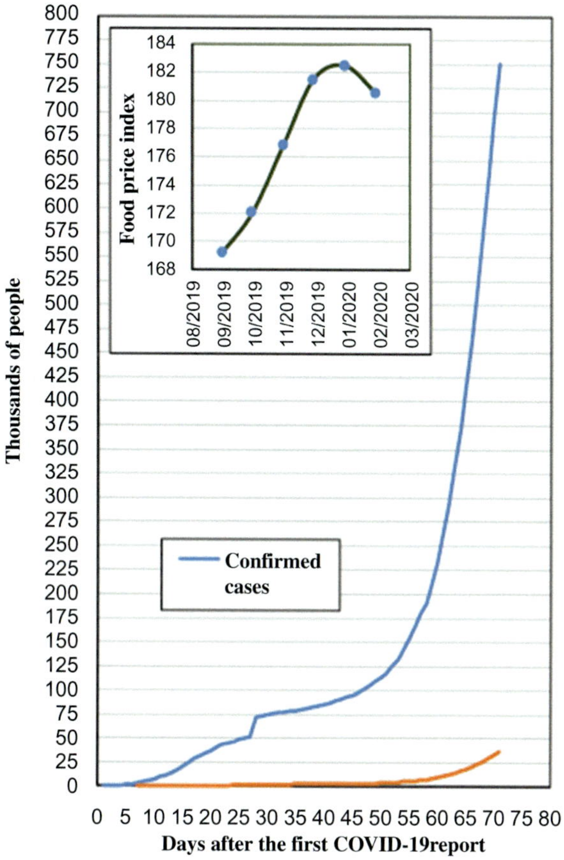

Fig. 2 Globally confirmed cases, deaths, and Food Price Index by the effect of COVID-19.[20]

restrictions[24] in addition to the earlier aspects. Due to the lack of up-to-date surveys in most countries, it is impossible to estimate COVID-19 effects on global poverty and food insecurity accurately. However, the evaluation of simulation models shows that 90 to 150 million people can fall into extreme poverty due to COVID-19.[24] Although such estimates are very vague due to the rapid onset of the disease, these projections estimate a significant increase in global poverty between% 15 and 24%. The highest increase in poverty is in sub-Saharan Africa and South Asia.[24] Poor people do not have enough financial resources to buy food for the prevention of hunger and malnutrition.

For this reason, they tend to buy cheaper and less nutritious foods to meet their needs. Even if the recession is short time, the effects of malnutrition can be long, especially in young children.[24] Of the four dimensions of food security, food availability is probably the most important.[27]

4. COVID-19 and food hygiene

The food supply chain is a complex global network that includes producers, consumers, agricultural and fishery products, processing and storage, transportation and marketing, etc.[28] The more the world as a village connects, the more likely it is that all countries will be exposed to this disease crisis. Therefore not preventing the spread of the disease in one country means that the world is at risk. The consequences of an epidemic disease negatively affect health and lead to unpleasant economic, social, and political crises.[29] A recent report by the United Nations Sustainable Development Goals (UNSDGs, 2019) found that about 55% of the world's population, especially in developing countries, lacks social protection. This vulnerability exacerbates socioeconomic harms that, in addition to weakening the diet and promoting malnutrition of the poor people, spread to the human rights and education sectors.[29]

However, the outbreak of COVID-19 has raised public health concerns, economic and food crises. During the quarantine, the food sector was severely affected, with the greatest impact on vulnerable groups. The agricultural and aquaculture economy in the last quarter of 2020 showed a significant decline that affected millions of people worldwide. This could be because of health concerns about the transmission of the virus through food.[12] Since the effects of this epidemic began in the food market, it is anticipated that food processing and production policies could be revised. Unless new methods of cooperation and action are adopted between government, industry, and individuals, the world will be even less prepared for the next epidemic in the future.[12]

Since the COVID-19 pandemic, the demand for higher nutritional value foods has increased compared to low-value and processed ones. Also, due to the widespread restrictions on food choices, such as the closure of restaurants, families have more opportunities to prepare and consume more healthy and nutritious home-cooked foods. Public and private organizations also present the necessary advice and training through social media to promote healthy behaviors about healthy food according to the limitations of the disease.[30] Recent research on COVID-19 has clearly shown that the virus remains active on plastics and stainless steel for up to 72 h, compared to 24 h on cardboard.[31–33]

Therefore due to the rate and routes of transmission of this virus, it is necessary to provide special health measures for the food industry. Although health concerns are a top priority in the COVID-19 epidemic, livelihoods and food insecurity should not be ignored. The world is currently on the brink of worsening unemployment and food security crises. Policymakers need to keep in mind that the COVID-19 threat still exists worldwide. Therefore they must be careful not to repeat the mistakes that occurred in the food crisis of 2007–08.[28] Food factories should take steps to preserve food products and distribute goods properly following WHO recommendations. However, packaging may be a suitable place for virus transmission.[34]

5. COVID-19 and food production

Globally, it has been estimated that drought and heat can reduce crop production by approximately 10% nationally. According to the Global Food Crisis Report (2020), severe weather events in 2019 have significantly affected food security in the Horn of Africa, South Africa, Central America, and Pakistan. However, the food security crisis still affects the ongoing economic crisis in Venezuela, Haiti, Sudan, and Zimbabwe.[35] The COVID-19 pandemic, in addition to the threat to health and the great damage it has done to countries' economies, has clarified other things. In addition to being a serious threat to health, the COVID-19 pandemic has also caused significant damage to countries' economies. The inadequacy of the global food production and distribution system has disrupted food supply in some parts of the world and wasted food in other parts. This is while world hunger is increasing with the COVID-19 crisis.[36]

The impact of COVID-19 on the food and agriculture parts has revealed the vulnerabilities of the agri-food supply chain, although the extent of disruption varies widely across the world.[37] In many developing countries, including Mexico, Peru, India, Thailand, South Africa, Nigeria, Ghana, and Zimbabwe, an important part of the country's economy is associated with the informal preparation and distribution of food. At the micro-level, the economies of many families also depend on this sector, and the challenges facing informal food preparation directly impact the families' economies.[38] Although restricting the activities of informal food preparation and distribution centers can be effective in preventing the spread of COVID-19, on the other hand, it creates two major problems in the field of food security. First, the livelihoods of many families involved in food preparation and distribution are at risk. Second, because the informal food centers provide cheaper foods, the food access of many families living in poorer areas, such as suburbs, villages, and low-income areas, decreases.[38]

Food security crises often occur due to a sharp decline in food production.[26] The prolonged COVID-19 pandemic has delayed the transport of seeds and fertilizers and thus slowed down the global agricultural process. Livestock farmers in the United States and the United Kingdom were forced to discard their food products due to decreasing customer demand, including schools and restaurants.[36] In rich countries, major crops, especially corn, wheat, and soybeans, are highly mechanized.[26] The presence of COVID-19 up to the planting season could affect the production of major food crops such as wheat, rice, and vegetables, because it is unclear whether agricultural inputs can be distributed promptly. If the production of staple foods is affected, the impact on food security is enormous.[39] About 25% of the world's population is directly involved in agriculture. The highest agricultural rates in the world and Asia are for Burundi (92.02%) and Nepal (65%), respectively. In the most populous countries of the world, such as India (42.38%) and China (25%), a high percentage of people are dependent on agriculture.[40] Many reactions to the epidemic diseases have led to changes in agriculture and food production that may continue for a long time.

In some cases, more emphasis may be placed on the automation of food production and processing to avoid the risks of labor use due to disease transmission or transfer restrictions. This can lead to more investment in mechanization. The mechanization can eliminate food contamination during production.[41]

In developing countries, agricultural production is performed with a large labor force. Many processes, such as planting rice and harvesting basic crops, bring workers together. Although farmers in poorer countries are generally younger than in rich countries, the health systems are usually weaker in the poorer ones, and the health challenges may increase individuals' vulnerability to COVID-19.[26] In this regard, many agricultural producers face labor shortages. The travel prohibition has led to a shortage of seasonal and informal farmworkers. The International Labor Organization (ILO) estimates that COVID-19 affects about 81% (2.7 billion workers) of the workforce due to full or partial closure of the workplace.[24,42] Disruption of the aquatic supply chain also occurred due to restrictions on transportation, trade, and labor. Decreases in production due to reducing fishing efforts and delays in aquaculture systems led to reduced availability and consumption of these foods. The reduction in consumers' demand and increase

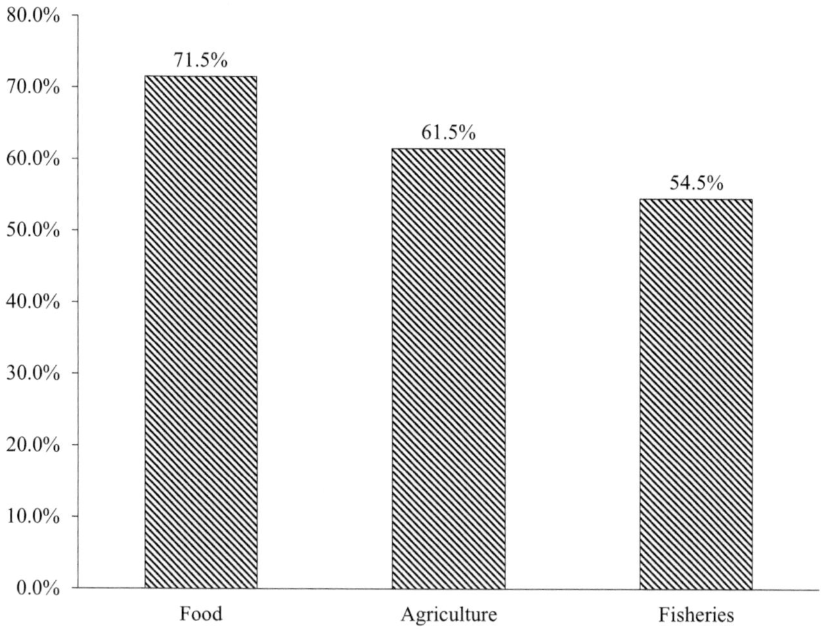

Fig. 3 Impact of COVID-19 lockdown.[34]

in maintenance costs have enhanced the price of aquaculture and reduced its cost-effectiveness for consumers. In India, fisheries are an important part of nutrition and food security. More than 9 and 14 million people depend directly on fisheries and are employed in this occupation, respectively, contributing to more than 1% of India's GDP.[34] Figs. 3 and 4 show the impact of COVID-19 lockdown on food, agriculture, and fisheries and the main factors for food contamination during food processes, factories, and stores, respectively.[34] To respond to such crises, food supply chain issues need to be addressed.

6. COVID-19 and the food crisis

The food crisis caused by COVID-19 does not mean a shortage of basic goods. During the disease pandemic, the share of grocery stores and retail markets has declined; however, large quantities of fresh products on farms have been spoiled and wasted.[43] COVID-19 has had many negative economic effects on people, leading to job losses and food insecurity, especially in low-income countries. These effects have led to a global food crisis.[44] COVID-19 has exacerbated the previous problems in the global food

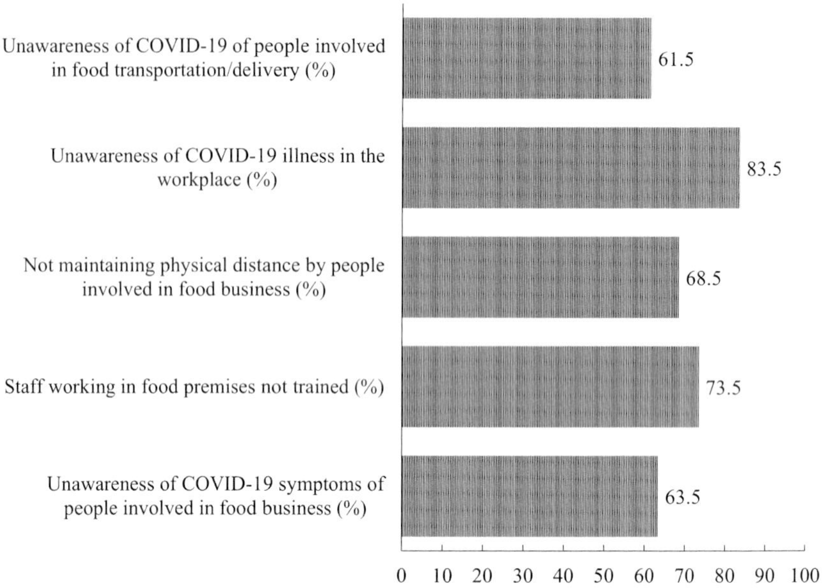

Fig. 4 COVID-19 and main factors for food contamination.[34]

system. Many of these problems were ignored or modified before the disease. The problems concerned with hunger, food deprivation, and food wastage have long been debated. However, the issue of food supply from farm to fork has never been so important and urgent.[36] The limitations of COVID-19 are severe, unfamiliar (for farmers), and completely unexpected to the food supply system.[45]

As reported in various researches, food anxiety and fears from food safety crises can change consumers' sensitivities and beliefs about food health and lead them to use natural and organic diets.[46] COVID-19 prevention measures such as closure, staying at home, public quarantine, and stopping transportation in communities are very challenging. With the approval of the first case of the disease, many developing countries imposed a short-term state of emergency. In some cases, the movement of imports and exports was slower or even stopped. During this economic crisis, countries must provide citizens with emergency packages that may not be enough to meet the needs of their vulnerable populations.[29] During the illness, the transport sector has shut down due to closures of various countries, which can disrupt the supply chain of basic goods, especially food and humanitarian aid. Under these circumstances, the developing countries, mainly dependent on agriculture, will probably run out of food. As a result, hunger and malnutrition put their health at risk due to poor and unhealthy eating habits. In addition, countries that are highly dependent on food imports and developing countries dependent on exports of raw materials such as oil are also affected.[29]

The COVID-19 crisis has shown that a coordinated local food distribution system is superior to the organizations that supply and distribute food. In the United States, the emergency food distribution system includes food banks that provide local food warehouses. During the disease, even reputable food banks, which depend on the help of retailers, are involved in this crisis and often fail to provide food stocks due to the slow assistance of retailers. In contrast, the food banks with wholesale suppliers have been better able to maintain access to food.[47] With the spread of the COVID-19, most countries have imposed higher customs controls on cargo ships, despite the risk of food spoilage as well as disruption of transport activities. Political measures have been taken to prevent the spread of COVID-19, which may globally reduce food production and increase prices.[14] Because the governments have imposed restrictions on food exports and nationwide closures, such reactions can cause food crises. For example, during the global economic downturn of 2007–08, the doubling of world food prices was largely due to trade restrictions imposed by the largest exporters of rice, wheat, and soybeans. These measures, intending to prevent shortages in some countries, helped supply basic foodstuffs in many national markets.[14] Various reports indicate that food insecurity caused by the COVID-19 crisis is rapidly increasing. The vulnerable population is more exposed to food insecurity. A study in the United States shows that 44% of low-income adults do not have food security and are mostly black and Hispanic.[48,49]

Although the effects of COVID-19 on food security in developed countries have been relatively minor so far, more serious problems are emerging in developing countries. In developed countries, the demand for some staple foods, such as rice, was initially very high, and the consumers bought many supplies due to the fear of food shortages. Some food consumption patterns have changed due to people being restricted to eating at home rather than in restaurants. In many developing countries, COVID-19 had a severe impact on employment and income, creating a major food crisis for many people who could not afford food.[41] With this crisis that led to unprecedented unemployment, people who had never experienced hunger before became vulnerable. It is estimated that 40% of people receiving services from food banks in recent weeks are first-time customers.[47] The studies have reported that about one-fifth of Africa's population (256 million people) is malnourished, and the number of hungry people increases. It is expected that Africa's population will double by 2050, and their food demand will triple. Therefore, to provide food to expand and have a healthy life and increase welfare based on the sustainable development goals (SDGs), it is necessary to preserve ecosystems and reduce inequalities.[11] Thus increasing the food stocks, especially in the agricultural off-season, may help reduce unpredictable shocks.

7. The impact of the COVID-19 epidemic on countries around the world

The impact of the COVID-19 epidemic on food insecurity and its health consequences in the world is very complex, multilevel (structural, familial, and individual levels), and two-dimensional.[50–52] After December 2019, the outbreak of COVID-19 increased the responsibilities of tackling global food insecurity. Given that most agricultural products are perishable in nature, this has led to changes in the amount of planting, harvesting, and storage of agricultural products, resulting in reduced food quality and increased production costs.[53]

From a macroeconomic point of view, the IMF estimates the loss of global GDP (GDP) caused by the COVID-19 epidemic at $ 9 trillion, a small portion of which could be highly cost-effective in preparing for an epidemic.[54] In a recent study (2020), Mauro and Baldwin reported that the outbreak of the coronavirus would cause economic collapse in countries such as the G-7, which has a 65% stake in the world's manufacturing units, as well as a 60% drop in global supply and demand. Forty-one percent of world exports are also affected by this outbreak.[55]

In 2020 UNICEF reported that approximately 820 million people were chronically hungry, and 113 million were experiencing severe insecurity.[42,53] More than 1.4 million people (14% of the population) in Bolivia suffer from food shortages due to financial constraints, and 7% suffer from chronic hunger. In India, approximately 16,500 farmers committed suicide even before the epidemic, for which the psychological and economic impact of COVID-19 could not be estimated (Fig. 5).[56]

UNICEF reports from the early months of the COVID-19 epidemic showed a 30% reduction in coverage of essential nutrition services in middle-income countries.[57] Researchers believe global trade in goods has fallen by 13%–22% due to COVID-19.[42] Kansiime et al.[58] online assessed the effects of the COVID-19 epidemic on household income and food security in Kenya and Uganda. This study showed that more than 67% of the

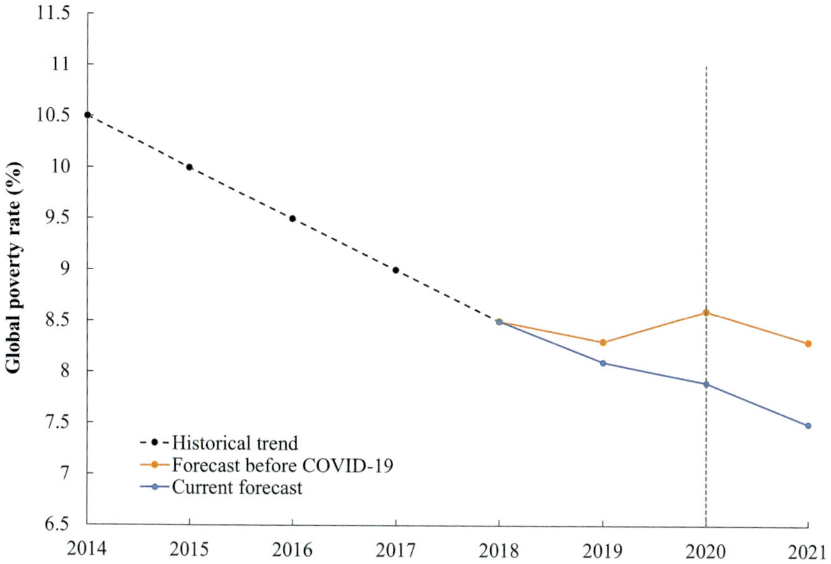

Fig. 5 Impact of COVID-19 on global poverty.[56]

participants were shocked by their income due to the COVID-19 crisis. Participants estimated that food insecurity increased by 38% and 44% in Kenya and Uganda, respectively, and that in both countries, regular fruit consumption decreased by about 30% compared to the normal preepidemic period.[58]

Risks of hunger and food security have also existed in Brazil since 2016 and are now exacerbated by the onset of the COVID-19 epidemic. This situation requires awareness of the scope and importance of the issue and the expression of measures in three government areas (federal, municipal, and state) to ensure access to adequate and healthy food and reduce the adverse effects of disease on diet, health, and nutrition among the most vulnerable.[59] A study conducted by UNICEF and the Brazilian Institute of Public Opinion and Statistics from July 3, 2020, to July 18, 2020, found that during the epidemic, one in five Brazilians aged 18 or over (33 million) has had no experience with money to buy food due to running out of income. The study also reported that about 9 million Brazilians could not even eat a meal due to a lack of money or food.[60]

According to the latest World Food Program (WFP) data, more than 368 million children are currently missing school meals due to the closure of schools in about 200 countries worldwide due to COVID-19.[61] About 25% of meat processing plants in the United States closed due to COVID-19 in 2 weeks in April 2020, and thousands of workers lost their jobs due to compliance with health protocols.[36] Recent two national surveys from the United States have shown that COVID-19 has led to increased food insecurity rates in families with children compared to previous years. The study of the effects of COVID-19 showed that 34.5% of households with children under 18 years of age and 34.4% of households with children under 12 years of age were food insecure by the end of April 2020, while these percentages were 14.7% and 15.1%, respectively.[1] Before COVID-19 pandemic, 1 in 9 households in the United States had food insecurity or limited or unreliable access to adequate food.[62,63]

In a survey, the Bangladesh Rural Advancement Committee reported that extreme poverty had increased by about 60% and that 14% of people had no food at home.[23] Also, the results of a study conducted on Romanian students showed that food wastage during the corona was significantly reduced in the study sample. Their awareness of the environmental consequences of food waste has also increased.[64] Hence, various studies have shown that COVID-19 has influenced people's behaviors to food preparation and consumption. Buying certain types of food that have a longer shelf life and higher nutritional value, storing food at home, as well as the tendency to consume home-cooked food are examples of these behaviors. This behavior led to higher food prices, and as a result, poor people were less able to buy these items. This is more evident in developing countries.[65]

The impact of the COVID-19 epidemic on food insecurity and poor health outcomes is due to previous economic and health inequalities, which are mainly driven by systemic racial discrimination.[51,66] Before COVID-19, black, Hispanic, and low-income households experienced food insecurity and chronic illness.[67] In 2018 the prevalence of food insecurity was highest among low-income households at 29.1%, non-Hispanic blacks at 21.2%, and Hispanics at 16.2%, while in the general population, it was 11.1%. Such disputes result from unequal access to resources, including employment, food, housing, education, and healthcare.[66,68]

Across Africa, high levels of malnutrition among women, children, and the elderly will be exacerbated by declining incomes in low-income families. Also, the livelihoods of farmers and suppliers are at greater risk due to restrictions and disruptions such as the closure of transportation routes.[4] However, most African countries have seen a steady decline in the prevalence of malnutrition since 2000. For example, the prevalence of malnutrition in Algeria, Morocco, Senegal, Cameroon, Togo, and Ethiopia increased from 10.7%, 6.8%, 28.7%, 30.8%, 31.1%, and 52% in 2000 to 3.9%, 3.4%, 11.3, respectively, 9.9%, 16.1%, and 21.4% in 2019. However, in countries such as

Uganda, Nigeria, and Madagascar, the prevalence rate of malnutrition increased from 27.7%, 9.3%, and 34.4% in 2000 to 41%, 13.4%, and 44.4% in 2019, respectively (Fig. 6).[69]

During the COVID-19 epidemic, India's economic loss is estimated at $ 234.4 billion, or 8.1% of GDP, assuming that India remains quarantined at least until the end of May 2020.[34] Figs. 7 and 8 show changes in GDP during the 5 weeks of quarantine in Nigeria and 7 weeks in Ethiopia.[70]

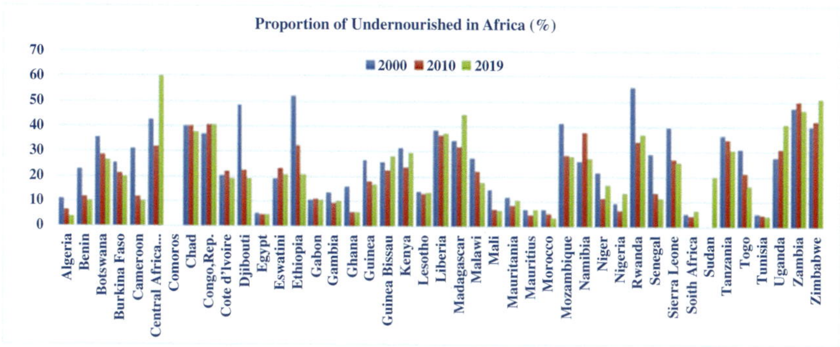

Fig. 6 Prevalence of Undernourished in African Population (%) 2000–19.[69]

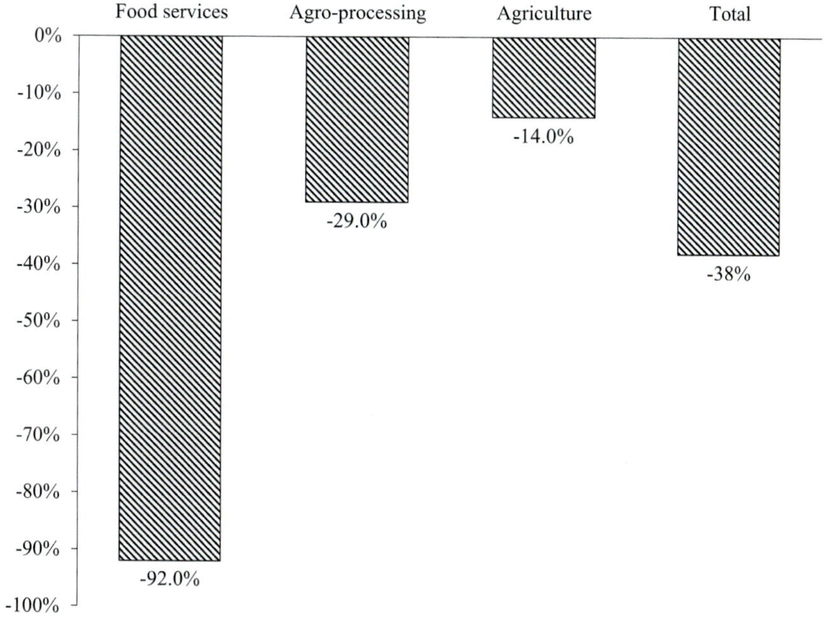

Fig. 7 GDP during the 5 weeks of quarantine in Nigeria.[70]

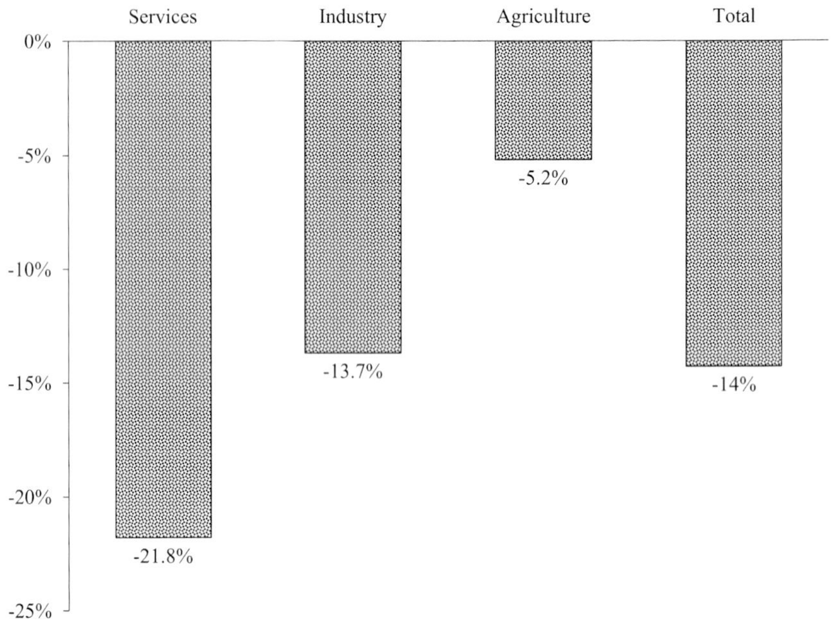

Fig. 8 GDP during the 7 weeks in Ethiopia.[70]

8. COVID-19, food insecurity, and its consequences

Food insecurity with cognitive and behavioral consequences such as skipping meals due to financial constraints, food hoarding, pressuring, or overfeeding children while preparing food due to concerns about food shortages, etc., has negative effects in child's health through family conflicts.[49] Although the distribution of food parcels by local and national governments and private donors among poor communities can help prevent acute starvation, the quality of food parcels should be evaluated as it may meet long-term nutritional needs. It is not enough and therefore has long-term negative effects on households that rely more on these food packages. In these packages, in addition to the amount of food, their type and number of calories are also very important.[71] The experience of food insecurity is stressful and, in the short and long term, is associated with many harmful physical and psychological consequences. Among children, food insecurity is also associated with adverse behavioral and educational outcomes.[72]

Short-term shortages of basic foodstuffs in shops, inability to access shops due to personal quarantine, and economic reasons were the three main factors in food insecurity. In particular, people from ethnic groups of blacks, Asians and minorities, unemployed adults, childcare charities, and people with health and disabilities were at higher risk.[13,73]

Previous research has shown that the health of older people is particularly endangered due to food insecurity, and given their vulnerability to the COVID-19 outbreak, this population needs to understand how food hardships occur. The elderly are generally not eligible for unemployment insurance, and the nutrition assistance program for the elderly is much smaller than for young adults.[74] Although the effects of food insecurity are heterogeneous within and across countries, the FAO believes that the consequences are for the unemployed, informal sector workers, families with children under 6, female-headed households, adults living alone, and adults. There will be more black families and low-income households.[75,76] Therefore, in conditions of food insecurity, children and adolescents with dietary deficiencies are exposed to developmental disorders, cognitive deficits, chronic physical and mental problems, and death.[77]

In the United States, about 38% of adults had experienced an increase in food insecurity since mid-March 2020, when COVID-19 was declared a national emergency.[78] This rate is likely to increase as the economic crisis continues and housekeeping orders continue. As a result of unemployment and declining incomes from the COVID-19 epidemic, millions of Americans struggled with the quantity and quality of food needed and the price of in-store food, accompanied by rising prices.[79] In addition, food insecurity in populations vulnerable to COVID-19 (for example, people with chronic illnesses and the elderly) increased due to fears of exposure to the virus.

A study of students in Texas found that 34.5% of them had experienced food insecurity over the past 30 days due to COVID-19, which is 15% more than food insecurity reported in previous US student reports.[15,48,80] Current lifestyle changes and the loss of part-time jobs were the most important predictors of food insecurity in students due to COVID-19. Also, in the Philippines, many industries have lost their incomes and purchasing power since the outbreak of the epidemic. As many as 7.3 million Filipinos are unemployed.[71] Since the epidemic, the Ministry of Welfare and Social Development has identified approximately 21 million low-income Filipino families needing immediate financial and food assistance from the government.[71]

In addition, students living with one parent were more than twice as likely as other students to experience food insecurity. This finding suggests that family support plays an important role in protecting students' food security in facing crises such as COVID-19. Family support increases food purchasing power and helps maintain a balanced diet, especially for students with lower nutritional literacy or lower cooking skills.[80–82]

Widespread food insecurity during the COVID-19 epidemic can have serious and long-term consequences for the health of low-income households. Food insecurity is associated with an increased risk of chronic diseases such as HIV,[83–86] type 2 diabetes,[87,88] cardiovascular disease,[89,90] hyperlipidemia, hypertension,[91] and high rate mortality.[92] In addition, given that chronic diseases such as diabetes and cardiovascular disease are risk factors for COVID-19 complications,[93] food insecurity can increase the risk of COVID-19 with a worse outcome.

The study of the impact of the first wave of COVID-19 on food insecurity during the epidemic crisis in the first week (April 20–26) of 2020 shows that a large proportion of respondents in April 2020 experienced food insecurity in the COVID-19 health emergency. Compared to March rates, food insecurity generally doubled in April and tripled among children. The rate of increase in food insecurity was higher than the projected increase in unemployment in April, especially for families with children. As a result, the number of economic problems families have experienced has increased and required an immediate and sustained response from the government.[94]

Therefore it is necessary to pay more attention to the relationship between eating pathology and food insecurity, especially in children and adolescents during pandemics. Although these times are uncertain, there are issues such as identifying the factors that exacerbate income and job inequality in the economic crisis that we must consider to protect the food security of children and adolescents now and shortly. Food security determines dignity, justice, life, and sustainable development.[1]

9. COVID-19 epidemic and food system

The world population is estimated to reach 10 billion by 2050, which raises significant concerns about food safety and adequate supply, hence the demand for foods such as meat, dairy products, as well as processed foods.[12] Before the epidemic, more than 80% of the Yemeni population was dependent on food aid and faced severe food insecurity. In Syria, 9.3 million people are insecure due to unprecedented inflation in food prices. Sudan is currently facing a strict travel ban, while food prices rose 82% in April from a month earlier. This will make it less likely to achieve the zero hunger target by 2030.[12]

Social justice and the goals of environmentally sustainable development are focused on reducing hunger, but the COVID-19 crisis has unprecedentedly affected these goals and disrupted the global food system. COVID-19 has tested the depth of global commitment to social justice and food sustainability and security.[36]

In addition, there is no specific system for the proper distribution of food in pandemic conditions. The COVID-19 pandemic made the defect more apparent. In general, based on food consumption, there are two types of food systems: one system that deals with the preparation and consumption of home food from grocery stores, farmer markets, and food centers, and the other system that is for consumption in institutions and outside the home like restaurants, schools, and businesses. The closure of restaurants, businesses, schools, and many institutions due to COVID-19 increased the demand for food at home, disrupting food supply in grocery stores.[95] Because food was originally prepared for use by farmers outside the home, and the consumption pattern changed due to COVID-19, large amounts of food were wasted.[96]

The food industry is a very important sector economically. However, the food sector faces various challenges compared to other areas of daily life, including tourism and aviation. The epidemic could lead to $ 113 billion in aviation losses and $ 80 billion in tourism.[97] Some food companies face various challenges due to declining revenues, while others work hard to meet retailers' growing demand. The fact is that this epidemic clearly shows that different companies from different industries around the world are closely related to each other. Hence, supply management strategies are also important to meet consumer needs. Maintaining the flow of food and goods across the supply chain must be ensured with the participation of all stakeholders. Ensuring consumer confidence is also essential for food safety and security.[97]

A study by Adhikari et al.[98] in Nepal showed that the COVID-19 pandemic had reduced the achievements of the SDGs as well as the negative impact on agricultural systems, food access, food consumption, and food security stability.[98] During an epidemic, continued supply flows in the agricultural and food sectors, are critical strategies to preventing a food crisis and reducing the negative impact on the global economy. As a result, every country has to realize the deterioration of the situation and sometimes, it has to tighten measures due to the prevalence of the epidemic. The supply chain must also be flexible enough to meet the challenges of the food supply chain.[97]

The vulnerability of food supply chains in food systems varies according to their priorities and structure. Their four important features can be as follows:

(i) Governments worldwide have made it a priority to ensure the delivery of staple foods to consumers.

(ii) In developing countries, traditional labor-focused food supply chains are more affected than modern ones.

(iii) Even modern food supply chains and systems can be severely affected by the closure or unemployment of labor and the severance of international connections.

(iv) COVID-19 has affected public food distribution systems. School closures, for example, deprive many poor children in the United States of public meals. Farmers and other suppliers struggle to find markets to replace institutions such as restaurants and schools, resulting in a significant amount of wasted milk and other micronutrient-fortified foods. Other food supply networks are also affected, including general nutrition programs for pregnant and lactating mothers.[24]

In high-income countries, perishable foods and their products have been significantly affected by COVID-19 due to their short shelf life and reliance on workers for storage and processing. Many farms employing migrant labor have faced labor shortages due to government restrictions on transportation to prevent the release of COVID-19, and the agricultural production cycle has been disrupted.[36] In summary, four major issues in the food industry and food supply chain have been addressed during the outbreak of COVID-19. First, people tend to follow a healthy diet to protect themselves and their immune systems. Second, food safety has received increasing attention among manufacturers, retailers, and consumers to prevent coronavirus transmission. Third, food security concerns have arisen due to traffic restrictions. Fourth, concerns about food stability have emerged during the epidemic.[97]

Thus the coronavirus (COVID-19) epidemic has shown how global food systems can become vulnerable, leading to increased food insecurity, malnutrition, and poverty, especially among vulnerable groups.[98]

10. Strategies to deal with the food crisis in the COVID-19 epidemic

Creating a global response to the impact of the COVID-19 pandemic on food insecurity and its consequences, including prolonged starvation and malnutrition, requires science-based solutions, informing policymakers, including governments, global organizations, and stakeholders.[1] However, various factors such as climate, geography, socioeconomic systems, healthcare systems, educational systems, and political structures must be considered for epidemics.[1]

However, being prepared for these patients, such as COVID-19, requires planning, organizing, investing, spending time and resources, as well as coordination between government agencies and the public. In addition, ensuring food availability, basic food supplies, and communicating with the public and teaching personal hygiene practices such as hand washing, masking, and physical distance are critical to COVID-19.[1,31,32]

Selective government policies to reduce the effects of COVID-19 on food security can include programs for food production, estimating food demand, appropriate methods of food distribution and storage, food processing and preparation, and a global food supply chain.[4]

Given that various issues affect food security, it is recommended to use the following approaches to create a food-resistant system against various threats:

- Provide innovation and low-cost or cost-effective methods to produce agricultural products that can increase production flexibility to be used against shocks and unpredictable consequences such as crop loss, epidemic conditions, market failure, etc.
- Creating associations of individuals and communities to effectively manage various innovations in agriculture.
- Interacting with decision-makers to support the implementation of robust political mechanisms that support appropriate agricultural solutions can increase flexibility in food systems.
- Support research that raises awareness of producers and consumers to strengthen the flexibility of food systems because it can, in addition to farmers' livelihoods and promote sustainable agricultural approaches, make healthy and nutritious food available to the community.[99]

11. Conclusion

COVID-19 showed that global food systems can become vulnerable, resulting in increased food insecurity, malnutrition, and poverty, especially among vulnerable groups. Therefore it is necessary to link the pathology of access to food and food insecurity, especially in children and adolescents during pandemics. In poor countries, agricultural production, from planting to harvesting, is done by labor. In these countries, health systems are usually weaker, and existing health challenges may increase people's vulnerability to epidemics such as COVID-19. Therefore many agricultural producers face labor shortages.

Due to the fact that in severe poverty there is not enough income to buy food to prevent hunger and malnutrition, poor people close to the poverty line turn to cheaper and less nutritious food. Although access to sources of income is short lived, the effects of malnutrition can be long lasting, especially for young children and adolescents. However, in these circumstances, among the four dimensions of food security, access to food is the most important.

International Labor Organization (ILO) surveys show that COVID-19 has affected more than 80% of the workforce due to complete or partial closure of the workplace. Although the timing of the epidemics is unclear, the identification of factors that exacerbate inequality in income, employment, and thus access to food should be considered to protect the food security of children and adolescents now and in the future.

Also, better management of food supply and demand can prevent an immediate food crisis for millions. During the crisis, various restrictions forced farmers to sell their products and dairy products while food banks faced shortages. Food distribution channels designed to bring fresh farm food to commercial customers could not easily feed the food banks, leaving farmers discarding the crop for not selling and leaving people hungry.

In an epidemic, the cooperation of most organizations in the distribution system and access to food is also very important. As the crisis has clarified, cooperation is much more vital in areas that are on the outskirts of cities or in rural areas. Because of these collaborations, the rate of food waste will reduce.

Responding to the impact of the COVID-19 pandemic on food insecurity and its consequences, including poverty, prolonged starvation and malnutrition, seems to require science-based solutions, informing policymakers, including governments and global organizations as well as stakeholders. However, various factors such as climate, geography, socioeconomic systems, healthcare systems, educational systems, and political structures must be considered for epidemics.

References

1. Paslakis G, Dimitropoulos G, Katzman DK. A call to action to address COVID-19-induced global food insecurity to prevent hunger, malnutrition, and eating pathology. *Nutr Rev* 2021;**79**(1):114–6.
2. Aborode AT, Ogunsola SO, Adeyemo AO. A crisis within a crisis: COVID-19 and hunger in African children. *Am J Trop Med Hyg* 2021;**104**(1):30.
3. Chang HH, Meyerhoefer CD. COVID-19 and the demand for online food shopping services: empirical Evidence from Taiwan. *Am J Agric Econ* 2021;**103**(2):448–65.
4. Otekunrin OA, Otekunrin OA, Fasina FO, et al. Assessing the zero hunger target readiness in Africa in the face of COVID-19 pandemic. *Caraka Tani J Sustain Agric* 2020;**35**:213–27.
5. Elsahoryi N, Al-Sayyed H, Odeh M, et al. Effect of Covid-19 on food security: a cross-sectional survey. *Clin Nutr ESPEN* 2020;**40**:171–8.
6. Nagata JM, Palar K, Gooding HC, et al. Food insecurity is associated with poorer mental health and sleep outcomes in young adults. *J Adolesc Health* 2019;**65**(6):805–11.
7. Reynolds C, Goucher L, Quested T, et al. Consumption-stage food waste reduction interventions—what works and how to design better interventions. *Food Policy* 2019;**83**:7–27.
8. Spang ES, Moreno LC, Pace SA, et al. Food loss and waste: measurement, drivers, and solutions. *Annu Rev Env Resour* 2019;**44**:117–56.
9. Assembly UGJUGA. *Universal declaration of human rights*. vol. 302. United Nations; 1948. p. 14–25 [2].
10. Chilton M, Rose D. A rights-based approach to food insecurity in the United States. *Am J Public Health* 2009;**99**(7):1203–11.
11. Chiwona-Karltun L, Amuakwa-Mensah F, Wamala-Larsson C, et al. COVID-19: from health crises to food security anxiety and policy implications. *Ambio* 2021;**50**(4):794–811.
12. Ma NL, Peng W, Soon CF, et al. Covid-19 pandemic in the lens of food safety and security. *Environ Res* 2021;**193**, 110405.
13. Barker M, Russell J. Feeding the food insecure in Britain: learning from the 2020 COVID-19 crisis. *Food Secur* 2020;**12**(4):865–70.
14. Erokhin V, Gao T. Impacts of COVID-19 on trade and economic aspects of food security: evidence from 45 developing countries. *Int J Environ Res Public Health* 2020;**17**(16):5775.
15. Wolfson JA, Leung CW. Food insecurity and COVID-19: disparities in early effects for US adults. *Nutrients* 2020;**12**(6):1648.
16. Béné C. Resilience of local food systems and links to food security—a review of some important concepts in the context of COVID-19 and other shocks. *Food Secur* 2020;1–8.
17. Grosso M, Falasconi L. *Addressing food wastage in the framework of the UN sustainable development goals*. London, England: SAGE Publications Sage UK; 2018.
18. Lemaire A, Limbourg S. How can food loss and waste management achieve sustainable development goals? *J Clean Prod* 2019;**234**:1221–34.
19. World Health Organization. *The state of food security and nutrition in the world 2019: safeguarding against economic slowdowns and downturns*. Food & Agriculture Org; 2019.

20. Siche R. What is the impact of COVID-19 disease on agriculture? *Sci Agropecu* 2020;**11**(1):3–6.
21. Kalichman SC, Grebler T, Amaral CM, et al. Food insecurity and antiretroviral adherence among HIV positive adults who drink alcohol. *J Behav Med* 2014;**37**(5):1009–18.
22. Leung CW, Epel ES, Ritchie LD, Crawford PB, Laraia BA. Food insecurity is inversely associated with diet quality of lower-income adults. *J Acad Nutr Diet* 2014;**114**(12): 1943–53.
23. Zabir AA, Mahmud A, Islam MA, et al. COVID-19 and food supply in Bangladesh: a review. *South Asian J Soc Stud Econ* 2020;**10**(1):15–23.
24. Laborde D, Martin W, Swinnen J, Vos R. COVID-19 risks to global food security. *Science* 2020;**369**(6503):500–2.
25. O'Hara S, Toussaint EC. Food access in crisis: food security and COVID-19. *Ecol Econ* 2021;**180**, 106859.
26. International Monetary Fund. A crisis like no other, an uncertain recovery. In: *World economic outlook update*. IMF; 2020.
27. Godfray HCJ, Crute IR, Haddad L, et al. *The future of the global food system*. The Royal Society; 2010.
28. Liu J, Liao X, Qian S, et al. Community transmission of severe acute respiratory syndrome coronavirus 2, Shenzhen, China, 2020. *Emerg Infect Dis* 2020;**26**(6):1320.
29. Workie E, Mackolil J, Nyika J, Ramadas S. Deciphering the impact of COVID-19 pandemic on food security, agriculture, and livelihoods: a review of the evidence from developing countries. *Curr Res Environ Sustain* 2020;, 100014.
30. Huizar MI, Arena R, Laddu DR. The global food syndemic: the impact of food insecurity, malnutrition and obesity on the healthspan amid the COVID-19 pandemic. *Prog Cardiovasc Dis* 2021;**64**:105.
31. Chen Y, Liu Q, Guo D. Emerging coronaviruses: genome structure, replication, and pathogenesis. *J Med Virol* 2020;**92**(4):418–23.
32. Bakhtiyari S, Mirzaei A, Jalilian M, Mazlomi S, Nourmoradi H, Kakaei H. The effects of personal, environmental, and genetic factors on epidemic of coronavirus disease-19: a review of the current literature. *Open Access Maced J Med Sci* 2020;**8**(T1):250–7.
33. Mousazadeh M, Naghdali Z, Rahimian N, Hashemi M, Paital B, Al-Qodah Z, et al. Management of environmental health to prevent an outbreak of COVID-19: a review. In: *Environmental and Health Management of Novel Coronavirus Disease (COVID-19)*. Academic Press; 2021. p. 235–67.
34. Bhat BA, Gull S, Jeelani G. A study on COVID-19 lockdown impact on food, agriculture, fisheries and precautionary measures to avoid COVID-19 contamination. *Galore Int J Appl Sci Humanit* 2020;**4**(2):8–18.
35. Udmale P, Pal I, Szabo S, Pramanik M, Large A. Global food security in the context of COVID-19: a scenario-based exploratory analysis. *Progr Disaster Sci* 2020;**7**, 100120.
36. Fleetwood J. Social justice, food loss, and the sustainable development goals in the era of COVID-19. *Sustainability* 2020;**12**(12):5027.
37. Fan S, Teng P, Chew P, Smith G, Copeland L. Food system resilience and COVID-19—lessons from the Asian experience. *Glob Food Sec* 2021;**28**, 100501.
38. Skinner C, Watson V. Planning and informal food traders under COVID-19: the south African case. *Town Plan Rev* 2020;1–7.
39. Hossain ST. Impacts of COVID-19 on the agri-food sector: food security policies of Asian productivity organization members. *J Agric Sci - Sri Lanka* 2018;**15**(2):116.
40. Timilsina B, Adhikari N, Kafle S, Paudel S, Poudel S, Gautam D. Addressing impact of COVID-19 post pandemic on farming and agricultural deeds. *Asian J Adv Res Rep* 2020;28–35.
41. Henry R. Innovations in agriculture and food supply in response to the COVID-19 pandemic. *Mol Plant* 2020;**13**(8):1095.

42. Poudel PB, Poudel MR, Gautam A, et al. COVID-19 and its global impact on food and agriculture. *J Biol Today's World* 2020;**9**(5):221–5.
43. FAO. *COVID-19 and the risk to food supply chains: how to respond?*. Rome; 2020. https://doi.org/10.4060/ca8388en.
44. Laborde D, Martin W, Vos R. *Poverty and food insecurity could grow dramatically as COVID-19 spreads.* Washington, DC: International Food Policy Research Institute (IFPRI); 2020.
45. Huss M, Brander M, Kassie M, Ehlert U, Bernauer T. Improved storage mitigates vulnerability to food-supply shocks in smallholder agriculture during the COVID-19 pandemic. *Glob Food Sec* 2021;**28**, 100468.
46. Xie X, Huang L, Li JJ, Zhu H. Generational differences in perceptions of food health/risk and attitudes toward organic food and game meat: the case of the COVID-19 crisis in China. *Int J Environ Res Public Health* 2020;**17**(9):3148.
47. Bublitz MG, Czarkowski N, Hansen J, Peracchio LA, Tussler S. Pandemic reveals vulnerabilities in food access: confronting hunger amidst a crisis. *J Public Policy Mark* 2021;**40**(1):105–7.
48. Dunn CG, Kenney E, Fleischhacker SE, Bleich SN. Feeding low-income children during the Covid-19 pandemic. *N Engl J Med* 2020;**382**(18), e40.
49. Jones AD. Food insecurity and mental health status: a global analysis of 149 countries. *Am J Prev Med* 2017;**53**(2):264–73.
50. Weiser SD, Palar K, Hatcher AM, Young SL, Frongillo EA. Food insecurity and health: a conceptual framework. In: *Food insecurity and public health.* CRC Press; 2015. p. 23–50.
51. Seligman HK, Berkowitz SA. Aligning programs and policies to support food security and public health goals in the United States. *Annu Rev Public Health* 2019;**40**:319–37.
52. Hamid MZBSA, Karri RR. Overview of preventive measures and good governance policies to mitigate the COVID-19 outbreak curve in Brunei. In: *COVID-19: systemic risk and resilience.* Cham: Springer; 2021. p. 115–40.
53. Poudel PB, Poudel MR, Gautam A, Phuyal S, Tiwari CK, Bashyal N, et al. COVID-19 and its global impact on food and agriculture. 5. *J. Biol. Today's World.*, 9; 2020. p. 221–5.
54. Lele U, Bansal S, Meenakshi JV. Health and nutrition of India's labour force and COVID-19 challenges. *Econ Polit Wkly* 2020;**55**(21):13.
55. Baldwin R, Di Mauro BW. *Economics in the time of COVID-19: a new eBook.* VOX CEPR Policy Portal; 2020. p. 2–3.
56. Hossain MM, Purohit N, Sharma R, Bhattacharya S, McKyer EL, Ma P. Suicide of a farmer amid COVID-19 in India: perspectives on social determinants of suicidal behavior and prevention strategies. *SocArXiv* 2020;1–8.
57. UNICEF. *Situation tracking for COVID-19 socio-economic impacts.* New York: UNICEF; 2020.
58. Kansiime MK, Tambo JA, Mugambi I, Bundi M, Kara A, Owuor C. COVID-19 implications on household income and food security in Kenya and Uganda: findings from a rapid assessment. *World Dev* 2021;**13**:105199.
59. Ribeiro-Silva RD, Pereira M, Campello T, et al. Covid-19 pandemic implications for food and nutrition security in Brazil. *Cien Saude Colet* 2020;**25**:3421–30.
60. de Carvalho CA, Viola PC, Sperandio N. How is Brazil facing the crisis of food and nutrition security during the COVID-19 pandemic? *Public Health Nutr* 2021;**24**(3):561–4.
61. Pérez-Escamilla R, Cunningham K, Moran VH. *COVID-19 and maternal and child food and nutrition insecurity: a complex syndemic.* Wiley Online Library; 2020.
62. Coleman-Jensen A, Rabbitt MP, Gregory CA, Singh A. *Household food security in the United States in 2018, ERR-270.* US Department of Agriculture, Economic Research Service; 2019.

63. National Research Council. *Food insecurity and hunger in the United States: An assessment of the measure*. National Academies Press; 2006.
64. Burlea-Schiopoiu A, Ogarca RF, Barbu CM, Craciun L, Baloi IC, Mihai LS. The impact of COVID-19 pandemic on food waste behaviour of young people. *J Clean Prod* 2021;**294**:126333.
65. Mouloudj K, Bouarar AC, Fechit H. The impact of COVID-19 pandemic on food security. *Cah cread* 2020;**36**(3):159–84.
66. Bailey ZD, Krieger N, Agénor M, Graves J, Linos N, Bassett MT. Structural racism and health inequities in the USA: evidence and interventions. *Lancet* 2017;**389**(10077): 1453–63.
67. Control CfD, Prevention. *Diabetes report card 2017*. Atlanta: Centers for Disease Control and Prevention, US Dept of Health and Human Services; 2018.
68. Berkman LF, Kawachi I, Glymour MM. *Social epidemiology*. Oxford University Press; 2014. p. 615.
69. von Grebmer K, Bernstein J, Mukerji R, et al. *Global hunger index: The challenge of hunger and climate change*. Bonn: Welthungerhilfe; 2019.
70. Swinnen J, McDermott J. COVID-19 and global food security. *EuroChoices* 2020;**19**(3):26–33.
71. Ong MM, Ong RM, Reyes GK, Sumpaico-Tanchanco LB. Addressing the COVID-19 nutrition crisis in vulnerable communities: applying a primary care perspective. *J Prim Care Community Health* 2020;**11**, 2150132720946951.
72. Wolfson JA, Leung CW. Food insecurity during COVID-19: an acute crisis with long-term health implications. *Am J Public Health* 2020;**110**(12):1763–5.
73. Power M, Doherty B, Pybus K, Pickett K. How COVID-19 has exposed inequalities in the UK food system: the case of UK food and poverty. *Emerald Open Res* 2020;**2**.
74. Ziliak JP. Food hardship during the COVID-19 pandemic and Great Recession. *Appl Econ Perspect Policy* 2021;**43**(1):132–52.
75. Smith MD, Wesselbaum D. COVID-19, food insecurity, and migration. *J Nutr* 2020;**150**(11):2855–8.
76. Coleman-Jensen A, Nord M. Food insecurity among households with working-age adults with disabilities. In: *USDA-ERS economic research report*; 2013. p. 144.
77. Dahir AL. *Instead of Coronavirus, the Hunger Will Kill Us.'A Global Food Crisis Looms*. 22. The New York Times; 2020.
78. Schanzenbach D, Pitts A. *Food insecurity in the census household pulse survey data tables*. Institute for Policy Research; 2020. p. 1–5.
79. FAO. *Summary findings: food price outlook, 2020*. USDA; 2020.
80. Moore CE, Davis KE, Wang W. Low food security present on college campuses despite high nutrition literacy. *J Hunger Environ Nutr* 2020;1–7.
81. Nikolaus CJ, Ellison B, Nickols-Richardson SM. Are estimates of food insecurity among college students accurate? Comparison of assessment protocols. *PLoS One* 2019;**14**(4), e0215161.
82. Freudenberg N, Manzo L, Mongiello L, Jones H, Boeri N, Lamberson P. Promoting the health of young adults in urban public universities: a case study from City University of new York. *J Am Coll Health* 2013;**61**(7):422–30.
83. Chop E, Duggaraju A, Malley A, et al. Food insecurity, sexual risk behavior, and adherence to antiretroviral therapy among women living with HIV: a systematic review. *Health Care Women Int* 2017;**38**(9):927–44.
84. Weiser SD, Leiter K, Bangsberg DR, et al. Food insufficiency is associated with high-risk sexual behavior among women in Botswana and Swaziland. *PLoS Med* 2007;**4**(10), e260.
85. Borges ÁH, O'Connor JL, Phillips AN, et al. Factors associated with plasma IL-6 levels during HIV infection. *J Infect Dis* 2015;**212**(4):585–95.

86. Tenorio AR, Zheng Y, Bosch RJ, et al. Soluble markers of inflammation and coagulation but not T-cell activation predict non-AIDS-defining morbid events during suppressive antiretroviral treatment. *J Infect Dis* 2014;**210**(8):1248–59.
87. Seligman HK, Bindman AB, Vittinghoff E, Kanaya AM, Kushel MB. Food insecurity is associated with diabetes mellitus: results from the National Health Examination and Nutrition Examination Survey (NHANES) 1999–2002. *J Gen Intern Med* 2007;**22**(7):1018–23.
88. Fitzgerald N, Hromi-Fiedler A, Segura-Pérez S, Pérez-Escamilla R. Food insecurity is related to increased risk of type 2 diabetes among Latinas. *Ethn Dis* 2011;**21**(3):328.
89. Ford ES. Food security and cardiovascular disease risk among adults in the United States: findings from the National Health and Nutrition Examination Survey, 2003–2008. *Prev Chronic Dis* 2013;**10**:E202.
90. Ridker PM, Hennekens CH, Buring JE, Rifai N. C-reactive protein and other markers of inflammation in the prediction of cardiovascular disease in women. *N Engl J Med* 2000;**342**(12):836–43.
91. Gundersen C, Ziliak JP. Food insecurity and health outcomes. *Health Aff* 2015;**34**(11):1830–9.
92. Anema A, Chan K, Chen Y, Weiser S, Montaner JS, Hogg RS. Relationship between food insecurity and mortality among HIV-positive injection drug users receiving antiretroviral therapy in British Columbia, Canada. *PLoS One* 2013;**8**(5), e61277.
93. CDC COVID-19 Response Team. Preliminary estimates of the prevalence of selected underlying health conditions among patients with coronavirus disease 2019—United States, February 12–March 28, 2020. *MMWR Morb Mortal Wkly Rep* 2020;**69**(13):382–6. https://doi.org/10.15585/mmwr.mm6913e2.
94. Schanzenbach D, Pitts A. *Estimates of food insecurity during the COVID-19 crisis: results from the COVID impact survey*. Institute for Policy Research Rapid Research Report; 2020.
95. Lakhani N. *A perfect storm: US facing hunger crisis as demand for food banks soars*. The Guardian; 2020. Retrieved from: https://www.theguardian.com/environment/2020/apr/02/us-food-banks-coronavirus-demand-unemployment.
96. Yaffe-Bellany D, Corkery M. *Dumped milk, smashed eggs, plowed vegetables: food waste of the pandemic*. The New York Times; 2020. p. 11.
97. Aday S, Aday MS. Impact of COVID-19 on the food supply chain. *Food Qual Saf* 2020;**4**(4):167–80.
98. Adhikari J, Timsina J, Khadka SR, Ghale Y, Ojha H. COVID-19 impacts on agriculture and food systems in Nepal: implications for SDGs. *Agr Syst* 2021;**186**, 102990.
99. Shilomboleni H. COVID-19 and food security in Africa: building more resilient food systems. *AAS Open Res* 2020;**3**.

CHAPTER TWO

Effects of COVID-19 on the availability of clean water and sanitation

Abbas Ostadtaghizadeh[a], Lara Hamdanieh[a], and Simin Nasseri[b]
[a]Department of Health in Emergencies and Disasters, School of Public Health, Tehran University of Medical Sciences, Tehran, Iran
[b]Department of Environmental Health Engineering, School of Public Health, Tehran University of Medical Sciences, Tehran, Iran

1. Importance of water for health

Water is required for drinking, cooking, personal hygiene, washing, cleaning, agriculture, sanitation, etc.[1] The international human rights law states that it is the right of all to have access to adequate water and sanitation. It includes access to safe, affordable, and sufficient water supply as well as to appropriate sanitation facilities. This is vital to ensure humans survival, prevent death due to dehydration, and reduce diseases related to water, sanitation, and hygiene (WASH).[2] Supplying water means treating raw water and distributing it to the customers. Sanitation means collecting and treating wastewater to become safe products that can be discharged to the environment or used for other purposes.[3] Hygiene includes water (such as ensuring the safety of water supplies), personal, domestic, and environmental hygiene.[4]

Inadequate sanitation, limited water supplies, and poor hygiene can contribute to the spread of diarrheal and infectious diseases. Most public health problems, mainly in crises, occur due to inadequate quality and quantity of water.[2] Infectious diseases can be either transmitted by direct contact between the community members or from the environment (contamination of water, food, soil, or from insects). Four water-related transmission routes lead to the spread of diseases[5]:

(a) Water-borne diseases: caused by ingesting polluted water containing pathogens (e.g., diarrheal diseases, cholera, typhoid).

(b) Water-washed diseases: caused by inadequate personal hygiene due to lack or scarcity of water (e.g., scabies, trachoma, skin infections).

COVID-19 and the Sustainable Development Goals
https://doi.org/10.1016/B978-0-323-91307-2.00001-8

(c) Water-based diseases: caused by the intermediate host that lives in water and carries the pathogenic agent (e.g., schistosomiasis).

(d) Water-related vector-borne diseases: caused by vectors of communicable diseases that develop in or near water (e.g., malaria, yellow fever, dengue fever).

In addition, diseases may occur due to a combination of these causes. For instance, amebiasis is caused by inadequate personal hygiene and polluted water.

The water crisis is defined as "a significant decline in the available quality and quantity of freshwater, resulting in harmful effects on human health and economic activity." According to the World Economic Forum, the water crisis is the number five global risk in terms of impact on society. Water scarcity affects a quarter of the world's population, which is expected to worsen with time.[6] Today, 785 million people (1 in 9), 2 billion people (1 in 3), and 3 billion people (2 in 5) globally lack access to safe water, adequate sanitation, and soap and water for handwashing at home, respectively.[7] Furthermore, the United Nations states that nearly 22% of the healthcare facilities globally do not have access to the required water and sanitation services.[3] The water crisis is also a health crisis. WASH-related diseases cause about 1 million deaths annually.[7] In European countries, 31 and 48 million people do not have access to basic sanitation and piped water, respectively, and the unsafe water supply is leading to 14 deaths daily.[8] According to World Health Organization (WHO), poor water and sanitation services accounted for 829,000 deaths due to diarrheal diseases in 2016, equal to 1.9% of the global disease burden.[3] Also, a child dies from a water-related disease every 2 min.[7] More than 90,000 deaths and 2.8 million cases of cholera are reported each year. If untreated, patients die from dehydration within hours. However, with treatment, the case fatality rate can be decreased to less than 1%.[9] Moreover, global warming, urbanization, the rapid growth of megacities, more people living in areas with water stress, and aging infrastructure are major problems that the water sector is facing worldwide.[3] Sometimes, natural disasters further worsen the situation as they result in biological or chemical contamination of water and food, disruption of water supply, damage of the water sources and wastewater treatment services, and electricity cut off, which interrupts pumping water. Hence, an outbreak of water and sanitation-related diseases and a nutrition emergency might occur some weeks or months later after a disaster happens. Climate change is exacerbating the situation. It is leading to more floods and longer droughts. The latter dries up the springs, and floods pollute the water sources.[10]

Knowing that many outbreaks can be prevented, Water, Sanitation, and Hygiene (WASH) interventions play an important role in reducing the burden of these diseases.[9] Pathogens can infect humans through different pathways such as food, flies, fingers, fluid, and feces. In order to reduce public health risks, WASH programs create barriers along these main pathways.[2] There are three main components of WASH interventions in outbreak response: (a) Water: increase its quantity and quality; (b) Sanitation: isolate feces from the environment, assure appropriate feces management, lessen open defecation, and minimize exposure to infectious waste; and (c) Hygiene: promote awareness, distribute hygiene kits, and ensure environmental hygiene.[9] Handwashing with soap mitigates and controls the spread of a wide spectrum of communicable diseases (such as respiratory infections and gastrointestinal diseases). Previous studies ensured that the global burden of disease could be reduced by promoting hand hygiene and is considered a cost-effective measure. In addition, personal hygiene reduces the effects of Severe Acute Respiratory Syndrome (SARS) and is highly recommended to deal with the risk of influenza pandemics.[11]

To have a healthy community, it is critical to promote hygiene practices, supply safe drinking water, provide sanitation facilities, and reduce environmental health risks.[2,12] Key components for strengthening communities before and during an emergency are continuous public education about household water treatment, food hygiene, hand washing, waste disposal, and latrines usage. The top public health priorities in emergencies are (a) having access to healthcare, shelter, food, water supplies, and sanitation facilities; (b) controlling communicable diseases; and (c) having public health surveillance in place.[10]

This chapter aims to discuss the effects of COVID-19 on the water and sanitation sectors. It highlights the challenges that SARS-Cov-2 posed to these sectors by giving examples from different countries and state the related lessons learned.

2. Effect of COVID-19 on water

2.1 Characteristics of SARS-CoV-2

The severe acute respiratory syndrome coronavirus 2 (SARS-CoV-2), the virus that causes COVID-19, can be transmitted from human to human via direct contact with infected person/surfaces and infective respiratory droplets.[13] To protect the human health during the COVID-19 outbreak, like in any other infectious disease outbreak, appropriate WASH conditions should be provided.[14] According to the WHO, hand hygiene at the right time and correctly using soap and water or alcohol-based hand rub is one of the preventive measures against SARS-CoV-2.[13,15] Soap can destroy the lipid bilayer surrounding SARS-CoV-2, and the water removes the remaining inactivated virus.[16] Therefore the spread of COVID-19 is influenced by water availability and accessibility.[17]

SARS-COV-2 is an enveloped virus consisting of a fragile external membrane that can become quickly inactive, since it is less stable and very sensitive to oxidants than viruses with water-based transmission (such as rotavirus, norovirus, adenoviruses, and hepatitis A virus).[15] Enveloped viruses are known to be less stable in the environment than nonenveloped human enteric viruses (such as rotavirus, adenovirus, and hepatitis A). The virus can be easily inactivated by chlorine, heat, ethanol, ultraviolet (UV) rays,[18] low or high pH, and sunlight.[13] The presence of organic matter in the water increases the virus's survival.[19] There is no evidence about the persistence of SARS-CoV-2 in treated drinking water, although its presence in untreated drinking water is possible. According to the current evidence, the fecal-oral transmission pathway, i.e., SARS-CoV-2 transmission from the feces, seems to be low.[13]

2.2 Vulnerabilities

COVID-19 hit the vulnerable the most. Those who rely on water tankers, private vendors, water points, and toilets in the community will be more vulnerable than others. The high cost of water and waiting for hours to collect water where physical distancing is not feasible can further increase the vulnerability. Also, having limited household budgets might lead some families to consider hand sanitizer and soap a burden and not a priority.[20]

It is very challenging to contain the virus where there is lack of reliable and good quality WASH services, which is the case in many underdeveloped and developing countries.[3] These countries have limited wastewater treatment capacities, and untreated wastewater is usually directly discharged into the water bodies. India, Vietnam, Pakistan, Philippines, and Indonesia treat only 38%, 10%, 8%, 4%, and 1% of their wastewater, respectively. More than 85%, 80%, and 50% of households in sub-Saharan Africa, Asia, and Latin America are not connected to the sewerage network. In addition, if the wastewater treatment facilities are present, they often do not meet the required national standards due to unsafe management leading to environmental contamination. In many areas, surface or groundwater is directly used (without treatment) by households for daily activities, posing a public health risk. Slums and informal settlements are deprived of their basic needs (clean water, drainage, waste collection, toilets, and sewers) that foster the spread of the diseases.[19] For example, in India, the sewage treatment capacity is very limited such that only 38% of the generated sewage is treated. This means that more than 38,000 million liters of untreated sewage is directly discharged into the rivers daily. The rivers are also polluted by industrial effluents.[15] In the Indian urban areas, about 70% of the sewage goes directly to the water bodies without being treated, and the remaining treated sewage water is used in irrigation.[15] In Brazil, it was reported that the COVID-19 cases and deaths were in municipalities having very limited access to safe water or sewerage system.[21]

COVID-19 pandemic highlighted the importance of providing safe water, sanitation, and hygiene for all to protect their health. Although handwashing seems to be a simple recommendation to prevent being infected by SARS-COV-2, it is very complicated in regions with water scarcity. Eighteen out of 22 Arab countries suffer from water scarcity.[22] 1700 m^3/person/year is the threshold of renewable water. Countries whose annual renewable water supplies are between 1000 and 1700 m^3/person/year, below 1000 m^3/person/year, or below 500 m^3/person/year are considered to be experiencing water stress, water scarcity, and absolute scarcity, respectively.[22,23] Annually in the Arab countries, more than 362 million people have access to less than 1000 cubic meters of freshwater per individual. Knowing the importance of hand hygiene during the pandemic, the water demand is expected to increase by 9 to 12 L per person daily. In this region, more than 74 million people are more susceptible to get infected by COVID-19, because they do not have access to basic handwashing facilities. Seventy million people have interrupted water supply in 10 Arab countries. The Arab region must spend approximately $150–250 million each month to meet the increased domestic water demand. Furthermore, over 87 million people do not have access to drinking water through taps. Some purchase drinking water from private vendors, while others cannot afford this option and have to collect water from public sources (wells and standpipes), which poses a risk of COVID-19 transmission. The latter mainly occurs in informal settlements where they are not connected to water supply networks. Curfews and mobility restrictions can worsen the situation since these people will not be able to access the standpipes, and delivering water through tanker trucks might be interrupted. About 26 million refugees and internally displaced persons lack adequate WASH services, making them vulnerable to

COVID-19. Sometimes water supply is intentionally interrupted because of political and military reasons. About 1.8 million Palestinians do not have access to their water resources and need WASH services. In Gaza Strip, the quantity and quality of water are very limited, and only 1 out of 10 has access to safe water.[22] It is important to note that due to the economic crisis, increased unemployment rate, and limited financial resources, the default on water bills will be very high.[22,24] Consequently, fewer resources will be available for operating, managing, and conducting repairs in the water sector.[22]

The sources of water bodies' contamination include open defecation by an infected person, infected wastes, infected sewage, untreated wastewater, and infected personal protective equipment (PPE).[19] Excessive usage of disinfectants and disinfection by-products further deteriorate the quality and safety of the water. Noteworthy, more antiviral drugs are being used to treat patients, and when its residues are discharged into the wastewater then to the water bodies, it will have a detrimental effect on the ecosystem. The demand for PPE has increased since the beginning of the pandemic; however, their safe disposal is challenging. It will be dangerous to enter the water bodies since plastics can be transferred to microplastics, an emerging pollutant. Also, it is predicted that over 1.56 billion masks could end up in oceans in 2020, posing a threat to the ecosystem.[25]

COVID-19 exacerbated the impact of drought and water shortage in countries that are already experiencing climate variation and decrease in rainfall like Ireland, the United Kingdom, Turkey, Ethiopia, Kenya, Syria, Poland, Romania, Kosovo, and India.[8]

2.3 COVID-19 and water availability

Overusing water during handwashing and keeping the tap on will pose excess pressure on the water sector. A study in Bangladesh measured the consumption of water per person while handwashing. It showed that keeping the tap on while handwashing led to the overuse of 1.7 L of water per handwash and 14.9 L of water per day. During the pandemic, hand washing while keeping the tap on led to 13-fold overuse of water in Bangladesh. Compared to the prepandemic situation, each participant used 12.8 times more water per day during the pandemic. It was concluded that keeping the tap on while handwashing will account for 1179% of water loss during this public health emergency.[26]

In low- and middle-income countries, where water scarcity is a critical problem and more than a billion live in informal settlements, people might prioritize using water for activities other than hand hygiene. Some households tend to store large quantities of water, which leads to viral and bacterial illnesses if it was not properly stored. Water sharing between neighbors might increase to cope with the situation, thus increasing the risk of getting infected due to physical contact. Some people who do not have enough time to wait for hours to collect water or for other reasons might use water from nearby surface water or water tanker with low quality and high prices. Some might seek another place to live where water is more available, increasing the risk of COVID-19 transmission to the new destination.[16]

As this pandemic evolves worldwide, some countries might increase local food production since food-producing countries reduced their food exports. In this way, the already scarce water resources will shift toward the agriculture sector. As a result, more water will be pumped from surface and groundwater resources to meet the demand of the domestic and agriculture sectors leading to water stress.[22] Thus water insecurity will contribute to food insecurity.[16]

2.4 Effect of COVID-19 lockdown on water quantity and quality

Locking down cities and shutting down businesses increased the domestic water demand and decreased the nondomestic (i.e., industrial, commercial, public, and institutional) demand.[24] Domestic water refers to water provided for houses and apartments. The industrial category refers to factories and industrial parks. The commercial category includes malls, stores, restaurants, hotels, and others. General category means healthcare and governmental facilities, schools, and universities.[27] In a survey by Global Water Leaders Group, they estimated an average of 27% decrease in water demand by industries due to the pandemic. Notably, many governments excluded the employees in the water sector from movement restrictions policies to maintain service continuity. Nevertheless, disruptions in logistics and supply chains were reported.[3]

Lockdown contributed to the increased domestic water demand since people had to stay home, and handwashing is considered one of the most important measures to prevent infection by the coronavirus.[15] For example, some municipalities in India (e.g., Kozhikode and Ahmedabad) reported up to 25% increase in domestic water usage. Similar results were reported in Joinville city in Brazil, where residential buildings consumed more water than the public buildings and industries (comparing periods before and after the lockdown).[15] This might be due to excess water flow from the tap while handwashing.[26]

The effect of change in water demand depends on the relative proportion of domestic and nondomestic water use and how much each nondomestic sector contributes to the economy, which usually varies between countries. Concerning nondomestic water demand, some sectors were more affected than others.[24] For the majority of the water utilities, there was a drop in the revenues due to a decrease in the total water use[24] (mainly by industries and commercial centers[3]). The change in water demand affected the expenditure and revenue of utilities, water bills, water quality in the buildings, and conditions for using water and wastewater. It is important to note that these effects are short term, and after few months, in some areas, the water demand will go back to the normal conditions (pre-COVID-19 levels).[24]

In the Malaysian river, the water quality index had improved during the lockdown.[28] In India, during the COVID-19 lockdown, many industries were closed from March to September 2020, which led to the short-term improvement of the water quality and quantity in many rivers.[15] The transformation in water quality is expected to go back to its normal condition after businesses reopen.[29] Also, in the same period, the excess rainfall increased the discharge that increased the volume of the water flow in rivers and increased the dilution of the pollutants.[15,30] However, no significant water quality improvement was reported in some rivers where most of the pollution comes from domestic sewage rather than industrial effluents. This ensures the importance of treating the industrial and domestic wastewater before discharging it to the rivers.[15] Moreover, industries located near rivers should abide by the environmental guidelines.[31]

Suspending some agricultural activities during the lockdown led to less water used in irrigation and an increase in the average river discharge and water quantity in reservoirs. For example, in the first 3 months of lockdown in India, the status of the stored water in 123 reservoirs was 159% more than the last 10 years' average storage in the same duration.[15]

During the lockdown, electricity demand in some countries decreased, so less water was consumed for electricity generation. Therefore to reduce the pressure on the water resources, it will be better to shift toward less water-intensive technology for generating electricity.[32]

During COVID-19 lockdown, many private and public buildings will close for a few weeks or months. This means that there will be limited or no water flow in these premises, leading to water stagnation in the building plumbing. Thus the quality of the water will decrease as mold, Legionella bacteria (that causes Legionnaires' disease), or microbial pathogens grow because of corrosion, chlorine decay, or harmful metals leaching from the

Table 1 Change in domestic and nondomestic water demand during COVID-19 lockdown.

City/country	Increase in domestic water demand (%)	Decrease in nondomestic water demand (%)	References
Portsmouth, England	15%	17%	24
San Francisco, California	10%	32%	24
Kozhikode and Ahmedabad, India	25%	–	15
Joinville, Brazil	11%	53%, 42%, and 30% in the industrial, commercial, and public categories, respectively	27
Ireland	20%	–	8

pipes. When premises open again, the deterioration of water quality due to chemical and microbiological contaminants will pose public health risk.[13,24,25] Several measures can be undertaken to minimize the risks within these premises before reoccupancy, including testing the water quality to ensure that it meets the national standards.[13,24]

Table 1 presents the change in demand for domestic and nondomestic water in some cities during the lockdown, and Fig. 1 summarizes the effect of COVID-19 lockdown on water.

2.5 COVID-19 and water bills

Major revenue loss is predicted in the water supply chain. During the pandemic, governments took different measures to ensure water services continuity among low-income customers and vulnerable groups. It included, but is not limited to, suspending meter reading and invoicing, moratoriums on cutting off water services, postponing or exempting paying bills, or donating water tanks. All these measures contributed to revenue losses in the water sector. Global Water Leaders Group expects an average of 15% revenue reduction in water and wastewater utilities.[3]

Moratoriums are not a sustainable option, and many water utilities cannot financially afford them. After a short period of time when lifting moratoriums, plans should be in place to prevent the vulnerable members from being disconnected from water. Therefore water utilities can eliminate late

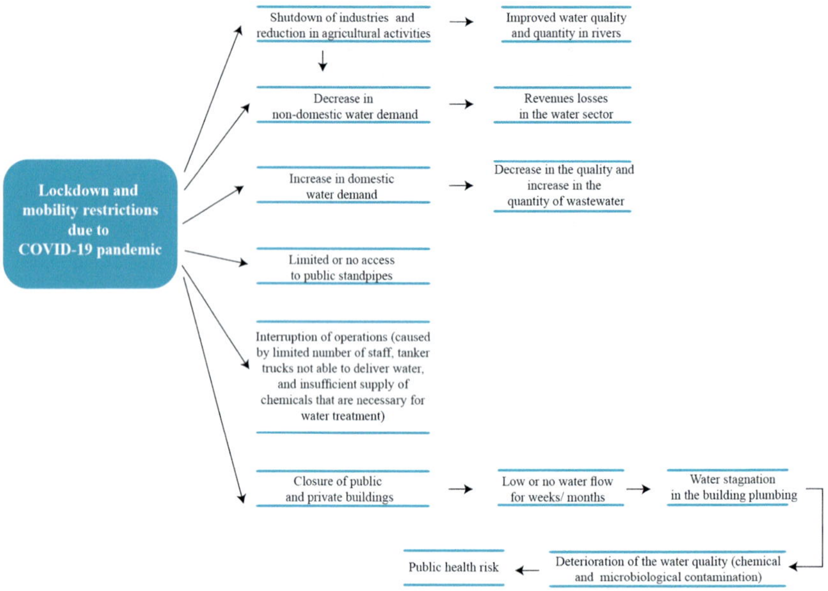

Fig. 1 Effect of COVID-19 lockdown on water.[3,8,13,15,17,22,24,25,28]

fees and expand repayment options to ease the burden on those facing financial hardships.[33]

Some utilities benefit from the revenue that is gained by selling water to businesses in order to subsidize the household water cost. However, this was greatly impacted in the pandemic, affecting the ability to continue providing affordable water for consumers.[24]

After COVID-19 spread worldwide, all countries introduced new policies to respond to this pandemic; however, little attention was given to the water sector. Only 11 out of 27 European countries implemented short-term policy interventions regarding the water sector, focusing mainly on the payment of water bills. Thus there was absence of major intervention and change in the water sector. This sector faced interruption in operations due to labor cost, absenteeism, inability to buy PPE for all the workers, and shortage of chemicals necessary for treating water.[8]

3. Effect of COVID-19 on sanitation

Abdominal pain, vomiting, and diarrhea are among the gastrointestinal symptoms of SARS-CoV-2.[34] SARS-CoV-2 is excreted via the gastrointestinal tract of COVID-19 patients into the wastewater.[18,35] It can be present in an infected person's feces, urine, or vomit.[25,36] Even after the nasopharyngeal samples tested negative for COVID-19-infected patients, SARS-CoV-2 RNA was still detected in their feces for days, suggesting that the virus might be replicating in the gastrointestinal tract.[35] SARS-CoV-2 was detected in raw (untreated) wastewater in Netherlands, Italy, the United States of America, France, Australia, Spain,[35,37] and Iran.[18] In addition, a study done in Iran reported the presence of SARS-CoV-2 RNA in raw and treated wastewater.[18]

One of the pathways of SARS-CoV transmission was fecal-oral, and SARS-CoV-2 is genetically similar to it.[19] SARS-CoV-2 RNA was detected in fecal and urine samples in several studies. These samples were either collected from wastewaters of the affected community or directly from COVID-19 patients. For these reasons, SARS-CoV-2 might be transmitted via the fecal-oral route. Although there is no reported case of fecal-oral transmission of COVID-19, studies show that it is possible mainly in areas with poor wastewater management.[18,19,35] The pandemic hotspots were identified in crowded areas (i.e., large population density and informal settlements), mainly with limited waste management and sanitation services like in Cairo and Mumbai.[3] It is important to point out that the majority of the studies about detecting SARS-CoV-2 in wastewater were conducted in developed countries.[19]

Viral RNA was also detected in Monterrey's surface water and groundwater samples during a SARS-CoV-2 peak phase. Leaked sewage system or contaminated surface water by sewage might be the possible routes that led to the groundwater contamination.[38] Fig. 2 summarizes the possible sources of surface water contamination with SARS-CoV-2.

Several factors determine the degree to which the coronavirus remains infectious in wastewater, including how long it stays in the water, treatment type, and environmental conditions. According to WHO, the human coronaviruses can live for only 2 days in the hospital wastewater (at approximately 20°C) or dechlorinated water.[15] Another study ensured that SARS-CoV-2 could survive in untreated wastewater for a few hours to days, posing public health risks through aerosolized wastewater or water-borne transmission.[18]

An increase in the water demand means consumption of more water with soap or disinfectants, which in return decreases the quality and increases the quantity of wastewater. Thus it requires additional costs to increase capacities for the drainage structures and treatment facilities to safely collect

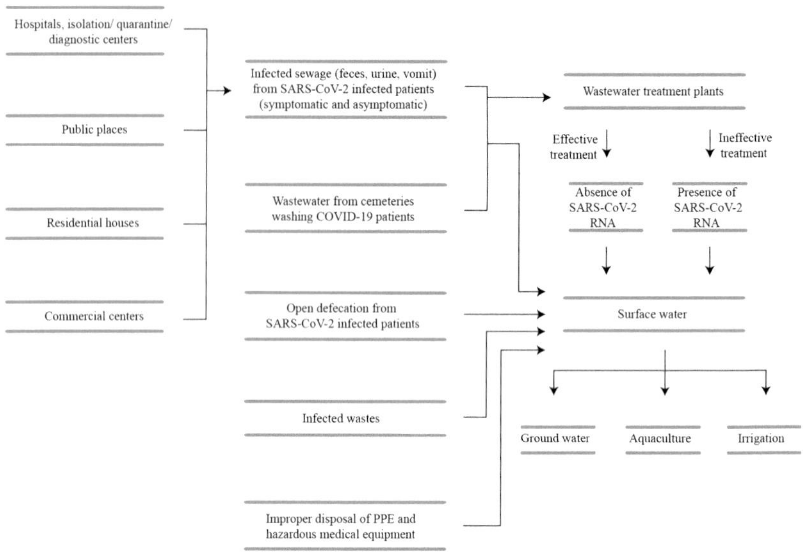

Fig. 2 Possible sources of surface water contamination with SARS-CoV-2.[13,18,19,22,25,29,35,36,38,39]

and treat the large quantity of wastewater before being discharged and reused.[17,22] This is challenging in areas with limited wastewater treatment, thus increasing the risk of polluting the surface water that might permeate into the groundwater. The same applies to hazardous medical equipment that is not safely disposed of. Therefore the collected wastewater from areas having COVID-19 patients should be appropriately treated rather than only filtered and discharged into the environment.[22]

One of the studies concluded that using UV for wastewater disinfection is more effective than chlorine. Also, for effective chlorine disinfection, the wastewater treatment plant (WWTP) operators should ensure that the free residual chlorine complies with the international standards at specific conditions.[18]

Available evidence ensures that wastewater monitoring for the virus can help determine the total number of COVID-19 symptomatic and asymptomatic cases in the community.[40] Studies showed a relation between SARS-CoV-2 RNA concentrations in wastewater and the number of reported COVID-19 cases. Also, concentrations of SARS-CoV-2 RNA in wastewater can give information about the COVID-19 cases few days (4 to 7 days) ahead of the results of the COVID-19 clinically confirmed cases. Environmental surveillance for SARS-CoV-2 was used in several developed countries.[37] Effective surveillance can be applied when populations are connected to WWTPs to identify the infection hotspots.[40] However, this is very challenging where populations are not connected to sewers; rather, they use septic systems, pit toilets,[19,37] or open drains, which is the case in many developing countries.[40] In this situation, testing surface water for sewage contamination is one of the options. Environmental surveillance for SARS-CoV-2 can be used for early warning, detection in areas with limited clinical surveillance capacities and limited access to health facilities, and detection of SARS-CoV-2 from animal sources.[37] Wastewater-based epidemiology (WBE) is an effective surveillance tool for monitoring the virus circulation in the community.[18] It has been applied in several countries and used as an early warning since it can identify the extent of virus spread in the community. The WBE functions by collecting wastewater samples from WWTPs and detecting the presence of viral RNA in order to determine whether the infection rate is increasing or decreasing.[15] Nevertheless, cost-benefit analysis for investing in environmental surveillance versus strengthening WASH and essential surveillance activities should be done, especially in developing countries.[37]

During the pandemic, using treated or untreated wastewater in irrigation will pose public health threat[18] and increase the possibility of foodborne transmission of SARS-CoV-2.[41] To provide reliable data about SARS-CoV-2 transmission, the physical and chemical properties of the wastewater should be studied. Moreover, operation and maintenance standards in WWTPs should be met to prevent the wastewater from contributing to disease transmission.[18] While the wastewater is transported to the WWTP, airborne transmission of SARS-CoV-2 might occur.[19] Aerosolization might occur not only in WWTPs but also in flushing at homes.[40]

WHO recommends sanitation workers to follow standard operating procedures at the workplace that include wearing PPEs, following COVID-19 general mitigation measures, minimizing spills, getting the vaccines for diseases related to sanitation, and self-monitoring for infectious disease symptoms. These people, as well as those promoting hygiene in the community, should be allowed to resume their work during the lockdown and movement restrictions since they are providing extremely important services.[13]

Indeed, wastewater has destroying effects on human health, economy, and ecosystem.[4] Since the excreta from SARS-CoV-2 infected patients might threaten the environment and the public, wastewater should be treated in well-managed WWTPs. Decrease in exposure risk and pathogen reduction can be only be guaranteed by effective treatment and disinfection of wastewater. Water safety plans should be in place to ensure the safety of the water. Centralized water treatment can decrease the SARS-CoV-2 concentration. In areas lacking centralized water treatment and not connected to safe water pipes, other measures can be applied to destroy the viruses, such as boiling, using ultrafiltration or nanomembrane filters, solar or UV irradiation, and chlorine products with appropriate dose.[13]

4. Sustainable development goal 6 in the context of COVID-19 pandemic

The impact of COVID-19 on sustainable development goal (SDG) 6 (clean water and sanitation) and the possibility of achieving this goal by 2030 need to be studied in depth.[15] From the positive side, governments are now more than ever aware of the importance of providing clean water for all, and they are trying their best to do so based on the recommendations for combatting the COVID-19 pandemic. Furthermore, this has driven many international organizations to assist less developed countries in increasing water access.[15] The global water demand, before the pandemic, was mainly for the agricultural sector (70%) and other sectors like domestic use and industries (30%). However, the pandemic shifted the water demand and supply patterns for hygiene and protecting human health. Therefore there might be a higher possibility for achieving the SDGs.[15] Also, water directly affects the cities' resilience and sustainability[42] and SDG 11 (sustainable cities and communities) focuses on the importance of having resilient and sustainable cities and human settlements.[43]

On the other side, the Sustainable Development Goals Report 2020 mentions that achieving SDGs is challenging in the COVID-19 pandemic.[44] Knowing that a quarter of the people worldwide do not have a reliable water supply shows that SDG 6 is far from being achieved by 2030.[3] COVID-19 pandemic led to an economic crisis and high rates of unemployment that will affect SDG 1 (no poverty), SDG 2 (Zero Hunger), and SDG 3 (public health) that will definitely affect governments' actions regarding SDG 6.[15] The pandemic will slow down the progress in this goal since water utilities are facing losses in revenues which hinder their ability to do further capital investments. Lower investments in the water sector are expected globally.[3] In some countries, there is a 61% funding gap that hinders them from achieving SDG 6.[45]

In 2021 a report assessing the progress in the Asia-Pacific region regarding SDGs showed that it is far from achieving any of the SDG targets by 2030. The progress regarding Goal 6—clean water and sanitation—is still slow. Water stress is the main obstacle in this region hindering from achieving several targets.[46] In addition, there is a lack of data that can help track the progress in SDG 6 in the European Union.[47]

While meeting the water demands, it is also vital to secure the irrigation. The indirect effect of COVID-19 that countries should be aware of is food insecurity. Due to lockdown and physical distancing protocols, many workers will not be able to participate in harvesting, which might, in the worst scenario, contribute to famine. In this way, SDG 2 will be severely impacted. Thus authorities should ensure the stability of the food system and prevent the disruption of the agricultural supply chain.[42]

COVID-19 deepened the already existing inequalities. SDG 12 (responsible consumption and production) will not be achieved if the human right to water management was not respected and applied. COVID-19 and climate change are threat multipliers that affect the water sector for the dream of having a sustainable world.[42] Good water management is the basis for climate change adaptation and consequently achieving SDG 13 (climate action).[48]

Water is critical for ecosystems, health, eradicating poverty, food security, peace and human rights, and education.[44] Thus responding to the pandemic should pave the way toward the 2030 Agenda.[46] The pandemic is a great chance to build forward better by changing the threats into opportunities to achieve SDG 6 and other SDGs by 2030.[49]

5. Lessons learned regarding water and COVID-19

Raising awareness about human health and the environment is the pillar to have a sustainable environment.[31] To prevent and combat future outbreaks, water security has to be strengthened globally. Water security is not only critical for public health but also for food security, economic growth, protecting livelihoods, and increasing resilience to climate change.[20] Water governance, policy-making, and financial investments should be strengthened to increase water sector resilience amid the COVID-19 pandemic, climate change, and freshwater scarcity. No matter what interventions are implemented, COVID-19 recovery will only be shortened if access to clean water and sanitation increases.[8] The SDG 6 Global Acceleration Framework, coordinated by UN-Water, considers that actions toward achieving SDG 6 are driven by optimizing finance, data and information (to measure progress and do more research), developing capacities (more skilled staff), innovation (use of new technologies), and governance (collaboration and cooperation between countries and different sectors).[50]

Improving and strengthening the water quality monitoring system at the national level by conducting frequent water sampling and having satellite- and ground-based water quality monitoring is needed. These systems are the base for accurate data and conducting detailed analysis about the anthropogenic effects on water quality. The lockdown is considered an opportunity to effectively manage the water resources by monitoring their quality as well as water quantity and biodiversity. The resilience of municipalities in dealing with fluctuating water demands should be assessed. Evaluating the water consumption patterns is indispensable to maintain the water utilities, manage the water requirements, and create policies. To deal with future pandemics, suitable wastewater treatment and surveillance technologies (such as artificial intelligence and the Internet of Things) should be in place to collect comprehensive data, trace the viruses, and determine their threat. Also, there is a need to improve or build infrastructure that connects rural and urban places to WWTPs, upgrade the treatment methods, and use computing techniques for monitoring. It is important to determine the consequences of using water for irrigation and crop production. There is a need to quantify water demand in all sectors, improve safe water supply for all, and strengthen the government capacities to deal with unprecedented events.[15] To manage outbreaks more effectively, having small decentralized WWTPs could be a good option.[40] Moreover, service providers should be able to supply all the chemicals needed to test and treat the water and wastewater to ensure that people are receiving water of high quality.[22] Reusing safely treated wastewater is one of the solutions to cope with water scarcity.[49]

Water and sanitation services should be available for all, including those who cannot afford to pay the water bills. Cutting off the water because of economic problems should be prohibited, and governments and utility operators should reconnect services and set measures such as waiving tariffs to help people.[22] WHO considers that cutting off the water because of inability to pay the bills is not acceptable, and governments should take immediate actions to ensure all have access to water (for example, use tanker trucks or extend pipes for water supplies).[13] To ensure continuity of services, paying the water bills online and remote technologies should be introduced (since sometimes mobility restrictions delayed collecting bills).[22]

Increasing awareness of water conservation by changing behavior is the basis for sustainable actions. Decreasing water flow in the taps, efficiently using water in the agriculture sector,[22] replacing taps with sensor taps, and changing people's behavior to turn the tap off while handwashing are effective options to mitigate water overuse.[26]

Responding to water changes during the pandemic requires the use of new technologies, demand forecasting systems, and remote monitoring and leak detection systems.[24] Having automated systems that can be remotely controlled will facilitate the operations and lead to efficient response if an unprecedented event occurs. Automated and digitalized industries were able to easily cope with the pandemic's changes, such as social distancing and restrictions.[3] Water utilities should enhance their resilience in order to continue providing water and wastewater services during unexpected events (infrastructure failure, health threats, and extreme climate conditions). Therefore more funding is needed by governments and international organizations to bolster water utility resilience.[24]

WASH recommendations can also be applied during the pandemic, mainly hand hygiene; safely managing excreta, dead bodies, medical wastes (from COVID-19 patients); frequently cleaning the environment, and applying disinfection practices. Untreated wastewater, including wastewater from healthcare facilities, should not be discharged to be used for producing food and aquaculture. In healthcare facilities, excreta must be considered a biohazard and should be treated based on that.[13] The procedures of disaster and emergency prevention can be utilized to maintain access to good water quality. Public health engineering professionals and other responders play a vital role in managing the impact of the environment on public health.[4]

According to WHO, handwashing facilities should be present everywhere, such as in front of public buildings, toilets, and transport stations, to ensure access for all. These facilities should be functioning and have soaps, not necessarily the antibacterial one since the normal soap is enough to inactivate the enveloped viruses.[13]

Countries should cooperate with one another to share the lessons learned and best practices for safely and sustainably managing the water sector.[22] COVID-19 is an opportunity for countries to cooperate and support one another for shared water resources and other basic water needs. For example, six countries (over 60 million people) benefit from the Mekong River. Regional water-sharing governance and solidarity are the keys to ensure that no one will be affected and all have access to rivers passing in different countries, mainly in conflict-affected areas.[42] It is critical to prohibit destroying or interrupting water services in conflict-affected areas.[22]

It is the time to ensure good governance, invest in the water sector, build capacities, address the most vulnerable groups, and focus more on research. If we did not increase the resiliency in water and sanitation, we would always be vulnerable to another pandemic.[49]

6. Limitations

Although the pandemic, directly and indirectly, affected the water and wastewater sectors, the extent of the impact is still unclear. There are limited data and monitoring systems to track the water quality in all rivers during lockdowns and movement restrictions.[15] Although many countries already have policies and plans for hygiene, implementing them is hindered due to limited financial and human resources.[52] Available data about hygiene is few and often with poor quality. There is not a standardized definition for hygiene, which is challenging when it comes to reporting or comparing data about hygiene. WHO is willing to develop the hygiene definition. To improve public health, investing in infrastructure should be considered when speaking about hygiene rather than just focusing on handwashing with soap and changing behavior.[51]

7. Conclusion

Water has a pivotal role in combatting COVID-19 and achieving sustainable development. COVID-19 dramatically affected the water sector, and the improper management of water will lead to the spread of this disease. This vicious cycle will only stop if strict measures were set. Investing in the water sector and ensuring all have access to safe water and sanitation is no longer an option; rather, it is fundamental for survival. Fig. 3 summarizes the challenges in finance, research, and water and sanitation services that were highlighted during the pandemic and should be tackled in the future to end up with resilient communities.

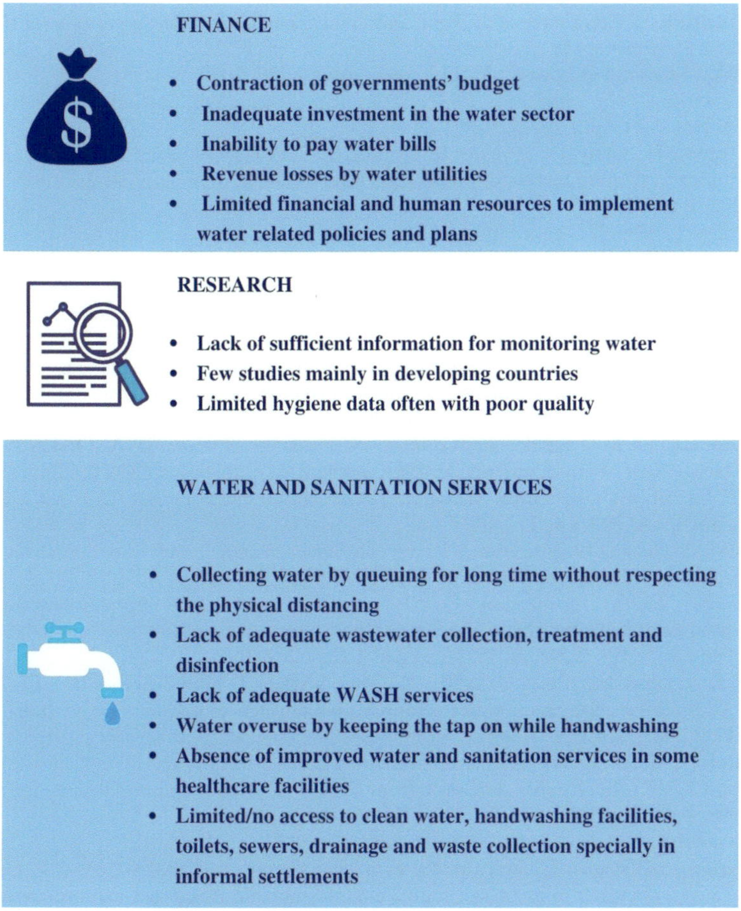
FINANCE
Contraction of governments' budget
Inadequate investment in the water sector
Inability to pay water bills
Revenue losses by water utilities
Limited financial and human resources to implement water related policies and plans
RESEARCH
Lack of sufficient information for monitoring water
Few studies mainly in developing countries
Limited hygiene data often with poor quality
WATER AND SANITATION SERVICES
Collecting water by queuing for long time without respecting the physical distancing
Lack of adequate wastewater collection, treatment and disinfection
Lack of adequate WASH services
Water overuse by keeping the tap on while handwashing
Absence of improved water and sanitation services in some healthcare facilities
Limited/no access to clean water, handwashing facilities, toilets, sewers, drainage and waste collection specially in informal settlements

Fig. 3 Challenges highlighted during COVID-19 pandemic.[3,7,8,15,19-22,24,26,49,51]

References

1. Davey K, Shaw R. *A hierarchy of water requirements based on Maslows hierarchy of needs*; 2019 https://repository.lboro.ac.uk/articles/figure/A_hierarchy_of_water_requirements_based_on_Maslows_hierarchy_of_needs/8059565/1. [Accessed 28 April 2021].
2. Sphere Association. *The sphere handbook: humanitarian charter and minimum standards in humanitarian response*. 4th ed. Geneva, Switzerland: Practical Action Publishing; 2018.
3. International Finance Corporation. *The impact of COVID-19 on the water and sanitation sector*. IFC; 2020. https://www.ifc.org/wps/wcm/connect/126b1a18-23d9-46f3-beb7-047c20885bf6/The+Impact+of+COVID_Water%26Sanitation_final_web.pdf?MOD=AJPERES&CVID=ncaG-hA.
4. Khorram-Manesh A, Goniewicz K, Burkle FM. Unrecognized risks and challenges of water as a major focus of COVID-19 spread. *J Glob Health* 2021;**11**:03016. https://doi.org/10.7189/jogh.11.03016.

5. International Committee of the Red Cross. *Health emergencies in large populations (H.E.L.P.): public health course in the management of the humanitarian aid.* ICRC; 2001. Geneva, Switzerland.
6. World Economic Forum. *The global risks report 2020*; 2020.
7. Water.org. *The water crisis 2021*; 2021 https://water.org/our-impact/water-crisis/. [Accessed 29 April 2021].
8. Antwi SH, Getty D, Linnane S, Rolston A. COVID-19 water sector responses in Europe: a scoping review of preliminary governmental interventions. *Sci Total Environ* 2020;143068.
9. Yates T, Allen J, Leandre Joseph M, Lantagne D. *WASH interventions in disease outbreak response.* Oxfam; 2017.
10. Wisner B, Adams J, World Health Organization. *Environmental health in emergencies and disasters : a practical guide / edited by B. Wisner, J. Adams.* WHO; 2002. https://apps.who.int/iris/handle/10665/42561.
11. Freeman MC, Stocks ME, Cumming O, et al. Systematic review: hygiene and health: systematic review of handwashing practices worldwide and update of health effects. *Tropical Med Int Health* 2014;**19**(8):906–16.
12. Mousazadeh M, Naghdali Z, Rahimian N, Hashemi M, Paital B, Al-Qodah Z, et al. Management of environmental health to prevent an outbreak of COVID-19: a review. In: *Environmental and Health Management of Novel Coronavirus Disease (COVID-19).* Academic Press; 2021. p. 235–67.
13. World Health Organization. *Water, sanitation, hygiene, and waste management for SARS-CoV-2, the virus that causes COVID-19*; July 29, 2020.
14. World Health Organization. *WASH and COVID-19*; 2020 https://www.who.int/teams/environment-climate-change-and-health/water-sanitation-and-health/burden-of-disease/wash-and-covid19. [Accessed 1 May 2021].
15. Balamurugan M, Kasiviswanathan K, Ilampooranan I, Soundharajan B. COVID-19 lockdown disruptions on water resources, wastewater and agriculture in India. *Front Water* 2021;**3**:24.
16. Stoler J, Miller JD, Brewis A, et al. Household water insecurity will complicate the ongoing COVID-19 response: evidence from 29 sites in 23 low-and middle-income countries. *Int J Hyg Environ Health* 2021;**234**:113715.
17. Sivakumar B. *COVID-19 and water.* Springer; 2020.
18. Nasseri S, Yavarian J, Baghani AN, et al. The presence of SARS-CoV-2 in raw and treated wastewater in 3 cities of Iran: Tehran, Qom and Anzali during coronavirus disease 2019 (COVID-19) outbreak. *J Environ Health Sci Eng* 2021;1–12.
19. Pandey D, Verma S, Verma P, et al. SARS-CoV-2 in wastewater: challenges for developing countries. *Int J Hyg Environ Health* 2020;113634.
20. Cooper R. *Water security beyond Covid-19.* Lancang-Mekong Water Resources Cooperation; 2020.
21. Silva RR, Ribeiro CJ, Moura TR, Santos MB, Santos AD, Tavares DS, et al. Basic sanitation: a new indicator for the spread of COVID-19? *Trans R Soc Trop Med Hyg* 2021;**115**:832–40.
22. UN ESCWA. *The impact of COVID-19 on the water-scarce Arab region*; 2020.
23. World Bank. *Making the most of scarcity: accountability for better water management in the Middle East and North Africa.* The World Bank; 2007.
24. Cooley H, Gleick PH, Abraham S, Cai W. *Water and the COVID-19 pandemic: impacts on municipal water demand.* Pacific Institute; 2020.
25. Ji B, Zhao Y, Wei T, Kang P. Water science under the global epidemic of COVID-19: bibliometric tracking on COVID-19 publication and further research needs. *J Environ Chem Eng* 2021;105357.

26. Sayeed A, Rahman MH, Bundschuh J, et al. Handwashing with soap: a concern for overuse of water amidst the COVID-19 pandemic in Bangladesh. *Groundw Sustain Dev* 2021;**13**:100561.
27. Kalbusch A, Henning E, Brikalski MP, de Luca FV, Konrath AC. Impact of coronavirus (COVID-19) spread-prevention actions on urban water consumption. *Resour Conserv Recycl* 2020;**163**:105098.
28. Praveena SM, Aris AZ. The impacts of COVID-19 on the environmental sustainability: a perspective from the Southeast Asian region. *Environ Sci Pollut Res* 2021;1–8.
29. Gude VG, Muire PJ. Preparing for outbreaks—implications for resilient water utility operations and services. *Sustain Cities Soc* 2021;**64**:102558.
30. Dutta V, Dubey D, Kumar S. Cleaning the river ganga: impact of lockdown on water quality and future implications on river rejuvenation strategies. *Sci Total Environ* 2020;**743**:140756.
31. Chakraborty B, Roy S, Bera A, et al. Eco-restoration of river water quality during COVID-19 lockdown in the industrial belt of eastern India. *Environ Sci Pollut Res* 2021;1–15.
32. Roidt M, Chini CM, Stillwell AS, Cominola A. Unlocking the impacts of COVID-19 lockdowns: changes in thermal electricity generation water footprint and virtual water trade in Europe. *Environ Sci Technol Lett* 2020;**7**(9):683–9.
33. Shimabuku M, Diringer S, Feinstein L, et al. *Water and the COVID-19 pandemic: ensuring access to water as shutoff moratoriums lift*; 2020 https://pacinst.org/publication/ensuring-access-as-moratoriums-lift/. [Accessed 10 May 2021].
34. Villapol S. Gastrointestinal symptoms associated with COVID-19: impact on the gut microbiome. *Transl Res* 2020;**226**:57–69.
35. Langone M, Petta L, Cellamare C, et al. SARS-CoV-2 in water services: presence and impacts. *Environ Pollut* 2020;115806.
36. Buonerba A, Corpuz MVA, Ballesteros F, et al. Coronavirus in water media: analysis, fate, disinfection and epidemiological applications. *J Hazard Mater* 2021;125580.
37. World Health Organization. *Status of environmental surveillance for SARS-CoV-2 virus*. World Health Organization; August 5, 2020.
38. Mahlknecht J, Alonso-Padilla D, Ramos E, Reyes LM, Álvarez MM. The presence of SARS-CoV-2 RNA in different freshwater environments in urban settings determined by RT-qPCR: implications for water safety. *Sci Total Environ* 2021;147183.
39. Iranian Association for Popularization of Sciences, UNESCO. *International workshop on COVID-19 and water consumption pattern*; 2020.
40. Siddique A, Shahzad A, Lawler J, et al. Unprecedented environmental and energy impacts and challenges of COVID-19 pandemic. *Environ Res* 2021;**193**:110443.
41. Aboubakr HA, Sharafeldin TA, Goyal SM. Stability of SARS-CoV-2 and other coronaviruses in the environment and on common touch surfaces and the influence of climatic conditions: a review. *Transbound Emerg Dis* 2021;**68**(2):296–312.
42. United Nations. Ensure availability and sustainable management of water and sanitation for all. https://sdgs.un.org/goals/goal6 (accessed 5 May 2021).
43. United Nations. *The 17 goals*; 2021 https://sdgs.un.org/goals. [Accessed 5 May 2021].
44. United Nations. *The sustainable development goals report 2020*; 2020.
45. United Nations. *Ensure availability and sustainable management of water and sanitation for all*; 2020 https://sdgs.un.org/goals/goal6. [Accessed 5 May 2021].
46. United Nations. *Asia and the Pacific SDG progress report 2021*; 2021.
47. European Union. *Sustainable development in the European Union overview of progress towards the SDGs in an EU context*; 2020.
48. UN Water. *Climate change adaptation is mainly about water.* United Nations; 2022.

49. UN Water. *UN-Water joint statement: 31st special session of the general assembly in response to the COVID-19 pandemic*; 2020 https://www.unwater.org/un-water-joint-statement-31st-special-session-of-the-general-assembly-in-response-to-the-covid-19-pandemic/. [Accessed 10 May 2021].
50. UN Water. *SDG 6 global acceleration framework—action space*; 2022 https://www.unwater.org/sdg6-action-space/. [Accessed 10 May 2021].
51. World Health Organization, UN-Water. *Hygiene UN-water GLAAS findings on national policies, plans, targets and finance*. World Health Organization; 2020.
52. Hamid MZBSA, Karri RR. Overview of preventive measures and good governance policies to mitigate the COVID-19 outbreak curve in Brunei. In: *COVID-19: systemic risk and resilience*. Cham: Springer; 2021. p. 115–40.

CHAPTER THREE

Effect of COVID-19 on future education: Reimagining tomorrow's lessons

Lim Suzylily[a] and Syazana Abdullah Lim[b]
[a]General Studies Division, Politeknik Brunei, Bandar Seri Begawan, Brunei Darussalam
[b]Food Science and Technology, School of Applied Sciences and Mathematics, Universiti Teknologi Brunei, Mukim Gadong A, Brunei Darussalam

1. Introduction

The United Nations Educational, Scientific, and Cultural Organisation (UNESCO) is a dedicated agency for the United Nations (UN) to contribute peace, encourage sustainable developments, and put an end to poverty. Formed in 1946 and based in France, the organization currently has 193 members and 11 Associate Members. In September 2015, 2030 Agenda for Sustainable Development that comprises of 17 goals was introduced in New York, United States of America. The goals ranging from eradicating extreme poverty to fighting climate change were developed and monitored closely by UNESCO to achieve better lives and future for all. Each of these goals consists of several targets with the aim of monitoring progresses toward the goal. In addition, the 2030 Agenda for Sustainable Development and its Sustainable Development Goals (SDGs) provides a theme of Leave No One Behind (LNOB) to include individuals of all genders and abilities. The promise epitomizes the commitments of UN members to include all in terms of eradicating poverty, putting discrimination and exclusion to an end, and reducing the inequalities and vulnerabilities.

SDG framework is a guide to achieving a sustainable future in areas of poverty, health, education, forests, oceans, climate change, and cities. The success of the SDGs will depend on the benchmark of each goal and every tier of government will assess the progress of each goal. Achieving the targets of the goals is a collaborative effort; government and non-government organizations are involved in working toward the targets. The examples of agencies are UNICEF (also known as the United Nations International Children's Emergency Fund) and accountable for running

COVID-19 and the Sustainable Development Goals
https://doi.org/10.1016/B978-0-323-91307-2.00009-2

humanitarian and developmental assistance to children worldwide and the Food and Agriculture Organization of the UN (FAO) and the World Bank have come together to fight against hunger and poverty.

Specifically, SDG4 is a universal education goal with a vision of ensuring inclusive and unbiased education and to encourage lifelong learning, which is the primary focus of this chapter. SDG4's targets emphasize mainly on quality education and gender equalities, and they are extended to an entire stage of formal education: from preprimary, primary, secondary technical and vocational, as well as higher education. The goal has seven targets with three means of implementation with the vision to be attained by 2030. All UN SDG goals are interconnected with education being the central subject that connects to other goals. For SDG4, four SDGs were identified to be closely impacted by the progress of SDG4.[1] Those goals are SDG10 (Reduced inequalities), SDG9 (Industry, innovation, and infrastructure), SDG13 (Climate action), and SDG5 (Gender equality). To monitor the progress of SDG4, indicators have been established, as depicted in Fig. 1, although there have been arguments on how these indicators are open to interpretations. Fig. 1 also shows the common theme found in all SGD4's targets which are equality, free access, and growth.

While Unterhalter[2] criticizes the narrow indicator of measuring equity in the SDG4's targets that does not serve the Leave No One Behind theme, SDG4's vision nonetheless strongly reaffirms that all individuals have the right to access knowledge. The power of having the right and quality education is undeniable as it improves one's socioeconomic status particularly in escaping poverty. UN reported that although substantial progress on school enrolment's rate can be observed over the past 10 years, statistics in 2018 demonstrated that around 260 million children were still not in school. Additional concern is the proportion of children (more than 50% of world's population) still lacking in the literacy and numeracy competence.[3] Albeit disturbing statistics, the achievements of SGD4 seem to be heading in the right direction.

In December 2019, COVID-19, a highly infectious disease, was first reported in China, which quickly spread around the world. Soon after, World Health Organisation (WHO) declared the virus COVID-19 as a pandemic on 11th of March 2020. It is now known that this disease can be transmitted from person to person mainly via droplets of saliva or nasal discharge when people infected with COVID-19—mostly do not display any symptoms—sneezes, coughs, or exhales droplets. Due to the novel strain of coronavirus, a huge portion of the world's population is not immune

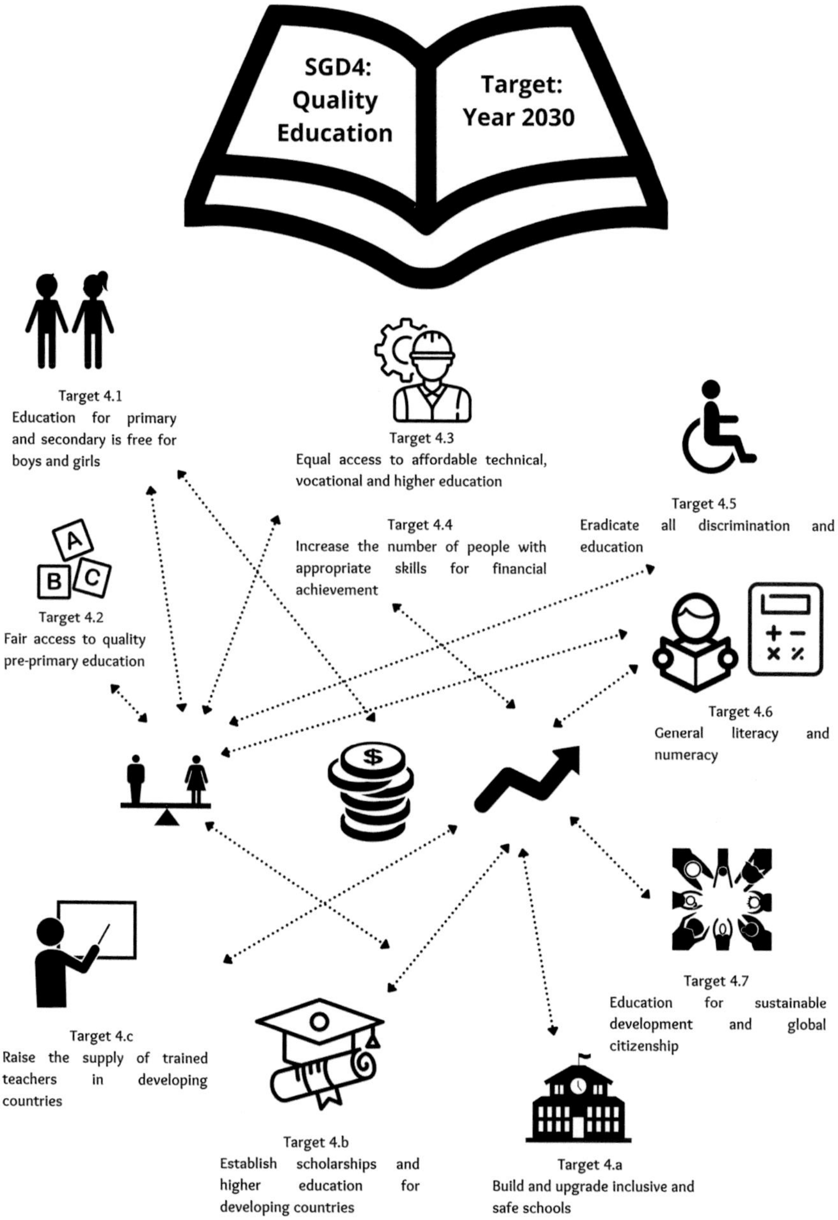

Fig. 1 Specific targets of SDG4.

to COVID-19 and can be easily infected. The large-scale community transmission of the virus forces the community to practice social distancing, isolation, enforce travel bans, and lockdowns which consequently instills social insecurity. As a result, the emergence of COVID-19 has threatened the progression of the SDG both directly and indirectly. Years of hard work in accomplishing the goals have been stalled or regressed. UNESCO sheds a negative light on COVID-19 where economies are weakening, triggering agonized society and turning people's lives in an unexpected way. With the presence of COVID-19, the future targets to be achievable in less than 10 years' time seem bleak, and time is running out. The aftermath of COVID-19 is obscure and difficult to measure and thus, countless research has been conducted on the issue of COVID-19 in various fields in the hope of reporting on the latest trend and phenomenon as a lesson learned for the future. Due to the fluctuating number of cases in different countries, government ministries are responding to actions varies in a bid to keep the countries going. Multiple sectors have been hit hard by the pandemic. Efforts have been taken by various governments and private agencies to reduce the burden caused by the COVID-19 pandemic.[4] Fig. 2 illustrates the COVID-19 management in different sectors. Interested readers could refer other materials for in-depth information as COVID-19 management is beyond the scope of this chapter.

As of April 10, 2020, UNESCO reported that nearly 190 countries instructed schools and universities to close, impacting over 90% students worldwide. Fast forward a year later (the year 2021), schools in some countries are still shut down and some have begun to allow students to return to school with conditions and strict safety measures. A significant impact of this global health crisis is the alarming rate of students returning to schools after the crisis. As illustrated by the Ebola virus (2013–16) epidemic in Africa, five million students were driven out of school for as long as 9 months in the West African nations of Sierra Leone, Guinea, and Liberia.[5] The sad reality is that many never went back to schools. Due to this, it is hoped that history does not repeat, and the likelihood of school dropouts is minimized when schools are safe to be fully reopened.

This chapter will examine the ongoing practices in schools as an effort to continue learning and the aftermath of COVID-19 in academic practices. This chapter will be divided into two sections: (i) the ongoing practices in schools during the pandemic where current issues affecting the students are raised in this section and (ii) the possible trends in adopting the best

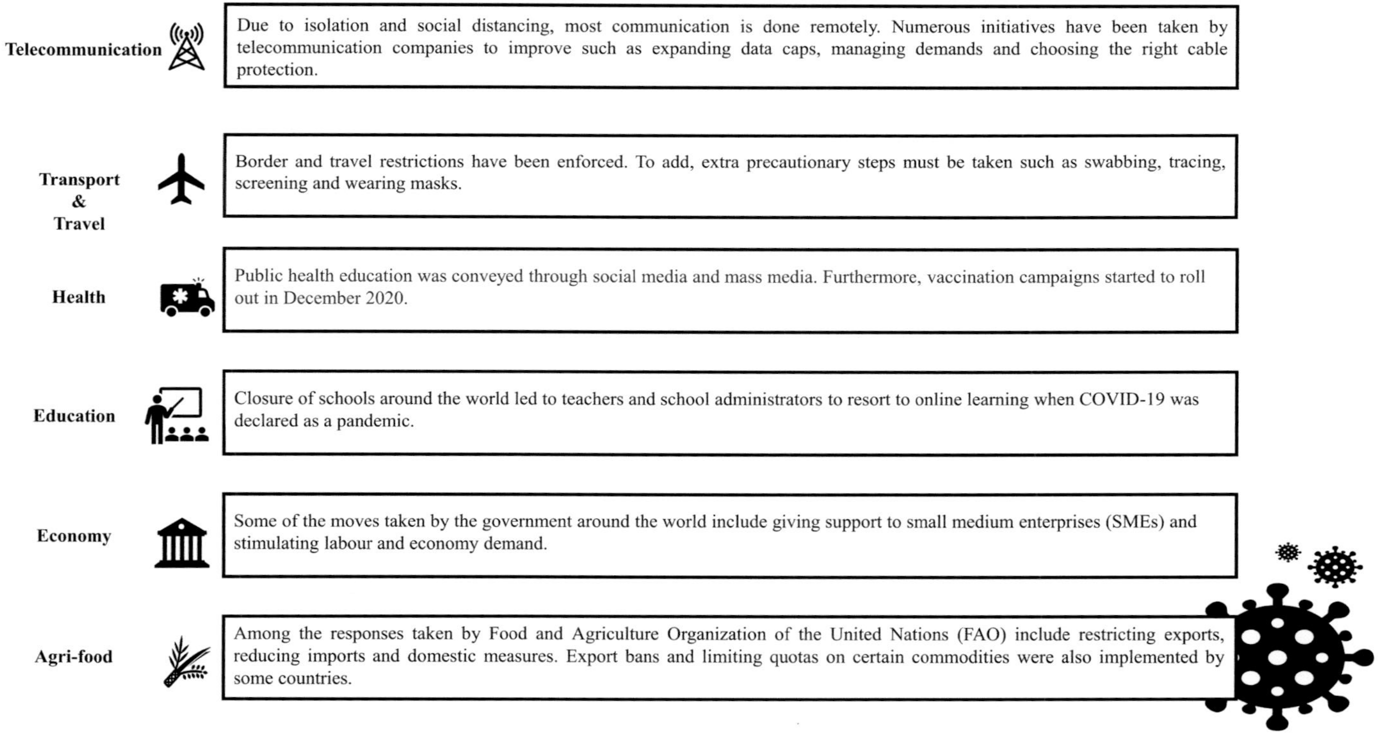
Telecommunication
Due to isolation and social distancing, most communication is done remotely. Numerous initiatives have been taken by telecommunication companies to improve such as expanding data caps, managing demands and choosing the right cable protection.
Transport & Travel
Border and travel restrictions have been enforced. To add, extra precautionary steps must be taken such as swabbing, tracing, screening and wearing masks.
Health
Public health education was conveyed through social media and mass media. Furthermore, vaccination campaigns started to roll out in December 2020.
Education
Closure of schools around the world led to teachers and school administrators to resort to online learning when COVID-19 was declared as a pandemic.
Economy
Some of the moves taken by the government around the world include giving support to small medium enterprises (SMEs) and stimulating labour and economy demand.
Agri-food
Among the responses taken by Food and Agriculture Organization of the United Nations (FAO) include restricting exports, reducing imports and domestic measures. Export bans and limiting quotas on certain commodities were also implemented by some countries.

Fig. 2 The COVID-19 management in different sectors.

practices in schools post-COVID-19. It is worthwhile to note that this chapter has been written from teachers' and students' perspectives.

2. Pre-COVID-19 vs now: The situation

Education is dynamic and every now and then, new strategies are being employed to boost students' learning. Strategies such as collaborative learning, inquiry-based learning, and differentiation including incorporation of technology have been proven to be effective and typically employed in traditional face-to-face classrooms prior to COVID-19. For instance, diversified teaching and learning strategies have been employed to enhance students' motivation and learning experience. In Quebec universities, lectures were often used to deliver lesson instructions and now, methods such as debates, group discussion, and role plays have become alternative methods.[6] The increasing popularity of incorporating technology in learning activities has also made such pedagogies to be carried out online. The move to digital classrooms has made web-based interactive learning possible. Moreover, online learning is widely accessible and easy, making it to be widely adopted and practiced.[7,8] In the case of Ghana, the implementation of online teaching and learning was stationary, despite the efforts made by the Government of Ghana to provide for laptops. Although hybrid learning is not a new concept in education, some students still perceive online learning to be a less effective method than the traditional face-to-face interactions due to lack of ICT skills, tools, and even, electrical supplies.[9]

2.1 COVID-19 and SDGs

Ironically, COVID-19 presents both challenges and opportunities in the education sector. The rise of COVID-19 cases in 2020 ultimately forces schools to continue lessons online as human contacts are to be made as limited as possible. As the situation rapidly worsens in the earlier stage of the outbreak and unbeknownst when the pandemic will end, the nation frantically searches for options to continue formal education. Teachers are forced outside their comfort zones, sending them into panic modes and now need to become active learners of technology leading to "panic-gogy." The term "panic-gogy" describes teachers being pressed to go online and consequently, resulting in them facilitating teaching and learning in an environment they are not familiar with.[10] With limited social and physical contact, schools globally have resorted to online platforms. In theory, online learning proves to be the most feasible alternative as various video conferencing platforms such as Zoom and Google Meet have come together to ensure that face-to-face interactions and access to education are not denied. However, factors such as access to internet, digital infrastructure, and economic inequality in most areas render it difficult to implement distant learning in most areas.[11] Fig. 3 shows a simple flowchart on the effect on students' learning if adequate technological infrastructure is not provided.

Infrastructures and services that are normally provided in schools have been greatly reduced and furthermore, digital divide proves to be an even greater challenge. Nonetheless, various free and open resources have been provided to continue learning away from schools permitting chat and collaborations across various devices such as desktops, mobile phones, laptops, and tablets through a convenient cloud system. Abundant resources have been listed out to support teachers, school administrators, students, and parents including[12]

1. Resources offered for psychological assistance (e.g., WHO mental health and psychological guidance).
2. Online learning management system (e.g., Century Teach, Google Classroom).
3. Systems available for simple mobile phones (e.g., Ustad Mobile).
4. Systems with robust offline functionality (e.g., Kolibri, Rumi).

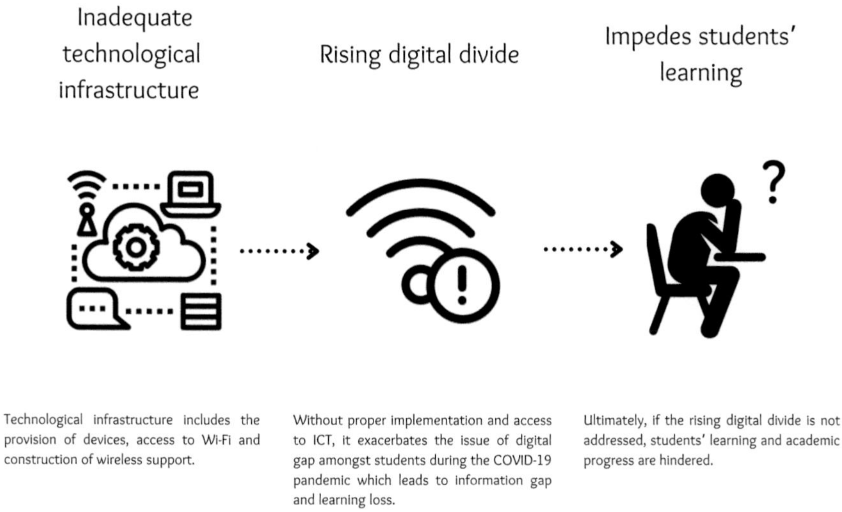

Fig. 3 A flowchart on the effect of a student's learning due to the inadequacy of technological infrastructure.

5. Massive open online course (MOOC) programs (e.g., Alison, Canvas Network).
6. Self-directed learning content (e.g., ABRA, British Council).
7. Mobile reading applications (e.g., African storybook).
8. Partnership platforms that provide for live-video communication (e.g., DingTalk and Lark).
9. Means to generate digital learning content for teachers (e.g., ThingLink, Trello).
10. A read-only repositories of remote learning solutions (e.g., Brookings).

2.2 Online learning—A new normal in schools and institutions

Online learning is growing each day with educators around the world trying to implement technology in students' learning. This is especially true in this era of modern technology where online learning has gained a massive popularity as a learning platform due to several benefits including improvement in quality of learning, enhancement of students' interest in learning, convenience in assessing online materials, and the opportunity for students to learn at their own pace.[13] The definition of online learning differs and terms such as "e-learning," "remote learning," "digital learning," and "distant learning" are often used interchangeably. For this chapter, we use the term *online learning* throughout with the definition: "Online learning is described by most authors as access to learning experiences via the use of some technology."[14] Online learning can either be asynchronistic (e.g., email, web board, web blogs) or synchronistic (e.g., audio-video conferencing, chat, and instant messaging), where communication between users takes place in a virtual setting.[15,16] The availability of online learning platforms and tools is abundant nowadays with their preferred choice of tools often dictated by teacher's creativities and objectives of lessons. Proper implementation of online learning tools, applications, and platforms helps to enhance learning outcomes through collaborative learning and engagement. For instance, the employment of social media as a synchronistic tool has allowed users to collaborate by sharing and exchanging user-generated content.[17] Social media applications are convenient and user-friendly, which are especially useful in the development of educational environment[18] since these applications encourage interactivity, a primary feature that appeals to majority of millennial students.[19] These positive outcomes ultimately attribute to satisfaction, perceived ease of use, and perceived usefulness of social media among students.[20] The perceptions of learners on the use of online learning have been researched and reported in many contexts. In one study by Peart and colleagues, the use of Twitter demonstrated less rating than the use of ShowMe, Panopto, and MCQ on Blackboard based on 210 undergraduates taking BSc Applied Sport and Exercise Science; BSc Sport, Exercise and Nutrition; and BSc Psychology with Sport Sciences.[21] Perhaps it is worth to note that the positive effects of COVID-19 on teaching and learning are still insufficiently researched as more emphasis is given on the struggles of learning online. Generally, it can be summarized that online learning can be a useful platform in our current learning environment, but suitable steps must be taken to ensure learning is successful and inclusive for all. The merit of online learning is undeniable but there are some drawbacks noted by the authors. Fig. 4 illustrates some of the benefits and drawbacks from the perspectives of teachers and students alike.

Since the transition from physical classrooms to online learning caused by COVID-19 outbreak was abrupt, this has created anxiety among students and parents alike and forcing them to adapt to the new normal. A year (at the time of writing) after the drastic decision of shutting down schools due to COVID-19 pandemic, some countries have now begun to ease their restrictions and slowly letting students to come back to schools. Full and

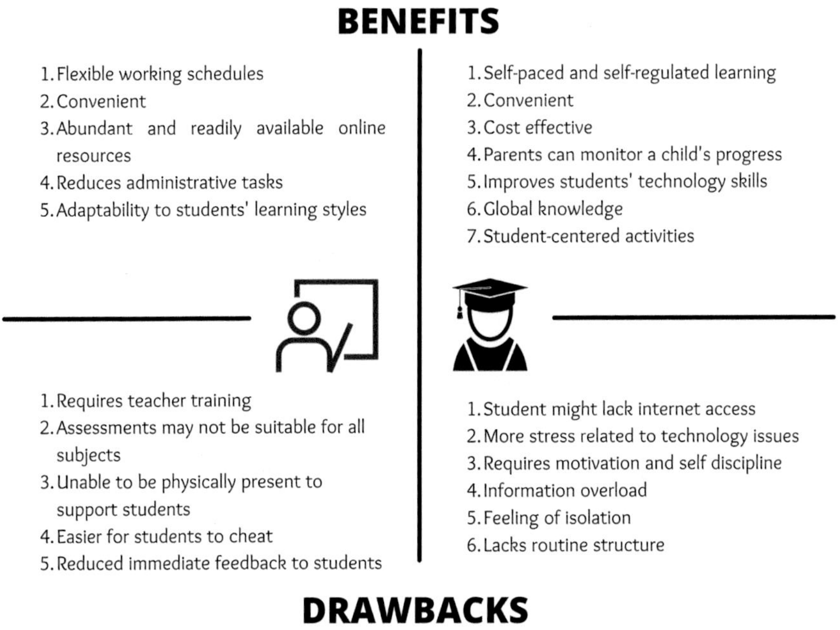

BENEFITS
1. Flexible working schedules
2. Convenient
3. Abundant and readily available online resources
4. Reduces administrative tasks
5. Adaptability to students' learning styles
1. Self-paced and self-regulated learning
2. Convenient
3. Cost effective
4. Parents can monitor a child's progress
5. Improves students' technology skills
6. Global knowledge
7. Student-centered activities
1. Requires teacher training
2. Assessments may not be suitable for all subjects
3. Unable to be physically present to support students
4. Easier for students to cheat
5. Reduced immediate feedback to students
1. Student might lack internet access
2. More stress related to technology issues
3. Requires motivation and self discipline
4. Information overload
5. Feeling of isolation
6. Lacks routine structure
DRAWBACKS

Fig. 4 The benefits and drawbacks of online learning.

partial closures vary, depending on the severity of the situation. UNESCO provides a constantly updated interactive map on its website to monitor school opening and closure around the world. Fig. 5 summarizes the status of school opening and closure based on the number of countries, between the year 2020 and 2021 at a 3-month interval.

Society is well aware that reopening of schools will not experience the same level of normalcy before its closure. On the surface, we see that schools are taking the necessary steps such as wearing face masks, reduction in class size, and a greater emphasis on hygiene, in trying to curb the spread of COVID-19. However, we must dig deeper to fully understand how the new normal has affected those in the education sector. Factors such as motivation and teachers' preparedness need to be considered in the implementations of the new normal.

School administrators and educators might have difference course of actions in tackling continuity of learning from home. Besides issues pertaining to gender, age differences also play a main role in education. Younger learners might need more support than adult learners. In higher education institutions, students are already familiar with the implementation of online learning where one of the examples is the widely practiced and use of Learning Management System (LMS) sites such as Canvas, Blackboard, Google Classroom, and Moodle that were designed to meet the learning needs of students in higher education.[22] However, one of the main challenges in the delivery of lessons online for educational institution, particularly in an unexpected crisis, is the preparedness of teachers and students as this will determine its success and the type of experience to students.[23] In a research study to determine areas of preparedness at higher institutions in e-learning by Parkes et al.,[23] they highlighted a low level of preparedness of students in relation to e-learning competencies, such as including writing, reading, and providing clear responses. On the other hand, these students demonstrated relatively high levels of preparedness in terms of technology and internet usage. A few studies[24,25] have also shown that the success of online learning is not merely due to individual factors but also considers social factors. Therefore understanding the factors that would affect user's acceptance of online learning will help to enhance students' learning experience.[24] For instance, a study conducted by Ngampornchai and Adams[26] in Thailand explored the acceptance and readiness of 98 undergraduates on e-learning. It was revealed that students in a higher academic year tend to accept online learning readily and showed a positive correlation between self-regulation and acceptance of e-learning. Additionally, the role of

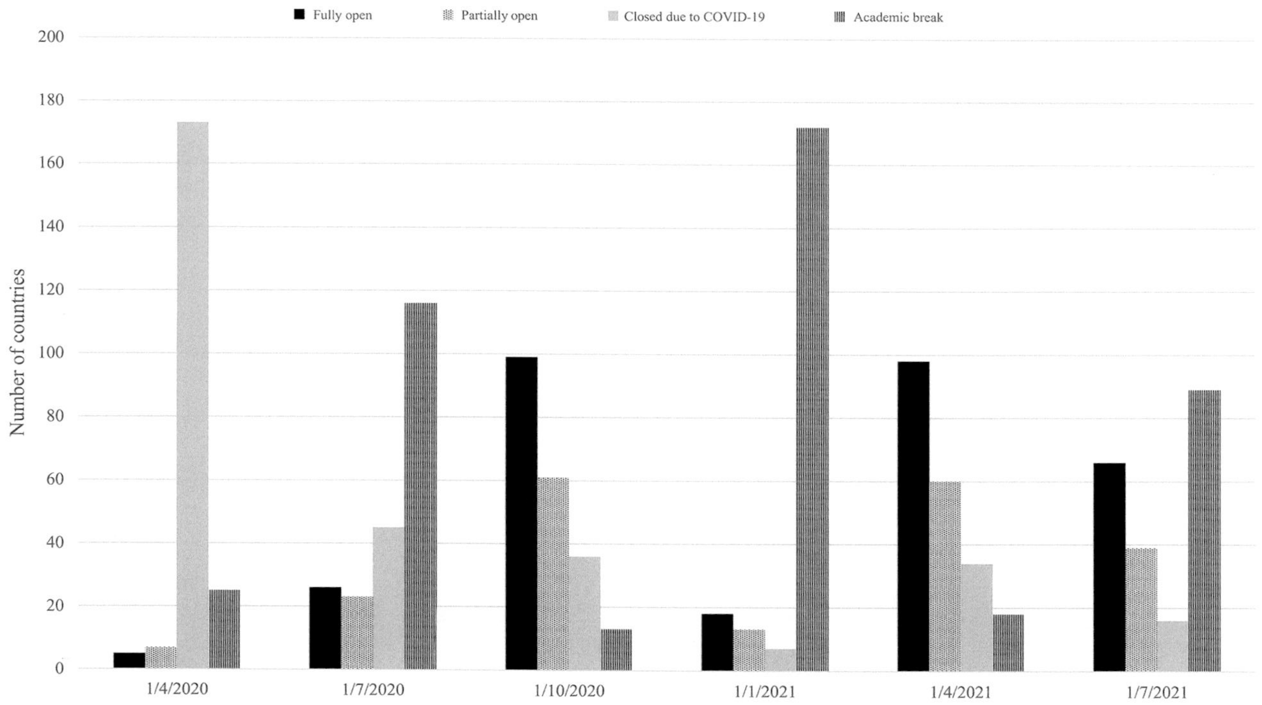

Fig. 5 The status of school opening and closure between the year 2020 and 2021 at a 3-month interval.

educators and instructors for online learning must switch from "knowledge-giver" to "facilitator" as to encourage collaboration and an ambient learning environment.[16] Instructors should be able to ascertain student learning from a distance and encourage communication to ensure a satisfying experience for students.

The world of education is vast. Alas, vocational education (VET) is one of the areas hit hard by COVID-19. In Target 4.3, it is aimed that by 2030, equal access for all women and men to affordable and quality technical, vocational, and tertiary education, including university, is targeted. A central pathway between education and work, vocational education prepares the students for the transition by providing practical and hands-on learning. To prepare the younger generations for the jobs of tomorrow, hands-on learning is highly highlighted albeit the issue surrounding this target now is not merely equal access but rather, the access itself. In most VET fields, the use of tools and machineries is necessary, and this proves to be particularly difficult in times when lessons are delivered online. The limitations caused by COVID-19 also set restrictions on the opportunities of apprenticeship. Organisation for Economic Co-operation and Development (OECD) has suggested some measures to be taken by vocational learning in the continuation of VET: flexible skills assessment and awarding of assessments, leveraging links between school- and work-based VET, wage support for apprenticeship, and allowing training breaks or extensions.[27] A similar concern was raised by students in the health sectors where clinical understanding and realization of bodily structures might be affected by the lack of practical training and thus, it must be ensured that the online materials match the application of clinical theories.[28] Adult learners are more self-regulated and self-sufficient, and it seems that despite obtaining higher grades, students have negative views on their learning, communication with other students, career preparation, as well as their social activities.[29] Perhaps the students need time to adjust to online learning. It is also worth mentioning that this might be a different case for younger learners where they need a greater support system. In Sri Lanka, it seems that the quality of TVET learning has been greatly reduced due to the use of low-tech online medium such as social media and emails.[27]

2.3 Digital divide

Prior COVID-19, it was reported by UNESCO that inclusive and equitable education was too slow, with over 200 million children being out of school in 2030.[30] Unfortunately, school closures further hinder the rate of inclusive and equitable education for children worldwide especially in socioeconomically diverse countries. Disadvantaged students are at a greater risk of being left out and further exacerbated by the pandemic as such students have significantly been affected by digital access. Inequalities in digital dimensions and ownerships of digital devices have been a concern in the implementation of online learning.[31,32] In 2017 it was reported by UNESCO that "six out of ten children and adolescents are not learning globally."[33] The statistic is worrying especially when access to education is much emphasized to achieve other goals in SDGs. The first target (Target 4.1) in SGD4 was to ensure quality primary/secondary education for all. Equality is not to be mistaken with equity. Adding complexity to this inequitable equation, teachers in low-income schools, less likely than their peers at high-income schools to have computers and internet in their classrooms, are thus less likely to develop comfort, competence, and confidence with the technology.[34] Gillett-Swan[35] also questions, "... whether providing flexibility in ways to access education (i.e., online rather than face-to-face) can provide students with as complete an education as if they were participating in a distraction-free environment." Furthermore, it is emphasized that in any learning context, unstable internet connectivity could stall online teaching and learning,[36] causing wasted time and frustration among students. One of the most important factors to be considered when contemplating the implementation of online learning is the ease and accessibility to the internet. The bridge of digital divide is widening as a result of COVID-19 but it is hopeful that the relevant agencies can come up with the best solutions to provide the right access to education.

From a sociological standpoint, several authors have pointed out that for teachers and learners, school is a secondary digital environment, after the home, where uses of digital technology are richer, more diverse, and spontaneous.[37,38] Across continents, gender differences in attitudes toward technology have also been reported: differences are significant among North American students but smaller differences are seen among Asian and European students.[39] In Greece, female youths have lower self-efficacy and are less positive toward technology than their male counterparts, citing more parental and peer support for the boys.[40] Across all developing areas, the main hindrance to digital inclusion is unaffordability. Several factors play into the role for not adopting technologies such as expensive devices, lack of access, and connectivity. These factors are common worldwide and it hits the women in the regions of Africa and Asia, in particular. It seems that women are less aware of mobile internet, and some believed that mobile internet is of no relevance to them in their lives. From here, it can be deduced that support from home as well as the social environment has an influence on the use of digital technologies.

A further distinction on digital divide is made between technology in the developed and developing countries. It has been observed that studies exploring teachers' access to digital technologies need more investigation and to compare those in developing countries such as Pakistan, the report is close to nonexistent. To add, more consideration in the existing literature is placed on physical access. In actuality, various dimensions can be investigated, from motivational use to skills of ICT.[41]

To summarize, digital divide is not merely referring to the access to technologies, but it also relates to the meaningful use of its access. Perhaps the provision of digital infrastructure is the first step of bridging the gap of digital divide. The next step is to cater to the needs of the users by providing the right trainings on using technologies.

3. Post-COVID-19: Lessons learnt

3.1 Redesigning the curriculum and pedagogy

A transformation in lesson design due to the pandemic has given an unprecedented prospect for educators and academic administrators to search for innovative approaches in teaching and learning in a short period of time. Although the transition was hurried, the limitations from online learning have provided a pathway to reexamine alternative learning instructions assuming that access to technologies is readily available to all students and teachers. The implementation of online learning quickly makes the school administrators and educators realize that delivering lessons face-to-face and trying to achieve the same objectives online are different. Learning materials should be redesigned to match lesson delivery: from high dependency of classroom-based teaching such as textbooks, support system, and roles of teaching staff to address the needs of online learners.[42] Transforming traditional teaching materials for online learning can be labor intensive and exceptionally tough for instructors who are not familiar with online technology.[43] In this regard, online learning has its own perceived perks, teachers and students must take on technology willingly. Carrying out an effective online learning will require the students to be ready with technology, learning supervision, pedagogical training, and social roles and responsibilities.[44]

Although online learning has been practiced in line with the advancement of technologies, the objective is different. Prior to the pandemic, one purpose is to deliver lesson instructions. Now, the main goal of implementing online learning is to ensure continuity of learning to ensure the learning environment reaches the students.[45] From this, a series of activities and resources were shifted to meet the objective of online learning. Perhaps the shift from teacher-led classrooms to virtual ones was too sudden that throws the students in disarray. One study focuses on students' perceptions and preferences about agriculture in India. Through an online survey, it was reported that more than half of the respondents were prepared in taking on online learning because of the convenience and flexibility of online classes. The students reported that the taped lessons and quizzes at the end of each class improved the efficiency of the lessons.[46] The strategy can be one of the many ways of assessing the students as it might help the students to retain information better in virtual classrooms, keeping them engaged throughout as well.

When schools were shut down, one critical task was to make sure that learning is uninterrupted.[47] Hence, most, if not all, turned to online learning to continue learning. The statement "learning goes on" or the trendy hashtag #learningneverstops is often used to avoid learning loss. Academic results were also affected by school disruptions. To observe the relationship between results and school disruptions, there must be a wide discrepancy where interruptions such as long holidays, students taking gap year, and disasters causing students to be displaced must be considered.[48] However, the question of how learning is measured and assessed still stands. In many practices before the pandemic, passing written exams is required to progress to another academic level. On the height of the pandemic, alternative assessment and evaluation methods were suggested to reduce the burden of teachers by substituting written examinations with assessments such as presentations and projects.[49] The methods of assessments range from quizzes, group discussion, and asynchronous discussion. An advantage of the mentioned assessment methods is the flexibility of allowing the students to be assessed in a calmer and less competitive environment. Perhaps this lets the students to be more creative as it allows a better freedom of expression on their abilities. In turn, this kind of skills will be carried on to their adult lives, promoting lifelong learning. Yet, the challenges of online assessments are to be evident too. Several obstacles have been identified such as difficulty in conveying precise instructions and intentions, struggles in providing feedbacks to help students in reaching their objectives, and hardship in monitoring participations.[50] Further concern of online assessments includes cheating that consequently threatens academic integrity.[51,52] Hence, methods such as take-home examinations[53] and infographic projects[54] have been employed to reduce the risk of cheating.

When the Ministry of Education of China introduced the policy "Suspension of classes without suspending schooling" as the consequence of the pandemic, a variety of online instructions and methods were implemented by teachers. Li et al.[55] studied the method of Thinking-Based Instruction Theory (TBIT) as a curriculum design and innovation. The TBIT theory, derived from the well-known theories of Piaget's cognitive development theory and Vygotsky's constructivist theory, encourages students to perform instructional activities, promoting their thinking skills. The TBIT-based course design focuses on three vital characteristics: curriculum objective, curriculum implement, and curriculum contents. The curriculum objective focuses on the goals of the lessons. Meanwhile, the curriculum implement pays attention to how the objectives are achieved. Lastly, the curriculum contents are the design of the contents and how it can be organized to maintain students' interest and develop their skills. In the study, three primary schools in Hunan, Beijing, and Guangzhou affected by COVID-19 were chosen to design three courses (Home + X course, 551-course, and Flower-centered) based on the TBIT theories. The results showed that besides increasing students' motivation and learning behavior, the TBIT micro-courses also showed improvement in terms of quality. As a result, the study has an influence on the design of successful and exciting online classes appropriate in the current pandemic situation which may ultimately change students' thinking skills.

Another proposed learning design is the introduction of integrating student pods (students gathering in small groups for collaborative learning) using a digital interactive Maths tool called GeoGebra Classes.[56] Students in GeoGebra Classes can share working spaces and feedbacks on their work. Through this model, blended learning is applied, and this diversifies online learning methods.

Redesigning the curriculum to ensure equity requires a major shift[57] and the author suggested a small number of adaptations in his teaching: the right trainings for teachers, necessary modifications to special needs students, and not to replace face-to-face interactions with computer-mediated communication. Online learning should lead to autonomous learning and teachers should be guiding the students rather than leading them on what to do.[58] Redesigning teaching and learning methods also raises the question on the value of instructional time: will prolonged Zoom sessions be valuable or motivational if they are forced interactions?[39]

Digital media undoubtedly provides greater opportunities for youth to learn autonomously. Since SDG4 targets heavily on the notion of equality, therefore the need for support system to enhance the use of digital media cannot be ignored to ensure that all students are learning correctly as some reported issues on students' lack of autonomous learning and teachers lacking in delivering effective instructions to students. Digital divide is an important issue that is repeatedly emphasized in this chapter, which worries the front-runners of SDGs affecting lower income households the most. Efforts should also be taken from the government, nongovernmental organizations, and private companies alike to reduce inequality. One action proposed by UNESCO is to offer "free and open-source technologies to teachers and students."[12] This requires a great collaboration between agencies but essential for the betterment of the societies. The use of modern technologies is changing our lives and how we live. Due to this, technologies are constantly updated to meet human's needs. To stay current, technology skills need to be refreshed every three years[59] and hence, continuous attempts and collaborations must be carried out.

One case study[60] was presented in the Philippines at the University of Santo Tomas in the context of teaching and learning of Physical Chemistry 1 and Analytical Chemistry for Chemical Engineering students. A five-component blended learning strategy was employed during the period of COVID-19. The strategy was referred to as Discover, Learn, Practice, Collaborate, and Assess (DLPCA). The asynchronous method consists of pre-recorded lecture videos and these were uploaded on YouTube to allow students to rewatch and learn at their own pace. As for the synchronous part, video conferencing platforms were used. Some challenges were brought up in the study such as the stability of internet network, instructor's knowledge in using the available teaching and learning tools, and maintaining students' engagement and interest. Even with the stated challenges, DLPCA strategy was proved to be an effective method and could be another successful strategy to be implemented in blended classrooms.

The rise of COVID-19 provides time for deep reflection on our education system. The materials and lesson designs that would have worked in the past might not be suitable now or in a postpandemic world.

3.2 Online learning as the way forward

Online learning was once an alternative pathway and now, it could be the main method of teaching and learning. Tremendous change has happened in how education is managed during the COVID-19 period. Anderson et al.[61]

suggest that the world will be more tech-driven by 2025, binding economic, social, and healthcare transactions together. If the implementation of digital technologies is done correctly, positive impacts can be seen on the students. Lin et al.[11] reported that digital learning, learning motivation, and outcome prove to be positive and consequently, resulting in positive learning gains. Full online learning might not be a feasible option as it is believed that traditional learning cannot be fully replaced. Hence, blended learning will be accelerated to prepare for any future risks. The concept of blended learning was introduced more than a decade ago and it is a model which combines online and offline teaching and learning methods, aiming to enhance learning and to cater to distant leaners. From this practice, blended learning proves to be a practical model post-COVID-19.[62]

Swan[63] also supports that frequent and helpful feedback with the students lead to a positive achievement in online learning. In theory, an excellent group work relies on collaboration and equality. Group work calls for collaboration and equality from all members. Unfortunately, complete fairness is commonly not achievable due to different skillsets and characters of the students.[64]

Nijakowski et al.[65] present the case of blended learning in conservative dentistry with endodontics where theoretical classes were held online while practical lessons were conducted with patients, following the standard of safety procedure of COVID-19. The students acknowledged the increase in learning effectiveness during the pandemic and are in favor to continue after the pandemic.

Hew et al.[66] examined the outcomes of fully online flipped classes on student learning performance during the pandemic. Two stages were examined: (1) using the 5E (engage, explore, explain, elaborate, and evaluate) framework and (2) the transformation of two flipped classes into fully online flipped classes. The authors revealed that the students' final scores in the fully online flipped classes showed the same effectiveness in the normal flipped classes. Moreover, seven good practices were also identified when using videoconferencing platforms. These practices can help to support online classrooms and be used as a guideline for other interested instructors. The seven procedures are as follows:

1. To remove unnecessary background noise during the session, members are reminded to switch off their microphones.
2. Switching on webcams before the start of the session.
3. Managing the transition to the online flipped classroom approach for students.
4. Instructors should use dual monitors to simulate, as close as possible, the look and feel of a face-to-face class—one monitor to view all the participants in "gallery view," and the other to view the presentation material.

5. Activating and evaluating students' preclass learning with a short review.
6. Using an MIM app on mobile phones to foster quicker online response times and to communicate with students during their online breakout sessions.
7. Using a variety of presentation media as well as a variety of activities to sustain student interest.

Game-based learning (GBL)—a physical and mental stimulation—is another strategy that is slowly being accepted as a teaching and learning method. The idea of play in learning is not a recent phenomenon and it is now extended to today's digital society. Games can enhance learning in ways of increasing social engagement and giving paths to social interactions among peers.[67] A stream of studies focuses on the existing theories and models in education in relation to using games to promote learning. For example, a quasiempirical study[1] was conducted to test the motivation, engagement, and academic performance of students on Arabic language grammar course at Ajman University. A popular tool, Kahoot!, was used as a formative assessment. A conclusion was made: students who used Kahoot! in the experiment performed better and has higher motivation than those who do not.

3.3 Lifelong learning

It has been mentioned earlier that COVID-19 can present unique opportunities in expanding our comfort zones. The current situation also preps the students with skills such as resilience and adaptation. When students were to learn online, the students had to quickly adapt. There is no doubt that this goes together with the aim of SDG4 which is to promote lifelong learning. Although this is not an ideal path of achieving or promoting lifelong learning, this should be a takeaway lesson in developing one's skills and competencies. A "Learning-Integrated Life" concept was put forward by government investors where individuals are supposed to engage in skills which allows them to have the right employability skills and purpose during and after the pandemic.[68] The COVID-19 threats resulted in a system's vulnerability and yet, it shows how important the role of determination is in a cluster and in an individual. Social and emotional support became a central theme in avoiding learning loss.

About 50 years ago, lifelong learning became an essential concept in global policy which called attention to the idea that learning continues until children reach adulthood and, the concept of how learning is all around us and not limited to just physical classrooms.[69] Another remarkable outcome of COVID-19 affecting the education sector is how human relationship is tested. The center of any educational process is the human relationship between a student and a teacher.[70] Collaborative learning, coupled with good communication, develops an individual's critical reasoning skills.[71] This unprecedented event has shown teachers' commitment and their capacity in ensuring students' learning goes on smoothly. Additionally, it is evident that students' collaboration with their teachers is highly needed, and this cannot be done individually. COVID-19 also calls for "a global solidarity" which enhances the need to acknowledge equality. After all, just as working toward the goals of SDG is a shared responsibility, humankind should also move toward equality in every aspect of the goals.

Although many[72,73] have said that traditional classroom is still considered to be irreplaceable as communicating online can be an inhibiting aspect where some issues must first be tackled, the continuation of learning still must be emphasized, and cooperation and all individuals are responsible for their own progress. When doing a full online learning, there is a need to put an emphasis on self-efficacy. The notion of self-efficacy has been put forward by Bandura,[74] well before the popularity of online learning. Self-efficacy is a human factor where it depends on an individual effort to accomplish a task. In the case of this chapter, students had to rely on themselves to complete a single task as all face-to-face interaction was eliminated. One of the ways to support students' self-efficacy is to provide constant supervision on their work and by this, any difficulties in completing online tasks can be immediately addressed.

Due to the unusual circumstance, it seems that there is a need to act on renewing the commitments to the SDGs. Reassessing the targets of SDGs will hopefully allow young individuals to succeed in schools and to be equipped with appropriate skills, knowledge, and principles to succeed later in life. Ultimately, it is also hoped that these individuals will be able to contribute to the society which is core of the global agenda. The current predicament has revealed our capabilities in surviving and shows our resilience in building a better society.

4. Physical infrastructure

Thus far, this chapter focuses on different aspects of online learning and its effects in the education sector. One crucial characteristic to be discussed revolving post-COVID-19 crisis is a school's physical infrastructure. Physical facilities have a fundamental role in the achievement of educational goals and objectives by meeting the physical and emotional needs of those in the school community.[75] The needs of these two factors are met following certain conditions. A few aspects are considered to meet the physical needs which include providing safe physical structures, appropriate sanitary amenities, and spaces with a balanced visual and temperature conditions. The emotional needs, on the other hand, are achieved by creating enjoyable and welcoming settings.[76] Target 4.a states the importance of building inclusive and safe schools. Physical learning spaces affect learning outcome, as better provision of infrastructure leads to better attendance to school and increase teacher's motivation. This results in positive academic results. Although precautionary measures have been taken, the use and setup of physical space still needs to be taken into consideration. To encourage learning, this target ensures that satisfactory and safe physical infrastructure is provided for students from all background and status. The learning environments mentioned in this target include digital infrastructure such as the availability of computers and internet, access to adapted learning materials such as textbooks and lastly, the supply of electricity and water as basic amenities.

COVID-19 has reminded the society on the importance of hygiene and self-care. Since the pandemic is a global health crisis which restricts societal movement, it is crucial to consider this aspect in post-COVID-19 reimagination as investment in infrastructure will help in building resilience. The lack of basic sanitation and water faced by students puts them at a greater jeopardy of infection and diarrheal diseases, making them more likely to miss schools. Currently, literature on physical infrastructure is very limited considering the pandemic situation, as most literature is focused on technological infrastructure instead. The director of the UNESCO Institute for Statistics reported that about half of the schools around the world have no access to handwashing amenities and some lacks in basic water, sanitation, and hygiene (WASH) facilities.[77] Once again, we are reminded of how schools in less fortunate areas have less access to these facilities and thus, making them more vulnerable to the exposure of diseases, especially the deadly COVID-19. This highlights the urgency to solve sanitation crises in underprivileged schools.

Providing sufficient physical infrastructure alone is not enough as all individuals are required to have the right training about safety of operational procedures and learning practices. Efforts must be collectively given from teachers, parents, students, and administrators. Once again, we are prompted to remember that having access to amnesties alone is not enough and it has to be concurrent with knowledge and practice. UNICEF's response in tackling the said issues includes spreading awareness such as the Global Handwashing Day, transporting purified water to refugee camps, and working closely with front liners and providers during COVID-19 pandemic.

The provision of better infrastructure requires additional financing, and it might burden an already weakened economy due to COVID-19. Extra financing is needed to ensure that the right facilities are provided when students are ready to fully return to schools, especially the access to hygiene amenities and additional learning spaces. The new 2020 Global Education Monitoring (GEM) Report predicts that school shutdowns in poorer countries could lead to an increase of annual funding for up to US $200 billion annually.[78]

Overall, COVID-19 not only has changed how teachers and students learn and teach, but it also affects learning spaces. Perhaps the greatest challenge is the additional funding required to provide for the students and yet again, this requires the collaboration from various government and non-government agencies to provide for the schools to their best abilities.

5. Conclusion and future outlook

At the time of writing, nothing is certain as the pandemic outbreak is still an ongoing worry, albeit in a recovery phase, in many countries. Perhaps a future update is required to see the longitudinal trend. As of now, it can be seen how COVID-19 has impacted the world in various sectors and thus, directly affecting the success of SDGs. As a result, the targets of SDGs might be altered accordingly to suit the current situation to still achieve the aims of SDGs. From the education aspect, it can be concluded that it is likely that schools and institutions will blend online and physical learning for better preparation for any future crisis. As the world advances and evolves, students' learning techniques should be dynamic for continued relevance. Unfortunately, the pandemic accelerates the change in ways no one could have imagined. We have already seen that digital divide does not only affect developed and developing countries, but it also affects gender. If the issue of digital divide is not addressed quickly, the transition to full or partial online learning might create more setbacks on inclusivity, quality, and (in)equalities on education. However, with proper planning and policies, these gaps can be narrowed to ensure the access to education is attainable, in line with SGD4's goals. Now more so than ever, there is an urgent need to address the issues on social and economic inequalities. The use of physical spaces should also be considered to ensure the society's comfort. Nonetheless, call for actions to align the current pandemic situation with the future goals is much needed to achieve sustainable learning and education. As the world is holding on by a threat due to COVID-19, it is hoped that transformative recovery and efforts to reduce risks among students will bear a fruitful outcome for the education sector.

References

1. Shulla K, Voigt BF, Cibian S, et al. Effects of COVID-19 on the sustainable development goals (SDGs). *Discov Sustain* 2021;**2**(15). https://doi.org/10.1007/s43621-021-00026-x.
2. Unterhalter E. The many meanings of quality education: politics of targets and indicators in SDG 4. *Global Pol* 2019;**10**:39–51.
3. OECD. *VET in a time of crisis: building foundations for resilient vocational education and training systems*; 2021 https://read.oecd-ilibrary.org/view/?ref=132_132718-fdwmrqsgmy&title=VET-in-a-time-ofcrisis-Building-foundations-for-resilient-vocational-education-and-training-systems. [Accessed 25 May 2021].
4. Hamid MZBSA, Karri RR. Overview of preventive measures and good governance policies to mitigate the COVID-19 outbreak curve in Brunei. In: *COVID-19: systemic risk and resilience*. Cham: Springer; 2021. p. 115–40.
5. Smith WC. Consequences of school closure on access to education: lessons from the 2013–2016 Ebola pandemic. *Int Rev Educ* 2021;**67**:53–78. https://doi.org/10.1007/s11159-021-09900-2.
6. Tremblay-Wragg É, Raby C, Ménard L, Plante I. The use of diversified teaching strategies by four university teachers: what contribution to their students' learning motivation? *Teach High Educ* 2019;1–18. https://doi.org/10.1080/13562517.2019.1636221.
7. White C. Innovation and identity in distance language learning and teaching. *Innov Lang Learn Teach* 2008;**1**(1):97–110. https://doi.org/10.2167/illt45.0.
8. Atmojo AP, Arif N. EFL classes must go online! Teaching activities and challenges during COVID-19 pandemic in Indonesia. *Reg J* 2020;**13**(1):49–76.
9. Adarkwah MA. "I'm not against online teaching, but what about us?" ICT in Ghana post Covid-19. *Educ Inf Technol* 2021;**26**:1665–85. https://doi.org/10.1007/s10639-020-10331-z.
10. Baker KJ. Panic-gogy: a conversation with Sean Michael Morris. *Nat Teach Learn Forum* 2020;**29**(4):1–3. https://doi.org/10.1002/ntlf.30239.
11. Lin MH, Chen HG, Liu KS. A study of the effects of digital learning on learning motivation and learning outcome. *Eurasia J Math Sci Technol Educ* 2017;**13**(7):3553–64. https://doi.org/10.12973/eurasia.2017.00744a.
12. UNESCO. *Distance learning solutions*; 2020. Available at: www.en.unesco.org/covid19/educationresponse/solutions. [Accessed 22 September 2021].
13. Panigrahi R, Srivastava PR, Sharma D. Online learning: adoption, continuance, and learning outcome—a review of literature. *Int J Inf Manag* 2018;**43**:1–14.
14. Benson A. Using online learning to meet workforce demand: a case study of stakeholder influence. *Q Rev Dist Learn* 2002;**3**(4):443–52.
15. Ally M. Foundations of educational theory for online learning. In: *Theory and practice of online learning*. vol. 2. Athabasca University Press; 2004. p. 15–44.
16. Sitthirak C. Social media for language teaching and learning. *Thammasat J* 2013;**31**(1):611–9.
17. Kaplan A, Haenlein M, Mason R. *E-learning and social networking handbook: resources for higher education*. Routledege; 2018.

18. Hamidi H, Chavoshi A. Analysis of the essential factors for the adoption of mobile learning in higher education: a case study of students of the University of Technology. *Telematics Inform* 2018;**35**(4):1053–70.
19. Alabdulkareem SA. Exploring the use and the impacts of social media on teaching and learning science in Saudi. *Procedia Soc Behav Sci* 2015;**182**:213–24.
20. Al-Rahmi WM, Alias N, Othman MS, Marin VI, Tur G. A model of factors affecting learning performance through the use of social media in Malaysian higher education. *Comput Educ* 2018;**121**:59–72.
21. Peart DJ, Rumbold PL, Keane KM, Allin L. Student use and perception of technology enhanced learning in a mass lecture knowledge-rich domain first year undergraduate module. *Int J Educ Technol High Educ* 2017;**14**(1):1.
22. Ghilay Y. *Online learning in higher education*. Nova Science Publishers; 2017.
23. Parkes M, Stein S, Reading C. Student preparedness for university e-learning environments. *Internet High Educ* 2015;**25**:1–10.
24. Tarhini A, Hone K, Liu X. The effects of individual differences on e-learning users' behaviour in developing countries: a structural equation model. *Comput Hum Behav* 2014;**41**:153–63. https://doi.org/10.1016/j.chb.2014.09.020.
25. Liaw S, Huang HM. A study of investigating learners attitudes toward e-learning. In: *The fifth international conference on distance learning and education*. vol. 12; 2011. p. 28–32.
26. Ngampornchai A, Adams J. Students' acceptance and readiness for E-learning in northeastern Thailand. *Int J Educ Technol High Educ* 2016;**13**(1):34.
27. Hayashi R, Garcia M, Jayasundara HDSA, Balasuriya A, Hirokawa T. *COVID-19 impact on technical and vocational education and training in Sri Lanka*. Asian Development Bank; 2021.
28. Turney BW. Anatomy in a modern medical curriculum. *Ann R Coll Surg Engl* 2007;**89**:104–7.
29. Supriya K, Mead C, Anbar AD, et al. COVID-19 and the abrupt shift to remote learning: impact on grades and perceived learning for undergraduate biology students. *bioRxiv* 2021. https://doi.org/10.1101/2021.03.29.437480.
30. United Nations. *Ensure inclusive and equitable quality education and promote lifelong learning opportunities for all Infographic*; 2021 https://www.un.org/sustainabledevelopment/wp-content/uploads/2019/07/E_Infographic_04.pdf. [Accessed 20 May 2021].
31. Bell S, Cardoso M, Giraldo JP, El Makkouk N, Nasir B, Mizunoya S, et al. *Can broadcast media foster equitable learning amid the COVID-19 pandemic?*; 2020. Available at: https://blogs.unicef.org/evidence-for-action/can-broadcast-media-foster-equitable-learning-amid-the-covid-19-pandemic/. [Accessed 1 June 2021].
32. Buchbinder N. *Digital capacities and distance education in times of coronavirus: insights from Latin America*. World Education Blog; 2020. Available at: https://gemreportunesco.wordpress.com/2020/05/12/digital-capacities-and-distance-education-in-times-of-coronavirus-insights-from-latin-america/. [Accessed 6 June 2021].
33. UNESCO. *More than one-half of children and adolescents are not learning worldwide*; 2021 http://uis.unesco.org/sites/default/files/documents/fs46-more-than-half-children-not-learning-en-2017.pdf. [Accessed 20 May 2021].
34. Gorski P, Clark C. Multicultural education and the digital divide: focus on race 1. *Multicult Perspect* 2001;**3**:15–25. https://doi.org/10.1207/S15327892MCP0304_5.
35. Gillett-Swan J. The challenges of online learning: supporting and engaging the isolated learner. *J Learn Des* 2017;**10**(1):20–30.
36. Esewe R, Adejumo O. Challenges in ICT experienced by nurse educators in tertiary institutions in Edo State, Nigeria. *Afr J Phys Health Educ* 2014;50–60.
37. Buckingham D. Digital media literacies: rethinking media education in the age of the internet. *Res Comp Int Educ* 2007;2. https://doi.org/10.2304/rcie.2007.2.1.43.

38. Furlong J, Davies C. Young people, new technologies and learning at home: taking context seriously. *Oxf Rev Educ* 2012;**38**:45–62. https://doi.org/10.1080/03054985.2011.577944.
39. Lockee BB. Online education in the post-COVID era. *Nat Electron* 2021;**4**:5–6. https://doi.org/10.1038/s41928-020-00534-0.
40. Vekiri I, Chronaki A. Gender issues in technology use: perceived social support, computer, self-efficacy and value beliefs, and computer use beyond school. *Comput Educ* 2008;**51**(3):1392–404. https://doi.org/10.1016/j.compedu.2008.01.003.
41. Soomro KA, Kale U, Curtis R, et al. Digital divide among higher education faculty. *Int J Educ Technol High Educ* 2020;**17**:21. https://doi.org/10.1186/s41239-020-00191-5.
42. Chabbott C, Sinclair M. SDG 4 and the COVID-19 emergency: textbooks, tutoring, and teachers. *Prospects (Paris)* 2020;1–7. https://doi.org/10.1007/s11125-020-09485-y.
43. Motiwalla L, Tello S. Distance learning on the Internet: an exploratory study. *Internet High Educ* 2000;**2**:253–64. https://doi.org/10.1016/S1096-7516(00)00026-9.
44. Vonderwell S, Zachariah S. Factors that influence participation in online learning. *J Res Technol Educ* 2005;**38**:213–30.
45. Squelch J. Do school governing bodies have a duty to create safe schools? An education law perspective: current issues in education law and policy. *Perspect Educ* 2001;**19**(1):137–49.
46. Muthuprasad T, Aiswarya S, Aditya KS, Jha GK. Students' perception and preference for online education in India during COVID-19 pandemic. *Soc Sci Human Open* 2021;**3**(1):100101.
47. Popa S. Reflections on COVID-19 and the future of education and learning. *Prospects (Paris)* 2020;1–6. https://doi.org/10.1007/s11125-020-09511-z.
48. Smith WC. Consequences of school closure on access to education: lessons from the 2013–2016 Ebola pandemic. *Int Rev Educ* 2021;1–26. https://doi.org/10.1007/s11159-021-09900-2.
49. Hughes C. COVID-19 and the opportunity to design a more mindful approach to learning. *Prospects* 2020;**49**:69–72. https://doi.org/10.1007/s11125-020-09492-z.
50. Hannafin M, Hill J, Oliver K, et al. Cognitive and learning strategies in web-based environments. In: *The handbook of distance education*. Erlbaum; 2003. p. 245–60.
51. Lewis SE. Chemistry assessments through the sudden implementation of online instruction. *J Chem Educ* 2020;**97**(9):3418–22.
52. Nguyen JG, Keuseman KJ, Humston JJ. Minimize online cheating for online assessments during Covid-19 pandemic. *J Chem Educ* 2020;**97**(9):3429–35.
53. Jacobs AD. Utilizing take-home examinations in upper-level analytical lecture courses in the wake of the COVID-19 pandemic. *J Chem Educ* 2020;**97**(9). https://doi.org/10.1021/acs.jchemed.0c00768.
54. Grieger K, Leontyev A. Student-generated infographics for learning green chemistry and developing professional skills. *J Chem Educ* 2021;**98**(9):2881–91. https://doi.org/10.1021/acs.jchemed.1c00446.
55. Li Y, Zhang X, Dai DY, Hu W. Curriculum innovation in times of the COVID-19 pandemic: the thinking-based instruction theory and its application. *Front Psychol* 2021;**12**:601607. https://doi.org/10.3389/fpsyg.2021.601607.
56. Stahl G. Redesigning mathematical curriculum for blended learning. *Educ Sci* 2021;**11**(4):165.
57. Gorski P. Education equity and the digital divide. *AACE J* 2005;**13**(1):3–45.
58. Warschauer M. The paradoxical future of digital learning. *Learn Inq* 2007;41–9. https://doi.org/10.1007/s11519-007-0001-5.
59. Grand-Clement S. *Digital learning: education and skills in the digital age*. RAND Europe; 2017. https://www.rand.org/pubs/conf_proceedings/CF369.html.

60. Lapitan Jr LDS, Tiangco CE, Sumalinog DAG, Sabarillo NS, Diaz JM. An effective blended online teaching and learning strategy during the COVID-19 pandemic. *Educ Chem Eng* 2021;**35**:116–31. https://doi.org/10.1016/j.ece.2021.01.012.
61. Anderson J, Rainie L, Vogels EA. *Experts say the 'new normal' in 2025 will be far more tech-driven, presenting more big challenges*; 2021. Available at: https://www.pewresearch.org/internet/2021/02/18/experts-say-the-new-normal-in-2025-will-be-far-more-tech-driven-presenting-more-big-challenges. [Accessed 18 May 2021].
62. Güzer B, Caner H. The past, present and future of blended learning: an in depth analysis of literature. *Procedia Soc Behav Sci* 2014;**21**(116):4596–603.
63. Swan K. Virtual interaction: design factors affecting student satisfaction and perceived learning in asynchronous online courses. *Distance Educ* 2001;**22**(2):306–31.
64. Chang B, Kang H. Challenges facing group work online. *Distance Educ* 2016;**37**(1):73–88.
65. Nijakowski K, Lehmann A, Zdrojewski J, Nowak M, Surdacka A. The effectiveness of the blended learning in conservative dentistry with endodontics on the basis of the survey among 4th-year students during the COVID-19 pandemic. *Int J Environ Res Public Health* 2021;**18**:4555. https://doi.org/10.3390/ijerph18094555.
66. Hew K, Jia C, Gonda D, Bai S. Transitioning to the "new normal" of learning in unpredictable times: pedagogical practices and learning performance in fully online flipped classrooms. *Int J Educ Technol High Educ* 2020;**17**. https://doi.org/10.1186/s41239-020-00234-x.
67. Squire K. From content to context: videogames as designed experience. *Educ Res* 2006;**35**(8):19–29.
68. D2L. *The future of lifelong learning: designing for a learning-integrated life*; 2021. Available at: https://www.d2l.com/wp-content/uploads/2020/02/Future-of-Lifelong-Learning-D2L-2020-Digital-Edition.pdf. [Accessed 24 May 2021].
69. Bjursell C. The COVID-19 pandemic as disjuncture: lifelong learning in a context of fear. *Int Rev Educ* 2020;1–17. https://doi.org/10.1007/s11159-020-09863-w.
70. UNESCO. UNESCO: International Commission on the Futures of Education. *Education in a post-COVID world: nine ideas for public action*. UNESCO; 2020. Website Updated June 19, 2020 https://en.unesco.org/futuresofeducation/news/nine-ideas-for-public-action. [Accessed 28 May 2021].
71. So HJ, Brush TA. Student perceptions of collaborative learning, social presence and satisfaction in a blended learning environment: relationships and critical factors. *Comput Educ* 2008;**51**:318–36.
72. Palloff RM, Pratt K. *Building cyberspace learning communities: effective strategic for the online classroom*. Wiley Publishers; 2002.
73. Zhang D, Zhao JL, Zhou L, Nunamaker JF. Can e-learning replace classroom learning? *Commun ACM* 2004;**47**(5):75–9. https://doi.org/10.1145/986213.986216.
74. Bandura A. *Self-efficacy: the exercise of control*. W.H. Freeman; 1997.
75. Squelch J. Do school governing bodies have a duty to create safe schools? An educational law perspective. *Perspect Educ* 2001;**19**:137–49.
76. Lupinacci J. *A safe haven*. vol. 75. American School and University; 2002. p. 20–5. 8.
77. Montaya S. *Rethinking school infrastructure during a global health crisis*; 2020. Available at: http://uis.unesco.org/en/blog/rethinking-school-infrastructure-during-global-health-crisis. [Accessed 31 May 2021].
78. UNESCO Global Education Coalition. *UNESCO warns that the funding gap to achieve SDG4 in poorer countries risks increasing to US$ 200 billion annually due to COVID-19 if we do not take urgent action*; 2020. Available at: https://en.unesco.org/gem-report/sites/default/files/covid_cost_Press_Release_EN.pdf. [Accessed 4 June 2021].

CHAPTER FOUR

Effect of the COVID-19 on access to affordable and clean energy

Knawang Chhunji Sherpa[a], Gour Gopal Satpati[b], Navonil Mal[c], Agatha Sylvia Khalko[d], and Rajiv Chandra Rajak[d]

[a]Microbial Processes and Technology Division, CSIR-National Institute for Interdisciplinary Science and Technology (NIIST), Thiruvananthapuram, Kerala, India
[b]Department of Botany, Bangabasi Evening College, University of Calcutta, Kolkata, West Bengal, India
[c]Department of Botany, University of Calcutta, Kolkata, West Bengal, India
[d]Department of Botany, Marwari College, Ranchi University, Ranchi, Jharkhand, India

1. Introduction

The present pandemic situation caused by severe acute respiratory syndrome coronavirus 2 (SARS-CoV-2) shows rapid loss in human civilization. The current data (10th September 2021) shows 4,602,882 confirmed deaths and 223,022,538 active cases around the world due to this deadly virus.[1] Report says, human-to-human transmission is the most causing factor of this disease, which resulted in complete lockdown of town and cities globally.[2,3] Several researches have been performed on restoration of civilization in terms of social, environmental, and economic aspects.[4–6] Public health management during coronavirus disease-19 (COVID-19) is one of the most concerned topics, which leads the developments in medical technology including molecular-based technology, nanotechnology, advanced biosensing, and immunotherapeutics.[4,7–9]

The concept of sustainability in the recent decades has attracted global attention focusing on protecting the environment while providing socio-economic benefit and development to the present as well as future generations which is based on the concept of social, economic, and environmental sustainability.[10] Several goals and targets have been implemented in global political agendas toward the adoption of a sustainable route. Keeping this objective in mind, the United Nations in September 2015 adopted the 17 interlinked sustainable development goals (SDGs) that were designed as a shared blueprint for achieving a sustainable future for the people and the planet under the 2030 Agenda for Sustainable Development. The partnership among developed and developing countries came up in the form of

COVID-19 and the Sustainable Development Goals
https://doi.org/10.1016/B978-0-323-91307-2.00011-0

SDGs for putting an end to poverty, reducing inequality, stimulating the growth of the economy, and tackling with climate change and preservation of forests and oceans.

The 17 SDGs consist of 169 targets with 1256 publications, 3031 organized events, and 5414 actions taken so far.[11] These goals under the 2030 Agenda are universally applicable taking the policies and concerns of different nations into consideration. The intention of these goals ranges from eliminating hunger in the world to reducing inequalities and building sustainable societies. Balance and integration of social, economic, and environmental dimensions are necessary for implementing the SDGs.[12] However, the progress of these goals has been falling short of achieving the targets by 2030. In addition to the insufficient progress, the outbreak of coronavirus has been a major setback to the progress of achieving the SDG targets. The year 2020 witnessed the outbreak of coronavirus disease 2019 (COVID-19) with the World Health Organization declaring it a global pandemic by March 2020.[13] The novel coronavirus was first reported to have been emerged in Wuhan, China, in December 2019 which spread rapidly to other parts of the world impacting the global economy, energy systems, and overburdening the healthcare system worldwide.[2,4] The novel coronavirus is a zoonotic disease with high reproductive rate thus spreading faster than other coronavirus variations such as Severe Acute Respiratory Syndromes (SARS) and Middle East Respiratory Syndrome (MERS).[14,15] The COVID-19 is a subtype of coronavirus with single stranded RNA enclosed by spike glycoproteins that facilitate the entry of virus into the host cells leading to symptoms such as common cold to respiratory diseases in humans.[8,9] The contagious nature of the virus and the rapid rate of transmission are reported to be the primary cause of the outbreak of the disease.[16] Such transmission from one human to another arises due to human contact directly or indirectly via infected respiratory droplets either through inhalation or contact with contaminated surface or body fluid.[17] Such unprecedented catastrophe has taken the lives of more than 3 million with huge impact on the global economy and imperiling the progress of SDG targets.[18]

Achieving the 17 SDGs with its 169 targets is even more critical and necessary now than before which would require worldwide solidarity and prioritizing the susceptible socioeconomic sections of the world as well as the environment.[19] Among the 17 goals, SDG7's main goal is to encourage sustainable approach toward reliable and affordable energy. SDG7 encompasses the goal of ensuring inexpensive, dependable, sustainable, and modern renewable energy for all from resources such as wind, solar, and thermal.

It has 5 targets with 8 publications and 8 events that have been organized and 696 actions taken so far. Continuous rise in population and economic development have caused fossil fuel reserves to dwindle owing to overconsumption. This, in turn, has led to an increase in greenhouse gas emissions harming the environment. To counter the issue of global warming and removing our dependency on fossil fuels, the implementation of alternative renewable energy resource has become necessary. Socioeconomic development is constrained owing to the lack of access to clean and sustainable energy. People around the world require a reliable source of energy for their day-to-day activities, such as power for hospitals and schools, for cooking, heating, or cooling their homes. Earlier, the use of fossil fuels may have been cheaper than clean energy; however, with technological advancement and innovative research, renewable energy has become more affordable.

To mitigate the above-mentioned issues, progress of SDG7 and achieving the set targets is important. Efforts are being made to promote the use of renewable energy but the development has been slow. To fulfill the energy demand, a significant boost in renewable energy production across the globe is much needed. Infrastructure expansion and technology progression for providing clean energy in developing countries is essential for economic development and reducing the gap between rich and poor countries. The present chapter discusses the progress and challenges in achieving SDG7 and the impact of a pandemic on the goal's momentum.

2. SDG7 targets: Access to energy, renewable energy, and energy efficiency

SDG Goal 7 was framed to ensure inexpensive, reliable, and sustainable energy that is accessible to all. Easy accessibility to energy and power would help in providing smooth functioning in different sectors ranging from medicine to businesses, education, agriculture, communications, infrastructure, and other technology-related areas. There has been promising development in the accessibility of sustainable energy around the world over the last decade. Inaccessibility to electricity improved from 1.2 billion in 2010 to 789 million in 2018.[20] It has been reported that more than 2.3 billion people are dependent on wood, charcoal, waste from animal and crop, and other solid fuels for cooking and heating their homes The use of combustible fuels resulted in 4.3 million deaths in 2012.[21] The practice of using combustible fuels causes indoor air pollution that affects humans and the environment. Such practices have resulted in 4.3 million deaths in 2012.[21] Energy efficiency enhancement with the usage of renewable energy can help in a 40% reduction in emissions globally.[22]

Therefore to ensure that the SDG7 objectives are met, five energy targets were created to attain universal access to sustainable energy. The five targets are as follows:

- Target 7.1 was formulated to guarantee universal access by 2030 to modern energy in the form of electricity and clean energy for cooking.
- Target 7.2 was aimed at increasing the renewable energy shares substantially by 2030.
- Target 7.3 was created for doubling the energy efficiency progress by 2030.
- Target 7.A was aimed at promoting access to research and technology of clean energy by enhancing international cooperation. Promoting investment in improving infrastructure and clean energy technology that included renewable energy, energy efficiency, and advanced and cleaner fossil-fuel technology.
- Target 7.B by 2030 was created for expanding the infrastructure and technology upgradation for supplying modern and sustainable energy services in developing countries following the respective countries' programs of support. Priority would be given to least developed countries, Small Island developing states, and landlocked developing countries.

With the advent of different targets of SDG7, renewable energy has played an instrumental role in helping toward achieving this goal. By 2018 around 136 million people received electricity from off-grid renewables. Thus more efforts are needed so that around 620 million people who are still devoid of electricity can access affordable energy services by 2030.[23]

3. Why affordable and clean energy matters?

Energy is an important aspect of our everyday lives, especially for the poor, since it is needed for doing the most basic things like cooking food, lighting homes, and heating purposes. A major percentage of the vulnerable section's income is taken up by energy for basic needs. The rise of energy prices owing to the change in government policies not only affects their income but also their health and creates inequality which is a matter of social concern. Moreover, inaccessibility to affordable energy also impacts the environment. Difficulty in studying and improper storage of temperature-sensitive vaccines or medicines in hospitals are some of the issues faced by people owing to the lack of electricity. Lack of access to clean cooking is of grave concern as the use of solid fuels exposes people to high level of indoor air pollution that can have serious implications on their health causing respiratory or cardiovascular diseases, thereby increasing their susceptibility to diseases like coronavirus.[24] Thus modern electricity services are crucial for powering healthcare facilities to prevent an outbreak of disease and fighting off pandemics. It is also necessary for providing clean water to maintain hygiene and to enable communication for connecting people through technology. To prevent harmful consequences owing to the lack of access to energy, the adoption of the SDG7 is necessary to mitigate these issues. The targets formulated under the SDG7 further help in accelerating the progress to meet the goal by 2030.

Under SDG7, Target 7.1 which is subdivided into 7.1.1 and 7.1.2 focuses on accessibility to electricity and clean cooking, respectively. Over the years there has been considerable development in deploying inexpensive electricity to the people including on- and off-grid solution. People lacking electricity dropped from approximately 860 million in 2018 to 770 million in 2019.[26] However, the progress is unequal as sub-Saharan Africa shares about 75% of the population that still lacks access to electricity. Developing Asian countries have shown improvement with 96% of the section gaining access to electricity in 2019 which was much lesser in 2000 with 67%.[26] In India, the government launched Saubhagya Scheme in October 2017 which was able to provide 99% of the population with electricity in 2019.[25] Africa also witnessed a surge in electricity accessibility, doubling from 9 million from 2000 to 2013 to 20 million from 2014 to 2019 due to the deployment of on- and off-grid connection.[26]

Unlike the progress made in the accessibility of electricity, solution to clean energy for cooking purposes is still falling short. The access rate to clean cooking and technologies worldwide attained 63% in 2018.[27] Around 2.6 billion people still require access to clean cooking worldwide and suffer from household air pollution that has been the cause for approximately 2.5 million untimely deaths annually with women and children being affected the worst. This occurs due to the dependence on solid fuels like biomass and coal or the use of kerosene for cooking. Programs for using liquefied petroleum gas (LPG) and policies for promoting clean air have helped countries like India and China in providing access to clean cooking since 2010. The rate of access to clean cooking attained 49% for India and 71% for China in 2018. In contrast, sub-Saharan Africa rate of access was slow with only 17% of their population having access to clean cooking in 2018 from 15% in

2015.[26] Owing to the population growth outpacing the efforts, urgent actions need to be taken to tackle the rate of access.

Target 7.2 which aims at increasing the share of renewable energy in the total final energy consumption (TFEC) has progressed from 16.3% in 2010 to 17.3% in 2017 owing to the use of modern renewable energy.[20] The power sector witnessed a major increase with a 24.7% share of consumption of electricity globally in 2017 which surpassed the heating sector shares for the first time due to solar photovoltaic (solar PV) and wind energy. The renewable share in the transport sector was 3.3% in 2017 which was majorly contributed by liquid biofuels like biodiesel and bioethanol. The transport sector's share of renewable electricity consumption was at 0.3% globally. Sub-Saharan Africa had the largest renewable energy share in 2017 although the region accounted for about 85% of its renewable energy usage owing to the use of conventional biomass. To improve the consumption of renewable energy and to fulfill the objectives of the climate goals of SDG 7 by 2030, decarbonization in heat and transport sectors electrification is the sought after solution in terms of energy scenarios in the long run. Brazil leads in modern renewable with a 45% share followed by Canada (23%).[20] Policies formulated for renewable energy usage are important as they aid in procuring renewable electricity at a minimum price through auctions thus creating increase consumption and opportunities for local industry development through job openings.

The aim of target 7.3 under the SDG7 is to double the efficiency of energy globally by 2030. Measurement of energy efficiency is conducted in terms of energy intensity which is a percent decrease in the ratio of the total primary energy supply globally per unit of wealth produced or gross domestic product (GDP). Social and economic parameters are influencing factors in measuring the energy intensity which is inversely proportional to improvement in energy efficiency. Primary energy intensity worldwide in 2017 was 5.01 megajoules per US dollar with a 1.7% rate of improvement. A yearly improvement rate of 2.6% was estimated by United Nations to achieve the target by 2030; however, due to the slower progress rate than projected, the yearly average improvement rate was to be no less than 3% for achieving the SDG target.[28] Asia showed the highest improvement in energy intensity rate while the lowest was the Middle East region. The variations in efficiency among the different regions are most probably due to the economy of the region and the easy supply of energy. Efficient measures through policies and investment can help in gaining pace to double the rate by 2030. Implementation of policies such as minimum energy performance standards (MEPS) has proven to be successful in encouraging energy efficiency and being cost effective.[29] The government could help in easing the bulk procurement of equipment that is energy efficient, thus reducing its cost and providing financial incentives. Steps for strict policy action encourage global investment in energy efficiency measures and favor clean and efficient operations. According to the Sustainable Development Scenario conducted by IEA, an average improvement rate of 3.6% in energy intensity is possible with the right policy measures and digital technology.[26]

4. Modern renewable energy technologies

Renewable energy has been used for a long time in the form of solid fuels such as biomass for burning and hydropower for the generation of electricity. Renewable energy plays an important role in developing countries responsible for the final energy utilization of more than 50%.[30] Renewable energy is defined as energy derived from natural processes sustainably through different forms of energy, such as geothermal, bioenergy, solar, biofuel hydropower, and wind energy. Renewable energy has shown progress in recent years driven by SDGs and policy support by the government. Modern renewable energy (without the inclusion of conventional biomass usage) accounted for 11% of TFEC in 2018 which was slightly higher than 2013 with 9.6%.[31] Owing to the replenishing nature of renewable energy resources, it can be deployed over vast geographical regions resulting in significant economic progress and energy security. Renewable energy can help mitigate climate change, reduce air pollution caused by the burning of fossil fuels, reduce premature deaths caused due to household air pollution, and improve the health of people. Different renewable technologies that have been contributing to the progress of SDG7 are solar, wind power, hydropower, bioenergy, and geothermal power and heat.

(a) Solar technology utilizes sunlight for the direct conversion of light into electricity. Solar photovoltaic (PV) is a promising solar technology that is made up of cells. These solar PV cells are made of semiconductor materials that utilize sunlight for the separation of electrons from atoms for creating an electric current. For boosting the power of PV cells output, they are interconnected to form larger units called modules or panels. Several modules connect to form arrays. These arrays are connected to the electrical grid as a component of a complete PV system. The manufacture of solar PV module is possible in large plants thus allowing economies of scale. Another added advantage of using solar PV is the modular technology that allows it to be deployed in small quantities at a time. These advantages give the system the freedom to be used for personal electronics or the generation of utility-scale power. Other established solar technology such as solar thermal electricity or concentrating solar power (CSP) uses mirrors to concentrate the sunlight into a solar beam that heats up the working fluid in the solar receiver causing the heat engine to generate electricity.

The global market for solar PV in 2019 was reported to grow around 44%. A total of 627 gigawatts (GW) including on- and off-grid capacity was reported globally which was much higher when compared to 23 GW a decade earlier. As solar PV plays an important role in the generation of electricity, by 2019 around 22 countries had enough power owing to solar PV to meet around 3% of their electricity demand while 12 countries were able to meet 5% of the electricity demand. Electricity generation using solar PV claimed high shares in different countries like Honduras (10.7%), Italy (8.6%), Greece (8.3%), Germany (8.2%), and Chile (8.1%).[31]

To become the major source of electricity worldwide, solar PV are still faced with challenges such as instability of policy and regulatory frameworks and stress to the economy since electricity generated from nuclear and fossil fuel attracts more investors. Despite the challenges, corporate purchase of solar PV extending significantly and personal usage were important factors for the system distribution in many countries. China was reported to account for about 26% of new installation which was the highest share worldwide for the year 2019. In 2018 five countries, i.e. China, the United States, India, Japan, and Vietnam, collectively contributed to 56% of the newly installed capacity.

(b) Wind power uses wind turbines for the generation of electricity. When the wind hits the turbine's blades, the blades rotate and turn the turbine connected to it, thus changing the kinetic energy into rotational energy by moving the shaft. This shaft which is connected to the generator helps in the generation of electricity through electromagnetism. Consumption of wind energy is on the rise owing to its cost-effective technology. Onshore wind is an established technology with a supply chain worldwide while offshore wind is projected to progress rapidly. As per the IRENA's recent report, onshore and offshore wind generation capacity has increased by a factor of about 75 in the last 20 years with its growth from 7.5 GW in 1997 to around 564 GW by 2018.[32]

(c) Hydropower generates electricity from the potential energy of flowing water from a height. Conventional hydropower projects comprise run-of-the-river system, reservoir system, and low-head in-stream facility. Hydropower expands from large-scale projects (more than 10 MW capacities) to micro/mini capacity. This technology remains the largest renewable electricity source in the world and plays an integral role in the decarbonization of power system and improving their flexibility. Hydropower generation globally was approximated to be 4306 TWh in 2019 which was an increase of 2.8% from 2018. In 2019 Brazil took a lead in the commission of new hydropower capacity followed by China, Lao PDR, Bhutan, and Tajikistan.[33] Hydropower production varies yearly in the world not only because of modification in installed capacity but also due to changes in the weather pattern and local operations. Climate change poses a risk to the hydropower industry owing to which climate variability and its effect are being included in planning of projects, design, and operational arrangements. System integration with other renewable technologies like solar PV and wind energy can help in reducing the risk and aid in building a resilient system.

(d) Bioenergy encompasses the utilization of biological materials for a wide range of energy purpose. The energy derived from biomass can be converted to energy for use in heat and power generation and transport sector. Many bioenergy pathways have been well established and technically proven for commercial purpose. Biomass contributes to the largest share among all the renewable resources in the world energy supply. Bioenergy accounted for about 12% of the TFEC in 2018. Modern bioenergy excluding the conventional biomass usage accounted for around 5.1% of the total final energy demand globally in 2018.[34]

The contribution of modern bioenergy is significant in all sectors with a five-fold higher contribution than solar PV and wind power combined. Owing to strong policy support, bioenergy has shown accelerated progress. The electricity sector reported an increase of about 6.7% annually, while the transport sector showed an increase of 4.4% and about 1.1% for bio-heat. The liquid biofuels industry is more focused on bioethanol, biodiesel, and hydrotreated vegetable oil (HVO) and hydrotreated esters and fatty acids (HEFA). Ethanol production in 2019 was reported to be around 114 billion liters which was 2% higher than ethanol production in 2018 with 111 billion liters.[35] Biodiesel production increased to 47.4 billion liters in 2019 with Indonesia leading as the largest producer of biodiesel in the world.[31]

(e) Geothermal power and heat can be used for electricity generation or it can be directly used for heating purposes such as space heating and heat input for industries. Heat energy is generated from the earth's crust as hot water and steam which can be converted into electricity in a thermal power plant. Geothermal electricity generation was around 95 TWh (terawatt hour) and direct usage of thermal output was around 117 TWh in 2019.[36] Geothermal plants located near the source can cogenerate both electricity and heat for different applications. Thermal application from geothermal energy has grown over the years to nearly 8% on average with the space heating segment growing 13% annually. Geothermal energy found its direct use in swimming and bathing followed by heat spacing, greenhouse heating, industrial purposes, aquaculture, agriculture, melting snow, etc. The active markets for geothermal energy are spread across regions of Europe and China. Countries with the major supply of geothermal power in 2019 were the United States, Indonesia, the Philippines, Turkey, New Zealand, Mexico, Kenya, Italy, Iceland, and Japan. The United States leads in the area for the largest geothermal power capacity installation with a net operating capacity of 2.5 GW in 2019.[31]

The year 2019 saw progress for the geothermal industry with construction activity and government support. However, the industry still is faced with challenges of high project cost, inadequate funding, and risk mitigation. In-depth research and innovative technologies can aid geothermal energy in pushing forward toward an optimistic future.

5. Impact of COVID-19 on SDG7

The world has been facing climate and socioeconomic crises which can be addressed through the low-carbon energy transition. As per the Intergovernmental Panel on Climate Change (IPCC), 70%–85% of the global electricity by 2050 should be supplied by renewable energy to mitigate the pressing issue of global warming and steps toward decarbonization.[37] The UN Secretary-General in September 2019 initiated a decade of action to speed up the progress of SDGs. Unfortunately, within 6 months of its initiation, the world faced a global pandemic that impacted all sectors and the 17 SDGs. The COVID-19 pandemic highlighted the vulnerability of our society depicting how a health crisis quickly turned into a socioeconomic crisis. The government now faces the challenge of framing economic policies and recovery plans to bring back the pace of the economy and energy market. Progress in the renewable energy sector plays a crucial part in the low- and middle-income countries for socioeconomic development.[38]

The governments worldwide were compelled to undergo lockdown to mitigate the spread of the virus. The world witnessed a halt in the economy and a drop in energy demand. During the complete lockdown, the monthly demand for electricity reduced by 20% on average. The worldwide electricity demand reduced to 2.5% in the first few months of 2020 while oil and coal demand fell by 5% and 8%, respectively.[31] Amid the crisis, renewable electricity was the only resource that showed growth in demand owing to the low operating expenditure and access to the electricity system. This pandemic has highlighted the essential role that electricity accessibility plays in saving lives, sustaining the essential services, supply chains, and the livelihood of the people. Such circumstances have made the case even stronger as to why efforts on energy accessibility need to be accelerated.

Although restrictions on mobility and safety rules were able to slow the spread of the virus such measures delayed the construction of renewable energy installations of solar PV and onshore wind temporarily as well as interrupted the supply chains. Renewable projects, supply of equipment, policy execution, and investments were affected owing to the pandemic. During the first wave of COVID-19, cases rose rapidly spreading across the world. Europe witnessed a rapid surge in COVID-19 cases by the end of summer. Even with such a surge in cases, most countries did not introduce or reintroduce lockdown measures keeping the economy of the country in mind. With movement restriction and tightened quarantine rules, the manufacture of renewable equipment and construction activities were minimal. Investments in renewable projects and incentives also took a setback during the crisis with the government focusing the incentives on fighting against the virus. According to the International Energy Agency, the governments were advised to extend the warranty and contract of the projects for reducing the financial risk of the investors.[39]

In the first half of 2020, the electricity generation from renewable sources was reported to be 11% lower when compared to the first half of 2019. The solar PV and wind expansion were found to be 17% and 8% less than 2019, respectively. Unlike solar and wind, hydropower saw an increase in the first 6 months owing to the large-scale project commissioned in China. Thermal power production fell to 9% in the beginning months of 2020 in China. It also witnessed a decline in installation for wind by 50% and solar PV by 25% owing to shortage in manpower and limited construction activity. Similarly, Europe also reported lower renewable energy capacity addition in the first quarter of 2020 than 2019; however, it gained pace for installation during the second quarter with lockdown relaxations.[40]

Conversely, United States reported a twofold increase in the renewable capacity addition in the first 6 months of 2020 compared to 2019. As the wind and solar PV development is dictated by policy deadlines, the developers sped up the commissioning of the projects for meeting the deadline of federal tax incentives. India, on the other hand, had a slow growth of renewable energy capacity even before the lockdown was imposed. This was due to financial instability and project setbacks. Likewise, the ASEAN countries also reported 60% lower installation capacity in 2020 compared to 2019.

Distributed renewable for energy access (DREA) is a separate off-grid system capable of producing and distributing energy independent of a centralized electricity network. This system played an integral role during the beginning of the crisis by providing energy to rural and remote places, thus powering essential services and health facilities. But strict lockdown caused its operation to a halt as it did not come under essential services. Suppliers and project developers faced a shortage in cash as there was an economic recession and unavailability of the credit system. The fall in oil and gas prices put a lot of pressure on renewable technologies.

The energy demand in world was reported to fall by 6% in 2020. Restricted activity owing to lockdown during the pandemic projected a drop in the CO_2 emissions by 8% in 2020 however, such restriction resulted in economic adversity and rise in unemployment.[41] Such fall in CO_2 emissions and reduced usage of coal are temporary circumstances which would eventually rise as economy rises. Thus, to reach climate goals of Paris Agreement, the government needs to formulate policies and regulations that are sustainable and is able to cover all sectors. Amid the crisis, renewable electricity has been resilient; however, other renewables were not able to sustain their growth. Biofuel production was projected to fall by 13% in 2020 which is the lowest in 20 years. Of all the renewable energy, biofuels were greatly impacted mostly due to restriction in movement and plummeting oil prices. The production of biofuels was projected to reduce to 11.5% in 2020 compared to 2019.[40]

Consumption of renewable heat owing to restricted activity also declined in 2020. Before the pandemic itself, the energy efficiency progress was slow and below 3% annual rate improvement. Now with the pandemic situation, the efficiency has dropped sharply due to reduction in investments, construction activity, and decrease in equipment manufacture and purchase. Prioritizing sustainable renewable energy and efforts to bring in energy project investments are important for energy transition and recovering from economic and financial damage caused by the pandemic. Therefore, to overcome from this crisis, the government should come up with post-COVID-19 recovery plans that would help the SDG7 come back on track and accelerate its progress so as to achieve its targets by 2030.

6. Role of energy in COVID-19 response and post-COVID-19 scenario

Due to the pandemic nature of COVID-19, humanity faces a herculean challenge. This crisis has confined the world indoors, thereby impelling an existential economic downfall. One of the major stepping stone of world economy is the energy sector. To restrain the disease transmission, almost half of the world inexplicably followed a lockdown from the middle of March 2020, impacting the economic trajectory at a cosmic scale. This quarantine period associated with different socioeconomic restrictions, including the work-from-home policy, has declined the normal industrial strategies, curbing the energy demand sharply. Most of the agencies, including institutional, industrial, as well as the business sectors, which occupy the lion's share, reduced the manual mode of operation, wherever possible and shifted to the digital platforms. This transition diverted the commercial energy load toward the residential side, which ultimately altered the energy requirement profile of the society. Hence, the governments and the power sectors should join hands to nullify the effects of this drastic shift in power demand along with the development of new strategies to dodge any other future pandemic scenario. On the flip side, this lockdown period had positive impact over several environmental concerns at an unprecedented level as the sharp decline in energy demand, transport, and industrial operations have led to a remunerative output over air quality control and greenhouse gas emissions.

Elavarasan et al.[42] explicitly illustrated the pandemic footprints over the energy sectors and allocated them into two major categories, i.e., direct and indirect impact. Direct impact instigates the consequences of the energy requirement shift over the existing power grid industry. Each and every sector ranging from industrial, commercial, residential, or agriculture has its exclusive energy load quota, but the drastic energy demand variation during pandemic constrained the power operators to modify the power load pattern and generation accordingly. The industrial and transport sectors, which demand major share from the energy sector, had to halt their operations during COVID-19 outbreak. This led to a substantial downturn in the energy demand, resulting in the curtailment of energy market valuation.[42] In several European countries like Belgium, France, Spain, Netherlands, and Italy, the market figure of power exchange has diminished by 23%, 20.1%, 17.4%, 18.2%, and 17.7%, respectively.[43,44] Oil price collapse at global scale during March 2020 was the lowest reported since 2003 due to the consequence of COVID-19, causing a fall in the demand of oil and due to business-related issues among Saudi Arabia, Russia, and USA.[45] As a result of remarkable transposition in the energy currency, the existing power system management becomes a cumbersome task to administer. The governments of the countries affected by the pandemic should plan an emergency roadmap for utility operators by collaborating with their policy-making stakeholders to overcome the post-COVID-19 implications.

The indirect impact implies the roundabout effects of this pandemic scenario over several platforms like research investments and consumer relations which influence the energy and power division. Power generation based on fossil fuels witnessed low energy demand during COVID-19 but increase in grid from renewable energy.[46] Council of European Energy Regulators (CEER) in association with International Renewable Energy Agency (IRENA) has tried to mitigate these issues by stressing the relevance of power source diversification integrated with the environmental concerns to establish a "clean energy system".[47]

6.1 Indian perspective

The power distribution system of the world's third most power demanding country (about 1.54 trillion kWh per year) is divided into five regional segments: North Eastern Region (NER), Eastern Region (ER), Northern Region (NR), Western Region (WR), and Southern Region (SR).[42] These segments were monitored and controlled by India's Power System Operation Corporation (POSOCO) in its entirety.[48] Indian government imposed 'Janata Curfew' on 22nd March 2020 and nationwide lockdown from 25th March 2020 which was maintained in a full-fledged manner till 17th May (as per announcement by Government of India). The national energy demand decreased from around 3500 GWh (prior to the Janata Curfew) to 3000 GWh and reached the lowest at 2500 GWh on 1st April 2020. The regional power demand declined in NER and ER to about 22.5% and 20%, respectively, while the WR and SR witnessed a moderate reduction of 14.5% and 16%, respectively, and the least in the NR region with 10% drop, causing adverse effect on the power sector both economically and technically. Drastic decrease in the demand of power led to the Under Frequency-based load shedding (UFLS) due to mass disturbances in the frequency stability and generation schedule variation in the national power grid system, as encountered by the Frequency Variation Index (FVI),[42] which was mitigated and stabilized meticulously by Deviation Settlement Mechanism (DSM), regulated under Central Electricity Regulatory Commission in association with National Load Dispatch Centre, State Load Dispatch Centre, and Southern Regional Load Dispatch Centre through efficient generation according to the demand forecasting.

6.1.1 The famous "light-off event" in India

Indian prime minister addressed the nation to switch off their lights on 9th April at 9 pm for 9 min for cataloging the country's fight against COVID-19 and the largest democracy welcomed this note with immense pleasure. A preparatory practice was performed on 4th April 2020 to make a precision about the total power consignment abatement at the time of actual event. On the time of the actual event, total demand declination has been figured to be 31,089 MW with a minimum of 85,799 MW, documented at 21:10 h. POSOCO deduced earlier about the drastic fluctuations due to this abrupt change and the aftermath payload and had taken several controlled measures to diminish the consequences of this drastic shift. Hydrogeneration started to ramp down to 17,543 MW (from 25,559 MW to 8016 MW) at 20:45 h. This hydrogeneration was again ramped up from 8016 MW to 19,012 MW from 21:10 h to 21:27 h to meet the increase in demand after the event. Reduction of total 10,950 MW generation was achieved through thermal (6992 MW), gas (1951 MW), and wind generation (2007 MW) from 20:45 h to 21:10 h.[42]

6.1.2 Post-COVID-19 socioeconomic challenges for India

Increased unemployment, truncated transportation along with the work-from-home policy transpose and taper the energy exigency in India under the COVID-19 scenario, which has not only imposed a lot of hurdles to the stakeholders to uplift the economy during the post-COVID-19 platform but also created budgetary burden, perturbing the Indian socioeconomic standpoint as follows:

6.1.2.1 Downfall in the earning trajectory

As a result of massive work loss and gross downfall in the industrial as well as commercial belt, the earning trajectory of a large population dropped down severely, thereby making them impotent to pay the electricity bill. Under such circumstance, the revenue of the energy sector is adversely affected, thus triggering the increment in the electricity tariffs, which may cause future burden.

6.1.2.2 Dilution in the investments and subsidy relaxation over renewable energy projects

The pandemic has exposed the vulnerability of health sector with an overwhelming fiscal expenditure being expected during COVID-19 period as well as in the post-COVID-19 scenario. So the chance of curtailment in the funding and subsidy outlay in the research about renewable energy generation can be speculated for near future. In addition, the COVID-19-related financial liquidity crunch, agitation in the supply chain, and the labor-poverty also have slowed down the thriving advancement of the renewable energy sector intensively. For example, Indian solar energy sector relies over the Chinese supply chain for the production of photovoltaic solar panels and modules. Needless to say, this pandemic, with its origin in China, will delay the acquirement of the sourcing materials.[49] Indian distribution companies have faced 7.2 billion US dollars financial liquidity crunch, in addition to 4 billion US dollars revenue loss, during this crisis period.[50]

6.2 Post-COVID-19 challenges in the global context

A strong realization is essentially needed to combat with various post-COVID-19 challenges in the energy sector, although nobody can guarantee about exactly when we can add the 'post' prefix before the phrase 'COVID-19 scenario.' So it is high time to amalgamate the business game plan with the scientific strategies to settle down the concerning global turmoil. Some implementation measures are recommended as follows (Fig. 1).

6.2.1 Quality control and continuous monitoring over the fuel foundation

The pandemic situation restrained the movement of people with strict lockdown rules diminishing the mutual integration between certain parts of the world, from national to international level. Therefore it is extremely necessary for the stakeholders to realize the fuel potential of their own at its entirety for minimizing their dependence over other nations for fuel exchange. It will be challenging for the developing countries to stake the sourcing materials like LPG, LNG, coal, and crude oil from the international business market in post-COVID-19 period. In addition, fuel transportation can become another obstacle for power generation, as transport sector is affected by the pandemic. Thus focus should be given in finding indigenous

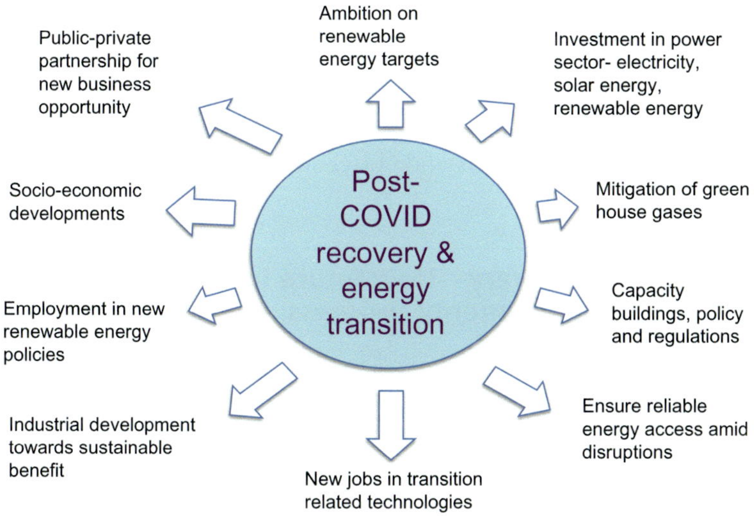

Fig. 1 Some implementation measures for post-COVID-19 energy crisis.

fuel sources and to install renewable energy generation systems to mitigate any sort of energy crisis during postpandemic times.

6.2.2 Concentrating hydrogen-based generations

We can efficiently decarbonize the transportation sector through hydrogen-based fuel generation as the source material can be generated in a clean and green way, i.e. through electrolysis of water (as this process does not rely upon the production of CO_2), and can effectively substitute the fossil fuel-based generations. As a result of COVID-19, EU and Germany focused their attention toward hydrogen production which was able to uplift their fiscal share in the energy sector.[46]

6.2.3 Imprisonment of the solar energy

Solar photovoltaic systems can be installed in the rural settings, where the demand is relatively less, which can be immensely helpful to reduce the postpandemic extended power burden. This can make village life independent of the worldwide fuel price fluctuation, thereby ensuring rural fuel security. For example, Bangladesh government has implemented a total of about 4.13 million solar home systems (SHS) in the rural belts, which have lasted long at about 7–8 years without any tussle.[42]

6.2.4 Step-by-step acceleration of the power load

It is expected that there will be an extreme overburden in the energy sector when everything will be opened up. To control this, the load should be enhanced gradually to maintain the grid viability, otherwise this tripping may cause derogatory system-wide blackout.

7. Green recovery—How future investment can drive sustainable energy progress, energy gap, and how to close them?

Under the present scenario, the billion-dollar question is when this crisis will come to an end and what will be the exact strategies of the policymakers and the stakeholders for the power sector to cope up with the curse of this satanic 'Lilliput.' To combat with this ongoing economic lethality, it is very much important to ignite the flame of sustainable and net-zero emissions economy to perpetuate the future climatic caliber. So, policymakers may view this as the two sides of the same coin; the long-term panacea to drive no-emission economy and the emergency of exigency to resist the economic swing in the new normal, but the uncertainty remains inherent in the questions about whether the urgent surge for a clean and green recovery will fuel up this process or the pandemic stretch will detain the metamorphosis of power industry.[51] Henceforth, the gradually amplified frustrations from the orthodox energy system drive the diversion in the world energy landscape. Undersupply of fossil-based source materials and reasonable cost of renewable resources have compelled several countries (for example, about 60% in Denmark) to complement the gap at a reasonable manner.[52] However, it is essential to say that, this renewable endeavor will definitely not make the industries qualitatively poor, in order to be renewably rich. Consistently, the investment tendencies have also been diversified to reach a sustainable goal.

For example, the Confederation of British Industry, Energy UK, the energy utility SSE, and the National Farmers' Union astonishingly received the 'building back better' motto, to stay tuned with the 'green' struggle. So, needless to say, recent jobs reboot, essence of clean air, government priorities along with the consumer concern are the battery for these low-carbon transitions in the low-contact future.[53] The possible ways for post-COVID-19 recovery are summarized in Fig. 2.

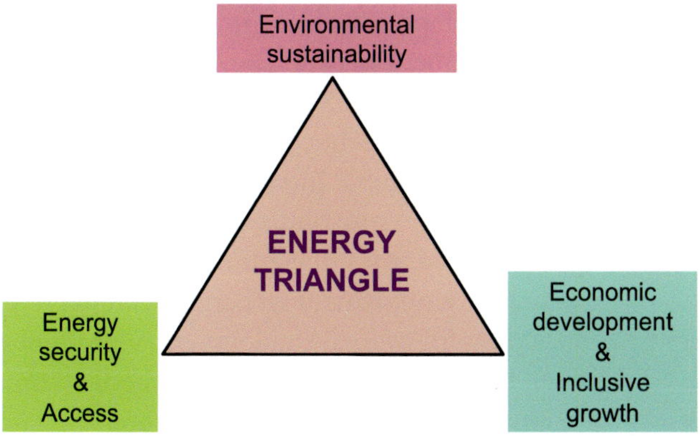

Fig. 2 Possible ways for post-COVID-19 recovery and sustainable energy transition.

7.1 Post-COVID-19 renaissance in the electricity sector

The sectorial twist in the energy stipulation pattern in association with a sharp demand declination has paved the potential for clean energy transition. Emerging needs in the new normal, like virtual smart-working, work from home, and online education,. can be regarded as the key players of this twist and the assumed hike in the post-COVID-19 energy demand. However, it is very easy to dilute these demands for the economic giants, as they cherish abundant, reliable electricity services, but for the developing countries this is not going to be a cakewalk. To drive out a sustainable recovery, European countries brought down fossil-based generations to about 25% during the first quarter of 2020 and renewable candidates, attaining 43% share of the total production during this period, efficiently complement this. In Italy, during March 2020, 45% of the national production has been contributed from renewable generations. According to IRENA, utility-scale wind and solar photovoltaic generation has the potential to outcompete and substitute the fuel-based power plants in a cost-effective way.[52] Another study, conducted by Enel foundation over Brazil, Chile, Argentina, Colombia, Peru, and Ecuador, has advocated mainly the Latin American trends and the results suggested that "almost 50 gigawatt (GW) of photovoltaic and 71 GW of wind can be installed by 2030, covering about 25% (up from today's 1%) of the total electricity demand, with economic benefits estimated at about US$3.6 billion by 2030, considering the fuel savings and the annuity of the investments needed for the additional renewable capacity." Among the developing nations, majorly in some sub-Saharan Africa as well as some Latin American countries, still there are several lacunae in electric accessibility. So on the whole, investment in renewable priorities can support the balance between technologies and operational approaches even in the poorest parts of the globe. Interestingly enough, the dynamism in the world's energy landscape, as outlooked by IRENA, particularly among the Latin American countries, these transition-associated technologies significantly expand the employment scenario, assuming to provide 3.2 million jobs by 2050, almost 8% of total employment opportunities over the continent.[52] Likewise, The Global Commission on the Economy and Climate[54] reports have estimated about 65 million job opportunities and $26 trillion financial yield by 2050, in this low-carbon economy.[53]

"Looking at the full year, the IEA (International Energy Agency) foresees a scenario where global energy demand contracts by 6%, the largest fall in percentage terms since World War II. Fossil fuels have been the most impacted: oil demand for the full year could drop by 9%, coal by 8%, and natural gas by 5%. Even nuclear could see a drop of 2.5%. The only energies not negatively affected are renewables, which could see their production increase by 0.8% as a result of new investments".[22]

7.2 Conclusion in the combustion engine era—A new engine for future

In order to restrain the dirty vehicles, several cities have introduced electrification policy in the transportation sector. To pass the eligibility test, set by EU car CO_2 rules, cars sold throughout 2020 have to restrict their CO_2 emission level below 95 g CO_2/km. Consistent with that, European car market has been shined by 8% share of the electricity-driven vehicles, among the total retail between January and May 2020. The best example is the Zwickau plant, the electric vehicle manufacturer from the Volkswagen factories.[55] Throughout Europe, transport industries are ready to produce 3.5 million electric vehicles in 2020–21 and about 12 battery gigafactories are going to be functional by 2023. In order to achieve the EU car CO_2 rule, it is necessary to grab 30%–40% of the new vehicles to be electrically mobile by 2030, which would be expected to reduce 11% of the total oil demand. German government decided to reduce taxes over the e-mobility sector and related areas. Likewise, US government has launched a benefit-in-kind regime for the e-mobility sector. Most devastatingly, restrain in the international travel policies severely hampered the aviation industry. However, this is not only the European scenario but Asian and American stories are also somewhat same.

7.3 Shift in the business blueprint of the oil companies—Signals for recovery

The international oil market has already started to accustom with the post-COVID-19 decarbonization policies to achieve competitive fitness against the low-emission perceptions. Indian Oil Corporation (IOC) has also taken new business opportunities, focusing on lower emission of toxic gases through restoring carbon, reducing methane emissions, decarbonizing natural gas, etc. The feasibility and competitiveness for decarbonization at a scalable way did not receive much attention by the political leaders, hence public-private partnerships are the only option to promote innovation.

7.4 Vaporization of the global gas markets

According to the IEA, the volatilization of gas market remains less (4% fall by 2020, in comparison with 8% in coal and 9% in gas industry) severe than the other power source sectors, because of its potential for low CO_2 production operations than other fuel-based emissions.[22] In Australia, pandemic became responsible for a drop of about AUD$80 billion of investments in gas and LNG projects. Russian government also decided to invest in this sector for high-speed economic retrieval. United Nations planned on adopting a zero-emission target from 2020 by declining the usage of natural gas and decarbonization through carbon capture utilization and storage (CCUS).

7.5 Recommendations—A ray of hope

For the sake of a quick economic upswing, the Energy Transitions Commission (ETC) keeps faith over several master policies to foster the economic stimulus packages. According to the perception of ETC, there will be four to fivefold increase in the energy demand, so it is extremely necessary to fuel up the renewable generations by at least 10-fold. The regeneration capacity should be uplifted at a level of 1500 GW per year on average within next 30 years to fine-tune this upcoming global energy hunger in addition to improving the grid armature. Needless to say, besides sustaining a low-emission future, investments in the renewable energy sectors can also elaborate the societal economic footprints through incepting job opportunities. Taking lessons from history, after the financial catastrophe in 2008, US government revived 9,00,000 jobs within a five-year time span through massive investments in clean energy projects. Likewise, another forecasting from IRENA recommends about the possibility of 17 million jobs throughout the world in this platform by 2030.[52] The transportation sector also becomes severely standstill by the hit of disease transmission. For the ease of urban transport, two conflicting issues, one is the biasness toward private vehicles over public commute and the environmental safety concerns, can make the electric vehicles winner in the rivalry with its combustion-based cousins. Therefore it is high time to diversify our perceptions toward the never-ending, eco-friendly resources to ensure a green future, with serenity in its entirety.

8. Conclusion and future perspectives

The worldwide emergency of COVID-19 and the incurred economic backwash have increased the worry of policymakers of various developed as well as developing nations, triggering a scout for recovery efforts about the economic frame shift consolidated with environmental sustainability. Capital investment may be the major driving force for technological propagation and to fine-tune the grievance. For the perspective of post-COVID-19 energy landscape, there is an array of options toward the low-emission future, but not all the options will go well at every part of the world. Due to differences in geographical location and topography, advantages vary from place to place. While some regions are suitable for building intermittent renewable resources which can be connected to larger hydropower resources for load stabilizing, some regions have abundance of solar resources along with natural gas. Geological advantages alongside industrial complexes having the capacity to make hydrogen with carbon capture and sequestration are also viable. With rapid exhaustion of fossil fuels a demand for low-cost and renewable energy resources will increase among various sectors too.

The European Union (EU) aimed at increasing their renewable energy share to 32% gross final consumption of energy by 2030 for the purpose of reaching the SDG7 target and decarbonizing its energy system. The EU underlines the significance of renewable energy usage in comparison to fossil fuels that take million years to renew itself and are the cause for greenhouse gas emissions in the atmosphere leading to global warming.[56,57]

IThe stimulus packages, in addition, can help in strengthening the fiscal policies in alignment with climate-neutral policies/targets and alleviating the disruption in the economic frameshift due to COVID-19 pandemic. To materialize all the efforts, boosting the shift in a more coordinated and integrated manner toward the zero carbon energy shift is absolutely necessary along with continuation of fiscal investments in a multilateral approach. Needless to say, COVID-19 strongly exposes the laxity of global economy at a time of system crises associated with an abrupt collapse in international trade as well as in GDP. Besides environmental concerns, the sectorial shift toward clean energy generation may be an excellent platform for short-term job creations promoting a long-term, sustainable economic growth.

The dispute for the establishment of a universal principle and approaches varies across groups, disciplines, and countries. In a broad term, energy shift can be accounted as timely and effective progress of the energy triangle: environmental sustainability, economic development and inclusive growth, and energy security and access. While the long-term impact of COVID-19 on energy systems remains to be seen, lessons can be learned from individual behaviors and international cooperation. Energy transition is the need of the hour with emerging and changing economies. Keeping the future in mind we must persist in our endeavors to overcome any upcoming situation.

References

1. WHO. *WHO coronavirus (COVID-19) dashboard*; 2021 https://covid19.who.int. [Accessed 10 September 2021].
2. Baranwal A, Mahapatra S, Purohit B, Roy S, Chandra P. Insights into novel coronavirus and COVID-19 outbreak. In: Chandra P, Roy S, editors. *Diagnostic strategies for COVID-19 and other coronaviruses. Medical virology: from pathogenesis to disease control.* Singapore: Springer; 2020. p. 1–17. https://doi.org/10.1007/978-981-15-6006-4_1.
3. Satpati GG. Algal sulfated polysaccharides: potent immunomodulators against COVID-19 in pandemic 2020. *Biosci Biotechnol Res Asia* 2020;**17**(3):601–5.
4. Dastidar MG, Roy S. Chapter 13—Public health management during COVID-19 and applications of point-of-care based biomolecular detection approaches. In: Dehghani MH, Karri RR, Roy S, editors. *Environmental and health management of novel coronavirus disease (COVID-19)*; 2021. p. 345–78. https://doi.org/10.1016/B-978-0-323-85780-2.00009-3.
5. Satpati GG. A preliminary report on plant based immunity against SARS-CoV-2 (COVID-19) in pandemic 2020. *Res J Biotechnol* 2020;**15**(10):174–6.
6. Hamid MZSA, Karri RR. Overview of preventive measures and good governance policies to mitigate the COVID-19 outbreak curve in Brunei. In: *COVID-19: systemic risk and resilience.* Cham: Springer; 2021. p. 115–40.
7. Mahapatra S, Baranwal A, Purohit B, Roy S, Mahto SK, Chandra P. Advanced biosensing methodologies for ultrasensitive detection of human corona viruses. In: Chandra P, Roy S, editors. *Diagnostic strategies for COVID-19 and other coronaviruses. Medical virology: from pathogenesis to disease control.* Singapore: Springer; 2020. p. 19–36. https://doi.org/10.1007/978-981-15-6006-4_2.
8. Roy S, Baranwal A. Diverse molecular techniques for early diagnosis of COVID-19 and other coronaviruses. In: Chandra P, Roy S, editors. *Diagnostic strategies for COVID-19*

and other coronaviruses. Medical virology: from pathogenesis to disease control. Singapore: Springer; 2020. p. 135–59. https://doi.org/10.1007/978-981-15-6006-4_7.
9. Sampath Kumar NS, Chintagunta AD, Jeevan Kumar SP, Roy S, Kumar M. Immunotherapeutics for COVID-19 and post vaccination surveillance. 3. *Biotech* 2020;**10**:527. https://doi.org/10.1007/s13205-020-02522-9.
10. Halkos G, Gkampoura EC. Where do we stand on the 17 sustainable development goals? An overview on progress. *Econ Anal Policy* 2021;**70**:94–122. https://doi.org/10.1016/j.eap.2021.02.001. https://www.volkswagen-newsroom.com/en/zwickau-3755.
11. https://sdgs.un.org/goals. (Accessed on 1-05-2021).
12. UN-ESCAP United Nations Economic and Social Commission for Asia and the Pacific. Integrating the three dimensions of sustainable development: a framework and tools. United Nations publication 2015, ST/ESCAP/2737.
13. WHO. Director-General's opening remarks at the media briefing on COVID-19 - 11 March 2020. URL. https://www.who.int/dg/ speeches/detail/who-director-general-s-opening-remarks-at-the-mediabriefing-on-covid-19—11-march-2020. [Accessed 10-05-2020].
14. Berchin, Guerra JBSOA GAIA. 3.0: effects of the coronavirus disease 2019 (COVID-19) outbreak on sustainable development and future perspectives. *Res Glob* 2020;**2**:100014. https://doi.org/10.1016/j.resglo.2020.100014.
15. Khan AH, Tirth V, Fawzy M, Mahmoud AED, Khan NA, Ahmed S, et al. COVID-19 transmission, vulnerability, persistence and nanotherapy: a review. *Environ Chem Lett* 2021;**7**:1–15. https://doi.org/10.1007/s10311-021-01229-4.
16. Mousazadeh M, Naghdali Z, Rahimian N, Hashemi M, Paital B, Al-Qodah Z. Management of environmental health to prevent an outbreak of COVID-19: a review. *Environmental and Health Management of Novel Coronavirus Disease*; 2021. p. 235–67.
17. Roy S, Ramadoss A. Chapter 1—Updated insight into COVID-19 disease and health management to combat the pandemic. In: Dehghani MH, Karri RR, Roy S, editors. *Environmental and health management of novel coronavirus disease (COVID-19)*; 2021. p. 3–39. https://doi.org/10.1016/B978-0-323-85780-2.00017-2.
18. UN (United Nations). Progress towards the sustainable development goals. Report of the General Secretary, E/2021/58, 30th April 2021.
19. Ranjbari M, Shams Esfandabadi Z, Zanetti MC, Scagnelli SD, Siebers PO, Aghbashlo M, et al. Three pillars of sustainability in the wake of COVID-19: a systematic review and future research agenda for sustainable development. *J Clean Prod* 2021;**297**:126660. https://doi.org/10.1016/j.jclepro.2021.126660.
20. Tracking SDG 7. *The energy progress report 2020, Washington DC*; 2020 https://trackingsdg7.esmap.org/downloads. [Accessed 10 April 2020].
21. IEA. *World energy outlook 2019*; 2019 https://www.iea.org/reports/world-energy-outlook-2019. [Accessed 10 March 2021].
22. IEA. *Global energy reviews*; 2020 https://www.iea.org/reports/global-energy-review-2020. [Accessed 20 April 2021].
23. IEA. *Africa energy outlook 2019*; 2019 https://www.iea.org/reports/africa-energy-outlook-2019. [Accessed 10 March 2021].
24. UN Environment programme, https://www.unep.org/explore-topics/sustainable-development-goals/why-do-sustainable-development-goals-matter/goal-7 [Accessed 4-05-2021].
25. REMAG. Transcending barriers to energy access through renewables. In: *Souvenir of the 8th annual technical symposium. Department of Energy and Environment TERI School of Advanced studies*; 2018.
26. IEA. *SDG7: data and projections*. Paris: IEA; 2020. https://www.iea.org/reports/sdg7-data-and-projections. [Accessed 20 April 2021].

27. WHO. *Building country capacity towards clean cooking solutions: the importance of setting standards.* Kampala, Uganda: Expert Consultation; 2019. https://www.who.int/airpollution/events/standards_workshop_kampala/en/. [Accessed 22 July 2020].
28. IEA. *Global Energy Review 2019: The latest trends in energy and emissions in 2019*; 2020 https://www.iea.org/reports/global-energy-review-2019. [Accessed 20 April 2021].
29. IEA. *Achievements of appliance energy efficiency standards and labelling programs. international energy agency technology collaboration programme on energy efficient end-use equipment (4E-TCP), Paris*; 2016 https://www.iea-4e.org/files/otherfiles/0000/0377/4E_2016_S_L_Report_Final.pdf. [Accessed 20 May 2020].
30. The World Bank Annual Report; 2018 https://documents1.worldbank.org/curated/en/630671538158537244/pdf/The-World-Bank-Annual-Report-2018.pdf. [Accessed 12 June 2020].
31. REN21. Renewables 2020c Global Status Report (Paris: REN21 Secretariat). 2020. https://www.ren21.net>gsr-2020. [Accessed 20 June 2020].
32. IRENA. *Renewable capacity statistics 2019.* Abu Dhabi: International Renewable Energy Agency (IRENA); 2019. p. 2–47.
33. IHA. *Global capacity based on International Hydropower Association (IHA), Hydropower Status Report (London: 2020)*; 2020 https://www.hydropower.org/sites/default/files/publications-docs/2020_hydropower_status_report_-_28_may_2020.pdf. [Accessed 20 May 2021].
34. IEA. *World energy outlook 2019*; 2018 https://www.iea.org/reports/world-energy-outlook-2018. [Accessed 10 March 2021].
35. IEA. *Oil 2020 (Paris: 2020)*; 2020 https://www.iea.org/reports/oil-2020. [Accessed 15 May 2021].
36. IEA. *International Energy Agency (IEA) Geothermal, 2019 Country Reports (Taupo, New Zealand: February 2020)*; 2019 http://iea-gia.org/publications-2/annual-reports. [Accessed 10 March 2021].
37. IPCC. *Summary for policymakers of IPCC special report on global warming of 1.5°C approved by governments*; 2018 https://www.ipcc.ch/2018/10/08/summary-for-policymakers-of-ipcc-special-report-on-global-warming-of-1-5c-approved-by-governments/. [Accessed 18 March 2021].
38. Cantarero MMV. Of renewable energy, energy democracy, and sustainable development: a roadmap to accelerate the energy transition in developing countries. *Energy Res Soc Sci* 2020;**70**:101716. https://doi.org/10.1016/j.erss.2020.101716.
39. IEA. *Put clean energy at the heart of stimulus plans to counter the coronavirus crisis.* Paris: IEA; 2020. https://www.iea.org/commentaries/put-clean-energy-at-the-heart-of-stimulus-plans-to-counter-the-coronavirus-crisis. [Accessed 15 May 2021].
40. IEA. *Renewables 2020: analysis and forecast to 2025.* International Energy Agency; 2020. https://www.iea.org/reports/renewables-2020. [Accessed 15 May 2021].
41. IEA. *The impact of the Covid-19 crisis on clean energy progress.* Paris: IEA; 2020. https://www.iea.org/articles/the-impact-of-the-covid-19-crisis-on-clean-energy-progress. [Accessed 15 May 2021].
42. Elavarasan RM, Shafiullah GM, Raju K, Mudgal V, Arif MT, Jamal T, et al. COVID-19: impact analysis and recommendations for power sector operation. *Appl Energy* 2020;**279**(1):115739. https://doi.org/10.1016/j.apenergy.2020.115739.
43. European Power Exchange (EPEX SPOT) SE; 2020 https://www.epexspot.com/en. [Accessed 19 April 2020].
44. The Iberian Electricity Market; 2020 https://www.mibel.com/en/home_en/. [Accessed 19 April 2020].
45. AEMO. *Australian energy market operator, quarterly energy dynamics Q1 2020, market insights and WA market operations.* AEMO; 2020. https://aemo.com.au/-/media/files/major-publications/qed/2020/qedq2020.pdf?la=en&hash=490D1E0CA7A21DB537741C5C18F2FF0A. [Accessed 25 April 2020].

46. McGrath M. *Five key questions about energy after Covid-19*; 2020 https://www.bbc.com/news/science-environment-52943037. [Accessed 27 June 2020].
47. IRENA. *COVID-19 and renewables- impact on the energy system, international renewable energy agency*; 2020 https://www.irena.org/events/2020/Jun/COVID-19-and-renewables-impact-on-the-energy-system. [Accessed 20 June 2020].
48. POSOCO. *Power system operation corporation limited (2020b)*. India: National Load Despatch Centre; 2020. https://posoco.in/. [Accessed 27 April 2020].
49. Sasi A. *Solar imports soar, it's now more make-in-China than make-in-India*. The Indian Express; 2020. https://indianexpress.com/article/business/solar-imports-soar-itsnow-more-make-in-china-than-make-in-india-6222146/. [Accessed 19 April 2020].
50. https://energy.economictimes.indiatimes.com.
51. Agrawala S, Dussaux D, Monti N. *What policies for greening the crisis response and economic recovery?: lessons learned from past green stimulus measures and implications for the COVID-19 crisis*. OECD Environment Working Papers, No.164, Paris: OECD Publishing; 2020. https://doi.org/10.1787/c50f186f-en.
52. IRENA. *The post-COVID recovery: an agenda for resilience, development and equality*. Abu Dhabi: International Renewable Energy Agency; 2020. p. 1–143.
53. http://newclimateeconomy.net.
54. The Global Commission on the Economy and Climate; 2018 http://newclimateeconomy.net. [Accessed 10 April 2021].
55. https://www.volkswagen-newsroom.com/en/zwickau-3755.
56. European Parliament and the Council of the European Union. *Directive 2009/28/EC on the promotion of the use of energy from renewable sources*; 2009.
57. European Parliament and the Council of the European Union. *Directive (EU) 2018/2001 on the promotion of the use of energy from renewable sources*; 2018.

CHAPTER FIVE

Impact of COVID-19 on decent work, economic growth, and world trade

Shirsendu Nandi[a] **and Chetna Chauhan**[b]
[a]Quantitative Techniques and Operations Management Area, FORE School of Management, New Delhi, India
[b]School of Management, Universidad de Los Andes, Bogotá, Colombia

1. Present status of the world economy

As the pandemic continues, it is going to decide the fate of global economic activity. In 2021 the world economy is set to step toward the strongest postrecession recovery in the last 80 years.[1] The recovery will be nonuniform across nations as it is anticipated that the major economies may register strong progress while most developing economies may experience lag. This year the growth in the global economy is predicted to accelerate to 5.6%, capitalizing on the potential of major economies of the world, namely, the United States and China. The world economy has picked up in 2021; however, the global GDP level will be 3.2% lower than the forecasts before the pandemic. The developing countries are going to face the slump for a much extended period.

It is expected that a quarter of growth in 2021 would come from China and the United States.[2] The strength of the US economy lies in substantial financial support and widespread vaccination drive, which contributed to a 6.8% GDP growth, which is the highest since the 1980s. China has already shifted its focus toward its economic stability and is expected to see an 8.5% growth.[1] A surge in outside demand and increased prices may lead to GDP growth in emerging market economies. It needs to be noted that the economic recovery depends on reappearances of COVID-19 waves, imbalances in vaccination drives, and measures by the governments.[3] In addition to the direct effects of the pandemic, the developing economies are struck with dampening skills due to loss of jobs and obstructed education, lesser investment, greater debts, and vulnerable economic structure.[4]

COVID-19 and the Sustainable Development Goals
https://doi.org/10.1016/B978-0-323-91307-2.00002-X

The experts have been optimistic about the ability of major emerging markets to cope with the pandemic and reduce new cases. Except for China, the growth among emerging market economies is expected to be 4.7% in 2022 in light of the withdrawal of support from the government. This perception rests on substantial uncertainty. The economy can be disrupted with pandemic waves, an environment filled with bankruptcies, stress, and social discontentment. Nevertheless, spillovers from developed countries have the potential to generate more dynamic growth globally.

All things considered, the pandemic is relied upon to have made genuine difficulties in the context of development.[5] The per capita pay growth rate is projected to be 4.9% among developing and emerging economies.[6] However, per capita pay lost in 2020 won't be completely recovered by 2022 in around 66% of developing and emerging economies, including 3/4 of struggling low-income nations. Before the current year is over, around 100 million individuals might have fallen once again into outrageous neediness while so-called weakest communities would have felt the majority of these antagonistic effects—females, kids, and casual laborers.[6]

The operations of almost all sectors have been affected by the pandemic. Lockdowns, supply chain interruptions, social distancing, and the issues of migrant laborers have led to changes in the functioning of the businesses. In light of the earlier discussion, the present chapter sets out to Impact of COVID-19 on Decent Work, Economic Growth, and World Trade. Section 2 examines the effect of the pandemic on economic growth. In Section 3, the effects on the trade have been discussed by highlighting the specific issues faced by the production sector and international trade including foreign direct investment (FDI) concerns. Section 4 presents an overview of decent work across key sectors. In Section 5, policies for recovery have been discussed. Section 6 concludes with future perspectives.

2. Pandemic crisis on the economic growth

The growth in the low-income countries (LICs) has been about 2.9% owing to lower vaccination. On comparing the per capita gains, it can be easily recalled that these are similar to what was two decades back in this set of nations. This is the highest sluggishness that the world has ever observed in the last two decades if the dip in 2020 is ignored. The output of LICs has been much lesser than what was forecasted before the COVID-19. The worst impact of the virus has been observed in LICs and the areas under conflict. However, it is expected that Asia and the Pacific regions would recover soon, especially the eastern part of Asia, mainly due to the power portrayed by China.[7] On the other hand, severe rebounds of the pandemic in India, Pakistan, and Nepal, particularly the second wave, would hamper the recovery in South Asia. The Middle East would see growth; however, this growth might not be enough to offset the effects of the earlier shrinkage.

Coming to Latin America and the Caribbean, it can be anticipated that they would also not be able to overcome the ill effects on their economy that happened in 2020.[8] The recovery in the sub-Saharan region is affected by the lower vaccination and subsequent delays to major investments in infrastructure and the extractives sector. However, these regions might be supported by the externalities of the recovery across the globe. It needs to be noted that, though the challenges have been anticipated, the picture will be clear only in the longer run. Several other issues pose a major threat to these countries, particularly after the COVID-19 crisis.[9] For example, the unmanageable burden of debt due to increased borrowing to fight the pandemic. With sluggishness on account of economic activities, a gradual recovery in 2021, and enhanced health-related social and economic spending, the burden of debts on low-income developing counties has risen to unsustainable levels. Therefore servicing obligations related to external debt will represent a big task.

A suspension, recently extended by another 6 months to mid-2021, on debt service payments of bilateral loans to 73 developing countries classified as least developed countries by the UN.[13] However, temporary postponement concerning service payments is not enough. Additional debt relief would be required to help the lower-income and least developed economies overcome the economic threat worsened by the pandemic. Furthermore, procedures for restructuring sovereign debt at the international level are fragmented and are insufficient to solve sovereign debt crises. With additional resources unlikely to be mobilized from other sources, such as Official Development Assistance, borrower countries will be left without additional external finance in a state of crisis when their citizens need support for healthcare and social well-being. Also, the debt servicing costs have been on the rise since 2012.[1]

Additionally, the developing nations face problems with repayments since the denomination of public debt in foreign currency. Fig. 1 shows the total amount of sovereign debt repayments due from different economies. The whopping amount due at the end of 2021 is about $2.7 trillion. A major proportion of this amount is due by governments in

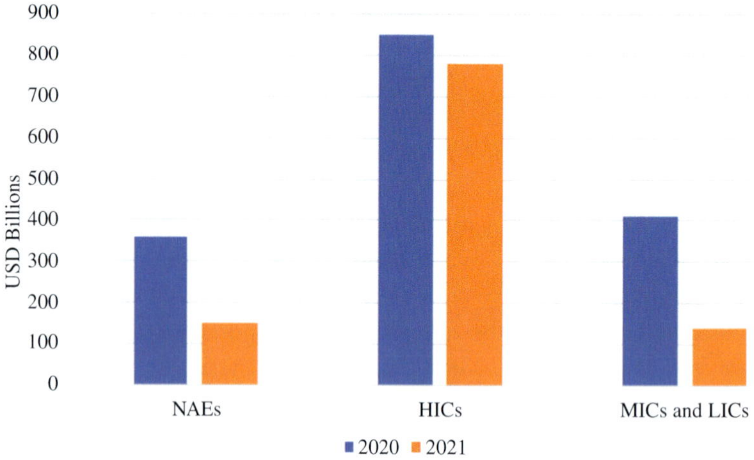

Fig. 1 Public external debt for MICs and LICs and Sovereign debt for HICs and NAEs (based on UNCTAD secretariat calculations). NAEs (new advanced economies): Russian Federation, Republic of Korea, Turkey, Hong Kong, Ukraine. HICs (high-income developing countries): Argentina, Lebanon, Brazil, Colombia, China, Chile, Mexico, Malaysia, Saudi Arabia, Thailand, UAE. MICs and LICs (middle- and low-income developing countries): India, Ghana, Egypt, Indonesia, Pakistan, Nigeria, Burkina Faso, Ethiopia, Philippines, Madagascar, Rwanda, Nepal, Sierra Leone, Yemen, Uganda, Belize, Bangladesh, Bolivia, Cameroon, Djibouti, Cote d'Ivoire, Fiji, Guatemala, Kenya, Honduras, Nicaragua, Paraguay, Papua New Guinea, Solomon Islands, Tonga.

low- and middle-income countries (MICs), as evident from Fig. 1. The possibilities of financing from external sources would be shrinking due to the pandemic. Therefore the repayment should be suspended for LICs and MICs for the current year to prevent any chances of widespread debt crises.

Another issue that required resolution in the short term is that of the migrant workers. There are 164 million migrant workers globally, and they constitute about 64% of total immigrants.[10] Millions of migrant employees were serving at the forefront during the pandemic as healthcare workers. It needs to be acknowledged that about 20% of doctors and 15% of nurses are immigrants. Migrant workers contribute to their homeland as well as the place they are employed. One of the major highlights of the COVID-19 crisis was the experiences of migrant workers across the world.[11] The scale at which the effects of pandemic-related crises affected this community was huge and created a debate in the global community. Especially, the healthcare and economic crises that these communities faced were huge. The COVID-19 pandemic has shed more light on the important role played by migrant workers in their destination. At the time of lockdown, several restrictions were imposed. Even then, several supply chains could resume operations due to migrant workers. However, obstructions in the movement of workers affected migration and thus cast an effect on other sectors. The agriculture sector was most affected as it is much more dependent on migrant workers as compared to other sectors. Seasonal farmworkers were affected due to the lockdown barricades and a record shortfall of about 1 million workers, which has been reported to affect Europe.[12]

3. Impact on trade

The dissent caused by the pandemic compelled business leaders across the globe to quickly adjust their systems for the well-being and security of their people. However, the survival of the organizations is another obvious test that business leaders have faced during pandemic times. The actions, such as lockdown, were taken to prevent the infection spread, which was followed by a scenario where production facilities halted, wrecking the whole worldwide network of value chains. It could be easily noticed that manufacturing has been one of the most noticeably hit sectors. The manufacturing industry represented almost 16% of the worldwide GDP in 2018.[13] Thus the focus of the government bodies across the nations essentially centers around empowering this sector leading to initiatives such as Make for India and Made in China 2025. Made in China 2025 has been the foundation strategy to transform China into a manufacturing hub. The strategy looks forward to moving China up the supply chain by using technological innovations or Industry 4.0 technologies. It is reported that 75% of organizations have one or more than one Tier 1 supplier from China.

Similarly, Make in India was launched in 2015 to invigorate the creation of products in India and diminish India's reliance on trading countries by production in their own country. Since then, FDI in the nation has trailed an ideal direction. The FDI got in the country since April 2000 is $592 billion, which was about double India's FDI from April 2014 to March 2019, i.e., $286 billion.[14] This brought about allowing FDI in various sectors along with venture-friendly policies. Unfortunately, the COVID-19 flare-up could cause worldwide FDI to contract by 5%–15% because of the plant closures that led to the shrinkage in the manufacturing sector.[1] The adverse consequences of COVID-19 on FDI ventures have been more in energy, auto, and aircraft businesses. Because of the plagues of COVID-19 across the globe, the makers of chemical, electronic gadgets, and airplanes confronted concerns in regard to the supply of inputs. Many of these companies initiated a decrease in underway activities and deferred the launch of new items, mainly due to the interrupted supply of components. The gadgets business is fundamentally influenced because of the COVID-19, as China is responsible for almost 85% of the worth of parts used in cell phones and almost 75% on account of televisions.[15] For example, every basic part, printed circuit sheets, LED chips, memory, TV panels, and capacitors, is imported from China. But, in January 2020, part costs increased by almost 2%–3% because of industrial facility closure, adversely affecting businesses across the globe.[15]

Looking at Europe, the automobile and gadget makers briefly shut their processing plants or limited their production, which brought about misfortune to the trade worldwide. For example, Daimler and Volkswagen announced as of late that they would briefly close down vehicle and motor manufacturing in their plants in Europe due to the COVID-19 episode to ensure the well-being of their laborers.[16] Companies such as Ford Motors Co.; Samsung Electronics Co., Ltd.; BASF SE; and Boeing Co. were badly hit by the pandemic. Further, these organizations also initiated moving their production facilities from the worst-hit nations to the nations with lesser COVID-19 plague. For example, in 2021, Ford Motors Co. cancelled a joint endeavor it had entered with Mahindra and Mahindra in 2019, referring to the reason that the COVID-19 pandemic exacerbated the situation for Ford.[17] The endeavor was pointed toward creating, promoting, and distributing Ford vehicles in India and some Ford and Mahindra items in the global markets. With that joint venture off the cards, Ford's odds of persistence in the Indian market became drearier and the company decided to exit India.

3.1 Production and international trade

The rate of decline of the industrial production index has slowed down in 2021. The average decline across nations concerning the industrial production index between March 2020 and June 2020 was 2.5%.[18] The average percentage decrease across lower- and middle-income nations fell in the first quarter of 2020 but was better in the next quarter of 2020. The index of industrial production recorded a lower decrease for upper- and middle-income countries in the first two quarters of 2020. The environment is full of uncertainties, and the impacts are going to be disproportionate across the sectors. United Nations Industrial Development Organization (UNIDO) compared production data between December 2019 and June 2020 for

62 nations that together account for about 9/10th of manufacturing value-added globally. The analysis shows that more than 50% of those nations have gone through a stretched economic downturn over January–June 2020. A few nations restricted their exports and accelerated their imports. Many nations did not apply trade policy.[19] Also, in most of the developed nations, capital spending is diminished by different extents. The majority of the countries saw a reduced investment in machinery and equipment.[18] This translates into a lower trade with other economies. Despite several measures, such as the introduction of liquidity and a reduction of borrowing, the investment was constricted in 2020. The hardships faced by international trade were worsened by a steep fall in the cost of energy. It needs to be noted that energy is an important component of most agricultural nations' trade. A particularly extreme fall in their unfamiliar trade profit added to the difficulties previously presented by money deteriorations vis-à-vis the US dollar.[20,21] In 2020 the effect of the pandemic on the trade volume of merchandise was different across geographies. Most countries recorded huge drops in both imports and exports.[22] The only exception was Asia. In Asia, the volumes of exports saw a surge of 0.3%. The volumes of imports were down by 1.3%. The strongest decline in imports was observed in the geographies which are rich in natural resources, namely, Africa, Middle East, and South America. This could be attributed to lower revenues in exports, with oil prices down by 35%. As compared to other geographies, North America saw a relatively lower decline in imports. Due to the large fiscal measures in the United States, the demand for merchandised products has been driven by North America, which is also motivating for other economies. South America and Europe are seeing an increase in imports with other regions following the league with slight improvement.[23]

Most of the worldwide demand for imports is being covered by Asian exports. The exports from Asia are anticipated to increase by 8.4% in 2021. The exports from Europe will also grow to the same extent. However, North and South America would see a smaller rise in exports compared to Asia and Europe in 2021. Exports from Africa and the Middle East depend on the travel sector as demand for oil would increase in that case.[24]

3.2 Foreign direct investment

Due to the sudden outbreak of the pandemic and subsequent lockdown, foreign direct investment (FDI) was instantly struck. Some of the expenditures related to the investment continued, but many of them were obstructed. A chain of events was triggered. A steep decline in FDI inflows worldwide was reported. According to the United Nations Conference on Trade and Development (UNCTAD), COVID-19 would lead to a downfall in FDI, which is mainly due to the contraction in the manufacturing industry and shutdowns.[25] This downfall is expected to be about 5%–15%. The FDI flows value in 2019 was about $1.6 trillion. The pandemic shed an adverse impact on FDI immediately after its commencement, leading to a downturn in economies. The incomparable pandemic circumstances led to the tardy execution of the investment projects. The new projects were shelved, and the foreign affiliate income saw a sharp decline. In 2020 the FDI was less than $1 trillion for the time ever (since 2005). It is anticipated that FDI will mark recovery only in 2022 or even after that. Various projects announcements were shelved. On similar lines, most of the mergers and acquisitions were postponed for uncertain times or even annulled. Even the hyped mergers were delayed in the United States and Europe due to issues with the approval.

4. Decent work: An overview

As per the investigations by International Labour Organization (ILO), 1.1 Mn of automotive manufacturing employees in the European Union were impacted due to the shutdowns in March 2020.[26] This is about 40% of the total population employed in the automotive sector. Most of these workers are German. These figures allude just to laborers straightforwardly working with car, truck, van, and transport producers. Nonetheless, considering the broader supply chain networks, the pandemic influences the entirety of the 13.8 million jobs in the EU. In the absence of new revenue streams, many organizations will confront huge liquidity issues in short to medium term. In the United States, the pandemic is influencing around 150,000 unionized laborers and countless nonunionized laborers in the industry.[27] The interruption in India's auto industry and its supply chain network is probably going to cost more than US$ 800 million by 2021. Contract laborers represent more than half of the labor force and are especially in danger in the near and medium term. A decline in manufacturing and demand cast a huge thump on the impact on laborers, both as far as business and working conditions in apparel manufacturing. An expected 200 manufacturing plants in Cambodia either deferred or reduced production, and more than 5000 employees have lost their positions.[26] In Myanmar, an absence of crude materials from China has prompted the shutdown of somewhere around 20 industrial facilities and acted as a hammer on about 10,000 jobs.[25] Simultaneously, the quantity of orders has plunged. In Vietnam, about 440,000–880,000 laborers could confront diminished hours or joblessness. In the direst outcome imaginable, this number could reach as high as 1.3 million. More than 2.17 million laborers in Bangladesh have been influenced by the emergency, with many confronting joblessness as orders are dropped, and production decays steeply. About 20% of firms were found to keep paying staff compensation for over a month under these conditions. Over 1,000,000 laborers have effectively been excused or furloughed.[25] Further, the impact on decent work across some of the sectors has been discussed.

4.1 Health sector

The healthcare industry is a significant wellspring of work. In many locales, business development rates for healthcare have been better as compared to other sectors. Healthcare and social work represented more than 105 million positions worldwide in 2013, 130 million positions in 2018, and an expected 136 million positions in 2020.[28] Moreover, well-being frameworks can create more good positions by animating development in different areas, like gear and mechanical production. In the United States, for instance, the healthcare sector was phenomenal in beating the 2007–2008 monetary emergency. Between 2006 and 2016, business development in medical care settings was 20%, in contrast to just 3% in the remainder of the economy. It is reported that 18 out of the 30 quickest developing occupations are in medical care and related occupations, adding an extended 3.4 million positions by 2028.[28] The United Nations High-Level Commission on Health Employment and Economic Growth perceived the healthcare area as a vital financial area and its interests in the well-being of the labor force. Moreover, the investment toward healthcare is expected to gain ground toward meeting the Sustainable Development Goals.[29] Data show, nonetheless, that practically all healthcare systems face difficulties finding, deploying, and holding adequate qualified, skilled, and motivated employees. Generally speaking, it is assessed that there will be a worldwide shortage of 18 million healthcare workers by 2030, which will principally influence low- and middle-income nations. The inconsistent spread of healthcare workers both between and inside nations establishes an obstruction to healthcare value.[30] Moreover, loopholes in healthcare would essentially influence the least fortunate populaces, especially in the countryside.[28] In 2014 the extent of the populace without admittance to healthcare administrations because of deficiencies was assessed at 84% in low-income nations. In some Asian and African nations, more than 90% of the populace had no admittance to medical services because of outrageous deficiencies in the number of healthcare workers (under three well-being laborers for every 10,000 individuals).

4.2 Agriculture

Various significant European agrarian nations, including France, Italy, Germany, Spain, and Poland, are especially frail. It is estimated that over a fourth of the food produced in the nation depends on roughly 370,000 normal occasional migrant agricultural laborers. The pandemic has likewise genuinely affected manpower-intensive harvest and because of deficiencies of manpower, lockdowns, and the brief discontinuance of farming. For instance, Europe's rural area is confronting extraordinary deficiencies because of terminated travel. Countless part-timers could not arrive at ranches that depended on their work during the reaping period. The effect on the sector is relied upon to be a long haul. Around 100,000 farmworkers will most likely be unable to come to Italy this year,[31] and the figure might be twofold that in France. In Germany, about 286,000 occasional transient laborers are locked inconsistently in organic product, vegetable, and wine creation; the government is investigating various methods of getting adequate laborers for the collection, including running nonstop flights for farmworkers and giving impermanent work licenses. On April 2, 2020, the European Commission had given viable direction for the Member States to work with cross-line travel for part-timers in basic occupations, which incorporate food area laborers, while setting up all vital means to stay away from the additional spread of the pandemic. The pandemic may likewise contrarily affect the livelihoods of millions of estate laborers occupied with exports. For instance, the new impermanent suspension of one of the world's biggest tea barters in Mombasa, Kenya, where tea from numerous eastern African nations is exchanged, whenever delayed, could devastatingly affect nearby economies. In Kenya alone, tea gives employment to somewhere in the range of 600,000 limited ranchers and daily wage earners. The immediate effect will be felt in different chain hubs, including processing plants, stockrooms, and carriers, just as homesteads, which might be compelled to stop production and lay off pluckers, who are frequently among the most burdened laborers and profoundly powerless against the financial inversion.

4.3 Construction

Construction laborers are among the weakest migrants who are confronting critical vulnerability and monetary difficulties because of the pandemic. Their everyday environments are such that social isolation to prevent the spread of the pandemic may not be possible, which has given rise to worry about the spread of the infection. Limitations on worldwide travel straightforwardly affected laborers' movement, prompting tough spots, for example, enrollment delays, questionable or unpredictable lawful status in nations, and being kept from getting back to homeland.[32] Besides, transient laborers are generally rejected from public reaction measures, for example, wage sponsorships, advantages of government-backed retirement, and social assurance measures. Continually changing travel and well-being necessities make it hard for enlistment offices to ensure laborers during movement and after their appearance in objective nations, placing laborers in powerless and now and then risky circumstances. Travelers who have lost their positions might be compelled to get back to nations previously confronting high joblessness and neediness, while others abandoned in host nations might be in danger of double-dealing and denials of basic liberties. Loss of pay is likewise bringing about a serious decrease in settlements sent home by traveler laborers generally. At last, the emergency can touch off or worsen complaints, segregation, doubt, and a feeling of unfairness over admittance to well-being administrations, nice positions.

5. Policies for recovery

In the present setting, tracking down the best way to a comprehensive recuperation requires managing the vulnerability of the planning process and execution of business policy framed by the government. The crossing point of the effect of the COVID-19 emergency and the continuous fate of work lies in the innovations, changes in demography, and environmental aspects. These factors ostensibly characterize the key strategic needs throughout the next few years. As highlighted by ILO's examination, the COVID-19 emergency has lopsidedly influenced females in various ways. The improvements concerning gender equality that were achieved in late many years have been nullified.

Moreover, the existing gender imbalances in the work market have intensified. The female workforce has been at far more serious risk than males, especially attributable to the slump effect on the service industry. It needs to be noted that females represent a huge proportion of the workforce in front-end occupations. For example, in the healthcare and well-being areas, females represent around 70% of all jobs. Simultaneously, ladies represent a huge extent of laborers in forefront occupations, particularly in the well-being and social consideration areas where ladies address around 70% of all specialists. To counter the gender-oriented impacts of the COVID-19 emergency, policymakers need to consider how gender equality can be incorporated into public work approaches as a central goal across various strategy areas. The policy measures need to be targeted at hard-hit areas (e.g., retail, convenience) and communities (e.g., ladies, youngsters, and others, like people with inabilities), particularly those in the casual economy, during the reactivation and recuperate.

The advancement of an approach with public monetary and work recuperation programs incorporating and organizing the commitment from various services and organizations is the key to thrive in the new normal. Focusing on the creation of relevant and useful positions, including reliable data on the figures and constant monitoring should be an integral part of recuperation packages. Useful change is a basic support to higher efficiency and quality positions. It should adjust admittance to primary worldwide sources of info, innovation, and information with designated backing to create and overhaul neighborhood creation limits. This works better by proceeding with changes and key connections between government and private enterprises. A cooperative and open participatory way is required to deal with procedures, plans and strategy execution. This encompasses social discourse and cooperation between governments, managers' and laborers' delegates, the scholarly community and common society—agreeing on key needs and acquiring resources for execution and further identification of responsibility. The intervention will, in general, can have a critical effect. At the end of the day, these arrangements or intercessions will, work preferably together. The experience of formalization scenes likewise shows that its requirements should set the specific mix of financial and institutional strategies in every area. The extent of 6:4 was demonstrated to be compelling in the Latin America and the Caribbean formalization scene of 2005–15.[1] The coordination of numerous intercessions is, in any case, an intricate test that public institutional settings should address.[1]

As the pandemic hit the nations, the governments focused primarily on interim policy measures to keep businesses going and retaining employment.[3] Immediate financial assistance was also given to businesses to deal with financial problems such as debts. The policies were framed to safeguard the workers and stimulate the rapid recommencement of domestic manufacturing. Several public procurement policies and subsidies for use were implemented.

Long- and medium-term policy measures are expected to take a forward seat as short-term measures in the COVID-19 did not prove their worth, as the world saw the dwindling traditional business models in the time of the pandemic. A review of African firms by UNIDO highlights that underlying changes in supply chains, like a change in demand patterns for the products and services and unmet demands, are to be impugned for the adverse effect on the industries. Therefore it is inevitable now to frame policies that strengthen the production and supply network alternatives. It is also important for the firms to invest in their production facilities and follow strategies that make them resilient for the future. The governments should frame policies that boost the efforts of the organizations to overhaul and revamp their operations toward being more resilient. Measures such as redeploying manpower, transitioning to new business models, improving productivity, and designing better products need to be implemented in full swing. The policymakers must therefore frame policies that are in line with the expected measures to transform the businesses. The case of Germany is worth mentioning in this regard. Germany, for example, has been a pioneer of Industry 4.0 and supports investments in cutting-edge technologies to foster growth and resilience.[33] New Zealand formulated a new manufacturing strategy as a result of COVID-19. The new policy focuses on making the energy, transport, and logistics sector more resilient. New Zealand too, like Germany, has been investing in Industry 4.0 technologies across all the sectors.[34] New business models' development would be in conjunction with the advancement in technological innovation, better products, and pushing these products into new markets.[35] All this can be achieved with the help of knowledge creation and the dissemination of technological know-how. University and industrial tie-ups would boost these initiatives. Therefore the tourism and education sector also need major attention shortly.

Recovery contributions would meet the extraordinary financial needs in the COVID-19. For example, a cess personal income tax for high-income groups can be incorporated.[36] Further, taxation on high profits would affirm that the organizations that prospered during and after the crisis contribute to building a better tomorrow.[37] The pandemic can accelerate permanent taxation movement in nations where it is desired to increase revenue for the government.[38]

6. Conclusions and future perspectives

It can be concluded that short-, medium-, as well as long-term policy measures for the industries with a spectrum of focus that ranges from relief measures to business model innovations would together pave the way for the development of a brighter future. The outcomes of the current policy reforms would be available in the medium term. The researchers and policymakers need to have a bird's-eye view of these outcomes and be ready for the iterations as required. Several unforeseeable issues would arise in the post-COVID-19 world, especially in developing countries. Continuing the businesses might be a challenge in the near future but is also a key for the well-being of the communities. To future-proof industry, policymakers need to outline the strategic fields that require immediate attention. The operations need to be made solid and should be able to withstand disruptions. Some of the action points for the manufacturing companies would include impetus on local inputs, developing local supply chains, development of new products, and reaching new markets. Technologies such as big data and predictive analytics can be utilized to locate the sources of potential disruptions and improve resilience.[39–41] By identifying the patterns in a vast amount of data flowing from the technology interventions can help to improve the availability of information for the key metrics and improve understanding of the complex workings of the organizations.[42] This could also be the first step on the way to autonomous systems that are resilient to shocks. As the restrictions that had been put in place to combat the spread of COVID-19 ease, transparency will become even more important. Companies will need to be flexible with their supply chain partners while they ensure that rising demand can be met. Therefore the foundation of the utility of technology capabilities would lie in collaboration and information sharing among the partners.[43,44] The internal and external actors can collaborate to make their organization equipped with information and communication technologies such as artificial intelligence, and the Internet of Things to increase collaboration.[45,46] The collaboration needs to be utilized in every aspect of the business, right from investing in technology capabilities to cocreation of sustainable outputs.[40] Therefore focusing on trust, collaboration, and technological capabilities, the global trade would be ready to face future contingencies as well.[47] As the United Nation (UN)'s SDGs propound to act as a guideline toward the achievement of sustainable development, SDG-17 particularly focuses on cross-sector as well as cross-country partnerships and cooperation for the achievement of goals. The measures highlighted earlier would reinforce the means of implementing and revitalizing the global partnership for sustainable development. The journey of driving the nations toward SDGs is grounded in unbiased sharing of risks and benefits and would require actions such as collaborative planning and development, exchange of information, and coordination at various levels among the different stakeholders in the global trade.[48] For a sustainable future, organizations need to align their goals with the SDGs not only at the strategic but also at the operational level.[49,50] Policies built upon shared vision, principles, and values at every level are inevitable to drive the agenda of revival successfully.

Acknowledgment

The infrastructural support provided by FORE School of Management, New Delhi in completing this book chapter is gratefully acknowledged.

References

1. UNCTAD. *Impact of the COVID-19 pandemic on trade and development: transitioning to a new normal*; 2020.
2. Worldbank. *Global economy on track for strong but uneven growth as COVID-19 still weighs*; 2021 https://www.worldbank.org/en/news/feature/2021/06/08/the-global-economy-on-track-for-strong-but-uneven-growth-as-covid-19-still-weighs. [Accessed 5 September 2021].
3. Hamid MZSA, Karri RR. Overview of preventive measures and good governance policies to mitigate the COVID-19 outbreak curve in Brunei. In: *COVID-19: systemic risk and resilience*. Cham: Springer; 2021. p. 115–40.
4. Harilal KN. World economy and nation states post COVID-19. *Econ Pol Wkly* 2020.
5. Legese FH. The world economy at COVID-19 quarantine: contemporary review. *Int J Econ Financ Manag Sci* 2020. https://doi.org/10.11648/j.ijefm.20200802.11.
6. International Monetary Fund. *Mitigating climate change—growth- and distribution-friendly strategies*; 2020 https://www.elibrary.imf.org/view/IMF081/29296-9781513556055/29296-9781513556055/29296-9781513556055.xml?language=en.
7. Vidya CT, Prabheesh KP. Implications of COVID-19 pandemic on the global trade networks. *Emerg Mark Financ Trade* 2020. https://doi.org/10.1080/1540496X.2020.1785426.
8. UNCTAD. *Economies in Latin America and the Caribbean urged to boost resilience to shocks following commodity price hikes*; 2021 https://unctad.org/news/economies-latin-america-and-caribbean-urged-boost-resilience-shocks-following-commodity-price. [Accessed 20 September 2021].
9. UNCTAD. *Global trade's recovery from COVID-19 crisis hits record high*; 2021 https://unctad.org/news/global-trades-recovery-covid-19-crisis-hits-record-high.
10. United Nations, Yearbook of the United Nations 1978, pp 1083-1092. December 1978. doi:10.18356/cfa20042-en.
11. Chakraborty I, Maity P. COVID-19 outbreak: migration, effects on society, global environment and prevention. *Sci Total Environ* 2020. https://doi.org/10.1016/j.scitotenv.2020.138882.

12. Foad HS, Katz R, Migration IO For. *World migration report 2020 (full report)*. vol. 54; 2015. https://publications.iom.int/books/world-migration-report-2020.
13. Dun & Bradstreet. *Business impact of the coronavirus (COVID-19) on regional logistics*; 2020. p. 2 [July] https://www.dnb.com/content/dam/english/economic-and-industry-insight/DNB_Business_Impact_of_the_Coronavirus_US.pdf.
14. Vet JMDE, Nigohosyan D, Ferrer JN, Gross A, Kuehl S, Flickenschild M. *Impacts of the COVID-19 pandemic on EU industries*. Publ Comm Ind Res Energy, Policy Dep Econ Sci Qual Life Policies, Eur Parliam; 2021. p. 1–83 [March] https://cdn.g4media.ro/wp-content/uploads/2021/03/IPOL_STU2021662903_EN.pdf.
15. Government of India. *Ministry of eletronics and information technology annual report*; 2020. Available at: https://www.meity.gov.in/writereaddata/files/MeitY_AR_English_2020-21.pdf.
16. Giroud A, Ivarsson I. *World investment report 2020: international production beyond the pandemic*. vol. 3; 2020. https://doi.org/10.1057/s42214-020-00078-2.
17. Indo-Asian News Service. *Ford India exit: what went wrong with Ford in India and who will benefit from its exit?* Auto News ET Auto; 2021. https://auto.economictimes.indiatimes.com/news/passenger-vehicle/cars/what-went-wrong-with-ford-in-india-and-who-will-benefit-from-its-exit/86120886.
18. Hartwich F, Hammer C. *Industrial production in LDCs and trade in the COVID era and resulting policy reactions*; 2021. Available at: https://www.unido.org/sites/default/files/files/2021-05/Keynote%20-%20LDC%20industrial%20performance%20in%20COVID%20era%20and%20resulting%20policy%20reactions%20%28final%29.pdf.
19. Evenett S, Fiorini M, Fritz J, et al. Trade policy responses to the COVID-19 pandemic crisis: evidence from a new data set. *World Econ* 2021. https://doi.org/10.1111/twec.13119.
20. United Nations. *The Covid-19 shock to developing countries : towards a "whatever it takes" programme for the two-thirds*. UNCTAD; 2020. p. 13.
21. Saif NMA, Ruan J, Obrenovic B. Sustaining trade during covid-19 pandemic: establishing a conceptual model including covid-19 impact. *Sustainability* 2021. https://doi.org/10.3390/su13105418.
22. Hayakawa K, Mukunoki H. The impact of COVID-19 on international trade: evidence from the first shock. *J Jpn Int Econ* 2021. https://doi.org/10.1016/j.jjie.2021.101135.
23. WTO. *World trade primed for strong but uneven recovery after COVID-19 pandemic shock*. WTO; 2021. https://www.wto.org/english/news_e/pres21_e/pr876_e.htm. Accessed 20 September 2021.
24. Obayelu AE, Edewor SE, Ogbe AO. Trade effects, policy responses and opportunities of COVID-19 outbreak in Africa. *J Chinese Econ Foreign Trade Stud* 2021. https://doi.org/10.1108/JCEFTS-08-2020-0050.
25. Espitia A, Mattoo A, Rocha N, Ruta M, Winkler D. Pandemic trade: COVID-19, remote work and global value chains. *World Econ* 2021. https://doi.org/10.1111/twec.13117.
26. ILO (International Labour Organization). *ILO sectoral brief: COVID-19 and the automotive industry*. ILO; 2020. p. 1–6 [April] https://www.ilo.org/wcmsp5/groups/public/—ed_dialogue/—sector/documents/briefingnote/wcms_741343.pdf.
27. Salvatore D. The U.S. and the world economy after Covid-19. *J Policy Model* 2021; **43**(4):728–38. https://doi.org/10.1016/j.jpolmod.2021.02.002.
28. ILO. *ILO sectoral brief: COVID-19 and the health sector 2020*; 2019. p. 1–12 [April].
29. Mousazadeh M, Naghdali Z, Rahimian N, Hashemi M, Paital B, Al-Qodah Z, et al. Management of environmental health to prevent an outbreak of COVID-19: a review. *Environmental and health management of novel coronavirus disease (COVID-19)*; 2021. p. 235–67.
30. Dehghani MH, Roy S, Karri RR. Novel coronavirus (COVID-19) in environmental engineering perspective. *Environ Sci Pollut Res* 2022;1–3.

31. Canevelli M, Palmieri L, Raparelli V, et al. COVID-19 mortality among migrants living in Italy. *Ann Ist Super Sanita* 2020. https://doi.org/10.4415/ANN_20_03_16.
32. ILO. *COVID-19 action checklist for the construction industry*; 2020. p. 6–9. https://www.ilo.org/wcmsp5/groups/public/—ed_protect/—protrav/—safework/documents/instructionalmaterial/wcms_764847.pdf.
33. Keenan JM. COVID, resilience, and the built environment. *Environ Syst Decis* 2020. https://doi.org/10.1007/s10669-020-09773-0.
34. Ministry of Economic Development. A refreshed industry strategy in response to COVID-19. *Portf Econ Dev* 2020;57–78.
35. Czifra G, Molnár Z. Covid-19 and industry 4.0. In: *Res Pap Fac Mater Sci Technol Slovak Univ Technol*; 2020. https://doi.org/10.2478/rput-2020-0005.
36. Collier R, Pirlot A, Vella J. *Tax policy and the COVID-19 crisis*. Intertax; 2020. https://doi.org/10.2139/ssrn.3646035.
37. Allain-Dupré D, Chatry I, Michalun V, Moisio A. *The territorial impact of COVID-19: managing the crisis across levels of government*. OECD Tackling Coronavirus; 2020.
38. Dun & Bradstreet. *Business impact of the coronavirus*. Dun Bradstreet Team; 2020.
39. Dubey R, Gunasekaran A, Childe SJ, et al. Examining the role of big data and predictive analytics on collaborative performance in context to sustainable consumption and production behaviour. *J Clean Prod* 2018. https://doi.org/10.1016/j.jclepro.2018.06.097.
40. Benzidia S, Makaoui N, Bentahar O. The impact of big data analytics and artificial intelligence on green supply chain process integration and hospital environmental performance. *Technol Forecast Soc Change* 2021. https://doi.org/10.1016/j.techfore.2020.120557.
41. Papadopoulos T, Gunasekaran A, Dubey R, Altay N, Childe SJ, Fosso-Wamba S. The role of Big Data in explaining disaster resilience in supply chains for sustainability. *J Clean Prod* 2017;**142**:1108–18. https://doi.org/10.1016/j.jclepro.2016.03.059.
42. PWC. *Making the leap to more digital, dynamic and efficient operations*; 2021 https://www.pwc.com/gx/en/industries/industrial-manufacturing.html. Accessed 3 September 2021.
43. Alkahtani M, Khalid QS, Jalees M, Omair M, Hussain G, Pruncu CI. E-agricultural supply chain management coupled with blockchain effect and cooperative strategies. *Sustainability* 2021. https://doi.org/10.3390/su13020816.
44. Kramer MP, Bitsch L, Hanf J. Blockchain and its impacts on agri-food supply chain network management. *Sustainability* 2021. https://doi.org/10.3390/su13042168.
45. Ayala NF, Le Dain MA, Merminod V, Gzara L, Enrique DV, Frank AG. The contribution of IT-leveraging capability for collaborative product development with suppliers. *J Strateg Inf Syst* 2020. https://doi.org/10.1016/j.jsis.2020.101633.
46. Chi M, Wang W, Lu X, George JF. Antecedents and outcomes of collaborative innovation capabilities on the platform collaboration environment. *Int J Inf Manage* 2018. https://doi.org/10.1016/j.ijinfomgt.2018.08.007.
47. Dubey R, Altay N, Blome C. Swift trust and commitment: the missing links for humanitarian supply chain coordination? *Ann Oper Res* 2019;**283**(1–2):159–77. https://doi.org/10.1007/s10479-017-2676-z.
48. Mehdikhani R, Valmohammadi C. Strategic collaboration and sustainable supply chain management: the mediating role of internal and external knowledge sharing. *J Enterp Inf Manag* 2019. https://doi.org/10.1108/JEIM-07-2018-0166.
49. Pohlmann CR, Scavarda AJ, Alves MB, Korzenowski AL. The role of the focal company in sustainable development goals: a Brazilian food poultry supply chain case study. *J Clean Prod* 2020;**245**. https://doi.org/10.1016/j.jclepro.2019.118798, 118798.
50. Silva ME, Figueiredo MD. Practicing sustainability for responsible business in supply chains. *J Clean Prod* 2020. https://doi.org/10.1016/j.jclepro.2019.119621.

CHAPTER SIX

Effect of the COVID-19 pandemic on the sports industry

Sara Keshkar and Gholam Ali Karegar
Faculty of physical education and sports sciences, Allameh Tabataba'i University, Tehran, Iran

1. Introduction

The COVID-19 crisis made all convinced of the interdependence of different elements of sustainability—ranging from ecosystem integrity to health, well-being, and subsequent socioeconomic prosperity. The response to the crises needs to be equally all-inclusive, with Sustainable Development Goals (SDGs) providing a suitable framework.[1]

The 2030 Agenda for Sustainable Development is a collection of 17 interlinked global goals prepared to be a blueprint for guaranteeing a more peaceful and sustainable future for the world's people. These goals show the roadmap and actions to be taken by all countries to provide a better world for their people.

Many organizations around the world have joined the United Nations Sustainable Development Program and have taken various steps toward fulfillment of the SDGs. Meanwhile, sports organizations have also joined the movement, while benefitting from the unique feature of sports as a valuable asset endeared by various social strata around the globe. The purpose of this chapter is to explain the role of sports in fulfillment of the goals of sustainable development and the actions that sports organizations can take to meet each of the 17 goals of sustainable development. Accordingly, the rest of this chapter deals with the importance of sport in the SDGs, as well as the various programs that sports organizations can implement to fulfill any of the SDGs in the world.

2. Sports and sustainable development

Sports play an important role in sustainable development. Since sports are very popular among the people of the world, it can play an effective role in meeting the global goals of sustainable development. This is a fact that the United Nations has acknowledged to from a long time ago. Therefore the

COVID-19 and the Sustainable Development Goals
https://doi.org/10.1016/B978-0-323-91307-2.00004-3

unique potential of sports and its important role in sustainable development are mentioned in the related documents, reports, and guidelines of the United Nations. The Sport for Development and Peace is one of the most important programs of the United Nations following the 2030 Agenda for the SDGs, in which sports are considered an important and effective tool for fulfillment of the goals of sustainable development. The Sport for Development and Peace programs respect and consider the rights of all people to participate in sports and leisure activities. These programs use sports, organized play, and any other physical activity to allow people to participate in sports and physical activity, thus strengthening social ties and cooperation among those groups involved in sports to achieve Sustainable Development Goals.[2]

The role of sports in improving people's lives is so important that the United Nations signed a contract with organizers of the Tokyo 2020 Olympics to send its global message of sustainable development through sports and athletes at the Olympics.[3] The Tokyo 2020 Olympics has been the greenest Olympics in world's sports history. Though the advent of the Corona pandemic has thwarted all the plans and efforts of the Olympic organizers, their programs have not lost their importance. The Tokyo 2020 Olympics was planned as a platform wherein the United Nations and other organizations, active in the field of health and well-being, can convey their messages to the international community. Dr. Tedros Adhanom Ghebreyesus, the director-general of the World Health Organization (WHO), participated in a news conference in Tokyo. During his speech to the International Olympic Committee (IOC) members, he emphasized the role of the Olympic Games in uniting the world and igniting the solidarity and determination necessary for ending the pandemic together. He said the world needed the Olympics amid the pandemic "as a celebration of hope."[4]

So, sports are the powerful driving force of the SDGs. Its contribution shows how different organizations, responsible for sustainable development, can get united, work with each other, and use sports for development and peace throughout the world. Sports and development experts believe that sports can best be used to contribute to the SDGs. Sports contributions to some sustainable development goals have had significant effects, while for others the sports have had weaker effect.[2] Table 1 presents the actions that sports can take about each of the sustainable development goals.

3. Effects of COVID-19 in the sports industry

The sudden emergence of the COVID-19 virus and its global outbreak inflicted great financial losses to the sports industry. Clubs were closed,

Table 1 SDGs and contribution of sports.

Goals No.	Goals	Contribution of sports
1	End poverty	• Employment productivity • Social security and the equal rights • Funds for poverty programs
2	Zero Hunger	• Mobilize resources for ending hunger • Healthy diets and nutrition • Raise awareness on food waste
3	Healthy lives and well-being	• Healthy lives through sports • Active and sustainable lifestyles • Health education
4	Quality education	• The equal right to education • Improvement of learning outcomes • Raising awareness about sustainability
5	Gender equality	• Advocacy and awareness-raising for gender equality • Equal participation of girls and women in sports • Empowerment and self-esteem increase of women and girls
6	Availability of clean water and sanitation	• Education for water management • Standards for water sanitation
7	Affordable and sustainable energy	• Energy provision systems • Renewable energy • Energy efficiency
8	Economic growth and decent work for all	• Economic growth and decent employment • Sport-based educational programs • Entrepreneurship
9	Resilient, sustainable industrialization, infrastructure and innovation	• Positively impact local and regional business • The labor market for youth • Capacity building, creating jobs • Responsible management of volunteers
10	Reduce inequality within and among countries	• Equality and respect for diversity • Platforms for human rights • Empowerment of people with disabilities

Continued

Table 1 SDGs and contribution of sports—cont'd

Goals No.	Goals	Contribution of sports
11	Sustainable cities and safe, resilient	• Green spaces • Athletic facilities • Fair and equal societies
12	Sustainable consumption and production patterns	• Provision of facilities in areas affected by poverty • Building green facilities • Green production
13	Climate action	• Nature-friendly lifestyles • The responsible use of natural resources • Climate change and protection education
14	Conserve and sustainably use the marine resources	• Innovative solutions to preserve the ecosystem • Protect the environment
15	Sustainable use of land	• The preservation of terrestrial ecosystems • Campaigns on biodiversity • The construction of green sports facilities and infrastructure
16	Peace, justice, and inclusive institutions	• Implementation of human rights and solidarity • Promote a culture of peace • National unity
17	Global partnership	• Build and strengthen multi-stakeholder networks and partnerships • Create synergies

competitions were not held, and sales of clothing and sports equipment decreased significantly. It was a great shock for the sports industry. Every element of sports has been affected, from athletes and clubs, sponsorships to the media coverage. Gradually, with COVID-19 having spread across the globe, the 2020 Olympic and Paralympic Games in Tokyo were postponed to 2021.[5]

Shortly afterward, as scientists became more aware of how coronavirus behaved and controlled it, sports organizations resumed implementing their programs with certain restrictions. The COVID-19 pandemic brought about many changes in the sports industry. Sporting events were held without spectators, which was the case at all sporting events, large and small. The

Olympics were held for the first time without the presence of foreign spectators; meanwhile, the Japanese people, worried about the further spread of the disease in their country through the Olympics, marched in the streets and called on the authorities to stop the Olympics.[6,7] The organizers of the Olympics endured a lot of financial, human, and energy cost to host the Olympics, yet the 2020 Olympics were not economically viable for the Japanese.[8] The coronavirus changed the Olympic slogan for the first time. The original Olympic motto, "Faster, Higher, and Stronger" was changed to "Faster, Higher, and Stronger-Together" at the suggestion of the International Olympic Committee. The slogan emphasized the message of unity and solidarity to encourage participating athletes and the world's people to work together to defeat the coronavirus and make the world a better place to live.[9]

The pandemic also affected the production of sports products. Customers' tastes in buying sports equipment changed due to the conversion of club sports to sports at home. People became more inclined to use sports equipment at home. At this time, sports clubs were closed, and the purchase of club sports equipment was stopped. Pools were also closed, and people used home pools, and manufacturers of hydrotherapy equipment began to produce small-sized equipment for home use. In this way, the manufacturers of sports equipment, in order not to suffer bankruptcy, changed their products according to the pandemic conditions and the new needs of the people.[10] Most sports manufacturers and retailers also sold their products in online stores, changing sales management practices and customer relationships.[11]

Another sports industry sector affected by the global coronavirus outbreak was the sports media, which was confused in the first months of the pandemic due to the closure of all sporting events and did not know what to do in the absence of live sports programs. For this reason, the sports competitions of previous years were repeated on television. Also, reporters did not know what to report or what news to publish. Therefore the pages of newspapers and magazines were devoid of sports news, and most of them focused on information and knowledge about the importance of sports during the pandemic. As a result, sports breakdown left serious negative impact on the performance of sports media.[12]

The COVID-19 pandemic had so extensive negative impact on the sports industry that it is impossible to predict to what extent and for how long these effects will last. However, it can be said with certainty that exercise and sports during the coronavirus outbreak have played an important role in developing physical and mental health and maintaining vitality and individual spirit.[13]

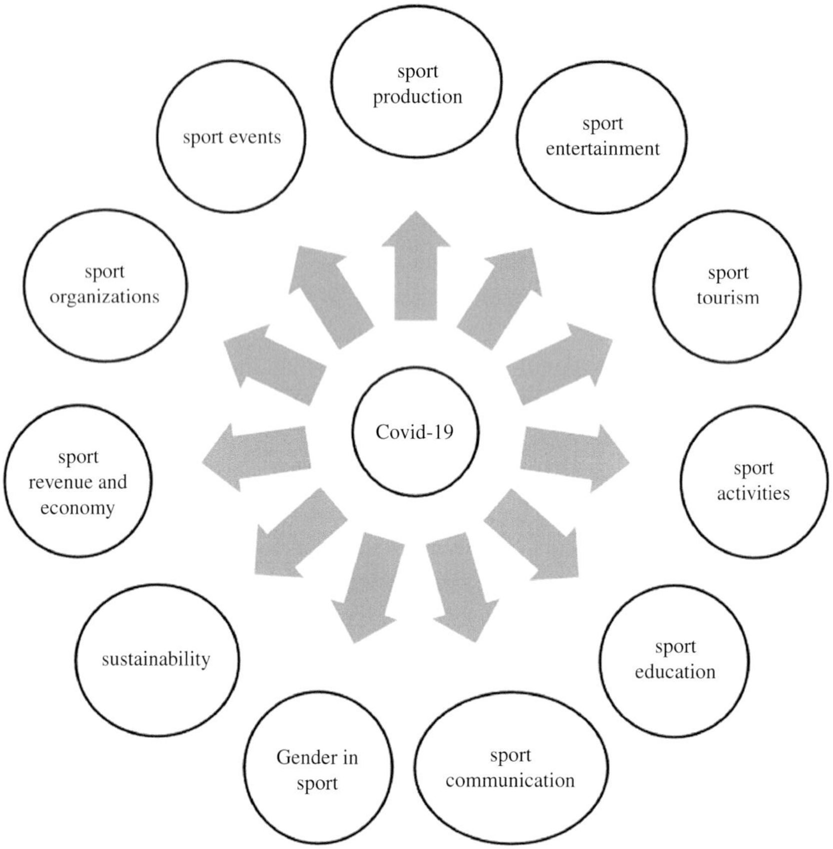

Fig. 1 Sections of sports industry affected by COVID-19.[14]

COVID-19 has affected various sectors of the sports industry, as shown in Fig. 1. Moreover, each section plays an important role in the development of the sports industry. The COVID-19 pandemic has affected the function of each of these sectors. In the rest of this chapter, the role of sports in contribution to the sustainable development goals and the effects of COVID-19 in the performance of sports organizations to address the 17 goals of sustainable development are discussed.

4. Sport and the sustainable development goals in pandemic era

As mentioned earlier, the sports industry can contribute to materialization of the SDGs. For this, it is necessary to discuss each sustainable development goal about how sports can be effective, especially in the pandemic era, which affected all sectors of sports industries. In the following, the role of sports in achieving each of the sustainable development goals and the COVID-19 pandemic intervention on it are discussed.

4.1 Goal 1: Sports can help end poverty

Sports can have a positive impact on international development and combating poverty. Everyone has the right to participate in sports activities, regardless of any sociological characteristics or physical ability. Also, large international sporting events can reduce poverty because such events can be a boon for the area's commerce and lessening poverty.[15] So, sport is a productive industry[16] that can help people and their local economy improve through the employment of unemployed people.

For this, sports industries consider people of all races and gender to be able to have a better life with a suitable income. COVID-19 and its global outbreak had a serious impact on the social and employment's economic situation. In the pandemic era, organizations reacted differently to improve the situation. Many reduced salary of their staff. So, some of the staff preferred to continue working with less payment or temporarily leave the work. Other organizations forced their staff to leave or be redeployed to other departments.[17] So, the pandemic changed the role of sports in combatting poverty because this time, poverty was generated in sports and now it was time to make new decisions to tackle the new problem. To solve the employees' financial problems, organizations started to use financial support on part of government. Later, gradually, sports administrations decided to hold sports events without any spectators in the stadiums, but they could buy tickets to watch the games through internet media and this way financial problems of sports clubs and their staffs could be solved. Also, organizations and athletes began to help poor people by charity contributions such as food distribution, helping the disabled in quarantine, fund-raising, donations, accompanying people in problems, and providing spiritual assistance to the community through social networks. So, athletes and sports organizations helped people to have better control over their lives.[3]

4.2 Goal 2: Role of sports in ending hunger

Elimination of hunger and malnutrition and ensuring access to safe, nutritious, and sufficient food for all is essential. Enabling people to feed themselves properly gives them the means to be healthy and to prosper in society. This requires implementing sustainable goals and setting up resilient agricultural production systems that generate sufficient income to local people while imparting basic nutritional knowledge. Nutrition plays a key role in sports performance and is an integral part of all sports training. Sports provides an ideal platform forraising public awareness, from an early age, of the link between health, nutrition, and sports, and the key principles of a healthy and balanced diet. Sports events also frequently spotlight local areas, producers, and products, thus offering many opportunities top-romote local agricultural production.[18] During the pandemic, many people lost their job and had no income to manage their family economy. So, some sports clubs and some elite athletes started to feed the hungry or help poor people financially. Kevin, the love of the Cleveland Cavaliers, Giannis Antetokounmpo of the Milwaukee Bucks, and others donated a considerable amount of money for those who had suffered from the pandemic. Also, some athletes began feeding the hungry people. For example, Steph Curry and his wife Ayesha donated to the Alameda County Community Food Bank and Feeding America to help ensure kids will not have to worry about where their next meal will come from.[19] Alireza Khadem, the former Iranian wrestler, prepared lots of food packages and took them to the poor people who were not in a suitable situation.[20]

4.3 Goal 3: Healthy lives, well-being, and sports

Physical activity is one of the most important tools for a healthy life, while inactivity is one of the greatest risk factors for global mortality.[21] New data suggests that inactivity drives 1 in 14 deaths globally. In other words, evidence shows that inactivity drives up to 8% of noncommunicable diseases and mortality in the world.[22] Also, there is evidence that shows a significant relationship between physical inactivity-related mortality and countries' income. In other words, physical inactivity is responsible for a substantial economic burden. Accordingly, the global burden, associated with physical inactivity, is substantial. The relative burden is greatest in high-income countries; however, the greatest number of people (absolute burden), affected by physical inactivity, live in the middle-income countries given the size of their populations.[23] High-income countries bear a larger proportion of economic burden (80·8% of healthcare costs and 60·4% of indirect costs), whereas the low- and middle-income countries endure a larger proportion of the disease burden (75·0% of DALYs).[24]

Policies that can encourage growing participation in sports and active recreation can reduce physical inactivity, while contributing to prevention of diseases and supporting realization of the SDGs.[25] Results of wide-scale research showed that sports for young people could lead to higher self-esteem, further empowering them to control stress, increased academic performance, and better family relationships.[26] These are protective factors or assets that can be potentially developed through sports and help prevent a range of problems. However, we should not forget that sports can itself lead to antisocial behaviors, including violence and hooliganism, drug abuse, cheating, and alcoholism.[27] Some athletes turn to drugs, including alcohol, to relieve stress and feel good.[28] Using drugs to improve performance in sports may lead to deprivation of an athlete from participation in a sport event. Drugs usage not only adversely affects health of the sportspeople but also harms reputation of the sports and sets a negative evidence to be considered by others. Sporting authorities have banned "performance-enhancing drugs" in sports. The World Anti-Doping Agency's (WADA) "Prohibited List" and the authorities that are in charge of ensuring its observation aim to guarantee integrity of sports and ensure clean and fair competition.[29]

The COVID-19 outbreak reduced drug testing in sports. In March, both the UK Anti-doping (UKAD) and the United States Anti-Doping Agency (USADA) announced a reduction in their testing programs.[30] Creative thinking, such as in-home self-drug testing by the U.S. Anti-Doping Agency, was controversial.[31] Athletes were required to complete their normal whereabouts, while a doping control officer connected via videoconference during a prescribed period. So, athletes provided their urine and blood samples at home while the doping control officer watched them virtually. Athletes also were responsible for packaging and sending their samples to the antidoping laboratory.[32] This has led many athletes to protest the new method of doping testing and saying: The reduction of drug testing during the coronavirus pandemic was a "let-down," "frustrating," and "disheartening" job.[30]

4.4 Goal 4: Quality education and sports

Good quality education provides all learners with the capabilities to become economically productive, develop sustainable livelihoods, respect peaceful and democratic societies, and enhance individual well-being.[33] Access to inclusive and sustainable education enables people to escape poverty, deepens our knowledge of the world around us, and provides better opportunities for all, particularly girls. Quality education is a right for everyone in the world, and Goal 4 emphasizes it. Inclusive sports activities have long been used to promote education. Everyone, especially children, needs daily physical activity. They can reduce their anxiety and stress, improve their fitness and self-confidence and self-esteem, and get a better lifestyle through using sports and physical activities. Also, sports can improve the quality of social communication. Thus sport is an important part of schools' curriculums. Results of various researches showed a linear relationship between physical activities and academic performance.[34–36] In other words, physical activities improve academic performance. It positively affects attention, concentration, and behaviors.[37] The COVID-19 pandemic forced an unprecedented global shutdown of schools for months. In many nations, schools were closed to students, and teachers directed educational activities remotely via digital devices or via the homeschooling resources. Also, the COVID-19 outbreak resulted in the cancelation of all organized after-school sporting activities.[38]

In the universities, COVID-19 had serious effects on all disciplines of sports education. Including sports coaching, class activities, students interaction with each other and also with their professors, sports and physical education activities, laboratory and clinical efforts. Despite the negative effects of a pandemic on sports education, some studies showed that most students had a good quality of life and high physical activity even with restricted education through online teaching and learning activities during the pandemic.[39] Even some were satisfied with the measures taken by the universities. However, some negative aspects were reported as lack of adequate infrastructure for some students, less effective teacher-student communication and interaction, the impossibility of performing practical applications, lack of socialization, lack of learning motivation, less objective examination, and the possibility of physical and mental health degradation.[40] Restricted education in the pandemic era created a "Knowledge gap" with the exchange of information between industry and education. The experts could not interact with students and discuss educational theories in practice, which could affect their future career.[41] Some experts believe that sports education in the postpandemic era will change, and it will most likely shift to more online education like every other academic discipline and using sports as an education tool will be an essential part of physical education. The sports industry will suffer, and this will result in a decreased demand for sports professionals. Those sports educators who are quick to adapt and have mastered the true online education are better positioned than their competitors.[41,42]

4.5 Goal 5: Sport and gender equality

In recent years, gender justice and women's empowerment in sports have received much attention. This is an interesting paradox because even though many cases of gender inequality are observed in sports, sports play an important role in creating gender equality and women's empowerment. The value of using sports-based approaches to empower women and girls is an important focus across many Sport for Development and Peace (SDP) initiatives in the Commonwealth. As mentioned before, there is increasing recognition and important critique of existing inequality and gender-based discrimination in sports. Attention to this dichotomy will contribute to the Commonwealth's consultation process that highlighted the importance of intensifying efforts to advance gender equality and women's empowerment in all sporting contexts, including the SDP programs and projects. It was argued that it is not enough to consider isolated gender issues only to make these advances. Rather, stakeholders across sports and the SDP must take a mainstreaming approach and make gender equality inherent in all the policy-making and programming, while stepping up efforts to reduce gender-based discrimination.[43]

Undoubtedly, COVID-19 has had more negative effects on women's sports than men's.[44,45] The impacts of COVID-19 on girls and women in the sports field can be evidenced in different areas, such as leadership, gender-based violence, economic opportunities, participation, and representation in the media.[44]

During the pandemic era, women were less present in the decision-making position for sports, and therefore women were less used in sports leadership. Women lost their jobs in sports and faced wage cuts or reductions more than men, and as a result, the economic situation of women in sports worsened compared to men. Even when it was decided to hold sporting events again, the women's sporting events were absent in the sports arena, and as a result, the media coverage of women's sports during the pandemic was significantly lower than that of men, and this had adverse effects on women's sports revenue.[46]

Women athletes in Islamic countries were in a more difficult situation during the pandemic. Because of the religious restrictions, these athletes usually had little media coverage, and during the pandemic, their competitions were closed and removed from many media reports.[47]

In the postpandemic era, it seems that the sports events program will continue to be in favor of men's sports, and women's sports events will have a tiny share in the programs. This will also harm women's sports sponsorship, and because media coverage will focus more on men's sports events in the future, sponsors will not be inclined to support women's sports. For this reason, it is necessary to pay special attention to women's sports in planning in the postpandemic era.[48,49]

4.6 Goal 6: Role of sports on availability of clean water and sanitation

Poor water supply is the reason for many people's death throughout the world. Therefore access to clean water is a vital need that the Goal 6 emphasizes. Access to clean water is such an important issue in sports that many sports celebrities promote it, and also it is a major challenge in the sports world, particularly for sports events organizers.[50] For instance, the Paris 2024 Olympic Games has joined the French Swimming Federation (FFN), the UNICEF, France, and thousands of people across the country to celebrate La Nuit de l'Eau (Night of Water), for improved access to swimming for all as a key legacy of its bid to host the 2024 Olympic and Paralympic Games. Le Nuit de l'Eau is an annual charity and sports event in France that, since 2008, has raised awareness on the importance of water as a vital resource and raised money to support the UNICEF's safe access to drinking water programs for children around the world.[51]

Sport can be an educational tool for managing water consumption considering the importance of using clean water. This important message can be conveyed to the community through sporting events, athletes, and various sports programs. For instance, the Football for Water, Sanitation and Hygiene (F4WASH) program in Kenya and Netherland[52] contributes to school children's improved access to water and sanitation. It thus provides a combination of hygiene education, safe water, and sanitation facilities, which give school children essential WASH services and an opportunity to nurture skills that they are likely to maintain as adults. They also use media in public education. In the Netherlands, water and sanitation facilities are installed at primary schools, and football coaches educate the children about using the facilities.[52]

Water use efficiency can be increased in sports facilities. In addition to the educational role of sports, as mentioned earlier, sports facilities can effectively manage water consumption and thus show the community that sports are not only a good educational tool for managing water resources and their proper use, but also being at the forefront of saving and managing water consumption.[53]

In some parts of the world, drought and water shortages are important issues of the future. For this reason, managing water consumption in sports venues, including the swimming pools, can be effective in preventing excessive consumption and optimal use of water. The results of Keshkar et al.[54] research showed that water pools in Tehran need to use water recycling systems, upgrade pool water technical systems, and provide general training on how to use water properly by users to manage water consumption better.[54]This example shows that sports venues can play an important role in managing water consumption. In this regard, some experts believe that irrigation is not just a matter related to water use at stadiums. Other sections like sinks, toilets, urinals, and running water for purposes of cleaning and cooking should be considered as the areas in which officials can consider optimal water conservation and management. Water is one of the main exigencies of sports teams to operate. For instance, in hockey, you need about 12,500 gal of water to make the ice.[55,56] Therefore, to effectively manage water consumption in sports venues, officials need to identify all forms of water consumption.

It seems that the outbreak of COVID-19 and the closure of sports and clubs have had a positive effect on water consumption because the absence of fans and spectators in sports venues reduced the amount of water consumption (e.g., waster used in toilets and restaurants, and for drinking, cleaning, and washing).[53]

4.7 Goal 7: Ensure access to affordable, reliable, sustainable, and modern energy for all

Access to energy for all is an essential element of sustainable development and constitutes one of the greatest challenges facing the world currently. The goal 7 highlights the need for universal access to clean and renewable energy to meet sustainable goals, guarantee inclusive communities, and combat climatic change.[2]

Sport and sports-based educational programs can support the initiatives that aim to ensure access to clean energy and promote energy efficiency. Sports facilities and events such as major international sports events can contribute to meeting the targets of generating renewable energy, ensuring energy efficiency, gaining access to the clean energy, and tackling climate change. Sustainable and inclusive sports infrastructure can promote organizational models that adopt clean and sustainable energy.[37]

The company Winwin Afrique has been tasked by the Côte d'Ivoire authorities to build a social and economic ecosystem through local sports centers. The aim is to encourage participation in sports and to use sports as a tool for development. The result is the AGORA program. The AGORA program, under which 91 complexes across Côte d'Ivoire are being built, is part of the country's 2016–2020 National Sports Policy, which aims to increase participation in sports in the country. The goals of this program include[57]:

- Promote participation in grassroots sports.
- Ensure that the population of Côte d'Ivoire lives within 3 km of a sports facility.

- Raise awareness among local people about the issues related to sustainable development (health, social innovation, and environmental protection).
- Stimulate the local economic fabric and create long-term local employment.
- Encourage the development of environmentally friendly facilities.[57]

Surprisingly, sports venues have been the pioneers in the promotion of sustainability. Many sports venues have jumped on the sustainability bandwagon to construct or renovate their structure in a race to minimize their carbon footprint, preserve their green legacy, and take the lead in innovation. The Amsterdam Arena is powered by more than 4200 solar panels and one wind turbine. The main building comprises an impressive energy-generating escalator. In November 2018, the Mercedes-Benz became the first professional sports stadium to receive a platinum Leadership in Energy & Environmental Design (LEED) certificate. Golden 1 Center, the home of the Sacramento Kings, was awarded the world's greenest and most technologically advanced sports and entertainment facility for 2017. Qatar's organizers for the 2022 football World Cup have pledged that all 12 venues will be zero-carbon emitting as an obligatory requirement from FIFA to deliver a zero-carbon tournament.[58] While many sports venues around the world are striving for sustainable development, some countries, including Iran, are not using renewable energy systems due to the economic hardships caused by global sanctions and some cultural and educational problems.[59]

Sport depends on the environment. This relationship is most obvious when the natural world is playing, and many of those sports see their playing conditions change. Winter sports need technology to recreate the playing surface, and indoor sports facilities require ventilation and lighting, which result in greenhouse gases. Therefore all sports activities have an impact on the environment. Before the COVID-19 pandemic, some sports organizations tried to meet the sustainable development goals in their initiatives. After COVID-19, the SDGs' values can be fully promoted in a healthier environment.[60]

Many researches showed that the COVID-19 pandemic caused a reduction of energy usage in sports venues. Chihib et al.[61] showed in their study on energy consumption in campus facilities that the situation of closing the campus facilities during the COVID-19 outbreak influenced the overall energy consumption of the campus. All facilities decreased their consumption value, and the majority of the facilities had a higher relative standard deviation in 2020 than in 2019. In their study, after analyzing the patterns and conducting the inventory in the university facilities, energy-saving measures such as switching off water heating systems in sports facilities for the swimming pool and showers and unplugging all the computers and other unused appliances such as vending machines when the university locations are inoperative (confinement, summer break) could have an important impact on energy savings in the future.[61]

4.8 Goal 8: Sport and economic growth

Sustained and inclusive economic growth is a prerequisite for sustainable development, which can contribute to improvement of public livelihoods worldwide. Economic growth can lead to new and better employment opportunities and provide greater economic security for all. Moreover, rapid growth, especially among the least developed and other developing countries, can help them reduce the wage gap relative to developed countries, thereby diminishing glaring inequalities between the rich and the poor.[62]

Sport is a driving force for the economy. The global growth of the sports industry and its relationship with other organizations will create new jobs. Sports and sporting events are very popular among the people of the world, and for this reason, hosting sporting events activates many nonsports organizations at the national or global level. Hotels, travel agencies, water, land and air transportation, leisure and entertainment centers, health centers, and sports organizations are involved in hosting sporting events. Hosting international sports events such as the Olympics, FIFA World Cup, or the Super Bowl is the reason for significant economic development in countries. Hosting sports events could secure foreign capital inflows, generate employment, and make people want to spend money.[63] Hosting sports events promotes sports tourism, global media communication, national and global marketing, healthcare services which each, in turn, creates new jobs nationally and internationally. If these activities adopt sustainable and inclusive measures, they can contribute to economic, social, and environmental development.[64]

In 2019, 1.37 million people were engaged in the field of sports in the EU-27. Regarding gender balance, men (54%) outnumbered women, which aligned with the one observed in total employment. The share of young people aged 15–29 was 35%—twice the share observed in overall employment, while the 30–64 age group accounted for 63%. In the EU-27, the number of people in sports employment grew by almost 200,000 more compared to 2014, equivalent to an overall increase of 17%.[65]

COVID-19 pandemic harmed employment in the sports industry. European Observatoire of Sport and Employment (EOSE) analyzed the EU-28 sports employment data for the first two quarters of 2020. Across the first two quarters of 2020, total sports employment in the EU-28 fell by 3.3%. By the end of Q2 of 2020, there were 9.6% fewer females and 17% fewer young people[15–24] sports workers than at the end of 2019. The female and young sports workforce appears to have been much harder hit by COVID-19 in the first half of 2020.[66] During the pandemic, many sports organizations stopped hiring new staff. Others fired employees or hired them part-time or without pay, all of which harmed the employees' financial situation.[16,67]

COVID-19 has impacted the future of sports careers. So, some jobs will be accompanied by many changes. Hosting sports events will require compliance with health protocols, which will indicate a change in the status of jobs related to the events. Some jobs will be held using the internet and cyberspace, and some services will be restricted. In such a situation, sports organizations should be careful about employees' and athletes' health and economic status. Special insurances should be provided for them with proper support, and they should also pay attention to improving the economic situation of organizations. In the future, the SDGs' implementation and observation of international human rights standards should be part of building, planning, and running mega-sporting events.[68]

4.9 Goal 9: The role of sports in achieving sustainable and resilient industrialization, infrastructure, and innovation

Investment in sustainable and resilient industrialization, infrastructure, and innovation are essential to achieve the SDGs.[69] Sustainable industrialization refers to the transformation toward an industrialized economy that can help to create wealth, social development, and environmental sustainability.[70]

Infrastructure such as the supply of drinking water and electricity, the disposal and treatment of wastewater, the mobility of people and goods, and the provision of information and communication technologies[71] represents the backbone of our economies. It powers our machines, creates networks that connect people, helps to transport goods, and enables services such as trade, healthcare, and education. In short, infrastructure largely determines our livelihoods today and in the future; it is key for safeguarding our environment and represents the seams of our societal fabric. These are the reasons that infrastructure also lies at the core of achieving the UN's Sustainable Development Goals.[72]

Resilience, as another important concept in Goal 9, in broad terms, is defined as the capacity to recover quickly from difficulties. Building resilience is crucial for organizations worldwide because they will always face challenges, big and small.[73]

The contribution of sport to the achievement of Goal 9 include: connecting with other sectors to grow the scale of the sports industry, organizing sports events regarding the local and regional business income, using labor standards for goods production, employing vulnerable groups, creating jobs and facilitating entrepreneurship, motivating community mobilization for economic growth, developing sports tourism, and encouraging volunteers.[74]

The COVID-19 pandemic had a significant impact on the sports' contribution to achieving Goal 9. Directions from public health organizations during the COVID-19 pandemic drastically altered the sports sector, prompting many sports decision-makers to reconsider what their organization does and how they do it. Although the full scope of the short- and long-term impacts is yet to be seen, some organizations have not survived. Others have used this period to adapt their operations, develop, and incorporate new ideas. To adapt themselves to crises, sports organizations need to undergo a dynamic process of learning, modification, and responsive decision-making to effectively respond to a changing and unpredictable environment.[75] At the beginning of the pandemic, sports organizations were forced to increase organizational resilience to prevent damage. They resisted pandemic threats by closing clubs and then hosting sporting events in a limited way. Sports organizations changed the process of providing sports services using digital media and in accordance with the environmental situation.[76]

Ghahfarokhi et al.[77] in their study on evaluating the challenges of sports businesses in the COVID-19 pandemic crisis, and introducing their resilience solutions, identified 11 challenges in two categories of "supply-side challenges" and "demand-side challenges." Also, 94 sports business resilience strategies for Corona and post-Corona eras were identified in four categories: "Marketing Mix Management," "Process Management," "Organizational Resource Management," and "Strategic Action Management." These operational strategies can save sports businesses from the risk of bankruptcy and exclusion from the sports ecosystem, while strengthening these firms to show growing resilience in the face of such crises in the future.[77]

4.10 Goal 10: Sport and inequality elimination

Many people face discrimination because of their gender, disability, or ethnicity. Sports can promote equality. Sport can also facilitate inclusion of persons with disabilities and vulnerable persons and the empowerment of women and girls.[78]

The pandemic negatively affected the lives of vulnerable groups, including children, the elderly, women, religious, ethnic and racial minorities, refugees and the homeless, the poor or the bankrupt, who suffered the greatest economic, social, and health damage during the pandemic era. Some damages include economic inequality, lack of equitable access to healthcare and sanitation services, and unequal access to safe working conditions and decent housing. In their research, Shur et al.[79] showed that COVID-19 affected older adults' health seriously. The elderly, those with chronic disease and lower socioeconomic groups, were disproportionately affected by restriction of movement, further widening the physical activity health inequality.[79] Also, COVID-19 restrictions have placed many different stresses and strains on the lives of people with disabilities. Social loneliness and social isolation had a significant impact on the health and well-being of every individual, especially for people with disabilities.[80]

Professional athletes and sports organizations can use their voices to raise awareness regarding the need to overcome the inequalities both demonstrated and exacerbated by COVID-19 and the types of measures that will need to be taken to do so.[68]

Sports in media can remove gender inequality by encouraging girls to participate in sports that boys traditionally play. Colombia instituted a quota rule that dictated that a certain number of football team members had to be girls, and the first goal had to be scored by a girl. This program educated girls on their capability and right to play any sports.[14]

4.11 Goal 11: Sustainable cities and communities

Every year, millions of people migrate to urban areas in search of a better life. By 2050 two-thirds of humanity—equal to 6.5 billion people—will be urban. According to evidence, more than 90% of all COVID-19 cases have occurred in cities, for example, highlightingsome of the difficulties of living in densely populated areas.[81]

Sport offers multiple solutions, helping make cities and human settlements more equal, resilient, and sustainable. Besides health and physical activity, sports generate momentum for more green spaces, athletic facilities, jobs, and economic growth.[82]

COVID-19 highlighted the role of sports and exercise in promoting community health. More interestingly, during the pandemic and staying in quarantine, it became possible for everyone to exercise through virtual media, regardless of age or gender, at home. For example, sports trainers made it possible for all family members to exercise using virtual sports classes. Also, sports equipment that could be used at home, such as dumbbells, stationary bikes, treadmills, and fitness equipment, were purchased for the family during the pandemic and could be used by all family members. So, participation in sports was provided equally to all family members. The pandemic caused people to take advantage of the antiinequality capacities of sports and use exercise for their health and family members.[83,84]

Sport has the potential to create public sports spaces in cities without discrimination. In public sports spaces in many cities worldwide, sports equipment and suitable space for the elderly, children, and the disabled and other social groups have been designed and built. This feature of sports helps to achieve the SDGs to create sustainable cities and communities.[85]

4.12 Goal 12: Responsible production and consumption

Sport can affect people's attitudes toward environmental protection and take the necessary measures to achieve the SDGs. Sports events are the best opportunity to show the importance of the environment and the use of green products, and the implementation of green management in front of the eyes of spectators who are either present at sports venues or watch it through the mass media.[86]

Sport can influence the behavior of people in society to achieve the goals of sustainable development. One of the most important problems in the world is the overuse of plastic. This substance is widely used in sports. Plastic is used in almost all sports equipment, from the floor of gyms to sports equipment and clothing, and finally containers and bottles of drinks and the cases of food for athletes. Usually, after sports events, venues are full of bottles or plastic bags. Therefore the sports itself pollute the environment with plastic. On the other hand, benefiting from green management, applying green products in sports venues, and recycling plastics that are used in stadiums will allow the sports to move toward meeting sustainable development goals.[87]

The Clean Seas Campaign, launched by the United Nations Environment Program in 2017, aims to engage governments, the general public, civil society, and the private sector in the fight against marine litter by addressing the root causes of the problem. The IOC is a member of Clean Seas alongside many sporting bodies and sponsors. Table 2 presents some actions taken in connection with this project.[88]

According to the Tokyo 2020 Olympics organizers' announcement, enough plastic was collected to create recyclable podiums. It collected

Table 2 The action of the clean sea campaign.

Process	Definition
Refuse	Stop using single-use plastic
Reduce	If plastic is necessary, find ways to use less
Reuse	Switch single-use items to reusable versions
Replace	Switch to plastic-free alternatives or select plastics that are recycled or easily recyclable
Recycle	Design your event to ensure that any plastic used gets recycled

Source: IOC & UN Plastic Game Plan for Sport 2020.

24.5 tons of used plastic and around 400,000 laundry detergent bottles for conducting the eco-friendly games. Major retailers and 113 schools from across Japan and Tokyo 2020 and Olympic Games sponsoring P&G Group helped the organizers make the initiative a success. The materials were collected over 9 months, and the campaign reached its goal in March 2020, the same month that the games were postponed to next year due to the COVID-19 pandemic.[89]

The outbreak of the COVID-19, resulting in the cessation of competitions or the restriction of spectators in stadiums, has reduced the consumption of plastic containers such as single-use water bottles in stadiums. However, on the other hand, the cessation of many trade relations between companies around the world has reduced the supply chain of raw materials for sports equipment that are made from recycled plastic materials.[90]

4.13 Goal 13: Sport and climate action

Climate change is one of the most important problems and the threat of the present century, which, if not addressed, will have adverse consequences for human life.[91]

COVID-19 and climate change both lead to global disruption that transcends borders and threatens the lives of millions of people and also are risk multipliers that exacerbate inequalities by disproportionately affecting the most vulnerable, each in its way. COVID-19 and climate change pose health threats of global magnitude.[92]

More than 50 million people were doubly hit in 2020 by climate-related disasters (floods, droughts, and storms) and by the COVID-19 pandemic. The COVID-19 and related quarantine worsened food insecurity and added another layer of risk to evacuation, recovery, and relief operations related to high-impact events. When disasters (storms, floods, and earthquakes) happened in different parts of the world in 2020, response and recovery operations were hampered, leading to delays in providing equipment and assistance.[93]

Athletes and sports organizations have an important role to play in the general response to climate change and the damage it causes. For example, in 2009, the Athlete for Earth Campaign was launched by the Earth Day Network, which featured many well-known professional athletes and Olympians. The campaign aimed to build solidarity between the people, sports organizations, and the environmental movement to counter destructive acts against the environment and natural resources.[94]

Human emissions of carbon dioxide and other greenhouse gases are a primary driver of climate change and present one of the world's most pressing challenges. This link between global temperatures and greenhouse gas concentrations—especially CO_2—has been true throughout the Earth's history.[95]

Based on a research conducted in 2020 on the greenhouse gas emissions, the global average temperatures have increased by more than 1°C since preindustrial times, and the concentration of CO_2 emissions has been reduced by almost 40%, compared to 2019.[96] However, during the pandemic, CO_2 emissions have declined by 25%, equal to 100 million tons of CO_2 emissions.[97]

Sports events constitute the ultimate product of the sports industry, and they are characterized by a large number of participants that attend or people who work for the event.[98,99] The massive production and overconsumption of sports products and services depend highly on thousands of sports events hosted annually across the world.[100,101] The main products of sports events include, but are not limited to, the merchandise of sporting goods and services, their delivery practices to facilitate sports consumption, and the implementation and practice of sports events.[99] Also, people who travel for sports events usually consume sporting goods and services in their daily lives. Consequently, these practices contribute to the vast majority of CO_2 emissions.

Moreover, the quantity of CO_2 emissions through sports production and consumption is associated with the type of sports events. For instance, the type of sports events that has the largest impact on the natural environment includes mega-scale sports events, such as the Olympics Games, the FIFA World Cup, the Super Bowl, and the collegiate football.[99] During such mega-scale sports events, spectators use different modes of transportation such as Single-Occupant Vehicles (SOV) and carpooling practices (e.g., traveling with family or friends).[102]

Given the outcome of COVID-19 restrictions toward the sports events, the limited transportation practices of sports teams and spectators, and the reduced functioning of sports facilities, it is vital to explore the CO_2 emissions that have been avoided during the COVID-19 crisis.[103]

Accordingly, in 2019, 278 million people attended sports events.[104] In 2020 the Statista forecast with the adjusted impact of COVID-19 predicted an average of 114 million people, which represents more than a 50% cut in attendance. Therefore, by calculating the annual impact of traveling behaviors in sports events, in 2019 spectators were responsible for 2.5 billion tons of CO_2 emissions, compared to the expected 912 million tons of CO_2 emissions in 2020. The statistics illustrate that more than 1.5 billion tons of CO_2 emissions will be avoided due to the controlled transportation variable.[104] Based on the most recent evidence, on average, industrial and human-induced practices emit 36 billion tons of CO_2 emissions in the atmosphere per year.[95] If we calculate that 2.5 billion tons of CO_2 are emitted by the spectators' transportation only during sports events, the sports industry might significantly impact the CO_2 emitted annually. Essentially, the sports industry, particularly the traveling behaviors of sports stakeholders, has a massive effect on the natural environment.[103]

4.14 Goal 14: Sports role in conserve and sustainably use the marine resources

Ocean acidification, illegal fishing and overfishing, and marine and water pollution are currently putting our marine and water ecosystems at risk.[50]

The role of sports to unite people in protecting our planet's biodiversity and in the fight against climate change could be a genuine game-changer. Why are sports beginning to adopt this cause as their own? It can be because of the natural fit between sports and the environment; Athletes needing clean air to train in, snow to ski on, reasonable temperature conditions to run or play in, and going forward. Commercial aspects of sports are likely to be more affected by stoppages in major tournaments because of adverse weather or unacceptable conditions.[105]

Numerous sports activities depend on the conservation of coastal, marine, and water-related ecosystems. The sports world is committed to addressing this challenge. Participation in sports, particularly water sports, enables us to learn about these ecosystems and the importance of conserving them. Furthermore, the sports industry, which involves athletes, event organizers, and companies, is developinginnovative solutions to preserve the ecosystems.[50]

The COVID-19 crisis and its consequences on aquatic sports are considerable. The Swimming, Diving and Water Polo Federation of Iran president said: "The outbreak of COVID-19 has greatly damaged the country's sports, especially water sports." He declared that aquatic sports in Iran had suffered the most from the COVID-19.[106] The COVID-19 crisis and its consequences for the swimming community have created a myriad of challenges for swimmers worldwide, including maintaining their fitness level and preparing to return optimally and safely to pool training and competitions. Several significant decisions were made to postpone or cancel major swimming events by FINA (Fédération Internationale de Natation). Swimmers were no longer allowed to continue their usual training in swimming pools and were confined to their homes.[107] Wendtlandt et al.[108] in a study on the Effects of Sports Activities and Environmentally Sustainable Behaviors on Subjective Well-Being before and during COVID-19 showed that nature-based and nature-neutral sports activities were significantly decreased during the first COVID-19 lockdown, while environmentally sustainable behaviors were increased. The regression analyses revealed that nature-based and nature-neutral sports activities and ecological consumption significantly added to individuals' subjective well-being in the pre- and during COVID-19 period. A decrease in nature-based and nature-neutral sports activities significantly predicted a decrease in individuals' subjective well-being.[108]

Anyway, though water sports may encourage people to take care of the environment on the other side, some water sports, for instance, boating, can damage the water environment through noise pollution, the deposits left from boats, sediment disruption, erosion, and disturbance of fish habitats[109,110] during COVID-19. This is while stoppage of water sports competitions in the pandemic era may have decreased some of these unfavorable impacts.[10]

4.15 Goal 15: Sport and sustainable use of land

The SDG 15 has the principle of protecting, recovering, and promoting the sustainable use of terrestrial ecosystems, while managing forests in a sustainable way, combating desertification, stopping and reversing land degradation, and stopping biodiversity loss.

Quality sports practice has always required access to a healthy natural environment. With the rise in outdoor sports in nature, the conservation of terrestrial spaces and ecosystems has become a major challenge for the sports world. Based on the example of events, labeled as "sustainable" or "zero waste" and initiatives combining sports and waste collection, the sports industry can be the source of innovative solutions for creating the eco-friendly practices. Sports events, and sports activities in general, provide a unique platform for raising public awareness since the early ages about the importance and the challenges of protecting forests and mountainous areas.[69]

Sport can play a very important role in the preservation and conservation of our land. In Tokyo 2020, activities to clean up forests and parks were so extensive to get prepared for the event.[111]

Compared to other SDG goals in sports, COVID-19 had the least pressure on the goal 15. However, the competitions in which people were invited to promote and preserve nature and ecosystems were stopped.[112]

4.16 Goal 16: The role of sports in peace, justice, and strong institutions

Remaining in quarantine and stopping the social and economic activities of the people during the pandemic increased the number of violent behaviors and human conflicts.[113]

Sport has always been used as the best solution to individual, national, or international conflicts. Sports diplomacy is a gateway for countries to confront their political problems through sports. This way, sport can help build bridges between communities in conflict.[68] The history of sports is full of examples in which sports and athletes have played an important role in solving the political problems of countries.[114]

Some of the most important examples of the role of sports in conflict resolution include ping-pong diplomacy, which was used to resolve the political dispute between the United States and the People's Republic of China in the 1970s. Didier Drogba, the football legend, is another example of sports that had an important role in stopping a civil war in the Ivory Coast in the 2000s. As other examples of athletes playing important roles in confronting political discriminations, reference should be made to a group of brilliant names in sports history such as Tommie Smith and John Carlos. The latter athlete took black-gloved stance against racial inequality in the 1968 Summer Olympics. Members of the Zimbabwean cricket team wearing black armbands citing the "death of democracy in our beloved Zimbabwe" should also be mentioned. Alternatively, the "hands up, do not shoot" gestures, made by the St. Louis Rams in their 2014 NFL game against the Oakland Raiders, is another example. In each case, these evidences demonstrate the unique position that athletes reserve, especially considering the press coverage of major events.[115] Sometimes it is sports organizations that play an effective role in solving the problems. For example, let's refer to the intervention of the World Football Federation to solve the problem of Iranian women attending football stadiums in 2019.[116]

In addition, sports culture has concepts and values such as self-sacrifice, chivalry, fair play, and teamwork, each of which can provide young people and adolescents with important learning for their social life.[117]

As mentioned, sport serves as a powerful means for bridging, bringing people together, and guaranteeing peace; it builds friendships and draws lines of respect across borders. Thomas Bach, the IOC president, declared: "The Olympic athletes show the whole world that it is possible to compete with each other while living peacefully together." Contributing to building a peaceful and better world through sports is a Fundamental Principle of the Olympic Charter, and it is why the IOC regularly joins the celebrations of the International Day of Peace, observed around the world on 21 September.[118]

The COVID-19 outbreak not only postponed the 2020 Olympics in Japan but also the competitions without spectators from different countries for a year, and this is the first time in the history of the Olympics that this important sporting event has been held without spectators from abroad. In fact, the peaceful and nondiscriminatory presence of the world's people on the Olympic scene has been stopped only because of the coronavirus pandemic.[119,120]

4.17 Goal 17: Sport and global partnership

Achieving sustainable development goals requires the cooperation and support of people, investors, organizations, and institutions. Sport can catalyze, build, and strengthen multistakeholder networks and partnerships for sustainable development and peace goals, involving and bringing together the public, governments, donors, NGOs, sports organizations, the private sector, academia, and the media. Sports can gather many supporters and create a network of sponsors who work to achieve sustainable development goals through the presence and support of sports.[68]

Global partnership in different parts of the sorting industry was affected by the COVID-19 outbreak. The World Federation of the Sporting Goods Industry (WFSGI) had challenging circumstances to work with their global communities, members, colleagues, partners, families, and friends whom the unprecedented spread of COVID-19 had impacted. About 30% of sporting goods-producing companies are looking to consolidate the supply base and keep only strategic partners. It means they have to decrease the number of their products and reduce their demand by canceling orders and restrict their global trading.[121]

Nike collaborated with the World Federation of the Sporting Goods Industry (WFSGI) and other member companies to launch a physical activity guide to support the World Health Organization's (WHO) work to promote physical activity. 'WHO Is Healthy at Home' campaign encouraged people to stay active while being at home during the COVID-19 crisis, and the guide provided resources to help. In the guide, the president of Nike declared: "We used NIKE's scale and influence to raise the bar for sustainability. We launched our Supplier Climate Action Program to develop pathways for carbon reduction for our materials and finished goods manufacturers".[122]

5. Cons and pros of COVID-19 for the sports industry and sustainable development

It could be argued that the global outbreak of COVID-19 was the most significant crisis of 2020 and 2021. This crisis in the sports industry is a turning point for the present and future of world sports. Although this crisis had unfortunate consequences for the people of the world, we should not forget that this crisis also led to good results, which are briefly discussed as follows. The crisis of COVID-19 taught us the following points:

- The world is truly a global village where good and bad events do not always remain within the confines of one country or region and can involve the whole world. So, think global and instead of improving the situation of a country, think about the welfare and health of the whole world. It reminds the great concept in Iranian poet, Saadi's famous poem: "Human beings are members of a whole, since in their creation they are of one essence, when the conditions of the time bring a member (limb) to pain, the other members (limbs) will suffer from discomfort."[123] So, if Olympic Games are stopped, it means sports in all the world are stopped, and it means that it is a common pain.
- To take potential risks seriously when planning for sports organizations to use Plan B when a crisis occurs and be able to manage the crisis. Lack of risk management programs in many sports organizations worldwide caused them serious economic, social, and organizational problems. This B plan can include organizational performance, production, human resource management, national and international communication, etc.
- To learn from each other in times of crisis and help each other keep world sports alive and active. When in a particular country, the sports

authorities decide a resistance program against pandemic to keep their sports alive, and they succeed, then other countries can follow suit and repeat their experience in their country.

- Human communication is essential for survival and sustainable development. During the pandemic era, social media was the best means of communication among people trapped in-home quarantine, and athletes around the world tried to use social media to help people maintain their physical and mental health through exercise. Many athletes became the social leaders of the people of the world and gave them morale and hope. It means that sports heroes belong to all the world.
- Education is a global requirement, and a pandemic with the help of digital media and platforms has helped professionals worldwide hold international webinars and global education through webinars and virtual conferences. Corona brought experts and scientists closer together and made scientific communication easier and wider in the world.
- Conservation of nature and the ecosystem is essential to guarantee better life for all the world people. Sports is always a good platform for guiding and teaching people to preserve nature. The pandemic has drawn the attention of sports organizations to sustainable development through sports more than before. Waste management in sports, use of natural energy and carbon dioxide, and prevention of environmental pollution, caused by holding sports competitions, need paying more attention in the postpandemic era to guarantee sustainable development and ecosystem preservation.
- Compared to other issues, central issues of sustainable development, i.e., social and economic justice, were affected the most in the pandemic era. Domestic violence against women, the economic losses of women's sports, discrimination against women, the poor economic situation of sports club staff, the bankruptcy of sports club owners, inadequate health insurance support, the disabled and the elderly sports, etc. are some of the most important harmful aspects of the pandemic. In the postcorona era, sports organizations need to pay more attention to them.
- Finally, although COVID-19 was a serious threat to all sports organizations and people around the world, organizations and intelligent people took advantage of the threat and, by carrying out social and economic activities tailored to the needs of today's society, became the leaders of organizational innovation in the sports world. Furthermore, the post-COVID-19 special sports products and activities that could engage individuals and organizations reaped unprecedented revenue for their producers and sponsors.

References

1. The Institute for European Environmental Policy (IEEP). *Global sustainable development in the aftermath of the COVID-19 pandemic*; 2020. MONDAY, 25 MAY 2020, 09:25 https://ieep.eu/news/global-sustainable-development-in-the-aftermath-of-the-COVID-19-pandemic. [Accessed 29 April 2021].
2. United Nations office on sport for development and (UNOSDP). *Sport and the sustainable development goals. An overview outlining the contribution of sports to the SDGs*; 2020 https://www.un.org/sports/sites/www.un.org.sports/files/ckfiles/files/Sport_for_SDGs_finalversion9.pdf. [Accessed 29 April 2021].
3. United Nations. *UN and Tokyo 2020, leverage power of Olympic Games in global sustainable development race*; 2018 https://news.un.org/en/story/2018/11/1025711. [Accessed 22 July 2021].
4. Grohmann K. *WHO head Tedros backs Tokyo games amid pandemic*. Reuters; 2021. https://www.reuters.com/lifestyle/sports/who-head-tedros-backs-tokyo-games-amid-pandemic-2021-07-21/. [Accessed 29 April 2021].
5. Krnjaic J. *The impact of the COVID crisis on the sport industry*. Marbella international university center; 2020. https://miuc.org/impact-covid-crisis-sports-industry/. [Accessed 28 April 2021].
6. Goldman T. *Protests have persisted outside of the Tokyo Olympics*. npr; 2021. https://www.npr.org/2021/07/23/1019892603/protests-have-persisted-outside-of-the-tokyo-olympics. [Accessed 28 April 2021].
7. Kiszla M. *As protest against Olympics raged outside a nearly empty stadium, all the fireworks in Japan couldn't stop opening ceremony from being a dud*. The Denver Post; 2021. https://www.denverpost.com/2021/07/23/kiszla-tokyo-olympics-opening-ceremony/. [Accessed 28 April 2021].
8. Statista. *Estimated economical loss of Tokyo 2020 Olympics in Japan as of January 2021*; 2021 https://www.statista.com/statistics/1105665/japan-estimated-economical-damage-of-tokyo-2020-olympics-cancellation-postponement/. [Accessed 28 April 2021].
9. International Olympic Committee. *Faster, Higher, Stronger—Together—IOC Session approves historic change in Olympic motto*; 2021 https://olympics.com/ioc/news/-faster-higher-stronger-together-ioc-session-approves-historic-change-in-olympic-motto. [Accessed 28 April 2021].
10. Keshkar S, Heidari M. *Challenges of marketing, attracting and loyalty of customers of hydrotherapy centers in Mashhad during COVID-19 pandemic*. MA. Thesis, Allameh Tabataba'i University.; 2021 [In Persian].
11. Happ E, Scholl-Grissemann U, Peters M, et al. Insights into customer experience in sports retail stores. *Int J Sports Mark Spons* 2021;**22**(2):312–29. https://doi.org/10.1108/IJSMS-12-2019-0137.
12. Clements D, Joyce L. *The impact of COVID-19 on sports media*. Seton Hall University; 2020. https://www.shu.edu/communication-arts/news/the-impact-of-COVID-19-on-sports-media.cfm. [Accessed 23 July 2021].
13. Hughes J. *How is the Coronavirus affecting sports? Keystone master studies*; 2020 https://www.masterstudies.com/article/how-is-the-coronavirus-affecting-sports/. [Accessed 29 April 2021].
14. Keshkar S. *The impact of COVID-19 on sports organizations performance. Research project*. Allameh Tabataba'i University; 2021 [In Persian].
15. Lexington Institute for Globally Transformative Technologies (LIGTT). *Using sports to combat poverty*; 2021 https://ligtt.org/using-sports-combatpoverty/#:~:text=Another%20important%20way%20that%20sports,that%20area%20and%20lessen%20poverty. [Accessed 28 April 2021].
16. Tate R. *A more productive, sustainable and responsible sport sector*. Sport and recreation alliance; 2016. https://www.sportandrecreation.org.uk/news/industry/a-more-productive-sustainable-and-responsible. [Accessed 29 April 2021].

17. Keshkar S, Dickson G, Ahonen A, et al. The effects of coronavirus pandemic on the sports industry: an update. *Ann Appl Sport Sci* 2021;**9**(1). https://doi.org/10.29252/aassjournal.964.
18. Sport en Commun.Zero hunger; 2018 https://www.sportencommun.org/en/impacts/zero-hunger. [Accessed 28 April 2021].
19. Elkins K. *NBA players, celebrities and others who are helping those most affected by the COVID-19 pandemic.* CNBC; 2020. https://www.cnbc.com/2020/03/17/celebrities-helping-those-most-affected-by-the-COVID-19-pandemic.html. [Accessed 28 April 2021].
20. Hamshahri. *This is how the Olympic champion helps the people of the border*; 2020 https://translate.google.com/523684. [Accessed 28 April 2021].
21. Silva DA, Tremblay MS, Marinho F, et al. Physical inactivity as a risk factor for all-cause mortality in Brazil (1990–2017). *Popul Health Metr* 2020;**18**:13. https://doi.org/10.1186/s12963-020-00214-3.
22. Swift D. *Inactivity drives 1 in 14 deaths globally*; 2021. New Data Suggest https://www.medscape.com/viewarticle/948439. [Accessed 23 July 2021].
23. Katzmarzyk PT, Friedenreich C, Shiroma EJ, et al. Physical inactivity and non-communicable disease burden in low-income, middle-income and high-income countries. *Br J Sports Med* 29 March 2021. https://doi.org/10.1136/bjsports-2020-103640. Published Online First.
24. Ding D, Lawson KD, Kolbe-Alexander TL, et al. *The economic* burden of physical inactivity: a global analysis of major non-communicable diseases. *Lancet* 2016;**388** (10051):1311–24. https://doi.org/10.1016/S0140-6736 (16)30383-X.
25. Lindsey I, Chapman T. *Enhancing the contribution of sport to the SDGs: commonwealth policy guide.* London, United Kingdom: Commonwealth Secretariat; 2017. p. 32.
26. Brettschneider W. Risks and opportunities: adolescents in top-level sport ñ growing up with the pressures of school and training. *Eur Phy Educ Rev* 1999;**5**:121–33. https://journals.sagepub.com/doi/10.1177/1356336X990052004. [Accessed 27 April 2021].
27. United Nations. *Policy brief: the impact of COVID-19 on women*; 2020. Retrieved from: https://www.unwomen.org//media/headquarters/attachments/sections/library/publications/2020/policy-brief-the-impact-of-COVID-19-on-women-en.pdf. [Accessed 22 April 2021].
28. U.S. Department of Justice. *The Coach's playbook against drugs. Portable guide*; 2021 https://www.ojp.gov/ondcppubs/publications/pdf/coach-a-thon.pdf. [Accessed 29 April 2021].
29. Health direct; 2019. Drugs in sports https://www.healthdirect.gov.au/drugs-in-sports. [Accessed 23 April 2021].
30. Walker-Khan M. *Reduced drug testing during coronavirus pandemic 'let-down', say athletes.* BBC sports; 14 June 2020. https://www.bbc.com/sports/athletics/53017626. [Accessed 28 April 2021].
31. Futterman M. *Doping tests go virtual. Is it temporary or a glimpse of the future?—The New York Times*; 2020 https://www.nytimes.com/2020/04/15/sports/olympics/coronavirus-drug-testing.html. [Accessed 28 April 2021].
32. Pitsiladis Y, Muniz-Pardos B, Miller M, et al. Sport integrity opportunities in the time of coronavirus. *Sports Med* 2020;**50**(10):1701–2. https://doi.org/10.1007/s40279-020-01316-6. Auckland, N.Z.
33. VVOB. *VVOB's definition of quality education*; 2021 https://www.vvob.org/en/education/our-vision-on-quality-education. [Accessed 20 July 2021].
34. Howie EK, Pate RR. Physical activity and academic achievement in children: a historical perspective. *J Sport Health Sci* 2021;**1**(3):160–9. https://doi.org/10.1016/j.jshs.2012.09.003.
35. Centers for Disease Control and Prevention (CDC). *The association between school based physical activity, including physical education, and academic performance.* Atlanta, GA: U.S. Department of Health and Human Services; 2010.

36. Morales J, Pellicer-Chenoll M, Garcia-Masso X, ai. Relation between physical activity and academic performance in 3rd-year secondary education students. *Percept Mot Skills* 2011;**113**(2):539–46. https://doi.org/10.2466/06.11.13.Pms.113.5.539-546.
37. Sport en common. *Quality education*; 2021 https://www.sportencommun.org/en/impacts/quality-education/. [Accessed 28 April 2021].
38. Roe A, Blikstad-Balas M, Dalland, et al. The impact of COVID-19 and homeschooling on students' engagement with physical activity. *Sports Act Living* 2021. https://doi.org/10.3389/fspor.2020.589227.
39. Nurhayati F, Wahjuni ES, et al. Quality of life and level of physical activity in sports education students during the COVID-19 pandemic. *Advances in Social Science, Education and Humanities Research*, 491; 2020. p. 1172–6. https://doi.org/10.2991/assehr.k.201201.196.
40. Radu MC, Schnakovszky C, Herghelegiu E, et al. The impact of the COVID-19 pandemic on the quality of educational process: a student survey. *Int J Environ Res Public Health* 2020;**17**(7770):1–15. https://doi.org/10.3390/ijerph17217770.
41. Schwarz E, Spittle S. Sport education. In: Keshkar, et al., editors. *The effects of coronavirus pandemic on the sports industry: an update*; 2021. p. 2–4. https://doi.org/10.29252/aassjournal.964. Ann Appl Sport Sci. 9 (1).
42. Wahlström T. *Post pandemic sport education*. The sports digest; 2020. http://thesportdigest.com/2020/04/post-pandemic-sports-education/. [Accessed 20 April 2021].
43. Dudfield O, Smith MD. *Sport for development and peace and the 2030 agenda for sustainable development*. UK: Commonwealth Secretariat. London; 2015.
44. Viteri A. *Impact of COVID-19 on women and girls in sports*; 2020. Retrieved from: https://theowp.org/impact-of-COVID-19-on-women-and-girls-in-sports/. [Accessed 29 April 2021].
45. Gillen N. *Nancy Gillen: how will coronavirus impact women's sports?*; 2020. Retrieved from: https://www.insidethegames.biz/articles/1093591/how-will-the-pandemic-affect-women-sports. [Accessed 20 April 2021].
46. European commission. *2021 report on gender equality in the EU*; 2021 https://ec.europa.eu/info/sites/default/files/aid_development_cooperation_fundamental_rights/annual_report_ge_2021_en.pdf. [Accessed 20 April 2021].
47. Iran Sport for all Federation (ISFAF); 2020. retrieved from http://www.isfaf.ir. [Accessed 20 April 2021].
48. UN Women. *COVID-19, women, girls and sport: build back better*; 2020. Retrieved from https://www.un.org/development/desa/dspd/wp-content/uploads/sites/22/2020/07/brief-COVID-19-women-girls-and-sport-en.pdf. [Accessed 20 April 2021].
49. Hilborne S. *What will COVID-19 mean for the future of women's sport?* Women in sport; 2020. https://www.womeninsport.org/opinion/COVID-19-future-of-womens-sport/. [Accessed 20 April 2021].
50. Sport en commun. *clean water and sanitation*; 2021 https://www.sportencommun.org/en/impacts/clean-water-and-sanitation/. [Accessed 20 April 2021].
51. Around the rings. *Paris 2024 Unites Behind La Nuit de l'Eau to Promote Swimming for All Legacy*; 2021 https://www.infobae.com/aroundtherings/federations/2021/07/12/paris-2024-unites-behind-la-nuit-de-leau-to-promote-swimming-for-all-legacy/. [Accessed 20 April 2021].
52. Beyond Sport. *Football for water. KNVB—Dutch FA project. Netherland*; 2015 https://www.beyondsport.org/project/f/football-for-water/. [Accessed 28 April 2021].
53. National Institute of Building sciences. *Taking the field: advancing energy and water efficiency in sports venues. A Report to U.S.* Department of Energy; 2014. https://www.brikbase.org/sites/default/files/NIBS_GSA_TakingTheField_Fina.pdf. [Accessed 20 April 2021].

54. Keshkar S, Afsharpour M. *Water management in Tehran's sports complexes under the conditions of the national water crisis.* M.A. Thesis, Faculty of sports sciences. Allameh Tabataba'i University; 2019.
55. Belson K. *Water waste: Go, Go.* New York Times; 2014. https://www.nytimes.com/2014/10/08/business/energy-environment/water-waste-going-going-.html?_r=0. [Accessed 29 April 2021].
56. Vero water. *How much water do stadiums and arenas use?* ; 2014 https://www.verowater.com/news/how-much-water-do-stadiums-and-arenas-use. [Accessed 25 April 2021].
57. Côte d'Ivoire Ministry of Sport. *Côte d'Ivoire—Youth, entrepreneurship, exchanges and more: an update on the Ouagadougou commitments*; 2019 https://www.diplomatie.gouv.fr/en/country-files/africa/after-the-ouagadougou-speech/article/cote-d-ivoire-youth-entrepreneurship-exchanges-and-more-an-update-on-the. [Accessed 20 April 2021].
58. Climate action. *The 5 most sustainable sports venues in the world*; 2018 https://www.climateaction.org/news/the-5-most-sustainable-sports-venues-in-the-world. [Accessed 28 April 2021].
59. Keshkar S, Ansari AA, Gh K. *Identifying the requirements and actions for green management in relation to the sustainable development of Iranian football stadiums.* Sport management studies; 2021. https://doi.org/10.22089/SMRJ.2021.10047.3312. (in press). [In Persian].
60. ITIK. *Sustainability and sports, an inseparable nexus*; 2021 https://www.itik.cat/uploads/files/IG_Sustainability%20and%20sport%2C%20an%20inseparable%20nexus.pdf. [Accessed 29 April 2021].
61. Chihib M, Salmerón-Manzano E, Chourak M, et al. Impact of the COVID-19 pandemic on the energy use at the University of Almeria (Spain). *Sustainability* 2021;**13**:5843. https://doi.org/10.3390/su13115843.
62. Unstat. *Goal 8: promote sustained, inclusive and sustainable economic growth, full and productive employment and decent work for all*; 2021 https://unstats.un.org/sdgs/report/2016/goal-08/. [Accessed 29 April 2021].
63. Yehia Y. *The costs and benefits of hosting international sports events.* Global edge, Michigan State University; 2018. https://globaledge.msu.edu/blog/post/55572/the-costs-and-benefits-of-hosting-intern. [Accessed 20 July 2021].
64. Sport en commun. *Decent work and economic growth*; 2020 https://www.sportencommun.org/en/impacts/decent-work-and-economic-growth/. [Accessed 21 April 2021].
65. Eurostat. *Employment in sports*; 2021 https://ec.europa.eu/eurostat/statistics-explained/index.php?title=Employment_in_sports. [Accessed 21 April 2021].
66. European Observatoire of Sport and Employment (EOSE). *Impact of COVID-19 on employment impact of COVID-19 on employment in sport debated at EU workshop*; 2021 https://eose.org/2020/12/impact-of-COVID-19-on-employement-in-sports-debated-at-eu-workshop/. [Accessed 28 April 2021].
67. Greni E. *That was my identity': COVID-19 pandemic costing stadium workers their jobs.* Cronkite News; 2020. https://cronkitenews.azpbs.org/2020/09/21/covid-cost-stadium-workers-jobs/. [Accessed 13 March 2021].
68. United Nations. *Recovering better: sport for development and peace. Reopening, recovery and resilience post-COVID-19*; 2021 https://www.un.org/development/desa/dspd/wp-content/uploads/sites/22/2020/12/Final-SDP-recovering-better.pdf. [Accessed 22 April 2021].
69. Sport en commun. *Industry, innovation and infrastructure*; 2020 https://www.sportencommun.org/en/impacts/industry-innovation-and-infrastructure/. [Accessed 28 April 2021].
70. United Nations (UNESCAP). *Transformations for sustainable development: promoting environmental sustainability in Asia and the Pacific.* United Nations publication; 2016. https://www.unescap.org/sites/default/files/Full%20report.pdf. [Accessed 28 April 2021].

71. Inter-American development bank. *What is sustainable infrastructure?* ; 2018 https://publications.iadb.org/publications/english/document/What_is_Sustainable_Infrastructure__A_Framework_to_Guide_Sustainability_Across_the_Project_Cycle.pdf. [Accessed 12 April 2021].
72. Wiener D, Didillon N, Nunez P, Downing L. *Financing sustainable and resilient infrastructure by creating a new asset class for institutional investors*. Switzerland: Global Infrastructure Basel Foundation; 2020.
73. Campelli M. *If sport wants a bright future, it has to build resilience*. The sustainability report, Sustainability.Sports; 2020. https://sustainability.sports/headline-if-sports-wants-a-bright-future-it-has-to-build-resilience/. [Accessed 25 April 2021].
74. European Football for Development Network. *GOAL 9: build resilient infrastructure, promote inclusive and sustainable industrialisation and foster innovation*; 2021 https://www.efdn.org/sports-addressing-sdg-goal-9/. [Accessed 11 April 2021].
75. Filo KE, Cuskelly G, Wicker P. Resource utilization and power relations of community sports clubs in the aftermath of natural disasters. *Sport Management Review* 2015;**18**(4):555–69. https://doi.org/10.1016/j.smr.2015.01.002.
76. Mutz M, Müller J, Reimers AK. Use of digital media for home-based sports activities during the COVID-19 pandemic: results from the German SPOVID survey. *Int J Environ Res Public Health* 2021;**18**(9):4409. https://doi.org/10.3390/ijerph18094409.
77. Alidoust Ghahfarokhi E, Sadeqi Arani Z. Sports business resilience in the COVID-19 crisis: the Delphi qualitative approach. *Iran J Manag Stud* 2021. https://doi.org/10.22059/ijms.2021.315742.674355 [In press].
78. Sport en commun. *Reduced inequalities*; 2020 https://www.sportencommun.org/en/impacts/reduced-inequalities/. [Accessed 28 April 2021].
79. Shur NF, Johns D, Kluzek S, et al. Physical inactivity and health inequality during coronavirus: a novel opportunity or total lockdown? *BMJ Open Sport Exerc Med* 2020;**6**. https://doi.org/10.1136/bmjsem-2020-000903, e000903.
80. Kamyuka D, Carlin L, McPherson G, Misener L. Access to physical activity and Sport and the effects of isolation and cordon sanitaire during COVID-19 for people with disabilities in Scotland and Canada. *Front Sports Act Living* 2020;**2**. https://doi.org/10.3389/fspor.2020.594501, 594501.
81. United Nations. *Policy Brief: COVID-19 in an Urban world*; 2020. Retrived from https://www.un.org/sites/un2.un.org/files/sg_policy_brief_covid_urban_world_july_2020.pdf. [Accessed 25 April 2021].
82. International Olympic Committee (IOC). *World cities day 2020: the power of sports to build healthier, more sustainable urban communities*. International Olympic committee; 2020. https://olympics.com/ioc/news/world-cities-day-2020-the-power-of-sports-to-build-healthier-more-sustainable-urban-communities. [Accessed 28 April 2021].
83. Chtourou H, Trabelsi K, H'mida C, Boukhris O, et al. Staying physically active during the quarantine and self-isolation period for controlling and mitigating the COVID-19 pandemic: a systematic overview of the literature. *Front Psychol* 2020;**11**(27). https://doi.org/10.3389/fpsyg.2020.01708.
84. Kaur H, Singh T, Arya YK, et al. Physical fitness and exercise during the COVID-19 pandemic: a qualitative enquiry. *Front Psychol* 2020;**11**. https://doi.org/10.3389/fpsyg.2020.590172, 590172.
85. United Nations. *Final report of the human rights council advisory committee on the possibilities of using sport and the Olympic ideal to promote human rights for all and to strengthen universal respect for them*. General Assembly, Human Rights Council; 2015. https://www.ohchr.org/EN/HRBodies/HRC/RegularSessions/Session30/Documents/A_HRC_30_50_ENG-.docx. [Accessed 25 April 2021].
86. Lim K, Ramely A, Wafi A. Make green growth a priority: issues and challenges in organising green sports tourism events. *Malays J Sustain Environ* 2020;**7**(1):53–68. https://doi.org/10.24191/myse.v7i1.8910.

87. Plastic Europe. *Plastics in sport and leisure applications*; 2021. Retrieved from: https://www.plasticseurope.org/en/about-plastics/sport-leisure. [Accessed 25 April 2021].
88. International Olympic Committee (IOC). *IOC's Plastic Game Plan for Sport to help sports organizations tackle plastic pollution*; 2020 https://olympics.com/ioc/news/ioc-s-plastic-game-plan-for-sports-to-help-sports-organisations-tackle-plastic-pollution. [Accessed 28 April 2021].
89. Bindiya S. *Eco-Friendly Tokyo Olympics: organizers collect 24.5 tons of plastic to create recyclable podiums.* Inside sports; 2020. September 29, 2020 https://www.insidesport.co/eco-friendly-tokyo-olympics-organisers-collect-24-5-tonnes-of-plastic-to-create-recyclable-podiums/. [Accessed 29 April 2021].
90. Alpin S. *Recycled materials: navigating globally changing markets during COVID-19*; 2020. Retrieved from https://www.anthesisgroup.com/recycled-materials-navigating-globally-changing-markets-during-covid-19/. [Accessed 25 April 2021].
91. United Nations. *Climate change 'biggest threat modern humans have ever faced'.* World-Renowned Naturalist Tells Security Council, Calls for Greater Global Cooperation; 2021. Retrieved from: https://www.un.org/press/en/2021/sc14445.doc.htm. [Accessed 21 April 2021].
92. Relief web. *COVID-19, Displacement and Climate Change, June 2020*; 2020 https://reliefweb.int/report/world/COVID-19-displacement-and-climate-change-june-2020. [Accessed 25 April 2021].
93. World meteorological organization (WMO). *Climate change indicators and impacts worsened in 2020*; 2021 https://public.wmo.int/en/media/press-release/climate-change-indicators-and-impacts-worsened-2020. [Accessed 20 July 2021].
94. Clinton foundation. *Athletes for the Earth*; 2021 https://www.clintonfoundation.org/clinton-global-initiative/commitments/athletes-earth. [Accessed 6 August 2021].
95. Ritchie H, Roser M. *CO_2 and greenhouse gas emissions*; 2020. Published online at OurWorldInData.org. Retrieved from: https://ourworldindata.org/co2-and-other-greenhouse-gas-emissions. [Accessed 20 April 2021].
96. Masson-Delmotte V, Zhai P, Pörtner H-O, et al. *Global Warming of 1.5°C.* Intergovernmental Panel on Climate Change; 2019. Retrieved from: https://www.ipcc.ch/site/assets/uploads/sites/2/2019/06/SR15_Full_Report_High_Res.pdf. [Accessed 22 April 2021].
97. Meng W, Xu L, Hu B, et al. Quantifying direct and indirect carbon dioxide emissions of the Chinese tourism industry. *J Clean Prod* 2020;**126**:586–94. https://doi.org/10.1016/j.jclepro.2016.03.177.
98. Collins A, Flynn A. Measuring the environmental sustainability of a major sporting event: a case study of the FA cup final. *Tour Econ* 2008;**14**(4):751–68. https://doi.org/10.5367/000000008786440120.
99. Triantafyllidis S. Carbon dioxide emissions research and sustainable transportation in the sports industry. *MDPI* 2018;**4**(4):57. https://doi.org/10.3390/c4040057.
100. Triantafyllidis S, Ries RJ, Kaplanidou KK. Carbon dioxide emissions of spectators' transportation in collegiate sporting events: comparing on-campus and offcampus stadium locations. *Sustainability* 2018;**10**(1):241. https://doi.org/10.3390/su10010241.
101. Chard C, Mallen C. Examining the linkages between automobile use and carbon impacts of community-based ice hockey. *Sport Management Review* 2012;**15**(4):476–84. https://doi.org/10.1016/j.smr.2012.02.002.
102. Triantafyllidis S, Davakos H. Growing cities and mass participant sports events: traveling behaviors and carbon dioxide emissions. *J Carbon Res* 2019;**5**(3):49. https://doi.org/10.3390/c5030049.
103. Triantafyllidis S. Environmental change, the sports industry, and COVID-19. In: Pedersen PM, Ruihley BJ, Li B, editors. *Sport and the pandemic, perspectives on*

COVID-19's impact on the sport industry. 1st ed. London: Routledge; 2020. https://doi.org/10.4324/9781003105916 [chapter 4].
104. Statista. *Sport events worldwide*; 2020. Retrieved from https://www.statistacom/outlook/272/100/sport-events/worldwide#market-revenue. [Accessed 22 April 2021].
105. International Union for Conservation of Nature. *Why sports is a home run for biodiversity protection*; 2018 https://www.iucn.org/news/business-and-biodiversity/201805/why-sports-home-run-biodiversity-protection. [Accessed 28 April 2021].
106. Islamic republic of Iran news agency (IRNA). *Rezvani: Water sports have suffered the most from Corona*; 2020 https://www.irna.ir/news/84106642. [Accessed 28 April 2021].
107. Haddad M, Abbes Z, Mujika I, Chamari K. Impact of COVID-19 on swimming training: practical recommendations during home confinement/isolation. *Int J Environ Res Public Health* 2021;**18**:4767. https://doi.org/10.3390/ijerph18094767.
108. Wendtlandt M, Wicker P. The effects of sport activities and environmentally sustainable behaviors on subjective well-being: a comparison before and during COVID-19. *Front Sports Act Living* 2021;**3**. https://doi.org/10.3389/fspor.2021.659837, 659837.
109. The land between. *Recreational boating and the environment—Tips and tricks for environmentally conscious boating*; 2019 https://www.thelandbetween.ca/2019/07/recreational-boating-and-the-environment-tips-and-tricks-for-environmentally-conscious-boating/. [Accessed 28 April 2021].
110. Environmental protection. *The environmental impacts of boating*; 2017 https://eponline.com/Articles/2017/03/27/The-Environmental-Impacts-of-Boating.aspx. [Accessed 28 April 2021].
111. Sport for sustainable development. *Global introduction of the goal with some statistics*; 2021 https://sport4sd.com/goal-15-life-on-land. [Accessed 28 April 2021].
112. Bates AE, Mangubhai S, Milanés CB, et al. The COVID-19 pandemic as a pivot point for biological conservation. *Nat Commun* 2021;**12**:5176. https://doi.org/10.1038/s41467-021-25399-5.
113. World Health Organization (WHO). *COVID-19 and violence against women what the health sector/system can do*; 2020 https://apps.who.int/iris/bitstream/handle/10665/331699/WHO-SRH-20.04-eng.pdf?ua=1. [Accessed 28 April 2021].
114. Jönsson K. *Sport and politics. An ethical approach*. Centre for Baltic and East European Studies, Södertörn University. Baltic Worlds; 2012. http://balticworlds.com/x/.
115. Maurice C. *Politics and sport: how FIFA, UEFA and the ioc regulate political statements by athlete*. Law in sports; 2016. https://www.lawinsport.com/topics/item/politics-and-sports-how-fifa-uefa-and-the-ioc-regulate-political-statements-by-athletes. [Accessed 24 July 2021].
116. Hyde M. *Iranian women allowed to watch football at stadium for first time in decades*. The Guardian; 2019. https://www.theguardian.com/football/2019/oct/09/iranian-women-allowed-to-watch-football-at-stadium-for-first-time-in-decades. [Accessed 28 April 2021].
117. Keshkar S. *The cultural differences in sports. Research project*. Allameh Tabataba'i University; 2018.
118. IOC. *Peace through Sport*; 2020 https://olympics.com/ioc/peace-through-sports. [Accessed 29 April 2021].
119. Yamamura E, Tsutsui Y. The impact of postponing 2020 Tokyo Olympics on the happiness of O-MO-TE-NA-SHI Workers in Tourism: a consequence of COVID-19. MDPI, *Sustainability* 2020;**12**, 8168. 1–16 https://doi.org/10.3390/su12198168.
120. Crowcroft O. *Tokyo 2020 Olympics postponed due to the coronavirus outbreak*. Euro news; 2020. https://www.euronews.com/2020/03/23/coronavirus-will-the-2020-olympic-games-be-delayed. [Accessed 28 April 2021].

121. World Federation of the Sporting Goods Industry. *Significant impact of COVID-19 on the global sporting goods industry*; 2020 https://www.theuiaa.org/uiaa-media-COVID-19/significant-impact-of-COVID-19-on-the-global-sporting-goods-industry/. [Accessed 23 April 2021].
122. Purpose. Nike. *A letter from our President and CEO*; 2020 https://purpose.nike.com/ceo-letter. [Accessed 29 April 2021].
123. Shirazi S. *The Gulistan of Saadi: in Persian with English translation (Persian Edition)*. Compiled by: Reza Nazari, CreateSpace Independent Publishing Platform; 2016.

CHAPTER SEVEN

Monetary quantification of COVID-19 impacts on sustainable development goals: Focus on air pollution and climate change

Hemant Bherwani[a,b], Dhanya Balachandran[a], Alaka Das[a], and Rakesh Kumar[b,c]
[a]CSIR-National Environmental Engineering Research Institute (CSIR-NEERI), Nagpur, Maharashtra, India
[b]Academy of Scientific and Industrial Research (AcSIR), Ghaziabad, Uttar Pradesh, India
[c]Council of Scientific and Industrial Research (CSIR), Anusandhan Bhawan, New Delhi, India

1. Introduction

The presence and spread of the novel coronavirus have affected several regions throughout the world.[1,2] The epidemic began in Wuhan City in December 2019 and quickly spread to other regions of the world.[3,4] In light of the current crisis, the government agencies of the afflicted nations have devised initiatives to limit COVID-19 prevalence among their citizens. The Government of India implemented a series of curfews in this reference, which includes self-lockdown—"Janta Curfew" on 22nd March 2020, lockdown-1 that was declared from 24-03-2020 to 14-04-2020 and extended to lockdown-2 (15-04-2020 to 03-05-2020), lockdown-3 (04-05-2020 to 17-05-2020), and lockdown-4 (18-05-2020 to 31-05-2020). It is followed by Unlock 1 which started on 1-05-2020 and continues to Unlock 14 till 31-07-2021.[5] COVID-19 was lowered by these lockdowns and control measures, whose impacts can also be seen in social, economic, and environmental aspects with a positive drift associated with ambient air quality in national or state sectors.[6,7] Air quality is a crucial problem for residents' health as well as the economy.[6,8] An instantaneous strategic move of COVID-19-related lockdown may have helped to improve air quality; however, there are intensifying impacts associated with various sustainable development goals (SDGs).[5] During the pandemic, energy demands and production cycle drastically altered and became an insurmountable problem.

COVID-19 and the Sustainable Development Goals
https://doi.org/10.1016/B978-0-323-91307-2.00018-3

Further the healthcare services got skewed towards COVID-19, resulting in the deterioration of other healthcare services. The pandemic has made hindrances in delivering essential services to the society by restricted capacity which it has formerly provided smoothly. Owing to disturbances in logistics and supplies of material and equipment, the services of the health system have been seriously affected due to this pandemic.[9] The Centre for Monitoring Indian Economy (CMIE) indicated an increase in poverty, unemployment, labor scarcity, and other information. The troubling state of economics and e-commerce hurt Indian citizens' livelihoods.[5]

According to recent research findings, the control strategies used during the COVID-19 outbreak had a significant influence on SDGs, particularly SDG-3 (Good Health and Wellbeing) and SDG-13 (Climate Action). The epidemic's social isolation, lockdown, and quarantine were all new to civilization, and they all harmed the society's equilibrium in every way. It did, however, provided some paybacks in terms of better air quality and reduced carbon footprint. Pandemic risk increases if accessibility to clean water for drinking and sanitation gets limited. However, the pandemic-triggered nationwide lockdown also delivered some benefits, such as decreased pollution rate in water resources. The longest freshwater lake in India (Vembanad lake) showed an approximate decrease in suspended particulate matter concentration by one-third in 2020 compared to 2019 which is a record lower rate of pollutants within the past 7 years.[10] Reduced industrial activities and consequent decrease in wastewater discharge during the lockdown period resulted in a 50% decline in the concentration of groundwater-borne cationic solutes, e.g., Se, As, Fe, and Pb, as well as NO_3, total and faecal coliform in the coastal city of Tuticorin. Approximately 50% of reduction in air pollution was evident in New York and Delhi from the previous year, with a considerable reduction in PM_{10}, $PM_{2.5}$, CO, and NO_2 which adds to the positive aspects of impacts of COVID-19.[3,10] According to data analyzed using statistical approaches, such as analysis of variance and regression models, air pollution in a specific place is increasing the risk factor of death due to COVID-19.[11] Particulate matter (PM) can play a prominent role in the spread of disease via the atmosphere, water, and touch due to its chemical characteristics, shape, and particle size, as well as its ubiquitous dispersion on virtually all objects.[12] An additional problem related to the outbreak is frontline staff's proper disposal of personal protective equipment (PPE), which can be a contaminant.[13] Decentralized incineration of PPEs have been proven to be environmentally and human health-friendly, with the purpose of safe waste disposal and illness prevention from such equipment.[14]

$PM_{2.5}$ is a primary source of respiratory sickness in individuals, which became a serious condition during the COVID-19 outbreak, among the different air pollutants. However, due to the entire cessation of human activities during the pandemic, there was a significant reduction in its level as well as CO_2 emissions, which became a blessing for addressing severe environmental concerns such as air pollution and climate change. The decrease in environmental pollution should be studied in light of forward-thinking initiatives and strategies aimed at achieving a truly sustainable community.[15] Analysts are now focusing their attention on the pandemic's mortality and economic implications. Assessing the economic impacts of ceasing human activities during such an outbreak shows a detailed picture of the changes in damage to the environment and public health. Such monetary evaluations can serve as a foundation for assessing the effects of a pandemic on various SDGs with a view that the efforts have taken now and in the future must be focused on creating a more fair, comprehensive, and resilient environment and communities that are more robust to epidemics, climate change, as well as many other worldwide problems that humankind addresses.[16] The valuation methodologies described in the subsequent sections can help policymakers comprehend the scale of COVID-19's implications on SDGs, as well as serve as a foundation for valuing other SDGs, allowing for adequate action to be taken to maintain a strong and sustainable community. Furthermore, it indicates the magnitude of losses the country incurs due to health and climate change burdens and underlines the bare minimum levels one can reach by using the example of COVID-19 lockdowns. This should convince policymakers about the cost of environmental deterioration to the country and should drive positive action for the betterment of the environment.

By using air pollution and human health as assessing metrics, the major objective of this chapter is to explain how to measure the effects of COVID-19-induced resource limits and lockdowns on SDGs. The study further determines the reduction in concentrations of $PM_{2.5}$ using advanced tools like geographic information system (GIS) and remote sensing (RS) data from moderate resolution imaging spectroradiometer (MODIS) along with CO_2 emissions statistics collected from various resources. Econometric tools and methods are used to calculate the monetary value of reduced morbidity and mortality linked with COVID-19 management efforts. The localized value of the social cost of carbon (SCC) is used to monetize CO_2 emission reductions.

2. Methodology for the assessment of $PM_{2.5}$ and CO_2 emissions

2.1 Assessment of $PM_{2.5}$

Annually, air pollution causes massive deaths and disabilities among the population, making it one of the leading sources of health concerns. It has ecological effects such as acid rain and poor vision, but it has a greater and much more substantial effect on public health. $PM_{2.5}$ is a key air pollutant that causes and worsens respiratory ailments in people. As a result, studying its prevalence in the environment is essential during a pandemic, because the virus harms people who have a respiratory illness. As explained earlier the control strategies adopted during the COVID-19 bought $PM_{2.5}$ levels in the environment to a lower figure. This reduction has a significant positive impact on a community's health. Recent research studies taking Delhi, Paris, London, and Wuhan as the study area show a substantial reduction in the concentration of various air pollutants from 2019 to 2020 related to COVID-19 control strategies. Accordingly, a total reduction of morbidity values from 167.29 to 102.97 Million \$ and mortality values from 12.83 to 6.50 Billion \$ has been reported for Delhi city.[3]

In this study, the assessment of $PM_{2.5}$ is done for a slot of two periods to understand its effect on the environment. The study period was from prelockdown phase (April–September 2019) to initial lockdown phase (April–September 2020) and from lockdown phase (April 2019–March 2020) to postlockdown phase (April 2020–March 2021). The lowered impacts of lockdown on $PM_{2.5}$ concentration are analyzed using GIS and remote sensing data from the MODIS, which is detailed later.

RS technology has a wide range of applications, but it can be particularly useful in predicting the environmental effects of a pandemic. The application of RS to extract aerosol optical depth (AOD) and $PM_{2.5}$ levels in India during the prelockdown, lockdown, and postlockdown periods is shown in this section. Ground-based monitoring stations that measure $PM_{2.5}$ levels in ambient air at higher frequencies have been established in most major cities across the world; however, these methods are insufficient to comprehend its spatial distribution.[17,18] In this study, a new approach for predicting $PM_{2.5}$ levels in the environment is applied by integrating AOD and meteorological data. Traditional $PM_{2.5}$ field measurements are hard to acquire spatial data, particularly at the accurate scale necessary to determine the volatility of high-density cities. Where ground estimations are not possible, RS technology can be used to estimate aerosols and aid in $PM_{2.5}$ evaluation.[18,19] The AOD has been the most often utilized technique in statistical models to forecast $PM_{2.5}$ levels in the environment since it is the easiest to generate.[20,21]

MODIS AOD data is extracted for the appropriate study period from Level 1 and Atmosphere Archive and Distribution System Distributed Active Archive Center (LAADS DAAC) for India, and AOD is computed accordingly. The Simplified Aerosol Retrieval Algorithm (SARA) binning model with the low surface pressure period equation [$PM_{2.5} = 110.5$ [SARA AOD] + 12.56] is used to convert AOD data to $PM_{2.5}$ measurements and the model has been verified.[22] The model relies on meteorological data and has a high degree of correlation between AOD and $PM_{2.5}$ observations. It also improves the regression coefficients of the $PM_{2.5}$ prediction model while incorporating meteorological dimensions. To accurately predict $PM_{2.5}$ data, several equations are established for each meteorological component in the binning approach.[23,24] Among these, the earlier mentioned approach equation predicts best. The model has a high correlation, a precise slope, a lower intercept, and a low error, and it can accurately reflect the spatial distribution of $PM_{2.5}$ in metropolitan areas at 500 m resolution. Fig. 1(A)–(D) represents the $PM_{2.5}$ estimated for India for the study period selected, respectively, as (April–September) 2019, (April–September) 2020, (April 2019–March 2020), and (April 2020–March 2021).

The analysis of the maps prepared for the prelockdown period (April–September 2019) and lockdown period (April–September 2020) reveals the mean concentration of $PM_{2.5}$ levels in the environment to be 64.95 and 62.55 $\mu g/m^3$, respectively. A reduction of a value of 2.40 $\mu g/m^3$ in $PM_{2.5}$ levels occurred during the lockdown period which is caused mainly due to cessation of all anthropogenic activities in the country resulting in an improvement in air quality. Moreover, the analysis of the maps prepared for the period of April–March in 2019–20 and April–March in 2020–21 shows values of $PM_{2.5}$ level to be on a higher side in 2020–21. This is because due to the unlock process numerous activities are carried out within a shorter duration and hence higher values of $PM_{2.5}$ for the period 2020–21.

2.2 Assessment of CO_2 emissions

Carbon dioxide emissions are a primary cause of climatic change and global warming. It is emitted into the environment by numerous sectors of society

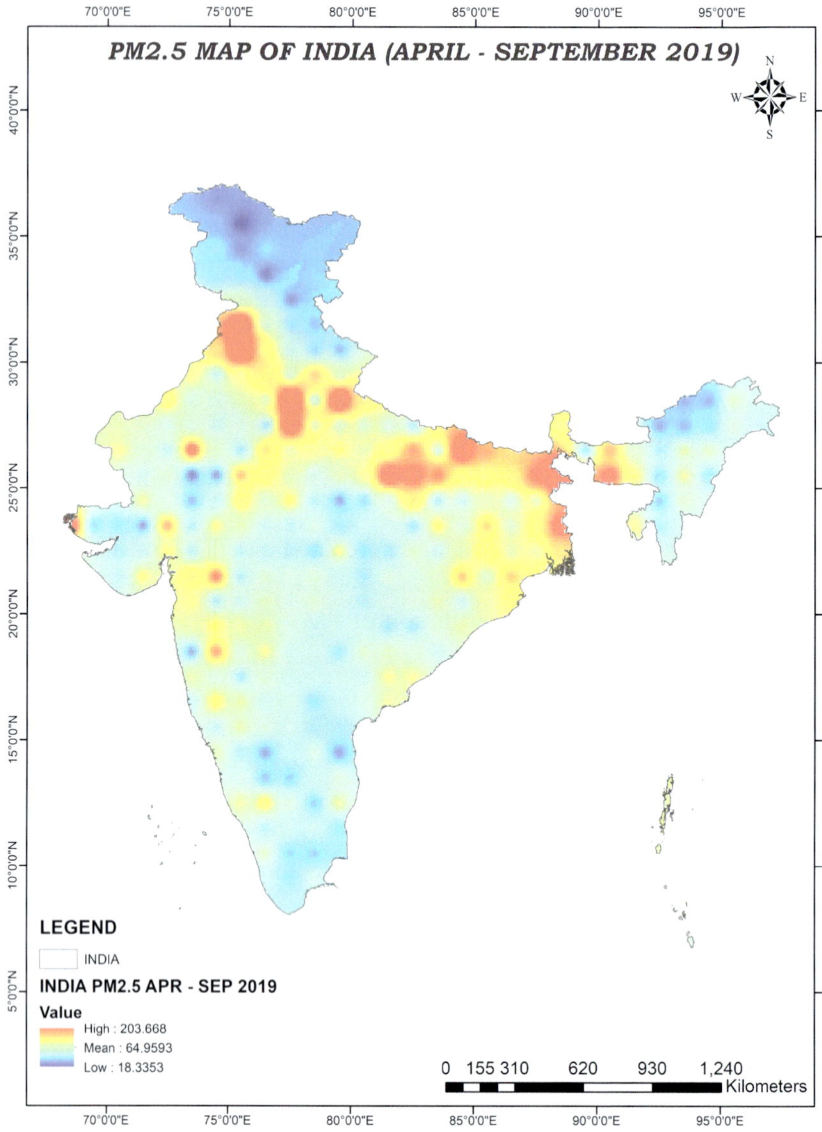

(a)

Fig. 1 $PM_{2.5}$ Maps of India for (A) (April—September) 2019,

(Continued)

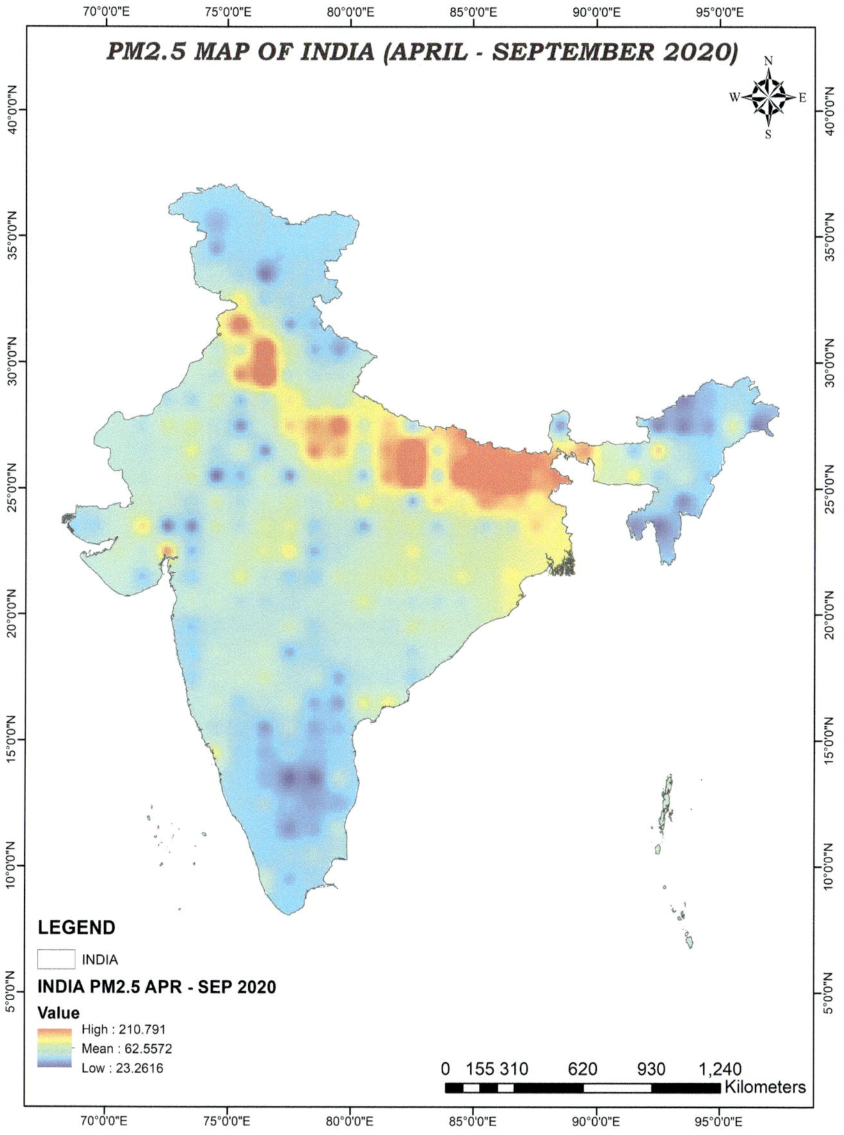

(b)

Fig. 1, cont'd (B) (April—September) 2020,

(Continued)

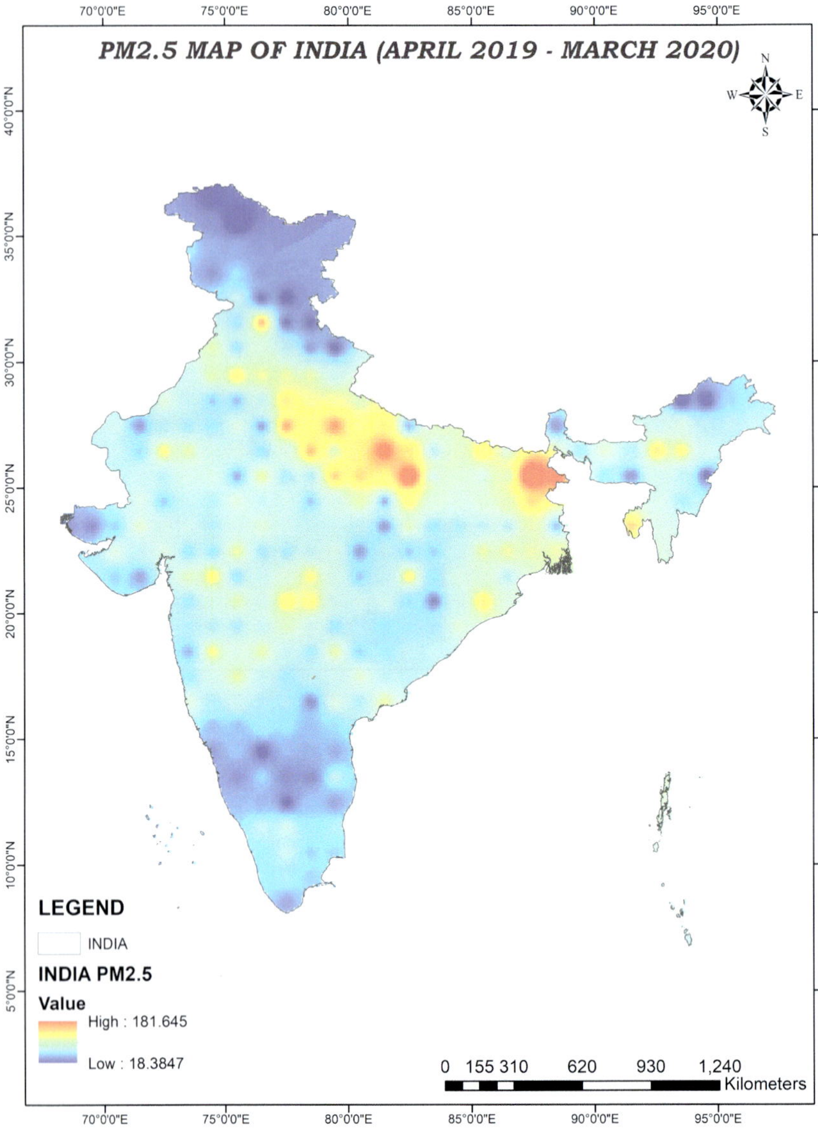

(c)

Fig. 1, cont'd (C) (April 2019—March 2020),

(Continued)

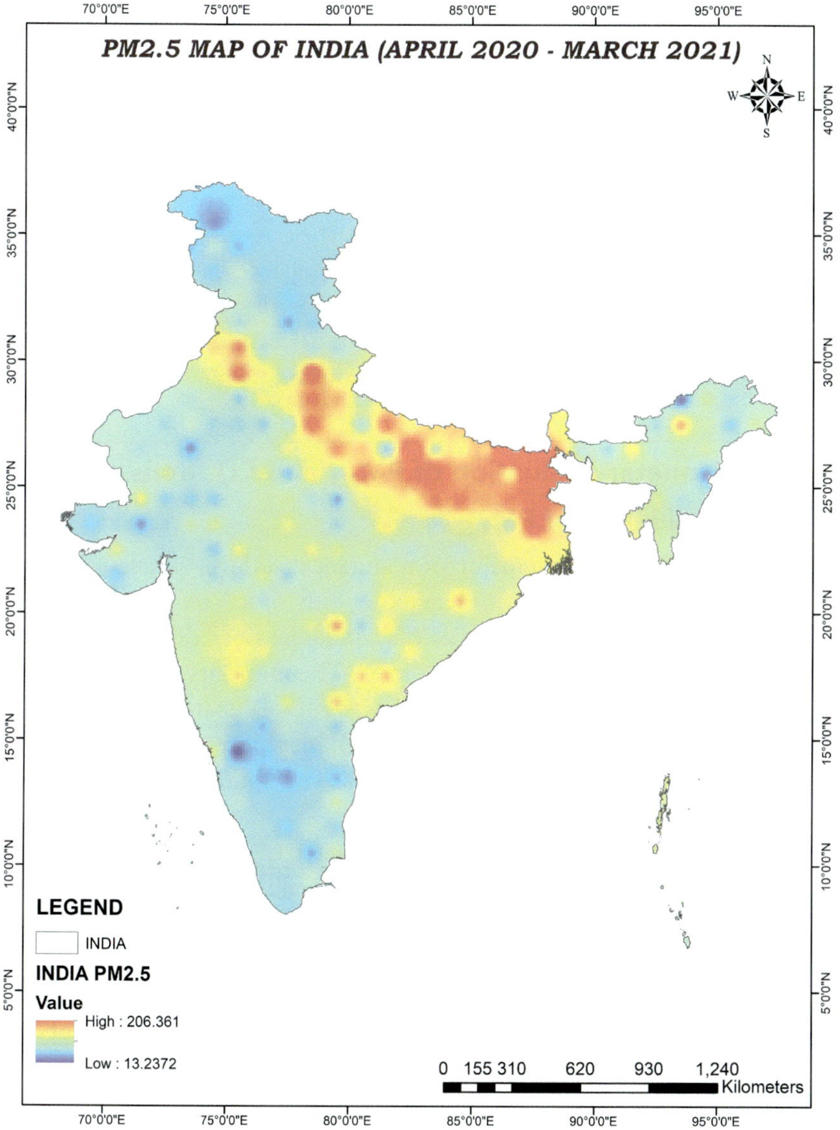

(d)

Fig. 1, cont'd and (D) (April 2020—March 2021).

and as a result of a country's economic operations. It was observed that due to the control techniques adopted during the COVID-19 epidemic, there was a significant reduction in these emissions due to the complete cessation of anthropogenic activities. According to a recent study outlining the impact of COVID-19 on SDGs, there was 26% reduction in CO_2 emissions during the lockdown period compared to 2019 levels.[5] As a result, there was an improvement in the weather conditions. For the assessment of improvement in these climatic conditions and their impact on the SDGs, the CO_2 emissions from fossil fuel use in India for the years 2019 and 2020 are considered and the annual changes in the emissions that occurred due to pandemic management strategies are evaluated.

3. Monetary valuation of $PM_{2.5}$ and CO_2 emissions

3.1 Valuation of $PM_{2.5}$

$PM_{2.5}$ is considered to be a major air pollutant that develops and aggravates respiratory illnesses in humans. Hence the study of its concentration in the environment is important during such a pandemic since the virus adversely affects the person already having the illness. The monetary value of reduced morbidity and mortality associated with COVID-19 management efforts is evaluated using the cost of illness (COI), disability-adjusted life years (DALY), and value of statistical life (VSL). The valuation methodologies are explained as follows.

The morbidity damages are assessed using COI and DALY. The data required for estimating the reduced monetary value of morbidity using the COI approach are taken from the National Sample Survey Office (NSSO) reports specifying the average cost of treatment involved for various diseases.

The DALY assessment of the morbidity loss estimation uses the DALY values determined from the statistics provided in the Global Burden of Diseases study in India in 2019. The COI and DALY assessment gives the total morbidity-related damages that are reduced due to improved air quality from 2019 to 2020.

The valuation of mortality damages cost saved due to the same scenario uses the reference value of VSL from previous studies conducted from labor wages. All the reference values are inflated using average inflation rates and 100 percent exposure is considered. The corresponding assessment equations used for the estimation are detailed as follows:

$$\text{Morbidity damages COI} = \text{COI} \times I_{ne} \times \text{IR} \tag{1}$$

$$\text{Morbidity loss DALY} = \text{DALY} \times I_{ne} \times \text{PCR} \times \text{IR} \tag{2}$$

$$\text{Mortality damages VSL} = \text{VSL} \times I_{ne} \times \text{IR} \tag{3}$$

The different attributes considered for the assessment are relative risk of pollutant (R_r), population attribute risk (PAR), rate attribute to exposure in the population (I_e), estimated no. of cases of mortality/morbidity (I_{ne}), and the total population of the city (N). The following attributes are calculated using the equations mentioned below:

$$R_r = 1 + (C_a - C_w) \times \frac{(R_r - 1)}{10} \tag{4}$$

$$\text{PAR} = \left(\frac{\sum([R_r(c) - 1] \times \rho(c))}{\sum([R_r(c) - 1] \times \rho(c) + 1)} \right. \tag{5}$$

$$I_{ne} = I_e \times \text{PAR} \times \text{N} \tag{6}$$

3.2 Valuation of CO_2 emissions

The cost of environmental harm caused by CO_2 emissions is calculated using the SCC. SCC, sometimes known as carbon emission shadow pricing, is the most widely used methodology for calculating economic losses caused by carbon dioxide. It illustrates the economic impact of increased CO_2 emissions as a result of climate change. The cost of damage is calculated as the difference between a baseline change in the climatic pathway and an additional rise in CO_2. The assessment method adopted for the current study also utilizes the same approach. For this purpose, the annual changes in the emissions of CO_2 from fossil fuels used in India are considered and it amounts to 30 million tonnes.[25]

The impact of these emission reductions on SDGs are monetarily quantified using the SCC equation provided as follows:

$$\text{SCC} = \text{Quantity of } CO_2 \text{ emitted } (t_{CO_2}) \times \text{Cost of } CO_2 \text{ per tonnes} \times \text{Purchase power parity (PPP)} \tag{7}$$

4. Results and discussions

The valuations of reduced morbidity and mortality damages due to COVID-19 lockdown are carried out and explained in this section based

Table 1 Input values.

Categories	Mean value (PPM)	Population (millions)[26]	Population (lakhs)	Per capita income (INR)[27]
India $PM_{2.5}$ from April to September 2019 (Prelockdown period)	64.9593	1367.6	13,676	92,085
India $PM_{2.5}$ from April to September 2020 (Lockdown period)	62.5572	1378.6	13,786	94,954

Table 2 Relative risk (R_r) and baseline incidence (I_e).[3]

Parameter	Mortality/morbidity	Relative risk (R_r)	Baseline incidence (I_e)
$PM_{2.5}$	Total mortality	1.015	543.5
	Respiratory diseases	1.022	550.9
	Cardiovascular diseases	1.013	546
	Asthma attack	1.021	940
	Chronic bronchitis	1.029	694

Table 3 Reference values.

Parameter	Reference value	References
COI	21,706	28
DALY	0.039	29
VSL	15 Million INR	30

Table 4 Mortality and morbidity damage cost.

Parameter	COI (morbidity damages cost) (Million INR)	DALY (morbidity loss cost) (Million INR)	VSL (mortality damage cost) (Million INR)
PM2.5	934.29	9.76	733,016

on the input values provided in Tables 1–3 and the damage cost estimated are given in Table 4.

4.1 Morbidity and mortality damages assessment

The mean concentration values of $PM_{2.5}$ for the prelockdown and postlockdown period are 64.95 and 62.55 $\mu g/m^3$ which is estimated from the AOD and $PM_{2.5}$ maps prepared. The various health-related problems caused by $PM_{2.5}$ include respiratory diseases, cardiovascular diseases, asthma attacks, and chronic bronchitis. Hence the baseline incidence values for these diseases and for mortality are taken from research studies and the relative risk of each illness is calculated according to Eq. (4) and are provided in Table 2. The study is carried out with the assumption of 100% exposure and hence the population statistics along with the per capita income is given in Table 1 is collected accordingly and the total damage cost of reduced morbidity and mortality using the reference values of COI, DALY, and VSL for India provided in Table 3 is estimated as per Eqs. (1)–(3). The monetary value assessed for the reduced morbidity damages and losses due to COVID-19 lockdown amounts to 943.76 million INR and the total reduced mortality damage cost amounts to 733,016 million INR which is a huge reduction when analyzed and accounts for about 0.5% of the GDP of the country. This is nothing but an improvement in SDGs relating to human health and well-being in the context of air pollution reduction due to COVID-19 lockdown.

4.2 SCC method

The values for the cost of CO_2 per tonne emitted to the atmosphere are taken as per USEPA for the year 2020. Monetary assessment is carried out for average discount rates of 3% and also considering the high impact scenarios. The values taken for the assessment are provided in Table 5.

The annual changes in the emission of CO_2 for the study period are collected from respective references, and the SCC for an average impact scenario yielded a value of 27,707 million INR and the high impact scenario is 81,143 million INR. This monetary quantification of reduced

Table 5 Estimated social cost of carbon (SCC).

Specifications	Values
Annual changes in the emissions of CO_2 (2019–20) (million tonnes)	30[25]
SCC for carbon for 2020 as per USEPA on 3% average discount rates ($)	42[31]
SCC for carbon for 2020 as per USEPA for high impact scenario ($)	123[31]
Purchase power parity (PPP) for 2020	21.99[32]
Estimated social cost of carbon (SCC) for 3% avg discount rates (million INR)	27,707
Estimated social cost of carbon (SCC) for high impact scenario (million INR)	81,143

CO_2 emission reveals the avoided damages to the environment and change in climatic conditions which would occur due to these reduced CO_2 emissions having huge worth.

5. Conclusion

The concept of sustainability is currently gaining a lot of traction all around the world. The SDGs are a major gateway for achieving a brighter future by addressing the world's problems. In the current situation, the goals relating to human health and well-being (SDG-3), as well as climate action (SDG-13), are some of the most important goals. SDG-3 aims to discover and validate all strategies to enhance health and well-being at all stages of life. Its goals encompass facilitating remote healthcare, promoting infection prevention and control through wearable monitoring systems, and tracking aspects that impact human life and well-being, such as air quality and traffic. Climate change is also affecting people and places all around the world today. It is harming lives and destabilizing global markets, injuring individuals, towns, and nations now and even more in the future. SDG-13 calls for action to fight this climate change and its consequences.

The COVID-19, which emerged unexpectedly and without warning, has created some positive impacts in various aspects recently. Due to the control techniques stated to bring the spread of illnesses to a lower value, the world nations that have been actively participating in economic operations and living a frenetic busy existence came to a halt. The continued lockdown strategies of COVID-19 thus became a portal for reduced carbon footprint and improved air quality which resulted due to the termination of anthropogenic activities. Improved air quality and climate conditions due to COVID-19 lockdown have a positive influence on human health which is quantified in monetary terms in this chapter. The quantified positive outcomes have thus impacted and enhanced the targets of SDGs relating the health and climate concerns.

COVID-19's monetary impact on air quality improvement and human health preservation in terms of lower CO_2, $PM_{2.5}$ emissions, mortality, and morbidity presents a clear picture of its influence as a turning point in the stages of growth that contributes to the goals of sustainable development. A reduction of 2.40 $\mu g/m^3$ of $PM_{2.5}$ from prelockdown to lockdown period yielded a total value of 943.76 million INR of reduced morbidity and 733,016 million INR of reduced mortality. The reduction of 30 million tonnes of CO_{2e} emission created a value of 27,707 million

INR for an average impact scenario and yielded 81,143 million INR for the high impact scenario as the reduced damage cost. Hence the current study estimating these reduction impacts reveals that it has a worth of 0.56% of the country's GDP at present. This research demonstrates that the quality of air should be considered as part of a comprehensive strategy for preventing infectious propagation, protecting human life, and achieving long-term environmental sustainability.[33–35] The monetary assessment carried out based on gross calculations and under certain assumptions gives a detailed picture of the kind of losses countries incur regularly due to high air pollution and carbon footprint.

6. Suggestions and future perspectives

These types of estimating methodologies can aid policymakers in developing and implementing programs that promote environmental and human harmony without jeopardizing natural resources. The COVID-19 lockdown-related impacts on SDG-3 and SDG-13 quantified in monetary terms establish the baseline which is achievable through the halt of economic activities. However, halting is not the solution that is being proposed here, rather, it is important to find ways in which the footprint of material and energy extraction and use can be reduced, using mechanisms such as the circular economy. The assessment carried out here, although under certain assumptions and grossing of values, should be improved with robust data for better communication to policymakers. Furthermore, to assess the exact implications of SDGs on COVID-19-related variations, it is necessary to examine local variables in the field, such as socioeconomic class, microclimatic conditions, health and community well-being, available resources, and so on.[35,36] Research and developments in these evaluation approaches may assist in extending these methodologies to evaluate the impact on other SDGs and act as a framework for developing innovative programs to achieve the targets.

References

1. World Health Organization. *Coronavirus disease (COVID-2019) situation reports*. Geneva: World Health Organization; 2020. https://www.who.int/emergencies/diseases/novel-coronavirus-2019/situation-reports. [Accessed 23 March 2020].
2. Gautam S, Hens L. SARS-CoV-2 pandemic in India: what might we expect? *Environ Dev Sustain* 2020;**22**:3867–9. https://doi.org/10.1007/s10668-020-00739-5.
3. Bherwani H, Nair M, Musugu K, Gautam S, Gupta A, Kapley A, et al. Valuation of air pollution externalities: comparative assessment of economic damage and emission

reduction under COVID-19 lockdown. *Air Qual Atmos Health* 2020;**13**:683–94. https://doi.org/10.1007/s11869-020-00845-3.
4. Gautam S. The influence of COVID-19 on air quality in India: a boon or inutile. *Bull Environ Contam Toxicol* 2020;**104**:724–6. https://doi.org/10.1007/s00128-020-02877-y.
5. Bherwani H, Gautam S, Gupta A. Qualitative and quantitative analyses of impact of COVID-19 on sustainable development goals (SDGs) in Indian subcontinent with a focus on air quality. *Int J Environ Sci Technol* 2021;**18**:1019–28. https://doi.org/10.1007/s13762-020-03122-z.
6. Gautam S. COVID-19: air pollution remains low as people stay at home. *Air Qual Atmos Health* 2020;**13**:853–7. https://doi.org/10.1007/s1186 9-020-00842-6.
7. Hamid MZSA, Karri RR. Overview of preventive measures and good governance policies to mitigate the COVID-19 outbreak curve in Brunei. In: *COVID-19: systemic risk and resilience*. Cham: Springer; 2021. p. 115–40.
8. Nair M, Bherwani H, Kumar S, Gulia S, Goyal S, Kumar R. Assessment of contribution of agricultural residue burning on air quality of Delhi using remote sensing and modelling tools. *Atmos Environ* 2020;**230**:117504. https://doi.org/10.1016/j.atmosenv.2020.117504.
9. Khetrapal S, Bhatia R. Impact of COVID-19 pandemic on health system & Sustainable Development Goal 3. *Indian J Med Res* 2020;**151**:395–9. https://doi.org/10.4103/ijmr.IJMR_1920_20.
10. Mukherjee A, Babu SS, Ghosh S. Thinking about water and air to attain Sustainable Development Goals during times of COVID-19 pandemic. *J Earth Syst Sci* 2020;**129**:180. https://doi.org/10.1007/s12040-020-01475-0.
11. Gupta A, Bherwani H, Gautam S, Anjum S, Musugu K, Kumar N, et al. Air pollution aggravating COVID-19 lethality? Exploration in Asian cities using statistical models. *Environ Dev Sustain* 2021;**23**:6408–17. https://doi.org/10.1007/s10668-020-00878-9.
12. Wathore R, Gupta A, Bherwani, Labhasetwar N. Understanding air and water borne transmission and survival of coronavirus: insights and way forward for SARS-CoV-2. *Sci Total Environ* 2020;**749**:141486. https://doi.org/10.1016/j.scitotenv.2020.141486.
13. Mousazadeh M, Naghdali Z, Rahimian N, Hashemi M, Paital B, Al-Qodah Z, et al. Management of environmental health to prevent an outbreak of COVID-19: a review. In: *Environmental and health management of novel coronavirus disease (COVID-19)*; 2021. p. 235–67.
14. Kumar H, Azad A, Gupta A, Sharma J, Bherwani H, Labhsetwar NK, et al. COVID-19 creating another problem? Sustainable solution for PPE disposal through LCA approach. *Environ Dev Sustain* 2021;**23**:9418–32. https://doi.org/10.1007/s10668-020-01033-0.
15. Filho WL, Azul AM, Wall T, Vasconcelos CRP, Salvia AL, et al. COVID-19: the impact of a global crisis on sustainable development research. *Sustain Sci* 2021;**16**:85–99. https://doi.org/10.1007/s11625-020-00866-y.
16. Frederick S. *Impact of COVID-19 on the sustainable development goals: pursuing the sustainable development goals (SDGs) in a world reshaped by COVID-19*. UNDP; 2020.
17. Gomišček B, Hauck H, Stopper S, Preining O. Spatial and temporal variations of PM1, PM2. 5, PM10 and particle number concentration during the AUPHEP—project. *Atmos Environ* 2004;**38**(24):3917–34. https://doi.org/10.1016/j.atmosenv.2004.03.056.
18. Al-Saadi J, Szykman J, Pierce RB, Kittaka C, Neil D, Chu DA, et al. Improving national air quality forecasts with satellite aerosol observations. *Bull Am Meteorol Soc* 2005;**86**(9):1249–62. https://doi.org/10.1175/BAMS-86-9-1249.
19. Gupta P, Christopher SA, Wang J, Gehrig R, Lee Y, Kumar N. Satellite remote sensing of particulate matter and air quality assessment over global cities. *Atmos Environ* 2006;**40**(30):5880–92. https://doi.org/10.1016/j.atmosenv.2006.03.016.

20. Clarke AD, Collins WG, Rasch PJ, Kapustin VN, Moore K, Howell S, et al. Dust and pollution transport on global scales: aerosol measurements and model predictions. *J Geophys Res-Atmos* 2001;**106**(D23):32555–69. https://doi.org/10.1029/2000JD900842.
21. Holben BN, Tanre D, Smirnov A, Eck TF, Slutsker I, Abuhassan N, et al. An emerging ground-based aerosol climatology: aerosol optical depth from AERONET. *J Geophys Res-Atmos* 2001;**106**(D11):12067–97. https://doi.org/10.1029/2001JD900014.
22. Bherwani H, Kumar S, Musugu K, Nair M, Gautam S, Gupta A, et al. Assessment and valuation of health impacts of fine particulate matter during COVID-19 lockdown: a comprehensive study of tropical and sub tropical countries. *Environ Sci Pollut Res* 2021;**28**(32):44522–37. https://doi.org/10.1007/s11356-021-13813-w.
23. Bilal M, Nichol JE, Spak SN. A new approach for estimation of fine particulate concentrations using satellite aerosol optical depth and binning of meteorological variables. *Aerosol Air Qual Res* 2016;**17**(2):356–67. https://doi.org/10.4209/aaqr.2016.03.0097.
24. Bherwani H, Anjum S, Kumar S, Gautam S, Gupta A, Kumbhare H, et al. Understanding COVID-19 transmission through Bayesian probabilistic modeling and GIS-based Voronoi approach: a policy perspective. *Environ Dev Sustain* 2020;**23**:5846–64. https://doi.org/10.1007/s10668-020-00849-0.
25. *Annual change in carbon dioxide (CO_2) emissions in India.* https://www.statista.com/statistics/1119152/annual-carbon-dioxide-change-in-india/. [Accessed 13 July 2021].
26. *Estimated total population in India.* https://www.statista.com/statistics/263766/total-population-of-india/. [Accessed 13 July 2021].
27. *Value of per capita income across India.* https://www.statista.com/statistics/935754/india-per-capita-income-value/. [Accessed 13 July 2021].
28. *Health in India.* India: National Sample Survey Office, Ministry of Statistics and Programme Implementation, Government of India; 2014.
29. Madheswaran S. Measuring the value of statistical life: estimating compensating wage differentials among workers in India. *Soc Indic Res* 2007;**84**(1):83–96. https://doi.org/10.1007/sll205-006-9076-0.
30. India State-level Disease Burden Initiative Air Pollution Collaborators. *Lancet planet health*; 2021. e25 – 38:5.
31. Bherwani H, Gupta A, Nair M, Sonwane H. *Framework for environmental damages cost assessment with examples. Special report on monetising damages.* Nagpur: CSIR-National Environmental Engineering Research Institute [NEERI]; 2019.
32. *Purchasing power parity values for India.* https://data.oecd.org/conversion/purchasing-power-parities-ppp.htm. [Accessed 13 July 2021].
33. Chen H, Guo J, Wang C, Luo F, Yu X, Zhang W, et al. Clinical characteristics and intrauterine vertical transmission potential of COVID-19 infection in nine pregnant women: a retrospective review of medical records. *Lancet* 2020;**395**(10226):809–15. https://doi.org/10.1016/S0140-6736(20)30360-3.
34. Bherwani H, Gupta A, Anjum S, Anshul A, Kumar R. Exploring dependence of COVID-19 on environmental factors and spread prediction in India. *NPJ Clim Atmos Sci* 2020;**3**(38). https://doi.org/10.1038/s41612-020-00142-x.
35. Kaur S, Bherwani H, Gulia S, Vijay R, Kumar R. Understanding COVID-19 transmission, health impacts, and mitigation: timely social distancing is the key. *Environ Dev Sustain* 2020. https://doi.org/10.1007/s1066 8-020-00884-x.
36. Bherwani H, Singh A, Kumar R. Assessment methods of urban microclimate and its parameters: a critical review to take the research from lab to land. *Urban Clim* 2020;**34**(2):100690. https://doi.org/10.1016/j.uclim.2020.10069 0.

CHAPTER EIGHT

Air quality during COVID-19 lockdown and its implication toward sustainable development goals

Chimurkar Navinya[a], Suman Yadav[b], Rama Rao Karri[c], and Harish C. Phuleria[a,b]

[a]Interdisciplinary Program in Climate Studies, Indian Institute of Technology Bombay, Mumbai, Maharashtra, India
[b]Environmental Science and Engineering Department, Indian Institute of Technology Bombay, Mumbai, Maharashtra, India
[c]Petroleum and Chemical Engineering, Faculty of Engineering, Universiti Teknologi Brunei, Bandar Seri Begawan, Brunei Darussalam

1. Introduction

Governments of the various nations across the globe had to unwillingly shut down their nonessential economic activities by declaring lockdown as an initial preventive measure to tackle the novel coronavirus (COVID-19). It has impacted millions of lives, but this number could have been worst without the lockdown. Highly populated countries such as China and India have implemented the longest lockdown spanning more than six weeks.[1,2] Almost every country has implemented lockdown as their first response to the COVID-19 pandemic in order to lower the spread rate and develop the necessary health infrastructure to deal with the cases. Further, additional measures such as social distancing, lockdowns, stay-at-home orders, and mandatory use of masks in public places have been implemented by all the countries to reduce the spread of the disease.[3] Air-conditioned restaurants, malls, theaters, and institutions remained closed as these places are considered to be potential spreaders. Public gatherings and religious events are banned over most of the regions, besides weddings and funerals are allowed with a very limited number of attendees.[4] Nonessential small industries; information technology firms; and the air, rail, and road transport sector also stopped their operations during the lockdown. As a result, these measures led to a decline in air pollutants and greenhouse gas (GHG)

COVID-19 and the Sustainable Development Goals
https://doi.org/10.1016/B978-0-323-91307-2.00008-0

emissions and thus air quality improvement around the world.[5,6] However, this has also shown our vulnerability toward the global crisis forcing the governments as well as the scientific community to rethink our pace and choices toward sustainable life.[7]

Several studies across the world have quantified the significant decline in the concentrations of different air pollutants during the lockdown.[1,6,8–15] Primary air pollutants, such as $PM_{2.5}$, PM_{10}, NO_2, and CO which are largely associated with vehicular emissions in urban areas, have observed the highest decline (>50%) across all regions, with a higher decline in more polluted cities. One of the key regions in the air pollution study, the Indo-Gangetic Plain (IGP), reported air quality below the permissible limits after many decades.[1]

Aerosols remained the highly discussed topic during the pandemic for their involvement in the spread of the virus, as evidences showed, not just the physical contact but droplets from coughing/sneezing and inhalation of small airborne particles can transmit from an infected to an uninfected person.[16] A two-meter distance protocol only works when the mask is on; otherwise, even 6 m may not be enough to avoid the spread of the virus.[17] Although engineering controls can prevent the spread,[18] but studies have strongly suggested about airborne transmission route of COVID-19 as well.[19] On the other hand, long-term exposure to bad air quality may increase the vulnerability of people with preexisting and compromised lung conditions.[20,21] It has been reported that regions with higher $PM_{2.5}$ could potentially result in threefold higher mortality.[22] Similar risk associations have also reported during the SARS pandemic in 2003.[23]

A few epidemiological studies have examined the environmental conditions which could affect the spread of the virus, primarily examining the association of temperature and relative humidity with daily new cases.[24–26] However, the role of meteorology on air quality vis-à-vis the effect of lockdown has been quantified by a handful of studies only.[1,27]

All of these choices during the lockdown affect our commitment toward 17 SDGs (169 SDGs-related targets) decided by the United Nations (UN) under the *Transforming Our World: The 2030* agenda in 2015.[28] Air pollution and GHGs are considered as one of the significant indicators to monitor the progress of four SDGs, which include SDG3 (Good health and well-being), SDG7 (Clean energy), SDG11 (Sustainable cities), and SDG13 (Climate actions).[28,29] Two of the SDG targets explicitly highlight the importance of air pollution: SDG 3.9 targets a substantial reduction in the number of deaths and illnesses from hazardous chemicals and air, water, and soil pollution and contamination by 2030, while SDG 11.6 targets reduction in the adverse per capita environmental impact of cities, including by paying special attention to air quality, municipal and other waste management.[28,30] The complexity to understand the consequences of SDG-related decisions is somewhat seen during the pandemic and exploitation of the available data can help in future policy-making.

Thus, to understand future measures to improve air quality and mitigate the adverse health and climate effects, it is necessary to exploit the current scenario. This chapter explores the impact of the national lockdowns on urban air quality across the globe and discusses future policy implications toward improving air quality from the learnings of this natural intervention.

2. Lockdown measures adopted around the world

Affecting more than 200 countries as of Sep 07, 2020,[31] the pandemic has forced every country to restrict their internal as well as external movements. Activities were only allowed locally based on the absolute essentials so that this restriction (also known as lockdown, stay-at-home, curfews, or shutdown) could reasonably reduce the spread of the virus at the initial stage and provide the governments a time window to establish and expand required health facilities. Countries such as Italy, India, China, and Mexico have declared some of the largest lockdowns in history (see Table 1). India

Table 1 Lockdown details of 20 worst-affected countries.

Sr. No.	Country	Start	End	Level	Reference
1	USA	19-Mar	11 May	Regional	32,33
2	India	25-Mar	07-Jun	National	34
3	Brazil	24-Mar	10-May	State	35
4	Russia	28-Mar	30-Apr	National	36
5	Peru	16-Mar	30-Jun	National	37
6	Colombia	6-Apr	15-Jul	National	38
7	South Africa	26-Mar	30-Apr	National	39,40
8	Mexico	23-Mar	01-Jun	National	41
9	Spain	14-Mar	09-May	National	42
10	Argentina	20-Mar	28-Jun	National	43
11	Chile	29-Jul	17-Aug	City	44
12	Iran	14-Mar	20-Apr	National	45,46
13	UK	23-Mar	30-Jun	National	27
14	Bangladesh	26-Mar	30-May	National	47

Continued

Table 1 Lockdown details of 20 worst-affected countries—cont'd

Sr. No.	Country	Start	End	Level	Reference
15	France	17-Mar	11-May	National	48
16	Saudi Arabia	23-Mar	20-Jun	National	49
17	Pakistan	24-Mar	09-May	National	50
18	Turkey	23-Apr	27-Apr	Cities	51
19	Italy	09-Mar	18-May	National	52
20	Iraq	22-Mar	11-Apr	National	53,54

USA: ~28 states declared regional lockdown; **India:** Some states have extended the lockdown; **Brazil:** São Paulo only declared lockdown; **Russia:** lockdown extended for Moscow till 12–05; **Chile:** 3 Metro areas, Nighttime curfew 22:00–06:00; **Bangladesh:** Nighttime curfew 20:00–06:00; **Turkey:** Major 31 Metro areas gone through lockdown; **Italy:** lockdown Started from Northern Italy.

recorded the biggest lockdown ever by restricting more than 1.3 billion population voluntarily in a house for "*Janta Curfew*" on March 22, 2020,[55] followed by six-week long strict lockdown across the country.[1] However, the length of the lockdown does not represent the effective prevention of the virus spread. Some countries such as South Korea and Sweden haven't introduced any lockdown during the pandemic,[56] while countries such as Brazil[35] implemented the lockdown in major cities and high-risk areas only. Chile[57] and Bangladesh[58] have also tried nighttime curfew to limit nocturnal movements (see Table 1). These lockdowns are implemented phase-wise to have a timely evaluation of the situation while considering the revival of economic activities.

Oxford COVID-19 Government Response Tracker (OxCGRT) is continuously monitoring the government policies of 180 different countries and classifying the publicly available information into 17 indicators which are further summed into four groups indicating health, economic, policy information, and overall effect.[59] Fig. 1, compiled from the OxCGRT, shows the stringency index of each country for the government policies, which is derived from the orders such as closure or restriction of school, workspace, public event, social gathering, public transport, internal movement, and international travel.[59] The majority of the strict protocols by various countries have been enforced between 15th March and 15th April and followed up to June 2020. Thus the period of April–May remained the most restricted months due to overlapping lockdown orders from various governments (Fig. 2). China was the first country to declare nationwide lockdown and successfully prevented the spread of the virus in Wuhan using early lockdown and exhaustive testing.[60] India expected to be the worst affected country, with the longest lockdown enforced by some of the state governments even after the reopening order from the central government.[61]

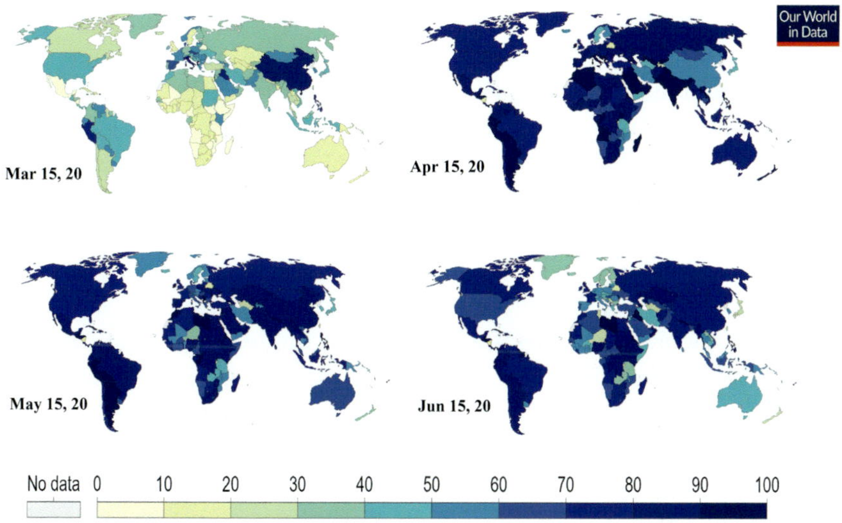

Fig. 1 COVID-19: Government response stringency index. As of Sep 07, 2020.[59] (This is a composite measure based on nine response indicators, including school closure, workplace closure, and travel bans, rescaled to a value from 0 to 100 (100 = strictest). The index simply records the number and strictness of government policies and should not be interpreted as "scoring" the appropriateness or effectiveness of a country's response. OurWorldInData.org/coronavirus CC BY.)

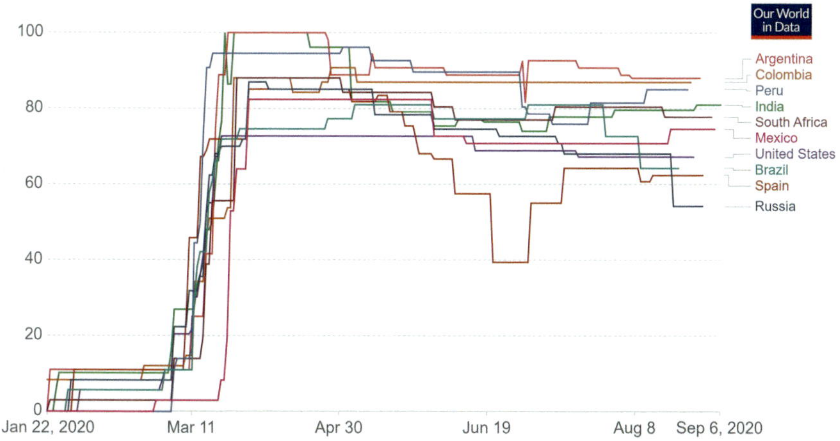

Fig. 2 Change in government response stringency index with the time for the top ten worst-affected countries. As of Sep 07, 2020.[59] (This is a composite measure based on nine response indicators, including school closure, workplace closure, and travel bans, rescaled to a value from 0 to 100 (100 = strictest). The index simply records the number and strictness of government policies and should not be interpreted as "scoring" the appropriateness or effectiveness of a country's response. OurWorldInData.org/coronavirus CC BY.)

Despite strict lockdown orders in many developing countries, the daily surge of new COVID-19 cases showed unconstrained growth.[62] Some studies have examined the effectiveness of these lockdowns by analyzing variability in the daily new cases, using various tools such as Growth Factor,[63] Daily Incidence Proportion, Daily Cumulative Index,[64] and Effective Reproduction Number.[65] These studies show that the lockdown in countries like Bangladesh, Brazil, Chile, Pakistan, and South Africa has failed to control the situation, where unbridled daily new cases have been observed during lockdown.[62] The effectiveness of the lockdown in the aforementioned developing countries also depends on the behavior of the citizens to understand the importance of social distancing and successful confinement of the key cities to prevent rural areas from getting infected. The economy of the developing countries heavily relies on the metropolitan cities, which in some way impacted the effectiveness of the lockdown, and virus infection spread to rural regions as most of the daily wage workers migrated to their hometowns due to unemployment. The prolonged lockdown with rising daily new cases can have socioeconomic consequences, while this unprecedented disruption in the major economic activities can ignite many issues such as unemployment.[66]

3. Air quality during COVID-19 lockdown

The economic growth of many developed and rapidly developing nations has aggravated air pollution levels, specifically in urban areas. Worsening air quality in many parts of the world is a severe threat to the human respiratory system considering the long-term exposure to the criteria air pollutants ($PM_{2.5}$, PM_{10}, NO_2, SO_2, CO, and O_3).[67–70] More than ~5 million deaths are annually attributed to air pollution.[71] These emissions are mainly due to vehicular, agriculture, residential, and industrial (including power) sectors.[72–76] These sources have been operating uninterrupted for many decades which has gradually degraded the air quality, but worldwide the lockdown due to the COVID-19 virus outbreak can be considered as the biggest hiatus for human activities and thus the emissions from these sources during the modern era.[77]

The unrestrained spread of COVID-19 with no vaccine available as of Sep 2020 forced everyone to stay indoors and the economic activities went down. As a consequence, the imposed lockdowns have provided a unique opportunity to examine the earth's atmosphere without the emissions from major sectors.[77,78] Thus this natural intervention across the globe presented a unique opportunity for the scientific community leading to numerous studies recording a marked decline in air pollution levels during the COVID-19 lockdown.

A majority of these studies are from India[1,8,9,12,79] and China.[80–84] The air quality impact of the lockdown has also been investigated in the USA,[85] Brazil,[10] Malaysia,[13,86] Spain,[11] Pakistan,[87] Kazakhstan,[88] Iran,[89] Tehran,[90] Ecuador,[91] Istanbul,[92] and UK[27,93] as well. The global decline in pollutants considering a common lockdown period is also analyzed by a few studies[6,94] and found a similar range of pollutant changes as observed by the regional or city/country-specific studies.

3.1 Change in air quality during lockdown

3.1.1 Asia

In the past few decades, (Indo-Gangetic Plain) IGP (India),[95] Beijing (China),[96] and Lahore (Pakistan)[97] are in discussion for their particulate pollution-related issues, owing to the aforementioned sectors along with some natural aerosols such as dust from long-range transport.

In Feb 2020, NASA had released the initial evidence showing the tropospheric NO_2 density $< 100\,\mu mol\,m^{-2}$ during the lockdown (Feb 10–25, 2020) in Wuhan, China; these values were fivefold lesser than the previous year.[98] Further, NASA released NO_2 and (Aerosol Optical Depth) AOD decline over the Indian region, clearly showing AOD reduction up to ~0.5, especially over the IGP region.[98] Researchers show a significant reduction in the major criteria air pollutants which is due to the lockdown effect leading to the closure of nonessential sectors and decreased vehicular mobility on the road.[1,9,79]Kumar et al.[99] reported considerable reductions in $PM_{2.5}$ in 5 major cities of India compared to the same period of the previous 5 years, where it reduced to 41%–53% (Delhi), 10%–39% (Mumbai), 19%–43% (Chennai), 26%–54% (Hyderabad), and 24%–36% (Kolkata). Navinya et al.[1] also reported a significant decrease in postlockdown $PM_{2.5}$ and PM_{10} in 17 cities across India. Mahato et al.[79] reported a decrease of more than 50% in $PM_{2.5}$ and PM_{10} concentrations over Delhi, India. Mitra et al.[100] reported $PM_{2.5}$ (39%), PM_{10} (60%), CO (30%), and NO_2 (53%) reduction during lockdown compared to 2019 in Kolkata, India. Many of the studies have reported different estimations of air pollutant reduction in the same cities due to the variation in selection of the number of days, stations, lockdown periods, and control periods. Saadat et al.[101] reported a 25% decrease in emissions at the start of the lockdown based on Chinese emission data, as coal usage decreased by 40% due to the slowdown of factories and power plants. They further estimated 11% improvement in air quality during lockdown compared to 2019 data from 330 cities of China. Major cities in China—Shanghai, Beijing, Wuhan, and Guangzhou—experienced a reduction in $PM_{2.5}$ by 6.4, 9.2, 30.8, and 5.4 $\mu g\,m^{-3}$, respectively, during the lockdown.[102] Kanniah et al.[103] reported a decrease in tropospheric NO_2 column density (27%–34%) in most South-East Asian countries. $PM_{2.5}$ and PM_{10} showed 23%–32% and 26%–31% decrease in urban, while 20%–42% and 28%–39% in industrial areas, respectively, compared with 2018 and 2019. A similar decrease of 40%–70% has also been observed in the AOD over urban areas of Malaysia during Mar–Apr 2020.

Overall, Ahmedabad (68%), Beijing (79%), Bangalore (87%), Nagpur (91%), and Zhejiang (69%) show the largest reduction for $PM_{2.5}$, PM_{10}, NO_2, SO_2, and CO, respectively, while Baghdad (225%), Delhi (37%), and Singrauli (35%) show increase in the ozone levels during the lockdown in Asia (see Table 2).

3.1.2 North and South America

NASA confirmed a 30% decline in atmospheric NO_2 over Northeastern USA during the lockdown.[117] A group of studies (Table 2) suggests that San Jose (45.0%), Las Vegas (41%), and Los Angeles (41%) showed the larger decline in $PM_{2.5}$, while sharp PM_{10} decline was observed over Los Angeles (57%), Las Vegas (54%), and Fresno (54%). Similar to Asia, the American continents also show a huge reduction in the atmospheric NO_2, with states such as Alabama (89%), California (89%), and Louisiana (83%) reported relatively very high reduction.[85] Similarly, a prompt reduction was observed in SO_2 over Quito (69%), Louisiana (61%), and Las Vegas (49%). The increase in O_3 is relatively lesser than in Asia, with Salt Lake (25%), Providence (20%), and Toronto (17%) showing a slight increase in surface ozone during the lockdown (see Table 2).

3.1.3 Europe

The Sentinel-5P, a European satellite mapped NO_2 over France and nearby, confirmed a significant reduction over Milan, Paris, and Madrid.[118] Similarly, NO_2 reduced by 56% over Scotland, with Glasgow showing ~39% decline (see Table 3). Reduction in the $PM_{2.5}$ is also significant over Vienna (57%), Paris (53%), and Scotland (48%). The highest reduction has been observed over Vienna (−61%) for PM_{10}. Surprisingly, SO_2 over the UK shows a significant and consistent increase by 82%–206%,[27] whereas surface

Table 2 Air quality change over major cities.

Continent	Country	City	Base time	$PM_{2.5}$	PM_{10}	NO_2	SO_2	CO	O_3
Africa	Ethiopia	Addis Ababa[104]	Pre-L	−5.4					
	Nigeria	Kaduna[105,a]	2004–19			−3.0	10.5		1.9
	Nigeria	Lagos[105,a]	2004–19			−1.4	54.0		2.2
	South Africa	Dublin[94]	2019	−45.2	−44.3				
Asia	Bangladesh	Dhaka[106,a]	Pre-L			−69.0	−66.6	−5.7	2.6
	China	Beijing[107]	2019	−6.5	−79.1	−25.6	−42.6	−11.0	
	China	Chengdu[94]	2019					−29.1	
	China	Nanjing[94]	2019	−31.3	−31.8		−46.1	23.8	
	China	Shanghai[107]	2019	−26.6	−29.1	−43.8	−31.2	−18.2	
	China	Suzhou[108]	2017–19	−33.5	−19.0	−36.5	−67.1	−5.8	−0.1
	China	Wuhan[80]	2017–19	−44.0	−47.9	−54.	−29.9	−16.2	27.1
	India	Ahmedabad[1]	2019	−67.7		−67.5	−33.4	−36.5	
	India	Bangalore[1,94]	2019	−45.4	−48.9	−86.7	−80.5	−24.2	−10.6
	India	Chennai[1]	2019	−30.2		−36.3	−69.2	−23.7	
	India	Delhi[1,109]	2019/Pre-L	−58.1	−70.5	−79.2	−53.2	−30.2	37.4
	India	Hyderabad[1]	2019	−19.4	−31.9	−35.0	26.0	−26.1	
	India	Jaipur[1,110]	2019/Pre-L	−50.5	−48.1	−68.4	−8.9	−55.0	−25.0
	India	Kolkata[1,111]	2019	−23.5	−24.2	−55.9	45.6	14.8	6.3
	India	Lucknow[1]	2019	−51.5		8.1	167.4	−30.1	
	India	Mumbai[1,109]	2019/Pre-L	−0.9	−27.3	−57.9	46.9	−45.6	20.7
	India	Nagpur[1]	2019	−52.6	−52.6	−49.9	−90.6	−63.0	
	Iran	Tehran[89,a]	2019	10.5	−11.3	−13.0	−12.5	−13.0	3.0
	Iraq	Baghdad[112]	Pre-L	0.0	55.0	−8.0			225.0
	Israel	Jerusalem[94]	2019					465.2	

Continued

Table 2 Air quality change over major cities—cont'd

Continent	Country	City	Base time	$PM_{2.5}$	PM_{10}	NO_2	SO_2	CO	O_3
	Japan	Tokyo[94]	2019						31.9
	Kazakhstan	Almaty[88]	2018–19/Pre-L	−21.0		−35.0	7.0	−49.0	15.0
	Malaysia	Kuala Lumpur[113]	Pre-L	−32.1		−65.6	38.5	−32.1	
	Malaysia	Seremban[113]	Pre-L	−16.8		−61.1	25.2	−21.0	
	Mongolia	Ulaanbaatar[94]	2019	−25.6	−43.4				
	Saudi Arabia	Al Ahsa[49]	Pre-L		−57.0	−34.0	128.0	0.8	27.0
	Saudi Arabia	Dammam[49]	Pre-L		7.8	−12.0	35.0	2.2	−82.0
	Saudi Arabia	Qatif[49]	Pre-L		−70.0	−26.0	−25.0	−42.0	35.0
	Singapore	Singapore[114]	2016–19	−29.0	−23.0	−54.0	−52.0	−6.0	18.0
	South Korea	Seoul[94]	2019					−13.4	
	Taiwan	Taipei[94]	2019					24.3	
	Thailand	Bangkok[94]	2019						−28.5
	UAE	Abu Dhabi[94]	2019	−32.4					
Asia/Europe	Turkey	Istanbul[92]	Pre-L	−33.0	−37.5	−36.5	−51.5	−49.0	
Australia	Australia	Sydney[94]	2019	−35.1					
Europe	Austria	Vienna[94]	2019	−57.1	−60.7	−18.1			
	France	Paris[94]	2019	−53.2	−52.7	−33.1			
	Netherlands	Amsterdam[94]	2019	−47.5				−35.1	
	Norway	Oslo[94]	2019			−28.3			
	Poland	Warsaw[94]	2019		−45.9			28.1	
Europe	Scotland[115]	–	2019	−48.4		−55.8			
	Spain	Madrid[94]	2019			−33.3			26.9
	Switzerland	Bern[94]	2019			−27.0			
	UK	Birmingham[27]	2013–19	−10.0		−34.0	117.0		34.0
	UK	Glasgow[27]	2013–19	−12.0		−39.0	152.0		50.3

	UK	London[27]	2013–19	−9.0		−35.0	82.0		35.0
	UK	Manchester[27]	2013–19	−10.0		−32.0	114.0		32.0
N. America	Canada	Toronto[94]	2019						17.8
	USA	Alabama[107]	2019	−30.7			−88.7		
	USA	Boston[85]	2017–19	−23.0		−36.0		−22.0	8.0
	USA	California[107]	2019	−27.7	−19.9	−44.2	−88.7		
	USA	Florida[107]	2019	−33.7	−32.3	−35.4	−73.3	−4.7	
	USA	Fresno[85]	2017–19	−25.0	−54.0	−42.0		−31.0	−9.0
	USA	Las Vegas[85]	2017–19	−41.0	−55.0	−49.0		−28.0	17.0
	USA	Lost Angeles[85]	2017–19	−41.0	−57.0	−34.0		−34.0	−17.0
	USA	Louisiana[107]	2019	−10.8	61.6	−61.2	−82.3	−33.3	
	USA	New York[85]	2017–19	−29.0		−40.0		−37.0	8.0
	USA	Providence[85]	2017–19	−31.0		−26.0			20.0
	USA	Salt Lake City[85]	2017–19	−5.0		−43.0			25.0
S. America	Brazil	São Paulo[116]	2015–19				−54.3	−64.8	30.0
	Colombia[94]	Bogota[94]	2019				−64.8	15.8	
	Ecuador	Quito[91]	Pre-L	−29.0		−68.0	−48.0	−38.0	
	Peru[94]	Lima[94]	2019		−25.7	−4.6	−75.2	−27.3	−42.5

[a]Satellite data used for the study, Pre-L stands for Prelockdown period of respective study region.

Table 3 Association of new COVID-19 cases with meteorological conditions.

Location	Date	Result	Reference
Jakarta, Indonesia	Jan 1–Mar 29, 2020	Temperature positively correlated with the daily new cases. ($r=0.392$)	119
122 cities, China	Jan 23–Feb 29, 2020	A unit rise in temperature (lag0–7) led to a 3.432% rise in daily new cases when the temperature is below 3°C.	120
166 countries (excluding China)	As of Mar 27, 2020	A unit increase in temperature and RH can reduce 5.94% and 1.23% daily new cases, respectively, at lag0–3.	121
Delhi, India	Mar 1–Jun 30, 2020	Strong Significant Correlation between Temperature and confirmed cases, 80% of the confirmed cases occurred when the temperature was higher than 30 deg. C.	122
Wuhan, China	Jan 20–Feb 29, 2020	A positive association with COVID-19 daily death counts was observed for the diurnal temperature range ($r=0.44$), but a negative association for relative humidity ($r=-0.32$).	123
World	Mar 25–Apr 18, 2020,	The temperature has −0.45, −0.42, and −0.50 correlation with total cases, active cases, and cases/per million, respectively.	124
China	Dec 1, 2019–Feb 11, 2020	A unit increase in temperature decreases the daily confirmed cases by 36%–57%, when RH ranges from 67% to 85.5%. A unit increase in RH decrease the daily confirmed cases by 11%–22% when temperature ranges from 5.04°C to 8.2°C	125
China	Jan 23–Mar 1, 2020	The doubling time correlated positively with the temperature and inversely with humidity ($R^2=0.18$)	126
New York, USA	Mar 1–Apr 12, 2020	The average temperature has a positive Kendall correlation ($r=0.29$) with total cases	127
World (Excluding, less 5 cases)	As of Mar 8, 2020	Cool and dry places will support the virus, while extremely hot, cold, and wet will suppress it	128
India	Mar 25–Apr 30, 2020	Regions with 28–34 deg. C. and RH 35%–80% have reported 91% of the total new cases	129

Table 3 Association of new COVID-19 cases with meteorological conditions—cont'd

Location	Date	Result	Reference
52 African States	Mar 30–Apr 29, 2020	COVID-19 growth correlated positively with the wind speed ($r=0.212$), while inversely with the temperature ($r=0.624$) and RH ($r=0.551$).	130
Lagos, Nigeria	Mar 9–May 12, 2020	Inverse correlation ($r=-0.356$) between new cases and temperature, suggesting higher temperature might have decreased the spread.	131

Wind speed, RH, pressure, and city are covariates for temperature–COVID-19 association[121]; RH is covariate for temperature–COVID-19 association; confounders controlled for, including, wind speed, median age, global health security index, human development index, and population density[132]; diurnal temperature range, RH, and absolute humidity are covariates for temperature–COVID-19 association, while air pollution is confounding variable[125]; RH is a covariate for temperature–COVID-19 association[126]; RH is covariate for temperature–COVID-19 association[130]; wind speed and RH are covariates for temperature–COVID-19 association, fixed effect of countries and days are confounder.

O_3 shows a consistent increase over Europe which is in agreement with the other regions. Further, CO showed a high reduction in London (48%).[94]

A present review suggests that changes in the SO_2 are much heterogeneous, while a consistent decline in PMs and NO_2 has been observed; similarly, O_3 showed an increase across the nations. As seen in Table 2, many cities from India, China, and the USA, such as Delhi, Bangalore, Beijing, Wuhan, Lost Angeles, Louisiana, and Las Vegas, have shown significant changes in concentration.

Venter et al.[6] have investigated 10,000+ air quality stations and TROPOMI onboard the Sentinel-5P satellite to quantify changes in $PM_{2.5}$, NO_2, and O_3 using weather benchmark model trained between 2017 and 2019 to ostracize meteorological impact on air pollution. As of 15th May 2020, NO_2 and $PM_{2.5}$ showed an average of 60% [48%–72%] and 31% [17%–45%] decline, respectively, while O_3 showed slight increase by 4% [−2% to 10%] over 34 countries. Except for Denmark and Australia, every country has reported a decline in NO_2 with Serbia and Croatia observed the highest decline (see Fig. 3). Similarly, except Switzerland and Australia, all nations have shown an appreciable reduction in $PM_{2.5}$. UAE (>40%) has recorded a maximum decline in O_3, while majority of the nations have shown a negligible or increasing effect on ozone.[6]

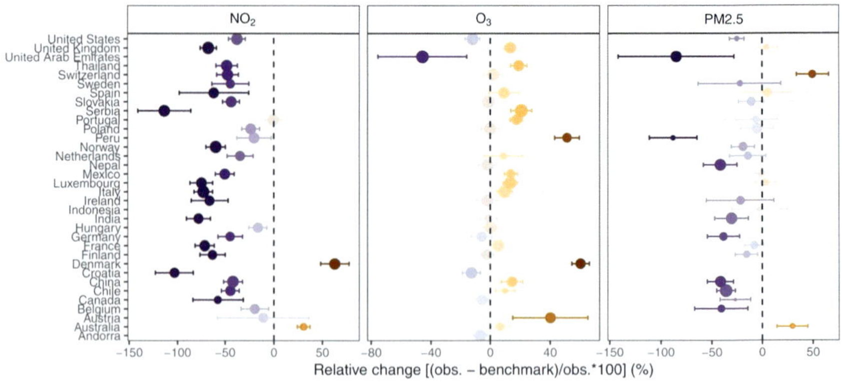

Fig. 3 Ground-level air pollution change during Jan–May 2020 with respect to the base year 2017–19.[6]

3.2 Emission sources during lockdown

Many previous emission studies have firmly agreed on the sectors primarily responsible for the unhealthy air quality, where transportation,[72,75] industries,[102] agricultural burning,[133] and residential biomass burning[73,134,135] head the list. The unprecedented reduction in air pollution during the lockdown periods owes to one of these sectors. A study conducted by Le Quere et al.[5] suggest that the power, industrial, surface transport, public, residential, and aviation activities changed by −7.4%, −19%, −36%, −21%, +2.8%, and −60%, which reduced daily CO_2 emission by 17% [11%–25%] during April 2020; however, they found that the contribution to the CO_2 reduction was mainly associated to the surface transport (43%), industry and power (43%), and aviation (10%) sectors.

In a Google mobility report (Fig. 4), it can be observed that the number of visitors in the workplaces, recreational zones, parks, public transits, and grocery stores dropped by 30% or more across many nations, while mobility increased in the residential areas by 10%, as April 2020 remained the most restricted month.[137] A policy brief over the Indian scenario by Phuleria and Navinya[77] suggests that NO_2 decline differs with the population of the city as a region with >5 million population showed ~70% decline, while <3 million showed only a 12% reduction, owing to the higher reduction in the mobility in larger cities. On the other hand, SO_2 which is primarily emitted from the power plants did not show a consistent drop during the lockdown. Activities in industries and power hubs showed some decrease, while SO_2 changes were not appreciable over the cities with no power plants

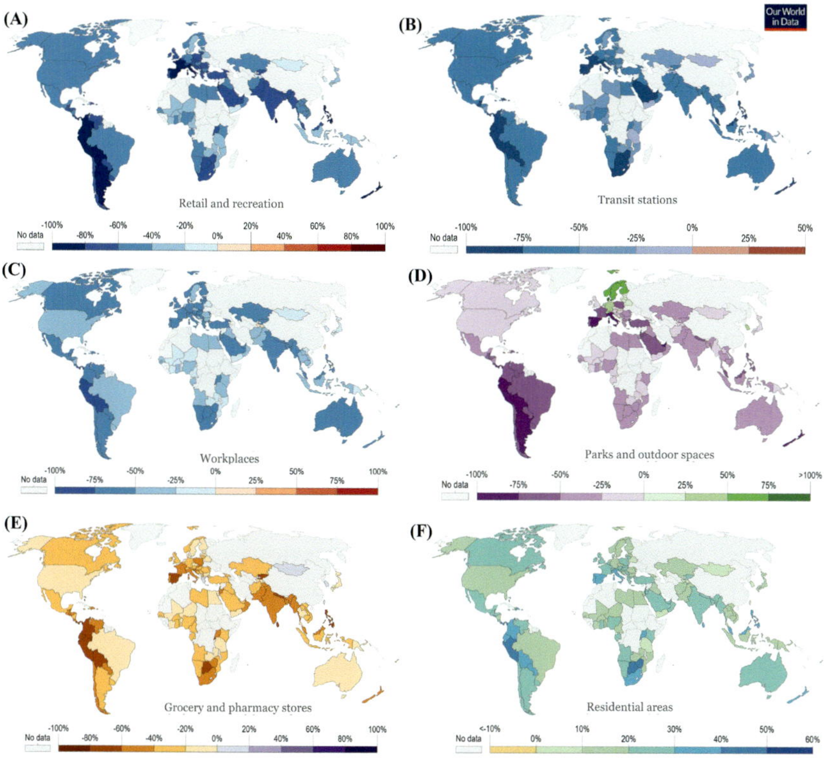

Fig. 4 Change in visitor numbers on Apr 15, 2020, relative to the baseline (Jan–Feb 6, 2020). (A) Retail and recreation, (B) Transit stations, (C) Workplaces, (D) Parks and outdoor spaces, (E) Grocery and pharmacy stores, (F) Residential areas.[136] (The index is smoothed to the moving 7-day average. Not recommended to compare levels across countries. (A) Includes restaurants, cafes, shopping centers, theme parks, museums, libraries, and movie theaters. (B) Includes public transport hubs such as subway, bus, and train stations. (D) Includes local parks, national parks, public beaches, marinas, dog parks, plazas, and public gardens. (E) Includes grocery markets, food warehouses, farmers' markets, specialty food shops, drug stores, and pharmacies. OurWorldInData.org/coronavirus CC BY.)

or industry nearby.[77] Some field burning events were observed over Central India, which suggests uninterrupted emissions from agricultural residue burning.[138] Central Electricity Authority of India (CEA) report showed the unchanged supply of electricity to the regions with respect to the requirement; however, the overall demand for the power fell down due to the shutdown of many public places during lockdown.[139] Venter et al.[6] also found the change in mobility is significantly associated with country-specific NO_2 but not with O_3 and $PM_{2.5}$. The majority of the reduction in air pollutant concentration during the lockdown has been observed between the peak traffic hours (7–10 am and 7–10 pm), which reflects the impact from the transport sector.[1] Several studies[1,5,6,10,77,140] unanimously suggest that reduced vehicular activities and power demand are the major contributors for such drastic improvement in the air quality.

3.3 Change in meteorology during lockdown and its impact on air pollution

Regional air pollution can also be influenced due to changes in meteorological parameters such as temperature, relative humidity, and wind speed.[1] However, the majority of the studies have reported the decline of major pollutants during the lockdown without considering the effect of meteorological differences.[15,80,81,84,85] Navinya et al.[1] examined the changes in temperature, relative humidity, and wind speed over 17 cities in India during the six-week long nationwide lockdown and found no significant difference between the lockdown and the previous year (2019) meteorology.[1] The magnitude of the change during the lockdown and the previous year period in temperature, wind speed, and relative humidity were ±3°C, $\pm 0.5\,\mathrm{m\,s^{-1}}$, and ±15%, respectively.[1] However, compared to the prelockdown period (Feb–Mar 2020), they observed the temperature and the wind speed to be increasing while relative humidity decreasing over India during the lockdown[1] indicating the seasonal shift from premonsoon to the summer/monsoon.

Fig. 5 shows the change in three major meteorological parameters over the globe for Apr 2020, the month when most countries had restricted their economic activities with the average for the same month during 2016–2019 given by the National Aeronautics and Space Administration's (NASA) Modern-Era Retrospective Analysis for Research and Applications, Version 2 (MERRA-2) data.[95,141–144] The changes in the meteorological parameters shown in Fig. 5 agree with Navinya et al.[1] for India. However, the changes in the meteorological conditions across the world seem heterogeneous—India, China, Eastern Europe, and Western Canada show a decrease in the temperature, while Northern Africa, Mexico, Western Australia, and central Russia show an increase. As temperature and relative humidity are inversely related, an opposite trend was observed for relative humidity, while the wind speed changed in a range of $\pm 1\,\mathrm{m\,s^{-1}}$ over lands, where India, China, Australia, and the USA experienced a decrease; meanwhile, Canada, Middle East, and Northern Europe observed gain (See Fig. 5).

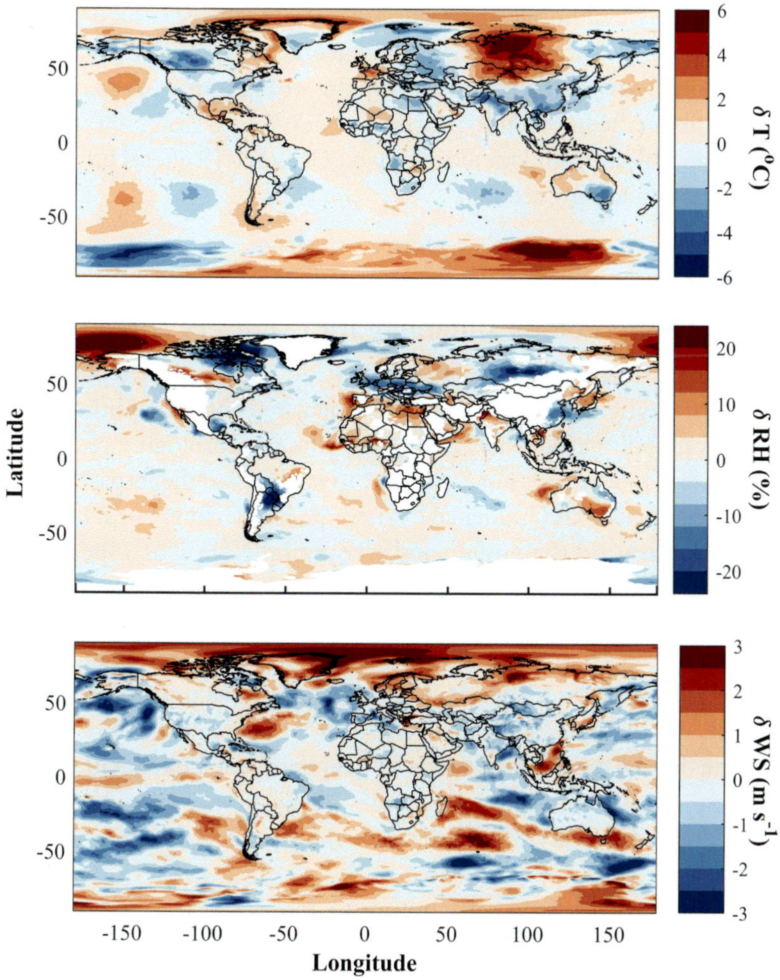

Fig. 5 Change in temperature, relative humidity (at 950hpa), and wind speed (top to bottom) during April 2020 compared to the average of the previous four years (2016–19) for April. *(Source: NASA's MERRA-2, Created by the authors using MATLAB 2017b.)*

As these meteorological changes were very small over the land, they do not seem to influence any large-scale air pollution declines across every region of the world. Hence it is very likely that these meteorological changes are not playing a vital role in air quality decline during lockdown.[145] It is accepted that the low temperature and wind speed and high relative humidity support stagnation of the air, which could lead to higher pollutant concentrations.[9] Although the regions like India observed such conditions during April 2020; however, the PMs concentration remained ∼50% lower than the previous years[1,8,9,12] indicating the strong impact of the lockdown over and above the meteorological differences. Additional discussion on the effect of air pollution and meteorology on COVID-19 effects has been provided in the following section.

4. Environmental cofactors during COVID-19

4.1 Meteorology suitability for COVID-19 spread

The earlier virus outbreaks such as SARS and influenza have been studied for understanding their growth under particular weather conditions and the seasonal variability in the daily new cases. The meteorological changes during the lockdown are not just important to understand the impact of slowed economic activities and influence over air quality decline, but it has a major contribution toward the growth and spread of the virus, as a specific combination of the temperature and humidity can affect the survival of the virus. In a retrospective study that has analyzed the postevent information of the SARS outbreak, a temperature between 16°C and 28°C is suggested to support the growth of the SARS virus.[146] Another study showed that the risk of influenza could significantly increase in low temperature and humidity, while the diurnal temperature range (DTR) positively linked with the infection rate.[147] A few other studies have also reported that the temperature,[148] DTR,[149] and humidity[150] can simulate the spread rate of the respiratory viruses.

In order to understand early outbreaks, experts across the globe started investigating the spread rate of COVID-19 under various temperatures and relative/absolute humidity conditions. The correlation coefficient with lag and generalized additive models (GAM) are used to examine the relation between daily surge and meteorological conditions. Contrasting findings are reported regarding the influence of the meteorological parameters on the spread of COVID-19 (see Table 3). The disagreement among these studies can be attributed to the time period considered, lockdown measures, and average temperature for that region (see Table 3). The tropical regions such as Indonesia and India reported a positive correlation between the temperature and COVID-19 spread,[119,122,151] while global studies showed that the cool and dry condition supports spread of the virus.[121,124,128] Mecenas et al.[25] reviewed the major published articles on the subject and concluded that the hot and wet conditions would suppress the virus spread; however, the quality of the results is graded low.[25] As the outbreak is still not under control, it could get worse as the Northern Hemisphere approaches toward winter.

4.2 Air pollution, a catalyst

As 90% of the world's population lives where air quality standards exceed WHO limits, air pollution remains the biggest culprit when it comes to the deaths related to respiratory system failure, with annually ~4.2 million deaths worldwide attributed to the exposure to outdoor air pollution.[71] During the SARS outbreak in 2003, the effect of aerosols was examined and it was found that regions with the worst air quality had high mortality.[23] Similarly, many studies have examined the COVID-19 mortality with long-term exposure to $PM_{2.5}$, PM_{10}, and NO_2, as it could develop an inflammatory condition of the lungs.[21,152–157]

A preexisting inflammatory lung condition due to exposure to poor air quality, with coexisting COVID-19 infection, could be fatal; thus, many studies have quantified the share of air pollution in the COVID-19 mortality during the pandemic across the world. Statistical tools such as generalized additive model[153], simple linear regression,[158] multiple linear regression,[154,156,159] and correlation coefficients[24,152,155,160,161] are used to understand share of air pollution in COVID-19 mortality.

Wu et al.[22] have reported that US counties were having average $PM_{2.5} < 8\,\mu g\,m^{-3}$ and $> 8\,\mu g\,m^{-3}$ have an average death rate of 1.6 and 4.7 (per 100,000), respectively, thus attributing a unit increase in long-term $PM_{2.5}$ exposure to 15% increase in COVID-19 death rate. Similarly, Italian region showed a strong association of $PM_{2.5}$ and COVID-19 deaths ($R^2 = 0.53$).[160] Strengthening the argument, Ogen (2020) reported 83% of COVID-19 deaths to be associated with the regions having NO_2 more than $100\,\mu mol\,m^{-3}$. However, a city-based study over Milan[152,155] and California[24] showed a negative association between air pollution and COVID-19 mortality, which can be plausibly explained by the nonconsideration of socioeconomic indicators.[24] A $10\,\mu g\,m^{-3}$ increase in $PM_{2.5}$, PM_{10}, and NO_2 attributes to 2.24%, 1.76%, and 6.94% increase, respectively, in daily new cases over 120 cities of China, considering wind speed, RH, temperature, and city as covariates.[153] Parallel to earlier studies, Li et al.[158] have found a significant positive correlation between the daily confirmed new cases and $PM_{2.5}$ ($R^2 = 0.23$), PM_{10} (0.158), and NO_2 (0.158) over Xiaogan and Wuhan. Spatial association between confirmed infections and air pollutants such as $PM_{2.5}$ ($R^2 = 0.34$), PM_{10} ($R^2 = 0.27$), and NO_2 ($R^2 = 0.25$) are also reported by Fattorini and Rengoli (2020). Many studies that have used spatial data homogeneously concluded that long-term exposure to poor air quality could be lethal if coexist with COVID-19 infection.[21,22,159–161] Evidences suggested that COVID-19 mortality and morbidity are strongly associated with $PM_{2.5}$ and NO_2, while to some extent PM_{10}, illustrating the impracticality of a larger particle to reach type II alveolar cells.[157] A decreased NO_2 and $PM_{2.5}$ helped to avoid 8911 [6950 10,866] and 3214 [2340 4087] deaths from cardiovascular diseases during the lockdown in China, which outnumbered COVID-19-related deaths (4633 as of May 4, 2020), that suggest air pollution control-related policies and laws could be more helpful toward avoiding future deaths.[162]

5. Preventive policies for COVID-19 spread and air pollution

Use of alcohol-based sanitizers, social distancing up to 6 ft, avoiding crowded places, use of masks, keeping hygiene, avoid touching the face, and lockdowns are some of the preventive measures advised by the WHO to reduce the spread of COVID-19.[163] Many countries have made it mandatory to follow the aforementioned advisory and penalized for noncompliance.[164,165] Rapid task forces have been established to track potential spread to avoid community transfer in many countries. Individual tracking applications (e.g., *Aarogya Setu* by India) have been developed to keep a record of infected persons and notifying users if a potential spreader is nearby.[166] However, multidimensional aspects of the pandemic need to be considered to effectively control the spread, contain morbidity and mortality, and revive economic activities.

5.1 Post-COVID-19 preventive measures

Reduced anthropogenic emissions during the lockdown have flourished the environment, but climate change is not totally arrested. Besides, the economic growth is severely hampered, and the livelihoods of millions of people (more so the poorest of the poor) across the globe are affected. However, this temporary decline in air emissions gave an opportunity to revisit national and global policies to improve air quality, avoid climate crises, and to reduce susceptibility toward such future global crises. The pandemic has also allowed us to examine our pace to adapt to any global change. For many decades scientists have been apprising the deaths associated with air pollution, but seriousness toward this issue, in low- and middle-income countries, in particular, remained low. About 1 million deaths (as of Sep 2020) during the ~8 months of a pandemic are four times lesser than the fatalities (~4.2 million annually) due to air pollution[71] and thus warranting concerted global efforts and attention to reduce air pollution.

Masks have become a new normal during the pandemic, although these are enforced by the regional authorities to minimize and slow down the spread, but now people are understanding its significance. However, wearing a mask would also help to reduce air pollution exposure to a certain degree. Thus the practice of using a mask in high-exposure environments, especially by those who are more susceptible, e.g., asthmatics, could be promoted even after the pandemic and will require a similar level of awareness campaign. However, these are short-term measures only and governments need to rethink about the post-COVID-19 policies to accommodate future global crises such as climate change and health effects due to air pollution. Activities such as agricultural burning that influences the regional air quality for considerable months every year need to be discouraged and alternate usage of the agricultural waste need to be identified. Similarly, Ujjwala Yojana, to provide clean cooking gas by the Government of India, needs to be accelerated to reduce the residential emissions due to solid biomass cookstoves.[167]

Emissions from the transport and industrial sector are likely to go up as government removes the lockdown restriction to revive the economy after controlling the COVID-19 situation. This sudden increase in the emissions due to a drastic shift in the demand as offices and institutes open would reasonably compensate for what has been achieved during the lockdown. The transport sector may feel higher pressure due to such change in demand, resulting in overloaded vehicles, longer routes to travel. Similarly, the nonessential industries which were closed or working with minimal employees will gradually shift toward a normal working load as COVID-19 comes under control. Open street waste burning for campfires, especially in rural regions, will also start as curfew eased. Many economic and social activities will trend toward normalcy; thus, emissions will also reach to prelockdown levels.[77]

Sustainable mitigation options such as work from home, public transport, promoting electric or hydrogen vehicles, and stringency toward solid waste burning are needed to be considered in the post-COVID-19 world.[77] Encouraging green industries, scrapping the old vehicle, eliminating harmful

Table 4 Examples of policy measures to reduce air pollution while reviving the economy.[167]

Sector	Measure to stimulate green production	Measure to stimulate green demand
Transport	Vehicle scrappage policy to enable the retirement of old vehicles	Cash for clunkers scheme to incentivize modernization of the vehicle fleet
Industry	Green certification and subsidized credit lines for green production	Green procurement scheme
Agriculture	Reduce/remove urea fertilizer subsidy (excessive use of urea fertilizer is a source of secondary $PM_{2.5}$) and divert subsidy toward organic farming	
Energy	Subsidized loans for renewable energy	Cap and trade program (to generate demand for clean energy)

chemicals, and more subsidies to renewable plants can be also pivotal to reduce air pollution while reviving the economy (see Table 4).[167]

The gain in the air quality will be lost soon as the restrictions will be eased, and the industrial production and commercial activities will boost to compensate for the economic loss during the lockdown.[168] Post-COVID-19 higher emissions and their interaction with the winter-time low temperatures could be critical,[169] as more evidences are supporting air-borne transmission and the link between air quality and mortality. In addition, cold and dry regions are considered to be favorable for the long-term survival of the virus,[25] with low immunity during winter.[170] These call for better preparedness toward the threat of COVID-19 under the favorable environmental conditions for the virus survival, spread, and potency.

6. Conclusions

COVID-19, since it is observed first in Wuhan, China, has claimed ~1 million lives as of Sep 27, 2020, despite global measures including strict lockdowns for several weeks. However, this number could have been worse without such preventive steps. Major developed and developing countries such as the USA, China, Italy, India, and Mexico chose to restrict their non-essential economic activities to avoid the unconstrained spread of the virus. The majority of the countries closed mobility within and out of the country by restricting transport and vehicular activities, IT hubs, shopping malls, parks, and even government offices. Thus Apr 2020 remained globally the idlest month due to overlapping lockdowns of many countries.

Numerous studies across the world have unanimously confirmed a decline in air pollution levels, especially for the $PM_{2.5}$, PM_{10}, and NO_2, while SO_2 showed a heterogeneous response mainly attributed to the thermal power generation sources nearby, whereas surface O_3 showed a slight but consistent increase. These changes are strongly associated with the reduced anthropogenic activities, especially road transport activities as evident by the empty roads during the lockdown everywhere. Highly polluted regions of Asia such as IGP showed significant improvement in the air quality, as well as, cleaner regions of Europe and the USA also reported similar changes. The decline in the pollution levels was observed despite the usual contribution from other anthropogenic sources such as power plants, agricultural burning, and residential biomass burning and other natural sources during the lockdown, highlighting the relatively large impact of transportation sources and commercial activities on urban air quality. These changes helped climate and environment-related SDGs to gain progress; however, the duration is very short, in particular for climate-related gains and air pollutant emissions quickly reached back to prelockdown levels once the lockdown was lifted or restrictions were eased. Meteorological changes during the lockdown seem low and heterogeneous to initiate such large and consistent air pollution decline. Though the lockdown provides a very short-term draconian solution toward improving air quality, it severely affected the economic growth and livelihoods of millions of people across the world; hence, learning from this natural experiment can be exploited to frame future sustainable policies to mitigate global crises such as human health.

Other factors such as meteorological suitability for virus spread and preexisting lung conditions likely due to prolonged exposure to poor air quality have influenced the regional mortality and morbidity of COVID-19. The role of meteorology indicates mixed effects, e.g., studies using global data find cool and dry places supporting virus spread, while studies over tropical regions show a positive correlation between temperature and COVID-19 spread rate. However, the general acceptance is that hot and humid conditions will suppress the spread. Similarly, regions with higher pollution indicate higher mortality, and it is likely that the preexisting lung conditions due to prolonged exposure to air pollution make us more susceptible to COVID-19 infection and death.

COVID-19 pandemic has shown our vulnerability toward the global crisis and questioned our pace toward achieving SDGs. Air quality and GHG reduction helped SDGs to gain some benefits but for a short duration; however, the experience gained during the lockdown could help to revise policies and our progress to meet SDG commitments. Moreover, air pollution acted as a catalyst during such pandemics and likely made high exposed populations more susceptible to corona virus infection and fatality. This reflects the importance of meeting SDGs to make humans less susceptible to such global crises, and more so for the low- and middle-income countries. Governments of various countries need to keep the future global crisis in their mind while restoring the economic activities, as the cost of overcoming the crisis could be more than the cost of prevention. Hence, future policies need to be built on current experiences, and perhaps concerted efforts are needed toward renewable energy, sustainable industrial production, and smart and efficient transportation.

References

1. Navinya C, Patidar G, Phuleria HC. Examining effects of the COVID-19 national lockdown on ambient air quality across urban India. *Aerosol Air Qual Res* 2020;**20**(8):1759–71. https://doi.org/10.4209/aaqr.2020.05.0256.
2. Express. *China lockdown period: this is how many days China was in lockdown—latest details | Travel News | Travel | Express.co.uk*; May 29 2020 https://www.express.co.uk/travel/articles/1288872/china-lockdown-period-details-coronavirus-uk-travel-advice-news-latest. [Accessed 18 September 2020].
3. Hamid MZSA, Karri RR. Overview of preventive measures and good governance policies to mitigate the COVID-19 outbreak curve in Brunei. In: *COVID-19: systemic risk and resilience*. Cham: Springer; 2021. p. 115–40.
4. The Hindu. *Wedding, funeral curbs to continue—The Hindu*; August 1 2020 https://www.thehindu.com/news/national/tamil-nadu/wedding-funeral-curbs-to-continue/article32244393.ece. [Accessed 22 September 2020].
5. Le Quéré C, Jackson RB, Jones MW, et al. Temporary reduction in daily global CO2 emissions during the COVID-19 forced confinement. *Nat Clim Chang* 2020;**10**(7):647–53. https://doi.org/10.1038/s41558-020-0797-x.
6. Venter ZS, Aunan K, Chowdhury S, Lelieveld J. *COVID-19 lockdowns cause global air pollution declines*; 2020. https://doi.org/10.1073/pnas.2006853117.
7. Mousazadeh M, Naghdali Z, Rahimian N, Hashemi M, Paital B, Al-Qodah Z. Management of environmental health to prevent an outbreak of COVID-19: a review. In: *Environmental and health management of novel coronavirus disease (COVID-19)*; 2021. p. 235–67.
8. Singh V, Singh S, Biswal A, Kesarkar AP, Mor S, Ravindra K. Diurnal and temporal changes in air pollution during COVID-19 strict lockdown over different regions of India. *Environ Pollut* 2020;**266**. https://doi.org/10.1016/j.envpol.2020.115368, 115368.
9. Sharma S, Zhang M, Anshika GJ, Zhang H, Kota SH. Effect of restricted emissions during COVID-19 on air quality in India. *Sci Total Environ* 2020;**728**. https://doi.org/10.1016/j.scitotenv.2020.138878, 138878.

10. Dantas G, Siciliano B, França BB, da Silva CM, Arbilla G. The impact of COVID-19 partial lockdown on the air quality of the city of Rio de Janeiro, Brazil. *Sci Total Environ* 2020;**729**. https://doi.org/10.1016/j.scitotenv.2020.139085.
11. Tobías A, Carnerero C, Reche C, et al. Changes in air quality during the lockdown in Barcelona (Spain) one month into the SARS-CoV-2 epidemic. *Sci Total Environ* 2020;**726**. https://doi.org/10.1016/j.scitotenv.2020.138540, 138540.
12. Jain S, Sharma T. Social and travel lockdown impact considering coronavirus disease (COVID-19) on air quality in megacities of India: present benefits, future challenges and way forward. *Aerosol Air Qual Res* 2020;**20**. https://doi.org/10.4209/aaqr.2020.04.0171.
13. Mohd Nadzir MS, Chel Gee Ooi M, Alhasa KM, et al. The impact of movement control order (MCO) during pandemic COVID-19 on local air quality in an Urban area of Klang Valley, Malaysia. *Aerosol Air Qual Res* 2020;**20**(March):1237–48. https://doi.org/10.4209/aaqr.2020.04.0163.
14. Isaifan RJ. The dramatic impact of coronavirus outbreak on air quality: has it saved as much as it has killed so far? *Glob J Environ Sci Manag* 2020;**6**(3):275–88. https://doi.org/10.22034/gjesm.2020.03.01.
15. Liu F, Page A, Strode SA, et al. *Abrupt declines in tropospheric nitrogen dioxide over China after the outbreak of COVID-19*; 2020. https://doi.org/10.1126/sciadv.abc2992.
16. Domingo L, Marqu M, Rovira J. Influence of airborne transmission of SARS-CoV-2 on COVID-19 pandemic. *A review* 2020;**188**(June):17–20. https://doi.org/10.1016/j.envres.2020.109861.
17. Setti L, Passarini F, De Gennaro G, Barbieri P, Piscitelli P, Miani A. *Airborne transmission route of COVID-19: why 2 meters/6 feet of inter-personal distance could not be enough*; 2020. https://doi.org/10.1038/d41586-020-01049-6.
18. Covaci A. How can airborne transmission of COVID-19 indoors be minimised? *Environ Int J* 2020;**142**(May). https://doi.org/10.1016/j.envint.2020.105832.
19. Morawska L, Cao J. Airborne transmission of SARS-CoV-2: the world should face the reality. *Environ Int* 2020;**139**(April). https://doi.org/10.1016/j.envint.2020.105730, 105730.
20. Conticini E, Frediani B, Caro D. Can atmospheric pollution be considered a co-factor in extremely high level of SARS-CoV-2 lethality in northern Italy?*. *Environ Pollut* 2020;**261**. https://doi.org/10.1016/j.envpol.2020.114465, 114465.
21. Ogen Y. Assessing nitrogen dioxide (NO2) levels as a contributing factor to coronavirus (COVID-19) fatality. *Sci Total Environ* 2020;**726**. https://doi.org/10.1016/j.scitotenv.2020.138605.
22. Wu X, Nethery RC, Sabath BM, et al. *Exposure to air pollution and COVID-19 mortality in the United States: a nationwide cross-sectional study*; 2020. https://doi.org/10.1017/CBO9781107415324.004.
23. Cui Y, Zhang Z-F, Froines J, et al. Air pollution and case fatality of SARS in the People's republic of China: an ecologic study. *Environ Health: Glob Access Sci Source* 2003;**2**:1–15. https://doi.org/10.1186/1476-069X-2-1.
24. Bashir M.F., Ma B., Bilal, K.B., Tan M.A.B.D., Bashir M. Correlation between climate indicators and COVID-19 pandemic in New York, USA, Sci Total Environ J 2020;728(January):138835. doi:https://doi.org/10.1016/j.scitotenv.2020.138835.
25. Mecenas P, Bastos R, Vallinoto A, Normando D. *Effects of temperature and humidity on the spread of COVID-19: a systematic review*; 2020. p. 1–31. https://doi.org/10.1101/2020.04.14.20064923.
26. Kumar S. Effect of meteorological parameters on spread of COVID-19 in India and air quality during lockdown. *Sci Total Environ* 2020;**745**. https://doi.org/10.1016/j.scitotenv.2020.141021, 141021.

27. Higham JE, Ramírez CA, Green MA, Morse AP. UK COVID-19 lockdown: 100 days of air pollution reduction? *Air Qual Atmos Health* 2020;1–8. https://doi.org/10.1007/s11869-020-00937-0.
28. WHO. Ambient air pollution: a global assessment of exposure and burden of disease. *Clean Air J* 2016;**26**(2):6. https://doi.org/10.17159/2410-972x/2016/v26n2a4.
29. Bherwani H, Gautam S, Gupta A. Qualitative and quantitative analyses of impact of COVID-19 on sustainable development goals (SDGs) in Indian subcontinent with a focus on air quality. *Int J Environ Sci Technol* 2021;**18**(4):1019–28. https://doi.org/10.1007/S13762-020-03122-Z.
30. Rafaj P, Kiesewetter G, Gül T, et al. Outlook for clean air in the context of sustainable development goals. *Glob Environ Chang* 2018;**53**:1–11. https://doi.org/10.1016/J.GLOENVCHA.2018.08.008.
31. Worldometers. *Coronavirus update (live): 30,702,361 cases and 956,506 deaths from COVID-19 virus pandemic—worldometer*; 2020 https://www.worldometers.info/coronavirus/?utm_campaign=homeAdvegas1?. [Accessed 19 September 2020].
32. Timeanddate. *First day of stay at home order in the United States*; 2020 https://www.timeanddate.com/holidays/us/lockdown-day-1. [Accessed 19 September 2020].
33. Economictimes. *US states begin easing lockdowns as virus weakens in Asia*; 2020 https://economictimes.indiatimes.com/news/international/world-news/us-states-begin-easing-lockdowns-as-virus-weakens-in-asia/articleshow/75370662.cms. [Accessed 19 September 2020].
34. Aljazeera. *India extends coronavirus lockdown to May 31 | India News | Al Jazeera*; May 17 2020 https://www.aljazeera.com/news/2020/05/india-extends-coronavirus-lockdown-31-200517163717633.html. [Accessed 19 September 2020].
35. Garda. *Brazil: quarantine in São Paulo extended through May 10 /update 13*; 2020 https://www.garda.com/crisis24/news-alerts/334111/brazil-quarantine-in-sao-paulo-extended-through-may-10-update-13. [Accessed 21 September 2020].
36. The Moscow Times. *Putin extends Russia's coronavirus lockdown as new infections continue to rise—The Moscow Times*; April 28 2020 https://www.themoscowtimes.com/2020/04/28/putin-extends-russias-coronavirus-lockdown-as-new-infections-continue-to-rise-a70130. [Accessed 19 September 2020].
37. Garda. *Peru: COVID-19 state of emergency extended until June 30 /update 16*; May 23 2020 https://www.garda.com/crisis24/news-alerts/344801/peru-covid-19-state-of-emergency-extended-until-june-30-update-16. [Accessed 19 September 2020].
38. Garda. *Colombia: COVID-19 lockdown extended until July 15 /update 18*; June 25 2020 https://www.garda.com/crisis24/news-alerts/354106/colombia-covid-19-lockdown-extended-until-july-15-update-18. [Accessed 21 September 2020].
39. SA Health. *Statement by President Cyril Ramaphosa On South Africa's response to the coronavirus pandemic, Union Buildings, Tshwane*; April 23, 2020 https://sacoronavirus.co.za/2020/04/23/statement-by-president-cyril-ramaphosa-on-south-africas-response-to-the-coronavirus-pandemic-union-buildings-tshwane/. [Accessed 21 September 2020].
40. Businesstech. *Ramaphosa announces 21 day coronavirus lockdown for South Africa*; March 23, 2020 https://businesstech.co.za/news/government/383927/ramaphosa-announces-21-day-coronavirus-lockdown-for-south-africa/. [Accessed 21 September 2020].
41. Medicalxpress. *Mexico begins reopening after two-month lockdown*; June 1, 2020 https://medicalxpress.com/news/2020-06-mexico-reopening-two-month-lockdown.html. [Accessed 21 September 2020].
42. NDTV. *Coronavirus updates: Spain to extend lockdown till may 9 As COVID-19 death count tops 20,043*; April 19, 2020 https://www.ndtv.com/world-news/coronavirus-updates-spain-to-extend-lockdown-till-may-9-as-covid-19-death-count-tops-20-043-2214257. [Accessed 21 September 2020].

43. Buenos Aires Times. *Buenos Aires Times | Lockdown extended until June 28, with "two types of quarantine."*; June 5, 2020 https://www.batimes.com.ar/news/argentina/lockdown-extended-until-june-28-with-two-types-of-quarantine.phtml. [Accessed 21 September 2020].
44. Garda. *Chile: Authorities to gradually lift lockdown restrictions in central Santiago from August 17 /update 24*; 2020 https://www.garda.com/crisis24/news-alerts/368666/chile-authorities-to-gradually-lift-lockdown-restrictions-in-central-santiago-from-august-17-update-24. [Accessed 10 September 2020].
45. Garda. *Iran: Natiowide lockdown implemented as over 11,300 COVID-19 cases confirmed March 13 /update 12*; March 14, 2020 https://www.garda.com/crisis24/news-alerts/322811/iran-natiowide-lockdown-implemented-as-over-11300-covid-19-cases-confirmed-march-13-update-12. [Accessed 21 September 2020].
46. Garda. *Iran: Authorities begin reopening highways, shopping centers following easing of COVID-19 restrictions April 20 /update 21*; April 20, 2020 https://www.garda.com/crisis24/news-alerts/334311/iran-authorities-begin-reopening-highways-shopping-centers-following-easing-of-covid-19-restrictions-april-20-update-21. [Accessed 21 September 2020].
47. The Hindu. *Bangladesh to extend shutdown till May 30—The Hindu*; May 14, 2020 https://www.thehindu.com/news/international/bangladesh-to-extend-shutdown-till-may-30/article31579303.ece. [Accessed 19 September 2020].
48. BBC. *Coronavirus: France eases lockdown after eight weeks—BBC News*; May 11, 2020 https://www.bbc.com/news/world-europe-52615733. [Accessed 21 September 2020].
49. Anil I, Alagha O. The impact of COVID-19 lockdown on the air quality of Eastern Province, Saudi Arabia. *Air Qual Atmos Health* 2020;1–12. https://doi.org/10.1007/s11869-020-00918-3.
50. Chandir S, Siddiqi DA, Setayesh H, Khan AJ. Impact of COVID-19 lockdown on routine immunisation in Karachi, Pakistan. *Lancet Glob Health* 2020;**8**(9):e1118–20. https://doi.org/10.1016/S2214-109X(20)30290-4.
51. Daily News. *Turkey to impose four-day lockdown—Turkey News*; April 20, 2019 https://www.hurriyetdailynews.com/turkey-to-impose-four-day-lockdown-154053. [Accessed 21 September 2020].
52. BBC. *Coronavirus: Italy's PM outlines lockdown easing measures—BBC News*; April 27, 2020 https://www.bbc.com/news/world-europe-52435273. [Accessed 19 September 2020].
53. The Star. *Iraq on total lockdown until March 28 over virus fears | The Star*; March 22, 2020 https://www.thestar.com.my/news/regional/2020/03/22/iraq-on-total-lockdown-until-march-28-over-virus-fears. [Accessed 21 September 2020].
54. CNN. *(151) Iraq extends country-wide curfew through April 11*; March 26, 2020 https://edition.cnn.com/world/live-news/coronavirus-outbreak-03-26-20-intl-hnk/h_f4ac339b0b21acdd555166640c374a00. [Accessed 21 September 2020].
55. The Hindu. *Janata Curfew | updates—The Hindu*; March 22 2020 https://www.thehindu.com/news/national/janata-curfew-march-22-live-updates/article31133447.ece. [Accessed 18 September 2020].
56. The Indian Express. *Explained: these are the countries that have not imposed lockdowns | Explained News,The Indian Express*; May 16 2020 https://indianexpress.com/article/explained/explained-the-countries-that-have-not-imposed-lockdown-and-why-6389003/. [Accessed 19 September 2020].
57. National Post. *Chile announces nationwide nightly curfew, coronavirus cases hit 632 | National Post*; 2020 https://nationalpost.com/pmn/health-pmn/chile-announces-nationwide-nightly-curfew-coronavirus-cases-hit-632. [Accessed 21 September 2020].

58. Garda. *Bangladesh: nationwide curfew in place until June 15; Cox's Bazar classified as a red zone /update 14*; June 7 2020 https://www.garda.com/crisis24/news-alerts/348671/bangladesh-nationwide-curfew-in-place-until-june-15-coxs-bazar-classified-as-a-red-zone-update-14. [Accessed 21 September 2020].
59. Hale T, Angrist N, et al. *Oxford COVID-19 government response tracker, Blavatnik School of Government*; 2020 https://www.bsg.ox.ac.uk/research/research-projects/coronavirus-government-response-tracker.
60. BBC. *Coronavirus: Wuhan draws up plans to test all 11 million residents—BBC News*; May 12, 2020 https://www.bbc.com/news/world-asia-china-52629213. [Accessed 21 September 2020].
61. Lockdown Extension in Bihar, Maharashtra: These states to impose total shutdown amid COVID-19 outbreak | full list. (n.d.), https://www.india.com/news/india/lockdown-extended-till-august-31-these-states-to-impose-total-shutdown-amid-covid-19-outbreak-full-list-4099385/. Accessed 2 October 2021.
62. Nabi KN, Islam MR. Has countrywide lockdown worked as a feasible measure in bending the Covid-19 curve in developing countries? *MedRxiv* 2020. https://doi.org/10.1101/2020.06.23.20138685.
63. Tang Y, Wang S. Mathematic modeling of COVID-19 in the United States. *Emerg Microbes Infect* 2020;**9**(1):827–9. https://doi.org/10.1080/22221751.2020.1760146.
64. Lai CC, Wang CY, Wang YH, Hsueh SC, Ko WC, Hsueh PR. Global epidemiology of coronavirus disease 2019 (COVID-19): disease incidence, daily cumulative index, mortality, and their association with country healthcare resources and economic status. *Int J Antimicrob Agents* 2020;**55**(4). https://doi.org/10.1016/j.ijantimicag.2020.105946.
65. Kohlberg E, Neyman A. *Demystifying the math of the coronavirus*; 2020 https://bit.ly/simpleR. [Accessed 7 September 2020].
66. Chitra J, Rajendran SM, Jeba Mercy J, Jeyakanthan J. Impact of covid-19 lockdown in Tamil Nadu: benefits and challenges on environment perspective. *Indian J Biochem Biophys* 2020;**57**(4):370–81.
67. Delfino RJ, Gong H, Linn WS, Pellizzari ED, Hu Y. Asthma symptoms in hispanic children and daily ambient exposures to toxic and criteria air pollutants. *Environ Health Perspect* 2003;**111**(4):647–56. https://doi.org/10.1289/ehp.5992.
68. Schikowski T, Sugiri D, Ranft U, et al. Long-term air pollution exposure and living close to busy roads are associated with COPD in women. *Respir Res* 2005;**6**(1):1–10. https://doi.org/10.1186/1465-9921-6-152.
69. Goss CH, Newsom SA, Schildcrout JS, Sheppard L, Kaufman JD. Effect of ambient air pollution on pulmonary exacerbations and lung function in cystic fibrosis. *Am J Respir Crit Care Med* 2004;**169**(7):816–21. https://doi.org/10.1164/rccm.200306-779oc.
70. Landrigan PJ, Fuller R, Acosta NJR, et al. The lancet commission on pollution and health. *Lancet* 2018;**391**(10119):462–512. https://doi.org/10.1016/S0140-6736(17)32345-0.
71. WHO. *Air pollution*; 2020 https://www.who.int/health-topics/air-pollution#tab=tab_1. [Accessed 1 July 2020].
72. Pandey A, Venkataraman C. Estimating emissions from the Indian transport sector with on-road fleet composition and traffic volume. *Atmos Environ* 2014;**98**:123–33. https://doi.org/10.1016/j.atmosenv.2014.08.039.
73. Pandey A, Sadavarte P, Rao AB, Venkataraman C. Trends in multi-pollutant emissions from a technology-linked inventory for India: II. Residential, agricultural and informal industry sectors. *Atmos Environ* 2014;**99**:341–52. https://doi.org/10.1016/j.atmosenv.2014.09.080.
74. Sadavarte P, Rupakheti M, Bhave P, Shakya K, Lawrence M. Nepal emission inventory—part I: technologies and combustion sources (NEEMI-tech) for 2001-2016. *Atmos Chem Phys* 2019;**19**(20):12953–73. https://doi.org/10.5194/acp-19-12953-2019.

75. Ramachandra TV, Shwetmala. Emissions from India's transport sector: Statewise synthesis. *Atmos Environ* 2009;**43**(34):5510–7. https://doi.org/10.1016/j.atmosenv.2009.07.015.
76. Guttikunda SK, Nishadh KA, Gota S, et al. Air quality, emissions, and source contributions analysis for the greater Bengaluru region of India. *Atmos Pollut Res* 2019;**10**(3):941–53. https://doi.org/10.1016/j.apr.2019.01.002.
77. Phuleria HC, Navinya C. *What did the lockdowns tell us about air pollution source contributions?* Collaborative Clean Air Policy Centre; 2020. https://ccapc.org.in/policy-briefs/2020/phuleria-navinya-commentary. [Accessed 10 September 2020].
78. Ching J, Kajino M. Rethinking air quality and climate change after covid-19. *Int J Environ Res Public Health* 2020;**17**(14):1–11. https://doi.org/10.3390/ijerph17145167.
79. Mahato S, Pal S, Ghosh KG. Effect of lockdown amid COVID-19 pandemic on air quality of the megacity Delhi, India. *Sci Total Environ* 2020;**730**. https://doi.org/10.1016/j.scitotenv.2020.139086, 139086.
80. Xu K, Cui K, Young L-H, et al. Impact of the COVID-19 event on air quality in Wuhan, Jingmen, and Enshi cities, China. *Aerosol Air Qual Res* 2020;**2**:915–29. https://doi.org/10.4209/aaqr.2020.04.0150.
81. Filonchyk M, Hurynovich V, Yan H, Gusev A, Shpilevskaya N. Impact assessment of COVID-19 on variations of SO2, NO2, CO and AOD over East China. *Aerosol Air Qual Res* 2020;**20**. https://doi.org/10.4209/aaqr.2020.05.0226.
82. Bao R, Zhang A. Does lockdown reduce air pollution? Evidence from 44 cities in northern China. *Sci Total Environ* 1954;**2020**(731). https://doi.org/10.1016/j.scitotenv.2020.139052, 139052.
83. Chen Q-X, Huang C-L, Yuan Y, Tan H-P. Influence of COVID-19 event on air quality and their association in Mainland China. *Aerosol Air Qual Res* 2020;**20**(7):1541–51. https://doi.org/10.4209/aaqr.2020.05.0224.
84. Cadotte MW. Early evidence that COVID-19 government policies reduce urban air pollution. *EarthArXiv Prepr* 2020;**1-9**. https://doi.org/10.31223/osf.io/nhgj3.
85. Chen LWA, Chien LC, Li Y, Lin G. Nonuniform impacts of COVID-19 lockdown on air quality over the United States. *Sci Total Environ* 2020;**745**:13–6. https://doi.org/10.1016/j.scitotenv.2020.141105.
86. Ash'aari ZH, Aris AZ, Ezani E, NIA K, et al. Spatiotemporal variations and contributing factors of air pollutant concentrations in Malaysia during movement control order due to pandemic COVID-19. *Aerosol Air Qual Res* 2020. https://doi.org/10.4209/aaqr.2020.06.0334.
87. Shareef A, Hashmi DR. Impacts of COVID-19 pandemic on air quality index (AQI) during partial lockdown in Karachi Pakistan. *J Health Environ Res* 2020;**6**:93–7. https://doi.org/10.11648/j.jher.20200603.17.
88. Kerimray A, Baimatova N, Ibragimova OP, et al. Assessing air quality changes in large cities during COVID-19 lockdowns: the impacts of traffic-free urban conditions in Almaty, Kazakhstan. *Sci Total Environ* 2020;**730**. https://doi.org/10.1016/j.scitotenv.2020.139179, 139179.
89. Broomandi P, Karaca F, Nikfal A, Jahanbakhshi A, Tamjidi M, Kim JR. Impact of COVID-19 event on the air quality in Iran. *Aerosol Air Qual Res* 2020;**20**. https://doi.org/10.4209/aaqr.2020.05.0205.
90. Faridi S, Yousefian F, Niazi S, Ghalhari MR, Hassanvand MS, Naddafi K. Impact of SARS-CoV-2 on ambient air particulate matter in Tehran. *Aerosol Air Qual Res* 2020;**20**. https://doi.org/10.4209/aaqr.2020.05.0225.
91. Zalakeviciute R, Vasquez R, Bayas D, et al. Drastic improvements in air quality in Ecuador during the COVID-19 outbreak. *Aerosol Air Qual Res* 2020;**20**(8):1783–92. https://doi.org/10.4209/aaqr.2020.05.0254.

92. Şahin ÜA. The effects of COVID-19 measures on air pollutant concentrations at Urban and traffic sites in Istanbul. *Aerosol Air Qual Res* 2020. https://doi.org/10.4209/aaqr.2020.05.0239 The.
93. Schäfer B, Verma R, Giri A, et al. *Covid-19 impact on air quality in megacities*; 2020 https://arxiv.org/abs/2007.00755.
94. Shrestha AM, Shrestha UB, Sharma R, Bhattarai S, Tran HNT, Rupakheti M. Lockdown caused by COVID-19 pandemic reduces air pollution in cities worldwide. *EarthArXiv Prepr* 2020. https://doi.org/10.31223/osf.io/edt4j.
95. Navinya C, Vinoj V, Pandey SK. Evaluation of pm2.5 surface concentrations simulated by nasa's merra version 2 aerosol reanalysis over India and its relation to the air quality index. *Aerosol Air Qual Res* 2020;**20**(6):1329–39. https://doi.org/10.4209/aaqr.2019.12.0615.
96. Yan D, Lei Y, Shi Y, Zhu Q, Li L, Zhang Z. Evolution of the spatiotemporal pattern of PM2.5 concentrations in China—A case study from the Beijing-Tianjin-Hebei region. *Atmos Environ* 2018;**183**:225–33. https://doi.org/10.1016/j.atmosenv.2018.03.041.
97. Lodhi A, Ghauri B, Rafiq Khan M, Rahman S, Shafique S. Particulate matter (PM2.5) concentration and source apportionment in Lahore. *J Braz Chem Soc* 2009;**20**(10):1811–20. https://doi.org/10.1590/S0103-50532009001000007.
98. NASA. *NASA earth observatory*; 2020 https://earthobservatory.nasa.gov/.
99. Kumar P, Hama S, Omidvarborna H, et al. Temporary reduction in fine particulate matter due to 'anthropogenic emissions switch-off' during COVID-19 lockdown in Indian cities. *Sustain Cities Soc* 2020;**62**. https://doi.org/10.1016/j.scs.2020.102382, 102382.
100. Mitra A, Chaudhuri TR, Mitra A, Pramanick P, Zaman S. *Impact of COVID-19 related shutdown on atmospheric carbon dioxide level in the city of Kolkata*; 2020. p. 84–92. https://sites.google.com/site/pjsciencea.
101. Saadat S, Rawtani D, Hussain CM. Environmental perspective of COVID-19. *Sci Total Environ* 2020;**728**. https://doi.org/10.1016/j.scitotenv.2020.138870, 138870.
102. Wang Q, Kwan MP, Zhou K, Fan J, Wang Y, Zhan D. The impacts of urbanization on fine particulate matter (PM2.5) concentrations: empirical evidence from 135 countries worldwide. *Environ Pollut* 2019;**247**:989–98. https://doi.org/10.1016/j.envpol.2019.01.086.
103. Kanniah KD, Kamarul Zaman NAF, Kaskaoutis DG, Latif MT. COVID-19's impact on the atmospheric environment in the Southeast Asia region. *Sci Total Environ* 2020;**736**. https://doi.org/10.1016/j.scitotenv.2020.139658, 139658.
104. Weyuma Bulto T, Kosa Chebo A, Gudisa Ede A, Chalchisa WB. *Implications of COVID-19 on the of fine particulate matter (PM2.5) in Ethiopia*; 2020. https://doi.org/10.21203/rs.3.rs-66750/v1.
105. Fuwape IA, Okpalaonwuka CT, Ogunjo ST. Impact of COVID -19 pandemic lockdown on distribution of inorganic pollutants in selected cities of Nigeria. *Air Qual Atmos Health* 2020;1–7. https://doi.org/10.1007/s11869-020-00921-8.
106. Islam MS, Tusher TR, Roy S, Rahman M. Impacts of nationwide lockdown due to COVID-19 outbreak on air quality in Bangladesh: a spatiotemporal analysis. *Air Qual Atmos Health* 2020;1–13. https://doi.org/10.1007/s11869-020-00940-5.
107. Shakoor A, Chen X, Farooq TH, et al. Fluctuations in environmental pollutants and air quality during the lockdown in the USA and China: two sides of COVID-19 pandemic. *Air Qual Atmos Health* 2020. https://doi.org/10.1007/s11869-020-00888-6.
108. Xu K, Cui K, Young L-H, et al. Air quality index, indicatory air pollutants and impact of COVID-19 event on the air quality near Central China. *Aerosol Air Qual Res* 2020;**20**(6):1204–21. https://doi.org/10.4209/aaqr.2020.04.0139.
109. Kumari P, Toshniwal D. Impact of lockdown measures during COVID-19 on air quality– A case study of India. *Int J Environ Health Res* June 2020;1–8. https://doi.org/10.1080/09603123.2020.1778646.

110. Sharma M, Jain S, Lamba BY. Epigrammatic study on the effect of lockdown amid Covid-19 pandemic on air quality of most polluted cities of Rajasthan (India). *Air Qual Atmos Health* 2020. https://doi.org/10.1007/s11869-020-00879-7.
111. Bera B, Bhattacharjee S, Shit PK, Sengupta N, Saha S. Significant impacts of COVID-19 lockdown on urban air pollution in Kolkata (India) and amelioration of environmental health. *Environ Dev Sustain* 2020. https://doi.org/10.1007/s10668-020-00898-5, 0123456789.
112. Hashim BM, Al-Naseri SK, Al-Maliki A, Al-Ansari N. Impact of COVID-19 lockdown on NO2, O3, PM2.5 and PM10 concentrations and assessing air quality changes in Baghdad, Iraq. *Sci Total Environ* 2020;**754**. https://doi.org/10.1016/j.scitotenv.2020.141978, 141978.
113. Ash'aari ZH, Aris AZ, Ezani E, Kamal NIA, Jaafar N, Jahaya JN, et al. *Spatiotemporal variations and contributing factors of air pollutant concentrations in malaysia during movement control order due to pandemic COVID-19*; 2020 https://aaqr.org/articles/aaqr-20-06-covid-0334. [Accessed 9 September 2020].
114. Li J, Tartarini F. Changes in air quality during the COVID-19 lockdown in Singapore and associations with human mobility trends. *Aerosol Air Qual Res* 2020;**20**(8):1748–58. https://doi.org/10.4209/aaqr.2020.06.0303.
115. Dobson R, Semple S. Changes in outdoor air pollution due to COVID-19 lockdowns differ by pollutant: evidence from Scotland. *Occup Environ Med* 2020;**0**:1–3. https://doi.org/10.1136/oemed-2020-106659.
116. Nakada LYK, Urban RC. COVID-19 pandemic: impacts on the air quality during the partial lockdown in São Paulo state, Brazil. *Sci Total Environ* 2020;**730**. https://doi.org/10.1016/j.scitotenv.2020.139087, 139087.
117. NASA. *Data shows 30 percent drop in air pollution over northeast U.S*; 2020 http://www.nasa.gov/feature/goddard/2020/drop-in-air-pollution-over-northeast. [Accessed 22 September 2020].
118. ESA. *ESA—Coronavirus lockdown leading to drop in pollution across Europe*; 2020 https://www.esa.int/Applications/Observing_the_Earth/Copernicus/Sentinel-5P/Coronavirus_lockdown_leading_to_drop_in_pollution_across_Europe. [Accessed 9 September 2020].
119. Tosepu R, Gunawan J, Effendy DS, et al. Correlation between weather and Covid-19 pandemic in Jakarta, Indonesia. *Sci Total Environ* 2020;**725**. https://doi.org/10.1016/j.scitotenv.2020.138436.
120. Xie J, Zhu Y. Association between ambient temperature and COVID-19 infection in 122 cities from China. *Sci Total Environ* 2020;**724**. https://doi.org/10.1016/j.scitotenv.2020.138201, 138201.
121. Wu Y, Jing W, Liu J, et al. Effects of temperature and humidity on the daily new cases and new deaths of COVID-19 in 166 countries. *Sci Total Environ* 2020;**729**:1–7. https://doi.org/10.1016/j.scitotenv.2020.139051.
122. Babu SR, Rao NN, Kumar SV, Paul S, Pani SK. Plausible role of environmental factors on COVID-19 transmission in the megacity Delhi, India. *Aerosol Air Qual Res* 2020;**20**. https://doi.org/10.4209/aaqr.2020.06.0314.
123. Ma Y., Zhao Y., Liu J., et al. Effects of temperature variation and humidity on the death of COVID-19 in Wuhan, China. Elsevier. (n.d.), https://www.sciencedirect.com/science/article/pii/S0048969720317393. Accessed 26 September 2020.
124. Mandal CC, Panwar MS. Can the summer temperatures reduce COVID-19 cases ? *Public Health* 2020;**185**:72–9. https://doi.org/10.1016/j.puhe.2020.05.065.
125. Qi H, Xiao S, Shi R, et al. COVID-19 transmission in mainland China is associated with temperature and humidity: A time-series analysis. *Sci Total Environ* 2020;**728**. https://doi.org/10.1016/j.scitotenv.2020.138778.

126. Oliveiros B, Caramelo L, Ferreira NC, Caramelo F. Role of temperature and humidity in the modulation of the doubling time of COVID-19 cases. *medRxiv* 2020. https://doi.org/10.1101/2020.03.05.20031872.
127. Bashir MF, Jiang B, MA B, et al. Correlation between environmental pollution indicators and COVID-19 pandemic: a brief study in Californian context. *Environ Res* 2020;**187**. https://doi.org/10.1016/j.envres.2020.109652.
128. Araujo M, Naimi B. *Spread of SARS-CoV-2 Coronavirus likely to be constrained by climate*; 2020. p. 1–15. https://doi.org/10.1101/2020.03.12.20034728.
129. Gautam S. The influence of COVID-19 on air quality in India: A boon or inutile. *Bull Environ Contam Toxicol* 2020;1–3. https://doi.org/10.1007/s00128-020-02877-y.
130. Adekunle IA, Tella SA, Oyesiku KO, Oseni IO. Spatio-temporal analysis of meteorological factors in abating the spread of COVID-19 in Africa. *Heliyon* 2020;**6**(8). https://doi.org/10.1016/j.heliyon.2020.e04749.
131. Ogaugwu C, Mogaji H, Ogaugwu E, et al. Effect of weather on COVID-19 transmission and mortality in Lagos, Nigeria. *Scientifica (Cairo)* 2020;**2020**:1–6. https://doi.org/10.1155/2020/2562641.
132. Ma Y, Zhao Y, Liu J, et al. Effects of temperature variation and humidity on the death of COVID-19 in Wuhan, China. *Sci Total Environ* 2020;**724**. https://doi.org/10.1016/j.scitotenv.2020.138226, 138226.
133. Guoliang C, Xiaoye Z, Sunling G, Fangcheng Z. Investigation on emission factors of particulate matter and gaseous pollutants from crop residue burning. *J Environ Sci* 2008;**20**:50–5. https://doi.org/10.1016/S1001-0742(08)60007-8.
134. Habib G, Venkataraman C, Shrivastava M, Banerjee R, Stehr JW, Dickerson RR. New methodology for estimating biofuel consumption for cooking: atmospheric emissions of black carbon and sulfur dioxide from India. *Glob Biogeochem Cycles* 2004;**18** (3):1–11. https://doi.org/10.1029/2003GB002157.
135. Lam NL, Chen Y, Weyant C, et al. Household light makes global heat: high black carbon emissions from kerosene wick lamps. *Environ Sci Technol* 2012;**46**(24):13531–8. https://doi.org/10.1021/es302697h.
136. Google Mobility Report. *Google community mobility report*; 2020 https://www.google.com/covid19/mobility/.
137. Rahman M, Thill J, Paul KC. *COVID-19 pandemic severity, lockdown regimes, and people's mobility: evidence from 88 countries. SSRN*; 2020. p. 1–17. https://papers.ssrn.com/sol3/papers.cfm?abstract_id=3664131.
138. Pandey SK, Vinoj V. *Surprising increase in aerosol amid widespread decline in pollution over India during the COVID19 Lockdown*; 2020. https://doi.org/10.31223/osf.io/5kmx2.
139. CEA. *Central electricity authority (CEA), ministry of power, government of india, power supply position—energy report*; 2020 http://cea.nic.in/monthlyarchive.html.
140. Mor S, Kumar S, Singh T, Dogra S, Pandey V, Ravindra K. Impact of COVID-19 lockdown on air quality in Chandigarh, India: understanding the emission sources during controlled anthropogenic activities. *Chemosphere* 2020;**263**. https://doi.org/10.1016/j.chemosphere.2020.127978, 127978.
141. He L, Lin A, Chen X, Zhou H, Zhou Z, He P. Assessment of MERRA-2 surface PM2.5 over the Yangtze River basin: ground-based verification, spatiotemporal distribution and meteorological dependence. *Remote Sens* 2019;**11**(4). https://doi.org/10.3390/rs11040460.
142. Gelaro R, McCarty W, Suárez MJ, et al. The modern-era retrospective analysis for research and applications, version 2 (MERRA-2). *J Clim* 2017;**30**(14):5419–54. https://doi.org/10.1175/JCLI-D-16-0758.1.
143. Randles CA, da Silva AM, Buchard V, et al. The MERRA-2 aerosol reanalysis, 1980 onward. Part I: system description and data assimilation evaluation. *J Clim* 2017;**30**:6823–50. https://doi.org/10.1175/JCLI-D-16-0609.1.

144. Bosilovich M, Akella S, Coy L, Cullather R, Draper C. *MERRA-2: initial evaluation of the climate*. NASA; 2015. p. 43. https://core.ac.uk/download/pdf/42697879.pdf.
145. Schiermeier Q. Why pollution is plummeting in some cities-but not others. *Nature* 2020. https://doi.org/10.1038/d41586-020-01049-6.
146. Tan J, Mu L, Huang J, Yu S, Chen B, Yin J. An initial investigation of the association between the SARS outbreak and weather: with the view of the environmental temperature and its variation. *J Epidemiol Community Health* 2005;**59**(3):186–92. https://doi.org/10.1136/jech.2004.020180.
147. Park JE, Son WS, Ryu Y, Choi SB, Kwon O, Ahn I. Effects of temperature, humidity, and diurnal temperature range on influenza incidence in a temperate region. *Influenza Other Respir Viruses* 2019;**14**(1):11–8. https://doi.org/10.1111/irv.12682.
148. de Araujo Pinheiro SDLL, PHN S, Schwartz J, Zanobetti A. Isolated and synergistic effects of PM10 and average temperature on cardiovascular and respiratory mortality. *Rev Saude Publica* 2014;**48**(6):881–8. https://doi.org/10.1590/S0034-8910.2014048005218.
149. Luo Y, Zhang Y, Liu T, et al. Lagged effect of diurnal temperature range on mortality in a subtropical megacity of China. *PLoS One* 2013;**8**(2). https://doi.org/10.1371/journal.pone.0055280.
150. Metz JA, Finn A. Influenza and humidity—why a bit more damp may be good for you! *J Infect* 2015;**71**(S1):S54–8. https://doi.org/10.1016/j.jinf.2015.04.013.
151. Gautam AS, Joshi A, Kumar S, Shinde M, Singh K, Nautiyal A. Variation of atmospheric parameters and dependent nature of Covid-19 pandemic in India during the lockdown period. *J Crit Rev* 2020;**7**(19):2445–53. https://doi.org/10.31838/jcr.07.19.297.
152. Zoran MA, Savastru RS, Savastru DM, Tautan MN. Assessing the relationship between surface levels of PM2.5 and PM10 particulate matter impact on COVID-19 in Milan, Italy. *Sci Total Environ* 2020;**738**. https://doi.org/10.1016/j.scitotenv.2020.139825.
153. Zhu Y, Xie J, Huang F, Cao L. Association between short-term exposure to air pollution and COVID-19 infection: evidence from China. *Sci Total Environ* 2020;**727**. https://doi.org/10.1016/j.scitotenv.2020.138704.
154. Jiang Y, Wu XJ, Guan YJ. Effect of ambient air pollutants and meteorological variables on COVID-19 incidence. *Infect Control Hosp Epidemiol* 2020. https://doi.org/10.1017/ice.2020.222.
155. Zoran MA, Savastru RS, Savastru DM, Tautan MN. Assessing the relationship between ground levels of ozone (O3) and nitrogen dioxide (NO2) with coronavirus (COVID-19) in Milan, Italy. *Sci Total Environ* 2020;**740**. https://doi.org/10.1016/j.scitotenv.2020.140005.
156. Vasquez-Apestegui V, Parras-Garrido E, Tapia V, et al. *Association between air pollution in Lima and the high incidence of COVID-19: findings from a post hoc Analysis*; 2020. https://doi.org/10.21203/rs.3.rs-39404/v1.
157. Copat C, Cristaldi A, Fiore M, et al. The role of air pollution (PM and NO2) in COVID-19 spread and lethality: a systematic review. *Environ Res* 2020;**191**. https://doi.org/10.1016/j.envres.2020.110129, 110129.
158. Li H, Xu XL, Dai DW, Huang ZY, Ma Z, Guan YJ. Air pollution and temperature are associated with increased COVID-19 incidence: A time series study. *Int J Infect Dis* 2020;**97**:278–82. https://doi.org/10.1016/j.ijid.2020.05.076.
159. Yao Y, Pan J, Wang W, et al. Association of particulate matter pollution and case fatality rate of COVID-19 in 49 Chinese cities. *Sci Total Environ* 2020;**741**. https://doi.org/10.1016/j.scitotenv.2020.140396.
160. Frontera A, Martin C, Vlachos K, Sgubin G. Regional air pollution persistence links to COVID-19 infection zoning. *J Infect* 2020;**81**(2):318–56. https://doi.org/10.1016/j.jinf.2020.03.045.

161. Fattorini D, Regoli F. Role of the chronic air pollution levels in the Covid-19 outbreak risk in Italy. *Environ Pollut* 2020;**264**. https://doi.org/10.1016/j.envpol.2020.114732.
162. Chen K, Wang M, Huang C, Kinney PL, Anastas PT. *Air pollution reduction and mortality benefit during the COVID-19 outbreak in China*; 2020. https://doi.org/10.1016/S2542-5196(20)30107-8. thelancetcom.
163. WHO. *Advice for the public.* World heal Organ; 2020. https://www.who.int/emergencies/diseases/novel-coronavirus-2019/advice-for-public.
164. The Hindu. *5,000 fine for SOP violations, 200 for not wearing mask—The Hindu*; September 5, 2020 https://www.thehindu.com/news/national/tamil-nadu/5000-fine-for-sop-violations-200-for-not-wearing-mask/article32527084.ece. [Accessed 22 September 2020].
165. Indian Express. *Jharkhand's 'no mask' penalty – up to Rs 1 lakh; here's how other states are dealing with Covid rule violators | India News, The Indian Express*; July 23, 2020 https://indianexpress.com/article/india/jharkhands-no-mask-penalty-up-to-rs-1-lakh-heres-how-other-states-are-dealing-with-covid-rule-violators-6520089/. [Accessed 22 September 2020].
166. AarogyaSetu. *Aarogya Setu App : COVID-19 Tracker launched to alert you and keep you safe. Download now! | MyGov.in. Government of India*; 2020 https://www.mygov.in/task/aarogya-setu-app-covid-19-tracker-launched-alert-you-and-keep-you-safe-download-now/. [Accessed 22 September 2020].
167. Narain U. *Air pollution: locked down by COVID-19 but not arrested.* WHO; 2020. https://www.worldbank.org/en/news/immersive-story/2020/07/01/air-pollution-locked-down-by-covid-19-but-not-arrested. [Accessed 10 September 2020].
168. Mehta S, Ganguly T, Matte T, Kass D. *Sustaining air quality gains during the COVID crisis.* Collaborative Clean Air Policy Centre; 2020. https://ccapc.org.in/policy-briefs/2020/mehta-ganguly-matte-kass. [Accessed 10 September 2020].
169. Brauer M. *COVID-19 only makes air pollution mitigation more urgent.* Collaborative Clean Air Policy Centre; 2020. https://ccapc.org.in/policy-briefs/2020/brauer-covid.
170. Eske J. What's the link between cold weather and the common cold. *Med News Today* 2018. https://www.medicalnewstoday.com/articles/323431.

CHAPTER NINE

COVID-19 pandemic: The fears and hopes for SDG 3, with focus on prevention and control of noncommunicable diseases (SDG 3.4) and universal health coverage (SDG 3.8)

Amirhossein Takian[a,b,c], Azam Raoofi[a,c], and Hajar Haghighi[a]

[a]Department of Health Management, Policy & Economics, School of Public Health, Tehran University of Medical Sciences (TUMS), Tehran, Iran
[b]Department of Global Health & Public Policy, School of Public Health, Tehran University of Medical Sciences (TUMS), Tehran, Iran
[c]Health Equity Research Centre (HERC), Tehran University of Medical Sciences (TUMS), Tehran, Iran

Key messages

- The emergence of the COVID-19 crisis has posed critical challenges to all aspects of development. The pandemic damaged many global public health achievements and impeded the pathways toward Sustainable Development Goals in almost all settings.
- Although the Noncommunicable diseases (NCD) mortality rate reduced during the last decade, the rapid spread of COVID-19 has led to widespread healthcare disruptions and long-term consequences for patients with NCD.
- Universal health coverage (UHC) will be able to strengthen the health system with enough resilience to strike a meaningful and efficient balance between essential healthcare services and additional requirements for crisis management.
- COVID-19 highlights the importance of meaningful intersectoral collaboration and a surveillance and response system in preparing for likely health emergencies of the future.
- The fragility and unpreparedness of the health systems in many countries during COVID-19 demonstrated UHC's fundamental role in achieving sustainable health development in all societies.

COVID-19 and the Sustainable Development Goals
https://doi.org/10.1016/B978-0-323-91307-2.00014-6

1. Introduction

Launched by the United Nations (UN) in 2015 and endorsed by 194 Member States, Sustainable Development Goals (SDGs) aim to scale up global cooperation to reduce poverty and achieve peace, prosperity, and health for all.[1–3] SDGs include 17 goals and 169 targets, of which SDG 3—ensuring a healthy life and promoting well-being for all ages—and its 13 targets are specifically focused on health (Box 1). Moreover, some other SDGs indirectly address health-related issues or their consequences may affect health (Fig. 1).[4]

Following the legacy of the millennium development goals (MDGs) and as a result of global focus on SDGs, in particular SDG 3, significant progress in global health has been achieved, i.e., maternal, infants, and the under-5 children mortality rate was declining; healthy life expectancy was increasing in 202 countries; access to safe drinking water and basic sanitation services was increasing; the share of current health expenditure as a percentage of Gross Domestic Product was increasing[5]; the Global Action Plan for the Prevention and Control of Noncommunicable Diseases (NCDs) was placed on the World Health Organization (WHO) agenda in 2013,[6] following which many countries developed national strategies to reduce the burden of NCDs and relatively good results have been achieved; the incidence of many infectious diseases was declining; many emerging and reemerging diseases such as poliomyelitis and malaria were on the edge of eradication, and chronic poverty and hunger were declining.[7] Besides, primary healthcare (PHC) and universal health coverage (UHC) were prioritized on the WHO agenda and subsequently on the agenda of many countries, so that 75% of the national health policies of the world were developed with the aim of moving toward UHC.[8]

Despite many achievements, the acceleration of many countries in achieving SDGs has been less than expected; for instance, food insecurity was on the rise in some countries.[9] In this regard, WHO, in collaboration with 11 other UN agencies, has developed a "Global Action Plan for Healthy Lives and Well-being for All" to facilitate global movement toward health-related SDGs. The program aimed to assist countries in implementing national health-related strategies to reach SDG 3, "Ensure healthy lives and promote well-being for all ages."

BOX 1 Targets of the sustainable development goals 3

3.1 By 2030, reduce the global maternal mortality ratio to less than 70 per 100,000 live births.

3.2 By 2030, end preventable deaths of newborns and children under 5 years of age, with all countries aiming to reduce neonatal mortality to at least as low as 12 per 1000 live births and under-5 mortality to at least as low as 25 per 1000 live births.

3.3 By 2030, end the epidemics of AIDS, tuberculosis, malaria and neglected tropical diseases and combat hepatitis, water-borne diseases and other communicable diseases.

3.4 By 2030, reduce premature mortality from non-communicable diseases by one-third through prevention and treatment and promote mental health and well-being.

3.5 Strengthen the prevention and treatment of substance abuse, including narcotic drug abuse and harmful use of alcohol.

3.6 By 2020, halve the number of global deaths and injuries from road traffic accidents.

3.7 By 2030, ensure universal access to sexual and reproductive health-care services, including family planning, information and education, and the integration of reproductive health into national strategies and programs.

3.8 Achieve universal health coverage, including financial risk protection, access to quality essential health-care services and access to safe, effective, quality and affordable essential medicines and vaccines for all.

3.9 By 2030, substantially reduce the number of deaths and illnesses from hazardous chemicals and air, water and soil pollution and contamination.

3.A Strengthen the implementation of the WHO Framework Convention on Tobacco Control in all countries, as appropriate.

3.B Support the research and development of vaccines and medicines for the communicable and noncommunicable diseases that primarily affect developing countries, and provide access to affordable essential medicines and vaccines, in accordance with the Doha Declaration on the TRIPS Agreement and Public Health, which affirms the right of developing countries to use to the full the provisions in the Agreement on Trade Related Aspects of Intellectual Property Rights regarding flexibilities to protect public health, and, in particular, provide access to medicines for all.

3.C Substantially increase health financing and the recruitment, development, training and retention of the health workforce in developing countries, especially in least developed countries and small island developing States.

3.D Strengthen the capacity of all countries, in particular developing countries, for early warning, risk reduction and management of national and global health risks.

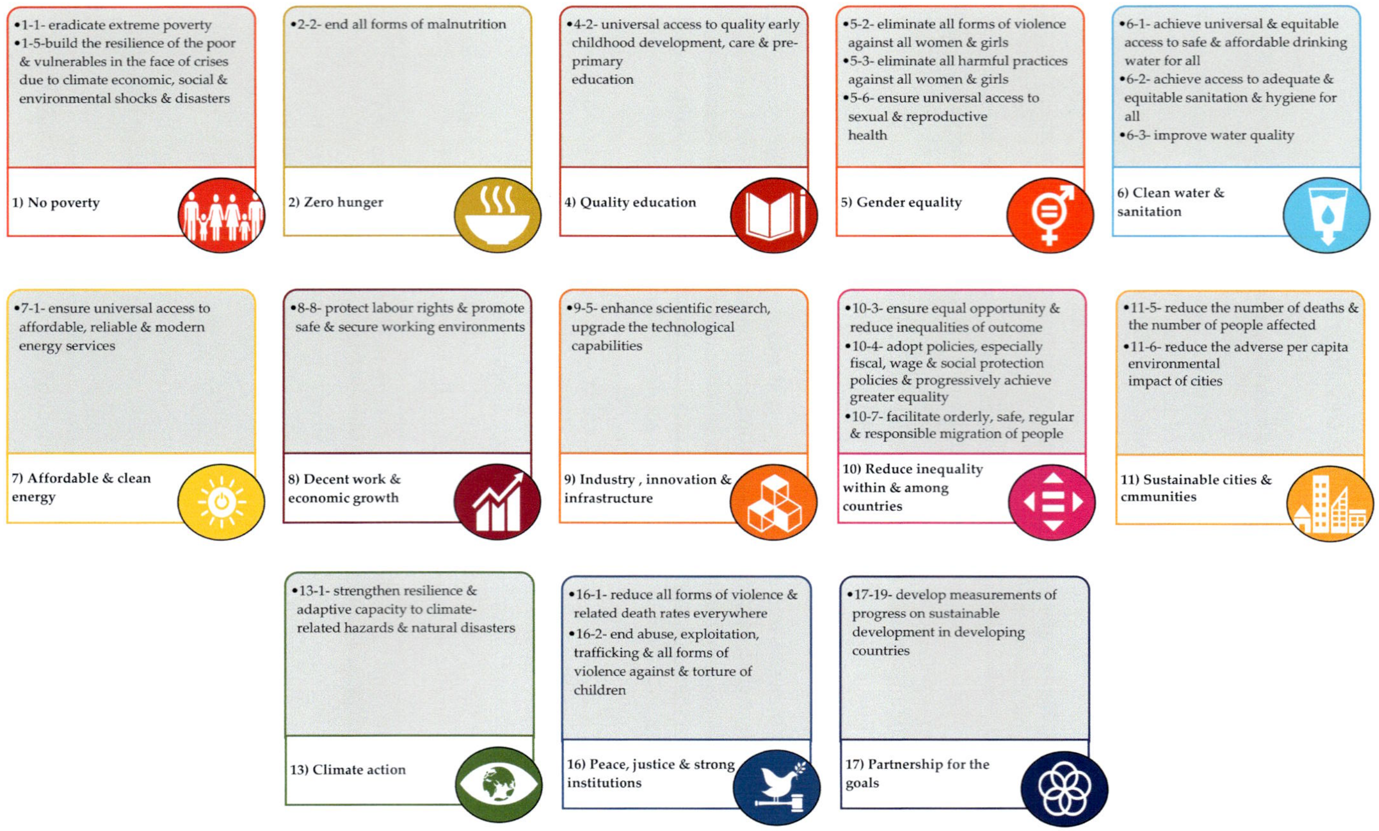

Fig. 1 Other sustainable development goals and targets that are indirectly related to health. *(Translated from "Takian A, Raoofi A. Covid-19 pandemic and global sustainable health development. In: Niknam MH, Azizi F, editors.* Health and covid-19 crisis in the Islamic Republic of Iran. *Tehran, IR Iran: Academy of Medical Sciences of the Islamic Republic of Iran; 2020. p. 62–97. With modification.)*

2. Global health in the COVID-19 pandemic

In December 2019, at a time when the world was only a third of the way to the sustainable development agenda, the COVID-19 crisis began, rather devastatingly, to shatter many achievements; posed challenges to global health and other social, economic, and developmental aspects; and created the most destabilizing conditions to global health in recent history.[1,10] According to the UN, the global community faced an unprecedented situation in the face of COVID-19, threatening many aspects of the population lives and leading to collapse in several global public health achievements of the past two decades, mostly related to the MDGs and SDGs.[10,11] This raises the question of whether SDGs are appropriate during the crisis and postcrisis eras.[12] The COVID-19 pandemic exacerbated poverty, hunger, shortage of clean water and sanitation, and inequitable access to education, which is also threatening the ongoing fragile progress toward sustainable societies.[1,13] The ever-increasing burden of COVID-19 has pushed the health systems of many countries to the brink of collapse,[3] particularly where the flow of resources to the basic health services has already been limited.[14] The provision of essential healthcare services, including cancer screening; prenatal care; family planning; diagnosis and treatment of infectious diseases other than COVID-19; and prevention, control, and treatment of NCDs, was disrupted or neglected.[3] According to the United Nations, during March and April 2020, child vaccination slowed in 70 countries to some degree and, in some cases, was completely suspended.[9]

Furthermore, safe delivery in health facilities in some African countries, e.g., Burundi, showed a reduction of up to 60% in 2020 compared to 2019.[15] Domestic violence against women and children also increased, and millions of unwanted pregnancies and unsafe abortions are expected due to women's lack of access to family planning services and safe delivery facilities.[9,15] Worse still, access to safe drinking water and basic sanitation has become difficult for billions of people due to COVID-19.[3]

Disruption in healthcare delivery and reduced access to food and nutrients resulting from the COVID-19 pandemic have posed serious risks to global health and well-being, i.e., increasing maternal, neonatal, and under-5 children mortality rates.[15,16] Further, the pandemic has caused decreased access to or delays in services related to early diagnosis, screening and treatment of NCDs, i.e., cancers and cardiovascular disease, which might have increased the morbidity and mortality of these diseases.[17] The same applies to infectious diseases. For instance, a 25% worldwide reduction in tuberculosis (TB) diagnosis within 3 months in 2020 may increase TB mortality rate by 13%. Similarly, 6 months' interruption in antiretroviral therapy for people living with HIV in sub-Saharan Africa in 2020 could lead to an additional 500,000 deaths from the disease.[15]

Many adverse consequences of COVID-19 result from years of limited investment in PHC and the provision of essential healthcare services, particularly in low- and middle-income countries (LMICs).[14] Such disruption will undermine decades of efforts to promote global health, the negative outcomes on population health may last for decades.[3] Nonetheless, many long-term negative impacts of COVID-19 on global health remain unclear.[10] These are testaments to the difficulty of achieving SDGs, especially SDG 3 in this difficult situation.[3,18] Under SDG 3, global leaders and the member states committed to nine targets and four tools. The main aim of this chapter is to discuss the intersections of COVID-19 and SDG 3 targets with a focus on two selected targets, including prevention and control of NCDs (SDG 3.4) and UHC (SDG 3.8).

3. COVID-19 and noncommunicable diseases

NCDs cover a range of long-term diseases resulting from biological, environmental, and behavioral risk factors. Tobacco use, air pollution, insufficient physical activity, unhealthy diet, overweight/obesity, and harmful alcohol use are the main risk factors of the five major NCDs, including cardiovascular diseases, cancers, diabetes, chronic respiratory diseases, and mental health disorders—all of which are preventable.[19] NCDs account for more than 70% of the world's causes of death each year (41 million out of 55 million in 2019), most of which are premature and occur before the age of 70.[20,21]

NCDs are major threats to achieving SDGs. These are neglected causes of poverty and obstacles to the economic development of countries.[21] The rapid rise of NCDs prevents poverty reduction (SDG 3.1), especially in low-income countries, associated with rising out-of-pocket (OOP) payments for health. Vulnerable people get involved with NCDs sooner than people of higher social status and die faster. This is due to the inconvenient truth that besides being more exposed to the risk factors, their access to health services is also more limited. The high cost of long-term treatment for NCDs, combined with the low income, plunges millions into poverty each year, which hinders countries' pathway toward sustainable development.[22]

In 2015 the UN General Assembly recognized NCDs as a major challenge to sustainable development and adopted SDG 3.4 to reduce premature mortality due to NCDs by one-third through prevention, treatment, and promoting mental health and well-being by 2030. Subsequently, WHO fostered its efforts to encourage member states to invest more in NCDs through enhancing their political support and technical capacity to reduce the burden of NCDs.[23,24] So-called best-buys, WHO introduced a list of evidence-based and cost-effective healthcare interventions, so the member states could choose them to deal with NCDs.[24,25] As a result of global efforts, steady progress was observed in NCD mortality rate before the COVID-19 pandemic.[21,26] The age-standardized NCD mortality rate dropped from 613.3 in 100,000 population in 2000 to 478.8 in 100,000 population in 2019 (Fig. 2). The UN SDG report 2021 has indicated that if the rate of decline has remained stable, Australia, New Zealand, Europe, and North America were on track to meet the SDG 3.4 target of a one-third reduction in premature NCD-related deaths.

COVID-19 exacerbated the complex challenges that people with NCDs face.[26] Due to the chronic nature of their disease, people with NCDs need to receive long-term essential healthcare or rehabilitation services. The rapid spread of COVID-19 has led to widespread healthcare disruptions and

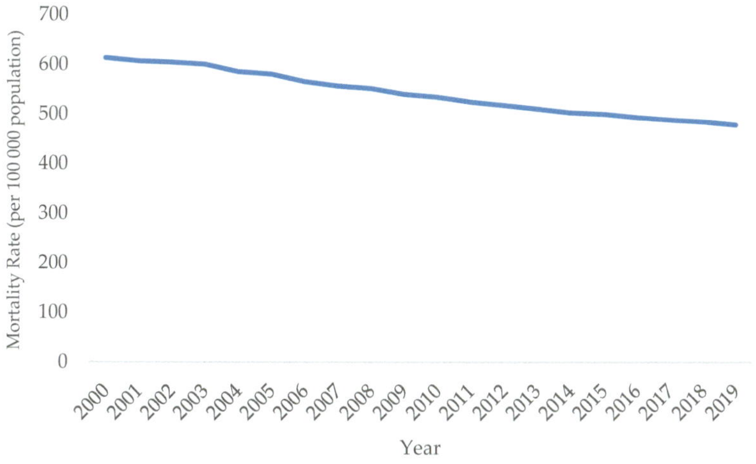

Fig. 2 Age-standardized NCD mortality rate (per 100,000 population). *(Reproduced from World Health Organization.* The Global Health Observatory. Noncommunicable diseases: mortality. *Geneva, Switzerland; 2021 [cited 2021 July 29]. https://www.who.int/data/gho/data/themes/topics/indicator-groups/indicator-group-details/GHO/gho-ghe-ncd-mortality-and-morbidity [Accessed 29 July 2021]. Copyright 2021.)*

long-term consequences for people with NCDs, especially those in need of regular or long-term care.[20] The available evidence suggests that people with NCDs are at higher risk for more serious types of COVID-19 and worse outcomes.[24] On the other hand, many people who die from COVID-19 are affected by NCDs,[24] which might represent a range of direct and indirect interactions between COVID-19 and NCDs. The direct effects are primarily because people with NCDs, if exposed, are more likely to get infected with COVID-19 more seriously with more severe consequences.[27] Therefore comorbidities may play an important role in increasing susceptibility to COVID-19, increasing the risk of severe disease progression, and exacerbating the COVID-19 crisis. This might be to the extent that if immediate action is not taken, a significant impact on health, economic, and social and political development would be unavoidable worldwide.[27,28] Indirect effects are due to not utilizing healthcare services by people with NCDs, which are far more difficult to measure than direct effects. This may lead to (a) delay in diagnosing acute conditions of the disease, (b) failure to perform routine screening, (c) prolonged waiting lists for diagnostic and therapeutic measures due to late referral,[27] and (d) increased morbidity and mortality in people with NCDs in the long run.[26]

A WHO rapid assessment based on a global survey of 163 countries during May 2020—the first global peak of the COVID-19 pandemic—showed partial or complete disruption of NCD services in 122 countries. Access to NCD outpatient services was completely restricted in 4% of the countries and partially restricted in 59% of countries, while inpatient services were open only for emergencies in 35% of countries. The survey also demonstrated that countries in the more severe phase of the COVID-19 pandemic had more disruptions in NCD services. Insufficient supplies of medicines, technologies, and diagnostics were the main reason for disrupting services to the people with NCDs in 20% of the countries under investigation.[29] The details of the NCD service disruptions are presented in Fig. 3. Another study reported the cancelation or postponement of 2.3 million cancer surgeries worldwide during the first COVID-19 lockdown.[30]

Worse still, some measures to combat COVID-19 may increase the risk factors for NCDs. For example, trade and movement restrictions within and between countries might reduce access to healthy medicines and foods and increase people's inclination toward unhealthy diets. It is also possible for people to be less physically active due to movement restrictions. In addition, staying home for long periods and the psychological consequences could increase the likelihood of turning to alcohol and tobacco. An increased

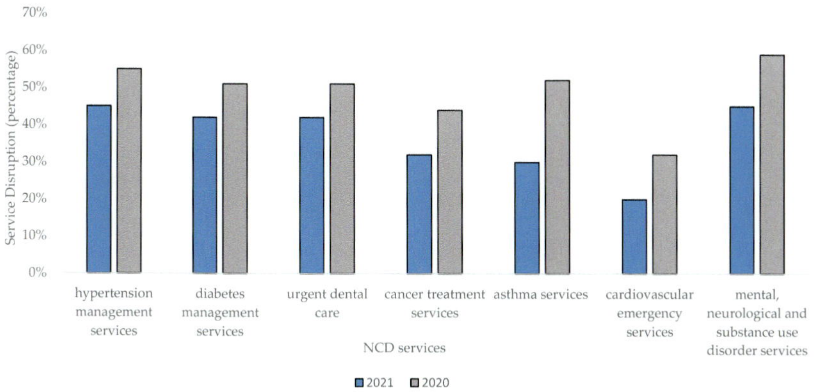

Fig. 3 NCD services disruption during 2020 and 2021. *(Adapted from World Health Organization.* Second round of the national pulse survey on continuity of essential health services during the COVID-19 pandemic. *Geneva: World Health Organization; 2021 April 23. License: CC BY-NC-SA 3.0 IGO.)*

prevalence of domestic violence has been reported following staying at home and unemployment. All of these might affect mental health and well-being and increase the overall risk of NCDs.[28] Therefore, while implementing the essential measures to mitigate, control, and minimize the serious consequences of COVID-19 is essential, strengthening the health system is also pivotal to maintain and resume the necessary measures for preventing and controlling NCDs and increasing patient access to health services.[28] The increasing evidence that demonstrates NCDs are associated with increased risk of death due to COVID-19 multiplies the need for a multidisciplinary approach with a focus on meaningful intersectoral collaboration and a robust surveillance and response system.[31,32] Simultaneously addressing both NCDs and COVID-19 contributes to the formation, maintenance, and promotion of long-term physical, mental, and social health and well-being, in addition to achieving SDG 3.4.[28] While the COVID-19 pandemic has caused devastating consequences for human civilization, it has also created a cosmopolitan moment to advocate more comprehensive policies and regulations to address NCDs and their related risk factors as the biggest threat not only to health and well-being but actually to the sustainable development of all societies. Therefore the need for effective and efficient programs to enhance primary and secondary prevention of NCDs as a national priority has become clear, now more than ever.[28] A summary of COVID-19 effects on NCD is illustrated in Fig. 4.

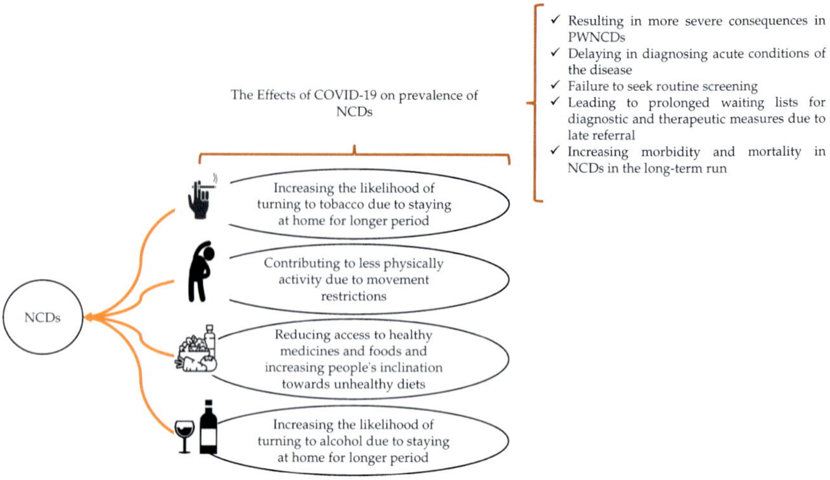

Fig. 4 COVID-19 impact on noncommunicable diseases.

4. Achieving universal health coverage in the COVID-19 era and after

UHC means that everyone should receive health services without any financial hardship whenever and wherever needed.[32] It emphasizes providing accessible, available, acceptable, affordable, and quality healthcare services for all citizens in an equitable manner to ensure no one is left behind.[33] The wide range of these services includes health promotion, prevention, treatment, rehabilitation, and palliative care.[32] Such comprehensive attention to all aspects of health was first reflected in the concept of PHC.[31] Accordingly, in the 2018 Astana Declaration, PHC was recognized as the most effective, efficient, and equitable health promotion and an essential tool for achieving UHC and health-related SDGs.[34] UHC will reduce health inequalities and lead to improved health indicators.[8,33] Effective protection of people from OOP payment and financial consequences of healthcare services will reduce the risk of being pushed into poverty. Otherwise, citizens may use their savings, sell their assets, or take out loans to pay for the services, which will ruin their future lives and those of their children.[32]

In line with SDGs, the WHO 13th General Program of Work (GPW) pursues three targets by 2023: one billion more people benefit from UHC, one billion more people better protected from health emergencies, and one billion more people enjoy better health and well-being.[32] Under SDG 3.8, endorsed by the GPW 13, UHC was placed on many countries' national agendas, leading to major global health achievements. The UHC Index of service coverage rose globally from about 45% in 2000 to 63.84% in 2015 and 65.74% in 2017 (Fig. 5).[35] Nevertheless, almost half of the world's population was not still fully covered by essential health services. Over 930 million people worldwide spent more than 10% of their household budget on health, while about 100 million people were driven into extreme poverty every year due to OOP payments for health.[8] This burden was more considerable in the LMICs, where a significant proportion of the population suffers from the lack of essential health services, insufficient financial protection, ineffective benefit packages, and a dysfunctional health insurance industry.[36] The essential need for UHC became more evident in the face of the COVID-19 pandemic when people with the highest need for appropriate, timely, and quality healthcare services suffered the most, paid extra from their pocket to receive care, and their access to required services declined

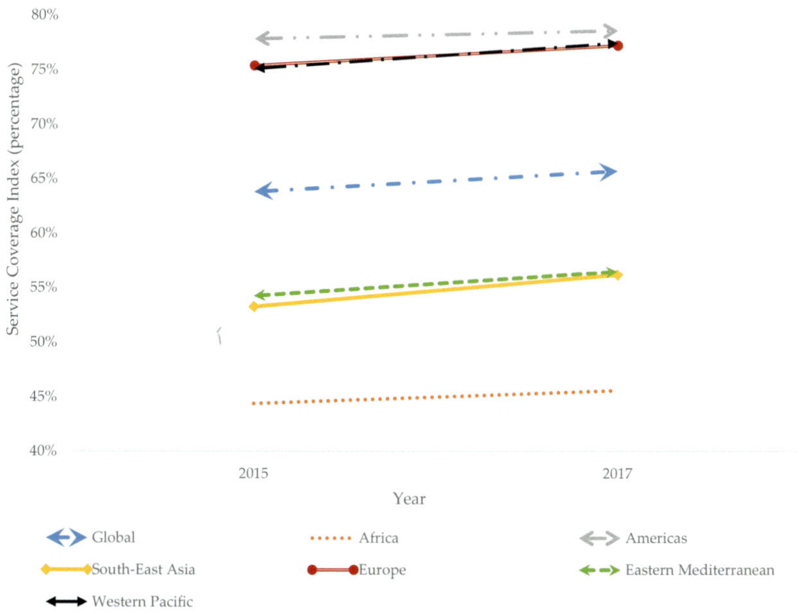

Fig. 5 UHC index of service coverage (SCI) trend. *(Reproduced from World Health Organization.* The global health observatory. UHC index of service coverage (SCI). *Geneva, Switzerland: World Health Organization; 2021 [updated 2019 September 6; cited 2021 July 30]. https://www.who.int/data/gho/data/indicators/indicator-details/GHO/uhc-index-of-service-coverage [Accessed 30 July 2021]. Copyright 2021.)*

dramatically, all of which led to slowing down the achievement of the SDGs and GPW 13 triple targets.

While many countries struggled to achieve UHC, the COVID-19 crisis continued to put tremendous pressure on health systems worldwide.[37] Access to essential healthcare services is the pillar of the health systems in the fight against COVID-19.[18] To minimize morbidity and mortality, maintaining accessibility, provision, and utilization of essential healthcare services during COVID-19 have been among major concerns for many member states and international organizations.[15,38] COVID-19 pandemic has caused a considerable decline in some major public health achievements of recent decades in a short period.[38] Disruption of healthcare services has slowed down people's healthcare-seeking behavior such as screening, vaccination, and even emergency medical care.[1] The ongoing decline and even collapse in essential healthcare services, from health promotion to palliative care, may seriously affect population health outcomes, particularly among the most vulnerable, e.g., women, children, the elderly, refugees, and minorities,[38,39] both in terms of supply and demand sides. People may avoid visiting healthcare facilities on the demand side due to fears of getting infected with COVID-19. Some people might not afford healthcare services because of losing their jobs or reduced income, which has been inevitable following COVID-19 restrictions. On the supply side, the availability of medical resources might have declined because most resources and equipment have been allocated to COVID-19 patients. Worse still, transportations and import of medicines and medical supplies have been disrupted due to borders' closure, reduced staff, declined production capacity, and political reasons, e.g., sanctions.[40] Finally, some mitigation strategies against COVID-19, i.e., quarantine and lockdown, can also hinder access to healthcare services[4,38]; hence they may lead to increased morbidity and mortality due to emerging communicable and noncommunicable diseases.[1] Indeed, an increasing trend in COVID-19 mortality and morbidity has been observed among people with underlying conditions, e.g., NCDs and immunodeficiency.[24]

Moreover, rising poverty and unemployment due to COVID-19 have increased OOP for health.[26] In both rounds of the WHO survey in 2020 and 2021, about 90% of the respondent countries reported substantial disruptions in access to healthcare services.[41] Nonetheless, many countries have developed policies, strategies, plans, and mechanisms to support essential healthcare services and reduce the negative impact of COVID-19.[26,38] A WHO survey revealed that almost 66% of responding countries have defined the set of essential healthcare services to be continued during the pandemic.

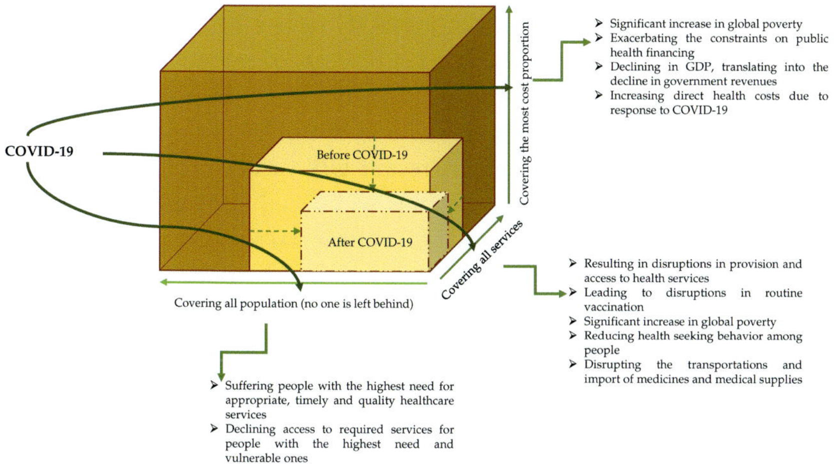

Fig. 6 COVID-19 impact on three dimensions of universal health coverage.

Approximately 55% of countries have allocated additional budgets to secure the continuity of essential healthcare services.[38] A summary of COVID-19 effects on UHC is illustrated in Fig. 6.

COVID-19 highlights the importance of UHC and intersectoral collaboration in preparing for health emergencies.[26] UHC will strengthen the health system with enough resilience to strike a meaningful and efficient balance between essential healthcare services and fighting against emergencies like COVID-19.[15,38] A resilient health system can respond to crises promptly through on-time detection and prevention while sustaining peace and protecting the economy.[42] The pandemic showed that health system resilience is a fundamental and cost-effective feature for overcoming complex health system challenges, as those countries that achieved UHC performed better against COVID-19.[42] Indeed, the COVID-19 crisis reindorsed that to achieve sustainable health development, UHC is needed, now more than ever.[43]

Viruses do not discriminate, meaning that although people of all races, ethnicities, genders, and nationalities are at the risk of being exposed to infection, the risk is not distributed equally among all humans, countries, and territories. Vulnerable population, including people with underlying diseases, the elderly, prisoners, migrants, refugees, and people with lower socioeconomic status, have been disproportionately suffering the most from COVID-19 due to their special health conditions; poor living conditions; and lack of access to high-quality public health services,[15,18,26] particularly within the LMICs.[1] According to the SDG report 2021, 76.4% of deaths from COVID-19 occur in people over 65 years of age, while only 14% of confirmed cases of COVID-19 occur in this age group.[26] Furthermore, the crises have exacerbated the previously disturbed living conditions and health of refugees and migrants. A recent UN survey revealed that about 5% of responded refugees and migrants who faced COVID-19 symptoms did not seek healthcare due to insufficient financial resources, fear of deportation, lack of access to healthcare, or depriving the right to receive these services.[26] These indicate the vulnerability of these groups to COVID-19 and its consequences and likely future pandemics.

In addition, universal coverage for affordable, safe, and effective COVID-19 vaccines, particularly for the most prioritized population, such as frontline health workers and its diagnostic and therapeutic methods, is crucial to overcoming the pandemic. To fulfill this, WHO has launched "The Access to COVID-19 Tools Accelerator (ACT-Accelerator)," consisting of four pillars, including diagnostics, treatment, vaccines (COVAX facility), and health system strengthening.[15,44] Nevertheless, the COVID-19 vaccine has not been distributed equitably. As of September 1, 2021, a total of 5.44 billion doses of the COVID-19 vaccine have been administered worldwide. Also, 3.15 billion people have received at least one dose of the COVID-19 vaccine, of which 63.5% were in high-income countries and 1.8% in low-income countries. Besides, 2.15 billion people globally were fully vaccinated against COVID-19, of which 53.3% are in high-income countries and only 0.6% in low-income countries (Fig. 7).

The COVID-19 crisis has exposed deep disparities in the societies and exacerbated the existing inequalities within and among countries,[1] which will endanger achieving UHC in many settings in the longer run.

5. COVID-19 and other SDG 3's targets

Undoubtedly, the COVID-19 pandemic has also severely affected other SDG 3's targets, which witnessed significant global improvements before the crisis.[45,46] For instance, before COVID-19, maternal and child mortality rate reduced, global HIV incidence among adults aged 15 to 49 declined, coverage of essential vaccination among children increased, the under-5 mortality rate fell from 76 death per 1000 live births in 2000 to 38 deaths per 1000 live births in 2019, the neonatal mortality rate (death in the first 28 days of life) approximately halved, falling from 30 death per

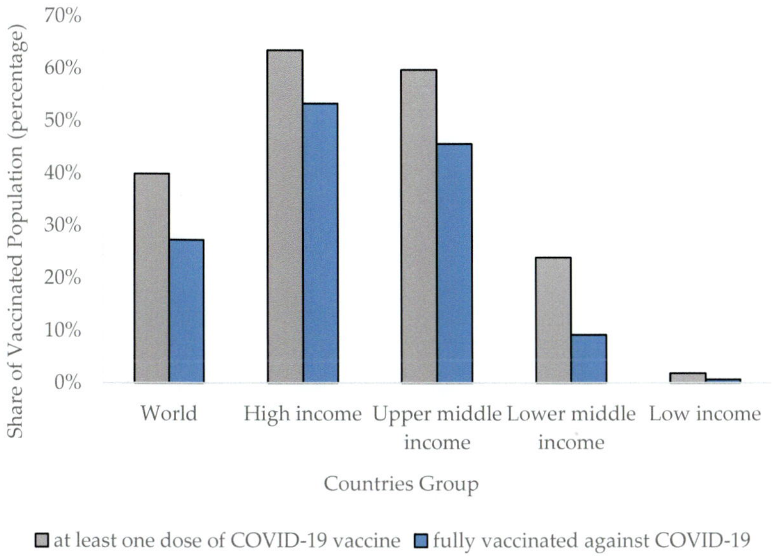

Fig. 7 Share of people received COVID-19 vaccine, as of September 1, 2021. *(Adapted from* Our world in data. Statistics and research, coronavirus (COVID-19) Vaccinations. *Oxford, UK: University of Oxford; 2021. https://ourworldindata.org/covid-vaccinations [Accessed 30 July 2021].)*

1000 live births in 2000 to 17 death per 1000 live births in 2019 (Fig. 8). COVID-19 and its imposing containment measures in most countries disrupted prenatal care services and supply of and access to reproductive health and family services.[47,48] Moreover, shortages in healthcare workers in most countries, along with a sudden increase in the number of COVID-19 patients, resulted in redeploying maternity staff to COVID-19 designated facilities, which inevitably reduced attention to maternal and child requirements.[47]

Although many countries, particularly the LMICs, suffered the most from the consequences of the recent pandemic, some high-income countries have endeavored to minimize the interruption in providing services for vulnerable groups via restructuring the service delivery system and tracking their health status remotely.[47] Nevertheless, 228,000 additional child deaths and nearly 11,000 further maternal deaths were only reported in south Asia in 2020, partially due to the allocation of most healthcare resources to combat the disruptive effects of the COVID-19 pandemic.[26] Patients with HIV/AIDS also experienced considerable disruptions in receiving preventive and treatment services, i.e., diagnostic tests and referral, during the crisis.[45] Similarly, the COVID-19 pandemic has disrupted

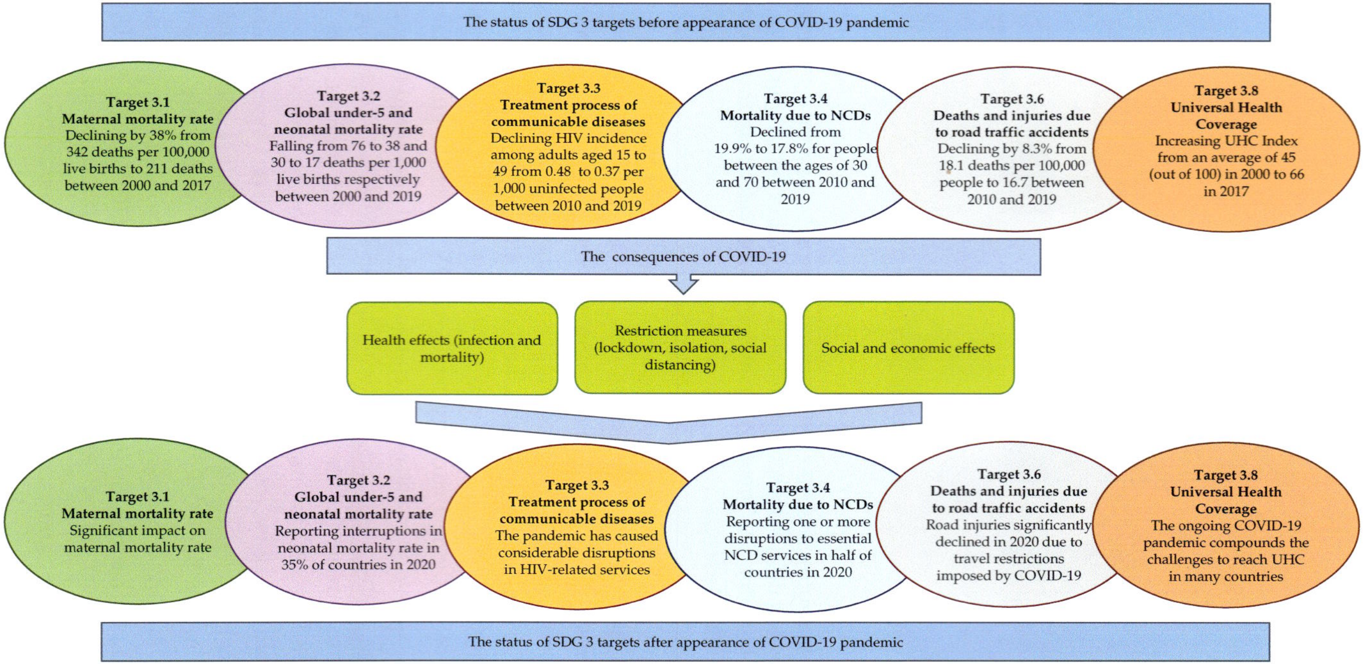

Fig. 8 The comparison of SDG 3's targets before and after COVID-19. *(This is an adaptation of an original work by United Nations.* The sustainable development goals report *2021. New York, USA: United Nations Publications; 2021.)*

finding new tuberculosis cases, as well as their follow-up and timely treatment.[49] Substance users and addicted persons are another most vulnerable group whose conditions worsened compared to other vulnerable groups during the COVID-19 pandemic. A growing body of evidence indicates that containment measurements might lead to intensifying drug abuse, making substance users more vulnerable to the risk associated with coronavirus.[50] Likewise, ample evidence illustrates many consequences on mental health and psychological damages, e.g., emotional distress, depression, stress, mood swings, irritability, insomnia, posttraumatic stress disorder, and anxiety, as a result of restriction measures, i.e., containment and lockdown uncertainty and unpredictability of the pandemic.[51] The recent survey by WHO reports that the unprecedented increase in mental illness and its devastating effects might have led to a significant increase in the global suicide death rate in 2019, due to which many member states decided to include mental health support into their COVID-19 plans in 2021.[26]

In summary, lack of resilience and unpreparedness in many health systems around the world has disrupted most healthcare services, e.g., promotion, prevention, treatment, and rehabilitation, particularly among the most vulnerable groups, i.e., women, children, people with NCDs, addicts, and people living with HIV/AIDS and tuberculosis[46] (Fig. 9).

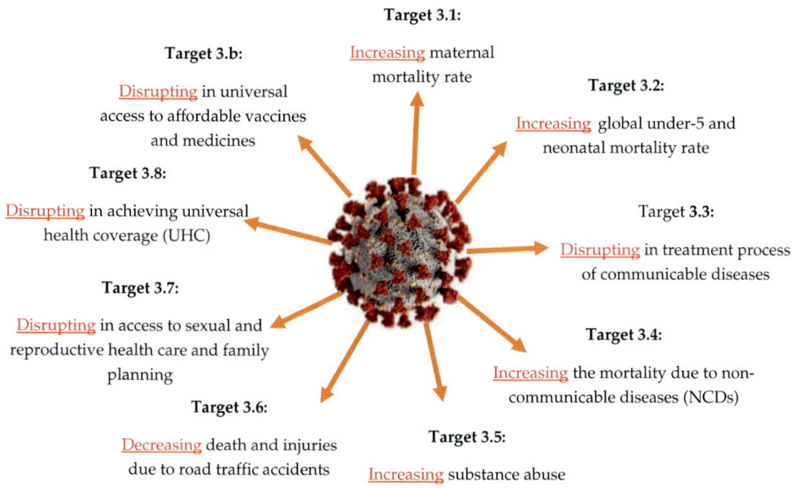

Fig. 9 The effects of COVID-19 on the targets of SDG 3.

6. Discussion

COVID-19 pandemic is still an unfolding story. Despite ever-growing evidence, the extent of the unknown about COVID-19 is still far more than what is known. The entire sustainable development agenda is at stake; hence timely and appropriate reforms in global governance are necessary to revert the derailed SDGs on track.[52]

The COVID-19 pandemic has set back global efforts to achieve SDGs. The crisis has reversed most progress made in ending hunger, eradicating poverty, and reducing inequality globally. This has caused the Human Development Index to lag behind for the first time since 1990.[15] It also threatens years of progress in improving global health. According to the UN SDG report 2021, evidence from countries that provide reliable and timely statistics shows that the COVID-19 pandemic has severely reduced life expectancy.[26] Many women have been denied access to family planning and reproductive health services during the COVID-19, which is predicted to lead to an additional 2.7 million unsafe abortions.[53] The UN Children's Emergency Fund has warned that almost 116 million infants and mothers will receive inadequate services under the COVID-19 pandemic.[54] A key informant survey conducted by WHO among the Ministry of Health's officials from 105 countries in 2020 revealed that even strong health systems could be rapidly affected by the COVID-19 outbreak.[38] In the shadow of the numerous catastrophic consequences of COVID-19 for the lives and health of millions worldwide,[1] strengthening strategic adaptations is necessary.[38]

COVID-19 demonstrates the fact that the health systems of many countries are not fully prepared to protect the health of their populations and highlights the importance of preparing for potential similar health crises in the future through strengthening national health systems.[55] It also reaffirmed that a strong and resilient health system based on PHC is the basis for an effective response to the crises and a reliable platform for progress toward health safety and UHC.[55] In fact, only by achieving UHC would it be possible to efficiently protect societies from the burning risks of potential future crises.[15] In such a situation, two basic components, including meaningful intersectoral collaboration as well as robust and accurate surveillance and response system, are crucial in understanding and managing the outbreak impact and adopting better decisions.[56] COVID-19 has proven that countries with the most efficient and effective outcomes in this fight have made extensive and precise use of these two basic components. We strongly recommend incorporating these two dimensions into the WHO's six building blocks along their pathway toward health system strengthening.[56]

Despite many catastrophes it has caused, the COVID-19 pandemic has also underscored the importance of SDG 3 for global public health, i.e., strong and resilient health systems, emergency preparedness, and a greater urgency to achieve UHC.[15] It has also shown that achieving sustainable development requires reforming global commitments and putting health at the heart of the agenda.[10,42] Health is both the result and the stimulus of socioeconomic progress; it is also the indicator of sustainable societies.[15] Even in times of recession, more investment in health leads to economic development due to protecting population lives.[57] Also, investing in health system functions, sustainable financing, and removing financial barriers to healthcare services accessibility are fundamental in laying the foundations for a better future, maintaining and promoting population health and ensuring a better response to potential future crises.[15,57]

The COVID-19 pandemic has also highlighted the fundamental role of UHC as the essential pillar of any health system to lead communities toward sustainable health development (SHD). We endorse the "Kampala Declaration on COVID-19 Vaccine Equity" that emphasizes the need to extend UHC to universal health preparedness (UHP), as well as universal health solidarity.[58] The COVID-19 crisis has shown that UHC is not enough without meaningful consideration of both UHP and the causes of causes, namely, Social Determinants of Health. This would not be achieved without a strong surveillance and response system as well as an effective intersectoral collaboration, in line with the whole-of-government and whole-of-society approach.[56]

Outbreak preparedness and response are among the health commodities that require macro-investments.[59] More than ever, the global community needs to unite to invest in public health goods as the basis for achieving UHC and health security. In addition to global unity, national strategic planning and countries' preparedness to respond to probable future crises are also critical.[60] Health system strengthening and sustainable efforts to achieve UHC, which guarantees equitable access to quality health services without financial risk for all people and effectively protects communities from future health crises, should be pushed on the country's national agenda.[15]

Although COVID-19 has shaken the move toward SDGs, it highlights the need for change to make them more attainable, even stronger than ever and makes a flip for more decisive and urgent progress toward it. Achieving UHC is crucial for preparing in the fight against any future crisis and move along the pathway toward SHD.[1,12]

7. Conclusion

Health is increasingly considered a fundamental human right and the backbone of sustainable societies and economies. Despite a great threat to decades of progress in health promotion, COVID-19 might become an opportunity to demonstrate the determination of nations to provide health services and achieve equitable and sustainable development. Moreover, fundamental reforms in governments' public policies and prioritizing health have become increasingly important. COVID-19 was a warning to awaken the world to the irreparable and difficult consequences of neglecting health. The COVID-19 crisis, exposing many aspects of global health threats that were overlooked, including poor health systems, lack of social support, and structural inequalities, showed that health as the engine of development must be at the forefront of policy-making. There is no longer any doubt that there is a close link between socioeconomic resilience and public health resilience. In other words, to achieve peace, prosperity, and sustainable development, it is essential that global health be clearly prioritized in all policies. To maintain sustainable social, economic, health, and well-being relations, it is crucial that all sectors of government, development partners, and civil societies show their solidarity and cooperation in combating the COVID-19 pandemic, existing crises such as NCDs and climate change, and any other potential future crises using the two approaches of the whole-of-government and the whole-of-society. Future pandemics are likely to occur, threatening societies and their sustainability. The fragility and unpreparedness of the health systems in many countries during COVID-19 demonstrated the fundamental role of UHP-oriented UHC to achieve SHD in all societies. We are all in this together. Indeed, we need to enhance global solidarity, unity, and social participation for a global mandate to reach UHC, now more than ever.

References

1. Min Y, Perucci F. *UN/DESA policy brief #81: impact of COVID-19 on SDG progress: a statistical perspective*; 2020 https://www.un.org/development/desa/dpad/publication/un-desa-policy-brief-81-impact-of-covid-19-on-sdg-progress-a-statistical-perspective/. [Accessed 8 January 2021].

2. Odey GO, Alawad AGA, Atieno OS, et al. COVID-19 pandemic: impacts on the achievements of sustainable development goals in Africa. *Pan Afr Med J* 2021;**38**:251.
3. The Lancet Public Health. Will the COVID-19 pandemic threaten the SDGs? *Lancet Public Health* 2020;**5**(9):e460.
4. Takian A, Raoofi A. Covid-19 pandemic and global sustainable health development. In: Niknam MH, Azizi F, editors. *Health and covid-19 crisis in the Islamic Republic of Iran*. Tehran, IR Iran: Academy of Medical Sciences of the Islamic Republic of Iran; 2020. p. 62–97.
5. World Health Organization. *Global Health Observatory (GHO) data. International Health Regulations (2005) monitoring framework*; 2020 https://www.who.int/gho/ihr/en/. [Accessed 16 September 2020].
6. World Health Organization. *Global action plan for the prevention and control of non-communicable diseases 2013–2020*. Geneva, Switzerland: World Health Organization; 2013.
7. United Nations. *The sustainable development goals report 2019*. New York, USA: United Nations Publications; 2019.
8. World Health Organization. *Universal health coverage*; 2021 https://www.who.int/health-topics/universal-health-coverage#tab=tab_3. [Accessed 4 July 2021].
9. United Nations. *The sustainable development goals report 2020*. New York, USA: United Nations Publications; 2020.
10. Holst J. The world expects effective global health interventions: can global health deliver? *Glob Public Health* 2020;**15**(9):1396–403.
11. Mejia R, Hotez P, Bottazzi ME. Global COVID-19 efforts as the platform to achieving the sustainable development goals. *Curr Trop Med Rep* 2020;1–5.
12. Time to revise the Sustainable Development Goals. *Nature* 2020;**583**(7816):331–2.
13. Heggen K, Sandset TJ, Engebretsen E. COVID-19 and sustainable development goals. *Bull World Health Organ* 2020;**98**(10):646.
14. World Health Organization. *Universal health coverage day 2020*; 2020 https://www.who.int/campaigns/universal-health-coverage-day-2020. [Accessed 29 July 2020].
15. United Nations Sustainable Development Group. *Policy brief: COVID-19 and universal health coverage*; 2020 https://unsdg.un.org/resources/policy-brief-covid-19-and-universal-health-coverage. [Accessed 1 January 2021].
16. Mousazadeh M, Naghdali Z, Rahimian N, Hashemi M, Paital B, Al-Qodah Z, et al. Management of environmental health to prevent an outbreak of COVID-19: a review. In: *Environmental and health management of novel coronavirus disease*; 2021. p. 235–67.
17. Mafham MM, Spata E, Goldacre R, et al. COVID-19 pandemic and admission rates for and management of acute coronary syndromes in England. *Lancet* 2020;**396**(10248):381–9.
18. Nhamo G, Chikodzi D, Kunene HP, Mashula N. COVID-19 vaccines and treatments nationalism: challenges for low-income countries and the attainment of the SDGs. *Glob Public Health* 2021;**16**(3):319–39.
19. Budreviciute A, Damiati S, Sabir DK, et al. Management and prevention strategies for non-communicable diseases (NCDs) and their risk factors. *Front Public Health* 2020;**8**:574111.
20. Pecout C, Pain E, Chekroun M, et al. Impact of the COVID-19 pandemic on patients affected by non-communicable diseases in Europe and in the USA. *Int J Environ Res Public Health* 2021;**18**(13):6697.
21. World Health Organization. *The global health observatory. Noncommunicable diseases*; 2021 https://www.who.int/data/gho/data/themes/noncommunicable-diseases. [Accessed 23 July 2021].
22. World Health Organization. *Noncommunicable diseases*; 2021 https://www.who.int/news-room/fact-sheets/detail/noncommunicable-diseases. [Accessed 23 July 2021].

23. Nugent R, Bertram MY, Jan S, et al. Investing in non-communicable disease prevention and management to advance the sustainable development goals. *Lancet* 2018;**391**(10134):2029–35.
24. Takian A, Bakhtiari A, Ostovar A. Universal health coverage for strengthening prevention and control of noncommunicable diseases in COVID-19 era. *Med J Islam Repub Iran* 2020;**34**(1):1050–3.
25. Bakhtiari A, Takian A, Majdzadeh R, Haghdoost AA. Assessment and prioritization of the WHO "best buys" and other recommended interventions for the prevention and control of non-communicable diseases in Iran. *BMC Public Health* 2020;**20**(1):333.
26. United Nations. *The sustainable development goals report 2021*. New York, USA: United Nations Publications; 2021.
27. Nikoloski Z, Alqunaibet AM, Alfawaz RA, et al. Covid-19 and non-communicable diseases: evidence from a systematic literature review. *BMC Public Health* 2021;**21**(1):1068.
28. Tin STW, Vivili P, Na'ati E, Bertrand S, Kubuabola I. Insights in public health: COVID-19 special column: the crisis of non-communicable diseases in the Pacific and the coronavirus disease 2019 pandemic. *Hawaii J Health Soc Welf* 2020;**79**(5):147–8.
29. World Health Organization. *The impact of the COVID-19 pandemic on noncommunicable disease resources and services: results of a rapid assessment*. vol. 2021. Geneva, Switzerland: World Health Organization; 2020.
30. COVIDSurg Collaborative. Elective surgery cancellations due to the COVID-19 pandemic: global predictive modelling to inform surgical recovery plans. *Br J Surg* 2020;**107**(11):1440–9.
31. Tumusiime P, Karamagi H, Titi-Ofei R, et al. Building health system resilience in the context of primary health care revitalization for attainment of UHC: proceedings from the fifth Health Sector Directors' policy and planning meeting for the WHO African region. *BMC Proc* 2020;**14**(Suppl. 19):16.
32. World Health Organization. *Universal health coverage (UHC)*; 2021 https://www.who.int/en/news-room/fact-sheets/detail/universal-health-coverage-(uhc). [Accessed 10 July 2021].
33. Hussain R, Arif S. Universal health coverage and COVID-19: recent developments and implications. *J Pharm Policy Pract* 2021;**14**(1):23.
34. World Health Organization. *Declaration on primary health care*; 2018 https://www.who.int/teams/primary-health-care/conference/declaration. [Accessed 15 July 2021].
35. World Health Organization. *The global health observatory. UHC index of service coverage (SCI)*; 2021 https://www.who.int/data/gho/data/indicators/indicator-details/GHO/uhc-index-of-service-coverage. [Accessed 30 July 2021].
36. World Health Organization. *Tracking universal health coverage: first global monitoring report*. World Health Organization; 2015.
37. Akinleye FE, Akinbolaji GR, Olasupo JO. Towards universal health coverage: lessons learnt from the COVID-19 pandemic in Africa. *Pan Afr Med J* 2020;**35**(Suppl. 2):128.
38. World Health Organization. *Pulse survey on continuity of essential health services during the COVID-19 pandemic*. Geneva: World Health Organization; 2020.
39. Takian A, Haghighi H, Raoofi A. Challenges, opportunities and future perspective associated with COVID-19 pandemic. In: Dehghani MH, Karri RR, Roy S, editors. *Environmental and health management of novel coronavirus disease (COVID-19)*. Philadelphia, USA: Elsevier; 2021. p. 443–78.
40. Takian A, Raoofi A, Kazempour-Ardebili S. COVID-19 battle during the toughest sanctions against Iran. *Lancet* 2020;**395**(10229):1035–6.

41. World Health Organization. *COVID-19 continues to disrupt essential health services in 90% of countries*; 2021 https://www.who.int/news/item/23-04-2021-covid-19-continues-to-disrupt-essential-health-services-in-90-of-countries. [Accessed 30 July 2021].
42. Takian A, Aarabi M, Haghighi H. The role of universal health coverage in overcoming the covid-19 pandemic. *BMJ Opin* 2020. https://blogs.bmj.com/bmj/2020/04/20/the-role-of-universal-health-coverage-in-overcoming-the-covid-19-pandemic/. [Accessed 20 April 2020].
43. Armocida B, Formenti B, Palestra F, Ussai S, Missoni E. COVID-19: universal health coverage now more than ever. *J Glob Health* 2020;**10**(1):010350.
44. World Health Organization. *What is the ACT accelerator?* ; 2020 https://www.who.int/initiatives/act-accelerator/about. [Accessed 1 January 2021].
45. Khetrapal S, Bhatia R. Impact of COVID-19 pandemic on health system & sustainable development goal 3. *Indian J Med Res* 2020;**151**(5):395–9.
46. Seshaiyer P, McNeely CL. Challenges and opportunities from COVID-19 for global sustainable development. *World Med Health Policy* 2020;**12**(4):443–53.
47. Chmielewska B, Barratt I, Townsend R, et al. Effects of the COVID-19 pandemic on maternal and perinatal outcomes: a systematic review and meta-analysis. *Lancet Glob Health* 2021;**9**(6):e759–72.
48. Mendez-Dominguez N, Santos-Zaldivar K, Gomez-Carro S, Datta-Banik S, Carrillo G. Maternal mortality during the COVID-19 pandemic in Mexico: a preliminary analysis during the first year. *BMC Public Health* 2021;**21**(1):1297.
49. The Global Fund to Fight AIDS TaM. *The impact of COVID-19 on HIV, TB and malaria services and systems for health: a snapshot from 502 health facilities across Africa and Asia.* Geneva, Switzerland: Global Health Campus; April 13, 2021.
50. Ornell F, Moura HF, Scherer JN, Pechansky F, Kessler FHP, von Diemen L. The COVID-19 pandemic and its impact on substance use: implications for prevention and treatment. *Psychiatry Res* 2020;**289**:113096.
51. Knolle F, Ronan L, Murray GK. The impact of the COVID-19 pandemic on mental health in the general population: a comparison between Germany and the UK. *BMC Psychol* 2021;**9**(1):60.
52. Fernandez-Portillo LA, Sianes A, Santos-Carrillo F. How will COVID-19 impact on the governance of Global Health in the 2030 agenda framework? The opinion of experts. *Healthcare (Basel)* 2020;**8**(4):356.
53. Wenham C, Smith J, Davies SE, et al. Women are most affected by pandemics—lessons from past outbreaks. *Nature* 2020;**583**(7815):194–8.
54. *Millions of pregnant mothers and babies born during COVID-19 pandemic threatened by strained health systems and disruptions in services.* New York, USA: UNICEF; May 7, 2020 [Press release] https://www.unicef.org/afghanistan/press-releases/millions-pregnant-mothers-and-babies-born-during-covid-19-pandemic-threatened.
55. Haldane V, De Foo C, Abdalla SM, et al. Health systems resilience in managing the COVID-19 pandemic: lessons from 28 countries. *Nat Med* 2021;**27**(6):964–80.
56. Takian A, Raoofi A. *We must redesign the WHO's building blocks to create more resilient health systems for the future.* BMJ; 2021. https://blogs.bmj.com/bmj/2021/04/14/we-must-redesign-the-whos-building-blocks-to-create-more-resilient-health-systems-for-the-future/. [Accessed 10 June 2021].
57. UHC2030. *International Health Partnership. Living with COVID-19: time to get our act together on health emergencies and UHC*; 2020 https://www.uhc2030.org/fileadmin/uploads/uhc2030/Documents/Key_Issues/Health_emergencies_and_UHC/UHC2030_discussion_paper_on_health_emergencies_and_UHC_-_May_2020.pdf. [Accessed 4 January 2021].
58. World Health Summit. *Kampala declaration on COVID-19 vaccine equity*; 2021 https://d1wjxwc5zmlmv4.cloudfront.net/fileadmin/user_upload/5_Regional_Meetings/

2021_Kampala/Kampala_Declaration_on_COVID-19_Vaccine_Equity_June_2021.pdf. [Accessed 10 July 2021].
59. Guterres A. *Scale up investment in Universal Health Coverage and in stronger health systems*; 2020 https://www.un.org/en/coronavirus/scale-investment-universal-health-coverage-and-stronger-health-systems. [Accessed 6 January 2021].
60. Schwartz J, Yen M-Y. Toward a collaborative model of pandemic preparedness and response: Taiwan's changing approach to pandemics. *J Microbiol Immunol Infect* 2017;**50**(2):125–32.

CHAPTER TEN

Effect of the COVID-19 pandemic on psychological aspects

Jaber S. Alqahtani[a], Ahmad S. Almamary[b,c], Saeed M. Alghamdi[b,d], Saleh Komies[e], Malik Althobiani[f], Abdulelah M. Aldhahir[g], and Abdallah Y. Naser[h]

[a]Department of Respiratory Care, Prince Sultan Military College of Health Sciences, Dammam, Saudi Arabia
[b]National Heart and Lung Institute, Imperial College London, London, United Kingdom
[c]Respiratory Therapy Department, King Saud Bin Abdulaziz University for Health Sciences, Ahsa, Saudi Arabia
[d]Faculty of Applied Medical Sciences, Umm Al-Qura University, Makkah, Saudi Arabia
[e]Faculty of Engineering, Department of Electrical and Electronic Engineering, Imperial College London, London, United Kingdom
[f]Department of Respiratory Therapy, King Abdulaziz University, Jeddah, Saudi Arabia
[g]Respiratory Care Department, Faculty of Applied Medical Sciences, Jazan University, Jazan, Saudi Arabia
[h]Department of Applied Pharmaceutical Sciences and Clinical Pharmacy, Faculty of Pharmacy, Isra University, Amman, Jordan

Chapter highlights

- The COVID-19 pandemic has emerged as a serious challenge to public health, medical staff, economic stability, and the functioning of governments.
- The COVID-19 pandemic has increased social solidarity, closeness, and a sense of support among the public, but more research is needed. That said, widespread psychological distress including stress, anxiety, and depression has been reported.
- Despite being trained to be resilient and emotionally reticent, medical staff regularly suffer heavily from psychological and emotional distress and frustration, yet during the COVID-19 pandemic, these feelings are aggravated.
- Depression, anxiety, obsession, insomnia, and posttraumatic stress disorder with higher risks of infection and mortality have been reported among medical care staff.
- Government guidelines and measures imposed during the COVID-19 pandemic have led to an economic crisis and recession, with jobs being lost or threatened across economic sectors.
- Unemployment has brought more stress, anxiety, fear, public dissatisfaction, and a higher mortality rate to the older group.
- The closure of schools, universities, and learning spaces during the COVID-19 pandemic has negatively affected educators, learners, and parents and caused the largest disruption in education systems in history, despite the introduction of distance learning.
- Alexithymia, inadequate supplies, and inadequate information are risk factors predisposing individuals to mental health and psychological disorders during the COVID-19 pandemic.

COVID-19 and the Sustainable Development Goals
https://doi.org/10.1016/B978-0-323-91307-2.00007-9

- Protective factors such as resilience, social support, and taking advantage of preventative strategies provided by healthcare organizations have been observed to maintain psychological stability for the public and medical staff, but more research is needed.

1. Introduction

In December 2019, a disease emerged from Wuhan, China, increasing the number of death cases caused by viral infection. When it was first discovered in 2019, the disease called COVID-19 was caused by severe respiratory syndrome coronavirus 2 (SARS-CoV-2).[1,2] COVID-19 started to spread rapidly to all continents in months. This deadly virus causes serious healthcare crises that affect all aspects of human life whether social, psychological, or clinical.[3–10]

Over 113 countries had been affected by COVID-19 when the World Health Organization (WHO) declared the quick and deadly virus a pandemic in March 2020.[11] The virus caused a considerable burden on the healthcare system, where hospitals suffered a shortage of critical care facilities and staff due to the vast number of cases admitted to hospitals daily.[12] Moreover, COVID-19 has vastly affected the world economy, education, and social life.[8,13,14]

With the rapid spread of COVID-19, countries took unprecedented protective measures to prevent and control the intensity of the spread. Governments banned human inbound and outbound travel, and countries took more serious measures like national lockdowns and 24-h curfews. Using a face mask and physical distancing when going out for essential needs were strictly implemented.[12] The WHO recommended all these actions to prevent the transmission of the virus among communities.[15]

The governments set rules to select the appropriate lockdown criteria for each country. These protective measures helped contain the rapid spread and effects of the virus, which allowed the countries to decrease the burden on the healthcare system. At the end of 2020, the first COVID-19 vaccine (Pfizer-BioNTech) was approved and used by the United States of America Food and Drug Administration.[16] Then, at the beginning of 2021, other vaccines started to be approved worldwide. However, new COVID-19 variants started to emerge in countries such as Brazil, South Africa, and England, which makes the effect of COVID-19 vaccination unclear.[17]

Through May 2021, the WHO reported 1,170,942,729 vaccine doses administered, 155,665,214 confirmed cases of COVID-19, and 3,250,648 deaths.[18]

COVID-19 risk factors can be categorized into two groups: demographics and comorbidity. From the literature, the demographic risk factors indicate that males are considered at high risk of COVID-19. Adults older than 65 years have a higher risk than younger adults.[19] Chronic conditions such as diabetes mellitus, chronic kidney disease, hypertension, respiratory system diseases, and cardiovascular diseases are considered risk factors for COVID-19.[20,21] Other factors such as obesity and smoking are likewise considered risk factors for COVID-19.[22,23]

COVID-19 has a significant impact on society and has caused more damage in low socioeconomic communities. The impact of COVID-19 on the low socioeconomic communities occurs due to crowded housing, poor housing conditions, and limited access to outdoor space.[24] Remote working has not been implemented in low-income societies due to limited resources.[24] Likewise, subcommunities are considered at a greater risk of COVID-19 due to race, ethnicity, and income disparity.[19] All the previous factors may reduce the benefits of the social distancing enforced by the governments. Thus individuals who live in communities that do not treat people equally depending on their race, ethnicity, and income status are more susceptible to COVID-19 infection and more likely to be at a greater risk of COVID-19 complications.[19]

The global economic decline due to the COVID-19 pandemic has reached an alarming level, which raises the concern of whether the current SDGs are suitable for the postpandemic period or not.[25,26] Although the SDGs were not planned to respond to the current pandemic, dealing with the pandemic should parallel the achievement of the SDGs. Dealing with the COVID-19 pandemic needs collaborative efforts that integrate the SDGs with healthcare decisions at the national level.[25]

The psychological burden caused by the COVID-19 pandemic is a well-recognized issue. Studies have investigated the negative psychological effects of the COVID-19 pandemic on the general population and healthcare providers. Xiong et al. conclude that depression, anxiety, posttraumatic stress syndrome, psychological distress, and overall stress have been higher in the general population during the pandemic than before the pandemic.[27] Females, people under the age of 40 years old, those with a history of psychiatric illness, the unemployed, students, and individuals who view news or social media frequently were considered vulnerable to developing psychological disorders.[27] Other studies have explored the psychological impact of the COVID-19 pandemic on healthcare providers. Luo et al. report an overall high psychological impact among healthcare providers caused by the COVID-19 pandemic.[28] da Silva and Neto compared the psychological effect of the pandemic on healthcare providers before and after the pandemic and conclude that healthcare providers who had higher exposure to COVID-19 cases are suffering more from anxiety, depression, and insomnia during the pandemic.[29] Thus it is evident that the COVID-19 pandemic is a severe burden on humans' psychological aspect.

The main aim of this chapter is to provide an overview of the psychological impact of the COVID-19 pandemic. This chapter first discusses the effect of the COVID-19 pandemic on the psychological aspects and reactions of the general population and healthcare providers. An in-depth overview of the psychological impact of COVID-19 on societies, including economic, education, and health, was conducted. Psychological risk factors that could increase the psychological burden of the COVID-19 pandemic and protective factors that may maintain psychological stability and achieve better health and community well-being for the general population and medical staff are explored and summarized.

2. Positive and negative psychological responses to the COVID-19 pandemic

COVID-19 has emerged as a serious challenge to public health, economic stability, and the functioning of governments. Studies have highlighted the effect of the pandemic on the public's psychological well-being, especially among healthcare workers, who are more likely to experience distress symptoms. While most studies focus on the pandemic's negative consequences, others have highlighted positive effects.[30]

2.1 The general public's psychological responses to the COVID-19

The spread of COVID-19 has resulted in an unprecedented number of lockdowns around the world. While the severity of these restrictions has differed from country to country, they have had a significant impact on people's everyday lives, impacting their jobs, leisure activities, livelihoods, and abilities to engage in social activities face to face. Fortunately, technology has quickly adapted to the current situation, and technical features have been implemented to help people cope with the ongoing pandemic. Since social distancing laws force people to depend more on telecommunications such as messaging, social media networking, and video conferencing, evidence indicates that positive attitudes arose during the introduction of lockdowns.[31]

People in the general population have improved their resilience. According to Serafini et al.,[32,33] psychological resilience is defined as the capacity to help or retrieve psychological well-being during or after addressing stressful and disabling conditions. Given the inability to meet face to face, the mutual experiences brought by the lockdowns have increased people's social solidarity and closeness[34–36] and their sense of support for each other. As a result, enhanced social and/or community support has been linked to a lower risk of developing psychological distress and psychiatric disorders.[37–39]

Despite this, studies have shown that lockdowns have caused widespread psychological distress among the general public, especially those who are more vulnerable to stress.[32–34,36,40] However, psychological distress may be caused by other factors than the fear of contracting the virus.[41] Stress, anxiety, and depression[16,42,43] are among the common signs of distress. The public's sense of helplessness[44–46] has grown because of separation from loved ones, loss of freedom, progression of the disease, and uncertainty about the future.[8,47]

Emotional distress, mood alterations and irritability, insomnia, post-traumatic stress symptoms, frustration, and emotional fatigue[33,48] have all been reported by individuals who have been quarantined.[33,48] Children and adolescents in particular are more susceptible to developing anxiety symptoms.[49] The slowing economy and the suspension of academic activities are two risk factors for college students who are stressed, anxious, or depressed.[44,50]

Overthinking and obsession with handwashing and an aversion to crowds have been identified as negative effects of lockdowns.[51] People exposed to possible infections may develop pervasive anxiety about infecting other people and their family members,[28,52,53] particularly if they have had symptoms that could be due to the coronavirus, which could lead to mental breakdowns.[54] Researchers have indicated that individuals without mental illness may experience new psychological symptoms, whereas those with mental illness may have their symptoms exacerbated. People who have already contracted the disease may experience shame, intense guilt, and social isolation.[55]

Cases of mental disorders and an increase in cases of suicide have been linked to the COVID-19 pandemic.[4,5,7,8,10,50,56] Boredom, frustration, anger, and loneliness are common signs of emotional and psychological distress in the general population. If these symptoms are heightened, they can increase the risk of suicidal ideation and, in the worst case, lead to suicide attempts.[57,58]

2.2 Healthcare professionals' psychological responses to the COVID-19

It is undeniable that the COVID-19 is a physiological and psychological health epidemic and that no one is immune to its effects. Apart from the immediate family members of those who contract the disease, healthcare staff are likely to be the most frequently affected simply because they are exposed to individuals who have contracted the virus. Although it is believed and expected that healthcare workers should have gained a certain level of endurance and resilience, it is understandable that they will eventually reach their breaking points. The surge in coronavirus cases, the constant exposure to deaths, the absorption of the emotional distress of patients and their families, and the exhaustion and social stigma they face may lead to considerable distress among healthcare workers.[10,52,59]

From a more optimistic perspective, reports show that during the current COVID-19 crisis, healthcare staff can still cultivate positive attitudes.[60,61] As a result, messages of hope and assurance of social security may aid healthcare workers in a more positive response to social threats. Unfortunately, only limited resources have looked at the potential positive effects of COVID-19 on healthcare staff, while reports have shown a slew of negative consequences that significantly affect the mental health of those employed in the healthcare sector.[28,62,63]

Luo and colleagues[28] conclude that the COVID-19 pandemic has caused a heavy psychological impact among medical workers and the general public. Despite being trained to become resilient and emotionally reticent, healthcare workers are vulnerable to developing psychological distress symptoms during the pandemic. A study shows that insomnia among healthcare workers is significantly higher compared to nonhealthcare workers.[64]

Aside from experiencing physical and emotional exhaustion, psychological stress, and burnout syndrome due to overwork,[62] healthcare professionals may experience posttraumatic stress disorder, depersonalization, and dissociation.[63,65,66] Healthcare workers have a higher risk and incidence of coronavirus infection and a higher mortality rate regardless of their staffing location.[63]

Healthcare providers may develop secondary stress disorders[67] due to daily exposure to traumatic scenarios and discomfort, especially when confronted with helpless situations. For instance, a lack of personal protective equipment (PPE),[32] treatment shortages, patient care prioritization, palliative care discontinuation, or life support termination of patient cases that have no chance of recovery may lead to secondary stress disorders. Like the general population, healthcare staff have experienced negative psychological symptoms such as depression, anxiety, insomnia, distress,[48] and post-traumatic stress disorder[49] due to their limited medical and social support access. Healthcare workers have developed pervasive anxiety and obsessive thoughts, limiting their ability to communicate with others.[68]

2.3 Implications

Governments worldwide have implemented social confinement as the most effective measure for preventing the spread of the coronavirus. However, as the world focuses on reducing the number of deaths and illness cases, therapeutic assistance seems to have been pushed to the sidelines. Inevitably, the pandemic has caused psychological and social distress among the public (Fig. 1). The virus causes constant anxiety, concern, and apprehension among the public, especially among the elderly, who are more vulnerable, and healthcare professionals working with coronavirus patients. Quarantines, changes in our daily lives, job loss, financial hardship, and grief over the death of a loved one may all influence people's mental health and

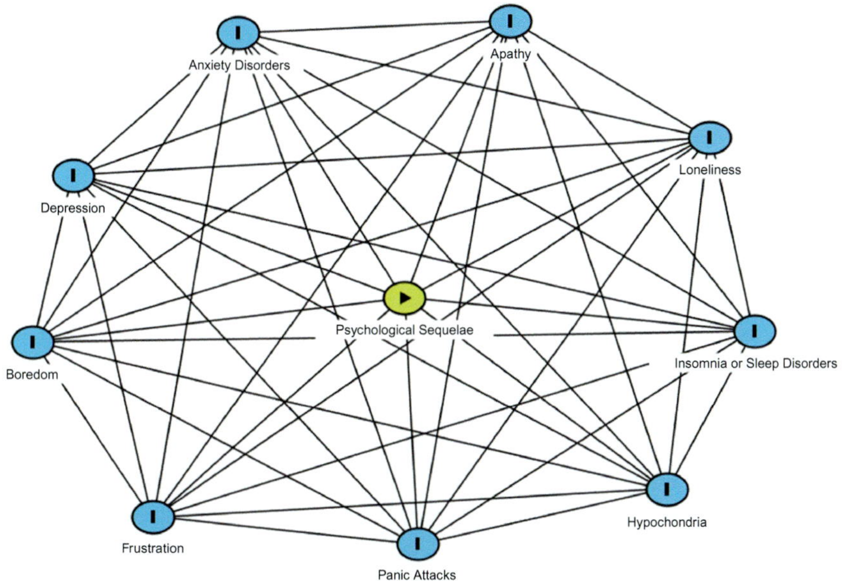

Fig. 1 Psychological sequelae of the COVID-19 pandemic on people.

well-being. To sum up, countries have made a tremendous effort to mitigate the undesirable effects of the COVID-19 pandemic. Nonetheless, it is critical that the public, especially healthcare professionals, receive sufficient psychological and social support to cope with and respond to the mental stresses brought on by the coronavirus pandemic, especially during the unprecedented period where all measures exist.[10,69,70]

3. The psychological burden of the COVID-19 pandemic on society

The coronavirus pandemic has financially impacted many individuals and resulted in a global economic crisis and recession. The government guidelines and measures imposed, including self-isolation, social distancing, and travel restrictions, have led to a reduction in the workforce across numerous economic sectors with jobs lost or currently being threatened. For example, in the United States, unemployment peaked at levels unheard of since 1948 during the recession.[71] Levels in April 2020 (14.8%) declined by December 2020 to 6.7%, although this was still elevated.[71] The American Psychological Association has reported a strong relationship between depression, stress, anxiety, and loss of life satisfaction and increased unemployment.[72] This trend is bidirectional between mental health and unemployment, whereby stable mental health is maintained by stable employment. In the long term, unemployment causes stress and anxiety, which eventually has a major effect on individual psychological health and can lead to negative consequences for public mental health.[72] The longer the stretch of unemployment, the worse people fare, with people out of work for 6 months or more experiencing significantly greater negative mental health outcomes.[73]

A previous metaanalysis study that included the psychological assessment of 63,439 participants from 10 countries reported that the prevalence of anxiety is 31.9% (95% CI: 27.5–36.7) of the general population. Additionally, the prevalence of depression among 44,531 participants was 33.7% (95% CI: 27.5–40.6). Table 1 presents the details of the included studies in this systematic review.

Individuals with low income and resources are more vulnerable to stress than individuals with a good average income.[74,75] Stress is strongly correlated to a decline in mental and physical health, even without considering financial conditions and strain. A study showed that, with respect to job loss during the COVID-19 pandemic, there was little comfort in solidarity; once

Table 1 Prevalence of depression, anxiety, and stress among the general population.

Study, date, country	Population	Male %	Tool	Score	Method	Depression % (*n*)	Anxiety % (*n*)	Stress % (*n*)
Amir Moghanibashi-Mansourieh, 2020, Iran	10,754	34.2%	DASS-21	28	Online survey	NA	50.9% (5472)	NA
M.Z. Ahmed et al., 2020, China	1074	53.2%	BAI BDI-II	23	Online survey	37.1% (399)	29% (312)	NA
C. Wang et al., 2020, China	1210	32.7%	DASS-21	22	Online survey	30.3% (367)	36.4% (440)	32.1% (389)
W. Cao et al., 2020, China[36]	7143	30.35%	GAD-7	20	Cluster sampling	NA	24.9% (1776)	NA
Y. Huang et al., 2020, China	7236	45.4%	GAD-7 CES-D	18	Web-based survey	20.1% (1454)	35.1% (2540)	NA
M. Ueda et al., 2020, Japan	1000	49.6%	GAD-7 PHQ-9	25	Online survey	43.1% (431)	33.2% (332)	NA
D. Liu et al., 2020, China	14,592	31.6%	GAD-7 PHQ-9	26	Online survey	53.5% (7503)	44.6% (6196)	NA
S.J. Zhou et al., 2020, China	8079	46.5%	GAD-7 PHQ-9	26	Online survey	43.7% (3533)	37.4% (3020)	NA
A. Sigdel et al., 2020, Nepal	349	54.2%	GAD-7 PHQ-9	29	Online survey	34% (119)	31% (109)	NA
S.S.H. Kazmi et al., 2020, India	1000	38%	DASS-21	19	Online survey	38.9% (389)	43% (430)	35.7% (357)
N. Othman et al., 2020, Iraq	548	49.6%	DASS-21	19	Online survey	44.9% (246)	47.1% (258)	17.5% (96)

Continued

Table 1 Prevalence of depression, anxiety, and stress among the general population—cont'd

Study, date, country	Population	Male %	Tool	Score	Method	Depression % (*n*)	Anxiety % (*n*)	Stress % (*n*)
Y. Wang et al., 2020, China	600	44.5%	SAS SDS	19	Online survey	17.17% (103)	6.33% (38)	NA
M. Qian et al., 2020, China	1011	50.44%	GAD-7	28	Telephone survey via random digital dialing	NA	26.6% (269)	NA
M. Shevlin et al., 2020, United Kingdom	2025	48%	GAD-7 PHQ-9	22	Online survey (quota sampling)	22.12% (448)	21.63% (438)	NA
P. Odriozola González et al., 2020, Spain	3550	35.1%	DASS-21	24	Social media	44.1% (1566)	32.4% (1150)	37% (1314)
Agberotimi et al, 2020, Nigeria	502	53.6%	GAD-7 PHQ-9	29	Respondent-driven sampling (RDS) technique and random survey sampling (RSS)	23.5% (118)	49.6% (249)	NA
C. Mazza et al., 2020, Italy	2766	28.3%	DASS-21	27	Online survey	32.8% (906)	18.7% (517)	27.2% (752)

DASS-21, the depression, anxiety, and stress scale; *GAD-7*, generalized anxiety disorder 7-item; *PHQ-9*, patient health questionnaire; *SAS*, Zung self-rating anxiety scale; *SDS*, Zung self-rating depression scale; *BAI*, the Beck Anxiety Inventory, *BDI*, Beck Depression Inventory, *CES-D*, Center for Epidemiologic Studies Depression Scale.

Modified from a study by Salari, N., et al. Prevalence of stress, anxiety, depression among the general population during the COVID-19 pandemic: a systematic review and meta-analysis. *Global Health* 2020;**16**:57.

people became reemployed, their mental health improved.[76] The age at which a worker loses a job can lead to greater damage in terms of wellness, with this being most severe between the age of 50 and 60. During a recession, job losses for this demographic result in an increase in mortality rate, which could be due to loss of health insurance.[77]

Several psychologists have described the emotional stages of someone who has experienced a job loss as similar to grieving. The emotional stages start with shock, then denial, anger, bargaining, and eventually acceptance and hope.[78]

Based on the Office for Budget Responsibility (OBR) projection, the UK's unemployment rate will reach 6.5% by the end of 2021, which amounts to around one million more unemployed people compared to the period before COVID-19. In another study, the OBR indicated that the associated length of unemployment would add an additional 200,000 people to the previous burden.[79] Finally, unemployment or seeking a job have a negative impact on both physical and mental health. The duration of time off work is directly proportionate to the negative health consequences for physical and mental health and life satisfaction.[80,81] Measures to combat COVID-19 have generally resulted in reduced income and job avalibality.[79]

Education plays a vital role in developing societies, qualifying, and preparing individuals for work. The largest disruption in history to education systems has occurred during the COVID-19 pandemic. Around 1.6 million learners have been affected in more than 190 countries, and 94% of the world's student population have been impacted by the closure of huge numbers of learning spaces.[82] Education disruption has substantial effects beyond education, although e-learning has been shown to have several advantages.

Children and adolescents have been the groups most affected by the closure of education campuses.[83] According to UNESCO, school closures occurred in more than 186 countries, resulting in 1.3 billion young people being affected. A study on parents who were obliged to care for their children in Japan showed that school closures led mothers with primary school children to have poorer mental health than other females.[83] In a survey conducted by the mental health charity Young Minds, which included 2111 participants in the UK presenting with an existing mental health condition, a total of 83% reported that the pandemic had made their conditions worse.[84] A survey carried out to investigate the impact of the COVID-19 pandemic on student mental health, which surveyed around 3239 high school and higher education students in April 2020, showed that 20% of college students' mental health had significantly worsened during COVID-19.[85] According to a later survey conducted in September 2020 that included 2051 students, 75% of students reported that their mental health had "worsened," "worsened somewhat," or "worsened significantly" since the beginning of the pandemic; 87.03% had experienced anxiety or stress; 78.06% had experienced sadness and disappointment; and 77.47% had felt lonely or isolated.[85] The majority of respondents reported that stress, anxiety, sadness, and depression had increased since the beginning of the pandemic. Another study conducted by Effective School Solutions found that educators, teachers, and professors had struggled as much as students with their mental health during the pandemic. In total, 84% of educators reported moderate to significant mental health challenges.[86]

Children were one of the most affected populations because of community-based mitigation programs, such as distance learning and closing playgrounds, among other life disturbances. These precautionary measures resulted in distress and confusion in both young and older children. They also resulted in annoyance, hostility, mental and physical violence, and disappointment, which could trigger adverse mental consequences in the long run.[87] Teachers also experienced more stress due to the increase in online classes, accompanied by symptoms of depression, lack of sleep, and anxiety due to increased workloads and working from home.[88,89] In another comprehensive study on the psychological impact of COVID-19 on secondary school teachers, 34% were found to be very anxious during the pandemic while 8% of teachers had experienced depressive emotions.[90]

Although distance learning has several advantages, most families are not able to sustain long-term distance learning due to varying education-based resources and connections. Families in poverty, working mothers, single parent families, and those with unstable employment may experience more psychological effects.[83] Many surveys across several educational systems indicated dissatisfaction with the one-way communication and teacher-control functionalities of the system.[91] Real-time interaction allows for the simulation of a real classroom learning situation, immediate interactive clarification of meaning, and higher quality discussion between groups.[92] However, students in online classes may experience headaches, lack of motivation, fatigue, avoidance/procrastination, ineffective time management, and isolation due to higher exposure to the personal computer screen.[93] The mismatch between reality and expectation can be difficult for students, especially younger learners, as children may experience a loss of motivation during interactive activities.[94–96]

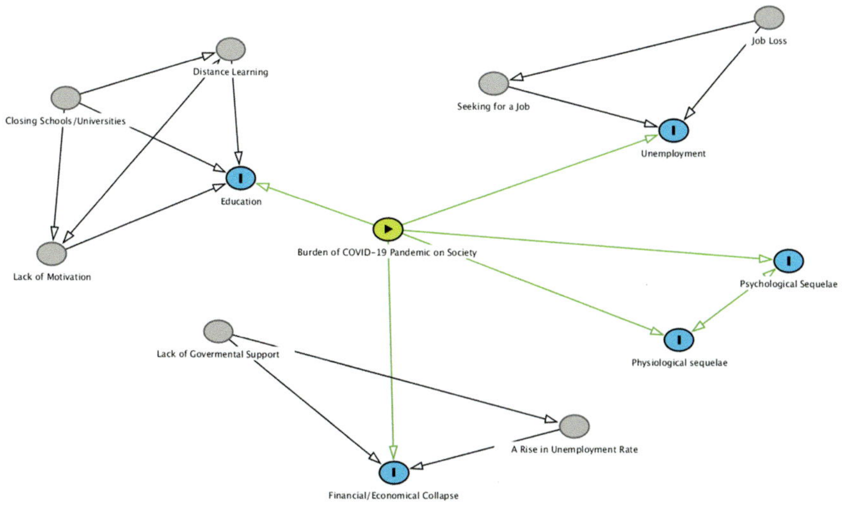

Fig. 2 The burden of the COVID-19 pandemic on society.

There was a strong association between job loss, personal economics, and level of education during COVID-19 and the impact on psychological health in all ages of societies. Fig. 2 outlines the most relevant and common psychological factors, such as education disturbance, unemployment and job loss, and financial situation, that affected and impacted the general population during COVID-19.

4. Risk and protective factors relevant to psychological reactions

4.1 Risk factors

The world has previously experienced several pandemics, such as the influenza virus (H1N1) in 1918, influenza virus (H2N2) in 1957, influenza virus (H3N2) in 1968, and flu pandemic (H1N1) in 2009. However, the COVID-19 pandemic has caused a global crisis that has affected every individual.[97] COVID-19 has caused not only deaths and physical harm but also fear and mental health problems.[4,5,7,8,10,50,96] This section highlights the risk factors of mental health problems based on current evidence, and protective factors that could mitigate the psychological burden of the COVID-19 pandemic.

During the past year, a growing body of research has been looking at the risk and protective factors that predisposed individuals to mental health disorders during the pandemic. Recent research has demonstrated several risk and protective factors,[32,98] such as alexithymia, inadequate supplies, and inadequate information. Individuals who experience these risk factors are more susceptible to mental health disorders. Resilience, social support, and taking advantage of preventative strategies provided by the healthcare organizations were protective factors that helped maintain psychological stability during the COVID-19 pandemic.[38,39] Fig. 3 shows a summary of the risk and protective factors relevant to psychological reactions.

4.1.1 Alexithymia

Studies of COVID-19 pandemic risk factors have uncovered a risk for individuals prone to alexithymia associated with mental health and psychological symptoms.[99,100] Alexithymia refers to emotional identification and expression deficiencies, and it includes externally oriented thinking, difficulty identifying feelings, and difficulty describing feelings.[101,102] Individuals prone to alexithymia fail to regulate their emotions and responses, which is associated with mental health problems.[103] Consequently, individuals

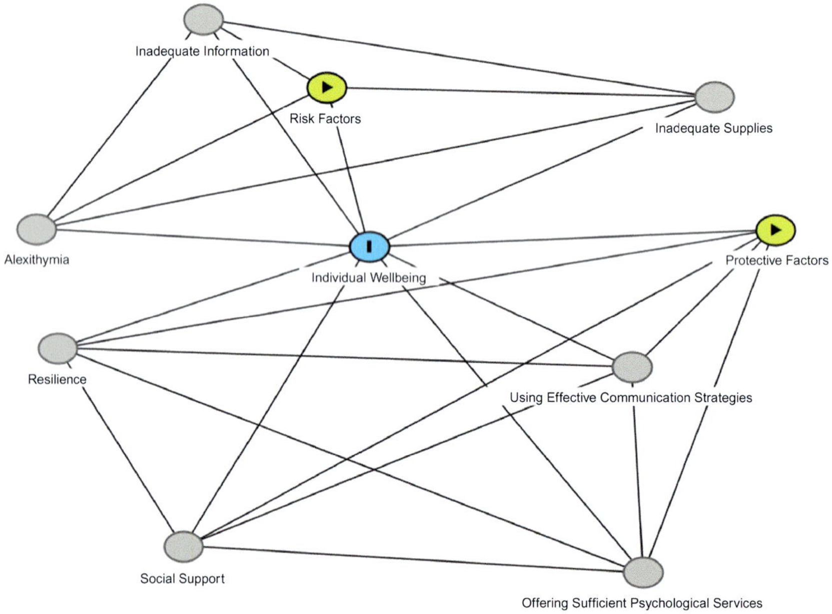

Fig. 3 Summary of the risk and protective factors that are relevant to psychological reactions.

with such traits fail to respond adequately and may show several psychological symptoms, such as depression, anxiety, and emotional distress.[104]

4.1.2 Inadequate supplies

Previous research has emphasized inadequate supplies and deficiency of necessities such as masks, food, water, and medication during the COVID-19 pandemic quarantine. This caused a great deal of frustration, fear, confusion, depression, stress, worry, anger, and uncertainty.[35,105] Various governmental systems introduced restrictions that impacted the food supply chain.[106] The food supply chain disruptions and food shortages placed substantial strain on governments, which induced panic.[107]

Unfortunately, countries were unprepared to protect healthcare providers and maintain adequate healthcare system supplies, resulting in uncertainty and panic. Alqahtani et al. conducted an international survey to explore the current global practices of ventilatory support management in COVID-19; in the study, the clinicians demonstrated that there was a shortage of PPE, testing, and mechanical ventilators.[108] Inadequate protective equipment and ventilator supply was a major emotional issue for frontline healthcare providers. The shortage of such critical equipment contributed heavily to them developing anxiety, losing control, having fear of spreading the virus to family, and feeling isolated.[109] Healthcare providers are vulnerable to emotional distress, frustration, anxiety, and depression on a normal basis; during the COVID-19 pandemic, because of increased workload and supply shortage, these feelings were exacerbated.[110] Healthcare providers were more vulnerable to burnout and increased workload during the pandemic due to increased cases and shortage of medical supplies.[52] Previous evidence showed that healthcare providers who worked during the SARS outbreak suffered posttraumatic stress disorder.[111] Posttraumatic stress disorder and mental health problems are associated with exposure to pandemics.[112–115]

4.1.3 Inadequate information

Other risk factors that jeopardized mental health during the COVID-19 pandemic, which several studies have suggested, are inadequate information, rumors, and conspiracy theories.[40,116–118] Bad news may cause fear, denial, anger, depression, and emotional distress. Despite extensive efforts from government leaders and health experts to create a clearer guide to mitigate the harm of COVID-19 and save individuals during quarantine, inaccurate information and its dissemination continued to undermine the global health response to control this pandemic.[119] Conflict guidelines by authorities confused the public and caused emotional distress. This caused confusion, insecurity, and isolation.[120]

Global health scientists and government healthcare authorities failed to provide clear advice and sufficient communication to ensure public mental health safety.[95–97] A massive flow of unverified information from television broadcasts, social media, and newspapers contributed to complex emotional distress for the public. The uncertainty and fear of the COVID-19 pandemic crisis have had serious health consequences, ranging from distress and anxiety to depression and panic.[121,122]

4.2 Protective factors

4.2.1 Resilience

Resilience is a key protective factor to strengthen individuals' approach to any challenging situation.[123,124] It is a personal attribute that promotes psychological stability during difficult situations and responding appropriately to difficult life events and future shock. It is the ability to anticipate, adapt, absorb, cope, and recover when traumatic events happen,[125] although some individuals are more likely to be rigid. Existing studies suggest that mindfulness and cognitive behavioral therapy techniques appear to improve individual resilience.[126] A survey in the United States found that resilient healthcare providers reported low levels of anxiety and depression.[98]

4.2.2 Psychological and social support

Another essential protective measure to maintain psychological stability is psychosocial support. Recent studies examined the role of social support during the COVID-19 quarantine and found that families and healthcare providers who received social support reported reduced anxiety and depression.[98] In nonpandemic situations, the study found a positive association between social support and individuals' general well-being.[127] An online survey in the United States found evidence of the association between social support and self-efficacy, lower levels of anxiety, and better sleep quality.[128]

4.2.3 Preventative strategies

We failed to learn a lesson from prior deadly pandemics such as H1N1, H2N2, H3N2, and the Middle East respiratory syndrome coronavirus MERS-CoV. The public, specifically healthcare providers, may have been protected better and the chaotic situation may have been prevented by learning the lesson and improving the healthcare system. Consequently, there was a lack of necessities (such as food, water, testing, PPE, oxygen, and mechanical ventilators), and conflicting public guidelines contributed to COVID-19 cases surging and the global crisis. These effects were a source of stress and triggered unstable emotional reactions. Global authorities, scientists, politicians, healthcare staff, social media, and the public all have crucial roles to play in maintaining stable and low-level sources of stress.[129]

Authorities, politicians, and news agencies should work closely with scientists and healthcare providers to understand their needs to support and empower them. The preparation and training of healthcare system management and personnel in psychosocial problems and implementing protocols would help reduce the risk of people developing mental health disorders.[130] Evidence-based resources that address mental health issues relating to disasters and the pandemic should be disseminated among staff. Furthermore, authorities should communicate effectively and implement clear and transparent guidelines for the public during quarantine.[131–135]

Providing alternatives that utilize online platforms to deliver psychological support during the COVID-19 quarantine to prevent mental health deterioration may be beneficial in gaining the public's trust. Integrating telehealth and home-based care is imperative to address psychological concerns in more vulnerable individuals, such as the elderly, people with immunosuppressant disorders, and those already living with mental health issues.[136] Telehealth plays an important role in addressing the needs of individuals with mental health instability without the need for physical contact.[137] Social media networks, telephone helplines, internet access, and informative TV programs should be implemented to minimize the level of loneliness and isolation.[138]

5. Conclusion

The negative impact of the COVID-19 pandemic was multidimensional and led to significant negative consequences on people's life. The prevalence of psychological disorders increased during the pandemic and varied significantly from one country to another and across different populations of the community, such as students, healthcare professionals, and the general population.[4,7,10] Since the emergence of COVID-19, governments have implemented restrictions, ranging from social distancing, quarantine, travel restrictions, curfews to complete national lockdown, to contain the rapid spread and effects of the coronavirus. These restrictions jeopardized global health by causing a severe physiological impact on the public and healthcare workers and creating an economic crisis. In addition, several risk factors, such as alexithymia, inadequate medical supplies, and lack of information, have caused mental health disorders and psychological impairment during the pandemic. Therefore individuals need to be resilient and benefit from social support and preventative strategies provided by healthcare organizations to maintain psychological stability. At the same time, government leaders and health experts should make an extra effort to provide clear advice and good communication to mitigate mental health issues caused by inaccurate and misleading information from television broadcasts, social media, and newspapers during the COVID-19 pandemic.

References

1. Huang C, et al. Clinical features of patients infected with 2019 novel coronavirus in Wuhan, China. *Lancet* 2020;**395**:497–506.
2. Cui J, Li F, Shi Z-L. Origin and evolution of pathogenic coronaviruses. *Nat Rev Microbiol* 2019;**17**:181–92.
3. Badr OI, et al. Incidence and outcomes of pulmonary embolism among hospitalized COVID-19 patients. *Int J Environ Res Public Health* 2021;**18**:7645.
4. Alyami HS, Naser AY, Dahmash EZ, Alyami MH, Alyami MS. Depression and anxiety during the COVID-19 pandemic in Saudi Arabia: a cross-sectional study. *Int J Clin Pract* 2021;**75**:e14244.
5. Varghese A, et al. Decline in the mental health of nurses across the globe during COVID-19: a systematic review and meta-analysis. *J Glob Health* 2021;**11**:05009.
6. Alwafi H, et al. Predictors of length of hospital stay, mortality, and outcomes among hospitalised COVID-19 patients in Saudi Arabia: a cross-sectional study. *J Multidiscip Healthc* 2021;**14**:839–52.
7. Alsairafi Z, Naser AY, Alsaleh FM, Awad A, Jalal Z. Mental health status of healthcare professionals and students of health sciences faculties in Kuwait during the COVID-19 pandemic. *Int J Environ Res Public Health* 2021;**18**(4):2203.
8. Naser AY, et al. The effect of the 2019 coronavirus disease outbreak on social relationships: a cross-sectional study in Jordan. *Int J Soc Psychiatry* 2020;**67**(6):664–71.
9. Shabrawishi M, et al. Clinical, radiological and therapeutic characteristics of patients with COVID-19 in Saudi Arabia. *PLoS One* 2020;**15**:e0237130.
10. Naser AY, et al. Mental health status of the general population, healthcare professionals, and university students during 2019 coronavirus disease outbreak in Jordan: a cross-sectional study. *Brain Behav* 2020;**10**:e01730.
11. World Health Organization. *WHO director-General's opening remarks at the media briefing on COVID-19—11 March 2020.* WHO; 2020.
12. Tangcharoensathien V, Bassett MT, Meng Q, Mills A. Are overwhelmed health systems an inevitable consequence of covid-19? Experiences from China, Thailand, and New York State. *BMJ* 2021;**372**:n83.
13. Schleicher A. *The impact of covid-19 on education insights education at a glance-2020.* The Organisation for Economic Co-operation and Development; 2021.
14. CRS Report. *Global economic effects of COVID-19.* Congressional Research Service; 2021.
15. World Health Organisation. *Coronavirus disease (COVID-19) advice for the public.* WHO; 2021.

16. Duan L, et al. An investigation of mental health status of children and adolescents in China during the outbreak of COVID-19. *J Affect Disord* 2020;**275**:112–8.
17. Mahase E. *Covid-19: what new variants are emerging and how are they being investigated?* British Medical Journal Publishing Group; 2021.
18. World Health Organization. *WHO coronavirus (COVID-19) dashboard*; 2021.
19. Raifman MA, Raifman JR. Disparities in the population at risk of severe illness from COVID-19 by race/ethnicity and income. *Am J Prev Med* 2020;**59**:137–9.
20. Zhang JJ, Lee KS, Ang LW, Leo YS, Young BE. Risk factors for severe disease and efficacy of treatment in patients infected with COVID-19: a systematic review, meta-analysis, and meta-regression analysis. *Clin Infect Dis* 2020;**71**:2199–206.
21. Gansevoort RT, Hilbrands LB. CKD is a key risk factor for COVID-19 mortality. *Nat Rev Nephrol* 2020;**16**:705–6.
22. Patanavanich R, Glantz SA. Smoking is associated with COVID-19 progression: a meta-analysis. *Nicotine Tob Res* 2020;**22**:1653–6.
23. Malik VS, Ravindra K, Attri SV, Bhadada SK, Singh M. Higher body mass index is an important risk factor in COVID-19 patients: a systematic review and meta-analysis. *Environ Sci Pollut Res* 2020;**27**:42115–23.
24. Patel J, et al. Poverty, inequality and COVID-19: the forgotten vulnerable. *Public Health* 2020;**183**:110.
25. Heggen K, Sandset TJ, Engebretsen E. COVID-19 and sustainable development goals. *Bull World Health Organ* 2020;**98**:646.
26. Nature. Time to revise the sustainable development goals. *Nature* 2020;**583**:331–2.
27. Xiong J, et al. Impact of COVID-19 pandemic on mental health in the general population: a systematic review. *J Affect Disord* 2020;**277**:55–64.
28. Luo M, Guo L, Yu M, Wang H. The psychological and mental impact of coronavirus disease 2019 (COVID-19) on medical staff and general public—a systematic review and meta-analysis. *Psychiatry Res* 2020;113190.
29. da Silva FCT, Neto MLR. Psychological effects caused by the COVID-19 pandemic in health professionals: a systematic review with meta-analysis. *Prog Neuro-Psychopharmacol Biol Psychiatry* 2020;**10**(104):110062.
30. Nelson B. The positive effects of covid-19. *BMJ* 2020;**369**:m1785.
31. Alvarez FE, Argente D, Lippi F. *A simple planning problem for covid-19 lockdown*. National Bureau of Economic Research; 2020.
32. Serafini G, et al. The psychological impact of COVID-19 on the mental health in the general population. *QJM* 2020;**113**:531–7.
33. Bai Y, et al. Survey of stress reactions among health care workers involved with the SARS outbreak. *Psychiatr Serv* 2004;**55**:1055–7.
34. Barbisch D, Koenig KL, Shih F-Y. Is there a case for quarantine? Perspectives from SARS to Ebola. *Disaster Med Public Health Prep* 2015;**9**:547–53.
35. Brooks SK, et al. The psychological impact of quarantine and how to reduce it: rapid review of the evidence. *Lancet* 2020;**395**:912–20.
36. Cao W, et al. The psychological impact of the COVID-19 epidemic on college students in China. *Psychiatry Res* 2020;**287**:112934.
37. Naser AY, et al. Knowledge and practices during the COVID-19 outbreak in the Middle East: a cross-sectional study. *Int J Environ Res Public Health* 2021;**18**:4699.
38. Gariepy G, Honkaniemi H, Quesnel-Vallee A. Social support and protection from depression: systematic review of current findings in Western countries. *Br J Psychiatry* 2016;**209**:284–93.
39. Zimet GD, Dahlem NW, Zimet SG, Farley GK. The multidimensional scale of perceived social support. *J Pers Assess* 1988;**52**:30–41.
40. Cava MA, Fay KE, Beanlands HJ, McCay EA, Wignall R. The experience of quarantine for individuals affected by SARS in Toronto. *Public Health Nurs* 2005;**22**:398–406.

41. Clemente-Suárez VJ, Dalamitros AA, Beltran-Velasco AI, Mielgo-Ayuso J, Tornero-Aguilera JF. Social and psychophysiological consequences of the COVID-19 pandemic: an extensive literature review. *Front Psychol* 2020;**11**:3077.
42. Courtet P, Olié E, Debien C, Vaiva G. Keep socially (but not physically) connected and carry on: preventing suicide in the age of COVID-19. *J Clin Psychiatry* 2020;**81**:20com13370.
43. Desclaux A, Badji D, Ndione AG, Sow K. Accepted monitoring or endured quarantine? Ebola contacts' perceptions in Senegal. *Soc Sci Med* 2017;**178**:38–45.
44. Engel-Yeger B, et al. Extreme sensory processing patterns and their relation with clinical conditions among individuals with major affective disorders. *Psychiatry Res* 2016;**236**:112–8.
45. Grassi L, Magnani K. Psychiatric morbidity and burnout in the medical profession: an Italian study of general practitioners and hospital physicians. *Psychother Psychosom* 2000;**69**:329–34.
46. Hall RC, Hall RC, Chapman MJ. The 1995 Kikwit Ebola outbreak: lessons hospitals and physicians can apply to future viral epidemics. *Gen Hosp Psychiatry* 2008;**30**:446–52.
47. Abrams E, Szefler S. COVID-19 and the impact of social determinants of health. *Lancet Respir Med* 2020;**8**:659–61.
48. Jeong H, et al. Mental health status of people isolated due to Middle East Respiratory Syndrome. *Epidemiol Health* 2016;**38**:e2016048.
49. Kang L, et al. The mental health of medical workers in Wuhan, China dealing with the 2019 novel coronavirus. *Lancet Psychiatry* 2020;**7**(3):e14.
50. Kawohl W, Nordt C. COVID-19, unemployment, and suicide. *Lancet Psychiatry* 2020;**7**:389–90.
51. Alqahtani J, et al. Sleep quality, insomnia, anxiety, fatigue, stress, memory and active coping during the COVID-19 pandemic. *Int J Environ Res Public Health* 2022;**19**(9):4940. https://doi.org/10.3390/ijerph19094940.
52. Lai J, et al. Factors associated with mental health outcomes among health care workers exposed to coronavirus disease 2019. *JAMA Netw Open* 2020;**3**:e203976.
53. Luchetti M, et al. The trajectory of loneliness in response to COVID-19. *Am Psychol* 2020;**75**:897–908.
54. Mache S, Vitzthum K, Klapp BF, Groneberg DA. Stress, health and satisfaction of Australian and German doctors—a comparative study. *World Hosp Health Serv* 2012;**48**:21–7.
55. Travaglino GA, Moon C. Compliance and self-reporting during the COVID-19 pandemic: a cross-cultural study of trust and self-conscious emotions in the United States, Italy, and South Korea. *Front Psychol* 2021;**12**:684.
56. Sher L. COVID-19, anxiety, sleep disturbances and suicide. *Sleep Med* 2020;**70**:124.
57. Neto MLR, de Oliveira Araújo FJ, de Souza RI, Lima NNR, da Silva CGL. When health professionals look death in the eye: the mental health of professionals who deal daily with the new coronavirus outbreak of 2019. *Front Med Case Rep* 2020;**1**:1–3.
58. Orgilés M, Morales A, Delvecchio E, Mazzeschi C, Espada JP. Immediate psychological effects of the COVID-19 quarantine in youth from Italy and Spain. *Front Psychol* 2020;**11**:2986.
59. Urzúa A, Samaniego A, Caqueo-Urízar A, Zapata Pizarro A, Irarrázaval Domínguez M. Salud mental en trabajadores de la salud durante la pandemia por COVID-19 en Chile [Mental health problems among health care workers during the COVID-19 pandemic]. *Rev Med Chil* 2020;**148**:1121–7.
60. Kanekar A, Sharma M. COVID-19 and mental well-being: guidance on the application of behavioral and positive well-being strategies. In: *Healthcare*. vol. 8. Multidisciplinary Digital Publishing Institute; 2020. p. 336.
61. Mohindra R, Ravaki R, Suri V, Bhalla A, Singh SM. Issues relevant to mental health promotion in frontline health care providers managing quarantined/isolated COVID19 patients. *Asian J Psychiatr* 2020;**51**:102084.

62. Øyane NM, Pallesen S, Moen BE, Åkerstedt T, Bjorvatn B. Associations between night work and anxiety, depression, insomnia, sleepiness and fatigue in a sample of Norwegian nurses. *PLoS One* 2013;**8**:e70228.
63. Saladino V, Algeri D, Auriemma V. The psychological and social impact of Covid-19: new perspectives of well-being. *Front Psychol* 2020;**11**:2550.
64. Pappa S, et al. Prevalence of depression, anxiety, and insomnia among healthcare workers during the COVID-19 pandemic: a systematic review and meta-analysis. *Brain Behav Immun* 2020;**88**:901–7.
65. Pompili M, et al. The associations among childhood maltreatment,"male depression" and suicide risk in psychiatric patients. *Psychiatry Res* 2014;**220**:571–8.
66. Richter F. *The video apps we're downloading amid the coronavirus pandemic*; 2020. Luettavissa https://www.weforum.org/agenda/2020/03/infographic-apps-pandemic-technology-data-coronavirus-covid19-tech. *Luettu* 3, 2020.
67. Salari N, et al. Prevalence of stress, anxiety, depression among the general population during the COVID-19 pandemic: a systematic review and meta-analysis. *Glob Health* 2020;**16**:1–11.
68. Vindegaard N, Benros ME. COVID-19 pandemic and mental health consequences: systematic review of the current evidence. *Brain Behav Immun* 2020;**89**:531–42.
69. Petzold M, Plag J, Ströhle A. Umgang mit psychischer Belastung bei Gesundheitsfachkräften im Rahmen der Covid-19-Pandemie [Dealing with psychological distress by healthcare professionals during the COVID-19 pandemia]. *Nervenarzt* 2020;**91**:417–21.
70. Blake H, Bermingham F, Johnson G, Tabner A. Mitigating the psychological impact of COVID-19 on healthcare workers: a digital learning package. *Int J Environ Res Public Health* 2020;**17**:2997.
71. Congressional Research Service. *Unemployment rates during the COVID-19 pandemic: in brief.* vol. 2021. CRS Report; 2021.
72. American Psychological Association. *The toll of job loss: the unemployment and economic crises sparked by COVID-19 are expected to have far-reaching mental health impacts.* vol. 2020. APS; 2020.
73. Pappas S. *The toll of job loss.* APS; 2020.
74. McKee-Ryan F, Song Z, Wanberg CR, Kinicki AJ. Psychological and physical well-being during unemployment: a meta-analytic study. *J Appl Psychol* 2005; **90**:53–76.
75. Paul KI, Moser K. Unemployment impairs mental health: meta-analyses. *J Vocat Behav* 2009;**74**:264–82.
76. David B. *Unemployment in the time of COVID-19: a research agenda.* 119. Sage; 2020. p. 103436.
77. Coile CC, Levine PB, McKnight R. Recessions, older workers, and longevity: how long are recessions good for your health? *Am Econ J Econ Pol* 2014;**6**:92–119.
78. Fowler D. *Unemployment during coronavirus: the psychology of job loss.* vol. 2021. BBC; 2021.
79. Thomson Kea. *Understanding the impacts of income and welfare policy responses to COVID-19 on inequalities in mental health: a microsimulation model.* University of Essex; 2021.
80. Holmes EA. Multidisciplinary research priorities for the COVID-19 pandemic: a call for action for mental health science. *Lancet Psychiatry* 2021;**7**:547–60.
81. Moore THM, et al. Interventions to reduce the impact of unemployment and economic hardship on mental health in the general population: a systematic review. *Psychol Med* 2017;**47**:1062–84.
82. United Nations. *Policy brief covid-19 and education.* August, United Nations; 2021.
83. Tsustsui Y. *Impact of closing schools on mental health during the COVID-19 pandemic: evidence using panel data from Japan.* University Library of Munich; 2020.

84. Lee J. Mental health effects of school closures during COVID-19. *Lancet Child Adolesc Health* 2020;**4**:421.
85. Mindes A. *The impact of COVID-19 on student mental health.* Stanford Education; 2020.
86. Young D. *Educators speak on mental health.* Effective School Solutions; 2020.
87. Dubey S, et al. Psychosocial impact of COVID-19. *Diabetes Metab Syndr* 2020;**14**:779–88.
88. Besser A, Lotem S, Zeigler-Hill V. Psychological stress and vocal symptoms among university professors in Israel: implications of the shift to online synchronous teaching during the COVID-19 pandemic. *J Voice* 2020;**36**(2):291.e9–291.e16.
89. Ng KC. Replacing face-to-face tutorials by synchronous online technologies: challenges and pedagogical implications. *Int Rev Res Open Dist Learn* 2007;**8**:335.
90. Stachteas P, Stachteas C. The psychological impact of the COVID-19 pandemic on secondary school teachers. *Psychiatriki* 2020;**31**:293–301.
91. Huber SG, Helm C. COVID-19 and schooling: evaluation, assessment and accountability in times of crises-reacting quickly to explore key issues for policy, practice and research with the school barometer. In: *Educ Assess Evaluation Account*; 2020. p. 1–34.
92. BC Children's Hospital. Impact of school closures on learning, child and family well-being during the COVID-19 pandemic. *B C Med J* 2020.
93. Wiles G. *Students share impact of online classes on their mental health.* The state News; 2021.
94. Züchner I, Jäkel H. Fernbeschulung während der COVID-19 bedingten Schulschließungen weiterführender Schulen: Analysen zum Gelingen aus Sicht von Schülerinnen und Schülern [Distance learning during the COVID-19-related school closings: the perspective of students from secondary schools]. *Z Erzieh* 2021;**26**:1–24.
95. Roe A, Blikstad-Balas M, Dalland C. The impact of COVID-19 and homeschooling on students' engagement with physical activity. *Front Sports Act Living* 2021;**2**:589227.
96. Zhao Y, et al. The effects of online homeschooling on children, parents, and teachers of grades 1-9 during the COVID-19 pandemic. *Med Sci Monit* 2020;**26**:e925591.
97. Liu Y-C, Kuo R-L, Shih S-R. COVID-19: the first documented coronavirus pandemic in history. *Biomed J* 2020;**43**:328–33.
98. Liu CH, Zhang E, Wong GTF, Hyun S, Hahm HC. Factors associated with depression, anxiety, and PTSD symptomatology during the COVID-19 pandemic: clinical implications for U.S. young adult mental health. *Psychiatry Res* 2020;**290**:113172.
99. Mannarini S, Balottin L, Toldo I, Gatta M. Alexithymia and psychosocial problems among Italian preadolescents. A latent class analysis approach. *Scand J Psychol* 2016;**57**: 473–81.
100. Paivio SC, McCulloch CR. Alexithymia as a mediator between childhood trauma and self-injurious behaviors. *Child Abuse Negl* 2004;**28**:339–54.
101. Sifneos PE. Affect, emotional conflict, and deficit: an overview. *Psychother Psychosom* 1991;**56**:116–22.
102. Taylor GJ. The alexithymia construct: conceptualization, validation, and relationship with basic dimensions of personality. *New Trends Exp Clin Psychiatry* 1994;**10**:61–74.
103. Hendryx MS, Haviland MG, Shaw DG. Dimensions of alexithymia and their relationships to anxiety and depression. *J Pers Assess* 1991;**56**:227–37.
104. Lankes F, Schiekofer S, Eichhammer P, Busch V. The effect of alexithymia and depressive feelings on pain perception in somatoform pain disorder. *J Psychosom Res* 2020;**133**:110101.
105. Pfefferbaum B, North CS. Mental health and the covid-19 pandemic. *N Engl J Med* 2020;**383**:510–2.
106. Bakalis S, et al. Perspectives from CO+RE: how COVID-19 changed our food systems and food security paradigms. *Curr Res Food Sci* 2020;**3**:166–72.
107. Singh S, Kumar R, Panchal R, Tiwari MK. Impact of COVID-19 on logistics systems and disruptions in food supply chain. *Int J Prod Res* 2021;**59**:1993–2008.

108. Alqahtani JS, et al. Global current practices of ventilatory support management in COVID-19 patients: an international survey. *J Multidiscip Healthc* 2020;**13**:1635–48.
109. Chen S, et al. Mental health status and coping strategy of medical workers in China during the COVID-19 outbreak. *medRxiv* 2020;20026872. https://doi.org/10.1101/2020.02.23.20026872.
110. Lee A, et al. Are high nurse workload/staffing ratios associated with decreased survival in critically ill patients? A cohort study. *Ann Intensive Care* 2017;**7**:46.
111. Wu P, et al. The psychological impact of the SARS epidemic on hospital employees in China: exposure, risk perception, and altruistic acceptance of risk. *Can J Psychiatr* 2009;**54**:302–11.
112. Lowe SR, Bonumwezi JL, Valdespino-Hayden Z, Galea S. Posttraumatic stress and depression in the aftermath of environmental disasters: a review of quantitative studies published in 2018. *Curr Environ Health Rep* 2019;**6**:344–60.
113. Mak IWC, et al. Risk factors for chronic post-traumatic stress disorder (PTSD) in SARS survivors. *Gen Hosp Psychiatry* 2010;**32**:590–8.
114. Wang C, et al. Immediate psychological responses and associated factors during the initial stage of the 2019 coronavirus disease (COVID-19) epidemic among the general population in China. *Int J Environ Res Public Health* 2020;**17**(5):1729.
115. Xiang Y-T, et al. Timely mental health care for the 2019 novel coronavirus outbreak is urgently needed. *Lancet Psychiatry* 2020;**7**:228–9.
116. DiGiovanni C, Conley J, Chiu D, Zaborski J. Factors influencing compliance with quarantine in Toronto during the 2003 SARS outbreak. *Biosecur Bioterror* 2004;**2**:265–72.
117. Braunack-Mayer A, Tooher R, Collins JE, Street JM, Marshall H. Understanding the school community's response to school closures during the H1N1 2009 influenza pandemic. *BMC Public Health* 2013;**13**:344.
118. Calisher C, et al. Statement in support of the scientists, public health professionals, and medical professionals of China combatting COVID-19. *Lancet* 2020;**395**:e42–3.
119. Mian A, Khan S. Coronavirus: the spread of misinformation. *BMC Med* 2020;**18**:89.
120. Center on International Cooperation. *Responding to COVID-19: the need for conflict sensitivity*. New York University; 2020.
121. Su Z, et al. Mental health consequences of COVID-19 media coverage: the need for effective crisis communication practices. *Glob Health* 2021;**17**:4.
122. Rosser BA. Intolerance of uncertainty as a transdiagnostic mechanism of psychological difficulties: a systematic review of evidence pertaining to causality and temporal precedence. *Cogn Ther Res* 2019;**43**:438–63.
123. Loprinzi CE, Prasad K, Schroeder DR, Sood A. Stress management and resilience training (SMART) program to decrease stress and enhance resilience among breast cancer survivors: a pilot randomized clinical trial. *Clin Breast Cancer* 2011;**11**:364–8.
124. Sood A, Prasad K, Schroeder D, Varkey P. Stress management and resilience training among Department of Medicine faculty: a pilot randomized clinical trial. *J Gen Intern Med* 2011;**26**:858–61.
125. Luthar SS, Cicchetti D, Becker B. The construct of resilience: a critical evaluation and guidelines for future work. *Child Dev* 2000;**71**:543–62.
126. Joyce S, et al. Road to resilience: a systematic review and meta-analysis of resilience training programmes and interventions. *BMJ Open* 2018;**8**:e017858.
127. Peirce RS, Frone MR, Russell M, Cooper ML, Mudar P. A longitudinal model of social contact, social support, depression, and alcohol use. *Health Psychol* 2000;**19**:28–38.

128. Xiao H, Zhang Y, Kong D, Li S, Yang N. The effects of social support on sleep quality of medical staff treating patients with coronavirus disease 2019 (COVID-19) in January and February 2020 in China. *Med Sci Monit* 2020;**26**:e923549.
129. The University of Melbourne. *Coronavirus (COVID-19): managing stress and anxiety*. The University of Melbourne; 2020.
130. Shanafelt T, Ripp J, Trockel M. Understanding and addressing sources of anxiety among health care professionals during the COVID-19 pandemic. *JAMA* 2020; **323**:2133–4.
131. Local Government Association. *Coronavirus (COVID-19) communications support and templates*. Local Government Association; 2021.
132. Reddy B, Gupta A. Importance of effective communication during COVID-19 infodemic. *J Family Med Prim Care* 2020;**9**:3793–6.
133. Forbes. *Three lessons communicators have learned during Covid-19*. Forbes Communications Council; 2021.
134. Abukhalaf AHI, von Meding J. Integrating international linguistic minorities in emergency planning at institutions of higher education. *Nat Hazards (Dordr)* 2021;1–25.
135. Abukhalaf AHI, von Meding J. Psycholinguistics and emergency communication: a qualitative descriptive study. *Int J Disaster Risk Reduct* 2021;**55**:102061.
136. Pfefferbaum B, et al. The H1N1 crisis: a case study of the integration of mental and behavioral health in public health crises. *Disaster Med Public Health Prep* 2012;**6**:67–71.
137. Monaghesh E, Hajizadeh A. The role of telehealth during COVID-19 outbreak: a systematic review based on current evidence. *BMC Public Health* 2020;**20**:1193.
138. Saltzman L, Hansel T, Bordnick P. Loneliness, isolation, and social support factors in post-COVID-19 mental health. *Psychol Trauma* 2020;**12**:S55–7.

CHAPTER ELEVEN

Effect of COVID-19 pandemic on social factors

Rohit Sindhwani[a], G. Pavan Kumar[b], and Venkataramanaiah Saddikuti[b]
[a]Operations Management, IMT Ghaziabad, Ghaziabad, Uttar Pradesh, India
[b]Operations Management, IIM Lucknow, Lucknow, Uttar Pradesh, India

1. Introduction

Human beings are social animals. Human beings carry out various activities, such as work, education, ensuring shelter for personal safety, following traditions, and use of social media, to satisfy their wants and desires. However, in the quest to satisfy their desires, human beings affected the environmental quality. A novel coronavirus, SARS-CoV-2, in early 2020 suddenly brought an upheaval to society. COVID-19 (the disease caused by SARS-CoV-2) demanded that humans become isolated and caused immeasurable problems to the social attitude of humans. Suddenly, the disease forced humans to carry out only the activities pertaining to basic needs such as food, cloth, shelter, and safety.[1] This decreased the purchasing behavior of humans, energy consumption, and transportation to a large extent. This has a positive impact on environmental quality in the short term. However, the negative impact of COVID-19 on society is immeasurable.[3]

The social impact of COVID-19 further enhanced the importance of achieving sustainable development goals (SDGs).[4] Governments and organizations realize that social responsibility measures improve society's overall well-being.[5] Responsible organizations are addressing the need to be beneficiary focused and build a community-focused approach.[7] The social performance of organizations is also linked to their economic performance.[8] Further, the social impact of COVID-19 is interlaced with the importance of values and ethics.[9] Many countries and organizations have repurposed resources and workforce to reduce the supply and labor shortage during a crisis. One of the most discussed topics during any crisis is the impact of such disruptions on social well-being. This leads to the topic of the social impact

COVID-19 and the Sustainable Development Goals
https://doi.org/10.1016/B978-0-323-91307-2.00003-1

of COVID-19 in this chapter. Broadly, six sectors are identified from the social progress index (SPI)[10] impacted during a crisis. These sectors are employment, education, healthcare, family, social media, and environment quality. The international governing bodies that manage these sectors are World Health Organization (WHO), International Labor Organization (ILO), United Nations Educational, Scientific and Cultural Organization (UNESCO), Intergovernmental Panel on Climate Change (IPCC), among others.[11] Each of these sectors is discussed in detail and their inherent characteristics during COVID-19 are understood.

To assess the social impact of COVID-19 on SDGs, the aim is to address portions of SDG 3, SDG 4, SDG 8, and SDG 11 through the study. The focus on good health and well-being of SDG 3 got severely compromised during COVID-19 as a number of essential health services got disrupted. The importance of universal health coverage (UHC) is essential for equitable access to healthcare to the society.[12] SDG 4 focuses on equitable quality education. Again, during COVID-19, education gains of past decades were severely hampered.[13] Lack of regular activities like attending schools and colleges, participating in co-curricular and extracurricular activities, and access to basic infrastructure resulted in reduction in proficiency levels of students. SDG 8 focuses on decent work and economic growth. There has been a loss of 255 million full-time jobs due to the pandemic in 2020.[14] While the impact was across the economy, majority of the workers in informal economy suffered. Finally, SDG 13 focuses on taking urgent actions to combat climate change. During the lockdown due to COVID-19, there was a reduction of pollution across the globe. However, the climate crisis continued in 2020, as the global average temperature remained above the preindustrial baseline. Accessing clean air in a unified world is still a distant dream.[15] The main objective of this study is to incorporate the challenges in the six sectors of the SPI during COVID-19 and highlight their significance with respect to the SDGs. The importance of country-specific requirements for the six sectors is elucidated through examples and cases in the chapter.

2. Employment

ILO has classified employment into three categories based on age: youth (15–24 years), adult (25–54 years), and old (>55 years). Among these categories, COVID-19 has impacted youth employment significantly. Youth are getting disproportionately unemployed since many works in the informal sector or the gig economy. Seventy-seven percent of youth hold informal jobs, and 126 million are extreme or moderate working poor. Many of the young population are migrants and work in different countries. In 2019, 70% of all international migrants are below 30 years of age, while 38% were below the age of 20 years. Further, youth in the 15–24 age group is 3 times more likely to be unemployed[16] (Fig. 1). In Southern Asia, South-Eastern Asia, and the Pacific, this ratio was more than six times in 2019. Many of these COVID-19-affected countries in South Asia have refugee problems that may affect these people's livelihoods during the crisis.[17]

During the pandemic in early 2020, ILO estimated a 5.3 and 24.7 million increase in the unemployment rate globally from a base level of 188 million in 2019 due to COVID-19.[18] However, the unprecedented scale of COVID-19 spread significantly disrupted the workplace. By the end of 2020, ILO estimated that 8.8% of the global working hours were lost, equivalent to 255 million full-time jobs (Fig. 2). This was roughly four times greater than the global financial crisis of 2009.[14] Further, 33 million full-time employees out of these 255 million were unemployed. Thus social protection is very important for young people who are at higher economic and social risk. However, incorporating the informal sector into social insurance programs is necessary to serve 77% of the youth. Countries need to monitor youth unemployment and underemployment and promote targeted recovery measures like youth innovation and social protection.[19]

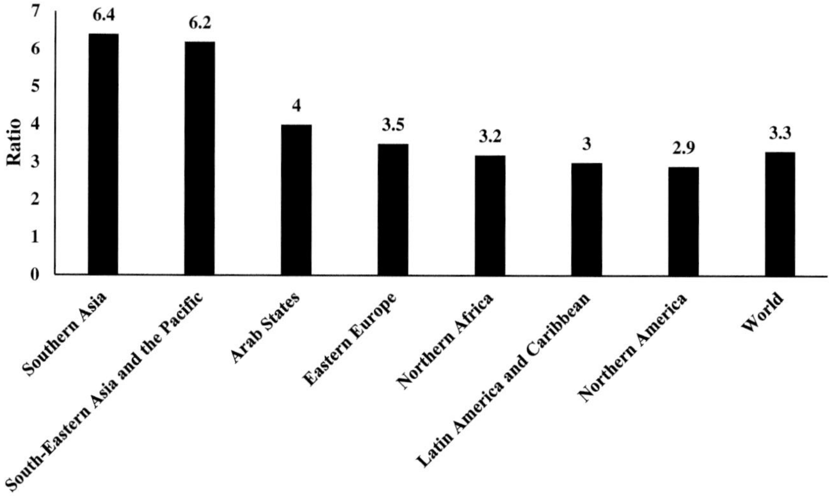

Fig. 1 Ratio of youth to adult unemployment rate in 2019.

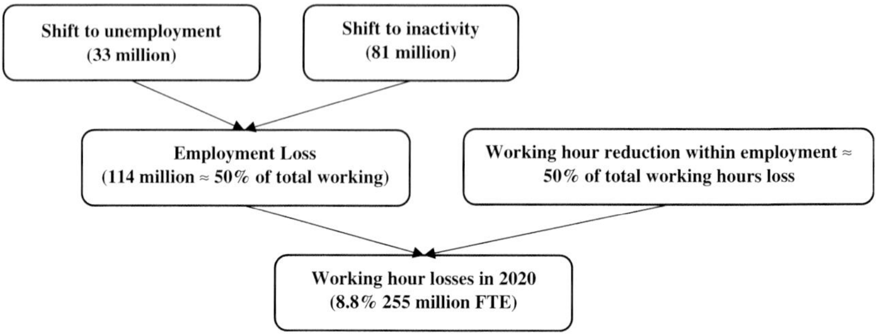

Fig. 2 Estimates of working hours and employment lost in 2020.

Looking into the specifics, the youth unemployment rate was expected to be almost constant in 2020 in the pre-COVID-19 era[18] (Table 1). This rate was expected to be between 13% and 14%. However, the employment-to-population ratio was already expected to decline pre-COVID-19 due to a decrease in labor force participation rates[16] (Table 2). Thus there was already a shortage of jobs for the youth. Similarly, as per the SPI, on average, 48% of people had vulnerable employment in the past decade before COVID-19[20] (Table 3). However, during COVID-19, the labor income lost in 2020 was estimated to be US$3.7 trillion or 4.4% of global GDP. The Americas experienced the largest labor income loss (10.3%) while the Asia Pacific registered the smallest loss (6.6%).[21] Overall, the global income declined by 8.3% in 2020 relative to 2019. The lower middle-income countries suffered the greatest losses in working hours in 2020, at 11.3%, well above the global average of 8.8%[14] (Fig. 3). The global labor force participation rate dropped

Table 1 World youth unemployment rate estimates pre-COVID-19.

Youth total %			Youth male %			Youth female %		
2019	**2020**	**2021**	**2019**	**2020**	**2021**	**2019**	**2020**	**2021**
13.6	13.7	13.8	14	14	14.1	13	13.1	13.2

Source: ILO.

Table 2 World youth employment-to-population ratio (EPR) globally pre-COVID-19.

Youth total %			Youth male %			Youth female %			Adults (%) 25+		
1999	**2019**	**2023**	**1999**	**2019**	**2023**	**1999**	**2019**	**2023**	**1999**	**2019**	**2023**
46.4	35.6	34.6	54.2	42.2	41	38.4	28.5	27.8	66	63.2	62.1

2023 are projections.
Source: ILO.

Table 3 Vulnerable employment in the world.

Year	**Vulnerable employment (% of employees)**
2020	46.7569
2019	46.8329
2018	47.1184
2017	47.4677
2016	47.8447
2015	48.2871
2014	48.7062
2013	49.0697
2012	49.7689
2011	50.2609

Source: socialprogress.org.

by 2.2%.[14] The working hour losses were majorly due to inactivity across the globe, but reduced working hours and unemployment also crippled the high-income countries (Fig. 4).

However, employment in information and communication, financial, and insurance activities increased in the second and third quarters. Employment also increased in mining, quarrying, and utilities in the third quarter of 2020[22] (Table 4). The magnitude of sectoral patterns varied across countries during the quarter. The construction, manufacturing, transportation, and

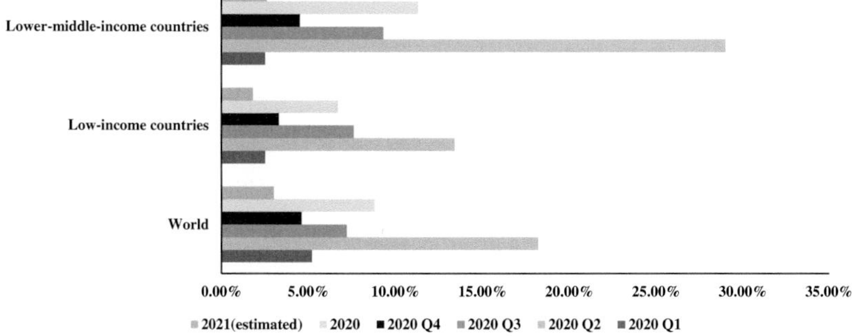

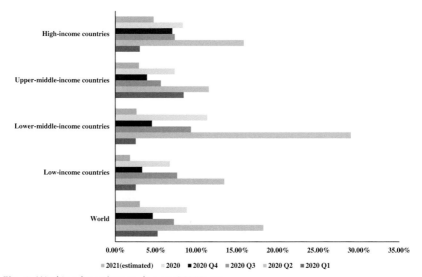

Fig. 3 Working hour losses due to COVID-19.

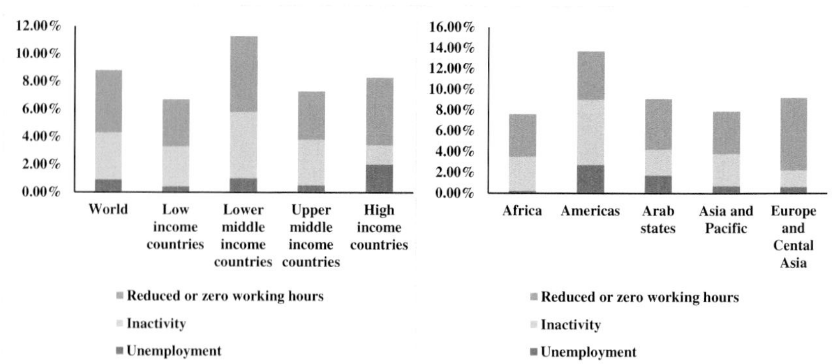

Fig. 4 Decomposition of working hour losses due to COVID-19 in 2020.

Table 4 Sectoral employment growth rates in second and third quarters of 2020.

		Growth of employment (year-on-year)%	
Sector	**At-risk status**	**2020 Quarter 2**	**2020 Quarter 3**
Accommodation and food services	High	−20.3	−13.6
Construction	Medium	−8.4	−2.2
Wholesale and Retail Trade	High	−7.2	−2.8
Manufacturing	High	−5.6	−2.5
Education	Low	−1.4	0.1
Transportation and Storage	Medium–High	−6.2	−6.1
Information and Communication	Low	5	7.3
Utilities	Low	0.1	1.1
Human health and Social work activities	Low	−0.8	0.5
Mining and Quarrying	Medium	3.6	2.8
Financial and Insurance Activities	Medium	3.4	3.5

Source: ILO.

storage sectors, which employ a large number of daily wage workers, continued to suffer over two quarters in 2020. This resulted in a mass exodus of workers from cities to villages in developing countries like India.[22]

ILO developed a policy framework, considering four key pillars to fight COVID-19 (Fig. 5). These pillars have been identified as follows[23]:

1. Stimulating economy and employment
2. Supporting enterprises, jobs, and incomes

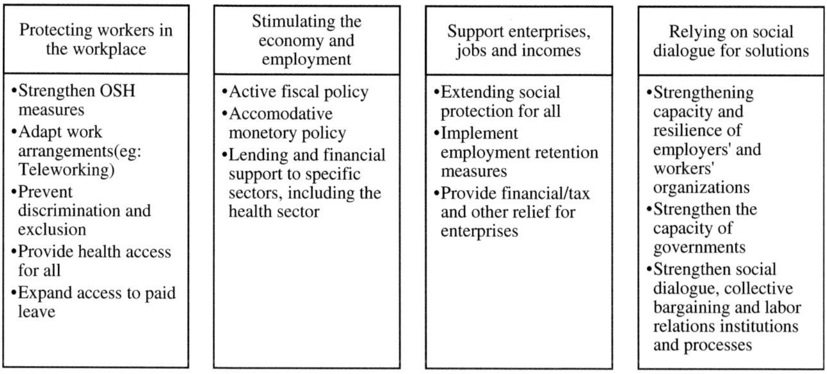

Fig. 5 Policy framework for employment to fight COVID-19.

3. Protecting workers in the workplace
4. Relying on social dialogue for solutions

The broad recovery strategies for employment as identified through the four pillars are mentioned as follows:

2.1 Working arrangements including telework

To promote teleworking, there is a need for simpler procedure, financial support, and IT capability at the national and workplace level. As per the US census bureau, the nonself-employed population of teleworkers has grown by over 102% from 2005 to 2014. This kind of adoption is fundamental during the current pandemic. There are some hazards of telework also which need to be addressed. Buomprisco et al.[24] stated that lack of dedicated working area, unavailability of ergonomic work equipment, and risk of overwork could have potential health implications.

2.2 Expanded access to paid sick leave

Provisions of paid sick leave are mandatory for workplace employees to promote the responsibility of the employers. Paid reduction in working time, employment retention, and unemployment benefits should be expanded to several countries. Social assistance benefits like cash transfers can enhance income security and boost demand. Heymann et al.[5] did their research on 193 UN member states in early 2020 and found that 27% of the countries did not guarantee paid sick leave from the first day of COVID-19 illness. Further, they found that 58% of countries did not have provisions for paid sick leave for self-employed and sharing economy workers.

2.3 Occupational health and safety (OSH) advice

Dedicated hotlines, websites, and information mediums need to be provided to disseminate advice on workplace OSH measures. Godderis and Luyten[25] stated that reduced income would translate to lower living standards, fewer tax resources, stress, and mental health issues. For example, Spain, which spent little on social protection during the economic crisis in the 1990s, had increased suicides and unemployment. Contrary to this, Sweden spent four times on social support programs, thus controlling the suicide rates. The authors reflected that the field of OSH should focus on social support and employment during and after the crisis.

2.4 Prevention of discrimination and exclusion

Many health workers in various countries have faced COVID-19-related harassment and bullying. As the coronavirus started to spread in 2020, Ely and Habibi[26] stated that social distancing might lead to stigmatization of already marginalized groups. Further, they reflected that nonuniversal systems based on legal entitlements of countries enhance the transmission of the virus and aggravate social and economic disruptions. Thus human rights protection cannot be an afterthought in epidemics.

2.5 Active fiscal policy and accommodative monetary policy

Central banks of countries need to cut interest rates, provide social security, and introduce tax breaks and waivers. Further, the deadline for repayment of mortgages needs to be extended. Chen et al.[27] did a cross-country comparative study of countries' fiscal policies during COVID-19. They identified that majority of countries had targeted the healthcare sector, business sector, individuals, or households. They suggested that countries should develop appropriate strategies and fiscal policies depending on the economic condition and severity of the COVID-19 crisis.[27]

2.6 Lending and financial support to some sectors

Financial support and subsidies to sectors making health-related items need to be provided. Sectors like tourism, aviation, and hotels need longer term support. Affected companies can benefit from the postponement of social or tax installments, and tax rebates. Also, expanding special financial support to MSMEs can help save a number of small businesses.[28]

3. Education

This pandemic has negatively impacted children and teenagers, including the closure of schools, isolation owing to government lockdown measures, and the collapse of the world economy. These negative impacts have short- and long-term effects on children, teenagers, families, teachers, and the educational ecosystem. Increased food insecurity and the onset of mental health problems are two more possible side effects.[29]

There was an impact of formal teacher-student and student-student interactions during the course of imparting education due to COVID-19. To mitigate the impact of COVID-19, several governments have stopped providing in-person schooling, which had affected the quality of education (Fig. 6). Initially, school closure was introduced by countries. Postlockdown, some countries resorted to impart online learning, and few countries resumed traditional in-person school teaching.[29]

School closure resulted in stress to parents, as children were spending most of their time using electronic devices. It also resulted in much stress for working women in healthcare, who could not attend their services when required. Finland allowed children whose parents work in essential services to attend preprimary and primary school until the third grade.[13]

The sudden closure of schools replaced in-person teaching with various forms of Information and Communication Technology (ICT)-based remote and distance education. Subsequently, after lifting the lockdown restrictions, many schools in several countries resorted to online learning

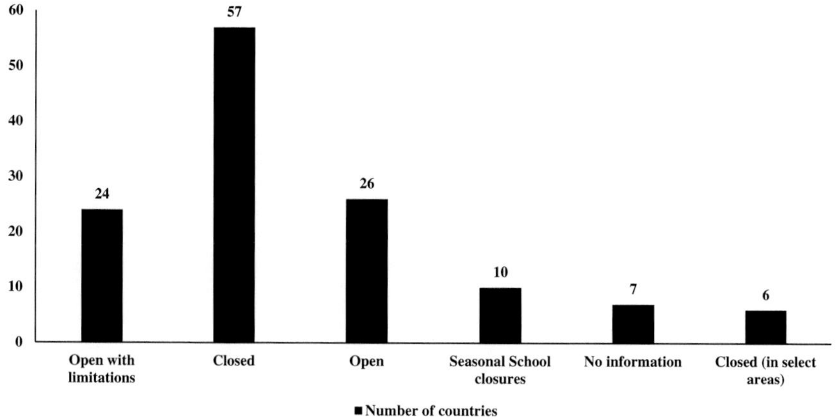

Fig. 6 Status of school closure in various countries due to COVID-19.

or distance education. This created a digital divide in Lower Middle Income and Lower Income countries. Digital Divide is a dynamic concept. It means the disparity between technology-rich and technology-poor. According to Cullen,[30] the digital divide is the disadvantage felt by individuals who are unable or unwilling to use ICT in their daily life. The OECD defined the "digital divide" in 2001 as "the gap between individuals, households, businesses and geographic areas at the different socio-economic levels concerning their opportunities to access ICTs and their use of the Internet." The digital divide has created major barriers such as the continuity of students' learning in urban versus rural areas and the digital readiness of government versus private educational institutions. The impact of the digital divide as shown by researchers is that students do not return for education is high[31] (Fig. 7).

Due to increased unemployment or not having access to digital technologies, an increasing trend of dropouts is observed in African countries.[32]

Teachers are also required to cope up with different platforms of teaching, controlling the students remotely, absenteeism of students, and ensuring proper attention from students. Their teaching skills are under constant watch by the parents and their supervisors. Teachers were made to ask to collect fees from the students, and retention of students was also made one of their responsibilities.[33]

Lack of exploitation of full potential, unfair competitive edge, and decreased productivity among the poor are the disadvantages of online teaching. The advantages include enhancement and convenience in learning due to the availability of reading materials online.[32]

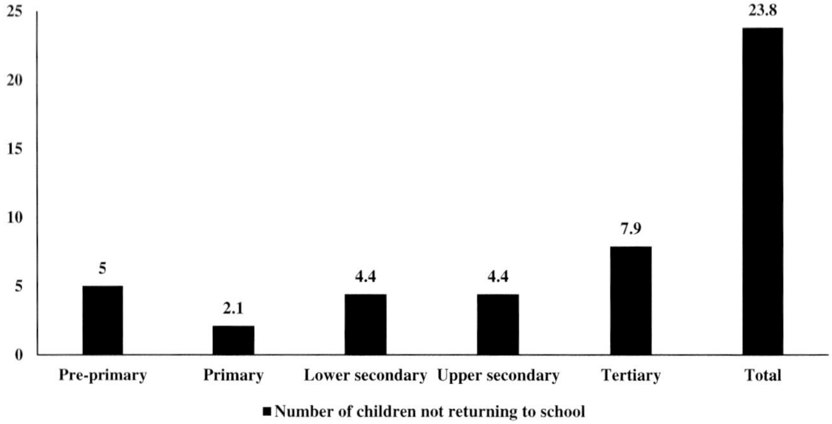

Fig. 7 Estimated students not returning for education. *(Source: Statista.)*

School reopening required the school authorities to take several precautionary measures such as physical distancing (e.g., by reducing class sizes) and other hygiene measures such as handwashing stations or mask wearing.[13] There was a lot of reluctance from the parents to send their children to school in some countries. However, as COVID-19 also impacted children in phase-2, many schools resorted to online education.[13]

COVID-19 ended children's regular activities like attending school, interacting with relatives and friends, playing outside, and experiencing nature and messed up the social and emotional benefits that come with them. Parents spent much more time in the company of their children during the COVID-19 quarantine, observing changes in behavior directly.[29]

Schools serve as safe havens for many children in addition to being places where they learn. Teachers and school staff perform a protective role for children's physical and mental safety by being in daily touch with them. They can warn authorities or parents in the event of violence or abuse.[29]

3.1 Early childhood education

Early childhood, the first 6 years of a child's life, is the most important development. According to neurobiology and cognitive development specialists, 90% of brain growth happens during the first 6 years of life. Center on the Developing Child at Harvard University indicates that mental and physical well-being, ability to be a good social being, and cognitive-linguistic abilities develop in early childhood. All of these skills are required for academic achievement and success in the workplace and community.[34]

Several parents have enrolled their children in online or home-schooling programs to continue their children's education during the COVID-19. Still, many parents experienced anxiety about the social and physical development of their children. There is evidence that excessive screen time can hurt children; however, the effects of zero learning years on a kid's long-term development are more detrimental and may have a multiplication effect.[34]

3.2 Primary education

Coronavirus's impact on primary education has made it more difficult for many students, particularly in developing countries. Many students in developing countries have limited access to the internet or internet-connected devices, making it difficult to keep up. By the age of 10, approximately 53% (2020) of children in low-income countries could not read, compared to 35% (2019) previously.[35] These children are classified as being in Learning Poverty. The amount of unsupervised time for these children will increase, and unless responsible adults ensure that the children focus on their studies, the percentage of Learning Poverty will rise. Furthermore, in 71 low-income countries, more than 30% of students lack internet access as of 2020.[36]

COVID-19 has affected female primary school enrollment significantly in developing countries. Girls, for example, have less access to digital platforms than boys. This disparity will only serve to increase the dropout rate among young females. Fewer girls in school correlate with an increase in teen pregnancy rates, which causes plenty of household issues. School closures also have a disproportionate impact on mothers. In 31 low-income countries, only 39% of women worked while caring for their children. As a result, women are pushed into the informal economy, earning less money and becoming desperately poor.[36]

3.3 Secondary education

In addition to the problems discussed by students in primary education, secondary students have another problem about their future educational prospects. Secondary students in their final year are concerned about their preparedness for college admission. Several colleges and universities closure have raised their anxiety levels about their plans. They will miss their final opportunity to evaluate their abilities if examinations are not held. There are no felicitations, no chance for demonstrating various leadership skills, no chance to attend Olympiad competition, and most importantly, loss of bonding between friends. Also, being in their teens, their anxiety levels are ever increasing, leading to increased stress levels, in case there are some disturbances in the parents' financial status.[37]

3.4 Tertiary education

Students live and study in the hostels (closed environments) in universities and colleges. They are also thriving cultural hubs, bringing students from all over the world together. Enrollment of international students has decreased as a result of class closures and the transition to an online mode of instruction. The foreign student population is about 5.5% of all the students in the United States, of which Chinese and Indians account for 51%. Although many tertiary education institutions worldwide provide few courses online, shifting all programs online may be extremely difficult. While few colleges may have well-developed online systems, smaller institutions may have difficulties. University and college administrators and their IT colleagues had to collaborate to bring the courses online. However, tertiary education institutions are well positioned to impart online education.[38]

3.5 Teachers and education systems

The lockdown and the public health situation, in general, had an emotional impact on teachers, professionals, and other adults. Moreover, as teachers have continued to work from home, their workload has increased. This is due to a lack of training in designing and implementing remote learning methodologies and the extra effort required by working from home during emergencies, where they must simultaneously respond to their obligations. Teachers must also maintain their physical and emotional health to work from home or participate in school reopening efforts. This presents educational institutions with another challenge.[39]

A substantial proportion of instructors belong to the age group that is most vulnerable to COVID-19 infection. As a result, even if schools reopen, it is unclear whether all teaching staff will be available to work in the classroom. Furthermore, teachers in various countries have expressed concerns about returning to work because of the risk of infection, resulting in a short-term scarcity of teaching staff. Also, in certain countries, offline teaching is opposed by teachers' unions.

Education funding is imperiled by the economic slowdown and the need for resources from the health and social security sectors. The education sector needs additional funds to expand the classroom, hostel, mess, and sports infrastructure, keeping in view of social distancing norms.[40] Hence, in a situation where government budgetary capacity is constrained, the following five reasons may result in increased financial pressure on educational institutions[41]:

- Reopening educational institutions will necessitate more resources to facilitate the implementation of new regulations.
- If the closure of schools continues, educational institutions are forced to expand and strengthen their remote teaching capabilities, which would require significant investment.
- Due to a shortage of instructors, systems require additional funding to hire new instructors.
- The health crisis will impact teachers' health, necessitating greater resources to cover their medical disabilities.

- In countries where private institutions dominate, parents who decide to transfer their children for financial reasons may demand more public institutions. Several private institutions may be forced to close as a result of this. Governments have to plan for the sustainability of public institutions due to this increased demand.

3.6 Research

University's operating budget is based on the following five important revenue sources: tuition and fees, hospitals and healthcare grants, externally financed research, state appropriations, and endowment. Most of these revenue streams are under jeopardy as a result of the pandemic's effects. Externally sponsored research has proven to be a reliable source of money so far, with no immediate threats to its continuation. Many institutions employed cost-cutting measures, which impacted funded research. However, at the start of the pandemic, governments gave institutions much flexibility in using research funds. Many traditional research activities were put on hold for the most part. Simultaneously, the COVID-19 situation prompted significant innovation in research collaboration and academic communication. Scientists who would never have met otherwise argued and discussed via videoconferences, shared data, ideas, and discoveries, and collaborated to find solutions. Coronavirus and associated research publications were made freely available by a number of publishers. Mendeley and ResearchGate, two scholarly collaboration networks, have created specific services to facilitate sharing and cooperation. The communication gap between professors and researchers has reduced dramatically. There was access to online software through virtual private networks, which otherwise, the IT department of the universities would have never allowed.[42]

However, the vast majority of research institutions have closed or gone virtual, and few are currently operating at lower levels due to social distancing. Another type of challenge has arisen as a result of lab equipment being shared among laboratories and in certain circumstances throughout the university. During the pandemic's peak, many scientific researchers were unable to travel internationally or to isolated locations, resulting in the loss of vital data and, in some cases, whole projects.[41]

4. Healthcare

The healthcare disaster due to COVID-19 has impacted the young and old households, male and female, rich and poor, and literate and illiterate. However, the adverse effects of the disease on older people are significant. Further, poor people lack the basic amenities like availing of healthcare resources, nutritious food, potable water, etc. Similarly, high levels of illiteracy have resulted in the exclusion or marginalization of those who lack access to technology. Gender also plays an important role. Globally, 70% of the healthcare workforce comprises female health workers.[43] Especially as the health systems get overloaded, the burden of home care largely landed on women and girls. The importance of human health and immunity during the pandemic disruption is discussed in subsequent sections.

4.1 Human health

When people are exposed to SARS-CoV-2, they are at risk of contracting COVID-19. Symptoms may or may not occur in a person who has been infected with this virus. SARS-CoV-2, like other coronaviruses, appears to transmit by respiratory droplets from person to person. Once inside the body, it predominantly affects the lungs. A persistent cough, shortness of breath, pain and tightness in the chest, fever, exhaustion, and a loss of taste and smell may develop over the course of 2–14 days. COVID-19 patients recover in less than 2 weeks in about 80% of cases without requiring special treatment. Some people may have mild flu-like symptoms. COVID-19, in some cases, has a serious effect on the lungs, causing breathing difficulties, low blood oxygen levels, lung damage, pneumonia, and pulmonary edema in certain patients. Experts are yet uncertain how the virus impacts lung cells. Furthermore, it seems that the body's immune response, the virus's impact on cells, and oxygen deprivation are all potentially fatal. People who require hospital treatment require extensive artificial breathing support, which puts them at risk of lung injury.[44]

COVID-19 can harm the blood, kidneys, nervous system, brain, cardiovascular, and gastrointestinal systems. Some people experience minor symptoms initially but eventually develop health issues that last weeks or months. Persistent symptoms include fatigue, shortness of breath, cough, joint discomfort, chest pain, headache, muscular soreness, and a fluctuating fever. Blood clots, brain fog, mood swings, vision problems, kidney damage, and heart palpitations are all possible side effects of COVID-19. There is also a possibility of hormonal, dermatological, and musculoskeletal issues, albeit there is not enough research to back this up yet.[45]

4.2 Human immunity

Boosting the immune system is found to be a useful option for COVID-19 patients. The immune system's processes and mechanisms are an important precursor to immune system development. The most recent observations on COVID-19 treatment could be the focus of future research. This would be a significant accomplishment if the various hurdles could be overcome.[46]

4.3 Universal health coverage

Countries have understood the importance of basic public health, stronger health systems, and contingency preparedness to bridge the structural inequality in healthcare systems. Accelerated UHC to promote and protect health and well-being should be a common goal for the international diaspora. In the short term, healthcare in countries should work based on the worst-case scenario. The aim should be to minimize morbidity and mortality while continuously maintaining essential health services. Those who are most vulnerable to COVID-19 need special attention. Hence, urgent response should be available for healthcare workers, frontline workers, people who are old, those with comorbidities, and those who are poor and live in crowded settlements. Also, the role of females in decision-making is crucial. Only 25% of the world's health ministers are women, and a similar proportion of women are in senior roles in health institutions. Thus the decision-making table does not reflect the women's role in the pandemic.[44] The United Nations have affirmed their stance on achieving UHC by 2030, as part of SDGs. The goal of UHC for individuals and communities is threefold[12]:

1. ***Equity in access***: Everyone in need of healthcare should have access irrespective of the income level of the person.
2. ***Sufficient quality***: Health services should provide sufficient quality healthcare to improve the health of the patient.
3. ***No undue financial risk***: Health services should not put anyone at financial risk due to the high cost.

However, during the COVID-19 crisis, UHC has been impacted for three reasons: transmission of the virus causing a large number of morbidity and mortality, the inability of the health systems to provide the essential health services due to resource constraints, and the socioeconomic impact. Countries can prevent healthcare disruptions if they are resilient enough to respond to these requirements.[47]

4.3.1 Transmission of the virus

Stringent public health measures are essential while preserving people's fundamental rights to reduce COVID-19 transmission. As the virus mutates and variants develop, addressing these restrictions across the time horizon is a tactical decision to be adopted by various governments. Contact tracing, testing, and isolation are critical together with age-specific interventions.[48]

4.3.2 *Essential health services*

Essential health services during the pandemic disruption are facing severe resource constraints. The requirement for doctors, nurses, and healthcare workers is crucial to sustaining the healthcare ecosystem. Similarly, the resource allocation of critical resources like beds, ventilators, and oxygen is crucial to maintain essential health services.[49]

4.3.3 *Socioeconomic impact*

The 26 richest people in the world hold wealth equivalent to half of the global population. Similarly, 70% of the world's population is living with wealth inequality. Gender, family, ethnic background, race, and culture also cause inequality. Clean water and sanitation, and nutrition are some of the important areas to improve socioeconomic impact.[50]

4.4 Clean water and sanitation

Inadequate access to clean water and disruptions in supply has also impacted socioeconomic well-being. Clean water for handwashing facilities is crucial to prevent COVID-19 as a nonpharmaceutical intervention. There is 40% of the population in the world who do not have access to clean water and sanitation (2.2 billion people lack access to water and 4.2 billion people lack access to sanitation). Populations living in slums have a higher risk of infection due to a lack of hygiene and sanitation standards.[50]

4.5 Nutrition

Nutrition and good health during COVID-19 are tightly interlinked. Unfortunately, volatility in demand, market tampering, supply disruptions, and stockpiling have impacted food prices. This has had negative effects on the nutrition of the vulnerable population. Further, there is a disruption in the meals of children and young people due to school closures impacting their nutrition. Around 320 million primary schoolchildren in 120 countries are not receiving school meals due to COVID-19. It is important to understand that the nutrition, health, and learning needs of the marginalized and vulnerable children are often interlinked. Policies need to address equitable solutions to address these challenges faced by countries.[50]

5. Family

The human need to feel safe, connected, hopeful, and calm is intensely important during crises and disasters. The importance of social well-being in family centered care revolves around open family presence at the bedside, morale booster of family members, physical presence, and caretaking. However, the principal mitigation strategy for pandemic disruption is isolation, physical distancing, and quarantine to prevent transmission. As highlighted by Hart et al.,[51] restrictions of COVID-19 should not in any way undermine the principles of family centered care. The authors stated that family centered care goals are based on respecting the role of family members as collaborators and care partners. Further, the collaboration of family members and healthcare staff is crucial to maintain the healthcare ecosystem. Thus "visitation" in family centered care should be replaced with "family presence" through nonphysical ways during COVID-19.

Our current generation is lucky to have timely support through technology, computers, mobiles, and broadband internet. Internet inequality has also reduced significantly in the past decade. Therefore technology laden family care strategies should be embedded in the policies of governments while addressing the needs of patients and their family members. Further, the policies need to be built for effective home care remedies through technology. The healthcare system should leverage the advantages of technology to help families during isolation and home care.

Further, access to CCTV cameras in the ICUs of hospitals should be provided to the family members of the patients. Daily videoconferencing and telephone contact are important for encouraging patients' morale and calming the nerves of suffering families.[52] The United States, for example, has permitted the use of technology, even though it is against compliance with HIPAA (Health Insurance Portability and Accountability Act Privacy, Security, and Breach Notification) Rules. Strong emotional contact is paramount to manage such a tragedy. Flexibility and resilience are key in improving the current situation. However, as Lebow[53] reflected, while telepresence is crucial, specific questions need to be asked about the impact of app-mediated prevention programs. It needs to be ensured that the privacy of the members of the family is not compromised. Further, these methods should not suddenly become the predominant methods of practice as family centered care in traditional settings has overarching benefits to the overall ecosystem of healthcare.

Another important concern, as addressed by Luttik et al.,[52] is the vulnerability and risk within the family during the COVID-19 crisis. Long-term care for ill parents, partners, and children during the pandemic requires good nurturing and values within the family. Children requiring specialized care would need guidance for medical nursery, daycare, and education. School closure has further exacerbated the situation. Family members having ill parents also require support and medical treatment. Finally, the partners living in confinement should improve their personal relationships to reduce stress and anxiety during the crisis. Beyond this, COVID-19 has also impacted community inclusiveness, the way traditions and marriages are performed and even limited personal freedom.[52]

6. Social media

Governments worldwide have used ICT to restore economic balance by granting exemptions and enacting legislation to aid in the fight against the pandemic's aftermath. During these times, the ICT industry experienced a rapid shift, with certain technologies finding new uses. Among the technologies that gained popularity were the over-the-top (OTT) services market, video conferencing technology, artificial intelligence (AI), video streaming platforms, team collaboration software, mobile security technology, video on demand (VoD) market, and cloud gaming business.[54]

COVID-19 cases are tracked in real time using AI-based solutions developed to combat the pandemic itself. Because people avoid crowded areas and prefer to shop online, the e-commerce sector has grown dramatically, fueling the proliferation of digital payment methods throughout the pandemic. Furthermore, the Voice over Long-Term Evolution (VoLTE) market has grown rapidly due to the growing adoption of WhatsApp, Messenger, Skype, Hangouts, and other similar platforms due to government regulations that encourage social isolation.[54]

7. Environmental quality

Lockdown has a short-term influence on criteria pollutants, sound pollution, GHG concentrations, overall cleanliness, and the threat to wild and domestic animals. Increased plastic and biomedical waste, decreased recycling, increased organic and inorganic pollutants owing to soap and sanitizer use, higher wastewater, and increased water usage are some of the long-term effects.[55]

7.1 Wildlife

During the lockdown, pollution levels plummeted, public spaces were abandoned, and human contact was restricted, allowing urban wildlife to go outside their regular habitat. In an effort to curb the spread of coronavirus, people have begun to confine themselves to the safety of their homes, and there have been tales of animals venturing into cities all over the world. This global slowdown also allows us to reconsider our relationship with nature and teaches us how to coexist to preserve our urban ecosystem. The fall in wildlife trade is another significant effect of the coronavirus outbreak. The COVID-19 epidemic is thought to have started at a wild animal market in Wuhan, China, putting the global wildlife trade in the limelight. Live animal markets have been recommended to be banned by governments worldwide, as well as illegal wildlife trafficking and poaching. Monkeys, stray dogs, elephants (tourism), and various other wildlife species that have adapted to live in urban areas and are strongly reliant on human-generated food waste to survive have been starved.[56]

7.2 Pollution

The COVID-19 pandemic has established a support system to aid in the cleanup of global air pollution. The cause of pollution in the air has also become evident during the lockdown in the respective countries[57]:

United Kingdom: During the COVID-19 lockdowns, commercial operations and international travel were suspended, resulting in a 20% reduction in electricity and gas use. As countries come out of lockdown, consumption is still 5%–10% lower than before, implying that the industry will not fully recover until the end of 2021 or 2022. COVID-19-induced consumption declines resulted in the highest reduction in greenhouse gas emissions since World War II, with emissions expected to drop by 8.5% in 2020. (Source: Capgemini report, National grid, UK.)

India: In India, the lockdown was imposed in the last week of March 2020 and extended up to May 2nd of 2020. Fig. 8 indicates a steep decrease in energy consumption in these months (Source: POSCO). The pollution levels are indirectly related to the consumption of electricity.

Australia: Victoria's commercial and industrial energy use dropped by 7% and 1%, respectively. Residential load demand increased by 14% in Victoria.[58]

United States: In some parts of the United States, residential energy demand has climbed by 8%. The need for educational and commercial buildings has decreased by 30%. (Source: Statista).

Particulate matter (PM) data levels have been rising in many cities before the lockdown began. However, as a result of the lockdown imposed by

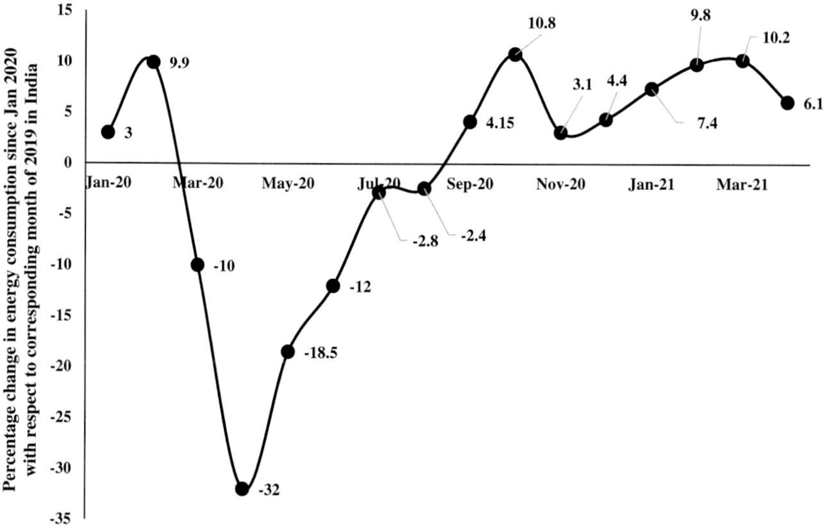

Fig. 8 Energy demand change in 2020 with respect to 2019. *(Source: POSCO.)*

COVID-19, PM data trended downward. It shows that the air quality in these major cities has greatly improved.[43]

As a result of the lockdown, offices, schools, movie theaters, malls, marketplaces, and "nonessential" service providers were all closed, forcing people to stay at home. All public transportation modalities for civilian travel have been stopped, including metro trains, buses, interstate trains, and international and domestic airplanes. As a result of decreasing automobile traffic and aircraft, dangerous nitrogen dioxide (greenhouse gases) and particulate matter produced by cars have dropped. Reduced economic and manufacturing activity also resulted in improvements in localized air quality. A reduction in nitrogen dioxide and methane is also witnessed as a result of a significant reduction in power output and construction activities. The amount of particulate matter in the air has decreased as construction and demolition operations have been reduced. Industry's reduction in energy demand reduced carbon emissions.[59] All these positive effects are short term, and governments should realize the harm caused by the factors discussed earlier and take suitable measures to eradicate them.

7.3 Negative effects

Extensive use of soap, sanitizers, PPE (gloves, masks, and body covers), and mass disinfection resulted in water pollution such as aquatic flora and fauna disturbances, increased wastewater, subsurface contamination, and water body pollution. The earlier mentioned activities also lead to soil pollution due to deteriorated soil quality and also affected plants. Air disinfectants are also observed due to these activities.[55]

7.4 Precipitation

Temperature and precipitation have been linked to the daily occurrence rate of COVID-19 infections. COVID-19 is positively correlated with maximum and normal temperatures. Precipitation, on the other hand, has a negative correlation.[60]

7.5 Human behavior

COVID-19 being an invisible threat has reduced people's trust in each other, making trust more vital than ever before. The forced move to virtual employment, consumption, and socializing will result in a large shift to virtual activity for everything. People believe they cannot rely on current health systems, which might lead to health being addressed in all parts of life, culminating in creating a healthy economy. People are willing to spend on the home and make at home as a result of self-isolation. Under the influence of travel restrictions, self-isolation, and lockdown required by many governments, a reinvention of authority is likely. It is possible that a greater understanding of the government and corporations' roles in society, as well as the value of collective behavior, will emerge.[61]

8. Conclusion

In this chapter, it is seen that the COVID-19 pandemic is impacting various dimensions of society. Six broad dimensions from the social development index, namely, Employment, Education, Healthcare, Family, Social Media, and Environment Quality, are identified to reflect the role of social impact. These factors are further magnified from the lens of SDGs. The data for the sectors suggests the positives and negatives for achieving the SDGs during COVID-19. The loss of working hours equivalent to 255 million full-time jobs has adversely impacted the SDG 8. However, during this period, people have realized the importance of health and family, thus giving importance to SDG 3. While 70% of the women are working for healthcare, there is a significant need to have gender equality at the leadership positions in healthcare. The importance of social media and education together to achieve SDG 4 cannot be overstated. The online education has become a challenge for 30% of students who lack internet access. Further, the opportunities for 51% of foreign students from China and India were also severely compromised during the pandemic. Finally, there have been some positives for SDG 13, as there is a highest reduction in GHG emissions since World War II. Overall, the statistics during the pandemic can help the decision-makers to plan better for the society in the future crisis.

Further, there is a need to address that countries may have conflicting goals during normal times versus during crises, while focusing on individual dimensions. Also, each crisis, earthquakes, cyclones, flood, draughts, and pandemic differ in severity and impact. Thus the policymakers should generate necessary scenarios depending on the severity of the crisis. Considering the challenge of inequality on the one hand and the severity of disease on the aging population, the topic will be receiving more attention in the future as well. Future research directions should integrate the role of community and culture, which act as a coherence for these six broad dimensions. While the pandemic disrupted the supply and demand of several businesses, the impact on society raised questions over international labor standards, worker health and safety, ethical sourcing, and corporate social responsibility. Likewise, future research in this area can address the micro level social needs of organizations within countries.

References

1. Dehghani MH, Roy S, Karri RR. Novel coronavirus (COVID-19) in environmental engineering perspective. *Environ Sci Pollut Res* 2022;1–3. https://doi.org/10.1007/s11356-022-18572-w.
2. Mousazadeh M, Naghdali Z, Rahimian N, Hashemi M, Paital B, Al-Qodah Z, et al. Management of environmental health to prevent an outbreak of COVID-19: a review. In: Dehghani MH, Karri RR, Roy S, editors. *Environmental and health management of novel coronavirus disease (COVID-19)*. Academic Press; 2021. p. 235–67. https://doi.org/10.1016/B978-0-323-85780-2.00007-X.
3. Lambert H, Gupte J, Fletcher H, et al. COVID-19 as a global challenge: towards an inclusive and sustainable future. *Lancet Planet Health* 2020;**4**(8):e312–4. https://doi.org/10.1016/S2542-5196(20)30168-6.
4. Sindhwani R, Saddikuti V. *Responsible supply chains: is COVID-19 a prescription for change?* Logisticsinsider.in; 2020. https://logisticsinsider.in/responsible-supply-chains-is-covid-19-a-prescription-for-change/.
5. Heymann J, Raub A, Waisath W, et al. Protecting health during COVID-19 and beyond: a global examination of paid sick leave design in 193 countries. *Glob Public Health* 2020;**15**(7):925–34. https://doi.org/10.1080/17441692.2020.1764076.
6. Hamid MZBSA, Karri RR. Overview of preventive measures and good governance policies to mitigate the COVID-19 outbreak curve in Brunei. In: *COVID-19: systemic risk and resilience*. Cham: Springer; 2021. p. 115–40.
7. Kovács G, Matopoulos A, Hayes O. A community-based approach to supply chain design. *Int J Logist* 2010;**5567**. https://doi.org/10.1080/13675567.2010.511609.

8. Tang CS. Socially responsible supply chains in emerging markets: some research opportunities. *J Oper Manag* 2018;**57**:1–10. https://doi.org/10.1016/j.jom.2018.01.002.
9. de los Reyes G, Scholz M, Smith NC. Beyond the "win-win": creating shared value requires ethical frameworks. *Calif Manage Rev* 2017;**59**(2):142–67. https://doi.org/10.1177/0008125617695286.
10. Stiglitz JE, Sen A, Fitoussi J-P. *Report by the commission on the measurement of economic performance and social progress*; 2009.
11. Martens K, Niemann D, Kaasch A. International organizations and the architecture of arguments in global social governance. *International organizations in global social governance. Global Dynamics of Social Policy*. Cham: Palgrave Macmillan; 2021. https://doi.org/10.1007/978-3-030-65439-9_14.
12. Schmidt H, Gostin LO, Emanuel EJ. Public health, universal health coverage, and sustainable development goals: can they coexist? *Lancet* 2015;**386**(9996):928–30. https://doi.org/10.1016/S0140-6736(15)60244-6.
13. UNESCO. *One year into COVID: prioritizing education recovery to avoid a generational catastrophe*; 2021 https://unesdoc.unesco.org/ark:/48223/pf0000376984.
14. International Labour Organization (ILO). *ILO monitor: COVID-19 and the world of work*. 7th ed; 2021. https://doi.org/10.1787/eco_surveys-nzl-2017-graph8-en.
15. Mukherjee A, Babu SS, Ghosh S. Thinking about water and air to attain sustainable development goals during times of COVID-19 pandemic. *J Earth Syst Sci* 2020;**129**(1). https://doi.org/10.1007/s12040-020-01475-0.
16. International Labour Organization (ILO). *Global employment trends for youth 2020: technology and the future of jobs*; 2020 https://www.ilo.org/wcmsp5/groups/public/—dgreports/—dcomm/—publ/documents/publication/wcms_737648.pdf.
17. Kluge HHP, Jakab Z, Bartovic J, D'Anna V, Severoni S. Refugee and migrant health in the COVID-19 response. *Lancet* 2020;**395**(10232):1237–9. https://doi.org/10.1016/S0140-6736(20)30791-1.
18. International Labour Organization (ILO). *COVID-19 and the world of work: impact and policy responses*. ILO; 2020. https://https://www.ilo.org/wcmsp5/groups/public/- - -dgreports/- - -dcomm/documents/briefingnote/wcms_738753.pdf.
19. Inanc H. Breaking down the numbers : what does COVID-19 mean for youth unemployment ? *Mathematica* 2020;1–22. https://www.mathematica.org/our-publications-and-findings/publications/breaking-down-the-numbers-what-does-covid-19-mean-for-youth-unemployment.
20. de Carvalho ÍCS, Di Serio LC, Guimarães CMC, Furlanetto KS. The social progress on the development of global competitiveness. *Compet Rev* 2020;**31**(4):713–28. https://doi.org/10.1108/CR-12-2018-0078.
21. International Labour Organization (ILO). *COVID-19 and the world of work: updated estimates and analysis*; 2020 https://www.ilo.org/wcmsp5/groups/public/@dgreports/@dcomm/documents/briefingnote/wcms_749399.pdf.
22. International Labour Organization (ILO). *ILO monitor: COVID-19 and the world of work*. 2nd ed; 2020. https://doi.org/10.18356/ba5cc386-en.
23. International Labour Organization (ILO). *COVID-19 and the world of work*. Int Labour Organ; 2020. p. 1–22 [April] https://www.ilo.org/wcmsp5/groups/public/@dgreports/@dcomm/documents/briefingnote/wcms_749399.pdf.
24. Buomprisco G, Ricci S, Perri R, De Sio S. Health and telework: new challenges after COVID-19 pandemic. *Eur J Environ Public Health* 2021;**5**(2). https://doi.org/10.21601/ejeph/9705, em0073.
25. Godderis L, Luyten J. Challenges and opportunities for occupational health and safety after the COVID-19 lockdowns. *Occup Environ Med* 2020;**77**(8):511–2. https://doi.org/10.1136/oemed-2020-106645.
26. Ely A, Habibi R. Human rights and coronavirus: What's at stake for truth, trust, and democracy? *Health Hum Rights* 2020;4–7.

27. Chen C, Shi Y, Zhang P, Ding C. A cross-country comparison of fiscal policy responses to the COVID-19 global pandemic. *J Comp Policy Anal Res Pract* 2021;**23**(2):262–73. https://doi.org/10.1080/13876988.2021.1878885.
28. Sahoo P, Ashwani. COVID-19 and Indian economy: impact on growth, manufacturing, trade and MSME sector. *Glob Bus Rev* 2020;**21**(5):1159–83. https://doi.org/10.1177/0972150920945687.
29. Jaramillo Sandra Garcia. *COVID-19 and primary and secondary education: the impact of the crisis and public policy implications for Latin America and the Caribbean.* UNDP; 2020, https:// https://www.undp.org/latin-america/publications/covid-19-and-primary-and-secondary-education-impact-crisis-and-public-policy-implications-latin-america-and-caribbean.
30. Cullen R. Addressing the digital divide. *Online Inf Rev* 2001;**25**(5):311–20. https://doi.org/10.1108/14684520110410517.
31. Ramsetty A, Adams C. Impact of the digital divide in the age of COVID-19. *J Am Med Inform Assoc* 2020;**27**(7):1147–8. https://doi.org/10.1093/jamia/ocaa078.
32. UNESCO. *A snapshot of educational challenges and opportunities for recovery in Africa*; 2021 https://unesdoc.unesco.org/ark:/48223/pf0000377513.
33. Huber SG, Helm C. COVID-19 and schooling: evaluation, assessment and accountability in times of crises—reacting quickly to explore key issues for policy, practice and research with the school barometer. *Educ Assess Eval Account* 2020;**32**(2):237–70.
34. Seshasai KVS. *Early childhood education: a silent victim of COVID-19?* Indianexpress.com; 2021. https://indianexpress.com/article/parenting/learning/early-childhood-education-a-silent-victim-of-covid-19-7300641/.
35. World Bank. *Learning poverty.* The World Bank; 2019. https://www.worldbank.org/en/topic/education/brief/learning-poverty.
36. Farr A. *The effects of the coronavirus on primary education.* Borgen Mag; November 2020. https://www.borgenmagazine.com/the-effects-of-the-coronavirus-on-primary-education/.
37. Kreitz M. *The impact of COVID-19 on high school students.* childandadolescent.org; 2020. https://www.childandadolescent.org/the-impact-of-covid-19-on-high-school-students/.
38. Times higher education. *The impact of coronavirus on higher education.* Times higher education; 2020. https://www.timeshighereducation.com/hub/keystone-academic-solutions/p/impact-coronavirus-higher-education.
39. Bishop PA. Middle grades teacher practices during the COVID-19 pandemic. *RMLE Online* 2021;**44**(7):1–18. https://doi.org/10.1080/19404476.2021.1959832.
40. Jiménez-Sánchez C. Impact of the SARS-CoV2 pandemic on education. *Rev Electron Educ* 2020;**24**(May):1–3.
41. Radecki J, Schonfeld RC. The impacts of COVID-19 on the research enterprise: a landscape review. *Ithaka S+R* 2020;**34**.
42. Ong AKS, Prasetyo YT, Young MN, et al. Students' preference analysis on online learning attributes in industrial engineering education during the covid-19 pandemic: a conjoint analysis approach for sustainable industrial engineers. *Sustainability* 2021;**13**(15). https://doi.org/10.3390/su13158339.
43. Gayen A, Haque SM, Mishra SV. COVID-19 induced lockdown and decreasing particulate matter (PM10): an empirical investigation of an Asian megacity. *Urban Clim* 2021;**36**(July 2020). https://doi.org/10.1016/j.uclim.2021.100786, 100786.
44. Gorman E, Connolly B, Couper K, Perkins GD, McAuley DF. Non-invasive respiratory support strategies in COVID-19. *Lancet Respir Med* 2021;**9**(6):553–6. https://doi.org/10.1016/S2213-2600(21)00168-5.
45. Knott M. *How do coronaviruses affect the body?* Medical News Today; 2021. https://www.medicalnewstoday.com/articles/coronavirus-effects-on-body#covid-19.

46. Chowdhury MA, Hossain N, Kashem MA, Shahid MA, Alam A. Immune response in COVID-19: a review. *J Infect Public Health* 2020;**13**(11):1619–29. https://doi.org/10.1016/j.jiph.2020.07.001.
47. Lal A, Erondu NA, Heymann DL, Gitahi G, Yates R. Fragmented health systems in COVID-19: rectifying the misalignment between global health security and universal health coverage. *Lancet* 2021;**397**(10268):61–7. https://doi.org/10.1016/S0140-6736(20)32228-5.
48. WHO. *Ethical considerations to guide the use of digital proximity tracking technologies for COVID-19 contact tracing*. World Health Organization; 2020. p. 6 [May] https://https://apps.who.int/iris/bitstream/handle/10665/332200/WHO-2019-nCoV-Ethics_Contact_tracing_apps-2020.1-eng.pdf.
49. WHO. *Operational guidance for maintaining essential health services during an outbreak*. World Health Organ; 2020. p. 1–10 [March] https://www.who.int/publications-detail/covid-19-operational-guidance-for-maintaining-essential-health-services-during-an-outbreak.
50. Butler MJ, Barrientos RM. The impact of nutrition on COVID-19 susceptibility and long-term consequences. *Brain Behav Immun* 2020;**87**:53–4.
51. Hart JL, Turnbull AE, Oppenheim IM, Courtright KR. Family-centered care during the COVID-19 era. *J Pain Symptom Manage* 2020;**60**(2):e93–7. https://doi.org/10.1016/j.jpainsymman.2020.04.017.
52. Luttik MLA, Mahrer-Imhof R, García-Vivar C, et al. The COVID-19 pandemic: a family affair. *J Fam Nurs* 2020;**26**(2):87–9. https://doi.org/10.1177/1074840720920883.
53. Lebow JL. Family in the age of COVID-19. *Fam Process* 2020;**59**(2):309–12. https://doi.org/10.1111/famp.12543.
54. ResearchAndMarkets. *Emergence of COVID-19: impact on ICT sector*; 2020 https://www.researchandmarkets.com/reports/5238702/emergence-of-covid-19-impact-on-ict-sector.
55. Ghafoor D, Khan Z, Khan A, Ualiyeva D, Zaman N. Excessive use of disinfectants against COVID-19 posing a potential threat to living beings. *Curr Res Toxicol* 2021;**2** (January):159–68. https://doi.org/10.1016/j.crtox.2021.02.008.
56. Sandilya A. *How COVID-19 pandemic has affected wildlife*; 2020 https://wildlifesos.org/chronological-news/how-covid-19-pandemic-has-affected-wildlife/.
57. Comunian S, Dongo D, Milani C, Palestini P. Air pollution and covid-19: the role of particulate matter in the spread and increase of covid-19's morbidity and mortality. *Int J Environ Res Public Health* 2020;**17**(12):1–22. https://doi.org/10.3390/ijerph17124487.
58. Madurai Elavarasan R, Shafiullah GM, Raju K, et al. COVID-19: impact analysis and recommendations for power sector operation. *Appl Energy* 2020;**279**(August). https://doi.org/10.1016/j.apenergy.2020.115739, 115739.
59. Suman R, Javaid M, Choudhary SK, et al. Impact of COVID-19 pandemic on particulate matter (PM) concentration and harmful gaseous components on Indian metros. *Sustain Oper Comput* 2021;**2**(October 2020):1–11. https://doi.org/10.1016/j.susoc.2021.02.001.
60. Menebo MM. Temperature and precipitation associate with Covid-19 new daily cases: a correlation study between weather and Covid-19 pandemic in Oslo, Norway. *Sci Total Environ* 2020;**737**. https://doi.org/10.1016/j.scitotenv.2020.139659, 139659.
61. Accenture. *COVID-19: 5 new human truths that experiences need to address*. Accenture; April 2020. https://www.accenture.com/in-en/about/company/coronavirus-human-experience.

CHAPTER TWELVE

The impact of COVID-19 in curbing the goals of ensuring sustainable development of life on land (SDG 15) and below water (SDG 14)

Louis Anto Nirmal and Samuel Jacob
Department of Biotechnology, School of Bioengineering, College of Engineering and Technology, Faculty of Engineering and Technology, SRM Institute of Science and Technology, Kattankulathur, Tamil Nadu, India

1. Introduction

In 2015 all the United Nations (UN) participant countries adopted the 2030 Agenda for sustainable development, ensuring an urgent action on the need of the hour crisis of life. Significant efforts to improve health and its infrastructure, tackle climate change, poverty eradication, ensure equality, and create opportunities for proper economic growth have been emphasized by the UN. To ensure all these needs, 17 sustainable developmental goals (SDG) were agreed by the world leaders and it's been already 6 years as of 2021 since being implemented and the goal is to fulfill all these goals by 2030.[1] Most of the key targets were supposed to be implemented by 2020. Despite progress within the extension of sustainable wildlife supervision and endangered area coverage for land, marine, and highland ranges, and the implementation of legislative, administrative, and accounting principles by various nations to guard ecosystems and biodiversity, the conservation goal remains threatened.[1]

In December 2019, severe acute respiratory syndrome coronavirus (SARS-CoV-2), named as novel coronavirus disease (COVID-19), originated and transmitted to major parts of the world with respiratory droplets from sneeze and cough between humans as a very common mode of transmission.[2] Some studies suggest that the spread of SARS-CoV-2 can be transmitted through contact with the COVID-19-infected person via object or airborne transmission.[3–5] Initially, the virus started affecting elders and

COVID-19 and the Sustainable Development Goals
https://doi.org/10.1016/B978-0-323-91307-2.00012-2

immune-compromised individuals severely.[6] As a result of its severity, COVID-19 was declared as a global pandemic and health emergency by the World Health Organization (WHO). SARS-CoV-2 in humans causes symptoms ranging from mild to severe symptoms depending on the individual's immune system. These symptoms include fatigue, high fever, abnormal respiratory functioning, sore throat, abnormal gastrointestinal behavior, loss of taste and smell for less severe cases, and acute-to-severe respiratory distress syndrome (ARDS) for very severe cases which required medical attention.[7] The implementation of these sustainable goals was affected due to the global pandemic. The world came to a halt, and it's been almost a year, and still, we are yet to recover from it. The worldwide pandemic has caused the closure of borders, reduced migration, and remote finances.[8,9] This worldwide pandemic affected global health and economic security.[10,11] The prospects of the second wave and the future waves have raised concerns about achieving these goals by 2030.

The world has been progressing to ensure better health infrastructure even in remote areas with the main aim of tackling COVID-19. The complete priority focus now is to eradicate COVID-19 by improving and implementing advanced technologies in vaccine manufacturing and medications.[12] Most countries were under lockdown for almost 3/4th of the year, while some countries are still following the lockdown restriction with only priorities being functioned.[13] The economic downfall for the countries could play a vital role in restricting the implementation of these targets in both developed and developing nations. The focus right now is to ensure increased job opportunities, establish healthcare technologies and facilities, poverty eradication, etc.[12] At the same time, the sustainability of terrestrial plants, animals, and the aquatic ecosystem is not prioritized.

Wildlife trafficking led to the ecosystem's disruption and a causative reason for spreading infectious diseases to animals. The UN stated that only 38 out of 113 nations were on track to integrate biodiversity with the national planning.[14] The SDGs are nonbinding treaties, and governments are likely to line their importance and target values. Their execution will mainly happen at the federal level, following the general steps of the policy-planning series, from priority setting of targets and indicators to policy assessment, judgment, and execution.[12,14]

SDG incorporation in curriculum nurtures students with contemporary education practices more than traditional methods of teaching instruction, research and undertaking more sustainable education methods is essential for helping scholars, and the larger community meet societal and environmental challenges and overcome socioeconomic development challenges both within the country and globally. The SDG tactics are rapidly getting modified to support the role of education institutions by making them the cutting edge of sustainable development.[15] Hence, by doing this, it offers a competitive benefit to education institutions. The UN has announced 2020–30 as the "Decade of Action" in attaining these SDGs.[16] SDG 14 emphasizes the preservation and sustainable usage of oceans and other marine supplies, including aquatic living. While SDG 15 emphasizes protecting, restoring, and encouraging the sustainable practice of maintaining terrestrial ecosystems, managing forests, fighting against desertification, and bringing land degradation to a standstill and thereby restricting the biodiversity loss (Table 1).[16] After COVID-19, due to the absence of additional financial funding allocated to achieve these goals, developing countries find it challenging to propose cost-effectively innovative policy mechanisms.[18]

COVID-19 has created both negative as well as positive opportunities in achieving the SDG goals. This chapter will elaborate on the impact of COVID-19 in implementing the goals of life on land (SDG 15) and life

Table 1 Agenda or targets of SDG 14 and SDG 15 between the years 2020 and 2030.[14,16,17]

SDG 14	SDG 15
Significantly reduce and prevent marine pollution from land-based activities and nutrient pollution	Conservation and sustainable use of terrestrial and inland freshwater ecosystems
Protect marine ecosystem and take actions on restoration for more productive oceans	Restore degraded forests and halt deforestation
Minimize ocean acidification	Battle desertification and restore degraded land which was due to drought and floods
Effectively regulate harvesting and prevent overfishing	Conservation of mountain ecosystem
Conserve 10% of coastal and marine ecosystem	Prevent the loss of biodiversity and extinction of threatened species
Eliminate fishery subsidies which are toward overfishing and unregulated methods	Sharing of the benefits from utilizing genetic resources and promote access to such resources
Increase economic benefits of developing countries through sustainable fishing and tourism	Take necessary actions to end wildlife trafficking and conserve the priority species

below water (SDG 14). Also, this chapter provides a clear understanding of how life on land and water influence each other in achieving the goals.

2. Key targets and impact of COVID-19 on SDG 14 (life below water)

Our oceans have a crucial role in making the earth habitable owing to the factors like the ocean's temperature, pressure differences, cyclones, chemistry, and their ecosystem. The rainwater we receive and the climate, oxygen, and food are provided and regulated by these water bodies.[19] Thus careful management of these resources below the water, by not affecting their ecosystem, is essential in creating a sustainable future.[19] There are few targets proposed by the UN to achieve in different target years as illustrated in Fig. 1 to ensure sustainability.

2.1 Reduction of marine pollution

This is one of the significant targets severely affected by COVID-19. The goal is to prevent and reduce substantial levels of marine pollution by

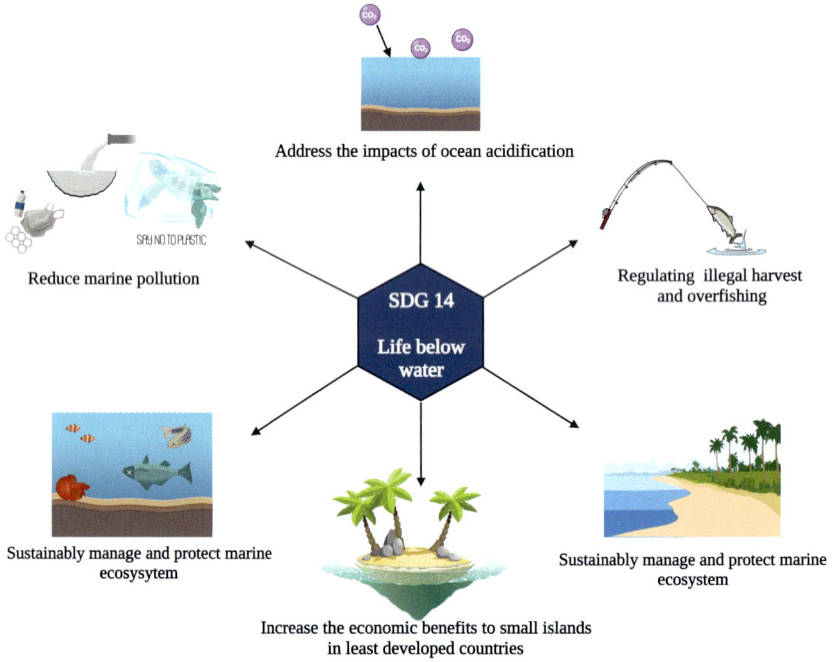

Fig 1 Key targets of SDG 14 (life below water) to be achieved by 2030.

2025. Studies have shown that tons of plastics that are used on land have made their way to the water bodies. It is estimated that an overall 4.8–12.7 million metric tons (MT) of plastic waste due to the waste disposal mismanagement of people on land entered the marine environment in a year.[20] Around half of these plastics are dumped into the oceans through rivers.[21] Eriksen et al.[22] stated that over 5 trillion plastics were floating in the oceans worldwide, leading to vast contamination of these water resources. The increased levels of plastic debris found in the oceans worldwide have created a major environmental and commercial crisis. Every year, a projected 5 to 12 million metric tonnes (MT) of plastic enters the ocean. As a result, the cleaning up cost and the financial loss in fisheries roughly cost about $13 billion every year. In this case, about 89% of plastic clutter identified on the ocean bed are Single-Use Plastics (SUP), primarily plastic bags.[23]

COVID-19 has majorly influenced this marine pollution since its arrival. The usage of N95 masks and other surgical masks were advised to reduce the transmission of COVID-19. This led to the extensive use of these masks, which are primarily made up of polyethylene terephthalate (PET) and polypropylene (PP). Even the gloves and other protective equipment were made up of these polymers like polyethylene (PE), PET, and PP. All these used plastic wastes were dumped into the rivers, which eventually reached the oceans, contaminating them. These plastics entering the oceans might degrade into microplastics.[24–26] Over a year, the demand for SUP has increased due to the usage of this personal protective equipment (PPE). The PP density for the surgical mask was about 20–25 g/m^2 in the case of the surgical mask, while the N95 masked had a PP density of 25–50 g/m^2. Those quantities of PP are very high for single use.[27,28] The degradation of these plastics into microplastics would be difficult to treat later due to their smaller size. Microplastics pose a severe threat to the marine ecosystem and also affects the food chain because of its longtime of decay.[28,29] It takes centuries to decay these plastics and will be a part of our environment for a more extended period. Studies have shown that these masks and plastics were already identified in major oceans, seas, shores, and other water bodies.[30,31] The fate of these microplastics is as follows: (i) plastics getting washed away onto beaches and shores, (ii) float on the oceans, (iii) deposit on the ocean bed, and (iv) ingested by living organisms like fishes and birds. The lockdowns, fewer workforce, and focus toward healthcare emergencies had let to this mismanagement and ultimately led to the disposal of these plastics without proper treatment into water bodies.[32] Though, the mismanagement of plastic disposal was understandable at the start of the pandemic due to the lack of awareness. Even after a year of learning to manage this pandemic, still, these masks are disposed of into the oceans raises a concern.[32] The mitigation of this plastic released into the marine environment requires massive government funding in order to achieve the SDG target. This particular target is scheduled to be accomplished by 2025.[17]

Not only microplastics but the untreated sewage discharge with increased nutrient concentration without prior treatment were released into oceans that could cause increased eutrophication and affects the aquatic animals and plants under water.[33] As the world was on a halt, the wastewater treatment plants were not functioning to its limit. The challenges and impacts of COVID-19 on this target would require immediate action and focus on achieving this goal within the stipulated time.

2.2 Rebuilding aquatic life

Intensive human activities have been reduced due to this pandemic. The water-based logistics haven't been in full swing as there are a lot of restrictions followed by each country. This has reduced the sound generated in these water bodies, which has benefited the aquatic organisms. It has been found that the organisms living under water moved toward the coast due to the lack of human and economic activities near the shore. Though these are few significant advantages, the land activities have had a significant impact on these species living below water. Plastic production has increased by 200 folds (2015) than it was in 1950.[34] The increased plastic production and the decreased recycling potential have affected the marine environment to an extent. Plastic litter reaching the marine bodies affected around 800 marine species in numerous ways like entanglement, ingestion, and harmful alteration of the environment.[35] Thus the main aim of the target (SDG 14.2) is to manage and protect all marine and coastal ecosystems in order to prevent adverse impacts, strengthen their resilience to fight, and conduct restoration plans to attain a health and more productive ecosystem.[36] The toxic chemicals released from land cause changes in the body and growth function of the aquatic organism. With 2020 being a crucial year for achieving this target, COVID-19 didn't help in attaining it. The research to develop a healthy aquatic environment has taken a hit as most of the research funding is prioritized for vaccines. It is difficult for developing nations to allocate funds for this research when all the funds are directed toward helping people getting back to their everyday life. In order to restore this marine system, proper research should be conducted in developing the scientific knowledge about the ecosystem and advance in research potential and marine transfer technology (Target 14.A). Indicator 14.A.1 is the proportion of the research budget allocated for research in the field of marine technology.[36] It has been estimated that over 3 billion people around the world depend on marine biodiversity for their living. There were very limited fishing activities that happened during the global pandemic affecting the livelihood of the people dependent on this. Key events in fisheries or aquaculture are fishing, fish farming, processing, transport of inputs, supply and circulation, and retail and wholesale marketing. All the activities of this supply chain process are deemed to be vital for success. Every phase of the supply chain is prone to be interrupted or hindered by the impacts and restrictive measures of COVID-19.[37] So once when the restrictions are being lifted, it is important to ensure that there is no such occurrence of overfishing. So, it is extremely important for the government to ensure the regulation of these activities after pandemic to avoid the prospects of overfishing, destructive fishing activities which would affect the ecosystem as per the target (SDG 14.4).

2.3 Ocean acidification

The early stages of the pandemic and lockdown restrictions showed positive signs in the reduction of global warming. With gradual reversal of lockdown and improper management of biomedical wastes that include hospital PPE kits disposed from viral infected environment has prompted attention from environmentalists and government towards negative impact on the ecosystem. Open incineration eventually increase the CO_2 levels in the atmosphere which in turn lead to ocean acidification thereby affecting the fulfilment if SDG 14.3 target. Acidification of oceans occurs as a result of the atmospheric CO_2 dissolved in water causing increased pH, making the water acid and also warmer. As a result of acidification, the oxygen levels start to dip and thus it suffocates some marine species and ultimately leads to shrinking their habitats. Increased temperatures could result in the surge of the speed of organisms or species within their thermal tolerance window but could also result in the rapid deterioration of cellular processes and functions when the temperature reaches higher than the tolerance limit.[38] Envisaging the collective effects of warming and acidification is hard, as ocean warming could either offset the results of marine acidification or intensify it through building up of stress effects.[39,40] Water with high pH affects crustacean animals which have shells like oysters and corals. The increased acidification of seawaters creates algal blooms, which make other marine animals sick. They will also prevent the sunlight from reaching the aquatic organisms. Thus it is essential to manage the disposal of wastes generated as a result of COVID-19, as the incineration of toxic substances from land can indirectly affect the marine water system and the organisms living in it.

3. Key targets and its impact of COVID-19 on life on land (SDG 15)

The priority aim of this goal is to protect and restore the resources on land and has vital targets to be accomplished in order to make this a success (Fig. 2). The aim of promoting sustainable use of land and ecosystem is not a cause, but it is essential for our survival on land. While its initial glance primarily focused on environmental matters, the goal is of much broader significance.

Together with Goals 6, 13, and 14, it can be considered central in the architecture of the 2030 Agenda, as natural resources and their sustainable

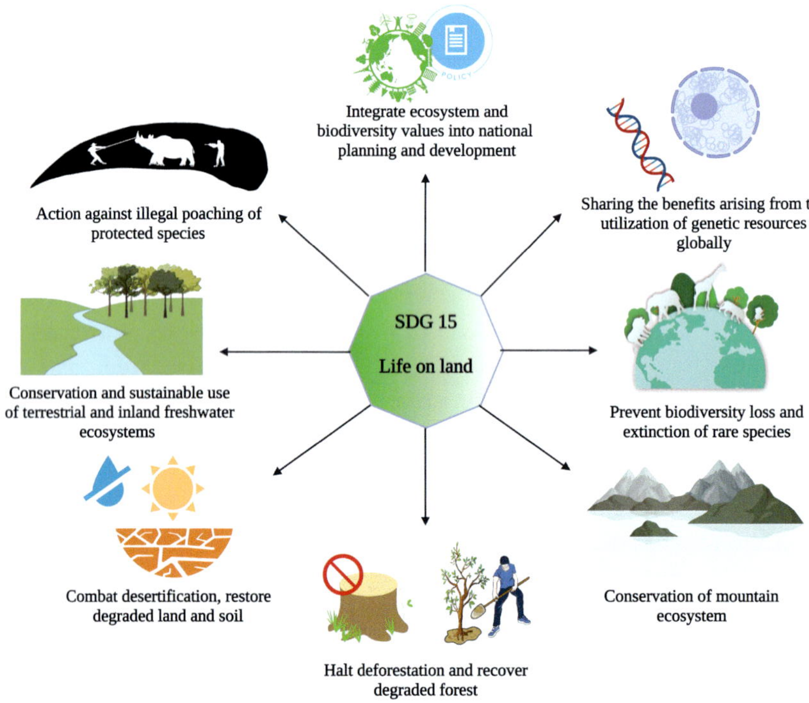

Fig 2 The proposed targets by the UN on SDG 15 (life on land).

management are relevant to achieving all SDGs and essential to avoid severe troubles to ecosystems, society, and economics.[41] It has been stated that almost 75% of the Earth surface has been altered by the humans. This leads to almost 1 million animal and plant species to the level of extinction.[42]

Forfeiture of biodiversity has the potential to have an effect on food security, economic and social welfare worldwide and particularly for people who heavily trust on local ecosystem which facilities their living.[42] In addition, global climate change and biodiversity are interrelated. Global climate change influences biodiversity. Biodiversity, through ecosystem services, can aid in climate change mitigation. Therefore ensuring sustainability, conservation, and restoration of biodiversity is a substantial tool to tackle global climate change. As we encroach and occupy fragile environments, this leads to the contact of humans with wildlife leading to the transmission of pathogens to humans, increasing and amplifying the risk of disease emergence. This emergence of zoonotic diseases, i.e., transmissible diseases between humans and animals, could affect the health of our planet in all major ways. Like SARS-CoV and MERS-CoV, SARS-CoV-2 is also an example of a zoonotic origin.[5]

The United Nations Environment Programme (UNEP) has provided four ways to support member countries to build back after COVID-19 pandemic. Its first aim is to help countries to manage COVID-19 waste followed by delivering a change of lifestyle for people and to conserve the nature. It also aims to guarantee economic recovery packages to fight the current pandemic and future crisis. It ensures revolutionizing worldwide environmental governance.

3.1 Factors causing zoonosis emergence

The COVID-19 outbreak threw some light on the future impacts of these zoonotic diseases. Through the global pandemic, the Earth has received its strongest warning to date to start addressing these issues seriously. The UNEP, in 2016, highlighted the emergence of zoonotic diseases worldwide as a major concern and stated that 75% of all infectious diseases affecting humans were zoonotic diseases. Coronaviruses are zoonotic which means it is transmitted between humans and animals. Severe Acute Respiratory Syndrome (SARS) and Middle East Respiratory Syndrome (MERS) were identified to be communicated from animals to humans.[43] Better forest management and supervision could play a vital role to limit the transmission of future zoonotic diseases. As a result of deforestation and green cover degrading, the buffer zones separating humans from animals decrease, thus increasing the probabilities of transmission of these zoonotic pathogens between the animal species as well as between animal species and humans.[44,45] The communication of these diseases to humans could be due to some animal attack, increased bushmeat hunting, killing animals, illegal wildlife trafficking—all these are related to wildlife fragmentation.[46–48]

Scientists believe that degraded wildlife habitats may boost quicker evolutionary processes as pathogens transmit easily to humans and other livestock. The factors causing zoonosis emergence were identified as follows: (i) increased deforestation, desertification, and other land alterations; (ii) increased agricultural cultivation and livestock production; (iii) poor monitoring and regulation laws for wildlife trade; (iv) the ineffectiveness of antibiotics due to its acquired antimicrobial resistance; (v) climate change.[49] Human intervention and wildlife trafficking could transmit infections from humans to animals too. Recent forest fragmentations are known as landscape processes which are interceded by human behaviors, and this enables direct transmission of zoonotic infections.[50,51] Especially, the spread of diseased bodily fluids from Nonhuman Primates (NHP) through direct contact has created the emergence of latest infections witnessed by human population, most particularly the origin of HIV almost 100 years before.[52] Numerous novel zoonotic disease-causing pathogens are the viruses that arise as humans and animals acquire increased interaction with wildlife animals which are the hosts of zoonotic pathogens. The danger for the exposure of latest zoonotic agents from wildlife depends mainly on three factors: (1) the range of microbes in a wildlife region, (2) the consequences of environmental modification on the occurrence of pathogens in wild populations, (3) the frequency of human and animal interaction of potential zoonoses within the wildlife regions.[53]

3.2 Emerging challenges in achieving SDG 15 due to COVID-19

One of the noticeable and immediate effects of COVID-19 was normally seen with the changes in policy as a response to the global epidemic like restricted budget sanction, allocation of environmental funds related to SDG to other pandemic relief sectors, forest restoration programs were on hold because of travel limitations, and simplification of environmental regulations, affecting forest protection and maintenance operations to a larger extent. For instance, countries like Ecuador and Mexico in Latin America have declared budget cuts that could directly impact organizations which enforce environmental guidelines and regulation in the aim of fighting global climate change.[54] Another consequence of the COVID-19 pandemic is the limited human resources availability.[55] Therefore several activities related to forest monitoring, management, and afforestation were affected, and these dangers are going to be soon seen in the aspect of unnoticed forest fires, agricultural farming or plantation extension, overgrazing, excessive plant growth, pest attack, and prohibited deforestation.[56,57] The highly increased infection and mortality rates, health issues, and other health concerns increase the limitations to the present labor scarcity. Recent on-field conservation surveys have been brought to halt as the experts and workers were either affected by COVID-19 or asked to return back to their home countries as a precautionary measure. This has brought a slowdown in conservation activities being conducted worldwide.[58] Protection and maintenance of the environment aided by the ecotourism sector have caused a major consequence owing to the fact that income source from the tourism will not be available due to COVID-19-related travel restrictions.[59,60] The idea of ecotourism, with the vision of sustainable development, started in the 1980s, to generate tourism revenues to be used in conservation and development plans.[61] As a result of COVID-19, the ecotourism, which is completely intertwined with nature, countries like Costa Rica and India faced complete shutdown for almost a year, and this could create negative effects on the same ecosystem and environmental-related benefits in the future.[61] Studies have revealed that the return of migrant workers back to their natives also created an excessive burden on the exploitation of the forest lands and caused uncontrolled forest alteration.[62] With migrant workers coming back to their natives, there is no doubt in observing a fall in their income levels and an increased need of agricultural supplies, which could increase the dangers of illegal deforestation.[62,63] Furthermore, rural families are expected to deal with income shortages by using additional forest resources, thereby being reliant and increased burden on wildlife forests.[64] COVID-19 emphasizes the need for careful observation of the changing ecological aspects of fragmented forests due to their potential to create hotspots displaying increased human-wildlife interaction.[65] The interaction with wildlife could create an opportunity for zoonotic transmission, leading to endless pandemics. Desertification, land degradation, and drought are associated with the loss of animal habitat and the transmission of diseases including COVID-19.[66] The rate of the next zoonotic disease emergence in the future will be very closely linked to the progression of the relationship shared between humans and the environment, predominantly in the growth of the agricultural frontier.[67]

The lockdown restrictions and the quarantine rules which were followed in most countries have caused an increase in consumers to buy things and food online. As a result, the organic wastes generated by each household increased drastically. Along with that, the food and things purchased is shipped packed, leading to inorganic waste generation.[67] The medical wastes are also on the increasing trend. Hospitals in Wuhan generated a mean of 247 metric tonnes (MT) of medical waste every day during the early pandemic, while their previous average before the pandemic was less than 50 tons.[68] In countries like the USA, India, and Brazil, where the population is comparatively higher, there has been a rise in garbage from PPE like masks and gloves.[69] The collection of the household wastes was not possible during the lockdown phases. Thus the disposal of wastes at that time was difficult to manage and was found to be disposed locally, causing contamination of the inland water bodies.

The World Health Organization (WHO) has announced that COVID-19, just like MERS, SARS, Ebola, and Bird Flu, originated from an animal. Scientists claim that the trafficking of pangolins in South East Asia could be a crisis, as these trafficked animals carry viruses very closely related to the current coronavirus. The unending COVID-19 crisis has brought attention to the wildlife trafficking of conserved species and other species (SDG Target 15.7) worldwide.[70] In general, pangolins were often illegally trafficked in South East Asia, as they are consumed as food and in traditional medicine. It is also said that the trade of wildlife and products has increased by shifting to online platforms as traffickers have initiated new methods to connect with interested buyers.[70] The lack of people monitoring due to COVID-19, health reasons, social distancing, time restrictions, and other precautions has made the process of wildlife trafficking and illegal export of conserved species easier.

Due to the increased consumption of plastics worldwide, an excess of SUPs would be expected to get accumulate as a result of mismanaged plastic wastes disposal. So, stress and strict laws should be in practice to reduce of intentional disposal of plastics before proper management. This could radically cut the countless PPEs which might have been littered into sewers, thus preventing the running waters from being blocked and overflowing of these waters into the streets of urban zones and supports reducing the spread of infectious diseases. Proper recycling of these PPE kits is essential in order to save the environment from plastics. Thus preserving various sorts of life on the terrestrial land requires meticulous planning of the targeted efforts to safeguard, reestablish, restore, and promote the preservation and sustainable use of terrestrial and other related ecosystems. Due to the overlaps between the goals, the crisis of SDG 15 has a cascading influence on other goals, particularly SDG 3 (Good Health and Well-being) and SDG 13 (Climate Action). Similarly, as shown in Fig. 3, the impacts of COVID-19 faced on land indirectly affect the life below water affecting SDG 14. Loss of biodiversity leans toward increasing pathogen spread and disease occurrence. Since forests hold 80% of the Earth's terrestrial species and contribute upto 1/3rd of carbon sequestration, it is essential to mitigate the global warming and curb the temperature-rise below 2°C. Immediate action on SDG 15 over the next 10 years should be mandatory despite arguments in certain quarters that developing nations are better off following economic and social policies in the short run.[71]

SDG 15 emphasizes precisely on managing forests sustainably, reversing and stopping land and natural habitation degradation, effectively avoiding

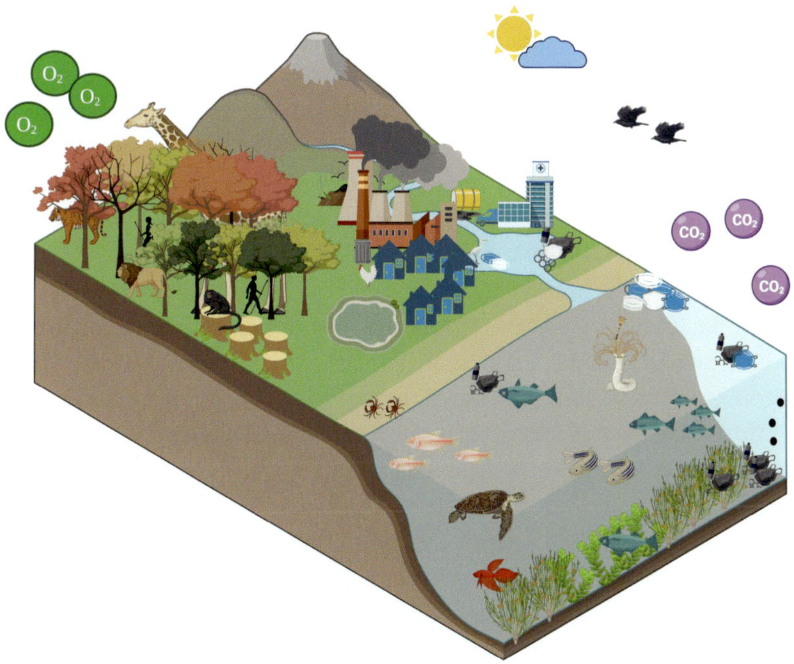

Fig 3 The impact of COVID-19 on land indirectly affecting life below water.

desertification, and ending biodiversity loss. Overall, all these efforts' collective purpose is to make sure that the rewards of terrestrial ecosystems, plus sustainable livelihoods, are going to be relished by future generations.

4. Efforts undertaken by the countries after COVID-19 crisis

Deforestation, degradation of forests, sustained biodiversity loss, and the continuing degradation of ecosystems have reflective consequences for human welfare and existence. The world countries fell short on the targets fixed for 2020 to stop biodiversity loss.[58] The decline in biodiversity is a factor in species extinction, leading to more delicate ecosystems and not affected disruptions. The risk of species extinction has increased by about 10% over the last 25 years globally.[36] The global pandemic COVID-19 has confirmed that by menacing biodiversity, humankind threatened its own survival. In spite of the losses that occurred in forest area, the forest biomass per hectare, the percentage of forest cover in conserved zones, and the certified forest area were increased significantly, indicating worldwide progress toward ensuring sustainable forest management. Till February 2021, 127 countries had pledged to fix their voluntary targets in order to achieve land degradation neutrality. While in 68 countries, the governments have authorized the targets officially.[36] The coronavirus pandemic and its consequent effects on humans and their economic welfare have blatantly shown the potential and threatening impact of zoonotic diseases. The cause for these diseases to spread has a major part to do with wildlife trade, no matter if it is legal or illegal, as it is a possible vector. While the illegal wildlife products are declining, for instance, there has been a 3.5-fold decrease in ivory products produced since 2013. Some species are under increasing threat, like Pangolins with a 10-fold increase in their products which is concerning.[36,72]

Efforts have been taken to reduce the pH of marine environments. Though the discharge of nutrient wastewater has been limited globally, eutrophication could not be substantially reduced yet. But observations in open oceans have shown a significant reduction in the overall pH in the last 20 years.[73] The UN, on the other hand, helps developing countries in mobilizing grants to support them to attain these goals. The organization has also introduced a new scheme for 2021–30 as "Decade on Ecosystem restoration," which is a globally coordinated program to reduce the degradation of habitat and improve the relationship between humans and nature.[74,75]

5. Conclusion

It is acknowledged that the threats and opportunities created in relation to the SDGs since the COVID-19 pandemic can only suggest an initial impression. It is important to assess the long-term impacts of the COVID-19 for every year of the SDG after the pandemic. As of now, both positives and negatives have been observed through this pandemic in relation to achieving these goals. Sufficient grants should be allocated to these goals after the crisis and fast-track the process in achieving this as these goals provide a sustainable future. Extensive research should be performed in maintaining and developing the ecosystem and not affect them nevertheless by the use of technology. SDG 14 and SDG 15 are interconnected, as the effect that happens on land will be reflected on the marine environment and vice versa. Thus it is important to create a balanced ecosystem which does not affect each other for any benefit. The accomplishment of these SDGs could prevent us from facing another global pandemic.

References

1. Bennich T, Weitz N, Carlsen H. Deciphering the scientific literature on SDG interactions: a review and reading guide. *Sci Total Environ* 2020. https://doi.org/10.1016/j.scitotenv.2020.138405, 138405.
2. Dastidar MG, Roy S. Public health management during COVID-19 and applications of point-of-care based biomolecular detection approaches. In: Dehghani MH, Karri RR, Roy S, editors. *Environmental and health management of novel coronavirus disease (COVID-19)*. Cambridge: Academic Press; 2021. p. 345–78. https://doi.org/10.1016/B978-0-323-85780-2.00009-3.
3. Shereen MA, Khan S, Kazmi A, Bashir N, Siddique R. COVID-19 infection: origin, transmission, and characteristics of human coronaviruses. *J Adv Res* 2020;**24**:91. https://doi.org/10.1016/j.jare.2020.03.005.
4. Mahapatra S, Chandra P. Clinically practiced and commercially viable nanobio engineered analytical methods for COVID-19 diagnosis. *Biosens Bioelectron* 2020;**165**. https://doi.org/10.1016/j.bios.2020.112361, 112361.
5. Khan AH, Tirth V, Fawzy M, Mahmoud AE, Khan NA, et al. COVID-19 transmission, vulnerability, persistence and nanotherapy: a review. *Environ Chem Lett* 2021; **7**:1–5. https://doi.org/10.1007/s10311-021-01229-4.
6. Roy S, Baranwal A. Diverse molecular techniques for early diagnosis of COVID-19 and other coronaviruses. In: Chandra P, Roy S, editors. *Diagnostic strategies for COVID-19 and other coronaviruses*. Singapore: Springer; 2020. https://doi.org/10.1007/978-981-15-6006-4_7.
7. Roy S, Ramadoss A. Chapter 1—updated insight into COVID-19 disease and health management to combat the pandemic. In: Dehghani MH, Karri RR, Roy S, editors. *Environmental and health management of novel coronavirus disease (COVID-19)*. Cambridge: Academic Press; 2021. p. 3–39. https://doi.org/10.1016/B978-0-323-85780-2.00017-2.

8. Arora P. *The impact of COVID-19 and the sustainable development goals*; 2020 https://www.voicesofyouth.org/blog/impact-COVID-19-and-sustainable-development-goals;. [Accessed 11 June 2021].
9. Baranwal A, Mahapatra S, Purohit B, Roy S, Chandra P. Insights into novel coronavirus and COVID-19 outbreak. In: Chandra P, Roy S, editors. *Diagnostic strategies for COVID-19 and other coronaviruses. Medical virology: From pathogenesis to disease control*, Singapore: Springer; 2020. https://doi.org/10.1007/978-981-15-6006-4_1.
10. Mahapatra S, Baranwal A, Purohit B, Roy S, Mahto SK, Chandra P. Advanced biosensing methodologies for ultrasensitive detection of human coronaviruses. In: Chandra P, Roy S, editors. *Diagnostic strategies for COVID-19 and other coronaviruses. Medical virology: from pathogenesis to disease control*, Singapore: Springer; 2020. https://doi.org/10.1007/978-981-15-6006-4_2.
11. Mousazadeh M, Naghdali Z, Rahimian N, Hashemi M, Paital B, Al-Qodah Z, et al. Management of environmental health to prevent an outbreak of COVID-19: a review. In: *Environmental and Health Management of Novel Coronavirus Disease (COVID-19)*; 2021. p. 235–67.
12. UN. *Impact of COVID-19 on SDG progress: a statistical perspective*; 2020 https://www.un.org/development/desa/dpad/publication/un-desa-policy-brief-81-impact-of-covid-19-on-sdg-progress-a-statistical-perspective/;. [Accessed 8 September 2021].
13. Hamid MZSA, Karri RR. Overview of preventive measures and good governance policies to mitigate the COVID-19 outbreak curve in Brunei. In: *COVID-19: Systemic Risk and Resilience*. Cham: Springer; 2021. p. 115–40.
14. SDG. *Goal 15 Protect, restore and promote sustainable use of terrestrial ecosystems, sustainably manage forests, combat desertification, and halt and reverse land degradation and halt biodiversity loss*; 2021 https://sdgs.un.org/goals/goal15;. [Accessed 9 June 2021].
15. Arana C, Franco IB, Joshi A, Sedhai J. SDG 15 life on land. In: Franco I, Chatterji T, Derbyshire E, Tracey J, editors. *Actioning the global goals for local impact*. Singapore: Springer; 2019. p. 247–64. https://doi.org/10.1007/978-981-32-9927-6_16.
16. Ford L. *Sustainable development goals: all you need to know*. The Guardian; 2015. https://www.theguardian.com/global-development/2015/jan/19/sustainable-development-goals-united-nations;. [Accessed 6 June 2021].
17. UN. *Goal 14: Conserve and sustainably use the oceans, seas and marine resources*; 2021 https://www.un.org/sustainabledevelopment/oceans/;. [Accessed 6 June 2021].
18. Barbier EB, Burgess JC. Sustainability and development after COVID-19. *World Dev* 2020;**135**. https://doi.org/10.1016/j.worlddev.2020.105082, 105082.
19. Ritchie RJ. Measurement of chlorophylls a and b and bacteriochlorophyll a in organisms from hypereutrophic auxinic waters. *J Appl Phycol* 2018;**30**(6):3075–87. https://doi.org/10.1007/s10811-018-1431-4.
20. Jambeck JR, Geyer R, Wilcox C, Siegler TR, Perryman M, Andrady A, et al. Marine pollution. Plastic waste inputs from land into the ocean. *Science* 2015;**347**(6223):768–71. https://doi.org/10.1126/science.1260352.
21. Lebreton LCM, van der Zwet J, Damsteeg JW, Slat B, Andrady A, Reisser J. River plastic emissions to the world's oceans. *Nat Commun* 2017;**8**:15611. https://doi.org/10.1038/ncomms15611.
22. Eriksen M, Mason S, Wilson S, Box C, Zellers A, Edwards W, et al. Microplastic pollution in the surface waters of the Laurentian Great Lakes. *Mar Pollut Bull* 2013;**77**(1–2):177–82. https://doi.org/10.1016/j.marpolbul.2013.10.007.
23. UNEP. *Plastic waste causes financial damage of US$13 billion to marine ecosystems each year as concern grows over microplastics*; 2014 https://www.unep.org/news-and-stories/press-release/plastic-waste-causes-financial-damage-us13-billion-marine-ecosystems;. [Accessed 8 June 2021].

24. Ajmeri JR, Joshi AC. 4—nonwoven materials and technologies for medical applications. In: Bartels VT, editor. *Woodhead publishing series in textiles*. India: Woodhead Publishing; 2011. p. 106–31. https://doi.org/10.1533/9780857093691.1.106.
25. Martínez Silva P, Nanny MA. Impact of microplastic fibers from the degradation of non-woven synthetic textiles to the Magdalena River water column and river sediments by the City of Neiva, Huila (Colombia). *Water* 2020;**12**(4):1210. https://doi.org/10.3390/w12041210.
26. Monteiro RC, do Sul JA, Costa MF. Plastic pollution in islands of the Atlantic Ocean. *Environ Pollut* 2018;**238**:103–10. https://doi.org/10.1016/j.envpol.2018.01.096.
27. Chowdhury H, Chowdhury T, Sait SM. Estimating marine plastic pollution from COVID-19 face masks in coastal regions. *Mar Pollut Bull* 2021;**168**, 112419.
28. Aragaw TA. Surgical face masks as a potential source for microplastic pollution in the COVID-19 scenario. *Mar Pollut Bull* 2020;**159**. https://doi.org/10.1016/j.marpolbul.2020.111517, 111517.
29. Godoy V, Prata JC, Blázquez G, Almendros AI, et al. Effects of distance to the sea and geomorphological characteristics on the quantity and distribution of microplastics in beach sediments of Granada (Spain). *Sci Total Environ* 2020;**746**, 142023.
30. De-la-Torre GE, Rakib MR, Pizarro-Ortega CI, Dioses-Salinas DC. Occurrence of personal protective equipment (PPE) associated with the COVID-19 pandemic along the coast of Lima, Peru. *Sci Total Environ* 2021;**774**. https://doi.org/10.1016/j.scitotenv.2021.145774, 145774.
31. Ardusso M, Forero-López AD, Buzzi NS, Spetter CV, Fernández-Severini MD. COVID-19 pandemic repercussions on plastic and antiviral polymeric textile causing pollution on beaches and coasts of South America. *Sci Total Environ* 2021;**763**. https://doi.org/10.1016/j.scitotenv.2020.144365, 144365.
32. Walker TR. Why are we still polluting the marine environment with personal protective equipment? *Mar Pollut Bull* 2021;**169**. https://doi.org/10.1016/j.marpolbul.2021.112528, 112528.
33. Wang B, Xin M, Wei Q, Xie L. A historical overview of coastal eutrophication in the China seas. *Mar Pollut Bull* 2018;**136**:394–400.
34. Our World in Data. *Plastic pollution*; 2018 https://ourworldindata.org/plastic-pollution?utm_source=newsletter. [Accessed 8 September 2021].
35. Sweet M, Stelfox M, Lamb J. Plastics and shallow water coral reefs. *Tech Rep* 2019. https://doi.org/10.13140/RG.2.2.29699.14880.
36. SDG. *Goals 14: Conserve and sustainably use the oceans, seas and marine resources for sustainable development*; 2021 https://sdgs.un.org/goals/goal14;. [Accessed 10 June 2021].
37. FAO. *How is COVID-19 outbreak impacting the fisheries and aquaculture food systems and what can FAO do*; 2020 http://www.fao.org/3/cb1436en/cb1436en.pdf;. [Accessed 10 June 2021].
38. Pörtner HO. Ecosystem effects of ocean acidification in times of ocean warming: a physiologist's view. *Mar Ecol Prog Ser* 2008;**373**:203–17. https://doi.org/10.3354/meps07768.
39. McCulloch M, Falter J, Trotter J, Montagna P. Coral resilience to ocean acidification and global warming through pH up-regulation. *Nat Clim Chang* 2012;**2**(8):623–7.
40. Anthony KR, Kline DI, Diaz-Pulido G, Dove S, Hoegh-Guldberg O. Ocean acidification causes bleaching and productivity loss in coral reef builders. *Proc Natl Acad Sci U S A* 2008;**105**(45):17442–6. https://doi.org/10.1073/pnas.0804478105.
41. Chazdon R, Brancalion P. Restoring forests as a means to many ends. *Science* 2019;**365**(6448):24–5. https://doi.org/10.1126/science.aax9539.
42. Schultz M, Tyrrell TD, Ebenhard T. *The 2030 agenda and ecosystems-A discussion paper on the links between the Aichi biodiversity targets and the sustainable development goals*. Stockholm, Sweden: SwedBio at Stockholm Resilience Centre; 2016.

43. Ahmad T, Khan M, Haroon, et al. COVID-19: zoonotic aspects. *Travel Med Infect Dis* 2020;**36**:101607. https://doi.org/10.1016/j.tmaid.2020.101607.
44. Bloomfield LS, McIntosh TL, Lambin EF. Habitat fragmentation, livelihood behaviors, and contact between people and non-human primates in Africa. *Landsc Ecol* 2020;**35** (4):985–1000. https://doi.org/10.1007/s10980-020-00995-w.
45. Brancalion PH, Broadbent EN, De-Miguel S, et al. Emerging threats linking tropical deforestation and the COVID-19 pandemic. *Perspect Ecol Conserv* 2020;**18**(4): 243–6. https://doi.org/10.1016/j.pecon.2020.09.006.
46. Plowright R, Reaser J, Locke H, et al. A call to action: understanding land use-induced zoonotic spillover to protect environmental, animal, and human health. *EcoEcoRxiv* 2020. https://doi.org/10.32942/osf.io/cru9w.
47. Aguirre AA, Catherina R, Frye H, Shelley L. Illicit wildlife trade, wet markets, and COVID-19: preventing future pandemics. *World Med Health Policy* 2020;**12**(3): 256–65. https://doi.org/10.1002/wmh3.348.
48. Banerjee A, Doxey AC, Mossman K, Irving AT. Unravelling the zoonotic origin and transmission of SARS-CoV-2. *Trends Ecol Evol* 2020. https://doi.org/10.1016/j.tree.2020.12.002.
49. UN. *Sustainably manage forests, combat desertification, halt and reverse land degradation, halt biodiversity loss*; 2021 https://www.un.org/sustainabledevelopment/biodiversity/;. [Accessed 12 June 2021].
50. Olivero J, Fa JE, Real R, Márquez AL, et al. Recent loss of closed forests is associated with Ebola virus disease outbreaks. *Sci Rep* 2017;**7**(1):1–9. https://doi.org/10.1038/s41598-017-14727-9.
51. Bausch DG, Schwarz L. Outbreak of Ebola virus disease in Guinea: where ecology meets economy. *PLoS Negl Trop Dis* 2014;**8**(7). https://doi.org/10.1371/journal.pntd.0003056, e3056.
52. Gonzalez E, Kulkarni H, Bolivar H, Mangano A, Sanchez R, Catano G, et al. The influence of CCL3L1 gene-containing segmental duplications on HIV-1/AIDS susceptibility. *Science* 2005;**307**(5714):1434–40. https://doi.org/10.1126/science.1101160.
53. Wolfe ND, Daszak P, Kilpatrick AM, Burke DS. Bushmeat hunting, deforestation, and prediction of zoonoses emergence. *Emerg Infect Dis* 2005;**11**(12):1822–7. https://doi.org/10.3201/eid1112.040789.
54. López-Feldman A, Chávez C, Vélez MA, et al. Environmental impacts and policy responses to COVID-19: a view from Latin America. *Environ Resource Econ* 2020;1–6. https://doi.org/10.1007/s10640-020-00460-x.
55. Corlett RT, Primack RB, Devictor V, et al. Impacts of the coronavirus pandemic on biodiversity conservation. *Biol Conserv* 2020;**246**. https://doi.org/10.1016/j.biocon.2020.108571, 108571.
56. Amador-Jiménez M, Millner N, Palmer C, Pennington RT, Sileci L. The unintended impact of Colombia's COVID-19 lockdown on forest fires. *Environ Resource Econ* 2020;**76**(4):1081–105. https://doi.org/10.1007/s10640-020-00501-5.
57. Farand C. *Forest destruction spiked in Indonesia during coronavirus lockdown*; 2020 https://www.climatechangenews.com/2020/08/18/forest-destruction-spiked-indonesia-coronavirus-lockdown/;. [Accessed 13 June 2021].
58. Mohan M, Rue HA, Bajaj S, et al. Afforestation, reforestation and new challenges from COVID-19: thirty-three recommendations to support civil society organizations (CSOs). *Environ Manage Today* 2021. https://doi.org/10.1016/j.jenvman.2021.112277, 112277.
59. Cherkaoui S, Boukherouk M, Lakhal T, Aghzar A, Youssfi L. Conservation amid COVID-19 pandemic: ecotourism collapse threatens communities and wildlife in Morocco. *E3S Web Conf* 2020;**183**:01003. https://doi.org/10.1051/e3sconf/202018301003.

60. Stronza AL, Hunt CA, Fitzgerald LA. Ecotourism for conservation? *Annu Rev Env Resour* 2019;**44**:229–53. https://doi.org/10.1146/annurev-environ-101718-033046.
61. Shah R. *A town in Costa Rica's faces an eco-tourism crisis: with its famed cloud forest closed, Monteverde fights for its life.* National Geographic; 2020. https://www.nationalgeographic.com/travel/2020/04/costa-rica-tourism-struggles-to-survive-during-coronavirus;. [Accessed 12 June 2021].
62. Fox JM, Yokying P, Paudel NS, Chhetri R. *Another possible cost of COVID-19: returning workers may lead to deforestation in Nepal East-West Centre, Honolulu, HI*; 2020 http://hdl.handle.net/10125/69942;. [Accessed 12 June 2021].
63. Chakraborty I, Maity P. COVID-19 outbreak: migration, effects on society, global environment and prevention. *Sci Total Environ* 2020;**728**. https://doi.org/10.1016/j.scitotenv.2020.138882, 138882.
64. Angelsen A, Jagger P, Babigumira R, Belcher B, Hogarth NJ, Bauch S, et al. Environmental income and rural livelihoods: a global-comparative analysis. *World Dev* 2014;**64**:12–28. https://doi.org/10.1016/j.worlddev.2014.03.006.
65. Mishra J, Mishra P, Arora NK. Linkages between environmental issues and zoonotic diseases: with reference to COVID-19 pandemic. *Environ Sustain* 2021;**29**:1–3. https://doi.org/10.1007/s42398-021-00165-x.
66. Perveen S, Orfali R, ul Azam MS, Aati HY, Bukhari K, Bukhari SI, et al. Coronavirus nCOVID-19: A pandemic disease and the Saudi precautions. *Saudi Pharm J* 2020;**28**(7):888–97. https://doi.org/10.1016/j.jsps.2020.06.006.
67. Ikiz E, Maclaren VW, Alfred E, Sivanesan S. Impact of COVID-19 on household waste flows, diversion and reuse: the case of multi-residential buildings in Toronto, Canada. *Resour Conserv Recycl* 2021;**164**. https://doi.org/10.1016/j.resconrec.2020.105111, 105111.
68. Singh N, Tang Y, Zhang Z, Zheng C. COVID-19 waste management: effective and successful measures in Wuhan, China. *Resour Conserv Recycl* 2020;**163**. https://doi.org/10.1016/j.resconrec.2020.105071, 105071.
69. Zambrano-Monserrate MA, Ruano MA, Sanchez-Alcalde L. Indirect effects of COVID-19 on the environment. *Sci Total Environ* 2020;**728**. https://doi.org/10.1016/j.scitotenv.2020.138813, 138813.
70. Abano I, Chavez L. *Wildlife trafficking, like everything else, has gone online during COVID-19*; 2021 https://news.mongabay.com/2021/06/wildlife-trafficking-like-everything-else-has-gone-online-during-COVID-19/;. [Accessed 13 June 2021].
71. Danda AA. *SDG 15 in the post-pandemic world: The Indian context*; 2021 https://www.orfonline.org/expert-speak/sdg15-post-pandemic-world-indian-context/;. [Accessed 13 June 2021].
72. Ingram DJ, Cronin DT, Challender DW, Venditti DM, Gonder MK. Characterising trafficking and trade of pangolins in the Gulf of Guinea. *Glob Ecol Conserv* 2019;**17**. https://doi.org/10.1016/j.gecco.2019.e00576, e00576.
73. SDG. *Goal 15 Protect, restore and promote sustainable use of terrestrial ecosystems, sustainably manage forests, combat desertification, and halt and reverse land degradation and halt biodiversity loss*; 2021 https://sdgs.un.org/goals/goal15;. [Accessed 12 June 2021].
74. ICUN. *The UN Decade on Ecosystem restoration*; 2021 http://www.onebigrobot.com/IUCN/. [Accessed 8 September 2021].
75. Mukherjee A, Babu SS, Ghosh S. Thinking about water and air to attain sustainable development goals during times of COVID-19 pandemic. *J Earth Syst Sci* 2020;**129**(1):1–8.

CHAPTER THIRTEEN

Global implications of biodiversity loss on pandemic disease: COVID-19

J. Brema[a], Sneha Gautam[a], and Dharmaveer Singh[b]
[a]Karunya Institute of Technology and Sciences, Coimbatore, Tamil Nadu, India
[b]Symbiosis Institute of Geoinformatics, Symbiosis International (Deemed University), Pune, India

1. Introduction

The emergence of coronavirus diseases—2019 (COVID-19), an emerging infectious disease (EID) has spread over 215 countries in a short span of 9 months.[1–4] EIDs [i.e., Ebola, H1N1, ZIKA, NIPAH, SARS, MERS, and, most recently, coronavirus (COVID-19)] cause large-scale morbidity and mortality, recession in the economy, and the emergence of poverty.[5–7] The impact on the economy is devastating when localized upsurges lead to regional outbreaks or global pandemics.[6,8] Severe Acute Respiratory Syndrome (SARS) outbreak in 2003,[9] the H1N1 (Influenza A virus subtype) pandemic in 2009,[10] the Ebola outbreak in West Africa during 2013–2016,[5] and the current outbreak of the novel coronavirus[11,12] have caused immeasurable economic damages.[13,14] This recent outbreak of "Novel Coronavirus" has kindled interest in analyzing the relationships between global environmental changes and human health.[15] Despite the clear evidences which clearly link these two phenomena, very little attention has been paid to understand the interactions between environmental changes and the EID.[16,17] It has been observed that around 70% of EIDs and almost all the recent emerging infectious diseases have originated from animals, and their emergence occurs due to complex interactions between animals and humans.[18]

Pandemic disease emergence is driven by anthropogenic factors such as deforestation and conversion of forest into agricultural lands, intensification of livestock production (toward food production), increased hunting and trading of wildlife, and it has an appalling effect on human population density and wildlife diversity.[16,19] For instance, the NIPAH (Nipah Virus encephalitis) virus outbreak in Malaysia in 1998 was due to the increase

COVID-19 and the Sustainable Development Goals
https://doi.org/10.1016/B978-0-323-91307-2.00006-7

in pig production nearer to the fringes of the tropical forests where the fruit bats (Pteropodidae) live; the sources of SARS and Ebola viruses have also been narrowed down to bats that are hunted for food.[5] The SDG goal 2 aims to increase agricultural productivity to achieve global food security, increasing agrarian lands, increased crop production, and livestock. The SDG goal 3 aims to ensure healthy life of human beings of all ages as referred by WHO. The SDG goal 13 aims at enhancing the resilience and adaptive capacity to climate-related hazards and natural disasters in all countries through national policies and strategies (UNDP). The SDG goal 15 aims at conservation of the world's terrestrial ecosystems as referred by UN. The agricultural land expansion and increased livestock production (SDG 2) lead to biodiversity loss.[20] In their study, Fitzherbert et al.[21] explained how oil palm expansions had caused significant biodiversity losses in South Asia. Similarly, Kehoe et al.[22] investigated the effect of agricultural expansion on the biodiversity in the Amazon and Afrotropics. They found a loss of 30% in species richness and 31% in species abundance because of the agricultural expansions. This suggests that strengthening of SGD2 leads to disturbances in the SDGs 3, 13, and 15. The SDGs 13 and 15 are closely related as climate change affects biodiversity and vice versa. The human developmental activities have triggered highly unfavorable changes in the biodiversity and earth ecosystems. Prevailing uncertainty and stressors like climate change and demographic changes have worsened the situation. In order to develop a secure sustained environment, the decision-makers are reconsidering development and environmental goals toward the achievement of strategic balance.[23–29] With reference to the interrelationship mentioned earlier, the initiatives taken by the various countries to achieve these SDGs interfere with one another. This interference of SDGs 2, 13, and 15 should be dealt with due consideration in framing the strategies to achieve SDG 3 (Human health).

Other drivers, such as livelihood aspects in the affected region, also exert a strong increased effect on the spread of emerging infectious diseases.[30] Initiatives toward drafting policies to decrease the rate of consumption of animal protein show a positive trend in developed countries.[31] These policies may slash down the risk of spreading emerging pathogens due to intensified livestock production.[18] Restoration of degraded natural habitats will help us to retain the original composition and wildlife dynamics, with added advantages such as water conservation, carbon sequestration, and drought management.[32] A measure for the inclusion of emerging infectious risk into sustainable development planning requires an interdisciplinary research approach. EID emergence involves livelihood, attitude of humans toward animals and forest cover, wildlife, livestock, and pathogen dynamics.[33,34]

There is an increased recognition that the United Nations has launched the 2030 agenda for sustainable development based on the following issues: human pressure leading to unprecedented environmental degradation, climate change, social inequality, and other matters which affect planet health. SDGs are interdependent,[34,35] and priorities (i.e., food security, protected ecosystem, and climate change mitigation) cannot be considered separately.[36–38] The objective of this study is to understand the relationship of the causes for the emergence of the pandemic diseases and its relationship with the changes in environment. The study also highlights the interference of one SDG with another and the need for framing the policies considering these interferences.

2. Climate change

Anthropogenic activities have largely impacted global environment that eventually led to the global warming.[39] Global warming of the earth's surface has occurred due to greenhouse gas emissions, especially carbon dioxide, which have exceeded their permissible level of concentration in the atmosphere.[39] Globally, an increase of ~1.0°C in the mean near air surface temperature of the earth is observed from 1850 to 2017.[40] This has led to climate change, which has affected the amount, intensity, and frequency of precipitation, and aggravated the extreme events of climate, e.g., heat waves, droughts, storms, and glacier lake outbursts. For instance, there has been an overall decrease in precipitation over land between 30°N and 10°S during the past few decades of the 20th century, with inevitable impacts on the ecological systems.[41,42] The vulnerability is high in terrestrial ecosystems as the climate change processes play a significant role in these ecosystems. Among the terrestrial ecosystems, forest cover constitutes the central part that influences climate change and, in turn, gets influenced.[43]

Climate change affects the forest and related ecosystems, and additionally more severe impacts are expected.[39] According to the latest report published by the Intergovernmental Panel on Climate Change (IPCC), global near air surface temperature is likely to increase by 1.5°C under a business-as-usual scenario by the end of 2050s; however, under higher emission scenarios, e.g., RCP4.5, RCP6.0, and RCP8.5, the mean temperature is predicted to likely be increased in the range of ~2–5°C by the end of 2100, with an associated increase in the number and frequency of extreme events,[42] with potential severe consequences for forest and ecological resources. Thus climate change may directly affect the ecosystem services provided by forest and will exacerbate the impacts of current natural and anthropogenic stress factors. Occurrence of wildfires, extreme weather changes, precipitation patterns, and nonnative and native invasive species are the deciding factors that make alterations within the forest cover.[44] Decay of certain tree species in North America has been associated with climate change.[45] This continuous process of climate change has the capacity to initiate/alter interacting processes within the forest ecosystem that may affect forest cover.[46]

The possible key drivers of forest cover change related to climate change are discussed as follows: upsurges in temperature, changes in precipitation, and increase in carbon dioxide (CO_2) level and food production.

a) Consequences of warming in the tropics: This gradually shifts the geographical location of some of the tree species toward north or to higher altitudes. Certain species may not be able to survive in the current locations. The species that exist in the higher altitudes may not be able to resist the increase in temperature nor shift to still higher altitudes. A number of biogeographical models demonstrate a polar ward shift of potential vegetation by 500 km or more for boreal zones.[47–49]

b) Consequences of extreme climatic conditions: Due to increased temperature, there is a considerable change in the extent of precipitation and flooding in streams. On the other hand, temperature fluctuation also leads to drought condition increasing the wildfire risk. The drought condition in the forestscape reduces the ability of trees to produce sap, which acts as a shield from destructive insects such as pine beetles. In 2011 due to warm temperature and drought condition in the early summer, more than 8 million acres of forest in the United States succumbed to wildfire. Increased temperature levels enhance the evapotranspiration rate leading to water loss from the forest soil. The soil moisture deficiency for an extended period indicates the onset of drought in a forest ecosystem. The soil moisture deficiency also results in reducing nutrient uptake by the trees, which causes a reduction in forest growth and productivity. The prolonged drought leads to species distribution and composition changes, habitat composition, and net primary productivity in a forest ecosystem.[50]

c) Availability of CO_2: With sufficient water and nutrients, increased atmospheric CO_2 may lead to more tree productivity, which alters the distribution of tree species in the forest.

d) Agricultural Production: It is estimated that the global population will reach to 11 billion people by 2100; accordingly the food production will be much more, accelerating the loss of biodiversity, which acts as a shield from zoonotic diseases. The United Nations Intergovernmental Science-Policy Platform on Biodiversity and Ecosystem Services (IPBES) has projected that 1 million species could become extinct within decades. The report says that the biodiversity loss will be a great threat to climate change pointing toward agriculture as the key factor.

3. Forest cover monitoring

Assessment of impact of climate change on landcover changes in the forest particularly concentrates on modeling and monitoring using remote sensing techniques. Remote sensing techniques are used to monitor the forest cover change, leaf area index (LAI), tree canopy height, and biomass content.[51] The utilization of satellite imageries and remote sensing techniques for the assessment of impact of climate change on forest cover has been gaining importance.[52] The remote sensing techniques allow the quantification of impact of climate change by way of monitoring the climate change-induced incidences, such as extent of degradation due to fire, shifting location of the tree species, and fluctuations in growth and productivity using satellite imageries. Normalized differential vegetation index (NDVI) is one of the key parameters to analyze the spatiotemporal changes in the forest cover.[51] There have been studies to understand the climate change on the phenology of vegetation in a forest cover based on NDVI.[53] LAI which is a vegetation parameter can be used as an indicator to monitor the climate change impacts and allied consequences in a forest cover using remote sensing techniques.[54,55] The rate of tree mortality due to thermal stress and effect of greenhouse gases can be seen as an indicator of climate change and the same can be monitored by color variation in remote sensing studies.[56,57] In recent days, the utilization of unmanned aerial vehicle (UAV) is one of the fruitful emerging technologies[58] that can practically be utilized for monitoring the ecophysiology of the forest cover affected by the climate change.[59] Despite the advantages of monitoring the forest degradation, the extent of shifting cultivation challenges do remain due to spatial limitations and temporal changes and unpredictable impacts on biomass.[60,61]

As per studies, it is observed that different types of forests respond differently to the drivers in forest areas. Therefore it can be concluded that more studies are needed to identify the optimal approach for monitoring forest degradation using remote sensing techniques based on the driver, the forest type, the intensity of impact, and the geographical location.[62]

3.1 Forest cover loss

Changes in land cover and land use from forested to nonforested regions have occurred due to natural causes, such as plant disease, increase in temperature, water stress, and fire; and human causes, such as land conversion for other purposes, timber harvesting, animal hunting, and infrastructure development. Changes from one to other land uses have links to a complex and multifaceted set of underlying driving forces, including population growth, poverty, livelihood changes, government policies, infrastructure development, and population migration.

The forests in humid regions of India such as the Western Ghats, western Himalayas, Eastern Ghats, and northeast India, are predicted to be highly resilient. These forests can be classified under the extremely resilient category to conditions such as large-scale precipitation fluctuations in addition to the shorter drought periods.

As per the studies conducted, it can be inferred that, in 2015, forest cover remained at 3999 M ha globally. The forest cover is approximately 31% of global land cover. Tropical and subtropical forests cover nearly 44% and 8% of the global area, respectively (Fig. 1). Twenty-six percent and twenty-two percent of the global forest area is occupied by temperate and boreal forest covers, respectively. Europe has the largest forest cover at 25% compared with other geographical subregions, followed by South America and North America with 25% and 21%, respectively.

As per Table 1, the changes according to the climatic domain are as follows: Between 1990 and 2015 the tropical forest area has declined by 195 M ha and forest in temperate countries has increased by 67 M ha, at an average of 2.7 M ha/year, but forest in the subtropical and boreal domains showed little change with 0.089 mHa/year (increase) and 0.084 mHa/year (decrease) during the period 2010–2015.

Southeast Asia (SEA) has lost maximum of 30% of its forests in the last 40 years.[64] In Cambodia, agricultural land area has doubled from 15% in the 1980s up to 30% in 2000. Still larger increase in agricultural land was observed in Vietnam with an increase from 20% in 1990 to 35% nowadays. The agricultural land growth rate has increased from 21% in the 1980s to 31.5% in the recent days in Indonesia. For example, in Sumatra region the deforested area has been converted into a growing suburban zone with intensive farming practices.

From Fig. 2, it is observed that annual deforestation rate has declined and increased during 2012 and 2014, showing that zero deforestation has not been adapted in a global manner.

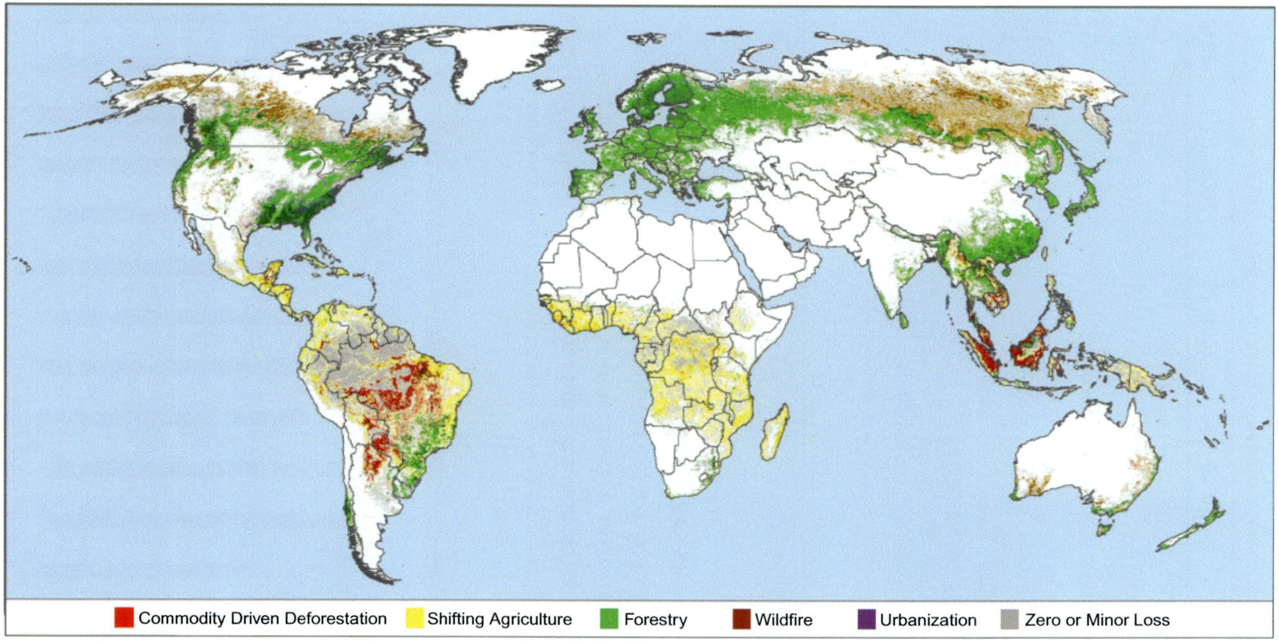

Fig. 1 Forest cover loss during the period 2001–15. Darker color intensity indicates a greater total quantity of forest cover loss.[63] *(Source: Curtis PG, Christy M, et al. Classifying drivers of global forest loss.* Science *2018;**361**:1108–11.)*

Table 1 Rate of change in forest cover.
Net rates of change in the areas of forest and other wooded land from 1990 to 2015 in different global climatic domains (M ha/year) (FAO, 2015)

	1990–00	2000–05	2005–10	2010–15
Forest				
Boreal (Inc. polar)	0.051	−0.193	1.204	−0.084
Temperate	2.290	3.657	2.851	2.208
Subtropical	−0.064	−0.173	−0.860	0.089
Tropical	−9.543	−7.863	−6.608	−5.520
Grand Total	−7.267	−4.572	−3.414	−3.308
Other wooded land				
Boreal (Inc. polar)	−0.348	0.371	0.482	−0.162
Temperate	−0.305	1.007	0.834	0.704
Subtropical	−0.104	1.460	−0.158	49.698
Tropical	1.644	1.989	2.936	4.178
Grand Total	−2.401	−0.151	4.094	46.062

Source: FAO (2015).

In the Western Ghats region of India, there is decrease in forest cover from 50,173 to 45,542.23 Hecs. during the period 2000–11 as shown in Fig. 3. It is projected that it will still decrease to 41,253.94 Hecs due to conversion of forest cover to plantation and built-up land.[65] Land use changes with respect to forest cover are unprecedented in the state of Kerala, India, during the past half century. A substantial increase in coconut and rubber

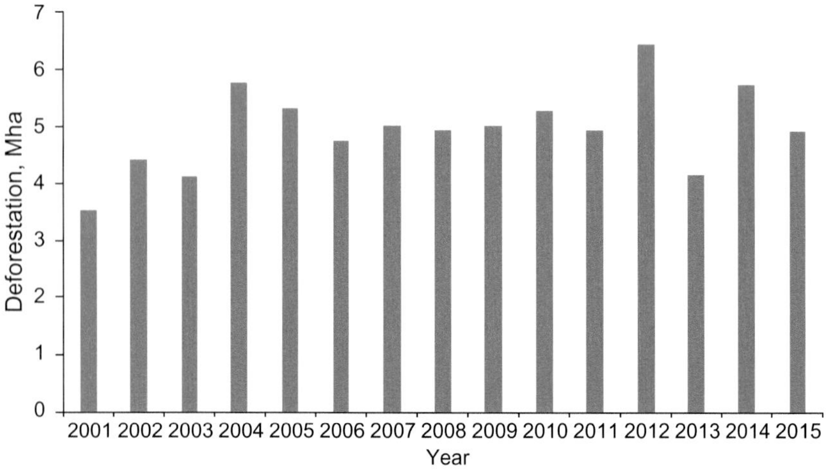

Fig. 2 Annual deforestation rate (2001–15).[63]

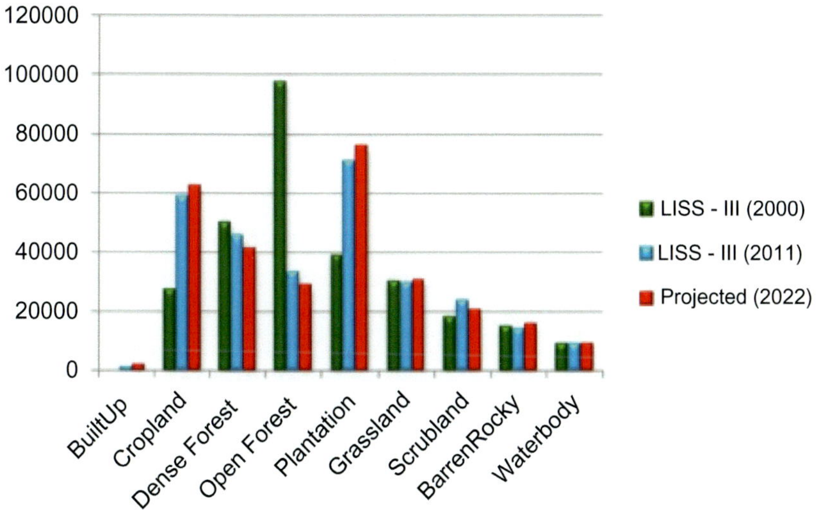

Fig. 3 Graph showing the variations in landcover classes in the Devikulam, Western Ghats, India. *(Source: Binutha C, Somashekar RK. Future prediction of Landcover in Devikulam Taluk, Kerala.* Int J Sci Nat *2014;**5**(4):677–83.)*

cultivation has been experienced in this region.[66] These studies explain the changes in biodiversity due to the expansion of area under food production in SEA.

4. Climate change and EID

The drivers leading to climate change are also causes for the increase of risk of EID. Loss of habitat forces animals to migrate and come in contact with other animals or human beings and transmit pathogens. Increase in production of livestock serves as a source of spillover of infections from animals to people. Decrease in livestock production could decrease the transmission of pathogens and also will lower the greenhouse gas emissions. Besides agricultural encroachment, construction of roads, dams, irrigation structures, mining activities, development of satellite townships, and coastal degradation also act as drivers for forest destruction and indirectly contribute to emerging infectious disease emergence. Unlike natural forest environments which are highly suitable for bat species, these altered forestscapes are more acceptable by a wide range of bat species. The bats find these environmental niches compatible for their resting and hunting needs.

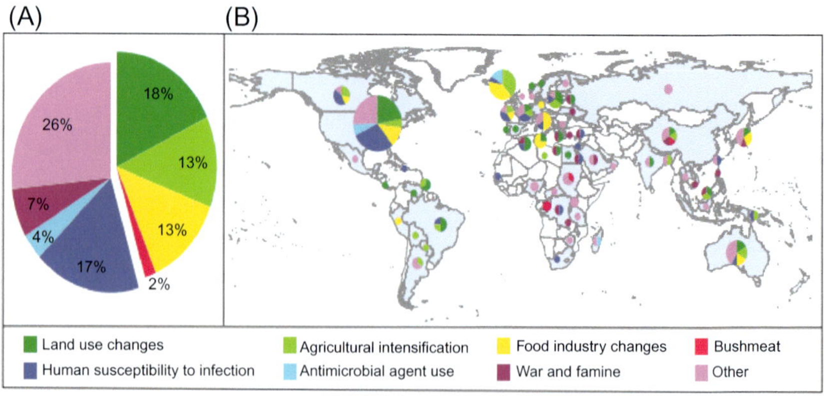

Fig. 4 Drivers and locations of emergence events of zoonotic diseases in humans from 1940 to 2005. *(Source: Keesing F, et al. Impacts of biodiversity on the emergence and transmission of infectious diseases.* Nature *2010;**468**:647–52.)*

Deforestation has increased steadily and is linked to spread of viruses like Ebola, Zika, and Nipah. Fig. 4 shows the distribution of outbreak of zoonotic diseases worldwide from 1940 to 2005. Deforestation pushes wild animals out of their natural habitats and drives them closer to human populations, creating more opportunity for the spread of zoonotic diseases (diseases that spread from animals to humans). There were 12,012 recorded outbreaks from 1980 to 2013. This comprises 44 million individual cases affecting every country globally. A number of factors have contributed to this increase in outbreaks, including globalization of travel, trade and connectivity, and thick populations living nearer to the fringes of devastated forests, but the links to climate change and biodiversity are the most striking. The occurrences of spillover of emerging infectious diseases to people are higher in the tropics, since the diversity of wildlife and pathogens is higher in these forests. For the pathogens to establish in a new species, it needs to cross multiple steps during the emergence process. The steps include initial invasion into the new host ("spillover"), the transmission stage in the new host, and the establishment of the pathogen in the host population in total.[67,68] In these steps, particular species in the biodiversity acts as a source for the initial invasion. Once the pathogen enters into a new host, thickly populated new host species may facilitate pathogen establishment and transmission within the new host habitat.[67] This hypothesis is supported by studies conducted on the jumping of the viruses leading to emerging diseases from animals to humans. Others such as environmental and socioeconomic factors such as clearing of forest for agriculture and wildlife hunting bring humans more into closer contact with new pathogens during the process.[69] In the case of Nipah virus, when it spilled over from wild fruit bats to domestic pigs, the proliferated population of pigs in local farms facilitated the establishment and transmission of the virus from pigs to human beings in Malaysia.[70] The mortality rate was high as 74% in humans due to the infection by Nipah virus. Such availability of high density of domesticated species normally occurs in the regions with low biodiversity conserved regions.

In Australia, the Hendra virus was detected in horses and human beings in 1994. This was reported due to spreading of aerosols from diseased horses which were initially contaminated by Pteropus bats. In the Ugandan forests it was observed that Zika virus infected millions since it could find a host in *Aedes aegypti*, a mosquito that lives in urban areas.

The existence of bat-borne virus like Australian Bat Lyssavirus (ABLV) and Duvenhage, which directly transmit virus to humans, has been studied. CoVs, zoonotic viruses find the wild animals and livestock as carriers for transfer to humans. During more than three decades, four human CoVs (HCoV-HKU1, HCoV-229E, HCoV-NL63, and HCoV-OC43) were identified as responsible for mild to moderate respiratory tract diseases, before the emergences of SARS-CoV and MERS-CoV in human beings.

5. Modeling the movement of pathogens and animals

Development of geographical information systems (GIS) tools and availability of satellite imageries with high spatial and temporal resolution satellites for Earth observation have made a tremendous or spectacular progress in the last three decades. This has made it possible to monitor weather, climate, environmental, and anthropogenic factors that help to forecast the occurrence or reemergence of epidemic diseases. Studies have been carried out to monitor the climatic, planetary health and biodiversity factors with high accuracy based on the techniques like combination of remote sensing data and GIS tools,[71,72] Studies have been carried out to monitor the factors that influence the vector-borne diseases such as malaria,[73,74] visceral leishmaniasis (VL),[75,76] Rift Valley fever,[77,78] schistosomiasis,[79–81] Chagas disease,[82,83] and leptospirosis.[84,85]

Predictive modeling may lead to improved understanding and will lead to planning proactive measures to prevent future epidemic diseases. The critical components to be included in a predictive model are temperature, humidity, chlorophyll content, soil moisture, vegetation indices, pathogen biology and ecology, and human host biology and ecology.[86]

With the availability of high-resolution satellite imageries and data processing techniques, a model has been developed to forecast the movement of forest pathogens using climate variables and real-time data. Support systems have been developed for the detection of movement of wild animals using hyperspectral remote sensing images. One such model has been developed to facilitate detection of moving wild animals (DWA) algorithm.[87] Studies have also been carried out to monitor the movement of wild animals using thermal remote sensing images.[88–91] There is a limitation in thermal remote sensing studies, where it applies only to limited and excellent areas.[89,91] Furthermore, it becomes difficult to differentiate animals from trees in thermal images as it requires a thermal level difference between the target and the background during observation.[88,90] The detection accuracy can be increased by way of developing ideal observation conditions and by processing the images using high-end techniques.

6. Research gaps, challenges, and recommendations for future

Foreseeing the changes shortly will support evidence-led policymaking toward the achievement of sustainability. With increasing uncertainties such as complex and multidimensional scenarios, critical research is needed to ensure balanced development in the life of humans and the sustenance of nature.

Moving forward, the researchers have excellent opportunities to make a definite contribution in facing the grand challenge toward development of sustainable environment without deviating from the SDGs. The responsible research community can take a lead in exploring ways of realizing the full potential of digital technologies toward the formation of a sustainable environment. The integration of SDGs 2, 3 13, and 15 toward achievement of sustainability is a challenging task. The imbalance created while meeting the SDG 2 (Food production) leads to negligence in the SDGs 3, 13, and 15. The clearance of land for agricultural and livestock production has disturbed the biodiversity, consequently the climate and humanitarian health. Suitable studies have to be taken up to reconsidering the targets defined in SDGs and related policy decisions.

7. Conclusions

Degradation of forests, changes in watercourses, and haphazard development toward food security and livelihood are disrupting ecosystems. In this regard, they are vanishing the boundaries between wild and human entities at an unprecedented scale. The studies show that the total forest area has declined by 3% between 1990 and 2015 and the loss of forest area is high in tropics when compared to the temperate. The tropics have lost the forest area by 196 Mha, whereas there is a gain in forest area by 66 Mha in the temperate region during the same period (1990–2015). The vulnerability and ingenuity of the planet toward climate change, degraded landscapes, and damaged ecosystems looks like our future. The emergence of COVID-19 crisis has depicted the relationships between the planetary health, human health, forestscapes, food security and livelihoods, allowing us to see in the real time and take proactive measures. Efforts are to be taken to closely correlate the changes in climatological parameters (like temperature, relative humidity, precipitation), forest cover change and biodiversity loss (endangered species wise), and EID. The efforts for surveillance of EID with related investigations need to be improvised. The surveillance methodology has to be implemented in the emerging disease hotspots especially in the fringes of the tropical forests. This will aid in identifying clusters of emergence in a large scale. This means that establishment of new approaches with explicit utilization of spatial data and computing techniques will lead to informed decisions on forest land cover management and food production. Policies need to be applied/developed to promote research on the interactions between climate change, biodiversity, food production, and EID (i.e., COVID-19) and this approach could provide better insights in integrated SDGs planning.

References

1. Bherwani H, Gautam S, Gupta A. Qualitative and quantitative analyses of impact of COVID-19 on sustainable development goals (SDGs) in Indian subcontinent with a focus on air quality. *Int J Environ Sci Technol* 2021;**18**:1019–28 [2021].
2. Gautam S. The influence of COVID-19 on air quality in India: a boon or inutile. *Bull Environ Contam Toxicol* 2020;**104**:724–6.
3. Gautam S. COVID-19: air pollution remains low as people stay at home. *Air Qual Atmos Health* 2020;**13**:853–7.
4. Gautam S, Samuel C, Gautam AS, et al. Strong link between coronavirus count and bad air: a case study of India. *Environ Dev Sustain* 2021. https://doi.org/10.1007/s10668-021-01366-4.
5. Cordelia EMC, Lindsey B, Ghinai I, Johnson AM, Heymann DL, et al. The Ebola outbreak, 2013–2016: old lessons for new epidemics. *Philos Trans R Soc Lond B Biol Sci* 2017;**372**(1721), 20160297.
6. Kissler SM, Christine T, et al. Projecting the transmission dynamics of SARS-CoV-2 through the postpandemic period. April 2020, *Science* 2020. https://doi.org/10.1126/science.abb5793.
7. Pike J, Bogich T, Elwood S, Finnoff DC, Daszak P. Economic optimization of a global strategy to address the pandemic threat. *Proc Natl Acad Sci U S A* 2014;**111**:18519–23.

8. Rajput H, Changotra R, Rajput P, et al. Correction to: the consequences of coronavirus outbreak on commodity markets. *Environ Dev Sustain* 2020;1–3.
9. Corman VM, Eckerle I, Memish ZA, Liljander AM, Dijkman R, Jonsdottir H, et al. Link of a ubiquitous human coronavirus to dromedary camels. *Proc Natl Acad Sci* 2016;**113**(35):9864–9.
10. Kshatriya RM, Khara NV, Ganjiwale J, Lote SD, Patel SN, Paliwal RP. Lessons learnt from the Indian H1N1 (swine flu) epidemic: predictors of outcome based on epidemiological and clinical profile. *J Fam Med Prim Care* 2018;**7**(6):1506–9.
11. Gautam S, Hens L. SARS-CoV-2 pandemic in India: what might we expect? *Environ Dev Sustain* 2020;**22**(5):3867–9.
12. World Health Organization. Coronavirus disease 2019 (COVID-19): situation report; 2020. 58 Retrieved April 04, 2020 from https://www.who.int/docs/defaultsource/coronaviruse/situation-reports/20200318-sitrep-58-covid-19.pdf?sfvrsn=20876712_2.
13. Changotra R, Rajput H, et al. Largest democracy in the world crippled by COVID-19: current perspective and experience from India. *Environ Dev Sustain* 2021;**23**:6623–41.
14. Zhou P. A pneumonia outbreak associated with a new coronavirus of probable bat origin. *Nature* 2020. https://doi.org/10.1038/s41586-020-2012-7.
15. Watts, et al. The lancet countdown on health and climate change: from 25 years of inaction to a global transformation for public health. *Lancet* 2018;**391**:581–630.
16. Allen T. Global hotspots and correlates of emerging zoonotic diseases. *Nat Commun* 2017;**8**:1124.
17. Keesing F, et al. Impacts of biodiversity on the emergence and transmission of infectious diseases. *Nature* 2010;**468**:647–52.
18. Morse SS, et al. Prediction and prevention of the next pandemic zoonosis. *Lancet* 2012;**380**:1956–65.
19. Jones K, et al. Global trends in emerging infectious diseases. *Nature* 2008;**451**:990–3.
20. Lanz B, Dietz S, Swanson T. The expansion of modern agriculture and global biodiversity decline: an integrated assessment. *Ecol Econ* 2018;**144**:260–77.
21. Fitzherbert EB, Struebig MJ, Morel A, Danielsen F, Brühl CA, Donald PF, et al. How will oil palm expansion affect biodiversity? *Trends Ecol Evol* 2008;**23**(10):538–45.
22. Kehoe L, Romero-Muñoz A, Polaina E, Estes L, Kreft H, Kuemmerle T. Biodiversity at risk under future cropland expansion and intensification. *Nat Ecol Evol* 2017;**1**(8): 1129–35.
23. Bai X, Van Der Leeuw S, O'Brien K, Berkhout F, Biermann F, Brondizio ES, et al. Plausible and desirable futures in the Anthropocene: a new research agenda. *Glob Environ Chang* 2016;**39**:351–62.
24. Haddad NM, Brudvig LA, Clobert J, Davies KF, Gonzalez A, Holt RD, et al. Habitat fragmentation and its lasting impact on Earth's ecosystems. *Sci Adv* 2015;**1**(2):1500052.
25. Harmáčková ZV, Vačkář D. Future uncertainty in scenarios of ecosystem services provision: linking differences among narratives and outcomes. *Ecosyst Serv* 2018;**33**: 134–45.
26. Johnson CN, Balmford A, Brook BW, Buettel JC, Galetti M, Guangchun L, et al. Biodiversity losses and conservation responses in the Anthropocene. *Science* 2017;**356** (6335):270–5.
27. MA. *Millennium ecosystem assessment. Ecosystems and human wellbeing: a framework for assessment.* Washington: Island Press; 2005.
28. Rockström J, Stefen W, Noone K, Persson Å, Chapin III FS, Lambin EF, et al. A safe operating space for humanity. *Nature* 2009;**461**(7263):472.
29. Mousazadeh M, Naghdali Z, Rahimian N, Hashemi M, Paital B, Al-Qodah Z, et al. Management of environmental health to prevent an outbreak of COVID-19: a review. *Environmental and health management of novel coronavirus disease (COVID-19).* Academic Press; 2021. p. 235–67.

30. Schneider MC, Aguilera XP, Smith RM, Moynihan MJ, da Silva Jr JB, Aldighieri S, et al. Importance of animal/human health interface in potential public health emergencies of international concern in the Americas. *Rev Panam Salud Publica* 2011;**29**:371–9.
31. Hamid MZSA, Karri RR. Overview of preventive measures and good governance policies to mitigate the COVID-19 outbreak curve in Brunei. In: *COVID-19: systemic risk and resilience*. Cham: Springer; 2021. p. 115–40.
32. Ricke KL, Caldeira K. Maximum warming occurs about one decade after a carbon dioxide emission. *Environ Res Lett* 2014;**9**, 124002.
33. Moreno DM, Michelle LB, Daszak P, et al. Opinion: sustainable development must account for pandemic risk. *Proc Natl Acad Sci U S A* 2020;**117**(8):3888–92.
34. Stafford-Smith, et al. Integration: the key to implementing the sustainable development goals. *Sustain Sci* 2017;**12**:911–9.
35. Nilsson M, Griggs D, Visbeck M. Policy: map the interactions between sustainable development goals. *Nature* 2016;**534**:320–2.
36. Hanspach J, et al. From trade-offs to synergies in food security and biodiversity conservation. *Front Ecol Environ* 2017;**15**:489–94.
37. Rohr JR, et al. Emerging human infectious diseases and the links to global food production. *Nat Sustain* 2019;**2**:445–56.
38. Springmann M, et al. Options for keeping the food system within environmental limits. *Nature* 2018;**562**:519–25.
39. IPCC. In: Parry M, et al., editors. *Climate change 2007: Impacts, adaptation and vulnerability. Contribution of working group II to the fourth assessment report of the intergovernmental panel on climate change*. UK: Cambridge University Press; 2007.
40. Ogunbode CA, Doran R, Böhm. G. Exposure to the IPCC special report on 1.5 C global warming is linked to perceived threat and increased concern about climate change. *Clim Change* 2020;**158**(3):361–75.
41. Hannah L. *Climate change biology*. 2nd ed. London, UK: Elsevier Academic Press; 2015.
42. IPCC. In: Stocker, et al., editors. *Climate change 2013: The physical science basis. Contribution of working group I to the fifth assessment report of the intergovernmental panel on climate change*. United Kingdom and New York, NY, USA: Cambridge University Press, Cambridge; 2013.
43. Settele J, Scholes R, Betts R, Bunn S, Leadley P, Nepstad D, et al. Terrestrial and inland water systems. In: Field CB, Barros VR, Dokken DJ, Mach KJ, Mastrandrea MD, Bilir TE, Kissel ES, editors. *Climate change: impacts, adaptation, and vulnerability. Part A: global and sectoral aspects. Contribution of working group II to the fifth assessment report of the intergovernmental panel on climate change*. Cambridge, UK/New York, USA: Cambridge University Press; 2014. p. 271–359.
44. Bhatti JS, Lal R, Apps MJ, Price MA. *Climate change and managed ecosystems*. Boca Raton, FL, USA: CRC Press; 2006.
45. Kurz WA, Dymond CC, Stinson G, et al. Mountain pine beetle and forest carbon feedback to climate change. *Nature* 2008;**452**:987–90.
46. Williamson CE, Saros JE, Vincent WF, Smol JP. Lakes and reservoirs as sentinels, integrators, and regulators of climate change. *Limnol Oceanogr* 2009;**54**(6 part 2):2273–82.
47. Cramer W, Bondeau A, Woodward FI, Prentice IC, Betts RA, Brovkin V, et al. Global response of terrestrial ecosystem structure and function to CO_2 and climate change: results from six dynamic global vegetation models. *Glob Change Biol* 2001;**7**:357–73.
48. Foley JA, Levis S, Prentice IC, Pollard D, Thompson SL. Coupling dynamic models of climate and vegetation. *Glob Chang Biol* 1998;**4**:561–79.
49. Solomon AM, Kirilenko AP. Climate change and terrestrial biomass: what if trees do not migrate? *Glob Ecol Biogeogr Lett* 1997;**6**:139–48.
50. Gustafson EJ, Shinneman DJ. Approaches to modeling landscape-scale drought-induced forest mortality. In: Perera AH, Sturtevant BR, Buse LJ, editors. *Simulation modeling of*

forest landscape disturbances. Switzerland: Springer International Publishing; 2015. p. 45–71.
51. Jones HG, Vaughn RA. *Remote sensing of vegetation: principles, techniques, and applications*. Oxford: Oxford University Press; 2010.
52. Boisvenue C, Running SW. Impacts of climate change on natural forest productivity—evidence since the middle of the 20th century. *Glob Chang Biol* 2006;**12**:862–82.
53. White MA, Hoffman F, Hargrove WW, Nemani RR. A global framework for monitoring phenological responses to climate change. *Geophys Res Lett* 2005;**32**: L04705. https://doi.org/10.1029/2004GL021961.
54. McDowell NG, Coops NC, Beck PSA, Chambers JQ, Gangodagamage C, Hicke JA, et al. Global satellite monitoring of climate-induced vegetation disturbances. *Trends Plant Sci* 2015;**20**(2):114–23. https://doi.org/10.1016/j.tplants.2014.10.008.
55. Smith AMS, Kolden CA, Tinkham WD, Talhelm AF, Marshall JD, Hudak AT. Remote sensing the vulnerability of vegetation in natural terrestrial ecosystems. *Remote Sens Environ* 2014;**154**:322–37. https://doi.org/10.1016/j.rse.2014.03.038.
56. Allen CD. Climate-induced forest dieback: an escalating global phenomenon? *Unasylva* 2009;**60**(231/232):43–9.
57. Schwantes AM, Swenson JJ, Jackson RB. Quantifying drought-induced tree mortality in the open canopy woodlands of Central Texas. *Remote Sens Environ* 2016;**181**:54–64. https://doi.org/10.1016/j.rse.2016.03.027.
58. Anderson K, Gaston KJ. Lightweight unmanned aerial vehicles will revolutionize spatial ecology. *Front Ecol Environ* 2013;**11**(3):138–46.
59. Zhang J, Hu J, Lian J, Fan Z, Ouyang X, Ye W. Seeing the forest from drones: testing the potential of lightweight drones as a tool for long-term forest monitoring. *Biol Conserv* 2016;**198**:60–9. https://doi.org/10.1016/j.biocon.2016.03.027.
60. Kissinger G, Herold M, De Sy V. *Drivers of deforestation and forest degradation: A synthesis report for REDD+ policymakers*. Vancouver, Canada: Lexeme Consulting; 2012.
61. Mertz O, Muller D, Sikor T, Hett C, Heinimann A, Castella J-C, et al. The forgotten D: challenges of addressing forest degradation in complex mosaic landscapes under REDD+. *Geol Tidsskr-Danish J Geogr* 2012;**112**:63–76.
62. De Sy V, Herold M, Achard F, Asner GP, Held A, Kellndorfer J, et al. Synergies of multiple remote sensing data sources for REDD+ monitoring. *Curr Opin Environ Sustain* 2012;**4**:696–706.
63. Curtis PG, Christy M, et al. Classifying drivers of global forest loss. *Science* 2018;**361**:1108–11.
64. Jukka M, et al. Remote sensing of forest degradation in Southeast Asia—Aiming for a regional view through 5–30 m satellite data. *Glob Ecol Conserv* 2014;**2**:24–36.
65. Binutha C, Somashekar RK. Future prediction of Landcover in Devikulam Taluk, Kerala. *Int J Sci Nat* 2014;**5**(4):677–83.
66. Kumar B. Land use in Kerala: changing scenarios and shifting paradigms. *J Trop Agric* 2005;**42**(1–2):1–12.
67. Hudson P, Perkins S, Cattadori I. In: Ostfeld R, Keesing F, Eviner V, editors. *Infectious disease ecology: effects of ecosystems on disease and of disease on ecosystems*. Princeton University Press; 2008. p. 347–67. 2008.
68. Wolfe N, Dunavan CP, Diamond J. Origins of major human infectious diseases. *Nature* 2007;**447**:279–83.
69. Woolhouse MEJ, Gowtage-Sequeria S. Host range and emerging and reemerging pathogens. *Emerg Infect Dis* 2005;**11**:1842–7.
70. Epstein JH, Field HE, Luby S, Pulliam JRC, Daszak P. Nipah virus: impact, origins, and causes of emergence. *Curr Infect Dis Rep* 2006;**8**:59–65.

71. Al-Hamdan MZ, Crosson WL, Economou SA, Estes Jr MG, Estes SM, Hemmings SN, et al. Environmental public health applications using remotely sensed data. *Geocarto Int* 2014;**29**(1):85–98.
72. Witt CJ, Richards AL, Masuoka PM, Foley DH, Buczak AL, Musila LA, et al. The AFHSC-division of GEIS operations predictive surveillance program: a multidisciplinary approach for the early detection and response to disease outbreaks. *BMC Public Health* 2011;**11**(Suppl 2):S10.
73. Baeza A, Bouma MJ, Dhiman RC, Baskerville EB, Ceccato P, Yadav RS. Long-lasting transition towards sustainable elimination of desert malaria under irrigation development. *Proc Natl Acad Sci U S A* 2013;**110**(37):15157–62.
74. Ceccato P, Connor SJ, Jeanne I, Thomson MC. Application of geographical information system and remote sensing technologies for assessing and monitoring malaria risk. *Parassitologia* 2005;**47**:81–96.
75. Bhunia GS, Kumar V, Kumar AJ, Das P, Kesari S. The use of remote sensing in the identification of the eco-environmental factors associated with the risk of human visceral leishmaniasis (kala-azar) on the Gangetic plain, in North- Eastern India. *Ann Trop Med Parasitol* 2010;**104**(1):35–53.
76. Sweeney A, Kruczkiewicz A, Reid C, Seaman J, Abubakar A, Ritmeijer K, et al. Utilizing NASA earth observations to explore the relationship between environmental factors and visceral leishmaniasis in the northern states of the republic of South Sudan. *Earthzine IEEE* 2014;**2014**.
77. Anyamba A, Chretien JP, Small J, Tucker CJ, Formenty PB, Richardson JH, et al. Prediction of a Rift Valley fever outbreak. *Proc Natl Acad Sci U S A* 2009;**106**(3):955–9.
78. Linthicum KJ, Anyamba A, Tucker CJ, Kelley PW, Myers MF, Peters CJ. Climate and satellite indicators to forecast Rift Valley fever epidemics in Kenya. *Science* 1999;**285**(5426):397–400.
79. Manyangadze T, Chimbari MJ, Gebreslasie M, Mukaratirwa S. Application of geospatial technology in schistosomiasis modelling in Africa: a review. *Geospat Health* 2015;**10**(2):326.
80. Simoonga C, Utzinger J, Brooker S, Vounatsou P, Appleton CC, Stensgaard AS. Remote sensing, geographical information system and spatial analysis for schistosomiasis epidemiology and ecology in Africa. *Parasitology* 2009;**136**(13):1683–93.
81. Walz Y, Wegmann M, Dech S, Raso G, Utzinger J. Risk profiling of schistosomiasis using remote sensing: approaches, challenges and outlook. *Parasit Vectors* 2015;**8**:163.
82. Kitron U, Clennon JA, Cecere MC, Gürtler RE, King CH, Vazquez- Prokopec G. Upscale or downscale: applications of fine scale remotely sensed data to Chagas disease in Argentina and schistosomiasis in Kenya. *Geospat Health* 2006;**1**(1):49–58.
83. Roux E, de Fátima VA, Girres JF, Romaña CA. Spatial patterns and ecoepidemiological systems—part I: multi-scale spatial modelling of the occurrence of Chagas disease. *Geospat Health* 2011;**6**(1):41–51.
84. Herbreteau V, Demoraes F, Khaungaew W, Souris M. Use of geographic information system and remote sensing for assessing environment influence on leptospirosis incidence, Phrae Province Thailand. *Int J Geomatics* 2006;**2**(4):43–50.
85. Skouloudis AN, Rickerby DG. In-situ and remote sensing networks for environmental monitoring and global assessment of leptospirosis outbreaks. *Procedia Eng* 2015;**107**:194–204.
86. Timothy E, Ford R, et al. Using satellite images of environmental changes to predict infectious disease outbreaks. *Emerg Infect Dis* 2009;**15**(9). 2009.
87. Oishi Y, Matsunaga T. Support system for surveying moving wild animals in the snow using aerial remote-sensing images. *Int J Remote Sens* 2014;**35**:1374–94.

88. Chretien L, Theau J, Menard P. Visible and thermal infrared remote sensing for the detection of White-tailed deer using an unmanned aerial system. *Wildl Soc Bull* 2016;**40**:181–91.
89. Christiansen P, Steen KA, Jorgensen RN, Karstoft H. Automated detection and recognition of wildlife using thermal cameras. *Sensors* 2014;**14**:13778–93.
90. Kissell Jr RE, Tappe PA. Assessment of thermal infrared detection rates using white-tailed deer surrogates. *J Ark Acad Sci* 2004;**58**:70–3.
91. Terletzky P, Ramsey R. Comparison of three techniques to identify and count individual animals in aerial imagery. *J Signal Inf Process* 2016;**07**:123–35. https://doi.org/10.4236/jsip.2016.73013.

PART TWO

Outbreak management and relevant case studies towards SDG's

CHAPTER FOURTEEN

Disaster risk management during COVID-19 pandemic

Shirsendu Nandi
Quantitative Techniques and Operations Management Area, FORE School of Management, New Delhi, India

1. Introduction

COVID-19, originated in Wuhan, China,[1,2] has caused a serious threat by claiming millions of human lives across the globe and posed serious social, economic, political, and environmental challenges on a long-term basis.[3] The disease is spreading daily[4] and this pandemic has been existing for the last 2 years or more across the world where some countries are battling with its 2nd wave (India and other south Asian countries) and some other countries have faced 3rd wave (European countries), and some are amid its 4th wave (Japan).[5] Recent pandemic caused by novel severe acute respiratory syndromes (SARS-CoV-2) shows similarity to these earlier CoVs such as SARS-CoV and MERS-CoV by causing mass mortality.[6] Due to the longer period of the pandemic, it is expected that multiple disasters and calamities will simultaneously hit areas already affected by COVID-19.[7] The urban population in various regions of Central and South America, South Asia, and Africa are more likely to be affected by flooding, and these flood-affected areas will, in turn, convert to an epicenter of the pandemic explosion, making the overall situation and disaster management far more challenging.[8] The COVID-19 situation of cities in Ottawa and Manitoba in Canada got worsened due to floods.[9,10] During the first wave of COVID-19, flood-affected East Africa observed increased vulnerability among people in terms of the death toll and rapid spread of the disease as social distancing and hygiene-related COVID-19 protocols could not be followed.[8,11] Concurrent hits of disasters during pandemic constrain and limit the effectiveness and application of prescribed mitigation strategies of disaster management.[12,13] There have been several other instances of multiple disasters during the current pandemic viz. COVID-19 coupled with cyclone in coastal areas of Cox's Bazar, Bangladesh[14]; COVID-19 coupled with cyclone (Yash) in coastal areas of West Bengal and Orissa, India;

COVID-19 and the Sustainable Development Goals
https://doi.org/10.1016/B978-0-323-91307-2.00013-4

COVID-19 coupled with a heat wave in Florida and other parts of the United States. Multiple disasters have reportedly caused a higher rate of fatality and comorbidity.[15] When Japan was hit by typhoon Hagibis during the phase of COVID-19, the disaster management, rehabilitation and recovery operation was jeopardized due to the lack of volunteers required to carry out these operations.[16–19] Though unprecedented or as extremely rare phenomena, governments and society at large across the world are facing natural disasters (viz. flood, drought, and cyclone) alongside combatting the pandemic COVID-19.[20] Collaboration among various public departments (viz. disaster management group, department of health, meteorology, irrigation, agriculture, and finance) and preparedness among government, civil society, and private sector are the keys to an integrated approach of mitigating the risk of disaster during COVID-19.[20,21]

The role of top government officials in the administration is pivotal in undertaking appropriate policies in disaster risk management during this pandemic. However, at the same time, successful implementation of those policies and strategies at an operational level requires strengthening the local bodies, local administration, and local communities by decentralization of power, particularly because of restrictions of travel during a pandemic. Okura et al.[22] describe how flood-prone rural areas of Nepal combatted multidisaster environment during COVID-19 by effective dissemination of information done through communication devices (mobile phone) and CDMC (community disaster management committee) regarding resilience, preparation for coordination, and practical action against hazards.

When COVID-19 is discussed concerning disaster management and lessons learned from the current pandemic, the traditional disaster risk management practice should be integrated via a bridge with a more resilient and modern 21st century disaster risk management approach having the ability to tackle risk unknown in nature or not fully understood.[23] According to Mishra,[23] this modern holistic disaster risk management approach considers unknown and rare events (pandemic created by an unknown virus) and the elements of risk inherent in our global system.

Disaster risk management in general, with greater priority during a pandemic, should not only stick to risk mitigation and action during the shock of the disaster but also consists of an effort of rehabilitation, reconstruction, and implementing of other relief measures enabling the affected people and locality to bounce back to its original shape. With due support of civil society and government, many localities and disaster-affected people have been able to build a resilient and robust future for themselves. A comprehensive disaster management plan must ensure timely help from the state and devise a method to compensate affected people for their economic losses due to disaster causing damage in the means of their livelihood. Similarly, in the context of health disasters like the current pandemic, lessons learned during COVID-19 guide us to include strategy and scientific recourse for the smooth recovery of affected people from COVID-19. The successful implementation of a strategy for recovery and rehabilitation of affected people will lessen the economic burden and promote a healthy social balance sheet on a long-term basis.

Disaster risk management as a discipline of interest both in the domain of academia and the practicing world is constantly evolving. From relatively less rigor it has grown tremendously, drawing heavily from STEM field, AI, and deep learning for more accurate technology-based scientific forecasting, viz. the end-to-end early warning system based on technology-based forecasting method launched in the Indian Ocean after the tsunami it suffered. It also requires knowledge and application of social and behavioral science for comprehensive management considering the human aspect.

The current chapter aims to develop a framework for integrating health or biological disaster management into the overall disaster risk management protocols and principles. It also suggests a shift from the traditional approach of reactive response after the outbreak/occurrence of the health disaster to a more proactive approach of health risk mitigation by building capabilities across the nation through the development of healthcare services and infrastructure to combat health disasters. Sustainable Development Goal-13 mentions the need for urgent actions to be taken and sets targets to combat the impact of climate change causing natural disasters. It is also discussed how to minimize risk and losses during COVID-19 and the required preventive measures to be taken during the pandemic in the light disaster risk reduction (DRR) framework.

2. The Sendai framework on the convention of disaster risk reduction

The Sendai framework for disaster risk reduction (SFDRR) and sustainable development goals (SDG) are two landmark achievements and steps the United Nations took in 2015. The Sendai framework recommends actionable steps to scale up risk mitigation strategies which in turn must build resilience against disasters across the world.[24,25]

The Sendai Framework on the convention of disaster risk reduction classifies different disaster events into two different categories of risk. (i) A hazardous event or disaster occurring with high frequency, low severity, and relatively less devastating was classified in an **extensive risk** category, e.g., landslides, localized draughts, and floods. (ii) A hazardous event or disaster occurring with low frequency, high severity, and relatively more devastating in nature, causing severe damage to lives and properties, was classified in an **intensive risk** category, e.g., tsunami, earthquake, and nuclear disasters. The convention opined that both these categories of events require comprehensive planning for management. There was an agreement regarding the possibility of efficient management and reduction of risk for these events as the risk is identifiable, quantifiable, and measurable, and an appropriate probabilistic risk evaluation may be carried out. According to the general disaster risk reduction principles, the impact of a disaster can be minimized and effectively managed by a multilevel, multidimensional, multidisciplinary coordinating approach.

However, the convention lacked broad-level discussion and fixing an effective protocol for combatting a black swan event.[26] A black swan event may be defined as a very rare event and has an impact on a large scale with widespread severe consequences.[27] The impact is extremely difficult to model as multiple disasters occur simultaneously in an almost unpredictable manner. The world has already witnessed black swan events having a catastrophic impact across the globe or inside a significantly large geographic region on most occasions. The Indian tsunami and earthquake in 2004, claiming nearly 230,000 lives and affecting countries like India, Maldives, Indonesia, Sri Lanka, Malaysia, and Thailand, is one of the well-known black swan events. The subprime crisis in the United States in 2008 led to a global economic crisis worldwide and impacted most of the countries in the world. Japan in 2011 faced a triple disaster one led to another, causing nearly 18,000 deaths. In an almost unpredictable and unprecedented manner, an earthquake led to a tsunami which in turn caused a nuclear disaster at the nuclear power plant at Fukushima.

Similarly, the COVID-19, which started during the latter half of 2019 in a small corner of the world, gradually spread worldwide and turned into a pandemic. Many countries have concurrently faced disasters like earthquakes, cyclones, chemical disasters, wildfire, drought, and floods during the COVID-19 pandemic. In Australia, the event of bushfires increased mortality and comorbidity during COVID-19.[28] In the United States, the firefighting to prevent wildfire was disrupted[29] and in Zimbabwe, social initiatives to combat the situation of lack of food grains caused by severe drought got hindered during the pandemic.[30] Although the probability of the individual disaster and the impact thereon can be computed, the risk analysis of the concurrent occurrence of the disasters, and therefore evaluating the larger impact of this event, is computationally very complex.

3. Principle lessons for combatting biological disasters like COVID-19 pandemic

The COVID-19 pandemic disaster did not discriminate between rich and poor or among people from different social strata and statuses. Effective management against this disaster requires a collective effort from everybody. In big nations like India and the United States, information sharing between the central government and state governments, among different state governments, between public authorities and civil society, is crucial for the exercise. While the hallmark of success in managing the pandemic disaster lies in the crucial role played by doctors, nurses, and other public and private health workers, it is equally important to engage community workers, civil society, and every citizen by specifying their roles and responsibilities in containing the pandemic. Researchers have established the necessity of building a resilient public health system to successfully implement the public health disaster risk reduction (DRR) program.[31,32] The principles of DRM (disaster risk management) must be integrated into the public health management system on a long-term basis.[33,34] Few underlying basic principles that need to be followed for this disaster management are as follows:

i. Acknowledging the role of government as a central body passing regulations and laws to manage and control the pandemic
ii. Acknowledging the role of society and every citizen and ensuring their strategic participation
iii. Reorganizing and repurposing critical resources, including human resources, capacities (hospital beds, medicine, medical equipment and aids, etc.)
iv. Repurposing and enhancing diagnostic and clinical management capacities
v. Appropriate use of technology within the constraints and focus on evidence-based research and dissemination of knowledge for information sharing

3.1 Risk assessment and evaluation by advanced mathematical modeling

One of the most important exercises of disaster prevention and mitigation is risk assessment. For this purpose, advanced probability-based dynamic epidemiological models (agent-based models or compartmentalized Markov chain-based models) may be used, drawing heavily from other related STEM fields (deep learning, artificial intelligence, advanced probability and stochastic process).[35] As evident, since the source of risk, nature of the virus, and many other things are unknown, it is extremely difficult to capture the entire risk through these models. Therefore the untapped risk may be reduced by reducing the vulnerability or enhancing people's resilience and the region's environment under risk. The risk assessment should consider the hazard, exposure, vulnerability, emergency response, and recovery capability for a catastrophic event like COVID-19. The tools used in risk assessment use input variables such as rate of spread of the disease, infection doubling rate, positivity rate, prevalence rate, demographic variables such as gender distribution, and distribution of different age groups among the affected population. The impact and consequence of the event may be analyzed by noting the mortality rate, rate of recovery, classification of severity of the disease, availability of health infrastructure, etc. Higher casualty and a less effective postdisaster recovery effort after Hurricane Katrina and Haiyan in New Orleans in the United States and the Philippines may be attributed to the fragile health infrastructure, lack of health insurance, and access of healthcare services to the public.[24,36,37] It is also important to enhance the capacity of providing healthcare services and optimally allocate scarce resources and thereby minimize the fatality.

The purpose of risk analysis and evaluation of impact in the context of disaster management is integrated planning and decision-making. Some major hindrances in the planning and decision-making process during the management of COVID-19 were observed.

a. Determination of a proper unit of analysis of a geographical area. It may be too small or too large. A large unit of analysis loses its characteristics of granularity. For example, a complete restriction or shutdown imposed in an entire subdivision might be useless since the actual source of infection might lie in a small corner of that region. Similarly, a chosen unit that is too small might lack several sufficient data points required for an appropriate decision.

b. Local factors or drivers of risk were dominant in determining the nature of spread and other variables on COVID-19. A management information system which does not consider the variety of controlling and risk factors specific to a particular zone or locality will lead to erroneous decision-making.

c. Since the disease and the nature of the virus are very dynamic, real-time updates of information need to occur within very small time intervals—failing which appropriate and timely decision-making for disaster management becomes impossible.

3.2 Importance of local administration and community involvement

All countries have issued guidelines on COVID-19 (symptoms, testing, prevention, quarantine and isolation, caregivers, treatments, etc.) and enacted laws and implemented them through administrative surveillance to contain the spread of this pandemic. The surveillance to contain the disease is largely done by using digital technologies. Tracking needs usage of tools like data dashboard, machine learning, and migration maps; contact tracing requires usage of global positioning systems and quarantine; and isolation makes use of artificial intelligence, global positioning systems, real-time monitoring of mobile devices, etc. Screening is done by using artificial intelligence, mobile phone applications, and digital thermometers. However, the role of community-based surveillance is far more important to contain the infection and manage this disaster. Areas where the community played the roles of ears to the government have managed the spread of COVID-19 efficiently. Risk reduction programs organized by community groups have been greatly beneficial for building awareness, scientific knowledge, and behavioral patterns as per COVID-19 protocol. Wearing masks, usage of sanitizers, and disinfecting the residence of infected people also helped to bring down the rate of infection to a great extent. Hence, community leadership has been instrumental in efficient disaster management by providing the authority with appropriate feedback from the ground level regarding any hindrances and negative consequences of implemented actions.

3.3 Managing risk versus managing uncertainty in managing the disaster of COVID-19

The current pandemic is known for a faster rate of spread of the disease, a differential rate of mortality and recovery rate, and a higher rate of mortality among older people and people with a weaker immune system.[38] As discussed, computation and capturing entire risk for managing the pandemic is extremely difficult since the scientific community is still pursuing scientific investigations to reveal facts on source of the virus, the emergence and characteristics of strains, etc. There exist uncertainty of effectiveness of various treatment protocols on people of different age groups, uncertainty concerning the opinion expressed by experts on acquired herd immunity, the effectiveness of different vaccines on generating sufficient antibody, and the timeline a vaccine can protect from the disease. Due to a lack of information on the virus and its different variants, most of the risk cannot be captured and remains unquantifiable for every pandemic. Risk analysis on any disaster is performed on past incidents and experience of that disaster, taking into account its impact, nature of devastation, frequency etc., future strategies for managing the disaster are prepared. Health hazards or biological disasters caused by pandemics require management of uncertainty. Hence, the management of health disasters warrants the advancement of risk analysis toward managing uncertainty and bridging the existing gaps.

3.4 Managing untapped global risk through reducing vulnerability or building local resilience

Today's open economy, the concept of the global village, and the interconnectedness within the world through fast connecting modes of transport have significantly contributed toward the fast spread of COVID-19 and ultimately turned into a pandemic. The impact and mortality rate in different parts of the world vary depending on the robustness of the public health system. Vulnerability in this context is defined as socioeconomic, physical, environmental, and other factors contributing positively to the population's susceptibility to hazards. During the monsoon, people in slum areas in India faced the dual hazards of flood and COVID-19 and were considered highly vulnerable under this pandemic.[39] Building resilience means reducing the vulnerability and thereby reducing the risk of a community from exposure to disaster. The vulnerable population, staff, and frontline warriors of COVID-19 may be considered groups at high risk,[17,40,41] and these groups must be given additional attention to get protection against the disease.

Considering the scale of impact of COVID-19, a good starting point of building resilience will be cooperation at a global level by sharing of information of outputs of research carried out worldwide and based on them deciding good practices to be followed. Those good practices might guide behavior and hygiene practices to be followed both at the individual and at the societal level, treatment protocols, diagnostic norms, repurposing, and optimal usage of resources. It is also further emphasized that resilience to health disaster decreases because of lack of access to good housing facilities, proper education, basic sanitation, clean water, social support, etc.[42,43] Role of communities and society, as well as individual factors like awareness, integration, diversity, self-regulation, and adaptability, plays a crucial role in building resilience.[44]

The branch of study called disaster risk management has come a long way. In the initial phase, postdisaster recovery and rehabilitation were of primary interest. From postdisaster recovery and crisis management, the branch evolved to disaster risk reduction and risk mitigation. The latest focus lies in building resilience. Building resilience requires building redundancy in social, economic resources, health system and infrastructure, and other capacities. The shock-absorbing capability or degree of resilience also depends greatly on systemic redundancy and modular approach—converting each locality to a self-reliant modular entity.

4. Planning, risk mitigation, resilience building: Methods of protection against a rare event like COVID-19

A pandemic in COVID-19 has disrupted planet earth which experienced the last pandemic almost a century back in the form of Spanish flu. Since a biological disaster and pandemic like COVID-19 is rare and highly improbable and uncertain, it may be termed a black swan event. From the perspective of disaster management, it is important to note certain characteristics of such disasters.

i. The highly unpredictable, unlikely, and high-profile event blows out of proportion very fast and shows the catastrophic impact

ii. Profiling the risk of such events is difficult as it exhibits a very small probability

iii. Exploration of causality and other facts are revealed after the disaster

The principle behind protection against this uncertain black swan event is learning from experience: investigating the source and main cause of the disaster. Extensive research and investigation must take place to find out how it spread and caused outsized impact at a global level, how it created disproportionate pressure on the existing medical resources and capacities, etc. The spread of the Ebola virus in Liberia, Guinea, and Sierra Leone weakened the existing public health system and resulted in the death of a large number of health workers.[45–48] Learning from the experience is not sufficient, but a forward-looking progressive philosophy to best prepare ourselves for the future is the key to prevent the disaster and limit its catastrophic impact. The latest philosophy lies in creating an antifragile system that works beyond building resilience. Resilience provides shock-absorbing capacity while the antifragile system promotes the evolution of the existing system as a better system. The objective is to absorb the shock of the disaster and minimize the damage and seek opportunities for the evolution of a new era of cultural changes; ideas; behavioral practices; social, economic, and political systems; and scientific and technological advancement. Because of the interconnected systems worldwide, penetration causing disaster to a particular system leads to failure of other connected systems located in other geographies very fast. (e.g., terrorized cyberattack). A country that wants to be better prepared for disasters like COVID-19 has to promote local resilience and build antifragile independent, modular, decentralized systems that can work as a self-sufficient unit.

4.1 Reinforcing risk management by implementing nationwide IT infrastructure, digitalization with local support

Digitalization nationwide is extremely important for managing risk arising out of a pandemic like COVID-19. It is essential to digitally capture data on various patient- and treatment-related information (demographics, symptoms, treatment protocols, test reports, finding responses to treatment, etc.) while treating patients of COVID-19 by creating and preserving relevant databases. The information may be used as inputs to appropriate models on predictive analytics to build a decision support system (DSS) necessary for strategic prioritization of resources and formulation of health policies. To gather data on each individual, the government must build IT infrastructure across the nation. People should have access to a device (smart phone or other handheld devices) connected to the internet. Penetration of internet and IT infrastructure is the necessary precondition for implementing tracking, tracing, and isolation—key steps to manage and contain the disease. This is more challenging because the asymptomatic people are spreading the disease without even knowing that they are transmitting it.[49] Community workers, organizations, and health workers at the local level may be deployed to successfully implement the digitalization process and establish a DSS. The local authority for disaster management and other related organizations and health institutions should be empowered for immediate response and recovery operations during postdisaster rehabilitation.

4.2 Resilience in supply chain through building robust infrastructure and redundancy

Keeping the supply chain disruption minimal is one of the important goals of disaster risk management during COVID-19. The Supply of essentials such as food items, groceries, medical equipment, and medicines was critical in combatting the disaster caused by COVID-19. During the phase of Ebola, some African countries experienced disruption in the supply and delivery of healthcare-related products and services due to weak supply chain and information systems.[50–52] During the outbreak of Yellow fever in countries like Angola, Uganda, and Congo, political unrest and warlike situations in different parts of Africa resulted in a larger death toll due to failure of supply chain infrastructure.[53–57] While restrictions in movement and lockdown created hindrances in supply, resilient businesses and firms made suitable adjustments in their operations including inbound and outbound logistics, inventory policies, and coordination strategies to provide uninterrupted supplies of essential items. The supply chain's resilience is also possible through redundancy in the mode of transportation and availability of strong infrastructural facilities to establish interconnectedness among various parts of a large nation through alternative modes of transportation (roads, railways, air, etc.). To ensure last mile delivery of food, vaccine at a doorstep government needs to scale up the capacity of the public distribution system by engaging human resources and efficient use of technology.

4.3 Economic, financial, and environmental resilience

During the phase of COVID-19, countries have faced natural disasters like floods, cyclones, and earthquakes. It is important to build and maintain disaster-resilient infrastructure for protecting life and properties from natural disasters. Building an economic resilience of a nation or the financial resilience of an individual is important for disaster management. It is more relevant in disaster management during COVID-19 because it has negatively affected the economy worldwide with rising unemployment and economic slowdown. Disaster management during COVID-19 requires financial resources to support the enhancement of capacities of healthcare services, undertake cutting-edge research, vaccinate people, provide food and economic support to marginalized, poor people. Instead of looking for financial resources after the disaster, a country should provide economic resources meant for disaster response as a part of long-term developmental planning. Countries that do not include the allocation of financial resources for disaster

Table 1 Different disasters, nunmber of affected people, number of deaths and economic losses from 1998 to 2017.

Type of disaster	Affected people (million)	Number of deaths	Economic losses (billion $)
Flood	2000	142,088	656
Draught	1500	21,563	124
Storm	726	232,680	1330
Earthquake	125	747,234	661
Extreme temperature	97	166,346	61
Landslide	4.8	18,414	8
Wild fire, volcanic activity	6.2	2398	68

Source: UNISDR (2017): Economic Losses. Poverty and disaster 1998–2017.

risk mitigation and management as a part of the national policy suffer from a financial crunch at the time of disaster. As disasters have become more frequent and are inevitable, countries should consider the financial allocation for disaster mitigation as the investment required to support long-term sustainable growth.[58] Literature is found on the impact of disasters on public health and clinical management-related matters.

Governments, NGOs, and civil society have come forward[59] and taken welfare measures for marginalized people, the weaker segment of the society, and people struggling for survival and livelihoods; arrangements for food, basic hygiene materials, healthcare facilities, and vaccination need to be done to extend support to people facing financial constraints due to restrictions imposed during COVID-19. One of the important measures of building economic resilience and providing social security is cash assistance and direct benefit transfer. This initiative also helps to boost up the demand side to provide resilience against economic slowdown. After due consultations with the central bank, the government may provide subsidies or loans at a cheaper rate to keep the businesses and affected industries running during the crisis period of COVID-19. Instead of looking for financial resources after the disaster, a country should provide for economic resources meant for disaster response as a part of long-term developmental planning (Table 1).

4.4 Sustainability practices, green initiatives, and conservation of scarce natural resources

It is well established that sustainability aspects are well connected in the prevention and mitigation of disasters.[60] Researchers may further explore the linkages of the current COVID-19 pandemic with violation of sustainability practices, deviation from green initiatives, and excessive consumption of scarce natural resources. However, urban areas exposed to pollution and coastal areas prone to natural disasters need to integrate sustainability initiatives on ecosystem restoration, plantation, hazard, risk mapping, vulnerability reduction, eco-friendly policies for disaster risk management. Rampant urbanization, indiscriminate use of natural resources, rapid industrialization, and deforestation have led to the loss of natural balance by destabilizing the proportional existence of natural gifts like rivers, mountains, springs, forests, and biodiversities. Sustainability efforts to reduce pollution, carbon footprints, and limit human activities causing the emission of greenhouse gases are welcome initiatives to reduce the risk of disaster. These kinds of sustainable and green practices in consumption and production naturally immune us from various risk factors.

5. Intersection of health and disaster risk management

There has been a lot of emphasis on research works, theory building, and policy implementation-related works in the interdisciplinary area of health and disaster risk management. In the context of disaster risk management, public health becomes a critical factor. The world health assembly, through its resolution, has also urged for strengthening of the disaster risk management system by integrating it into a national health policy.[61] A weaker public health creates a hindrance in attaining national, regional, and global developmental targets and goals.[62–64] Literature is found on the impact of the disaster on public health and clinical management-related issues, the commonalities and coordination between public health and crisis management, the impact of strengthening public health on disaster risk reduction, and the description of disaster management cycles applicable in case of an epidemic affecting public health. The Sendai framework for disaster risk reduction (SFDRR) has also given due consideration to health-related issues under disaster management.[65]

Health is considered one of the important outcomes of disaster risk management initiatives. In the context of the current pandemic COVID-19, health has emerged as a matter of concern and one of the critical goals to be achieved. In the African context, it has been strongly advised to use a strong public health system to mitigate the risk of health vulnerabilities and inequalities arising from the disaster.[66–68] Any natural disaster damages the physical, mental, and psychological well-being of individuals. It also causes significant morbidity and comorbidity among people affected by disasters. Therefore "Health-Emergency disaster risk management (Health-EDRM)," after adopting the health-related objectives from Sendai Framework, augments it further with its action and research agenda to decrease the risk of health hazards as a result of the disaster. It primarily encompasses focuses on the following:

a. A holistic approach to health-related interventions is required during all phases of disaster.

b. Cater to specific health needs of vulnerable sections of the population (people more likely to have health hazards), viz. children, elderly, differently-abled, and people having comorbidity, during a disaster.

c. Necessary steps to build health resilience among communities considering the entire spectrum of health hazards.

d. Internationally acknowledged standard of case-based reporting for measuring different health parameters during all phases of disaster (predisaster, during disaster, and postdisaster)

e. Agreed-upon guidelines regarding usage of terminologies and procedures for preparedness and building health resilience among communities should be prepared.

6. COVID-19: An economic disaster

COVID-19 pandemic has caused mortality and morbidity that keeps people out of work for a long period and slowed down the economy across the world. The pandemic also disrupted the global supply chain due to the lack of availability of inputs from major supplier countries caused by an interruption in production. Limited and restricted transportation among countries disrupted the global supply chain and logistics network, causing a further decline in economic activities. There has been supply and demand shock for various products and services, and regular consumption and production patterns were shattered due to the economic meltdown, lack of confidence among consumers, and other related reasons. As a consequence of the pandemic, there is an estimated loss of employment of 3%. Capital and labor being inputs of production, loss of confidence among investors, and lack of availability of labor have resulted in a supply shock.

An initial estimate predicted an average of 7% shrinkage for advanced economies, 2.5% contraction for developing countries and emerging economies, and an overall 4% contraction in the entire global economy. The actual contraction/growth of the first 10 countries (concerning nominal

Table 2 First 10 countries in terms of nominal GDP and their growth/contraction in GDP in 2020.

Country	Rank (nominal GDP)	GDP growth/ contraction (in %)
United States	1	−3.505
China	2	2.27
Japan	3	−4.83
Germany	4	−4.903
United Kingdom	5	−9.92
India	6	−7.965
France	7	−8.232
Italy	8	−8.871
Canada	9	−5.403
Korea	10	−0.958

Source: https://statisticstimes.com/economy/world-gdp-ranking.php.

GDP) in the world during 2020 has been presented in Table 2. The contraction in economic activities in many countries worldwide has led to a huge number of losses in jobs and livelihood, a decrease in per capita income. The vulnerability was more impactful among low-wage earners.

In order to effectively manage the negative impact of COVID-19 on the economy and trade, each country should administer certain steps on a short- and long-term basis. Figs. 1 and 2 show global deflated and normalized losses due to natural disasters. While the disaster in the form of a pandemic may continue its devastating impact for a longer period than expected, the government, treasuries, and central banks are expected to implement policies to continue their normal functioning. An initial response to combat this financial crisis may be cutting the bank rates by the government and policymakers. It is also equally important to determine appropriate monetary policy, health policy, and fiscal policy to regulate and control planned and unplanned expenditures to manage the financial distress caused by COVID-19. As long-term measures, the government has imposed restrictions on mass gatherings in public and workplaces, mobility of the public, and thereby limiting economic activities. Although these restrictions reflect efforts from the government to contain the spread of the virus, it has impacted all sectors of the economy. There has been an increase in the cost of imports and exports. Demand for travel and tourism dropped heavily. Demands for many services requiring close physical proximity also saw a decline.

The current pandemic has also demonstrated the need for an increase in healthcare expenditures. Previous researches have shown that a health

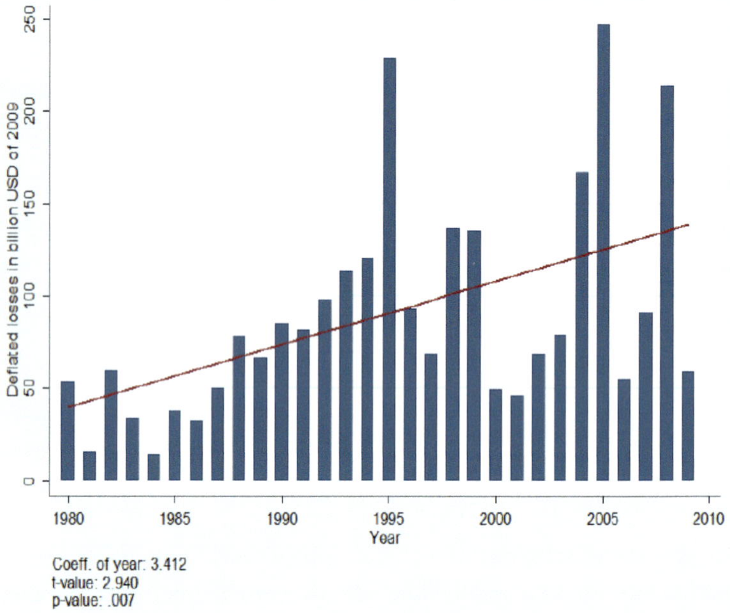

Fig. 1 Global deflated losses based on natural disasters. Note: based on 20,375 disasters. *(Source: Adopted from Neumayer E, Barthel F. Normalizing economic loss from natural disasters: a global analysis.* Global Environ Change *2011;**21**:13–24.)*

improvement improves GDP and vice versa.[69–71] Governments and policymakers must consider investment and increase aggregate expenditure in healthcare as a long-term strategy to manage a disaster like COVID-19. A nation consisting of a healthy population can cut down health expenses and experiences an increase in the productivity and earning potential of individuals.[72,73] Therefore the benefit of investment in healthcare can be observed both at an individual (micro) and country (macro) level. Another significant benefit of higher expenditure on healthcare is an increase in people's life expectancy, leading to an urge or motivation for future savings and investment in business activities resulting in economic progress. Many researchers have been conducted to explore the relationship between health and economic growth.[74–79] Various researchers have found a positive correlation between healthcare expenditures and personal income, per capita GDP, labor productivity, etc. Among the various predictors of per capita GDP, hospital expenditures and expenditures on personal healthcare are the two most important predictor variables of per capita GDP. However, there is

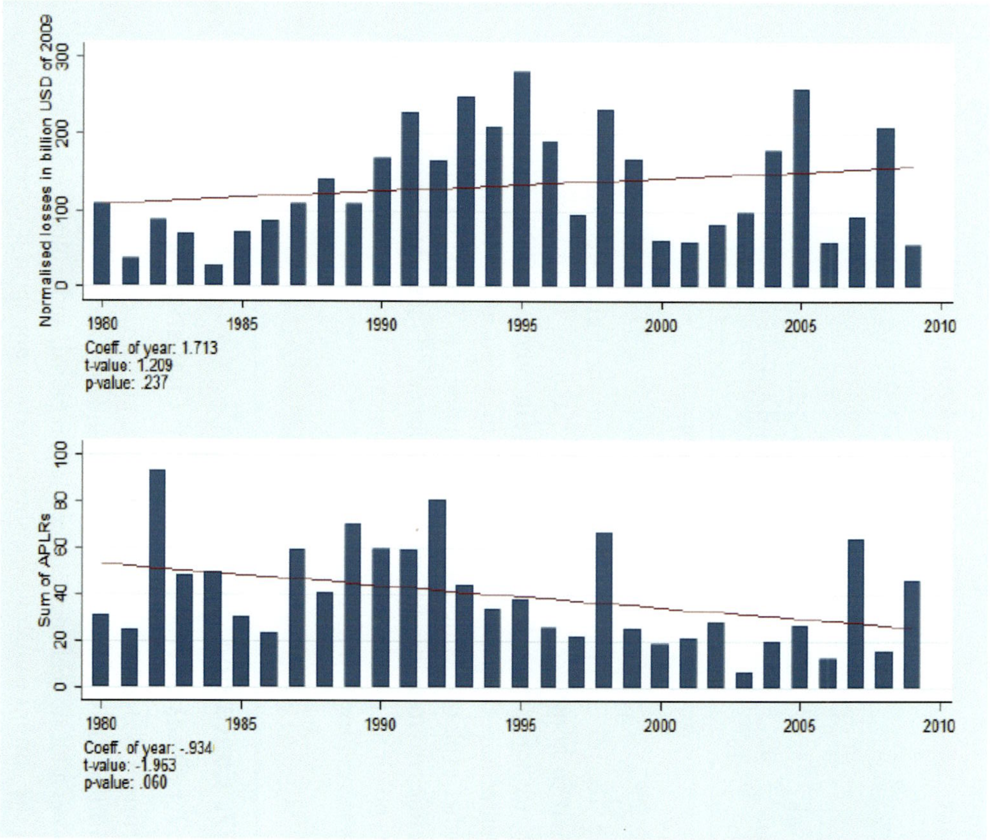

Fig. 2 Global losses from all natural disasters normalized with the conventional approach (top) and alternative approach (bottom). Note: based on 19,115 disasters. *(Source: Adopted from Neumayer E, Barthel F. Normalizing economic loss from natural disasters: a global analysis.* Global Environ Change *2011;**21**:13–24.)*

Table 3 Data of top 10 countries in terms of healthcare expenditures as % of GDP.

Countries	Rank (healthcare expenditure as % of GDP)	Healthcare expenditure as % of GDP (%)	Growth/ contraction in GDP (%) in 2020	Death/ million population	Deaths (absolute)
USA	1	16.9	−3.505	1838.57	603,491
Switzerland	2	12.2	−2.983	1270.7	10,896
Germany	3	11.2	−4.903	1096.41	91,148
France	4	11.2	−8.232	1628.25	109,190
Sweden	5	11	−2.818	1423.27	14,639
Japan	6	10.9	−4.83	117.59	14,848
Canada	7	10.7	−5.403	701.16	26,536
Denmark	8	10.5	−3.287	436.02	2537
Belgium	9	10.4	−6.424	2194	25,196
Austria	10	10.3	−6.59	1207.49	10,719

Source: https://www.statista.com/statistics/268826/health-expenditure-as-gdp-percentage-in-oecd-countries/.

debate regarding the optimal amount of healthcare-related spending required to boost economic growth.[80–82] Careful investment in various healthcare domains can boost productivity, income, and GDP of a country. It also promotes the general well-being of the population. Researchers need to further explore theories of welfare economics to decide how the scarce economic resources may be optimally allocated[83,84] after due consideration of data on GDP, per capita GDP, healthcare expenditures of different countries, etc., as provided in Table 3.

7. Conclusion

7.1 Disaster risk management: Challenges ahead

The current disaster of COVID-19 has taught us various lessons, and it is evident that disaster with its increased frequency and devastating capacity still poses a lot of challenges at the local, regional, and global levels. Especially, the current pandemic has shown how important it is to rethink the current approaches and mechanisms to combat and manage the risk of disaster. Researchers, administrators, and practitioners need to work together to find an efficient way of reducing the detrimental impact of disasters like COVID-19 on socioeconomic progress, poverty, and parameters of the human developmental index, security of life, livelihood, and property. The enormous pressure on healthcare facilities, and financial resources due to COVID-19 necessitates scientific research to invent models for intelligent usage of existing tools and methodologies to better forecast such events, compute risks, and prescribe measures to control risk and minimize losses.

Modern disaster management encompasses all phases of disaster but places relatively larger importance on disaster response and postdisaster rehabilitation and reconstruction. A public health disaster like COVID-19 demands more emphasis on planning and risk mitigation. There has been discussion on disaster management approach when there is a flood situation during COVID-19.[85,86] It is equally important to compute and control risk for concurrent multidisasters viz. COVID-19 is coupled with a flood, cyclone, drought, and chemical disaster.

The entire world can learn from the experience of the current pandemic and apply those learnings to build a better, comprehensive disaster management system[12,87] Gathering from the experience of managing the risk of a pandemic like COVID-19, researchers and experts have appreciated the importance of building modular, stand-alone, self-reliant, independent systems so that restrictions may be imposed when required in a particular region without affecting the normal functioning of other regions or systems. It restricts the propagation of risk from one system to another and contains the disease at a smaller region by allowing the independent functioning of individual systems.

8. Future risk management

The spread of COVID-19 has resulted in a heavy increase in mass mortality. While antiviral drugs and immune-based treatment have been able to provide positive results to some extent,[88] the key to successfully mitigating the future risk lies in the design and implementing vaccination among all. COVID-19 is a new disease and designing a vaccine and making it available after completion of clinical trial consumes a good amount of time. Therefore successful risk mitigation and management of health disasters like COVID-19 requires the usage of AI, deep learning, and other methods of predictive analytics to forecast its advent, characteristics, and capacity of causing damage. It is also required to successfully build probabilistic, AI, machine learning, or hybrid models to find the optimal strategies to prior track, trace, isolate, and treat people affected by pandemics to minimize the risk.

Acknowledgment

The infrastructural support provided to the author by FORE School of Management, New Delhi, in completing this Book Chapter is gratefully acknowledged.

References

1. Huang C, Wang Y, Li X, Ren L, Zhao J, Hu Y, et al. Clinical features of patients infected with 2019 novel coronavirus in Wuhan, China. *Lancet* 2020;**395**:497–506. https://doi.org/10.1016/S0140-6736(20)30183-5.
2. Zhu N, Zhang D, Wang W, Li X, Yang B, Song J, et al. A novel coronavirus from patients with pneumonia in China, 2019. *N Engl J Med* 2020. https://doi.org/10.1056/NEJMoa2001017.
3. UNDP. *COVID-19: UNDP's integrated response*. United Nations Development Programme; 2020. https://www.undp.org/. [Accessed 10 July 2021].
4. Mousazadeh M, Naghdali Z, Rahimian N, Hashemi M, Paital B, Al-Qodah Z, et al. Management of environmental health to prevent an outbreak of COVID-19: a review. In: Dehghani MH, Karri RR, Roy S, editors. *Environmental and health management of novel coronavirus disease (COVID-19)*. Academic Press; 2021. p. 235–67. https://doi.org/10.1016/B978-0-323-85780-2.00007-X.
5. Venkatachalam A. *Japan gets off its fourth wave*; 2021 Ha-asia.com. [Accessed 3 October 2021].
6. Khan AH, Tirth V, Fawzy M. COVID-19 transmission, vulnerability, persistence and nanotherapy: a review. *Environ Chem Lett* 2021;**19**:2773–87. https://doi.org/10.1007/s10311-021-01229-4.
7. Dehghani MH, Roy S, Karri RR. Novel coronavirus (COVID-19) in environmental engineering perspective. *Environ Sci Pollut Res* 2022;1–3. https://doi.org/10.1007/s11356-022-18572-w.
8. Marsham J. *East Africa faces triple crisis of Covid-19, locusts and floods*; 2020 https://www.climatechangenews.com/2020/05/11/east-africa-faces-triplecrisis-covid-19-locusts-floods. [Accessed 11 May 2020].
9. Ottawa: Ottawa City. *Flood preparations are well underway*; 2020 https://ottawa.ca/en/news/food-preparationsare-well-underway/. [Accessed 10 July 2021].
10. Manitoba. *High water response activity: COVID-19 pandemic adaptations*; 2020 https://www.gov.mb.ca/. [Accessed 10 July 2021].
11. Mousazadeh M, Naghdali Z, Rahimian N, Hashemi M, Paital B, Al-Qodah Z. Management of environmental health to prevent an outbreak of COVID-19: a review. In: Dehghani MH, Karri RR, Roy S, editors. *Environmental and health management of novel coronavirus disease (COVID-19)*. Academic Press; 2021. p. 235–67.
12. Chatterjee R, Bajwa S, Dwivedi D, Kanji R, Ahammed M, Shaw R. COVID-19 risk assessment tool: dual application of risk communication and risk governance. *Prog Disaster Sci* 2020;**7**. https://doi.org/10.1016/j.pdisas.2020.100109, 100109.
13. Phillips CA, Caldas A, Cleetus R, Dahl KA, Declet-Barreto J, Licker R, et al. Compound climate risks in the COVID-19 pandemic. *Nat Clim Chang* 2020;**10**:586–8. https://doi.org/10.1038/s41558-020-0804-2.
14. ISCG. *Cyclone emergency preparedness update*. Inter Sector Coordination Group; 2020. https://www.humanitarianresponse.info/en/operations/bangladesh/document/cyclone-emergency-preparedness-update-march-2020/. [Accessed 10 July 2021].
15. NOAA. *Global climate report—March 2020*. National Oceanic and Atmospheric Admiration; 2020. https://www.ncdc.noaa.gov/sotc/global/202003/. [Accessed 10 July 2021].

16. CB. *Damage by 2019 Typhoon no. 19.* Cabinet Ofce; 2020. http://www.bousai.go.jp/. [Accessed 10 July 2021].
17. CWSJ. *Lessons from Hagibis: learning to cope with intensifying disasters in the age of new normal.* Church World Service Japan; 2020. https://www.preventionweb.net/publications/view/70765/. [Accessed 10 July 2021].
18. NCSW. *Suspending volunteer center for disaster management.* Nagano Council of Social Welfare; 2020. https://www.csw-naganocity.or.jp/. [Accessed 10 July 2021].
19. Osumi M. *Experts urge rethink of disaster response measures as Japan battles coronavirus.* The Japan Times; 2020. https://www.japantimes.co.jp/news/2020/05/03/national/experts-urge-rethink-disaster-responsemeasures-japan-battles-coronavirus/. [Accessed 10 July 2021].
20. Amarnath G. *Why nations must prepare for natural disasters amid the current Covid-19 pandemic.* Water Risks and Development Resilience (WRDR), International Water Management Institute (IWMI); 2020. https://www.iwmi.cgiar.org/2020/04/why-nations-must-prepare-for-natural-disasters-amid-the-currentcovid-19-pandemic/. [Accessed 10 July 2021].
21. Hamid MZSA, Karri RR. Overview of preventive measures and good governance policies to mitigate the COVID-19 outbreak curve in Brunei. In: *COVID-19: systemic risk and resilience.* Cham: Springer; 2021. p. 115–40.
22. Okura Y, Neupane S, Rana B. *Avoiding a perfect storm: COVID-19 and floods in Nepal Findings from Community Disaster Management Committees*; 2020 https://europe.mercycorps.org/sites/default/files/2020-05/Avoiding_a_perfect%20storm_COVID-19_and_floods_in_Nepal.pdf. [Accessed 3 October 2021].
23. Mishra PK. COVID-19, Black Swan events and the future of disaster risk management in India. *Prog Disaster Sci* 2020;**8**, 100137.
24. *Sendai Framework for Disaster Risk Reduction 2015–2030*; 2015. Available from: http://www.unisdr.org/we/coordinate/sendai-framework.
25. Sustainable Development Goal 3. *Ensure healthy lives and promote well-being for all at all ages*; 2016. Available from: http://www.un.org/sustainabledevelopment/health/.
26. Basco GP. The coronavirus: Black swan and endowment shock. *Revista Galega de Economía* 2021;**30**(1):93–107.
27. Komljenovic D, Gaha M, Abdul-Nour G, Langheit C, Bourgeois M. Risks of extreme and rare events in asset management. *Saf Sci* 2016;**88**:129–45.
28. Wu X, Nethery RC, Sabath MB, Braun D, Dominici F. Exposure to air pollution and COVID-19 mortality in the United States. *Preprint Serve Health Sci* 2020. https://doi.org/10.1101/2020.04.05.20054502.
29. Groom N. *Trump administration halts wildfre prevention tool in California over coronavirus.* Reuters; 2020. https://www.reuters.com/article/. [Accessed 10 July 2021].
30. FEWSNET. *Zimbabwe famine early warning systems network.* Famine Early Warning System Network; 2020. https://fews.net/southern-africa/zimbabwe/. [Accessed 10 July 2021].
31. Aitsi-Selmi A, Murray V. The Sendai framework: disaster risk reduction through a health lens. *Bull World Health Organ* 2015;**93**(6):362. https://doi.org/10.2471/BLT.15.157362.
32. Bayntun C. A health system approach to all-hazards disaster management: a systematic review. *PLoS Curr* 2012;**4**. https://doi.org/10.1371/50081cad5861d, e50081cad5861d.
33. World Health Organization (WHO). Everybody's business. In: *Strengthening Health Systems to Improve Health Outcomes.* WHO's Framework for Action; 2007. Available from: http://www.who.int/healthsystems/strategy/everybodys_business.p.
34. UNISDR. *Terminology on disaster reduction.* United Nations Office for Disaster Risk Reduction (UNISDR); 2009. Available from: http://www.unisdr.

35. Jamshidi M, Lalbakhsh A, Talla J, Peroutka Z, Hadjilooei F, Lalbakhsh P, et al. Artificial intelligence and COVID-19: deep learning approaches for diagnosis and treatment. *IEEE Access* 2020;**8**:109581–95.
36. Casamina C, Lee C, Reyes R. Tropical cyclone Haiyan/Yolanda medical relief mission: perspectives of John A Bums School of Medicine 2nd year medical students. *Hawaii J Med Public Health* 2015;**74**(5):176–8.
37. Rudowitz R, Rowland D, Shartzer A. Health care in New Orleans before and after hurricane Katrina. *Health Aff* 2006;**25**(5):w393–406. https://doi.org/10.1377/hlthaff.25.w393.
38. Shaw R, Kim YK, Hua J. Governance, technology and citizen behaviour in pandemic: lessons from COVID-19 in East Asia. *Progr Dis Sci* 2020;**6**. https://doi.org/10.1016/j.pdisas.2020.100090, 100090.
39. Hollingsworth J. *How does India, a country of 1.3 billion people, have around 1,000 coronavirus deaths?* CNN; 2020. https://edition.cnn.com/. [Accessed 10 July 2021].
40. UNDRR. *Leave no one behind in COVID-19 prevention, response and recovery. United Nations Ofce for Disaster Risk Reduction*; 2020 https://www.undrr.org/. [Accessed 10 July 2021].
41. UN-Habitat. *UN-Habitat COVID-19: Key messages*. United Nations; 2020. https://unhabitat.org/. [Accessed 10 July 2021].
42. Acharya M. Ebola virus disease outbreak—2014: implications and pitfalls. *Front Public Health* 2014;**2**:263. https://doi.org/10.3389/fpubh.2014.00263.
43. Marmot M, Friel S, Bell R, Houweling TA, Taylor S. Commission on social determinants of health. Closing the gap in a generation: health equity through action on the social determinants of health. *Lancet* 2008;**372**(9650):1661–9. https://doi.org/10.1016/S0140-6736(08)61690-6.
44. Kruk ME, Myers M, Varpilah ST, Dahn BT. What is a resilient health system? Lessons from Ebola. *Lancet* 2015;**385**(9980):1910–2. https://doi.org/10.1016/S0140-6736(15)60755-3.
45. Cancedda C, Davis SM, Dierberg KL, Lascher J, Kelly JD, Barrie MB, et al. Strengthening health systems while responding to a health crisis: lessons learned by a non-governmental organization during the Ebola virus disease epidemic in Sierra Leone. *J Infect Dis* 2016;**214**(Suppl 3):S153–63. https://doi.org/10.1093/infdis/jiw345.
46. Kieny MP, Evans DB, Schmets G, Kadandale S. Health-system resilience: reflections on the Ebola crisis in western Africa. *Bull World Health Organ* 2014;**92**(12):850. https://doi.org/10.2471/BLT.14.149278.
47. Kieny MP, Dovlo D. Beyond Ebola: a new agenda for resilient health systems. *Lancet* 2015;**385**(9963):91–2. https://doi.org/10.1016/S0140-6736(14)62479-X.
48. World Health Organization. Health worker Ebola infections in Guinea. In: *Liberia and Sierra Leone—a preliminary report*. 2015; 2015. Available from: http://apps.who.int/iris/bitstream/10665/171823/1/WHO_EVD_SDS_REPORT_2015.1_eng.pdf?ua=1&ua=1.
49. Dastidar MG, Roy S. Public health management during COVID-19 and applications of point-of-care based biomolecular detection approaches. In: Dehghani MH, Karri RR, Roy S, editors. *Environmental and health management of novel coronavirus disease (COVID-19)*. Academic Press; 2021. p. 345–78. https://doi.org/10.1016/B978-0-323-85780-2.00009-3.
50. Bolkan HA, Bash-Taqi DA, Samai M, Gerdin M, von Schreeb J. Ebola and indirect effects on health service function in Sierra Leone. *PLoS Curr* 2014;6. https://doi.org/10.1371/currents.outbreaks.0307d588df619f9c9447f8ead5b72b2d.
51. Brolin Ribacke KJ, Saulnier DD, Eriksson A, von Schreeb J. Effects of the West Africa Ebola virus disease on health-care utilization—a systematic review. *Front Public Health* 2016;**4**:222. https://doi.org/10.3389/fpubh.2016.00222.

52. Elston JW, Cartwright C, Ndumbi P, Wright J. The health impact of the 2014–15 Ebola outbreak. *Public Health* 2017;**143**:60–70. https://doi.org/10.1016/j. puhe.2016.10.020.
53. Green A. Yellow fever continues to spread in Angola. *Lancet* 2016;**387**(10037): 2493. https://doi.org/10.1016/S0140-6736(16)30835-2.
54. Jones A, Howard N, Legido-Quigley H. Feasibility of health systems strengthening in South Sudan: a qualitative study of international practitioner perspectives. *BMJ Open* 2015;**5**. https://doi.org/10.1136/bmjopen-2015-009296, e009296.
55. Nishino K, Yactayo S, Garcia E, Aramburu GJ, Manuel E, Costa A, et al. Yellow fever urban outbreak in Angola and the risk of extension. *Wkly Epidemiol Rec* 2016;**91**(14): 186–92.
56. Omole O, Welye H, Abimbola S. Boko Haram insurgency: implications for public health. *Lancet* 2015;**385**(9972):941. https://doi.org/10.1016/S0140-6736(15)60207-0.
57. United Nations Office for Coordination of Humanitarian Affairs (UNOCHA). *Central African Republic Crisis and Its Regional Humanitarian Impact*; 2014. Available from: https://www.humanitarianresponse.info/system/files/documents/files/Central%20African%20Republic%20Crisis%20and%20its%20Regional%20Humanitarian%20Impact%20June%202014.pdf.
58. Kusumasari B, Alam Q, Siddiqui K. Resource capability for local government in managing disasters. *Disaster Prev Manag* 2010;**19**(4):438–51. https://doi.org/10.1108/09653561011070367.
59. Cai Q, Okada A, Jeong BG, Kim SJ. Civil society responses to COVID-19 pandemic: a comprehensive study of China, Japan and South Korea. *China Rev* 2021;**21**(1):107–37.
60. Peduzzi P. The disaster risk, global change, and sustainability nexus. *Sustainability* 2019;**11**:957. https://doi.org/10.3390/su11040957.
61. World Health Assembly Resolution; 2011. Available from: http://apps.who.int/iris/handle/10665/3566.
62. Dar O, Buckley EJ, Rokadiya S, Huda Q, Abrahams J. Integrating health into disaster risk reduction strategies: key considerations for success. *Am J Public Health* 2014;**104**(10):1811–6. https://doi.org/10.2105/AJPH.2014.302134.
63. Lamptey BJ, Awojobi ON. The spread of the Ebola virus disease and its implications in the West African sub-region. *Int J Innov Sci Res* 2014;**11**(1):130–43.
64. Michailof S, Kostner M, Devictor X. Post-conflict recovery in Africa: an agenda for the African region. In: *Africa Region Working Paper Series No 30*, World Bank; 2002. Available from: http://www.sergemichailof.fr/wpcontent/uploads/2010/02/postconflictrecoveryinafrica2002.pdf.
65. Aitsi-Selmi A, Murray V. Protecting the health and well-being of populations from disasters: health and health care in the Sendai framework for disaster risk reduction 2015–2030. *Prehosp Disaster Med* 2016;**31**(1):74–8. https://doi.org/10.1017/S1049023X15005531.
66. Barry SP, Somanje H, Kirigia JM, Nyoni J, Bessaoud K, Trapsida JM, et al. The Ouagadougou declaration on primary health care and health systems in Africa: achieving better health for Africa in the new millennium. *Afr Health Monit* 2010;**12**. Available from: https://www.aho.afro.who.int/en/ahm/issue/12/reports/ouagadougou-declaration-primary-health-care-and-health-systemsafrica-achieving.
67. Bayntun C, Rockenschaub G, Murray V. Developing a health system approach to disaster management: a qualitative analysis of the core literatureto complement the WHO Toolkit for assessing health-system capacity for crisis management. *PLoS Curr* 2012;**4**. https://doi.org/10.1371/5028b6037259a, e5028b6037259a.
68. World Health Organization (WHO). *Disaster risk management: a strategy for the health sector in the African region. Report of the secretariat.* Luanda, Republic of Angola: World Health Organization, Regional Committee for Africa; 2012. Available from: http://apps.who.int/iris/bitstream/10665/80238/1/AFR-RC62-6-e.pdf.

69. Bloom DE, Canning D. Health as human capital and its impact on economic performance. *Geneva Papers Risk Insur* 2003;**28**:304–15. https://doi.org/10.1111/1468-0440.00225.
70. Bloom DE, Canning D, Sevilla J. The effect of health on economic growth: a production function approach. *World Dev* 2004;**32**:1–13. https://doi.org/10.1016/j.worlddev.2003.07.002.
71. Öztürk S, Topcu E. Health expenditure and economic growth: evidence from G8Countries. *Int J Econ Empir Res* 2014;**2**:256–61.
72. Kurt S. Government health expenditures and economic growth: a federal-run approach for the case of Turkey. *Int J Econ Financ Issues* 2015;**5**:441–7.
73. Piabuo SM, Tieguhong JC. Health expenditure and economic growth—a review of the literature and analysis between the economic community for central African States (CEMANC) and selected African countries. *Heal Econ Rev* 2017;**27**:1–13. https://doi.org/10.1186/s13561-017-0159-1.
74. Aboubacar B, Xu D. The impact of health expenditure on the economic growth in sub-Saharan Africa. *Econ Lett* 2017;**7**:615–22. https://doi.org/10.4236/tel.2017.73046.
75. Bleakley H. Health, human capital and development. *Animal Rev Econ* 2010;**2**:283–310. https://doi.org/10.1146/annurev.economics.102308.124436.
76. Churchill SA, Yew SL, Ugur M. *Effects of government education and health expenditures on economic growth: a meta-analysis*. Report G9ERC21, London: Greenwich Political Economy Research Center; 2015.
77. Oni LB. Analysis of the growth impact of health expenditure in Nigeria. *IOSR J Econ Financ* 2014;**3**:77–84. https://doi.org/10.9790/5933-031 17784.
78. Wahab AA, Kefeli Z. Project citing a long-term expenditure growth in healthcare service: a literature review. *Procedia Econ Fin* 2016;**37**:152–7. https://doi.org/10.1016/S2212-5671(16)30106-X.
79. Wang F. More health expenditure, better economic performance? Empirical evidence from OECD countries. *Inquiry* 2015;**52**:1–5. https://doi.org/10.1177/0046958015602666.
80. Agenor PR. Health and infrastructure in a model of endogenous growth. *J Macroecon* 2008;**30**:1407–22. https://doi.org/10.1016/j.jmacro.2008.04.003.
81. Boucekkine R, Diene B, Azomahou T. Growth economics of epidemics: a review of the theory. *Math Popul Stud* 2008;**15**:1–26. https://doi.org/10.1080/08898480701792410.
82. World Health Organization. *How much should countries spend on health?* Geneva: World Health Organization; 2003.
83. Andrade JAS, Duarte APS, Simoes MCN. Education and wealth: welfare state composition and growth across country groups. *East J Eur Stud* 2018;**9**:111–44.
84. Beckerman W. From economic ‘efficiency’ to economic welfare. In: *Economics as applied ethics*. Cham: Palgrave Macmillan; 2017. https://doi.org/10.1007/978-3-319-50319-6_7.
85. Ishiwatari M, Koike T, Hiroki K, Toda T, Katsube T. Managing disasters amid COVID-19 pandemic: approaches of response to food disasters. *Progr Dis Sci* 2020;**6**. https://doi.org/10.1016/j.pdisa s.2020.100096, 100096.
86. Simonovic SP, Kundzewicz ZW, Wright N. Floods and the COVID-19 pandemic—a new double hazard problem. *WIREs Water* 2021;**8**:1509. https://doi.org/10.1002/wat2.
87. Quigley MC, Attanayake J, King A, Prideaux F. A multi-hazards earth science perspective on the COVID-19 pandemic: the potential for concurrent and cascading crises. *Environ Syst Decis* 2019;**40**:199–215. https://doi.org/10.1007/s10669-020-09772-1.
88. Sampath Kumar NS, Chintagunta AD, Jeevan Kumar SP. Immunotherapeutics for Covid-19 and post vaccination surveillance. *Biotech* 2020;**10**(3):527. https://doi.org/10.1007/s13205-020-02522-9.

CHAPTER FIFTEEN

A step toward better sample management of COVID-19: On-spot detection by biometric technology and artificial intelligence

Vivek Sharma[a], Monalisha Ghosh Dastidar[b], Sarada Sutradhar[c], Veena Raj[d], Kithma De Silva[e], and Sharmili Roy[f]

[a]Department of Chemical Engineering, Indian Institute of Technology Bombay, Mumbai, Maharashtra, India
[b]Research School of Engineering, College of Engineering and Computer Science, Australian National University, Canberra, ACT, Australia
[c]School of Pharmaceutical and Population Health Informatics, Dehradun Institute of Technology, Dehradun, Uttarakhand, India
[d]Faculty of Integrated Technologies, Universiti Brunei Darussalam, Gadong, Brunei Darussalam
[e]Department of Food, Plant and Environmental Sciences, Faculty of Agricultural, Dalhousie University, Halifax, NS, Canada
[f]Division of Oncology, School of medicine, Stanford University, Palo Alto, CA, United States

1. Introduction of SARS-COV2

The Severe Acute Respiratory Syndrome (SARS) is a form of beta coronavirus that caused the first outbreak in 2002 in China. In 2012 another outbreak named the Middle East Respiratory syndrome virus (MERS) was reported in Saudi Arabia. Seven years later, toward the end of 2019, a new mutation in the same family of viruses resulted in SARS-CoV-2 which caused a pandemic with irreversible lung damage and pneumonia-like symptoms in human population.[1] Till date, this virus has caused the most disastrous global health calamity of the century. More than 195 million people are affected with above 4.2 million deaths worldwide (https://www.worldometers.info/coronavirus/?utm_campaign=homeAdUOA?Si visited at 08.03.2021). According to some initial research data, SARS-CoV-2 was first detected at a live sea food wet market in Wuhan in the Hubei province of China.[2] Soon after that, the number of positive and critical cases mounted noticeably in China and across the world. On 30th January 2020, the World Health Organization (WHO) announced coronavirus outbreak as a public health emergency of international concern followed by

COVID-19 and the Sustainable Development Goals
https://doi.org/10.1016/B978-0-323-91307-2.00017-1

Table 1 Data given as per WHO report as on 24th June 2021.

Name	Confirmed cases—cumulative total	Confirmed death—cumulative total
Global	**179,241,734**	**3,889,723**
America	71,232,746	1,873,241
Europe	55,535,235	1,177,734
South-East Asia	34,351,183	478,700
Eastern Mediterranean	10,793,326	213,897
Africa	3,880,790	93,100
Western Pacific	3,447,690	53,038

declaration of a pandemic on 11th March 2020.[3] As of 24th June 2021, globally 179,241,734 confirmed cases have been reported along with 3,889,723 deaths (WHO report attached as Table 1, as on 24th June 2021) (Table 1).[4] In the past week (14th–20th June 2021), the number of cases and deaths continued to decrease worldwide with more than 2.5 million new cases weekly (COVID-19 Weekly Epidemiological Update: Edition 45, published 22 June 2021). Researchers are continuously working on epidemiological stories of this virus along with unknown activity and the origin of SARS-CoV-2 in detail. In the later sections of this chapter, the epidemiological features and structure of SARS-CoV-2 was discussed.

1.1 Epidemiological characteristic of SARS-CoV-2

SARS-CoV-2 is a member of the *Coronaviridae* family and is a genuine human pathogen like that of the other corona viruses such as HCoV-229E, HCoV-HKU1, SARS-CoV, MERS-CoV, HCoV-NL63, and HCoV-OC43.[5] In general, viral RNA was isolated from bronchoalveolar lavage (BL) as a fluid sample from infected individuals with severe pneumonia symptoms followed by using metagenomic RNA sequencing. Thus Chinese scientists identified that the beta-coronavirus is the causative agent of the recent outbreak that was not discovered earlier.[6,7] The whole genome sequencing (WGS) of this viral strain was performed for the first time to determine the genomic information. On 12th January 2020, the sequences closer to the whole genome were confirmed by various research institutes and those data were submitted to the GenBank (accession no. MN908947.2).[8,9] From those studies, a detailed epidemiologic structure was disclosed, indicating that different animals like bats, pangolins, and snakes may promote SARS-CoV-2 as an intermediate host for the transmission of human beta-coronavirus to the human.[8] So far, no conclusion has been drawn on when and where the virus first entered the human body.[10,11] On 2nd January 2020, the first human-to-human transmission occurred, where one of the family members was exposed to a close contact transmission with this virus and then the infection spread rapidly within the hospital in China.[12] Researchers have calculated the basic reproduction number (R0) based on transmission dynamics of COVID-19. Initially, China recorded the R0 to be 2.24–3.58.[13] The incubation period of SARS-CoV-2 is around 14 days with moderate time of 4–5 days. Various reports indicated that the upper respiratory tract has the highest viral shedding within the first three days of symptoms.[14] According to the researchers, SARS-CoV-2 is transmitted via aerosols in an enclosed space and urine, in addition to short distance and contact transmission. Recent investigations also indicated the transmission of this virus from a mother to her child.[15–17]

1.2 Structure of SARS-CoV-2

Researchers have studied the structure of SARS-CoV-2 via electron microscopy and found that this virus is made up of an icosahedral viral head with spherical structure. The diameter of the spherical head ranges from 100 to 200 nm containing a dense vitro-plasm and bounded by a lipid bilayer.[18] Further, studies mentioned that the virus is enveloped with four structural proteins such as the spike protein (S), the transmembrane glycoproteins (M and E), and the nucleocapsid protein (N). Each of them has a crucial function within the structure of the virus particle and also participate in the alternative aspects of the replication cycle[19] (Fig. 1B). The details of genomic organization of SARS-CoV-2 are stated as follows (Fig. 1A):

- The coronaviruses have a large envelope which carries a positive-sense single-stranded RNA (+ssRNA) sized around 30 kb which encodes 9860 amino acids as their genome. The content of G + C is 38%. It compromises 14 open reading frames (ORFs) with 9 subgenomic mRNAs units, which influence and conserve the spreadhead sequence, 9 transcription regulatory sequences, and 2 terminal untranslated regions.
- The 16 nonstructural proteins contain viral cysteine proteases such as NSP3 (papain-like protease) and NSP5 (main protease), NSP12 (RNA-dependent RNA polymerase, NSP13 (helicase), and other NSPs. These proteins help in transcription and replication of the virus.[20]
- Mutations have been detected in NSP2, NSP3, and the spike protein which show important role in SARS-CoV-2 infectivity.[21]

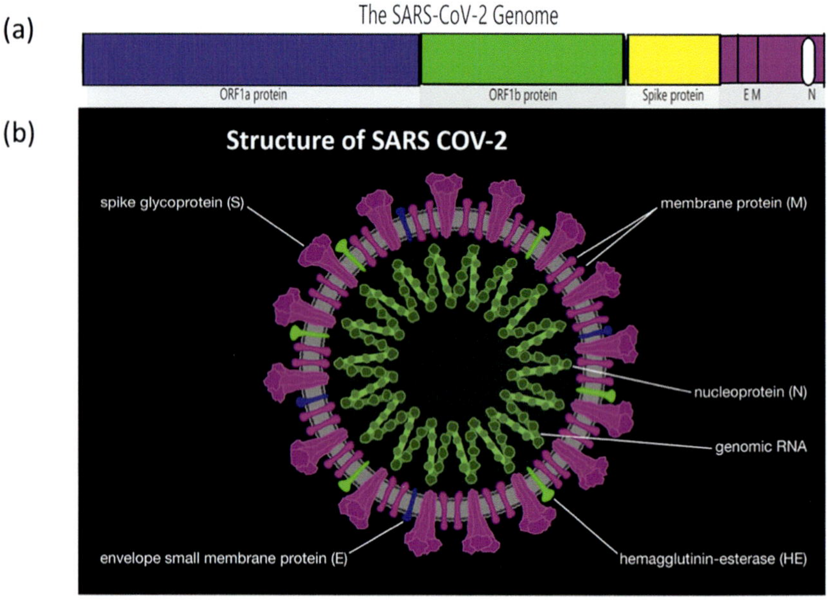

Fig. 1 Structural details of SARS-CoV-2. (A). Schematic illustration of SARS-CoV-2 genome. (B) The typical viral structure of SARS-CoV-2 with four kinds of protein component.

Molecular weight of the spike or S glycoprotein is around 150 kDa.[22] S glycoproteins create homotrimers on the viral surface and promotes the binding of enveloped virus onto the host cells through the angiotensin-converting enzyme 2 (ACE2).[23,24] In addition, S glycoprotein is cleaved by protease, which is a type of cell fusion into two subunits such as S1 and S2. S1 determines the host-virus range and cellular tropism with the receptor-binding domain. Almost 70% of coronavirus is shared by S1 subunit which contains a signal peptide, followed by an N-terminal domain and receptor-binding domain. On the other hand, the function of S2 is intermediate virus fusion into transmitting host cells and it shares 99% match with other coronaviruses like bats SARS-like CoVs and human SARS-CoV.[25] Besides, the nucleocapsid protein N is the structural component of CoV which influence this N protein to attach with nucleic acid, especially with RNA of the virus.[26,27] M protein is also a structural protein, and it is one of the key fragments of this virus that defines the envelope's structure.[28] The E protein is the smallest protein in the SARS-CoV-2 and it helps in the assembly and evolution of this virus.[29]

Further, the coronaviruses are classified under the subfamily of *Ortho-Coronaviridae*. Based on the genetic and antigenic principles, coronaviruses have been organized into 4 groups: alpha-coronavirus (α-CoV), beta-coronavirus (β-CoV), gamma-coronavirus (γ-CoV), and delta-coronavirus (γ-CoV).[30,31] There are 6 CoVs have been known as human-susceptible virus such as α-CoVs HCoV-229E, HCoV-NL63, β-CoVs HCoV-HKU1 and HCoV-OC43 with low pathogenicity, since it caused mild respiratory symptoms like a common cold. The other coronaviruses like β-CoVs, SARS-CoV, and MERS-CoV showed severe and potentially fatal respiratory tract infections in human beings.[32] About 79.5% of the SARS-CoV-2 genome sequence is identical with the other coronaviruses such as β-coronavirus, thus infecting human beings.

1.3 Current detection kits and technologies

Diagnosis plays an important role in a disease which outbreaks from any novel pathogen for which the population is not preimmunized. COVID-19 is among such infectious disease, which is highly contagious and lethal.[11,33,142] Later on, when the asymptomatic carriers of COVID-19 were reported, the scenario of symptom-based diagnosis changed. This eventually intensified the necessity for adequate diagnosis of majority of the population to combat the rapid transmission of the virus.[143] Collecting samples on proper time and accurate anatomical location is essential to determine the correct molecular diagnosis.[34–37] Prompt diagnosis and on-spot detection is of primary importance to combat the disease and reduce the transmission by quickly isolating the critical patients in intensive care.[38] Several detection methods (listed in Table 2) and kits (listed in Table 3) for SARS-CoV-2 are being used worldwide. These commercial kits received approval of an Emergency Use Authorization (EUA) from FDA. Thus these established processes can spot (i) specific viral gene regions by nucleic acid amplification techniques such as Real-Time Reverse Transcription Polymerase Chain Reaction [RT-PCR] and isothermal nucleic acid amplification mainly by loop-mediated isothermal amplification (LAMP)[39–43] along with other molecular diagnosis system, (ii) the antibodies produced by the immune system in response to the viral infection (serology/Immunoglobulin M (IgM)/Immunoglobulin G (IgG) tests), and (iii) the antigen testing by lateral flow assays.[44,45] Most of the COVID-19 diagnostic kits are based on genomic analysis, using RT-PCR assays, which is the usual gold standard for virus detection.[46] Nowadays on-spot detection techniques have become much easier and cost effective by using sensor-based diagnostic approaches. There are few readily available materials which made detection process much simpler than

Table 2 Detection methods of SARS-CoV-2.

Mode of detection	Detection methods
Radiology-based technology	• X-ray • Chest computed tomography
Culture-based detection	• Virus propagation in cell line
Molecular technology	• Real Time-RT PCR • Isothermal amplifications • CRISPR-Cas technology • Lab-on-chip
Immunoassay technology	• ELISA • Neutralization assay • Chemiluminescent assay • Lateral flow assay • Dip-stick
Alternative developing methods	• Aptameter • Molecular imprinting technology (MIT) • Microarray • Biosensor MALDI-TOP profiling
Sequencing technologies	• Sanger sequencing • Next generation sequencing • Nanopore sequencing

conventional methods, such as sensor chips and paper-based identification.[47–50] The antigen detection test is primarily based on the spotting of viral antigens by using specific antibodies. It is rapid, cost effective, usable at the POC and, therefore, is ideal for large-scale COVID-19 detection.[51,52] At-home COVID-19 detection kit such as RT-PCR Test-Home Collection Kit, developed by LabCorp, is used by the public to self-collect nasal samples at home.[53] The current market price of the collection kit is 119$ (USD). Hence, these kits are used for sample collection from infected individuals and sent back to diagnosis center and nearby hospitals for further analysis.[54]

Despite the challenges related to the cost and time, molecular test remains the most reliable technique due to its ability to find proper specificity and high sensitivity. Besides, the recent revolution in nanotechnology is also helping to reduce the cost and making the detection much simpler.[55–57] However, fast, portable, and accurate diagnostic tests are still vital and necessary because millions of people still need to be diagnosed. Therefore a cheap, reliable, and rapid test is needed. The recent revolution in nanoparticle-based

Table 3 Summarized list of commercially available SARS-CoV-2 detection kits approved by FDA and EUA for COVID-19 diagnosis.

Source of manufacturer/company	Name of diagnostic kits	Technology/platform	Regulation/validation	Collection process
Rutgers Clinical Genomics laboratory at RUCDR Infinite biologics—Rutgers University	Rutgers Clinical Genomics laboratory Taq Path SARS-CoV-2-Assay	rRT-PCR	EUA	Oropharyngeal (throat) swab, nasopharyngeal swab, anterior nasal swab, mid-turbinate nasal swab, and saliva specimens
Zymo Research Corporation	Quick SARS-CoV-2 rRT-PCR kit	rRT-PCR	EUA	Upper respiratory and lower respiratory systems
1 drop (Republic of Korea)	1 copy COVID-19 MDx Kit	rRT-PCR	CE Mark	Pharyngeal swab
Sherlock BioSciences, Inc.	Sherlock CRISPR SARS-CoV-2 Kit	CRISPR	FDA	Nasal swab, nasopharyngeal swab, oropharyngeal swab, or bronchoalveolar lavage (BAL) specimen
BioMerieux SA	SARS-CoV-2 RESPI-R-gene	rRT-PCR	EUA	Nasopharyngeal swab
Fast Track Diagnostics Luxembourg Sarl (A Siemens Healthineers Company)	FTD SARS-CoV-2	rRT-PCR	FDA and EUA	Nasopharyngeal swab and oropharyngeal swabs
Sansure BioTech Inc.	Novel Coronavirus (2019-nCoV)-Nucleic acid diagnostic kit (PCR-fluorescence probing)	rRT-PCR	FDA	Nasopharyngeal swabs, oropharyngeal (throat) swabs, anterior nasal swabs, mid-turbinate swabs, nasal washes, and nasal aspirates

Continued

Table 3 Summarized list of commercially available SARS-CoV-2 detection kits approved by FDA and EUA for COVID-19 diagnosis—cont'd

Source of manufacturer/company	Name of diagnostic kits	Technology/platform	Regulation/validation	Collection process
Bio-Rad Laboratories, Inc.	Bio-Rad SARS-CoV-2 ddPCR Test	Digital Droplet rRT-PCR	EUA and FDA	Nasopharyngeal swab and oropharyngeal swabs
Bio Fire diagnostics, LLC	Bio FireRespiratory Panel 2.1 (RP2.1)	rRT-PCR	FDA	Nasopharyngeal swab in transport media
Lab Genomics Co. Ltd.	Lab Gun COVID-19 RT-PCR kit	rRT-PCR	FDA	Nasopharyngeal swab and mid-turbinate swabs
Rheonix, Inc.	Rheonix COVID-19 MDx Assay	rRT-PCR	FDA	Nasopharyngeal swabs, oropharyngeal swabs, anterior nasal swabs, mid-turbinate nasal swabs, nasal washes, nasal aspirates, and bronchoalveolar lavage (BAL) fluid
Seasun Biomaterials	U-Top COVID-19 detection kit	rRT-PCR	FDA	Nasopharyngeal swabs, oropharyngeal swabs, anterior nasal swabs, mid-turbinate nasal swabs, nasal washes, nasal aspirates, as well as bronchoalveolar lavage (BAL) fluid and sputum specimen
Geno-Sensor LLC	GS COVID-19 RT PCR kit	rRT-PCR	FDA	Nasopharyngeal swabs, oropharyngeal swabs, anterior nasal swabs, mid-turbinate nasal swabs
Atila BioSystems Inc.	iAMP COVID-19 detection kit	Isothermal amplification (OMEGA), patented	FDA	Nasopharyngeal swab and oropharyngeal swabs

Becton, Dickinson and Company	BD SARS-CoV-2Reagents for BD MAX system	Antigen (chromatographic digital immunoassay)	FDA	Nasopharyngeal swab and oropharyngeal swabs
PerkinElmer. Inc.	PerkinElmer: New Coronavirus-nucleic acid detection kit	rRT-PCR	FDA	Nasopharyngeal swabs, oropharyngeal swabs, anterior nasal swabs
Mesa Biotech Inc.	Accula SARS-CoV-2 Test	PCR and lateral flow	FDA	Nasal swab
Thermo Fisher Scientific. Inc.	Taq Path COVID-19 combo kit	rRT-PCR	FDA	Nasopharyngeal swab, nasopharyngeal aspirates, and bronchoalveolar lavage
Centers for Disease Control and Prevention (CDC)	CDC-2019-nCoV-Real-Time RT-PCR diagnostic panel (CDC)	RT-PCR	FDA	Nasopharyngeal/Oropharyngeal swabs, lower respiratory tract aspirates, nasopharyngeal wash/aspirates or nasal aspirates, sputum, and bronchoalveolar lavage
Lucira Health, Inc. (Emeryville, CA, USA)	Lucira COVID-19—All in one single test kit	RT-LAMP	FDA	Self-collected nasal swab specimen
Detectachem Inc. (Sugar Land, TX, USA)	Mobile-Detect Bio BCC19 (MD-Bio BCC19) test kit	RT-LAMP	FDA	Nasopharyngeal swabs, oropharyngeal swabs, anterior nasal swabs, mid-turbinate nasal swabs
Seasun Biomaterials Inc. (Seoul, Korea)	AQ-TOP COVID-19 Rapid detection kit Plus	RT-LAMP	FDA	Oropharyngeal (throat) swab, nasopharyngeal swab, anterior nasal swab, mid-turbinate nasal, nasopharyngeal aspirate specimens, bronchoalveolar lavage, and sputum

Continued

Table 3 Summarized list of commercially available SARS-CoV-2 detection kits approved by FDA and EUA for COVID-19 diagnosis—cont'd

Source of manufacturer/ company	Name of diagnostic kits	Technology/platform	Regulation/ validation	Collection process
Abbott Diagnostics Scarborough, Inc. (Scarborough, ME, USA)	ID NOW-COVID-19	RT-LAMP	FDA	Nasal, nasopharyngeal, or throat swabs
Color Genomics, Inc. (Burlingame, CA	Color SARS CoV-2 diagnostic assay	RT-LAMP	FDA	Oropharyngeal (throat) swab, nasopharyngeal swab, anterior nasal swab, mid-turbinate nasal, nasopharyngeal aspirate specimens, bronchoalveolar lavage, and sputum
Euroimmun US Inc.	Anti-SARS-CoV-2 ELISA (IgG)	Serology (IgG)	FDA	Euroimmun US Inc.
Roche Diagnostics	Elecsys anti-SARS-CoV	Serology Antibody	EUA	Roche Diagnostics
Wadsworth Centre, New York State Department of Health	New York SARS-CoV Microsphere Immunoassay for Antibody detection	Serology Total antibody	FDA	Wadsworth Centre, New York State Department of Health
Wondfo (China)	Wondfo SARS-CoV-2 Antibody Test	Serology (IgG, IgM)	CFDA	Wondfo (China)
Rapid Test methods (Ireland)	COVID-19—IgG/IgM Lateral flow kit	Serology (IgG, IgM)	FDA	Rapid Test methods (Ireland)
CTK Biotech (USA)	On site COVID-19 IgG/ IgM rapid test	Serology (IgG, IgM)	FDA	CTK Biotech (USA)

Edinburg Genetics (UK)	COVID-19 colloidal Gold Immunoassay Testing kit	Serology (IgG, IgM)	FDA and EUA	Edinburg Genetics (UK)
Everest Links Pte (Singapore)	VivaDiag COVID-19 IgG/IgM rapid test	Everest Links Pte (Singapore)	FDA	Everest Links Pte (Singapore)
SD Biosensor (Korea)	Standard Q COVID-19 IgG/IgM duo	Serology (IgG, IgM)	FDA and EUA	Serum and plasma

EUA, FDA: U.S. Food and Drug Administration.

technologies is also very useful for any disease diagnosis as quickly as possible than any conventional process.[58–60] As this is a global challenge, science and research must pay close and continuous attention to the development and improvement of infectious disease detection at the POC.[46]

2. Biometric systems for COVID-19 management

In modern smartphones, we commonly see the authentication features like face detection and fingerprint sensors. These sensors are typically designed to detect certain features unique to a person and create a unique identity associated with the person. The authentication methods used by these systems are called biometric authentication. We can define biometric techniques as automated systems to verify and identify a living person using the person's physiological or behavioral features.[61,62] Biometric systems must not be confused with forensic methods which are also employed to detect a human or any other living organism. The key aspect which defines this field is the automated detection of only living humans.

Although these techniques essentially help in identifying people, they extensively help in other important aspects, viz. differentiating between a set of people, determining probabilistic similarity for a defined set of people.[63] The segregation of population can be done on the basis of any parameters, viz. gender, age, and nationality, and is done by externally making an entry for the biometric information. Due to this advantage, systems are often used by many states to control or monitor the spread of a disease. Especially during the current COVID-19 pandemic, these technologies have been extensively used in contact tracing, thereby helping in curbing the spread of the virus.[141] Essentially biometric data of citizens have been ethically linked with their geolocation to monitor whether they have been in contact with any potential COVID-19-infected person.[64–66] In this section we will specifically investigate the areas where biometric systems have been helpful in tackling the spread of the current pandemic. We describe their operation and discuss the concerns associated with data privacy.

2.1 Working mechanism of biometric devices

A biometric device can recognize either behavioral or physiological characteristics via handwriting, keystroke, retina, fingerprint, voice, face, etc.[67] Selection of a human characteristic from the above-mentioned list depends on the requirement and applications in places. However, few qualities such as robustness, accessibility, specificity, and availability must be considered before making a choice of the biometric system.[68] Robustness is measured by the number of times that matches a submitted input to a wrong identity. Accessibility can be attributed to the number of entries the device can process in a given amount of time. Even after identifying and quantifying the desired qualities, there still remains a void for the selection of best biometric system because all the biometric characteristics are explicitly dependent on the details of the purpose for which it is to be used.[69] Therefore it is very important to discuss the subsystems which fulfill the entire system. To build a biometric system for home security, designing the framework for contextual attributes is important to enhance the determination of a legitimate user. For that, servers need to be created separately with secure networking system and an end user smartphone, laptop, or any other electronic items need to be connected for continuous monitoring. For both the cases, backup storage is required to store daily incidents (Fig. 2).[70]

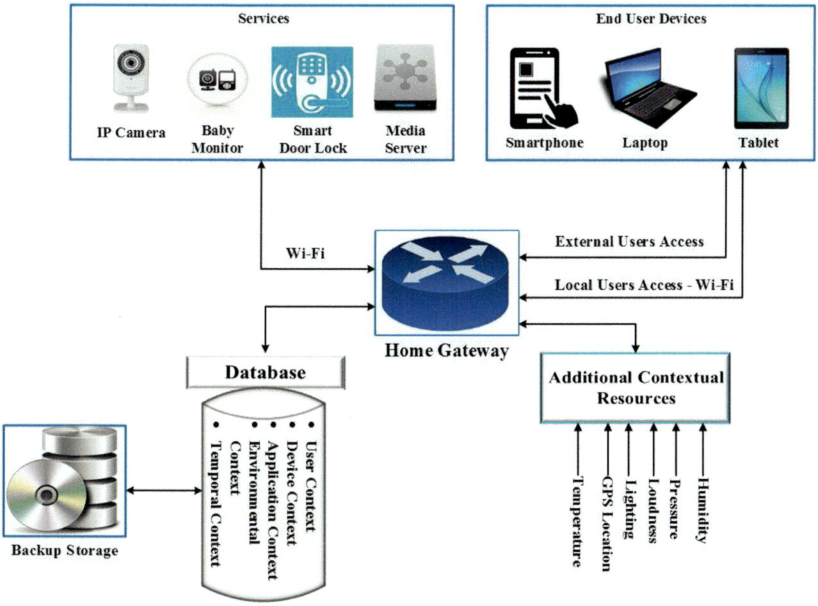

Fig. 2 A high level of proposed framework, where biometric devices show about the place of data collection, different circumstances, and potential determination to accomplish some information using biometric devices. *(This figure is adopted from Ashibani Y, Kauling D, Mahmoud QH. Design and implementation of a contextual-based continuous authentication framework for smart homes.* Appl Syst Innov *2019;***2** *(1) with permission.)*

Based on this concept, a biometric system can be divided into four components: data collection unit, signal processing, decision, and data processing. The data collection unit takes the defined user characteristic as an input which depends on factors like measurement, technical characteristic of the sensor, and the method for the measurement. Depending on the application of the system the data collected can be either kept enclosed or it might have to be first standardized (in case of open system where data collected from multiple systems must be matched) before sending it to signal processing unit. Optionally, a transmission system is often used post data collection to transmit the data to a centralized data processing unit. The user data tagged with the biometric characteristic received from the data collection unit is first segmented into different data sets based on the requirement. After segregation, the data is used in the pattern matching algorithms to distinctly distinguish individuals without error. Once data processing is done, the refined data is now stored into databases which can be localized or central[71,72] and is further used as a tool by the decision-making system. This system uses the fed data and matches it with the incoming user input to generate matched or no matched signal. Having discussed the basics of the structure and mechanism of a generic biometric system, it is important to discuss how it has been used in recent times to counter the spread of COVID-19.[73,74]

2.2 Application of biometric systems against COVID-19 vaccines

The most important implementation was to geo-tag a citizen to monitor whether they have come in close proximity of an infected individual or not. Meanwhile these apps are linked with an identity number of a citizen, when geotagged these applications can now spot a COVID-19 patient in proximity. Based on the range of proximity, viz. 500 m and 1 km., the citizen can now be classified under different threat levels.[75,76] Therefore if a person tests positive, all the citizens he/she might have come in contact with can be alerted. This directly impacts in reducing a further transmission of the virus, otherwise which could have been at an astronomical scale. Similarly, when the same user data is linked with the vaccination status, it gets much easier to track a vaccinated person.

2.3 Issues related to data privacy

Biometric systems have helped significantly in contact tracing and therefore, helping in curbing the spread of the virus. They have also helped in tracking a citizen's vaccination status which helps a lot in tracking the vaccination status of a country. However, with such huge pool of data generated from a country's citizens, some important concerns in the population are inevitable. For instance, to what extent states are using the user data, is the collected user data safe against cyberattacks, is it used for unethical surveillance on the citizen, etc.[77,78] Many countries that have deployed such systems during the current pandemic ensured that they are not collecting any personally identifiable information and only collecting geographical locations.[79,80]

3. Artificial intelligence and its applications for COVID-19 management

Adding to the earlier discussion on biometric systems, another great technological addition that can enhance the detection of viral transmission, identify the high-risk individuals, and assist with the real-time infection control is artificial intelligence (AI). AI is a technology that utilizes computer software to simulate human intelligence. It can correctly estimate the mortality risk based on historical data. AI is a proof-oriented clinical method which will help in the battle against SARS-CoV-2 by providing public monitoring, hospital care, notifications, and preventative guidance.[81–83] The common practice of AI and non-AI-related apps that aid general doctors in executing activities is depicted in Fig. 3.[84] Briefly, it depicts the flow of minimum non-AI therapies versus AI-based treatments. The flowchart also shows how AI is utilized in crucial stages of high-accuracy care, decreasing the complexity, and time it takes. Physicians may use AI technology not only to focus on the patient's treatment but also to improve illness prevention.

3.1 AI for early detection and diagnosis of COVID-19

AI can identify the usual and unusual symptoms of COVID-19, thereby alerting the patients and healthcare providers.[85,86] It supports a more cost-effective and quicker decision-making process. It aids in the identification and management of novel COVID-19 through the application of helpful algorithms. It can also aid in diagnosing infected persons using medical imaging technologies such as computed tomography (CT) and magnetic resonance imaging (MRI) scans of human body parts.

A false-negative result might prolong the diagnosis and treatment procedure, as well as raise the danger of viral transmission, therefore making early detection of COVID-19 patients very critical. Furthermore, not all hospitals

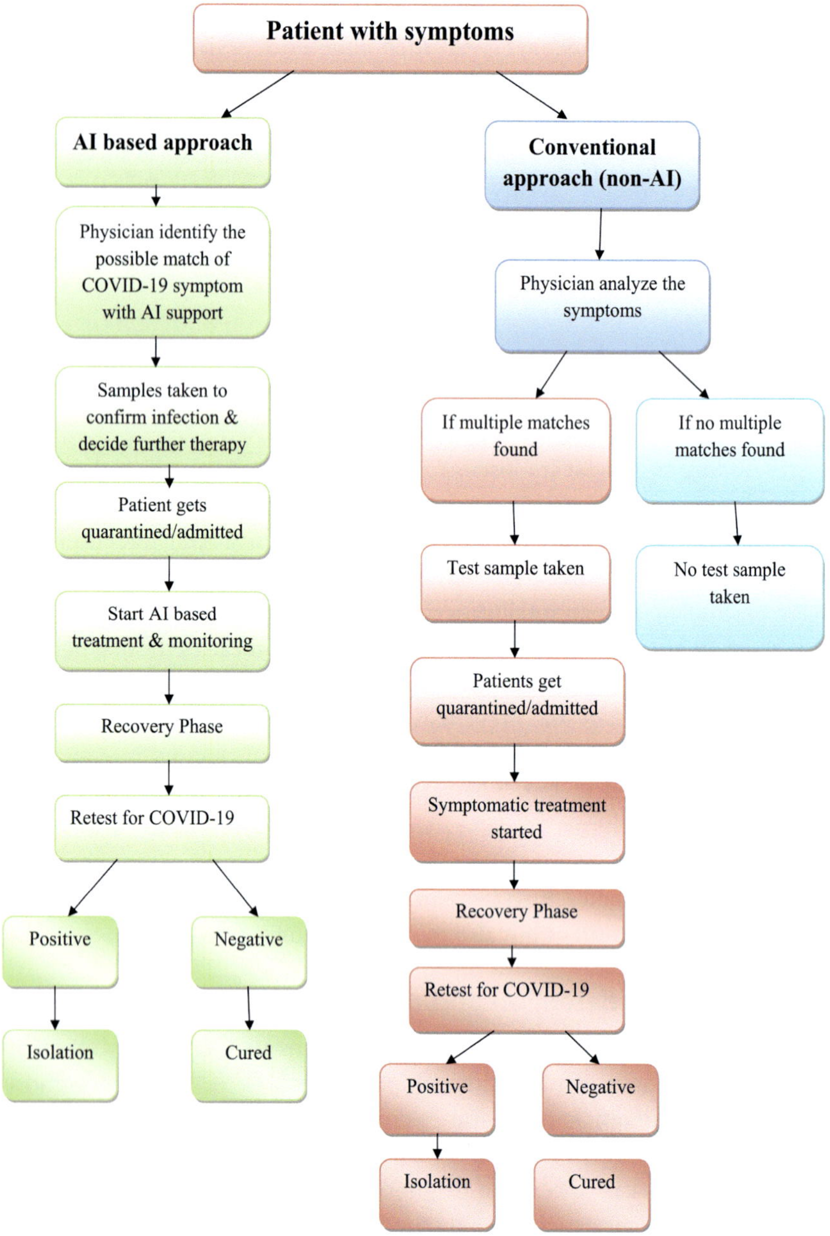

Fig. 3 AI- and non-AI-based applications that assist general practitioners in identifying COVID-19 symptoms. *(This figure is adopted with the permission from Vaishya R, et al. Artificial intelligence (AI) applications for COVID-19 pandemic. Diabet Metab Syndr Clin Res Rev 2020;**14**(4):337–9.)*

have radiologists with chest imaging competence, necessitating AI-assisted diagnosis.[86] This highlights the possible importance of a highly accurate AI system in quickly detecting patients. The suggested AI method by Mei et al.[87] includes CT imaging and medical information which has the same precision as a senior chest radiologist.

In the proposed technique, a deep convolutional neural network (CNN) was first designed to understand the radiological characteristics of patients with COVID-19 on the first CT scan.[87] They employed support vector machine (SVM), random forest, and multilayer perceptron (MLP) classifiers to categorize COVID-19 patients based on clinical data. MLP has the best tuning range performance. Therefore only MLP's output was recorded. Finally, utilizing radiological and medical records, they created a neural network[87] models to predict COVID-19 status. Three AI models are used to determine the likelihood of a patient having COVID-19: the first one is based on a chest CT scan, the next on clinical evidence, and the final is based on a combination of the chest CT scan. Moreover, the chance of possessing a parenchymal abnormality, as predicted by the CNN model (slice collection CNN), a comprehensive pulmonary tuberculosis (PTB) model that has a 99.4% accuracy in recognizing irregular lung slices from chest CT images. The 10 leading irregular CT images per patient were put into the next CNN (diagnosis CNN) to assess the chance of COVID-19 positive (P1). Demographic and medical data (the patient's age and sex, exposure history, symptoms, and laboratory tests) were input into a machine-learning model to differentiate COVID-19 positive cases (P2). To produce the joint model's final performance, an MLP network integrated the features provided by the diagnostic CNN model with the nonimaging clinical knowledge machine-learning model (P3). In a study, 279 patients achieved a zone under the 0.92 curve and had the good sensitivity as a senior thoracic radiologist in the thoracic system by AI models. The AI approach has improved the RT-PCR diagnosis of COVID-19 patients with routine CT scans by 68%.

3.2 AI for monitoring the treatment of COVID-19

AI can create an intelligent platform that can automatically track and forecast the progress of a virus. The visual characteristics of this condition can also be established by using a neural network which will help in tracking and managing the infected individuals.[88–90] It is capable of providing patients with regular reminders and remedies for the COVID-19 pandemic.

Current trends in machine learning (ML) and deep learning (DL) have increased the effect of imaging tools and are now being utilized for a variety of remote tasks that needs the presence of medical professionals. Rohmetra et al.[91] investigated the research possibilities for tracking COVID-19 contamination and quarantined individuals using DL and image/signal processing techniques. Most of these techniques could be implemented on a mobile device or a personal computer using simple cameras and sensors. Remote control on vital signs of health may be very useful for controlling the pandemic scenario. The vital signs of the patient can be routinely checked by physicians and taken care of when required. Their research shows how remote monitoring based on ML and imaging may be utilized to predict crucial indicators for early detection and to track remote patients on a regular basis.[91] In hospitals, contact-based monitoring equipment are utilized, although it is challenging to use them for active monitoring. Other challenges of AI technologies are for a specific domain in drug discovery and drug repurposing. With the implementation of this concept, the therapeutic processes will be robust, rapid, and cost effective. Combination of AI algorithms and network medicine for drug repurposing is a good prospect during the pandemic to combat SARC-CoV-2 (Fig. 4).[92]

The Massachusetts Institute of Technology's (MIT) Computer Science and AI Laboratory (CSAIL) has developed a system that can remotely follow individuals with the extremely infectious COVID-19 illness and thereby prevent the virus from spreading to healthcare workers.[93] The Emerald[94] is a new system that can not only measure critical patient parameters like breathing, but also monitor sleep patterns and send the information to the healthcare professionals through wireless signals. The Emerald was produced by a group headed by MIT scientist Dina Katabi.[95] It includes a WiFi-like box that detects wireless signals and tests them using AI. Emerald can reduce interaction and infection risk while simultaneously increasing healthcare capacity by allowing several patients to be watched at once.[96] This would also allow healthcare providers to evaluate and track fewer severe patients at home, instead of overburdening hospitals and health systems which could have been used exclusively for the most critical cases.[97] As a result, contact tracing by AI is a critical public health technique for controlling infectious disease. AI can aid in determining the depth of the virus's infection, finding clusters and "hot spots".[98–100] According to these studies, more than 36 countries (like Spain, Norway, Italy, Germany, Singapore, South Korea, and Israel) have successfully implemented automated contact tracing using centralized, decentralized, or a combination of both strategies to reduce effort and improve the efficacy of conventional healthcare diagnostic processes.

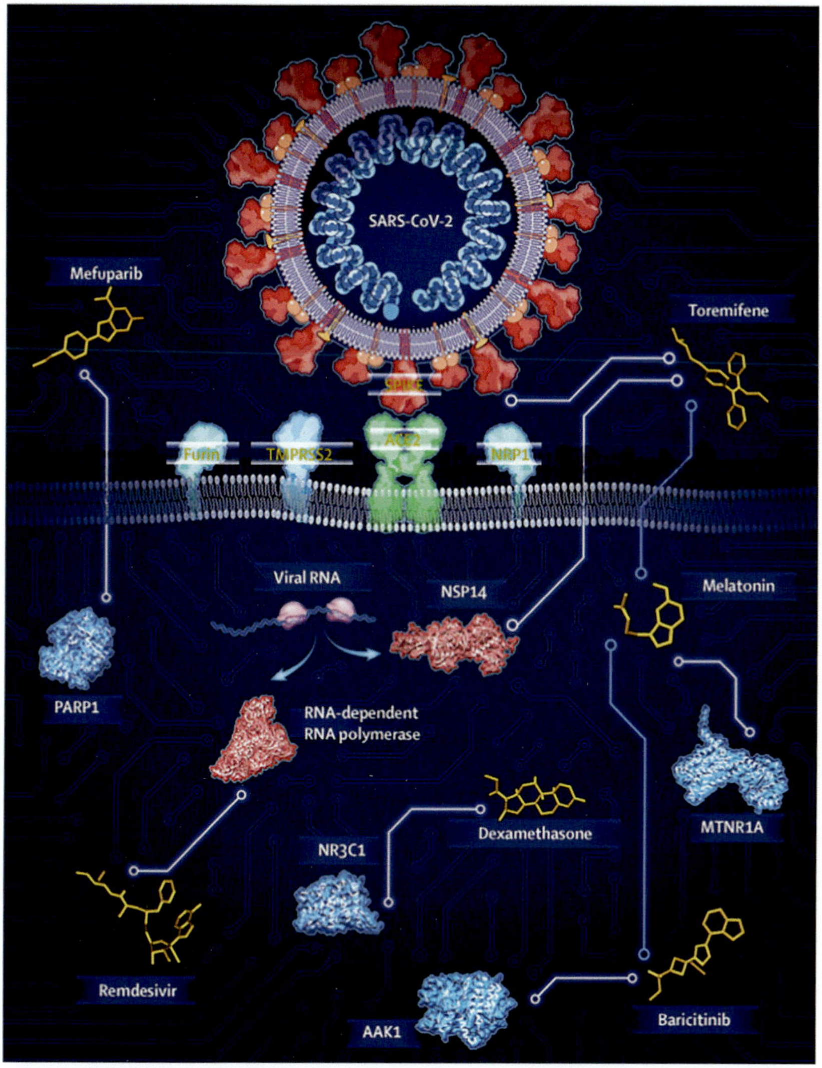

Fig. 4 An algorithm overview of AI-based concept that can be utilized for drug repurposing for COVID-19 that can make rapid and cost-effective way to invent the new therapy and many several options. *(This figure is adopted from Zhou Y, et al. Artificial intelligence in COVID-19 drug repurposing.* Lancet Digital Health *2020;***2***(12):e667–76 with permission.)*

3.3 AI for projecting the outbreak and mortality

Currently, only a few treatments are available for COVID-19. Ko et al.[101] have created a new model called EDRnet (ensemble learning model based on deep neural network and random forest models) to forecast in-hospital death using a regular blood test as an initial assessment in order to solve this problem. They chose 28 blood biomarkers and used patient's information such as age and gender as model inputs. They used an ensemble approach that combined both the models to enhance mortality prediction. EDRnet offered high sensitivity (100%), specificity (91%), and consistency in the testing data sets (92%). To enhance the amount of data points collected from patients, they created a web application (BeatCOVID19) that allows everyone to access the mortality prediction model and register their own blood laboratory results. This system could anticipate the presence of the virus, as well as the risk of disease transmission using accessible data, social networks, and news outlets. This system helps to identify the most susceptible areas, communities, and nations so that necessary measures can be implemented to prevent the spread.

3.4 AI for the development of drugs and vaccines

Scientists and medical practitioners have been asking for a feasible alternative to address the creation of a medicine and vaccine for the SARS-CoV-2. AI is used for drug research based on existing information on COVID-19. It may be used to create medication guidance systems and design them. AI-based technology helps to accelerate real-time drug testing in situations when traditional testing takes a lengthy period.[8,9] It could assist in the innovation of proper medicines for COVID-19 patients. Hence, it became an important method for producing screening tests and vaccinations.[102,103]

In biochemistry, AI aids scientists in better understanding the protein implicated in SARS-CoV-2 and identifying prospective threats.[104] ML leads to quick analysis of the complete viral proteins, enabling for more efficient and perhaps low-cost scientific investigation than prior vaccine development procedures.[104–106] Covax-19TM is a COVID-19 vaccine developed in Australia and developed using AI-based technology.[107,108] Vaxign-ML is a supervised ML algorithm that predicts the protegenicity score (the protegenicity score is the percentile rank score from the Vaxign-ML classification model) of all SARS-CoV-2 proteins.[109,110] Taiwanese scientists are doing research on a novel model on Deep Neural Network (DNN) to help in the development of COVID-19 medication such as homoharringtonine, salinomycin, boceprevir, tilorone, and chloroquine. Which were also shown to be effective on COVID-19 patients.[111]

Researchers from the United States and Korea proposed a novel molecular transformer-drug target interaction model[112] to address the need for an antiviral medication that could really treat COVID-19. The study compares AutoDock Vina, an open-source virtual screening and molecular docking tool, to a model based on a DL algorithm that uses COVID-19's 3C-like proteinase and FDA-approved 3410 existing medicines. Atazanavir (Kd of 94.94 nM), a common antiretroviral medicine used to treat HIV, was shown to be the best medicine for COVID-19 treatment, followed by Remdesivir (Kd of 113.13 nM). Moreover, after discovering a decade of medication research based on ML and AI technology, a merging of computational screening technique with docking application and machine learning for picking alternative medicine to research on SARS-CoV-2 was proposed.[113] Researchers point to the successful identification of Ebola[114] and the Zika virus[115] to conclude that the same technique might be used to identify drugs for COVID-19 and future viral pandemics.

4. Benefits and pitfalls of AI-based technologies

The COVID-19 pandemic has advanced the age of digital transformation. To combat the pandemic, AI and, in particular, ML and DL are being used in numerous fronts. However, in order to effectively manage the worldwide pandemic, several physicians and medical specialists have embraced the usage of AI. Following that, six areas have been identified where AI might help with successful pandemic management: early warnings and timely notifications, forecasting and monitoring illness prevalence, data dashboards, diagnosis and prognosis, treatment and cure, and social control. However, plenty of barriers stand in the way of widespread use of these cutting-edge technologies in larger scale clinical settings.

4.1 AI toward decreasing healthcare professionals' workload

Due to an unexpected and huge rise in the number of patients during the COVID-19 pandemic, medical personnel are overburdened. In this situation, AI is used to alleviate the strain on health professionals.[116–119] It assists in early diagnosis and intervention of this growing condition by employing digital methods and data analytics, as well as providing the best training to students and clinicians.[120,121] AI has the potential to improve future patient care and solve other potential issues, therefore decreasing the strain on clinicians. The introduction of robotics and AI can help considerably lower the risk of coronavirus transmission by decreasing human contact, safeguarding frontline healthcare professionals, administrative staff, and the general public. For instance, a trained DL system took

4.51 s on average to detect COVID-19 on CT chest, but a radiologist required 10 min and 9 s.[122,123] This indicates that if an AI software is trained to be as accurate as a radiologist, it will be able to provide findings 135 times quicker and operate around the clock without committing fatigue-related mistakes.[124]

Furthermore, AI can assist patients in getting into the proper position for computed tomography. Clinicians can place the patients appropriately in a control room with cameras, speakers, and AI-assisted positioning, eliminating personal contact with prospective victims and the risk of infection.[125] While AI is assisting in the optimization of healthcare operations by automating as many stages as feasible, it is not intended to replace human clinical reasoning and decision-making; rather, it is being utilized as a decision aid to improve efficiency, safety, and patient outcomes.

4.2 Challenges of large-scale screening

AI has the ability to analyze massive volume of data very efficiently. It is crucial in preventing the COVID-19 pandemic. As mentioned in the previous section, AI models are as effective as a skilled radiologist in diagnosing COVID-19.[87] Even if some COVID-19-infected people are asymptomatic, they do have the ability to spread the virus.[126,127] COVID-19 individuals with pneumonia-like symptoms could exhibit a pattern on their chest X-ray or CT imaging that only clinicians can understand.[128,129]

In the fields of biomedicine and cancer diagnostics, image processing techniques are interesting.[130] For the discovery of many illnesses, ML and DL approaches have proven to be useful.[131] Despite the fact that some people have been already diagnosed with SARS-CoV-2, their chest CT scans are normal. As a result, chest CT scans have a limited negative predictive value and do not clear out infection completely. The precision of a single AI diagnosis is currently being questioned. Thus, in order to meet clinical needs, AI algorithms must integrate chest imaging with clinical manifestations, exposure record, and clinical trials in the diagnosis of COVID-19.

However, before AI management, we need to think about appropriate clinical sample management such as proper packaging, less contamination, proper handling of the samples, proper media preparation to carry the samples from onsite to the hospitals or in any diagnostic center. In the following section, this chapter summarizes the clinical sample management and handling issues in detail.

5. Clinical sample management of infected patients

During the incubation phase of SARS-CoV-2, some infected individuals are symptomatic whereas some are asymptomatic. Hence, sample collection with proper expertise is important to diagnose the disease at an earlier stage. Collecting samples from COVID-19 patients is very challenging to handle and should be transferred as quickly as possible to the diagnostic centers.[2] The samples collected from nasopharyngeal swabs are highly recommended for confirmatory results, since the viral load is highest in the upper respiratory tract.[132] Sputum and blood samples are collected from the confirmed symptomatic patients with cough, high fever, and other general symptoms of COVID-19. In general, sputum samples are not recommended much due to aerosols production which can increase the chance of transmission.[132] For those patients who are in ventilators and/or in urgent care units, lower respiratory tract aspirate, BL fluids are recommended as samples for further assessment. In this section, we have discussed the sample collection process and on-spot collection challenges.

5.1 On-spot sample collection and laboratory confirmation

The main flow of sample gathering starts from swab collection from patients by a trained clinician who follows the proper guidelines by CDC, wearing personal protective equipment (PPE) and other safety measurements. Swabs are kept inside in a vial containing viral transport media and then transferred to nearby hospitals or diagnostic centers for various testing processes.[133] High amounts of viral RNA of SARS-CoV-2 are found in upper and lower respiratory tract of infected patients.[134] However, the viral load can be detected in stool and urine samples also. Samples from patients are collected by three main steps: (a) collection, (b) transport, and (c) storage. Quality of the samples depends on the operation and handling way of the collectors.[135] In general, first swabs are collected with cotton buds with plastic shafts and then kept into a sterile plastic container which contains viral transport media. It is highly recommended by WHO that any wooden shafts or calcium alginate swabs are not to be used as they may inactivate the virus and create false-negative results in RT-PCR test.[136] After the treatment and isolation, samples are repeatedly collected from the same infected patients to test until the result comes out to be negative. The frequency of sample collection should be every 2–4 days until two negative test results to confirm the patients are free from COVID-19.[137] Recently, there are many on-spot devices with advance protocol developed with biosensor technologies, molecular technologies, and antigen-based technologies for rapid confirmatory tests. Based on these technologies, many rapid kits (summarized in Table 3) are developed for quick and on-spot diagnosis for COVID-19. The most recommended test is RT-PCR test on respiratory samples. FDA has approved various rapid diagnostic tests which can provide on-spot and quick outcomes.[33]

5.2 Isolating high-risk groups

After sample management, the main critical step is to manage the infected patients. The patient management should be mainly done by isolation depending on the risk factors.[138] Soon after the confirmed test results, the patients need to be separated by 4 main categories such as extreme high-risk, high-risk, intermediate-risk, and low-risk case. Patients with extreme high-risk and high-risk need immediate medical support within 24 h.[139] Extreme high-risk patients may need invasive urgent care with ventilators, oxygen cylinders, and other life supports. Those patients need to be cared with high safety and precaution management since the viral loads of those patients could be extremely high and there could be a high chance of transmission from the patient to the caregiver. Isolating those patients completely in one cabin and providing them all separate facilities are highly recommended. Patients with intermediate-risk was evaluated by taking them in a separated and isolated area for further treatment with several RT-PCR tests. With the low-risk infected person, it is highly recommended that the action should be taken at home. They should be isolated at home with all immediate help from doctors over the phone. On the other hand, the hospital facilities such as number of beds, isolation rooms, ICU rooms, doctors, clinicians, nurses, and availability of oxygen cylinders need to be increased to handle the peak influx for COVID-19-infected patients.[140] Overall infrastructure and easy availability of laboratories and operators are needed to be very active due to the high demand of hospitalization of COVID-19 patients. Hence, the government, health sectors, and other frontline communities and individuals need to play a key role in terms of stopping this virus from spreading and to manage the crowd of patients properly. Healthcare workers should be more trained in the clinical and patient handling management. The healthcare professionals are actively participating during this pandemic and to control the infection, researchers are working continuously to mitigate the pandemic as early as possible. As a result, vaccination has been started and as per statistics shown in "Our world in data" 1.03 billion people worldwide which is around 13.2% of the world's population are vaccinated so far (https://ourworldindata.org/covid-vaccinations?country=OWID_WRL visited on 21.07.2021).

6. Conclusion and future prospective

Currently, there are numerous processes that have been developed to diagnose SARS-CoV-2 based on molecular and antigen-based technology. Nevertheless, concerning about time taking methodologies, the new approaches such as biosensor on-spot devices, biometric systems, and AI-based technologies are a quick mode of early detection during this pandemic situation. Several, AI- and biometric-based systems are forecasting about future probability of spreading this virus as well as providing the exact scenario of how many individuals are getting infected. The most important step is to geo-tag a citizen by a smartphone that has been considered very useful to monitor a COVID-19 patient for POC diagnosis as quick as possible. These contactless methodologies not only supply patient's field data but also provide risk-free direct contact between patients and clinicians. The AI- and ML-based technologies have also helped in identifying the existing and designing the new drugs which are effective against SARS-CoV-2. Perhaps, it is still important to have a precise, low-cost, reliable, rapid diagnostic method and testing kits to face this global pandemic. Scientists and researchers are still digging into these challenges and trying to solve them in order to fabricate a portable and user-friendly model for the accurate detection of COVID-19 which will help in enhanced management and prevention of any future pandemic.

References

1. Khan AH, et al. COVID-19 transmission, vulnerability, persistence and nanotherapy: a review. *Environ Chem Lett* 2021;**19**(4):2773–87.
2. Roy S, Ramadoss A. Chapter 1—Updated insight into COVID-19 disease and health management to combat the pandemic. In: Dehghani MH, Karri RR, Roy S, editors. *Environmental and health management of novel coronavirus disease (COVID-19)*. Academic Press; 2021. p. 3–39.
3. Park SE. Epidemiology, virology, and clinical features of severe acute respiratory syndrome -coronavirus-2 (SARS-CoV-2; coronavirus disease-19). *Clin Exp Pediatr* 2020;**63**(4):119–24.
4. Salzberger B, et al. Epidemiology of SARS-CoV-2. *Infection* 2021;**49**(2):233–9.
5. Gussow AB, et al. Genomic determinants of pathogenicity in SARS-CoV-2 and other human coronaviruses. *Proc Natl Acad Sci* 2020;**117**(26):15193.

6. Deng S-Q, Peng H-J. Characteristics of and public health responses to the coronavirus disease 2019 outbreak in China. *J Clin Med* 2020;**9**(2):575.
7. Jiang S, Du L, Shi Z. An emerging coronavirus causing pneumonia outbreak in Wuhan, China: calling for developing therapeutic and prophylactic strategies. *Emerg Microbes Infect* 2020;**9**(1):275–7.
8. Abduljalil JM, Abduljalil BM. Epidemiology, genome, and clinical features of the pandemic SARS-CoV-2: a recent view. *New Microbes New Infect* 2020;**35**, 100672.
9. Hu B, et al. Characteristics of SARS-CoV-2 and COVID-19. *Nat Rev Microbiol* 2021;**19**(3):141–54.
10. Buonaguro L, et al. SARS-CoV-2 RNA polymerase as target for antiviral therapy. *J Transl Med* 2020;**18**(1):185.
11. Baranwal A, et al. Insights into novel coronavirus and COVID-19 outbreak. In: Chandra P, Roy S, editors. *Diagnostic strategies for COVID-19 and other coronaviruses*. Singapore: Springer Singapore; 2020. p. 1–17.
12. Chan JF-W, et al. A familial cluster of pneumonia associated with the 2019 novel coronavirus indicating person-to-person transmission: a study of a family cluster. *Lancet* 2020;**395**(10223):514–23.
13. Zhao S, et al. Preliminary estimation of the basic reproduction number of novel coronavirus (2019-nCoV) in China, from 2019 to 2020: a data-driven analysis in the early phase of the outbreak. *Int J Infect Dis* 2020;**92**:214–7.
14. Malik YA. Properties of coronavirus and SARS-CoV-2. *Malays J Pathol* 2020;**42** (1):3–11.
15. Yang Y, et al. SARS-CoV-2: characteristics and current advances in research. *Virol J* 2020;**17**(1):117.
16. Amirian ES. Potential fecal transmission of SARS-CoV-2: current evidence and implications for public health. *Int J Infect Dis* 2020;**95**:363–70.
17. Wang M-Y, et al. SARS-CoV-2: structure, biology, and structure-based therapeutics development. *Front Cell Infect Microbiol* 2020;**10**:724.
18. Brahim Belhaouari D, et al. The strengths of scanning electron microscopy in deciphering SARS-CoV-2 infectious cycle. *Front Microbiol* 2020;**11**:2014.
19. Sarkar C, et al. Potential therapeutic options for COVID-19: current status, challenges, and future perspectives. *Front Pharmacol* 2020;**11**:1428.
20. Kumar S, et al. Morphology, genome organization, replication, and pathogenesis of severe acute respiratory syndrome coronavirus 2 (SARS-CoV-2). *Coronavirus Disease 2019 (COVID-19)* 2020;23.
21. Tang X, et al. On the origin and continuing evolution of SARS-CoV-2. *Natl Sci Rev* 2020;**7**(6):1012–23.
22. Ke Z, et al. Structures and distributions of SARS-CoV-2 spike proteins on intact virions. *Nature* 2020;**588**(7838):498–502.
23. Hatmal MMM, et al. Comprehensive structural and molecular comparison of spike proteins of SARS-CoV-2, SARS-CoV and MERS-CoV, and their interactions with ACE2. *Cell* 2020;**9**(12).
24. Singh V. A review on acute respiratory syndrome corona virus 2 (SARS-Cov-2) & its preventive management. *Asian J Pharm Res Dev* 2020;**8**(3):142–51.
25. Noman A, et al. Spike glycoproteins: their significance for corona viruses and receptor binding activities for pathogenesis and viral survival. *Microb Pathog* 2021;**150**, 104719.
26. Astuti I, Ysrafil. Severe acute respiratory syndrome coronavirus 2 (SARS-CoV-2): an overview of viral structure and host response. *Diabetes Metab Syndr Clin Res Rev* 2020;**14**(4):407–12.
27. Kang S, et al. Crystal structure of SARS-CoV-2 nucleocapsid protein RNA binding domain reveals potential unique drug targeting sites. *Acta Pharm Sin B* 2020;**10** (7):1228–38.

28. Lu S, et al. The SARS-CoV-2 nucleocapsid phosphoprotein forms mutually exclusive condensates with RNA and the membrane-associated M protein. *Nat Commun* 2021;**12**(1):502.
29. Sarkar M, Saha S. Structural insight into the role of novel SARS-CoV-2 E protein: a potential target for vaccine development and other therapeutic strategies. *PLoS One* 2020;**15**(8), e0237300.
30. Hsieh C-L, et al. Structure-based design of prefusion-stabilized SARS-CoV-2 spikes. *Science* 2020;**369**(6510):1501.
31. Florindo HF, et al. Immune-mediated approaches against COVID-19. *Nat Nanotechnol* 2020;**15**(8):630–45.
32. Guo Y-R, et al. The origin, transmission and clinical therapies on coronavirus disease 2019 (COVID-19) outbreak—an update on the status. *Mil Med Res* 2020;**7**(1):11.
33. Roy S, Baranwal A. Diverse molecular techniques for early diagnosis of COVID-19 and other coronaviruses. In: Chandra P, Roy S, editors. *Diagnostic strategies for COVID-19 and other coronaviruses*. Singapore: Springer Singapore; 2020. p. 135–59.
34. Mousazadeh M, Naghdali Z, Rahimian N, Hashemi M, Paital B, Al-Qodah Z, et al. Management of environmental health to prevent an outbreak of COVID-19: a review. *Environmental and health management of novel coronavirus disease (COVID-19)*. Academic Press; 2021. p. 235–67.
35. Dehghani MH, Roy S, Karri RR. Novel coronavirus (COVID-19) in environmental engineering perspective. *Environ Sci Pollut Res* 2022;1–3. https://doi.org/10.1007/s11356-022-18572-w.
36. Islam KU, Iqbal J. An update on molecular diagnostics for COVID-19. *Front Cell Infect Microbiol* 2020;**10**:694.
37. Chandra P, Roy S. *Diagnostic strategies for COVID-19 and other coronaviruses*. Springer; 2020.
38. Safiabadi Tali SH, et al. Tools and techniques for severe acute respiratory syndrome coronavirus 2 (SARS-CoV-2)/COVID-19 detection. *Clin Microbiol Rev* 2021;**34**(3), e00228-20.
39. Mahapatra S, et al. Advanced biosensing methodologies for ultrasensitive detection of human coronaviruses. In: Chandra P, Roy S, editors. *Diagnostic strategies for COVID-19 and other coronaviruses*. Singapore: Springer Singapore; 2020. p. 19–36.
40. Merkoçi A, et al. COVID-19 biosensing technologies. *Biosens Bioelectron* 2021;**178**, 113046.
41. Roy S, et al. Meat species identification using DNA-redox electrostatic interactions and non-specific adsorption on graphene biochips. *Food Control* 2016;**61**:70–8.
42. Roy S, et al. CHAPTER 16 isothermal DNA amplification strategies for food biosensors. In: *Food biosensors*. The Royal Society of Chemistry; 2017. p. 367–92.
43. Munirah H, et al. Rapid detection of pork DNA in food samples using reusable electrochemical sensor. *Scientia Bruneiana* 2016;**15**.
44. Roy S, et al. A novel, sensitive and label-free loop-mediated isothermal amplification detection method for nucleic acids using luminophore dyes. *Biosens Bioelectron* 2016;**86**:346–52.
45. Azam NFN, et al. Meat species identification using DNA-luminol interaction and their slow diffusion onto the biochip surface. *Food Chem* 2018;**248**:29–36.
46. Yüce M, Filiztekin E, Özkaya KG. COVID-19 diagnosis—a review of current methods. *Biosens Bioelectron* 2021;**172**:112752.
47. Dastidar MG, Roy S. Chapter 13—Public health management during COVID-19 and applications of point-of-care based biomolecular detection approaches. In: Dehghani MH, Karri RR, Roy S, editors. *Environmental and health management of novel coronavirus disease (COVID-19)*. Academic Press; 2021. p. 345–78.

48. Pérez-López B, Mir M. Commercialized diagnostic technologies to combat SARS-CoV2: advantages and disadvantages. *Talanta* 2021;**225**, 121898.
49. Roy S, Ahmed MU. *System and method for immobilization free electrochemiluminescence DNA detection using a luminophore dye for multi-species detection*; 2021. Google Patents.
50. Roy S, Rahman IA, Ahmed MU. Paper-based rapid detection of pork and chicken using LAMP–magnetic bead aggregates. *Anal Methods* 2016;**8**(11):2391–9.
51. Roy SXWS, Abd Rahman I, Ahmed MU. Based visual detection of Salmonella bacteria using isothermal DNA amplification and magnetic bead aggregation. *Malays J Microbiol* 2016;**12**(5):332–8.
52. Roy S, et al. Colorimetric nucleic acid detection on paper microchip using loop mediated isothermal amplification and crystal violet dye. *ACS Sensors* 2017;**2**(11):1713–20.
53. Antiochia R. Paper-based biosensors: frontiers in point-of-care detection of COVID-19 disease. *Biosensors* 2021;**11**(4):110.
54. Hilborne LH, et al. Linking statistics with testing policy to manage COVID-19 in the community. *Am J Clin Pathol* 2020;**154**(2):142–8.
55. Ravi N, et al. Diagnostics for SARS-CoV-2 detection: a comprehensive review of the FDA-EUA COVID-19 testing landscape. *Biosens Bioelectron* 2020;**165**, 112454.
56. Covid, L., n.d.RT-PCR test EUA summary. Accelerated Emergency Use Authorization (EUA) Summary COVID-19 RT-PCR Test (Laboratory Corporation of America). Available online: www.fda.gov (Accessed 20 March 2020).
57. Shetti NP, et al. 11—Electroanalytical techniques for investigating biofilms: applications in biosensing and biomolecular interfacing. In: Kanchi S, Sharma D, editors. *Nanomaterials in diagnostic tools and devices*. Elsevier; 2020. p. 293–329.
58. Kumar A, et al. Chapter 10—Nanotherapeutics: a novel and powerful approach in modern healthcare system. In: Maurya PK, Singh S, editors. *Nanotechnology in modern animal biotechnology*. Elsevier; 2019. p. 149–61.
59. Roy S, Arshad F, Eissa F, Safavieh M, Alattas SG, Uddin Ahmed M, et al. Recent developments towards portable point-of-care diagnostic devices for pathogen detection. *Sensors Diagnostics* 2022;**1**:87–105.
60. Roy S, et al. Recent nanobiotechnological advancements in lignocellulosic biomass valorization: a review. *J Environ Manage* 2021;**297**, 113422.
61. Kumar A, et al. Design and development of ultrafast sinapic acid sensor based on electrochemically nanotuned gold nanoparticles and solvothermally reduced graphene oxide. *Electroanalysis* 2020;**32**(1):59–69.
62. Roy S, et al. Modernization of biosensing strategies for the development of lab-on-chip integrated systems. *Bioelectrochem Interface Eng* 2019;325–42.
63. Tripathi KP. A comparative study of biometric technologies with reference to human interface. *Int J Comput Appl* 2011;**14**(5):10–5.
64. Zhang DD. *Automated biometrics: technologies and systems*. vol. 7. Springer Science & Business Media; 2013.
65. Jantz RL. Anthropological dermatoglyphic research. *Ann Rev Anthropol* 1987;**16** (1):161–77.
66. Hamid MZSA, Karri RR. Overview of preventive measures and good governance policies to mitigate the COVID-19 outbreak curve in Brunei. In: *COVID-19: systemic risk and resilience*. Cham: Springer; 2021. p. 115–40.
67. Xia Y, et al. Calming the cytokine storm in pneumonia by biomimetic nanoparticles. *Matter* 2020;**3**(1):18–20.
68. Wymant C, et al. The epidemiological impact of the NHS COVID-19 app. *Nature* 2021;**594**(7863):408–12.
69. Imran A, et al. AI4COVID-19: AI enabled preliminary diagnosis for COVID-19 from cough samples via an app. *Inf Med Unlocked* 2020;**20**, 100378.

70. Wayman JL. Fundamentals of biometric authentication technologies. *Int J Image Graph* 2001;**01**(01):93–113.
71. Jain AK, Flynn P, Ross AA. *Handbook of biometrics*. Springer Science & Business Media; 2007.
72. Wayman J, Jain A, Maltoni D, Maio D. An introduction to biometric authentication systems. In: *Biometric systems*. London: Springer; 2005. p. 1–20.
73. Ashibani Y, Kauling D, Mahmoud QH. Design and implementation of a contextual-based continuous authentication framework for smart homes. *Appl Syst Innov* 2019;**2**(1).
74. Wayman JL. Error rate equations for the general biometric system. *IEEE Robot Autom Mag* 1999;**6**(1):35–48.
75. de Boer J, Bazen AM, Gerez SH. Indexing fingerprint databases based on multiple features. In: *ProRISC the 12th Annual Workshop on Circuits, Systems and Signal Processing*; 2001.
76. Rahman A, et al. Adversarial examples—security threats to COVID-19 deep learning systems in medical IoT devices. *IEEE Internet Things J* 2021;**8**(12):9603–10.
77. Fritsch S, et al. Biometric covariates and outcome in COVID-19 patients: are we looking close enough? *medRxiv* 2020. p. 2020.11.04.20225961.
78. Bajpai N, Biberman J, Wadhwa M. *ICT initiatives in India to combat COVID-19*. Center for Sustainable Development, Earth Institute, Columbia University; 2020.
79. Mahroof A. Usage of IT interventions in the containment of Covid-19 spread. *Emerging trends and strategies for industry 4.0: during and beyond COVID-19*. Sciendo; 2021. p. 142.
80. Temiz S, Broo DG. Open innovation initiatives to tackle COVID-19 crises: imposter open innovation and openness in data. *IEEE Eng Manag Rev* 2020;**48**(4):46–54.
81. Van Natta M, et al. The rise and regulation of thermal facial recognition technology during the COVID-19 pandemic. *J Law Biosci* 2020.
82. Polidori MC, et al. COVID-19 mortality as a fingerprint of biological age. *Ageing Res Rev* 2021;**67**, 101308.
83. Okereafor K, et al. Fingerprint biometric system hygiene and the risk of COVID-19 transmission. *JMIR Biomed Eng* 2020;**5**(1), e19623.
84. Haleem A, Javaid M, Vaishya R. Effects of COVID-19 pandemic in daily life. *Curr Med Res Pract* 2020;**10**(2):78–9.
85. Bai HX, et al. Performance of radiologists in differentiating COVID-19 from non-COVID-19 viral pneumonia at chest CT. *Radiology* 2020;**296**(2):E46–e54.
86. Hu Z, et al. Artificial intelligence forecasting of COVID-19 in China. *arXiv* 2020. preprint arXiv:2002.07112.
87. Vaishya R, et al. Artificial intelligence (AI) applications for COVID-19 pandemic. *Diabetes Metab Syndr Clin Res Rev* 2020;**14**(4):337–9.
88. Ai T, et al. Correlation of chest CT and RT-PCR testing for coronavirus disease 2019 (COVID-19) in China: a report of 1014 cases. *Radiology* 2020;**296**(2):E32–e40.
89. Luo H, et al. Can Chinese medicine be used for prevention of Corona virus disease 2019 (COVID-19)? A review of historical classics, research evidence and current prevention programs. *Chin J Integr Med* 2020;**26**(4):243–50.
90. Mei X, et al. Artificial intelligence-enabled rapid diagnosis of patients with COVID-19. *Nat Med* 2020;**26**(8):1224–8.
91. Haleem A, et al. Artificial intelligence (AI) applications in orthopaedics: an innovative technology to embrace. *J Clin Orthop Trauma* 2020;**11**(Suppl 1):S80–s81.
92. Biswas K, Sen P. Space-time dependence of corona virus (COVID-19) outbreak. *arXiv* 2020. preprint arXiv:2003.03149.
93. Stebbing J, et al. COVID-19: combining antiviral and anti-inflammatory treatments. *Lancet Infect Dis* 2020;**20**(4):400–2.
94. Rohmetra H, et al. AI-enabled remote monitoring of vital signs for COVID-19: methods, prospects and challenges. *Computing* 2021;1–27.

95. Zhou Y, et al. Artificial intelligence in COVID-19 drug repurposing. *Lancet Digital Health* 2020;**2**(12):e667–76.
96. Lumb R, Lall V, Moreno A. The role of AI in testing, tracking and treatment of Covid-19. *Am J Manag* 2020;**20**(3):55–64.
97. Hardas BM, Damle NS. Enrich to rich—an indigenous model to combat COVID-19. In: *Health informatics and technological solutions for coronavirus (COVID-19)*. CRC Press; 2021. p. 13–26.
98. Aikat V. Interactive data validation and data preprocessing of contactless medical devices. *Thesis* 2020. https://doi.org/10.17615/zkpd-mw27.
99. Zhao M, et al. Assessment of medication self-administration using artificial intelligence. *Nat Med* 2021;**27**(4):727–35.
100. World Health Organization. *Contact tracing in the context of COVID-19: interim guidance, 10 May 2020 (No. WHO/2019-nCoV/Contact_Tracing/2020.1)*; 2020.
101. Lalmuanawma S, Hussain J, Chhakchhuak L. Applications of machine learning and artificial intelligence for Covid-19 (SARS-CoV-2) pandemic: a review. *Chaos, Solitons Fractals* 2020;**139**, 110059.
102. Bano M, Zowghi D, Arora C. Requirements, politics, or individualism: what drives the success of COVID-19 contact-tracing apps? *IEEE Softw* 2021;**38**(1):7–12.
103. Berglund J. Tracking COVID-19: there's an app for that. *IEEE Pulse* 2020;**11**(4):14–7.
104. Ko H, et al. An artificial intelligence model to predict the mortality of COVID-19 patients at hospital admission time using routine blood samples: development and validation of an ensemble model. *J Med Internet Res* 2020;**22**(12), e25442.
105. Sohrabi C, et al. World Health Organization declares global emergency: a review of the 2019 novel coronavirus (COVID-19). *Int J Surg* 2020;**76**:71–6.
106. Chen S, et al. COVID-19 control in China during mass population movements at New Year. *Lancet* 2020;**395**(10226):764–6.
107. Bobdey S, Ray S. Going viral–Covid-19 impact assessment: a perspective beyond clinical practice. *J Mar Med Soc* 2020;**22**(1):9.
108. Keshavarzi Arshadi A, et al. Artificial intelligence for COVID-19 drug discovery and vaccine development. *Front Artif Intell* 2020;**3**:65.
109. Gupta E, Mishra RK, Niraj RRK. Identification of potential vaccine candidates against *SARS-CoV-2*, a step forward to fight COVID-19: a reverse vaccinology approach. *bioRxiv* 2020. p. 2020.04.13.039198.
110. Chauhan N, et al. Interpretative immune targets and contemporary position for vaccine development against SARS-CoV-2: a systematic review. *J Med Virol* 2021;**93**(4):1967–82.
111. Sampath Kumar NS, et al. Immunotherapeutics for Covid-19 and post vaccination surveillance. *3 Biotech* 2020;**10**(12):527.
112. Ong E, et al. COVID-19 coronavirus vaccine design using reverse vaccinology and machine learning. *Front Immunol* 2020;**11**:1581.
113. Ong E, et al. Vaxign-ML: supervised machine learning reverse vaccinology model for improved prediction of bacterial protective antigens. *Bioinformatics* 2020;**36**(10):3185–91.
114. Ke Y-Y, et al. Artificial intelligence approach fighting COVID-19 with repurposing drugs. *Biom J* 2020;**43**(4):355–62.
115. Beck BR, et al. Predicting commercially available antiviral drugs that may act on the novel coronavirus (SARS-CoV-2) through a drug-target interaction deep learning model. *Comput Struct Biotechnol J* 2020;**18**:784–90.
116. Ekins S, et al. Déjà vu: stimulating open drug discovery for SARS-CoV-2. *Drug Discov Today* 2020;**25**(5):928–41.
117. Ekins S, Freundlich JS, Coffee M. A common feature pharmacophore for FDA-approved drugs inhibiting the Ebola virus. *F1000Res* 2014;**3**:277.

118. Ekins S, et al. Open drug discovery for the Zika virus. *F1000Res* 2016;**5**:150.
119. Chockanathan U, et al. Automated diagnosis of HIV-associated neurocognitive disorders using large-scale Granger causality analysis of resting-state functional MRI. *Comput Biol Med* 2019;**106**:24–30.
120. Gozes O, et al. Rapid AI development cycle for the coronavirus (covid-19) pandemic: initial results for automated detection & patient monitoring using deep learning ct image analysis. *arXiv* 2020. preprint arXiv:2003.05037.
121. Ting DSW, et al. Digital technology and COVID-19. *Nat Med* 2020;**26**(4):459–61.
122. Wan KH, et al. Precautionary measures needed for ophthalmologists during pandemic of the coronavirus disease 2019 (COVID-19). *Acta Ophthalmol* 2020;**98**(3):221–2.
123. Gupta R, Misra A. Contentious issues and evolving concepts in the clinical presentation and management of patients with COVID-19 infectionwith reference to use of therapeutic and other drugs used in co-morbid diseases (hypertension, diabetes etc). *Diabetes Metab Syndr* 2020;**14**(3):251–4.
124. Gupta R, et al. Clinical considerations for patients with diabetes in times of COVID-19 epidemic. *Diabetes Metab Syndr* 2020;**14**(3):211–2.
125. Li L, et al. Using artificial intelligence to detect COVID-19 and community-acquired pneumonia based on pulmonary CT: evaluation of the diagnostic accuracy. *Radiology* 2020;**296**(2):E65–71.
126. Sokolovskaya E, et al. The effect of faster reporting speed for imaging studies on the number of misses and interpretation errors: a pilot study. *J Am Coll Radiol* 2015;**12**(7):683–8.
127. Shi F, et al. Review of artificial intelligence techniques in imaging data acquisition, segmentation, and diagnosis for COVID-19. *IEEE Rev Biomed Eng* 2021;**14**:4–15.
128. Alimadadi A, et al. Artificial intelligence and machine learning to fight COVID-19. *Physiol Genomics* 2020;**52**(4):200–2.
129. Day M. Covid-19: identifying and isolating asymptomatic people helped eliminate virus in Italian village. *BMJ* 2020;**368**, m1165.
130. Huff HV, Singh A. Asymptomatic transmission during the coronavirus disease 2019 pandemic and implications for public health strategies. *Clin Infect Dis* 2020;**71**(10):2752–6.
131. Huang S, et al. Artificial intelligence in cancer diagnosis and prognosis: opportunities and challenges. *Cancer Lett* 2020;**471**:61–71.
132. Bastolla U. How lethal is the novel coronavirus, and how many undetected cases there are? The importance of being tested. *medRxiv* 2020. p. 2020.03.27.20045062.
133. Alam Khan F, et al. Blockchain technology, improvement suggestions, security challenges on smart grid and its application in healthcare for sustainable development. *Sustain Cities Soc* 2020;**55**, 102018.
134. Yang J, et al. Broad learning with attribute selection for rheumatoid arthritis. In: *2020 IEEE International Conference on Systems, Man, and Cybernetics (SMC)*; 2020.
135. Varghese GM, et al. Clinical management of COVID-19. *Indian J Med Res* 2020;**151**(5):401–10.
136. Cevik M, Bamford CGG, Ho A. COVID-19 pandemic—a focused review for clinicians. *Clin Microbiol Infect* 2020;**26**(7):842–7.
137. Ling Y, et al. Persistence and clearance of viral RNA in 2019 novel coronavirus disease rehabilitation patients. *Chin Med J (Engl)* 2020;**133**(9):1039.
138. Yan Y, Chang L, Wang L. Laboratory testing of SARS-CoV, MERS-CoV, and SARS-CoV-2 (2019-nCoV): current status, challenges, and countermeasures. *Rev Med Virol* 2020;**30**(3), e2106.
139. Centers for Disease Control and Prevention. *Interim guidelines for collecting, handling, and testing clinical specimens from persons under investigation (PUIs) for coronavirus disease 2019 (COVID-19)*; 2020.

140. World Health Organization. Clinical management of severe acute respiratory infection when novel coronavirus (2019-nCoV) infection is suspected: interim guidance. In: *Clinical management of severe acute respiratory infection when novel coronavirus (2019-nCoV) infection is suspected: interim guidance*; 2020. p. 21.
141. Neufeld Z, Khataee H, Czirok A. Targeted adaptive isolation strategy for COVID-19 pandemic. *Infect Dis Model* 2020;**5**:357–61.
142. Porter L. High risk or low worth?: A few practical and philosophical COVID-19 issues surrounding the isolation of high-risk senior women. In: *COVID-19*. Routledge; 2020. p. 256–69.
143. Williams SN, et al. Public perceptions and experiences of social distancing and social isolation during the COVID-19 pandemic: a UK-based focus group study. *BMJ Open* 2020;**10**(7), e039334.

CHAPTER SIXTEEN

Wearable body sensor network: SDGs panacea for an holistic SARS-CoV-2 mitigation, diagnostic, therapeutic, and health informatics interventions

Modupeola Elizabeth Olalere[a], Olusegun Abayomi Olalere[b], Chee-Yuen Gan[b], and Hamoud Alenezi[c]

[a]School of Computer Science, Universiti Sains Malaysia, Gelugor, Malaysia
[b]Analytical Biochemistry Research Centre, Inkubator Inovasi Universiti (I2U), Sains USM, Universiti Sains Malaysia, Penang, Malaysia
[c]Process Systems Engineering Centre (PROSPECT), Faculty of Chemical and Energy Engineering, Universiti Teknologi Malaysia, Johor Bahru, Johor, Malaysia

1. Introduction

The recent SARS-CoV-2 (i.e. COVID-19) was originally detected in the last quarter of the year 2019 as just a respiratory infection in Wuhan city of China.[1] This has since become a global pandemic involving over 150 countries all around the world. The World Health Organization (WHO) announced the epidemic as a pandemic on 11/03/2020 and advocated for concerted strategies to promote early warning systems all around the healthcare system.[2] The United States of America declared the disease outbreak to be a federal emergency. The SARS-CoV-2 virus is mostly spread between people through coughing or sneezing and direct interaction, as per current understanding.[3] Whenever droplets have a size greater than or equal to five micrometers, they are referred to as respiratory droplets; when they have a diameter smaller than five micrometers, they are referred to as droplet sections. The droplet portions may be referred to scientifically as "droplet nuclei" with transmission also possible via close contact with infected individuals, direct contact with things in the surrounding environment, and the use of goods on an infected people.[4] Emerging epidemiological evidence

https://doi.org/10.1016/B978-0-323-91307-2.00010-9

suggests that the geriatric, defined as those older than 75 years, are more susceptible to SARS-CoV-2 infection than other age categories.[5]

When examining the clinical features of COVID-19, it was found that the likely incubation time was 3 days, with mortality signs manifesting within 14 days in older people.[6] While SARS fatalities were examined in previous studies, it took between 4 and 17.4 days for the very first death signs to manifest.[6] Additionally, it is worth noting that SARS-CoV-2 has a much-reduced incubation time than the other 24 days. Furthermore, a period of toward with little action toward spreading has been reported. Additionally, another pattern found was that it takes a median of 20 days during the first death signs to manifest in those over the age of 70 years and 11.5 days for younger people. As a result of the above, it would seem that an old individual is more prone to get sick than others, necessitating the need for extra measures.

The United States-Centers for Disease Control and Prevention (US-CDC) reported that healthcare professionals faced very significant risks, even while wearing protective gear, due to their close contact with their patients.[7] Substances such as bodily fluids, infected surgical equipment and devices, contaminated surfaces, and aerosol transmissions provide a risk of direct or indirect transmission to victims.[8] SARS-CoV-2 infection results in a spectrum of symptoms comparable to past outbreaks, where moderate fever, coughing, and irregular gastrointestinal activity are described as the main symptoms. Additionally, several investigations have however documented asymptomatic instances.[9] As this outbreak keeps increasing, healthcare services are increasingly burdened with effective ways to respond to the rising operational demands.[1] The need, therefore, arises for the development of an effective healthcare information system capable of monitoring, supporting, treating, and managing the patient's electronic health record (HER).[10] The application of technology-based solutions can easily help health institutions in the process of managing pandemics by encouraging the rapid and widespread dissemination of data, real-time monitoring of transmission, and development of discussion groups and daily operations of essential services.[11] Take for example, information systems have been a crucial factor in China's reactions to the COVID-19 spread. In this instance, technological innovation, including prediction of spread, the monitoring of close contact, and remoteness, has been used at every point of the outbreak.[12] In response to the first wave of the COVID-19 pandemic, healthcare institutions have implemented many immediate solutions and complex technological resources in curtailing the spread. This, therefore, provoked a digital transformation that will always stay with us for a long time and can be subsequently applied as vital interventions to any future outbreaks. Wearable trackers can increase awareness of the health status of oneself, others, and the world and enable the users to choose more acceptable responses to new health scenarios. The wearable activity trackers (WAT) showed considerable benefit inpatient support and self-management in healthcare scenarios, especially in patients with dietary conditions such as hypertension and diabetes. Of the different wearable devices, wearable trackers are by far the most popular type. There are body-worn or handheld instruments or technologies that instantly capture data for improved knowledge of one, others, or the environment.

2. Diagnostic and therapeutic advances against SARS-CoV-2

Fatigue, fever, and pulmonary abnormalities are by far the most often seen SARS-CoV-2 beginning symptoms. The theorized group needed clinical tests or imaging techniques to establish the SARS-CoV-2 diagnosis after examining symptomatology and epidemiologic evidence.[13] COVID-19 victims' indications are inconsistent and cannot be utilized to diagnose the condition. COVID-19 has been diagnosed and screened using nucleic acid tests and computed tomography scans.[1] Upon obtaining the SARS-CoV-2 sequence of nucleotides from individual respiratory tract samples through deep sequencing analysis,[14] a range of RT-PCR-based diagnostic assays will be generated. The basic procedure is to collect RNA from the upper respiratory tract, separate it, and confirm its positivity using a particular primer during PCR. Additionally, there is serological testing. A computed tomography scan has been recommended to make a diagnosis of typical cases in epidemic areas, but chest CT screening is not recommended for population densities with minimal rates of infection due to its low good prognosis.[15] However, chest CT testing may be deemed a technique for existing COVID-19 diagnosis in outbreak zones.[15]

Along with nucleic acid PCR and serological screening, there are assays founded on other concepts, such as antigen-based testing, clustered regularly interspaced short palindromic repeats (CRISPR-based) technique, and physics-based procedures.[16] The rapidity with which antigens are detected is one of their primary benefits. Antigen analysis, on the other hand, is extremely specific for viruses but not as accurate as molecular polymerase chain reaction testing. Moreover, the s Specific High-sensitivity Enzymatic

Reporter is utilized to identify novel coronavirus gene sequences.[16] No equipment is needed, as it is comparable to the simple pregnancy test to rapidly identify the existence of a novel coronavirus ribonucleic acid sequence.[17] At the moment, the most often employed detection technique is a blend of nasopharyngeal swab nucleic acid PCR and serological detection using a nasopharyngeal swab.[17] The nucleic acid polymerase chain reaction (PCR) test findings remain the gold standard for COVID-19 detection, although serological testing may be performed in addition.[18,19] The sample location is also important in nucleic acid analysis. The virus is detectable in lungs, feces, blood, urinate, and testicular samples. The most practical specimens are spit or oropharynx swabs. Bronchoscopy is used by physicians to get samples from the lower respiratory system.[20] Nevertheless, this technique exacerbates the patient's discomfort and decreases the test's reliability. At the moment, research indicates that the precision of oropharyngeal swab sampling detection may be greater than that of nasopharynx testing, thus reducing the complexity of sample collection and the patient's discomfort.[20] Considering the lengthy process of developing new medicines from the bottom-up, many US food and drug administration pharmaceuticals previously used to treat other illnesses have been adapted to treating COVID-19 due to their antiviral characteristics. Interestingly, many anticancer agents have demonstrated the ability to treat acute COVID-19 by suppressing overactive immune function and are currently being studied in continuing clinical studies.

3. Impacts of SARS-CoV-2 on healthcare informatics

Thanks to the COVID-19 emergency, service distribution by health informatics applications has improved extraordinarily rapidly, demonstrating that WAT technologies have now attained the stage to be used in medical services at an unprecedented speed. It is possible that even at the end of this pandemic, digital interventions will remain in practice. The pandemic has contributed to rapid improvements in the scale of exchange of health records for both primary and indirect diagnosis. However how "emergency" health information systems will continue to work beyond interference with public confidence after the crisis is somewhat unclear. Several countries have enacted digital health policies for remote surveillance and telehealth systems to facilitate health-saving services to be provided and with no physical encounters.[21] The ability of digital health-related technology to shield patients, medical providers, and the population from disclosure has been universally acknowledged and facilitated. In the United Kingdom, primary healthcare has taken on telehealth on a comprehensive basis and has launched a modern, first-ever automated approach to handling digital treatment to the ideal location.

To improve pandemic monitoring, main screening, and accurate forecasts promptly, the disease prevention and information reporting process should be properly assessed. Government healthcare networks need to establish a multisource network that combines data analytics, sharing, integration, and input channels into profitable use. The unified system would improve the connection among different relevant agencies for disease control. COVID-19 detection and the database of all suspected cases can subsequently be used to evaluate and implement a national health information system for future interventions. It is important to know that many patients seen in primary and specialist hospitals can be remotely controlled. Also, this form of treatment can be given by care staff who quarantine following an infection or injury. This involves people with COVID-19 and other future pandemics who can be treated centrally with guidance on the signs of symptoms. The telehealth instruments have therefore taken a center stage and are being taunted as another form of "electronic personal protective equipment (PPE)" that can be applied for the acute medical condition without being physically proactive. Hence, the effect of the COVID-19 pandemic on healthcare informatics will undoubtedly have a long-term effect both on potential patients and health practitioners. By integrating health technologies with healthcare services, diagnostic performance and patients' treatment interactions can be enhanced, and online sharing of large medical resources and real-time knowledge exchange can also be accomplished. The interconnected framework will effectively mitigate the challenges of medical resource scarcity, unequal delivery of healthcare quality, and shortages of healthcare staff. The implementation of an interconnected intelligent healthcare framework for COVID-19 pandemic prevention and control would also provide a positive guide for the design and implementation of future intelligent healthcare frameworks for other public health emergencies.[11]

4. Sustainable development goals as panacea for holistic emergency response

The current COVID-19 healthcare emergency has had an overwhelming and detrimental effect on public and civil healthcare systems. This has generated several global healthcare problems and contributed in the past few months to the greatest humanitarian crises the world has ever experienced. These have put to test the competence of health practitioners on the tracking and exploration of modern approaches of digital health technology. The Millennium Development Goals (MDGs) are inextricably linked to efforts in decreasing the impact of infectious diseases. The 2030 Sustainable Development Agenda offers an impetus for policymakers and the global community to reiterate their commitment to supporting health as a core element of development.[22] According to the Sustainable Development Goal-3, the decline in the number of premature deaths and an improvement in life expectancy will only be ensured by the continuity, introduction, and application of a government program focused on public coverage, emergency response services, national health benefits, and accessible preventive care. The Goal-3 of the Sustainable Development Goals (SDGs) was to ensure healthier lifestyles and encourage well-being for every one of all ages with Target 3.8 focused on universal health coverage (UHC) which underscores the value of both individuals and families getting access to affordable health facilities without causing extreme burden.[22] MDG 6 emphasizes HIV/AIDS, influenza, and other illnesses, whereas MDG 4 (decreasing infant death), MDG 5 (enhancing maternal and newborn), and MDG 7C (increasing basic cleanliness and ensuring sustainable access to freshwater) all address infectious disease care. MDG 8E (ensure affordable access to needed drugs in underdeveloped nations in collaboration with pharma firms) and MDG 8F (enable access to the benefits of digital technologies, particularly information and communications technology, in collaboration with the private partners) not only collaborate with these goals but also recommend an improvisatory way to accomplish them.

These health programs also include those tailored to patients, such as curative treatment and community-based services, such as public health.[23] Improving UHC is an effective strategy for all nations to promote fair and safe health conditions and to increase the well-being of people and communities. The improvement of healthcare infrastructure is a part of attaining giant strides through UHC. A functional healthcare system is structured around individuals, organizations, and services required to strengthen, preserve, or rebuild the health of the population. Bolstering the health sector itself is a pathway in ensuring that the success of the system embraces the overarching goals of most government healthcare programs, initiatives, and strategies—consistency, fairness, effectiveness, transparency, efficiency, and sustainability.[23] The success of the MDGs proves that coordinated international intervention can be effective. Amid unparalleled advances in the healthcare system, more than 1 billion people, half of them in developing countries, have been unable to take advantage of the benefits of the MDGs. Infectious diseases make a significant contribution considerably to the global burden of disease in low- and middle-income nations. Annually, these nations lose well over 11 million individuals to major contagious illnesses ranging from AIDS, TB, and influenza to diarrheal infections, measles, and respiratory illnesses. Not only do certain nations bear a disproportionate share of the cost, but also susceptible sections of the society. Particularly, 95% of fatalities from respiratory infections and 98% of fatalities from diarrheal illnesses occur in low- and middle-income countries, while diarrhea, pneumonia, measles, and influenza claim the lives of a large number of infants below 5 years. The newly created SDGs are much more optimistic than their predecessors. SDG-3 provides importance to health and well-being for all populations in particular fields, such as infant mortality, communicable diseases, mental health, and occupational health.

5. Innovative technologies for diseases outbreak monitoring and control

5.1 Internet-based surveillance technology

Technological advancements play a critical role in the achievement of the SDGs by enhancing the quality and efficacy of modern and environmentally sustainable models of development. It is also important to develop innovative technology that encourages science and drives creativity.[24] These mechanisms can be improved by enhanced information exchange and cooperation between stakeholders in both national and international frameworks. It is also important to develop innovative technologies that encourage science and drive creativity. These mechanisms can be improved by enhanced information exchange and cooperation between stakeholders in both regional and global contexts. Healthcare quality is the degree to which the healthcare services are offered to people and patients and improve the expected survival rates, along with existing technical experience. Intermediate objectives of national health programs, plans, and initiatives were primarily instituted to achieve quality, equity, efficiency, accountability, resilience, and sustainability.[25]

Surveillance of emerging infectious diseases is critical for detecting public health risks early on. The emergence of new diseases is influenced by both human and natural factors, including population size, migration, and trade, as well as environmental issues and agricultural activities. A plethora of novel technologies are becoming increasingly more accessible for not just fast molecular characterization of microbes, but also more precise monitoring of infectious disease activities. An example of this technology is event-based surveillance, which is usually considered as conventional and passive surveillance since it is based on regular reporting of structured predefined information about occurrences and illnesses by healthcare institutions.[26] This kind of monitoring necessitates the presence of a public health network, is often costly, and results in a delay of about 2 weeks between data collection and dissemination. The development of computer science has resulted in the emergence of event-based surveillance as a complement to conventional early warning sign monitoring. Event-based systems are primarily used to gather and analyze unstructured data from a variety of sources, such as news stories, social media, and web searches. True, the bulk of data on initial reporting of infectious disease occurrences come from informal sources such as news reports and the internet. Digital surveillance systems are designed to identify potentially pandemic occurrences before official announcements. The Global Public Health Intelligence Network is one of the most valuable event-based surveillance technologies, scanning a variety of such private sources for unusual disease events and infestation speculations, such as websites, digital online forums, newspaper articles, and news websites.[26]

Remote sensing technology is another method of preventing disease outbreaks. Monitoring the environmental conditions with this technique may aid in illness prediction. Previous studies were able to build an environmental framework that correctly predicted the real incidence rate of a cholera epidemic using satellite imagery to gather data on ocean temperatures, surface height, and chlorophyll A levels. Except for water-borne illnesses, satellite imagery has been utilized to monitor vector movement, such as the location of the *Anopheles* species responsible for malaria incidence in Africa and to simulate Hantavirus pulmonary syndrome epidemics.[27] Vector-borne illness epidemics, on the other hand, are more difficult to forecast owing to the dynamics of vector ecology and human behavior, as well as the diversity of host immune systems among populations.[28] It is essential to closely monitor climatological factors (e.g., increase in sea surface temperature and prolonged rainfall) as well as vegetation and soil indicators to identify alterations that may lead to infectious disease outbreaks. By incorporating such data into prognostic mathematical modeling, signals may be generated to guide public health actions aimed at an epidemic abatement.

The use of mobile communication technologies through mobile phones creates new possibilities and difficulties in the monitoring of developing infectious diseases. Consider the Foodborne Chicago initiative, which was established by the Chicago Department of Public Health to track foodborne diseases through social media. It employs an algorithm to detect and react to tweets about food poisoning. Another new approach to event-based surveillance is "participatory epidemiology," which HealthMap illustrates with an example. The program, dubbed Flu NearYou, enables anybody over the age of 13 who lives in the United States or Canada to participate and submit questionnaires about influenza-like disease activity in their neighborhood. Besides providing information, social media may also aid in the data processing. HealthMap allows users to rate articles based on their importance, which may help to improve the quality of distributed data.[29] Mobile phone data is currently being recognized to monitor people's mobility to better understand the patterns of virus transmission and the pathways of disease importing from district to district.

Additionally, because of the widespread usage of cellphones and the expansion of internet connectivity, even in resource-constrained nations, mobile phone technology is being utilized for infectious disease monitoring. Mobile phones provide two-way communication and may be used to gather data for health monitoring as well as to disseminate critical public health data to the general population. A mobile tracking application such as the MySejahtera app, which was created by the Malaysian government to help in controlling the COVID-19 outbreak throughout their country. It enables users to self-assess their health and that of their family and friends, as well as track their health status during the COVID-19 epidemic. Additionally, MySejahtera allows the Malaysian Ministry of Health (MOH) to track users' health status and perform contact mapping for COVID-19, allowing them to take prompt action in delivering necessary remedies. MySejahtera is also the official channel for the Government of Malaysia's National COVID-19 Immunization Program, which provides vaccine enrolment, scheduling appointments, and the issuing of COVID-19 vaccination digital certificates.

5.2 Drawback of internet-based surveillance technology

While internet-based surveillance systems are rapidly utilizing more resources and advanced software for collecting and analyzing data, a regional monitoring disparity persists due to restrictions in communications networks, poor infrastructure and diagnostic capacity, a paucity of qualified staff, and significantly reduced awareness in these aspects, all of which contribute to disease underestimation. Additionally, underreporting and bureaucratic segregation impede attempts to monitor new infectious illnesses. National healthcare authorities must have access to real-time surveillance data on the internet to respond quickly and efficiently to an outbreak. Global cooperation should prioritize strengthening public health capabilities in elevated areas for the development of infectious diseases.

Additionally, concentrating on endemic monitoring concurrently in developing infectious disease "hotspots" would overcome some of the obstacles to early outbreak identification. This is especially true for illnesses in which animal instances precede human cases. Given that the majority of new infectious diseases including the one-health concept enable the development of shared fundamental capabilities for human disease monitoring. Technologies evolve at a breakneck pace as new capabilities become accessible, algorithms improve, and computing speed advances, enabling the creation of more complex surveillance techniques and more appropriate forecasting models. Coordination between agencies, institutions, researchers, and healthcare networks engaged in infectious disease monitoring, on the other hand, is critical for early detection and response to unique risks and, most critically, for the prevention of future pandemics.

6. Emergence of wearable activity trackers (WATs) technology

Wearable activity trackers (WATs) are electronic tracking tools that connect users to track and control their overall health measurements, including action taken, level of fitness, moving speed, blood pressure, and sleep quality. These WATs are usually connected to the body, especially the forearm, to help improve or enhance human health management functionality.[30] WAT frequently quantifies consumer activity and health status and instantly uploads the data to smartphone applications and relevant sites.[31] Examples of prominent items with these features include Apple Watch, Samsung Gear, Garmin, Fitbit, Xiaomi, and Jawbone. Given the deployment of these instruments in multiple disciplines of usage and growing scientific priorities, there is little awareness of the large research landscape. To create effective wearable trackers, it is important to consider the consumers of those trackers and their perspectives on designs and functionality by performing interviews or reviewing feedback as part of a user-centered design approach. The race for WAT advancement has begun since its launch, while many of them have not lasted for long, indicating the wearable movement we see today.

As wearable technology continues to advance, it has started to spread to other areas. The incorporation of wearable into healthcare services has become a topic of investigation and innovation in different organizations. Wearable continue to develop, evolving beyond smartphones and setting new frontiers, such as smart fabrics.[32] Technologies include the usage of cloth to execute a purpose such as the incorporation of a QR code into a garment or performance clothing that improves air movement during a workout.[33] Virtual reality is another highly common wearable tech. Stereo headsets have been produced by a variety of vendors for laptops, consoles, and handheld devices. This launching of Google headsets popularly known as the 'Google Daydream' is a practical example of how far wearable technology has evolved.[34] The detection systems for assisted care of the elderly are vital advancements in the field of wearable technology.[35]

The wearable sensors have an enormous capacity to generate large data, with high efficacy in the healthcare system.[36] With this justification, the investigator is turning their attention from information gathering to the development of smart machine learning capable of collecting useful information from data collected, using data mining methods such as statistical classification and neural networks. Other advances of wearable technology include the system that captures the biometric data directly from a patient's body such as body temperature, pulse rate, heart rate, brain wave, and muscle bio-signals to provide useful knowledge in the area of medical care and wellness.[37] Epidermal electronics is an emerging area in wearable technology. It is popularly known as epidermal technology since they are characteristically comparable to the epidermis skin layer. They are directly installed on the skin for active monitoring of physiological and metabolic functions.[38] The epidermal electronics are reportedly being established in the wellness and patient monitoring fields.

6.1 Wearable body sensor for tracking and control of COVID-19

Numerous studies on wearable development and execution aiming at sensing physiological characteristics from the human body have been reported. Mobile Wireless sensor systems are the ideal option for monitoring COVID-19 infection and preventing viral transmission.[39] This sensor is linked to a network edge in the internet-of-a-thing platforms, in which the processing takes place and is analyzed to identify the status of health.

The wearable sensor device can monitor and check the status of a COVID-19 patient at a remote location.[39] The IoT design architecture is compared to current technologies to determine the state of COVID-19 digital healthcare. Through all the foregoing research, it has been shown that the combination of IoT and deep learning techniques may successfully aid in tracking and alerting the human health condition.[39] The periphery and cloud computing components of the Internet of Things gather and analyze data in response to threshold circumstances. Deep learning may be utilized efficiently and reliably in strategic planning, therapy assistance, and monitoring and risk. Multimodal illness identification, monitoring, and therapy may all contribute to fulfilling real-time needs.[39] Previous wearable sensor design from previous studies (Table 1) is potent enough for the design of body sensors for the monitoring and control of COVID-19.

Table 1 Current adoption of wearable body sensor for health monitoring.

Body sensor design	Purpose of design and limitations	References
Visual interactive digital health monitor	To assess COVID-19 patients' physiological health indicators	[40]
IoT alert system	Emergency medical support	[41]
Convolutional neural network-based deep learning system	Obtaining patient X-ray scan data	[42]
Multilayered IoT-based deep learning with spatial pattern	Brain and central nervous system and data transmission through the skin into the cloud	[43]
API for the front end biomedical wearable	Dashboard for clinicians for EMG sensing utilized to aid in the detection of neuromuscular disorders	[44]
IoT devise with body area monitor	Capture data to give an advanced detection of a heart attack	[45]
IoT-based social distancing strategy	Contactless enclosed safety is achieved via social distance, mask sensing, and temperature monitoring	[46]
Geolocation and monitoring of COVID-19 areas	To keep an eye on individuals and send out alerts through cell phone	[47]
AI-based sensors for wearable health	It serves as a heart rate, temperature, and activity sensor.	[48]
Android web layer and Peripheral Interface (API) for cellular telephones	COVID-19 symptoms are monitored, managed, and analyzed	[39]

Bassam et al.[39] presented one of the most important reports on wearable design for COVID-19. The designed Internet of Things-based monitoring system is capable of measuring physiological indicators and symptoms in COVID-19-infected patients and transmitting them to a peripheral interface (API) that serves as a database for perusing and monitoring the infections threshold. Additionally, the work offered geographic information on potentially infectious patients who are quarantined or self-isolated. The archived database system can be utilized to notify medical personnel of a patient's condition, symptoms, and chosen spot. The suggested system comprises three stacks: wearable IoT, cloud, and mobile or online interface. Such layers operate independently and communicate with one another to enable wireless surveillance of COVID-19-infected individuals. Among the important features of the design, the study is that it has the potential to have a substantial effect on notifying health practitioners of possible infected individuals using geographic information to predict and assess the evidence. A database is built to hold all healthcare records of potentially infected patients and to retrieve data for analysis.

6.2 Current adoption and challenges of wearable activity trackers (WATs)

While wearable activity trackers (WATs) have been gaining traction since their commercial launch a decade ago and there is extreme demand in the usage and effect of these systems in various ways.[49] The demand for wearable emerging electronic technologies has dramatically grown and a variety of manufacturers have introduced the various design of wearable products. According to the International Data Corporation (IDC), the global demand for wearable tracking devices is anticipated to rise from 113.2 million products sales in 2017 to 222.3 million products sales in 2021.[50] A significant part of market analysis is the user willingness of adopting intelligent technologies which have profound consequences for firms to accelerate the process of diffusion. In the current sense, one of the main results of wearable activity trackers' acceptance and adoption is that its design as an all-purpose device is unrealistic and not economically feasible. Instead, the use of various designs and data structures can also be built that fit different user personal preferences.[51] Wearable activity trackers (WATs) growth has advanced quickly and accuracy testing has not maintained pace with the number of instruments in usage. The survey on the adoption and implementation of WATs is primarily based on the dialogue approach which makes it clear that a WAT gadget doesn't identify the desired outcomes in itself.

The confidentiality experience of wearable activity tracker may be influenced by attitude, personal confidence, and functionality of the device. For instance, more psychopathic users are more mindful of data privacy, while more secure users are less worried about confidentiality consequences. Based on an increase in user personality awareness, Karen et al.[52] proposed the customization options of developers and designers for different user groups with different secrecy preferences. While wearable healthcare technology has grown promisingly, its introduction has been delayed in contrast with other well-known portable technology devices such as mobile phones and tablets. This is because wearing healthcare technology is still being commercialized in a developmental stage, with most of the prestudies centered on its technical development, leading to insufficient comprehension of its spreading process.

7. Conclusion

The COVID-19 pandemic has underscored the need for more harnessing of digital infrastructure for remote monitoring. We see a need for more robust disease detection and monitoring of public health, which may be enhanced via wearable sensors since existing viral diagnostics and vaccinations are sluggish to develop. While this technology has been utilized to connect physiological measurements to everyday life and human performance, its use in forecasting the occurrence of COVID-19 remains a need. Wearable device users may be notified if alterations in their indicators match those linked with COVID-19. Anonymized data targeted to specific areas, like neighborhoods, may offer public health officials and academics a useful tool for tracking and mitigating the virus's transmission. As the world is being confronted with this deadly scourge, the utilization of wearable sensors has great potentials to help quickly build stable and secure information technology systems for the early detection, tracking, and control of SARS-CoV-2.

References

1. Zhou F, Yu T, Du R, Fan G, Liu Y, Liu Z, et al. Clinical course and risk factors for mortality of adult inpatients with COVID-19 in Wuhan, China: a retrospective cohort study. *Lancet* 2020;**395**:1054–62. https://doi.org/10.1016/S0140-6736(20)30566-3.
2. Gewin V. Five tips for moving teaching online as COVID-19 takes hold. *Nature* 2020;**580**:295–6.

3. Dehghani MH, Roy S, Karri RR. Novel coronavirus (COVID-19) in environmental engineering perspective. *Environ Sci Pollut Res* 2022;1–3. https://doi.org/10.1007/s11356-022-18572-w.
4. Mousazadeh M, Naghdali Z, Rahimian N, Hashemi M, Paital B, Al-Qodah Z, et al. *Management of environmental health to prevent an outbreak of COVID-19*; 2021. https://doi.org/10.1016/b978-0-323-85780-2.00007-x.
5. Khan AH, Tirth V, Fawzy M, Mahmoud AED, Khan NA, Ahmed S, et al. COVID-19 transmission, vulnerability, persistence and nanotherapy: a review. *Environ Chem Lett* 2021;**19**:2773–87. https://doi.org/10.1007/s10311-021-01229-4.
6. Sampath Kumar NS, Chintagunta AD, Kumar SJ, Roy S, Kumar M. Immunotherapeutics for Covid-19 and post vaccination surveillance. *3 Biotech* 2020;**10**:1–11.
7. Roy S, Baranwal A. Diverse molecular techniques for early diagnosis of COVID-19 and other coronaviruses. In: *Diagnostic strategies for COVID-19 and other coronaviruses*. Singapore: Springer; 2020.
8. Lim SA, Lim TH, Ahmad AN. The applications of biosensing and artificial intelligence technologies for rapid detection and diagnosis of COVID-19 in remote setting. In: *Diagnostic strategies for COVID-19 and other coronaviruses*. Singapore: Springer; 2020.
9. Dastidar MG, Roy S. *Public health management during COVID-19 and applications of point-of-care based biomolecular detection approaches*. Elsevier Inc; 2021. https://doi.org/10.1016/b978-0-323-85780-2.00009-3.
10. Ye Q, Zhou J, Wu H. Using information technology to manage the COVID-19 pandemic: development of a technical framework. Based on practical experience in China. *JMIR Med Inform* 2020;**8**, e19515.
11. Sohrabi C, Alsafi Z, O'Neill N, Khan M, Kerwan A, Al-Jabir A, et al. World Health Organization declares global emergency: a review of the 2019 novel coronavirus (COVID-19). *Int J Surgery* 2020.
12. Ye J. The role of health technology and informatics in a global public health emergency: practices and implications from the COVID-19 pandemic. *JMIR Med Inform* 2020;**8**, e19866.
13. Ye C, Qi L, Wang J, Zheng S. COVID-19 pandemic: advances in diagnosis, treatment, organoid applications and impacts on cancer patient management. *Front Med* 2021;**8**. https://doi.org/10.3389/fmed.2021.606755.
14. Lu R, Zhao X, Li J, Niu P, Yang B, Wu H. Genomic characterisation and epidemiology of 2019 novel coronavirus: implications for virus origins and receptor binding. *Lancet* 2020;**395**:565–74.
15. Xie X, Zhong Z, Zhao W, Zheng C, Wang F, Liu J. Chest CT for typical 2019-nCoV pneumonia: relationship to negative RT-PCR testing. *Radiology* 2020;**296**:E41–5.
16. Grant BD, Anderson CE, Williford JR, Alonzo LF, Glukhova VA. SARS-CoV-2 coronavirus nucleocapsid antigen-detecting half-strip lateral flow assay towards the development of point of care tests using commercially available reagents. *Anal Chem* 2020;**92**:11305–9.
17. Kellner MJ, Koob JG, Gootenberg JS, Abudayyeh OO, Zhang F. SHERLOCK: nucleic acid detection with CRISPR nucleases. *Nat Protoc* 2019;**14**:2986–3012.
18. Olalere OA, Tan MAF, Gan CY, Zafarina Z. Diagnostic advances for inborn error of metabolism (IEM) and screening interventions in selected Asian countries. *J Clin Biomed Sci* 2021;**6**:1–15.
19. Li Z, Yi Y, Luo X, Xiong N, Liu Y, Li S. Development and clinical application of a rapid IgM-IgG combined antibody test for SARS-CoV-2 infection diagnosis. *J Med Virol* 2020;**92**:1518–24.

20. Xu X, Chen P, Wang J, Feng J, Zhou H, Li X. Evolution of the novel coronavirus from the ongoing Wuhan outbreak and modeling of its spike protein for risk of human transmission. *Sci China Life Sci* 2020;**63**:457–60.
21. Golinelli D, Boetto E, Carullo G, Nuzzolese AG, Landini MP, Fantini MP. Adoption of digital technologies in Health Care during the COVID19 pandemic: systematic review of early scientific literature. *J Med Internet Res* 2020;**22**, e22280.
22. Kieny MP, Bekedam H, Dovlo D, Fitzgerald J, Habicht J, Harrison G, et al. Strengthening health systems for universal health coverage and sustainable development. *Perspectives* 2017;**95**:537–9.
23. Evans TG, Paule M. Systems science for universal health coverage. *Ed Bull Etin World Health Organ* 2017;**6736**:17889229.
24. Robinson-bassey GC, Edet OB. Nursing informatics education and use: challenges and prospects in Nigeria. *Glob J Pure Appl Sci* 2015;**21**:171–9.
25. World Health Organization. *Global action plan on the public health response to dementia 2017–2025: overview of the global situation*; 2017. p. 10–36.
26. Christaki E. New technologies in predicting, preventing and controlling emerging infectious diseases. *Virulence* 2015;**6**:558–65. https://doi.org/10.1080/21505594.2015.1040975.
27. Engelthaler DM, Mosley DG, Cheek JE, Levy CE, Komatsu KK, Ettestad P, et al. Climatic and environmental patterns associated with hantavirus pulmonary syndrome, four corners region, United States. *Emerg Infect Dis* 1999;**5**:87–94.
28. Ford TE, Colwell RR, Rose JB, Morse SS, Rogers DJ, Yates TL. Using satellite images of environmental changes to predict infectious disease outbreaks. *Emerg Infect Dis* 2009;**15**:1341–6.
29. Lyon A, Nunn M, Grossel G. Transbound. *Emerg Dis* 2012;**59**:223–32.
30. Graham Thomas CCC, Raynor HA, Bond DS, Luke AK, Gary RRW, Foster D. Weight loss in weight watchers online with and without an activity tracking device compared to control: a randomized trial. *Obesity* 2017;**26**:1014–21.
31. Kathryn Mercer ML, Giangregorio L, Schneider E, Chilana P. 188 Kelly Grindrod, acceptance of commercially available wearable activity trackers among adults aged over and with chronic illness: a mixed-methods evaluation. *JMIR Mhealth Uhealth* 2016;**4**, e7.
32. Sadanandan KS, Bacon A, Shin DW, Alkhalifa SFR, Russo S, Craciun MF, et al. Graphene coated fabrics by ultrasonic spray coating for materials., wearable electronics and smart textiles. *J Phys Mater* 2020;**45**:1–10.
33. Wang H, Han M, Song Y, Zhang H. Design, manufacturing and applications of wearable triboelectric nanogenerators. *Nano Energy* 2020;, 105627.
34. Stepanov D, Towey D, Chen TY, Zhou ZQ. A virtual reality OER platform to deliver phobia-motivated experiences. In: *2020 IEEE 44th Annu. Software, Appl. Conf. IEEE*; 2020. p. 1528–33.
35. Opoku Asare J, van Berkel N, Visuri A, Ferreira E, Hosio S, Goncalves DF, et al. CARE: context awareness for elderly care. *Health Technol* 2020;1–16.
36. Stavropoulos TG, Papastergiou A, Mpaltadoros L, Nikolopoulos S, Kompatsiaris I. IoT wearable sensors and devices in elderly care: a literature review. *Sensors* 2020;**20**:2826.
37. Khan S, Parkinson S, Grant L, Liu N, Mcguire S. Biometric systems utilising health data from wearable devices: applications and future challenges in computer security. *ACM Comput Surv* 2020;**53**:1–29.
38. He J, Xie Z, Yao K, Li D, Liu Y, Gao Z, et al. Trampoline inspired stretchable triboelectric nanogenerators as tactile sensors for epidermal electronics. *Nano Energy* 2020;, 105590.
39. Al Bassam N, Hussain SA, Al Qaraghuli A, Khan J, Sumesh EP, Lavanya V. IoT based wearable device to monitor the signs of quarantined remote patients of COVID-19. *Inform Med Unlocked* 2021;**24**, 100588.

40. Seshadri DR, Davies EV, Harlow ER, Hsu JJ, Knighton SC, Walker TA, et al. Wearable sensors for COVID-19: a call to action to harness our digital infrastructure for remote patient monitoring and virtual assessments. *Front Digit Health* 2020;**2**:8–16.
41. Nooruddin S, Islam MM, Sharna FA. An IoT based device-type invariant fall detection system. *IoT* 2020;**9**, 100130.
42. El-Rashidy N, El-Sappagh S, Islam SM, El-Bakry HM, Abdelrazek S. End-to-end deep learning framework for coronavirus (COVID-19) detection and monitoring. *Electronics* 2020;**9**:1439.
43. Dargazany AR, Stegagno P, Mankodiya K. WearableDL: wearable internet-of-things and deep learning for big data analytics-concept, literature, and future. *Mob Inf Syst* 2018;**4**:2.
44. Qureshi F, Krishnan S. Wearable hardware design for the internet of medical things (IoMT). *Sensors* 2018;**18**:3812.
45. Majumder AKM, ElSaadany YA, Young R, Ucci DR. An energy efficient wearable smart IoT system to predict cardiac arrest. *Adv Hum Comput Interact* 2019;**4**:56.
46. Petrović N, Kocić Đ. Iot-based system for COVID-19 indoor safety monitoring. In: *IcETRAN Belgrade*; 2020.
47. Lalitha R, Hariharan G, Lokesh N. Tracking the Covid zones through geo-fencing technique. *Int J Pervasive Comput Commun* 2020.
48. Asri H, Mousannif H, Al Moatassime H. Reality mining and predictive analytics for building smart applications. *J Big Data* 2019;**6**:1–25.
49. Ates HC, Yetisen AK, Güder F, Dincer C. Wearable devices for the detection of COVID-19. *Nat Electron* 2021;**4**:13–4.
50. IDC. *Worldwide wearables market grows 7.3% in Q3 2017 as smart wearables rise and basic wearables decline, says IDC*; 2017. Press Release from IDC November 30, 2017 https://www.idc.com/getdoc.jsp?containerId=prUS432.
51. Shin G, Jarrahi MH, Fei Y, Karami A, Gafinowitz N, Byun A, et al. Wearable activity trackers, accuracy, adoption, acceptance and health impact: a systematic literature review. *J Biomed Inform* 2019;**93**, 103153.
52. Karen Lamb MB, Huang H-Y, Marturano A. Users' privacy perceptions about wearable technology: examining influence of personality, trust, and usability. In: *Advances in Human Factors in Cybersecurity*; 2016. p. 55–68.

CHAPTER SEVENTEEN

The impact of COVID-19 on regional poverty: Evidence from Latin America

Ebru Topcu
Department of Economics, Nevsehir Haci Bektas Veli University, Nevsehir, Turkey

1. Introduction

The concept of sustainable development, which is expressed as "meeting the needs of the present generation while not compromising the ability of future generations to meet their own needs," was first used within the Brundtland Report published in 1987.[1] In 2015 a global call to action called the Sustainable Development Goals, was made by the United Nations. Sustainable development goals consist of 17 different targets that are aimed to be achieved by 2030. Ending all forms of poverty in all parts of the world is the first of the Sustainable Development Goals. Poverty is one of the key elements of the 2030 Agenda with the motto "Leave No One Behind."[2]

People in all countries and at all income levels are affected to varying degrees by the health and economic consequences of the COVID-19 pandemic. Various studies conducted during the pandemic period show that these effects lead to more serious problems for the poor and vulnerable people.[3] This situation is caused especially by the fact that the people in this group have lower income and education levels, are in precarious employment conditions, and are in lower-skilled occupational groups.[4,5]

Latin America is the region most affected by the COVID-19 pandemic. This health crisis has emerged after slow economic growth and limited progress in social indicators over the past few years. For this reason, it has led to sharp contractions in growth, which has a social and economic impact. All these negativities have caused some important social unrest in some countries in the region, especially in late 2019. Latin America, where vaccines and hospital beds are scarce, has been severely damaged by the intensity of the

COVID-19 and the Sustainable Development Goals
https://doi.org/10.1016/B978-0-323-91307-2.00016-X

pandemic and the deepest recession in the last two centuries. Although it corresponds to 8% of the population of the region, deaths from COVID-19 in the region constitute 30% of the deaths from COVID-19 in the world. In this context, the country's economy contracted by 7%. This rate is more than double when compared the declines in other regions.[5–7]

The most unequal region of the world is Latin America. From 2019 to 2020, 22 million people in the region are included in the category of the poor who cannot meet their basic needs.[a] In total, about a third of Latin America's 600 million residents live in poverty.[b] In other words, it is in the group defined by the United Nations as extreme poverty. Extreme poverty is defined as living on less than $1.90 per day. According to the UN (2020)[10] report, due to the pandemic, Latin America has reached the worst level of extreme poverty in the last 20 years. The number of poor in the region increased by 22 million in 2020 and reached 209 million. This situation is considered the highest level of poverty in the last 12 years.

The main purpose of this study is to examine the impact of COVID-19 on poverty in the Latin American region. In the light of the explanations earlier, it is possible to list the main reasons for choosing Latin America in the study as follows.

- Latin America is one of the regions with the highest income inequality[c] and poverty.
- Latin America is among the regions with the highest number of cases and deaths due to COVID-19.
- The negative effects of COVID-19 in the labor market have been predominantly on the informal sector. In this context, Latin America is one of the countries with the highest unregistered employment.

The remainder of the study is planned as follows: After the introduction, the second section gives brief information about COVID-19 in Latin America. The third section examines the impact of COVID-19 on poverty and some related macroeconomic indicators. The fourth section discusses recovery policies that can be implemented to reduce poverty in the post-COVID-19. Finally, the fifth section gives concluding remarks.

[a] Since 1999, the number of people living in extreme poverty worldwide has dropped by more than 1 billion. This achievement in reducing poverty has been turned back due to the COVID-19.[8]

[b] Poverty is not having enough money or access to resources to enjoy a decent standard of living.[9]

[c] Latin America is the region experiencing the highest income inequality in the world while 8 out of the world's top 20 countries are Latin American.[11]

2. COVID-19 in Latin America

An epidemic of unknown cause was reported in Wuhan, China, in December 2019. On February 11, 2020, the outbreak was named as COVID-19 by the World Health Organization (WHO)[12] COVID-19 has gained a global dimension as of February 2020. Novel coronavirus (COVID-19) is a new type of coronavirus that had impacted countries at a global scale. COVID-19, which is highly contagious and causes death rates, was declared a pandemic by the World Health Organization in March 2020. With the declaration of COVID-19 as a pandemic by the World Health Organization, governments have started to implement social distance and flexible working policies.[13]

The management of public health is extremely important during the pandemic period. Many restrictions are in place to control transmission within the population. In a process where there is no vaccine, these policies have been evaluated as effective solutions to prevent the spread of the pandemic. It has exacerbated the current situation of disadvantaged poor households, where informal work is common and there is no possibility to work from home. This process, in which restraint policies are implemented, has increased the risk of increasing absolute poverty in poor regions of the world.[14,15]

The World Health Organization declared Latin America as the epicenter of the pandemic in May 2020. More than 40% of the world's COVID-19 deaths occurred in this region. At the same time, the total infection rate has exceeded 6.5 million cases.[16]

Table 1 presents the number of COVID-19 cases and deaths from COVID-19 in selected Latin American countries. Brazil is the most affected Latin American country by the COVID-19. As of June 2021, the country reported nearly 16.8 million cases. It was pursued by Argentina, with 3.88 million confirmed cases of the pandemic. In total, the region registered over 33 million diagnosed patients, besides a growing number of fatal coronavirus cases. As of June 2021, a total of 1.2 million people died because of COVID-19 in Latin America and the Caribbean. Specially, Brazil reported approximately 470,000 deaths. In consequence of the COVID-19, Brazil's GDP forecast is expected to drop by nearly 6% in 2020. Also, Mexico ranked second in number of deaths, with 228,000 cases.

Table 1 Number of confirmed cases and deaths due to the novel coronavirus (COVID-19) in Latin America.

Country	Number of cases	Number of deaths
Brazil	16,803,472	469,388
Argentina	3,884,447	79,873
Colombia	3,488,046	90,353
Mexico	2,426,822	228,362
Peru	1,968,693	185,380
Chile	1,403,101	29,598
Ecuador	429,817	20,706
Bolivia	380,457	14,832
Panama	380,207	6388
Paraguay	364,702	9498
Costa Rica	325,779	4124
Dominican Republic	297,119	3642
Uruguay	304,411	4460
Venezuela	238,013	2689
Honduras	240,382	6415
Guatemala	258,633	8238
Nicaragua	7481	187
Cuba	145,852	985
El Salvador	74,141	2260
Jamaica	48,638	951

Statista. Number of confirmed cases of the novel coronavirus (COVID-19) in Latin America and the Caribbean. 2021. https://www.statista.com/statistics/1101643/latin-america-caribbean-coronavirus-cases/. [Accessed 5 June 2021].

3. The impact of COVID-19 on poverty

When the prepandemic period is examined, it is seen that the goal of ending poverty by 2030 is far from the target. Forecasts made in the pre-COVID-19 period show that 6% of the global population will live in extreme poverty by 2030. It is also predicted that an additional 71 million people will live in extreme poverty due to COVID-19. Although the policies implemented within the scope of the sustainable development goal reduce income inequality in some countries, the economic recession caused by the pandemic will push millions into poverty and inequality.[17]

In the prepandemic period, the slowdown in the progress of the goal of ending poverty, which is the first of the sustainable development goals, was remarkable. With the pandemic, the whole world has been facing the biggest economic recession since the Great Depression. This is expected to

Table 2 Proportion of people living below \$1.90 a day, 2010–2015, 2019 nowcast, and forecast before and during COVID-19 (percentage).

Years	Forecast before COVID-19	Current forecast
2010	15.7	
2011	13.7	
2012	12.8	
2013	11.2	
2015	10	
2018	8.4	
2019	8.2	8.2
2020 forecast	7.7	8.8
2021 forecast	7.4	8.7

United Nations. Sustainable development goals (SDGs) Report. 2020. https://unstats.un.org/sdgs/report/2020/goal-01/. [Accessed 20 June 2021].

make stable developments in poverty reduction even worse. Therefore the goal of ending poverty by 2030 is not likely to be achieved.

Health-related problems such as pandemics have an impact on the socioeconomic status of countries. Given that, the health problems experienced by individuals affect their productivity and lead to a decrease in employment rates. Income losses in parallel with these developments increase poverty rates. In Latin America, one of the most unequal regions of the world, COVID-19 has deepened the deterioration in macroeconomic indicators. Table 2 presents the extreme poverty rates over various years in the pre- and during COVID-19 periods.

According to Table 2, there has been a steady decline in poverty rates over the pre-COVID-19 period (2010–2019). The poverty rate, which was calculated as 15.7% in 2010, was calculated as 8.2% in 2019. In the pre-COVID-19 era, poverty rates are expected to be 7.4% and 7.2%, in 2020 and 2021, respectively. According to the poverty rate estimations based on the developments during COVID-19, the poverty rate is expected to increase to 8.8% in 2020. In 2021 it is foreseen that the poverty rate will be 8.7. Fig. 1 illustrates the mobility to workplaces by levels of regional poverty. In this figure, poverty is measured as the share of people in region living below national/international poverty lines.[d] As can be seen in the figure, poverty groups follow similar mobility patterns during the early COVID-19 era. Subsequent to COVID-19 measures taken, a sharp mobility drop has been experienced in particular for regions with lower poverty rates.

[d] Low % of poor is defined if region's poverty is below 25th; medium % of poor is defined if region's poverty rates is between 25th and 75th; high % of poor is defined if region's poverty rate is above 75th percentile.[14]

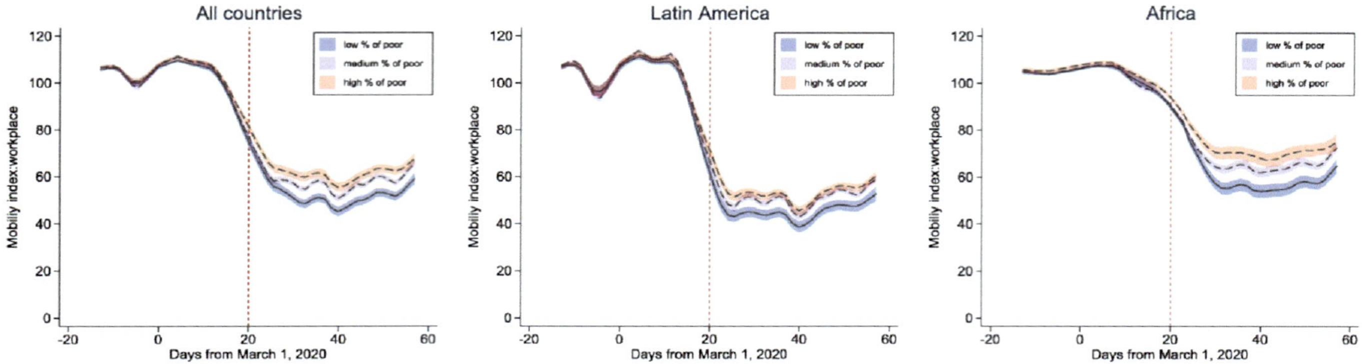

Fig. 1 Mobility to workplaces by levels of regional poverty.[14]

It is very important for effective policy choices to determine what factors lead to poverty or which factors deepen poverty. These factors may vary from country to country. Poverty is a complex phenomenon which leads to many problems such as income inequality, high vulnerability to disasters, unemployment, poor health, and lack of education.[18] Poverty is also affected by these problems. Therefore only macroeconomic indicators affecting poverty will be included herein.

3.1 Economic growth

When the negative effects of the pandemic began to appear in Latin America, the region was already facing some difficulties. Over the period 2014–2019, economic growth was 0.4% and this was the lowest level recorded since 1951.[10]

The expectations for the rise in poverty rates after COVID-19 are closely related to the economic growth rates in the region. For this reason, providing information about GDP rates in the region will contribute to a better understanding of the situation. Table 3 presents the gross domestic product (GDP) growth in selected Latin American countries.

Table 3 Gross domestic product (GDP) in Latin America.

	Years			
Countries	**2019**	**2020**	**2021**	**2022**
Argentina	−2.09	−9.96	5.84	2.48
Brazil	1.41	−4.06	3.66	2.57
Chile	1.02	−5.84	6.17	3.82
Colombia	3.28	−6.85	5.15	3.62
Costa Rica	2.17	−4.8	2.6	3.3
Dominican Republic	5.05	−6.73	5.48	4.96
Ecuador	0.01	−7.5	2.5	1.3
El Salvador	2.38	−8.58	4.2	2.84
Guatemala	3.85	−1.5	4.5	4
Honduras	2.65	−8	4.5	3.3
Mexico	−0.06	−8.24	5	3
Nicaragua	−3.88	−3	0.24	2.7
Panama	3.04	−17.95	12.05	5
Paraguay	−0.03	−0.9	4	4
Peru	2.23	−11.12	8.5	5.16
Uruguay	0.33	−5.7	3	3.1
Venezuela	−35	−30	−10	−5

Statista: Impact of the novel coronavirus (COVID-19) on gross domestic product (GDP) growth in selected countries in Latin America. 2021. https://www.statista.com/statistics/1105099/impact-coronavirus-gdp-latin-america-country/. [Accessed 28 June 2021].

According to Table 3, Mexico's GDP was forecasted to rise by 5% during 2021. Mexico was one of the Latin American countries that encountered the worst recession after the pandemic, as its GDP dropped 8% in 2020. Among the biggest economies in Latin America, Brazil was anticipated to experience one of the least GDP growth in 2021, about 3.7%.

The socioeconomic effects of the COVID-19 pandemic have led to some unprecedented developments in the region. Despite the heterogeneity between countries across the region, all countries have been affected by the COVID-19 crisis. On average, GDP growth declines by more than 9% in 2020. However, poverty rates will increase by 4.4% on average. The crisis in question will cause loss of income especially for approximately 40% of the workers who do not have any social assistance support and for the small firms that do not have the capacity to cope with this shock. 2.7 million businesses, mostly smaller ones, are likely to close. This will result in the loss of 8.5 million jobs. Due to the sharp decline in economic growth, the decline in poverty and income inequality is expected to reverse in 2020. Under the expectation of a 9% contraction in GDP, poverty in Latin America and the Caribbean is projected to increase by 6.9% year-on-year. Extreme poverty is likely to increase by 4.5%.[19]

3.2 Unemployment and labor sector

Job and income losses result in an increase in poverty. The economic contraction experienced during the pandemic has also an impact on the labor market. The quarantines, restrictions applied within the scope of the fight against COVID-19, and the resulting economic contractions have led to an increase in unemployment rates. It is important to consider the changes in the labor market while investigating the increase in poverty in the region.

One of the reasons why the pandemic crisis differs across countries is the rate of informal employment and the economic support mechanism provided to workers in this sector. In most Latin American countries, more than half of the workforce works informally. According to ILO estimations, the average informality rate in the region is 54%. This is an indication that the labor market has not been able to play a functional role. However, the low productivity performance of the region in the early 1990s draws attention as a characteristic feature that distinguishes Latin America from other developing regions in the world. Most of the workers in this sector lack access to quality healthcare. They are also at greater risk of infection due to the nature

Table 4 Estimates and projections for labor market.

	2019	2020	2021	2022
Unemployment rate (percentages)	8.0	10.3	11.1	8.9
Employment-to-population ratio (percentages)	59.2	52.9	54.7	58.1
Potential labor force rate (percentages)	4.9	7.2	6.1	5.0
Extreme working poverty (<US$1.90 PPP) (per day) (percentages)	3.0	3.8	–	–

International Labour Organization (ILO). World employment and social outlook: trends 2021. 2021. https://www.ilo.org/global/research/global-reports/weso/trends2021/lang–en/index.htm. [Accessed 30 June 2021].

of their jobs. In the pre-COVID-19 period (in 2019), the economy and labor market of the region were performing poorly (Table 4).[10,20,21]

In 2019 the unemployment rate in the region was 8%. In 2020 when the effects of the pandemic began to be seen, the unemployment rate rose to 10.3%. Unemployment rate is predicted to rise to 11.1% in 2021. The postpandemic recovery in the labor market is expected to take place in 2022. Although the unemployment rate is expected to be 8.9% in 2022, it is observed that unemployment rates have not returned to prepandemic conditions. While the employment to population ratio was 59.2% in 2019, it was 52.9% in 2020. Although this rate is expected to increase in 2021 and 2022, it is estimated that prepandemic rates will not be reached. While the potential labor force participation rate[e] was 4.9% in the prepandemic period, it increased to 7.2% in 2020. This rate, calculated when the effects of the pandemic began to be seen in 2020, is remarkable. The potential labor force participation rate, which was 7.2 in 2020, is expected to gradually decrease in 2021 and 2022. Extreme working poverty,[f] which was calculated as 3% in 2019, increased to 3.8% in 2020.

The contraction in economic activities resulting from the pandemics has particularly affected vulnerable groups. Most of these people are self-employed. Therefore these people are at risk of facing poverty. In the prepandemic period, 40% of total workers are not protected by safety nets such as labor-based social security insurance and basic supports. This situation has brought the risk of rising poverty and income inequality rates, which have been stable since 2014.[19]

[e] The potential labor force refers to nonemployed persons who are looking for a job but would become available to work only within a short subsequent period, or who are not currently looking but want to be employed and are available to do so.[22]

[f] Extreme working poverty rates refer to the shares of workers living in households with a daily per capita income or consumption less than US$1.90 in purchasing power parity (PPP).[22]

The impacts of the COVID-19 on the people's living conditions are deepened by the gradual rise in poverty and extreme poverty and the slowdown in the reducement of inequality in the 5 years prior to the pandemic. In spite of the development made in the reduction of poverty and inequality between 2002 and 2014, economic and social progress of region was already showing distinct indications of stagnation before the COVID-19.[23]

In some countries women may be suffering more exposure to the COVID-19 due to their overrepresentation in frontline health worker and their care liabilities in many households. Women meet other specific health risks as part of the coronavirus, because strict lockdown precautions may cause high levels of domestic violence.[24]

Considering the traditional and sexist role distribution, women have taken on a greater burden both physically and mentally than men during the pandemic period. Women are primary care providers in the region. At the same time, the daily time they allocate to unpaid home and care services is three times more than men. However, in some countries in the region, women are more likely to be employed in informal work. For this reason, they are more affected by decreases in economic activities. For example, in Mexico, 50% of men work in informal jobs, while 58% of women work in informal jobs.[16]

4. Postpandemic economic recovery for reducing poverty

Implementation of various economic policies is a necessity to reduce the poverty that has deepened with COVID-19. Sustainable development goals for poverty eradication should be addressed first in order to make policy implications for poverty alleviation after COVID-19. In this context, it is possible to summarize the sustainable development goals aimed at ending poverty as follows[18]:

- By 2030, reduce at least half the proportion of all men, women and children of all ages living in poverty in all its dimensions, according to national definitions.
- Implement nationally social protection systems and measures for all and achieve substantial coverage of the vulnerable and poor by 2030.
- By 2030, ensure that all women and men, particularly the poor and their defences, have equal rights over economic resources, access to basic services, ownership and control of land and other forms of property, inheritance, natural resources, new technologies and financial services.

Within the scope of sustainable development goals, improvement measures to reduce poverty that can be taken after COVID-19 can be listed as follows[10,19,22,23]:

- COVID-19 has affected the most poor and vulnerable groups in the region. Among this poor group, especially women, children, and immigrants have been the most affected segment. Therefore social protection and support assistance should be implemented for women, children, and underserved groups.
- In Latin America, one of the regions with the highest informal employment, labor policies, curfews, and restrictions applied due to COVID-19 have affected those employed in the informal sector the most. For this reason, policies that will reduce informal employment and provide new job areas that provide occupational safety and health support to these people should be implemented. In this context, investments in labor-intensive sectors should be increased.
- Reducing poverty should not be evaluated only from an economic perspective. Investments in human capital[g] such as health and education also directly or indirectly affect poverty. Latin America is the region where schools are closed the most during the pandemic period. In this context, compensatory education programs should be given to groups that cannot achieve equal opportunities in education.
- The COVID-19 pandemic has highlighted the importance of health infrastructure in a country. For this reason, investments should be made in the health sector for both physical and human capital.
- During the pandemic period, contractions were experienced in many branches of economic activity for various reasons, especially the disruptions in the global supply chain. This situation, which caused an increase in costs, led to contractions in production. At the end of this process, some workplaces were closed, while others reduced the number of employed workers. These sectors should be supported through subsidies.

5. Conclusion

COVID-19, which is an ongoing transmission across the globe, has directly or indirectly caused many economic and social problems.

[g] Health investments in human capital increase the productivity of labor. The productivity of healthier individuals and thus their contribution to production is higher. Health problems can lead to increased poverty. The inability of people to work due to health problems may affect their economic status and lead to inequalities.[25]

Although the COVID-19 pandemic affects all countries of the world, these socioeconomic effects have been felt more deeply, especially in developing countries. In this context, the aim of this study is to examine the impact of COVID-19 on poverty in Latin America given the worst income distribution and poverty across the globe as well as being the most affected region by COVID-19.

The region's economy, which was already fragile in the prepandemic period, experienced an economic contraction, as in the whole world, with the outbreak of the COVID-19 pandemic, and unemployment rates increased. The measures taken within the scope of combating the pandemic have had more negative effects, especially on the poor and vulnerable groups. The large number of labor force working in the informal sector can be seen as the reason of this situation.

With the gradual increase in poverty and extreme poverty and the slowdown in the reduction of inequality over the 5 years before the outbreak, the pandemic further deepened the deterioration in the living standards of the population across the region. Despite the positive developments such as the progress made in reducing poverty and income inequality and the expansion of the middle-income class over the 2002–2014 period, the economic development in the region was already in a stagnation period over the prepandemic period. These socioeconomic disruptions that emerged with the pandemic have led to the move away from the goal of ending poverty by 2030, which ranked first in sustainable development goals.

Experiences during the pandemic show that it is necessary to prioritize an inclusive development strategy. It is also noteworthy that the policies implemented either at the global or at the national level are less in solidarity with poorer nations and poorer people.[26] It can be suggested that the policies to be implemented within the scope of the goal of "ending poverty" should be sustainable policies that embrace all segments of the society.

In the postpandemic period, several policies should be implemented for economic recovery, primarily to reduce poverty. The first of these policies should be the social support and aid policies, especially for the poor and disadvantaged groups. The second should be devoted to labor market policies. In particular, policies that create new employment opportunities should be implemented. In this way, unregistered employment can be reduced and job opportunities that provide social security can be increased. Third, policies that support human capital, such as education and health, should be implemented. These policies will be effective in reducing poverty directly or indirectly. Finally, support should be given to sectors experiencing economic contraction. These support policies will be effective in both creating employment opportunities and reviving production.

References

1. Halkos G, Gkampoura E-C. Where do we stand on the 17 sustainable development goals? An overview on progress. *Econ Anal Policy* 2021;**70**:94–122.
2. Filho WL, Lovren VO, Will W, Salvia AL, Frankenberger F. Poverty: a central barrier to the implementation of the UN sustainable development goals. *Environ Sci Policy* 2021;**125**:96–104.
3. Mousazadeh M, Naghdali Z, Rahimian N, Hashemi M, Paital B, Al-Qodah Z, et al. Management of environmental health to prevent an outbreak of COVID-19: a review. In: *Environmental and Health Management of Novel Coronavirus Disease (COVID-19)*; 2021. p. 235–67.
4. Attanasio O, Rajan R. The invisible COVID-19 graveyard: intergenerational losses for the poorest young people and actions to address a human development pandemic. In: *UNDP Covid-19 policy document series*; 2020. LAC C19 PDS No. 26.
5. Lustig N, Tommasi M. Covid-19 and social protection of poor and vulnerable groups in Latin America: a conceptual framework. In: *UNDP Covid-19 policy document series*; 2020. UNDP LAC C19 PDS No. 8.
6. The Commonwealth Fund. *Latin America's COVID-19 crisis and implications for the rest of the world*; 2021 https://www.commonwealthfund.org/blog/2021/latin-americas-covid-19-crisis-and-implications-rest-world. [Accessed 25 September 2021].
7. Pan American Health Organization. *PAHO warns that only one in four people in Latin America and the Caribbean has been fully vaccinated against COVID-19*; 2021 https://www.paho.org/en/news/1-9-2021-paho-warns-only-one-four-people-latin-america-and-caribbean-has-been-fully-vaccinated. [Accessed 12 July 2021].
8. Mahler DG, Yonzan N, Lakner C, Aguilar RAC, Wu H. *Updated estimates of the impact of COVID-19 on global poverty: turning the corner on the pandemic in 2021?* World Bank Blogs; 2021. https://blogs.worldbank.org/opendata/updated-estimates-impact-covid-19-global-poverty-looking-back-2020-and-outlook-2021. [Accessed 6 June 2021].
9. Habitat for Humanity Great Britain. *What is poverty?*; 2022 *https://www.habitatforhumanity.org.uk/blog/2018/09/relative-absolute-poverty/*. [Accessed 18 September 2021].
10. United Nations (UN). *Policy brief: the impact of COVID-19 on Latin America and the Caribbean*; 2020 https://guyana.un.org/sites/default/files/2020-07/SG%20Policy%20brief%20COVID%20LAC%20%28English%29_10%20July.pdf. [Accessed 1 July 2021].
11. Amarante V, Galván M, Mancero X. Inequality in Latin America: a global measurement. *CEPAL Rev* 2016;**118**:25–44.
12. Mousazadeh M, Naghdali Z, Rahimian N, Hashemi M, Paital B, Al-Qodah Z, et al. Management of environmental health to prevent an outbreak of COVID-19: a review. In: Dehghani MH, Karri RR, Roy S, editors. *Environmental and health management of novel coronavirus disease (COVID-19)*. Academic Press; 2021. ISBN: 978-0-323-85780-2.
13. Lim SA, Lim TH, Ahmad AN. The applications of biosensing and artificial intelligence technologies for rapid detection and diagnosis of COVID-19 in remote setting. In: Chandra P, Roy S, editors. *Diagnostic strategies for COVID-19 and other coronaviruses. Medical virology: from pathogenesis to disease control*. Singapore: Springer; 2020.
14. Bargain O, Aminjonov U. Poverty and COVID-19 in Africa and Latin America. *World Dev* 2021;**142**, 105422.
15. Dastidar MG, Roy S. Public health management during COVID-19 and applications of point-of-care based biomolecular detection approaches. In: Dehghani MH, Karri RR,

Roy S, editors. *Environmental and health management of novel coronavirus disease (COVID-19)*. Academic Press; 2021. ISBN: 978-0-323-85780-2.
16. OECD. *Tackling Coronavirus (Covid-19) contributing to a global effort, COVID-19 in Latin America and the Caribbean: regional socio-economic implications and policy priorities*; 2020 https://read.oecd-ilibrary.org/view/?ref=129_129904-k3xp17fqbl&title=COVID-19-in-Latin-America-and-the-Caribb. [Accessed 15 July 2021].
17. The Lancet Public Health. Will the COVID-19 pandemic threaten the SDGs? *Lancet Public Health* 2020;**5**(9), e460.
18. United Nations. *Sustainable development goals, goal 1: no poverty*; 2022 https://www.undp.org/sustainable-development-goals#no-poverty. [Accessed 13 July 2021].
19. OECD. Overview: digital transformation for an inclusive and sustainable recovery post Covid-19. In: *Latin American economic outlook 2020: digital transformation for building back better*. Paris: OECD Publishing; 2020. https://doi.org/10.1787/329ec061-en [Accessed 19 June 2021].
20. Levy S. *Poverty in Latin America: where do we come from, where are we going?* ; 2016 https://www.brookings.edu/opinions/poverty-in-latin-america-where-do-we-come-from-where-are-we-going/. [Accessed 3June 2021].
21. Economic Commission for Latin America and the Caribbean (ECLAC)/International Labour Organization (ILO). *Employment situation in Latin America and the Caribbean, work in times of pandemic: the challenges of the coronavirus disease (COVID-19)*; 2020 https://repositorio.cepal.org/bitstream/handle/11362/45582/4/S2000306_en.pdf. [Accessed 7 June 2021].
22. International Labour Organization (ILO). *World employment and social outlook: trends 2021*; 2021 https://www.ilo.org/global/research/global-reports/weso/trends2021/lang-en/index.htm. [Accessed 30 June 2021].
23. Economic Commission for Latin America and the Caribbean (ECLAC). *Social Panorama of Latin America 2020*. (LC/PUB.2021/2-P/Rev.1), Santiago; 2021.
24. World Bank Group. *Poverty and shared prosperity 2020: reversals of fortune*; 2020 https://openknowledge.worldbank.org/bitstream/handle/10986/34496/211602ov.pdf. [Accessed 13 July 2021].
25. Shulla. The COVID-19 pandemic and the achievement of the SDGs. Virtual inter-agency expert group meeting on implementation of the Third United Nations decade for the eradication of poverty (2018–2027). In: *Accelerating global actions for a world without poverty*; 2021.
26. Gupta J, Bavinck J, Ros-Tonen M, Asubonteng K, Bosch H, Van Ewijk E, et al. COVID-19, poverty and inclusive development. *World Dev* 2021;**145**, 105527.

CHAPTER EIGHTEEN

Status quo of outbreak and control of COVID-19 in Southeast Asian Nations during the first phase: A case study for sustainable cities and communities

Malai Zeiti Binti Sheikh Abdul Hamid[a,b], **Rama Rao Karri**[b,c], **and Yajnasri Karri**[d]

[a]Centre for Communication, Teaching & Learning (CCTL), Universiti Teknologi Brunei, Bandar Seri Begawan, Brunei Darussalam
[b]Wellness Research Thrust, Universiti Teknologi Brunei, Bandar Seri Begawan, Brunei Darussalam
[c]Petroleum and Chemical Engineering, Faculty of Engineering, Universiti Teknologi Brunei, Bandar Seri Begawan, Brunei Darussalam
[d]Jerudong International School, Bandar Seri Begawan, Brunei Darussalam

1. Introduction

The Association of Southeast Asian Nations (ASEAN) is an important trading partner to other global countries, including the United States, China, Japan, the United Kingdom, Australia, and other leading countries. ASEAN has a GDP of 9.7 trillion and a total population of 655 million and a highly strategic territory of the South China Sea. Indonesia is the largest economy in Southeast Asia (SEA), the 16th largest economy in the world and home to the largest Muslim population of 270 million people worldwide. Three of the top 20 busiest ports in the world are located in SEA, with Singapore being the second busiest port globally.[1] Singapore is also the 4th largest exporter of high-tech products, while Brunei is the 4th largest producer of Liquefied Natural Gas (LNG) globally. Malaysia is one of the top exporters of natural rubber and palm oil. In terms of international trade, it is projected that by 2050, the collective economies of ASEAN are expected to grow into the 4th largest economies in the world. Currently, ASEAN represents the 4th largest import market from the United States[2] and continues to show trade growth yearly.

COVID-19 and the Sustainable Development Goals
https://doi.org/10.1016/B978-0-323-91307-2.00015-8

Since the global outbreak of the COVID-19 in Wuhan, China in December 2019, Thailand was the first country in SEA to record its first case. Singapore, Indonesia, and the Philippines have recorded the highest number of cases among ASEAN countries as of 24 June 2020 (global first phase), with Singapore having the highest number of cases, while Brunei, Vietnam, and Laos seem to have fully recovered and are virtually free of the COVID-19 virus.

Throughout the duration of the pandemic, ASEAN nations have received great support in terms of finance and health-related equipment and consumables from organizations and countries around the world, including the United States, China, Japan, South Korea, the World Bank, and the United Nations.[3]

Layos and Pena,[4] in their recent study, reviewed the role of innovation in mitigating the COVID-19 in ASEAN-5 economies. Their study has found a significant relationship between the level of innovation and a country's ability to respond to a crisis. Abuza's[5] assessment of the COVID-19 spread in Southeast Asia states that no government should be blamed for a pandemic, but they should be scrutinized for how they respond. This chapter further suggests that four interrelated criteria determine the success or disaster of the spread of the COVID-19 in each country, namely, leadership, government transparency, legitimacy, planning and preparedness.

The motivation of this chapter is to compare the assessment of COVID-19 cases within ASEAN countries in the first phase. Evaluating the virus spread in each country, and the outcomes provide insights into the strength and stability of a country's leadership, politics, and people, thus leading to sustainable cities and communities (SDG 11). This study is a test case to analyze the impact and recovery of COVID-19 cases in each country. So far, there is no article available in the open literature focused on analyzing the spread of COVID-19 in Southeast Asian nations. As the collective economies of ASEAN are projected to grow to the top 5 economies of the world, this study will present the overview of ASEAN countries in terms of controlling pandemics.

2. Methods

2.1 Study area

The research area reviews and analyzes the spread of COVID-19 cases among member countries of the Association of Southeast Asian Nations (ASEAN), namely, Brunei, Cambodia, Indonesia, Laos, Malaysia,

Fig. 1 Global distribution of ASEAN countries.

Myanmar, the Philippines, Singapore, Thailand, and Vietnam. Member countries of ASEAN are illustrated in Fig. 1.

2.2 Data collection

For this research study, the data set for COVID-19 is collected for all the ASEAN countries from the day of the first case to 24 June 2020 (tentative global first phase). Data was extracted from multiple sources of each respective ASEAN country. The sources are as follows:

(1) National Ministry of Health websites

(2) "Our World in Data" website that helped to provide graphs and charts for analysis

(3) Multiple COVID-19 dedicated articles in respective Southeast Asian nations

This data includes relevant information pertaining to the complete timeline of cases recorded, the number of infected cases, deaths, recoveries, active, serious, number of tests conducted, etc.

2.3 Data analysis

The analysis is conducted on available data as of 24 June 2020 derived from the total and daily infected COVID-19 cases of each ASEAN country. To understand the spread of COVID-19 for the foreseeable future in all Southeast Asian countries and estimate the lasting of the coronavirus pandemic in these countries, the Susceptible-Infected-Recovered (SIR) model, which is a well-known mathematical modeling of infectious diseases, is applied.[6,7,8] This model reasonably predicts the spread of contagious diseases transmitted from human to human.[9] This model works as a compartment model, as shown as follows:

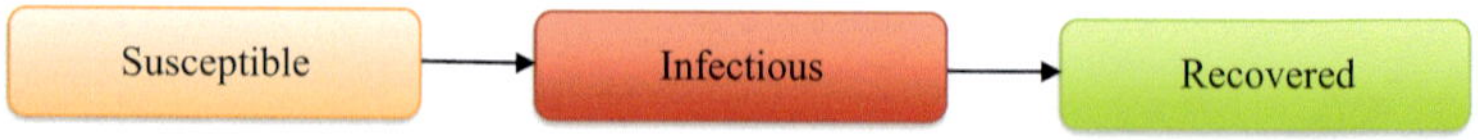

The SIR model is expressed as follows:

$$\frac{dS}{dt} = -\frac{\beta IS}{N}$$

$$\frac{dI}{dt} = -\frac{\beta IS}{N} - \gamma I$$

$$\frac{dR}{dt} = -\gamma I$$

where $S(t)$, $I(t)$, and $R(t)$ are the number of susceptible, infected, and recovered persons expressed as a function of time, t. The important model parameters of this model are the contact rate (β) and the average infectious period ($1/\gamma$). The total size (N) is computed as $N = S + I + R = constant$.

The earlier model equations are solved using the initial conditions: $S(0) = So$, $I(0) = Io$, $R(0) = Ro$.

The basic reproduction ratio ($Ro = \beta/\gamma$) is an important metric that is derived as the expected number of new infections from a single infection in a population where all subjects are susceptible.

This SIR epidemic model is a data-driven model that assumes a constant population, uniform mixing of the people, and eqi-likely infection.[10,11] The model parameters are obtained by minimizing of the objective function, which is the sum of the square of error (SSE). The schematic diagram of the epidemy evaluation graph is shown in Fig. 2. Here the epidemy evaluation graph regions (colors) are separated as epidemy phases. Here, light red represents the fast growth phase, yellow represents the transition to the steady-state phase, and green represents the pandemic ending phase.

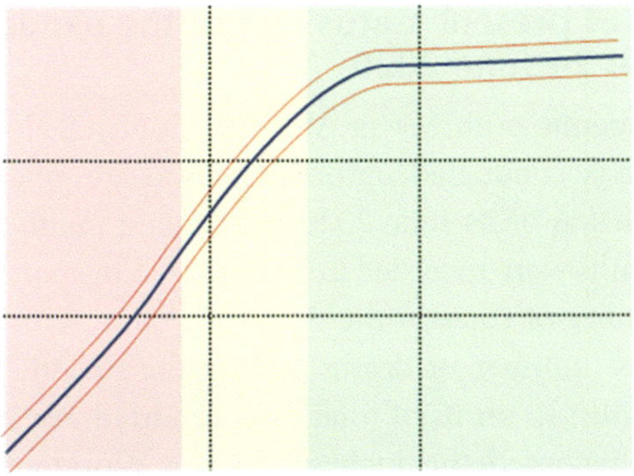

Fig. 2 Schematic representation of the epidemy evaluation graph resulted from the SIR model.

3. Results and discussion

3.1 Analysis of ASEAN countries

SARS-CoV2 (COVID-19) outbreak, which originated in Wuhan, China, has rapidly spread across the nations and devastated the world with human loss and derailed the economy of all nations. COVID-19 spreads from human to human, and the only way to limit the propagation within the community is to identify the people suffering from COVID-19 symptoms and isolate them, as shown in Fig. 3. This isolation is called a chain break, which is being followed by every country on this earth.[12]

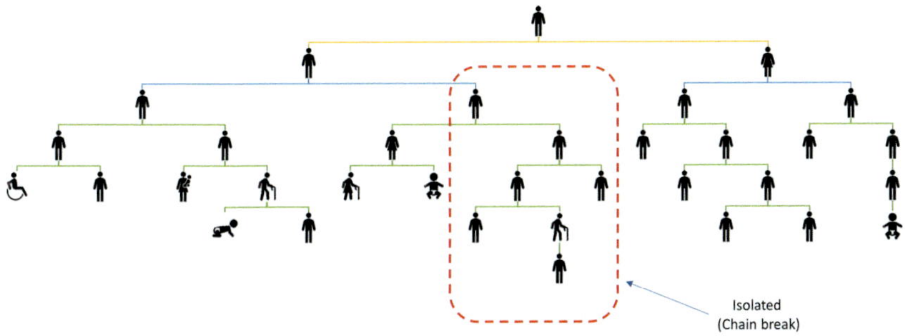

Fig. 3 Depiction of SARS-CoV2 (COVID-19) spread within the community.

3.2 Overview of present status quo of the pandemic outbreak in ASEAN as of 24 June 2020

The present pandemic outbreak in ASEAN countries, along with population and total tests conducted upto this period are given in Table 1. It can be noticed that as of 24 June 2020, the highest number of cases as well as the highest deaths were recorded in Indonesia. Singapore has reported the 2nd highest number of cases in the ASEAN region. However, it has also reported the least number of deaths among the nations, which reported around 3000 deaths. In terms of total cases reported per 1 million population, Singapore recorded the highest. As per Worldometers, Singapore has done more tests per 1 million people[13] than other ASEAN countries. Interestingly, Laos is the least affected country, among all the ASEAN countries. It can also be observed that Brunei and Laos have zero active cases, and Cambodia has only three active cases. In terms of recovery rate, Laos, Cambodia, Brunei, Malaysia, Thailand, and Vietnam have reported more than 90% recovery rate. There are 136,729 cases reported in ASEAN, and 76,703 cases recovered, meaning which that 56.1% of COVID-19 patients were entirely recovered.

3.3 Overview of the timeline of the pandemic outbreak

A review of the timeline of the first case reported and other vital statistics for ASEAN countries as of 24 June 2020 is presented in Table 2. Among the ASEAN countries, the first case was reported on 13 January 2020 in Thailand, whereas there was a rapid spread in ASEAN countries during the last week of January 2020. In Indonesia, even though the first case was logged on 2 March 2020, it can also be observed that the pandemic has extensively spread among the country within a short span. Cambodia has recorded a higher number of days, with zero cases per day. This number is a great sign to indicate that the pandemic is well in control in this country. Also, the metrics like total cases on day 30, 50, and 100 presented in Table 2 indicates the spread of COVID-19 cases. The number of cases in Singapore, the Philippines, and Indonesia has grown exponentially from day 50 to 100. A lower increase of cases indicates the rapid/controlled spread of infection. It was observed that Vietnam and Cambodia had reported more than 100 days with less than 5 cases reported/day, which indicates that the pandemic is well in control.

The spread of COVID-19 among these countries is shown in Fig. 4. This profile indicates the timelines and the total number of cases reported since

Table 1 Compilation of data for ASEAN countries as of 24 June 2020.

Country	Total cases	Total deaths	Total recovered	Active cases	Recovery (%)	Tot cases/1 M pop	Deaths/1 M pop	Total tests	Tests/1 M pop	Population
Indonesia	49,009	2573	19,658	26,778	40.1%	179	9	689,452	2521	273,468,761
Singapore	42,736	26	36,299	6411	84.9%	7306	4	684,359	116,994	5,849,533
Philippines	32,295	1204	8656	22,435	26.8%	295	11	631,063	5760	109,551,348
Malaysia	8596	121	8231	244	95.8%	266	4	704,336	21,767	32,357,654
Thailand	3158	58	3038	62	96.2%	45	0.8	468,175	6708	69,797,375
Vietnam	352	–	329	23	93.5%	4		275,000	2826	97,322,679
Myanmar	293	6	208	79	71.0%	5	0.1	66,353	1220	54,403,606
Brunei	141	3	138	0	97.9%	322[a]	7[a]	27,385	62,608	437,402
Cambodia	130	–	127	3	97.7%	8		33,211	1987	16,714,185
Laos	19	–	19	0	100.0%	3		13,507	1857	7,273,342
ASEAN	136,729	3991	76,703	56,035	56.1%	8433	36	3,592,841	224,248	667,175,885

[a]Extrapolated to 1 million population.
Source: Worldometers, 2020. Covid-19 Coronavirus pandemic. Worldometers.

Table 2 Review of COVID-19 growth of cases (as of 24 June 2020) in ASEAN, since the first case was reported.

Country	First case reported	Time period since first case	Total cases day 30	Total cases day 50	Total cases day 100	Total cases 24 Jun 2020
Thailand	13 Jan 20	5 M 0 W 4D	33 (12 Feb)	43 (03 Mar)	2811 (22 Apr)	3158
Singapore	23 Jan 20	4 M 3 W 4D	86 (22 Feb)	187 (13 Mar)	17,101 (02 May)	42,736
Vietnam	23 Jan 20	4 M 3 W 4D	16 (22 Feb)	44 (13 Mar)	270 (02 May)	352
Malaysia	25 Jan 20	4 M 3 W 2D	22 (24 Feb)	238 (15 Mar)	6298 (04 May)	8596
Cambodia	27 Jan 20	4 M 3 W 0D	1 (26 Feb)	12 (16 Mar)	122 (06 May)	130
Philippines	30 Jan 20	4 M 2 W 4D	3 (29 Feb)	202 (19 Mar)	10,463 (09 May)	32,295
Indonesia	2 Mar 20	3 M 2 W 1D	1528 (01 Apr)	6760 (21 Apr)	33,076 (10 Jun)	49,009
Brunei	9 Mar 20	3 M 0 W 8D	135 (08 Apr)	138 (28 Apr)	141 (17 Jun)	141
Myanmar	24 Mar 20	2 M 3 W 4D	132 (23 Apr)	180 (13 May)	N/A	293
Laos	24 Mar 20	2 M 3 W 3D	2 (24 Apr)	19 (14 May)	N/A	19

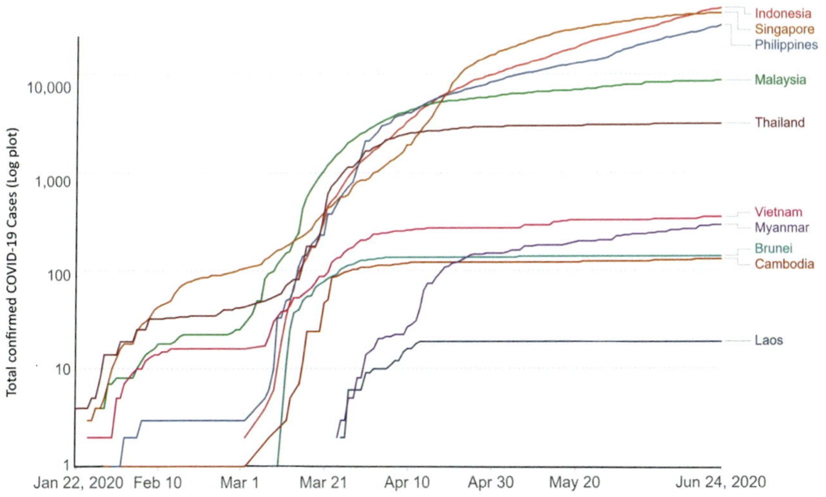

Source: https://ourworldindata.org/coronavirus-source-data [Date: 25 June 2020]

Fig. 4 Profile of spread of COVID-19 among the ASEAN countries.

the first case. It can be noticed that the spread of the pandemic was relatively low in the initial stages but picked up pace during the first week of March. This is due to the mass religious congregation in Kuala Lumpur, Malaysia, in late February and early March, where over 16,000 people attended, of which approximately 1500 people came from other parts of the world, including Brunei, Singapore, and Indonesia. This gathering has led to massive spikes in Malaysia as well as in neighboring countries.

3.3.1 COVID-19 outbreak doubling rate

The profile showing the COVID-19 outbreak doubling rate among the ASEAN countries is shown in Fig. 5. These profiles are visualized for the days since the 100th confirmed case is reported. The doubling rate was faster in the initial days, but it has slowed down. As per the profile, the highest doubling rate is recorded for countries like Indonesia, Singapore, and the Philippines. Countries like Myanmar and Vietnam have shallow doubling rates, and there were no new cases reported in Brunei and Cambodia for over a month. It indicates that the pandemic is entirely in control in these countries.

3.3.2 Review of deaths reported due to the COVID-19 outbreak

Since the COVID-19 outbreak, the number of infected cases has increased. Among the primary concern of the epidemic is the number of deaths that

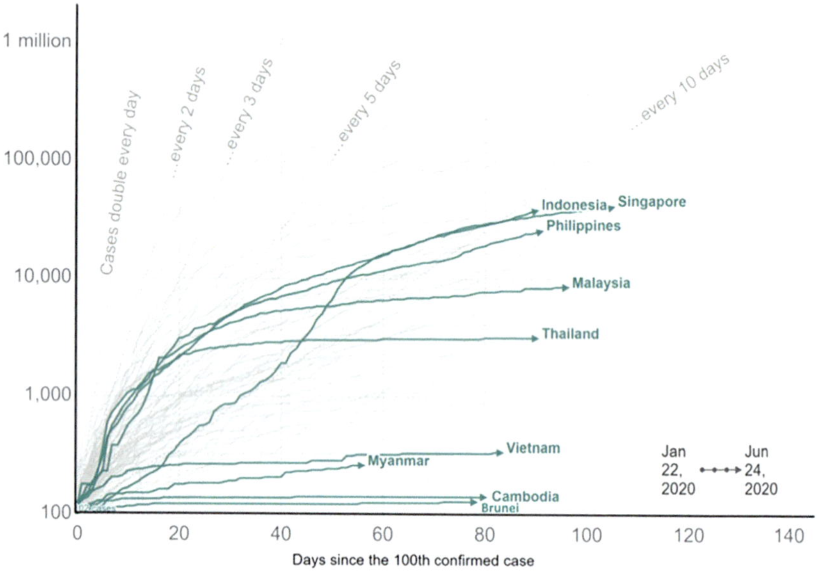

Source: https://ourworldindata.org/coronavirus-source-data [Date: 25 June 2020]

Fig. 5 Profile showing the case doubling rate among ASEAN countries.

occurred due to COVID-19. The overview of the number of deaths reported so far as of 24 June 2020 is given in Table 1. It can be noticed that among the ASEAN countries, the highest number of fatalities recorded were in Indonesia and the Philippines. Even though Singapore is steadily recording more cases, around 77.5% of infected cases are recovered, the fatality rate is only 0.06%.

The total number of confirmed cases against total confirmed deaths due to COVID-19 among ASEAN countries is shown in Fig. 6. It can be seen that Indonesia and the Philippines reported around 5% deaths out of the total confirmed cases, whereas Malaysia, Thailand, and Myanmar have reported around 2% deaths out of the total confirmed cases. Since there are no confirmed deaths reported yet in Cambodia, Laos, and Vietnam, these countries are not shown in the figure. Interestingly, even though the number of cases is high and increasing every day in Singapore, the number of deaths is very low. This may be due to the Singapore government's preventive measures and robust medical protocols in increasing the immunity in the infected patients, thus improving the recovery rates.

Case Fatality Rate (CFR) is the ratio between confirmed deaths and confirmed cases and is an essential statistical metric to evaluate the fatality rate. The comparison plot of CFR for ASEAN countries is shown in Fig. 7. The CFR is zero since Cambodia, Laos, and Vietnam have no recorded

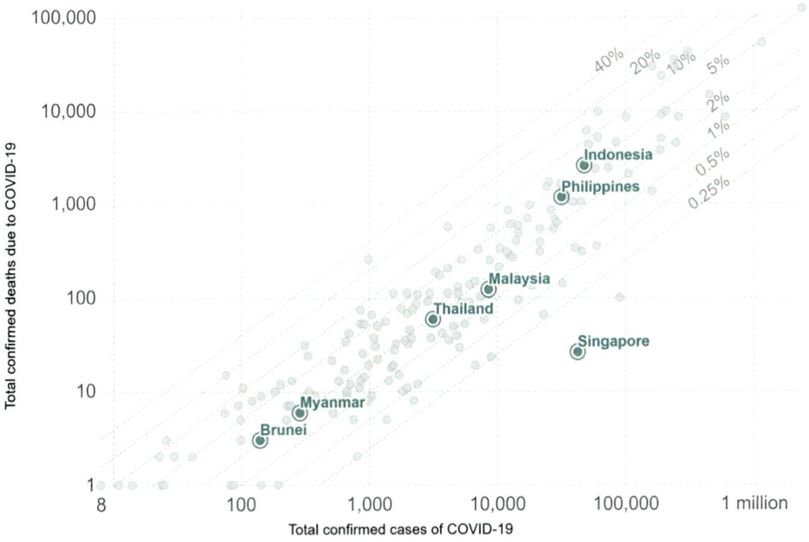

Source: https://ourworldindata.org/coronavirus-source-data [Date: 25 June 2020]

Fig. 6 Scatter plot showing the total confirmed cases vs total confirmed deaths due to COVID-19 among ASEAN countries.

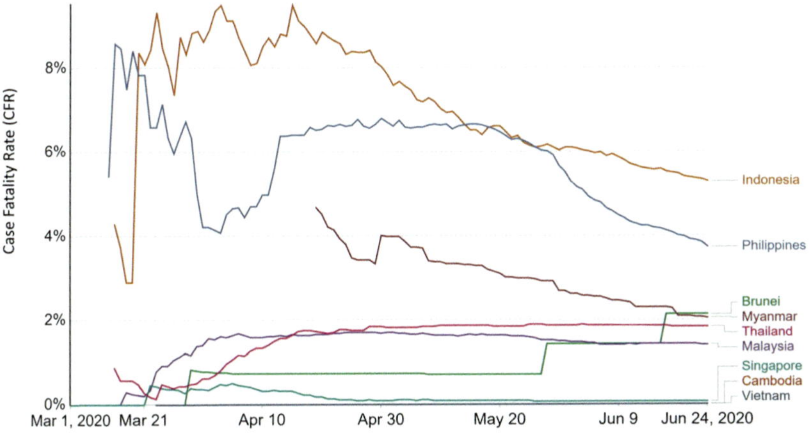

Source: https://ourworldindata.org/coronavirus-source-data [Date: 25 June 2020]

Fig. 7 Profile showing the case fatality rate (CFR) among ASEAN countries.

COVID-19 deaths. Even though the number of cases is high in Singapore, the number of deaths compared to the total number of cases is low; hence, the CFR is close to zero. Among the ASEAN countries, Indonesia and the Philippines have recorded a higher number of COVID-19 related deaths;

hence their respective CFR profiles are very high. However, thankfully, these profiles are lowering, which is a good sign.

3.3.3 Review of confirmed cases against the GDP per capita among ASEAN countries

To understand the relationship between the spread of pandemic (also control of spread) against the GDP per capita, the respective data of ASEAN countries are downloaded from https://ourwoldindata.org. The confirmed COVID-19 cases per million people vs GDP per capita among ASEAN countries are shown in Fig. 8. Here the GDP per capita income is based on 2017 statistics. This figure reveals interesting facts like the lower GDP per capita countries like Cambodia, Laos, Myanmar, and Vietnam have reported fewer COVID-19 cases per million people. Countries like Indonesia, Malaysia, and Thailand, with GDP per capita of more than $10,000, have reported a higher number of cases per million people. Singapore has the highest GDP per capita among the ASEAN countries and reported the highest number of cases per million people. Being the 2nd highest GDP per capita country, Brunei has relatively recorded a similar number of cases per million people as nations with $10,000 - $40,000 GDP.

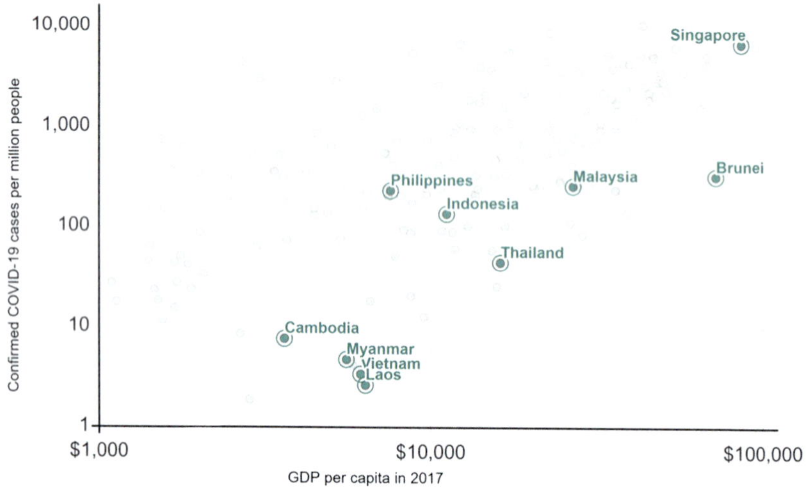

Source: https://ourworldindata.org/coronavirus-source-data [Date: 25 June 2020]

Fig. 8 Scatter plot showing the confirmed COVID-19 cases per million people vs GDP per capita among ASEAN countries.

3.4 Analysis of COVID-19 pandemic in Brunei Darussalam

3.4.1 The sequence of cases originated and government actions

The first COVID-19 case in Brunei was recorded on 9 March 2020, of a man who had returned to Brunei after attending a religious congregation with a group of other Bruneians in Kuala Lumpur, Malaysia. Of the 81 Bruneians who had attended, 19 Bruneians were found to be infected. This event eventually led to the infection of a total of 71 cases, which represents more than 50% of total cases in Brunei.

As of 24 June 2020, Brunei has recorded 141 confirmed cases, 138 recovered cases, and conducted 16,751 tests in the country.[14] There have been three deaths in total so far. The Brunei government has imposed numerous preventive measures including suspending public gatherings and events such as weddings and sporting events. Additionally, the government has restricted air travel, shut down public facilities such as mosques, and even closed all schools resorting to work and study from home measures. Brunei has not seen a case in the last 6 weeks.

3.4.2 Forecasting of COVID-19 outbreak using the SIR model

The growth of infections in Brunei has increased rapidly after the onset of the first case; after a month, the spread of infections has completely been arrested due to government preventive measures. The SIR model is simulated to forecast the outbreak spread, and the predicted profile is compared with the actual recorded cases, as shown in Fig. 9. The pandemic outbreak spread initially with a doubling time of 5.2 days. The estimated SIR model parameters are given in Table 3. The predicted total epidemic duration is 39 days, and the total growth phase duration is 18 days.

The SIR model simulation predicted that the end of the epidemic (5 cases) is estimated to be 9 April 2020, which is close to 30 March 2020 (real-time data). Similarly, the model predicted that the end of the epidemic (1 case) is 21 April 2020, which is very close to 20 April, when there were no cases reported for two weeks. However, there was one case on 7 May and 2 cases on 8 May, which was the last case in Brunei. Root mean square error (RMSE) of the model prediction is 2.198 with an R^2 of 0.994. According to Hamid,[15] there is unlikely to be a second local outbreak in the country unless the Brunei government is lax with air travel restrictions causing a resurgence in imported cases.

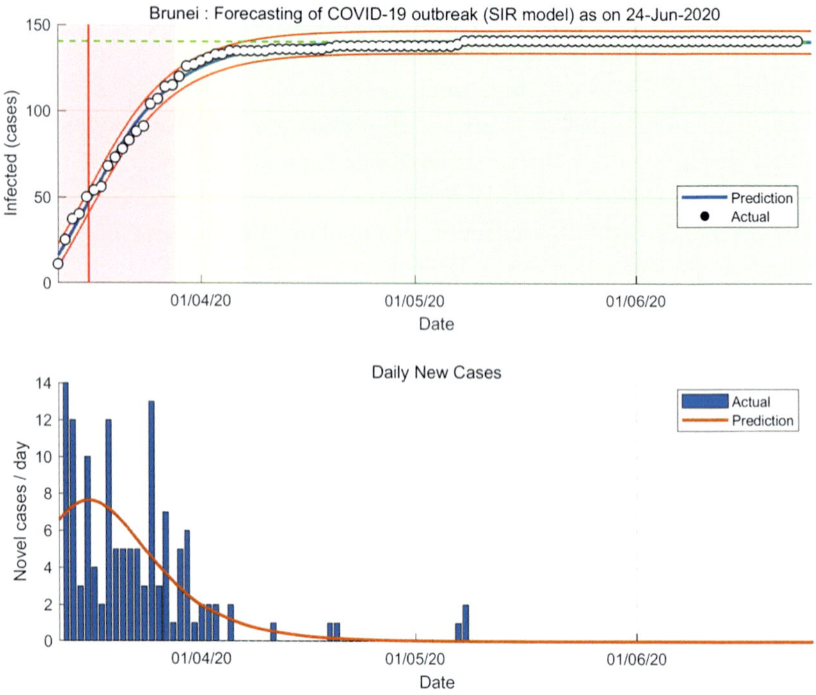

Fig. 9 Forecasting of COVID-19 outbreak using the SIR model for Brunei.

3.5 Analysis of COVID-19 pandemic in Cambodia

3.5.1 The sequence of cases originated and government actions

Cambodia saw the first COVID-19 case on 28 January 2020. Specifically, the first case was a man who was reported to have returned from Wuhan, China, with his family. In terms of COVID-19 cases, Cambodia has seen a total of 130 confirmed cases, 128 recovered cases, and no deaths as of 24 June 2020. In its efforts to combat the spread of COVID-19 in the country, the Cambodian government established a dedicated national committee and took measures including the closure of educational institutions nationwide, restriction of air travel, closing down border crossings with Vietnam, and introduced monthly allowances to unemployed workers caused by the virus.

Table 3 Epidemic modeling by susceptible-infected-recovered (SIR) model for ASEAN countries.

			SIR model parameters					
Country	Acceleration phase (days)	Deceleration phase (days)	Contact frequency (Beta) (/day)	Removal frequency (gamma) (/day)	Predicted total epidemic duration (days)	Root mean squared error	*P*-value	R^2
Brunei	6	12	0.437	0.304	39	2.2	9.137e−113	0.994
Cambodia	5	6	0.513	0.142	32	3.5	4.489e−82	0.986
Indonesia	57	66	0.097	0.062	568	125.0	5.512e−129	0.997
Myanmar	9	11	0.301	0.08	63	47.8	5.340e−21	0.701
Malaysia	21	25	0.159	0.059	236	435.3	2.037e−112	0.981
Philippines	74	83	0.131	0.104	666	741.6	1.369e−114	0.993
Singapore	23	28	0.163	0.075	305	861.6	4.937e−182	0.997
Thailand	11	14	0.306	0.123	143	56.6	5.648e−194	0.998
Vietnam	18	21	0.171	0.056	147	3.943	2.397e−11	0.983

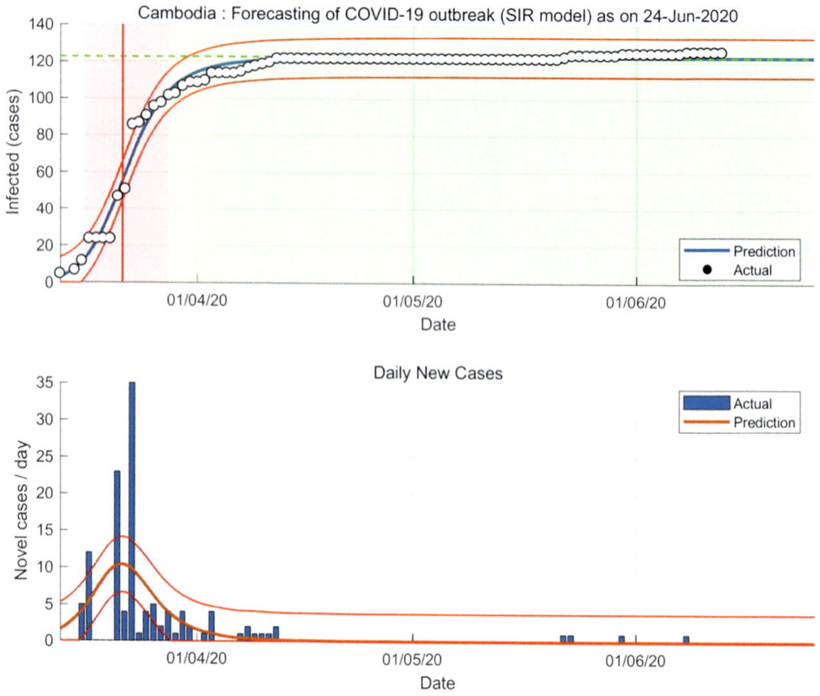

Fig. 10 Forecasting of COVID-19 outbreak using the SIR model for Cambodia.

3.5.2 Forecasting of COVID-19 outbreak using the SIR model

Using the SIR model, the outbreak's spread in Cambodia is forecasted. The SIR model-predicted profile is compared with the actual recorded cases, as shown in Fig. 10. The pandemic outbreak spread initially with a doubling time of 1.9 days. The estimated SIR model parameters are given in Table 3. The predicted total epidemic duration is 32 days, in which the total growth phase duration is 12 days.

The SIR model simulation predicted that the end of the epidemic (5 cases) is estimated to be 04 April 2020, which is close to 26 March 2020 (real-time data). Similarly, the model predicted that the end of the epidemic (1 case) is 14 April 2020, which is very close to 12 April, when there were no cases reported for 4 weeks. However, there were few cases (one per week) reported later. RMSE of the model prediction is 3.5, with R^2 of 0.986.

3.6 Analysis of COVID-19 pandemic in Indonesia

3.6.1 The sequence of cases originated and government actions

The first two COVID-19 cases in Indonesia were reported on 2 March 2020. These two cases were a dance instructor and her mother, who were suspected to be infected by a Japanese national. On 9 April 2020, the virus had spread to all 34 provinces of Indonesia, in which at least 500 cases were present in half of the provinces.

As of 24 June 2020, there have been a total of 49,009 confirmed cases in Indonesia, followed by 19,658 recovered cases and 2573 deaths. Additionally, there have also been 689,452 tests conducted. Indonesia has the highest number of COVID-19 cases among Southeast Asian countries.

Indonesia implemented a local lockdown as opposed to a national lockdown. Further, it introduced a national COVID-19 initiative called the "Large Scale Social Restriction" (LSSR), which includes the closure of public schools and facilities, restriction of public transport, and the control of public movement between provinces.

3.6.2 Forecasting of COVID-19 outbreak using the SIR model

Using the SIR model, the outbreak's spread in Indonesia is forecasted. The SIR model-predicted profile is compared with the actual recorded cases, as shown in Fig. 11. The estimated SIR model parameters are given in Table 3.

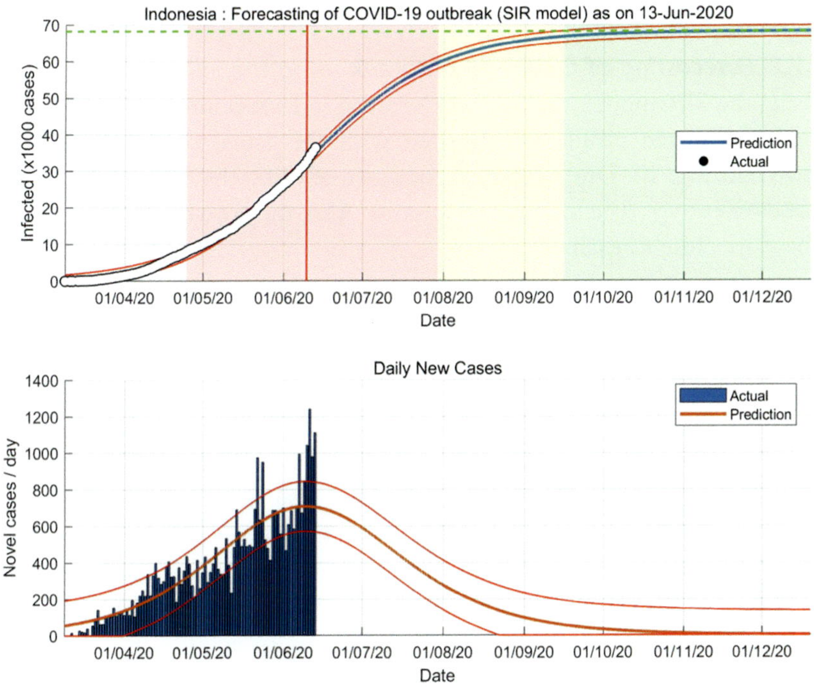

Fig. 11 Forecasting of COVID-19 outbreak using the SIR model for Indonesia.

The pandemic outbreak spread initially with a doubling time of 1.9 days. The estimated SIR model parameters are given in Table 3. With rising cases, the predicted total epidemic duration may last for 568 days, in which the total growth phase duration is 123 days. The SIR model simulation predicted that the end of the epidemic (5 cases) is estimated to be 11 February 2021, and the end of the pandemic (1 case) is 24 March 2021 as the cases increase. RMSE of the SIR model prediction is 125.0 with R^2 of 0.997.

3.7 Analysis of COVID-19 pandemic in Laos

3.7.1 The sequence of cases originated and government actions

On 24 March 2020, the first two cases of COVID-19 were reported in Laos. These two initial cases represented a man who had returned from Thailand and a female tour guide who was infected by a Cambodian tourist who tested positive. It should be noted that Laos was also the last country in Southeast Asia to have caught the spread of the virus.

On 29 March 2020, the Laos government imposed a national lockdown that effectively closed all country land borders in addition to air travel. By 18 May 2020, after many improvements in the daily number of cases in the country, the Laos government loosened its restrictions.

3.7.2 Forecasting of COVID-19 outbreak using the SIR model

Using the SIR model, the outbreak's spread in Laos is forecasted. The SIR model-predicted profile is compared with the actual recorded cases, as shown in Fig. 12. Due to the low number of cases, the SIR model could not have enough data to train and forecast. Also, the growth rate and ending phase are close to each other.

3.8 Analysis of COVID-19 pandemic in Malaysia

3.8.1 The sequence of cases originated and government actions

The first case of COVID-19 in Malaysia was reported on 25 January 2020. The first case was reportedly infected by travelers coming from China. In late February 2020, a religious congregation took place at the Jamek Mosque, attended by over 16,000 people worldwide. This mass gathering led to one of the largest initial outbreaks in the country and infected other attendees from other countries, including Brunei, Singapore, and Indonesia.

The actions of containing the outbreak in Malaysia occurred during a change in government leadership. In its efforts to combat the outbreak, the new Malaysian government had imposed the "Movement Control

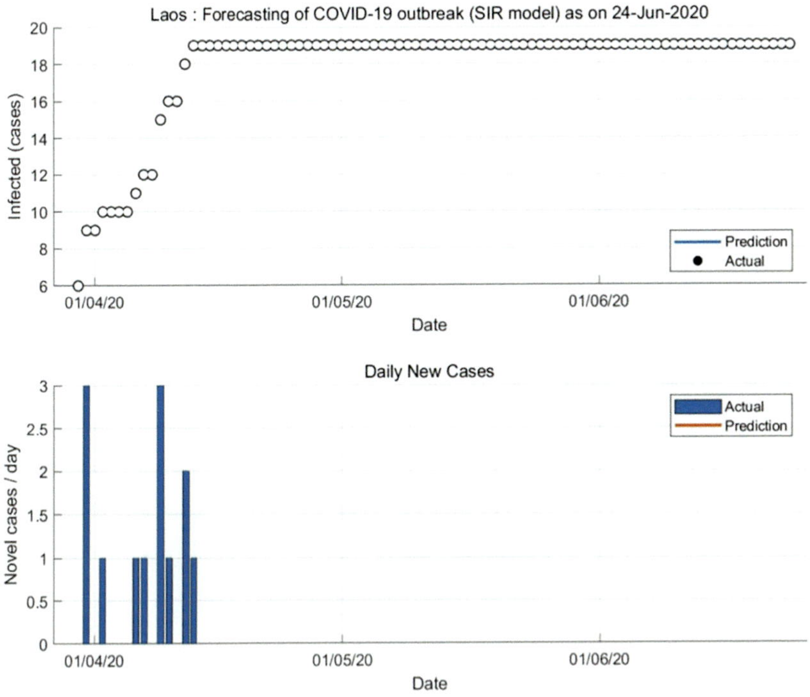

Fig. 12 Forecasting of COVID-19 outbreak using the SIR model for Laos.

Order" throughout the country. This included prohibiting of mass gatherings of events and activities such as sports, and cultural and religious activities, including attending Friday prayers at mosques and weddings. The government also restricted travel into the country and imposed mandatory quarantines for travelers who were allowed into the country. Other actions taken were the temporary closure of educational institutions nationwide and nonessential government offices and services. Though the Movement Control Order was a temporary periodical directive across the country, it had been extended four times. Other notable efforts taken by the government were the introduction of special allowances to be provided to low-income households during the pandemic. Despite that Malaysia initially had the highest number of cases in Southeast Asia, the growth of cases had significantly dropped due to the strong measures taken by the government. Malaysia currently stands as the 4th highest in cases within Southeast Asia with an outlook of recovery in the near future. As of 24 June 2020, Malaysia has confirmed a total of 8596 cases, 8231 recovered cases, 121 deaths, and has conducted 704,336 tests throughout the country.

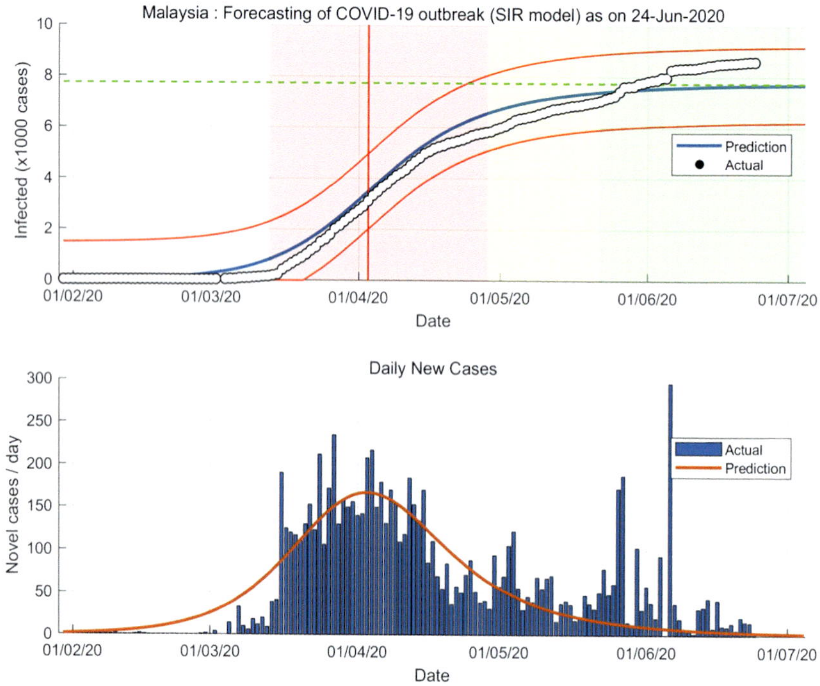

Fig. 13 Forecasting of COVID-19 outbreak using the SIR model for Malaysia.

3.8.2 Forecasting of COVID-19 outbreak using the SIR model

Using the SIR model, the outbreak's spread in Malaysia is forecasted. The SIR model-predicted profile is compared with the actual recorded cases, as shown in Fig. 13. The pandemic outbreak spread initially with a doubling time of 6.9 days. The estimated SIR model parameters are given in Table 3. With a growing number of cases, the predicted total epidemic duration may last for 236 days, in which the total growth phase duration is 46 days.

Based on the available data, the SIR model predicts that the end of the epidemic (5 cases) is estimated to be 18 August 2020, and the end of the epidemic (1 case) is 22 September 2020, as the cases are increasing. So far, the model predictions are perfect, resulting in an RMSE of 435.3 with an R^2 of 0.981.

3.9 Analysis of COVID-19 pandemic in Myanmar

3.9.1 The sequence of cases originated and government actions

In Myanmar, the first and second two cases were reported on 23 March 2020. As of 24 June 2020, there have been a total of 290 confirmed cases in Myanmar, 200 recovered cases, and 6 deaths. About 22,077 tests have been conducted.

Myanmar announced a community lockdown in one village in China state to combat the spread of the virus. On 30 January 2020, Myanmar formed a special committee to tackle the pandemic. On 1 February 2020, Myanmar suspended Chinese visas from entering the country and evacuated 59 students in Wuhan. By 14 March 2020, Myanmar set new bans and restricted travelers from China, South Korea, and parts of Europe, and by 21 March 2020, new restrictions were further imposed on all foreign nationals, including requirements of presentations of medical certificate and 14-day quarantine. Air travel is put on hold on 13 April 2020.

3.9.2 Forecasting of COVID-19 outbreak using the SIR model

Using the SIR model, the outbreak's spread in Myanmar is forecasted. The SIR model-predicted profile is compared with the actual recorded cases, as shown in Fig. 14. The pandemic outbreak spread initially with a doubling time of 2.6 days. The estimated SIR model parameters are given in Table 3.

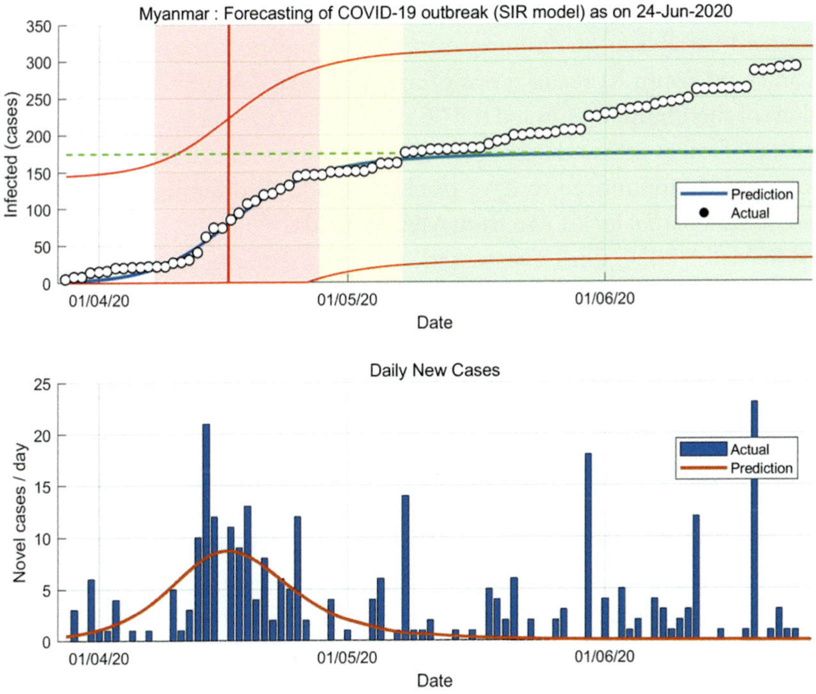

Fig. 14 Forecasting of COVID-19 outbreak using the SIR model for Myanmar.

The predicted total epidemic duration may last for 63 days, in which the total growth phase duration is 20 days. Based on the data available so far, the SIR model predicts that the end of the epidemic (5 cases) is estimated to be 7 May 2020, and the end of the epidemic (1 case) is 22 May 2020. So far, the model predictions are moderately good, resulting in an RMSE of 47.8 with R^2 of 0.701. SIR model predictions are not as good as for other ASEAN countries.

3.10 Analysis of COVID-19 pandemic in the Philippines

3.10.1 The sequence of cases originated and government actions

The first case confirmed in the Philippines was reported on 30 January 2020, involving a 38 year-old Chinese woman from Wuhan who arrived from Manila from Hong Kong while the second case was a 44 year-old Chinese man, reported on 2 February 2020, who had died 1 day earlier. As of 24 June 2020, there have been a total of 32,295 confirmed cases, 22,435 active cases, 8656 recovered cases, and 1204 deaths. About 631,063 tests have been conducted.

The Philippines recorded the highest number of cases in Southeast Asia, in which the largest single case increase in cases was reported on 23 June 2020 and had recorded 1186 new cases. The Philippines government has imposed travel bans on countries including mainland China, Macau, Hong Kong, and South Korea in terms of measures. On 7 March 2020, the president of the Philippines issued the "Code Red Sub Level 1," including procuring of safety gear and other preventive measures. By 12 March 2020, the country was announced to have reached "Code Red Sub Level 2," which including a partial lockdown from Metro Manila, which expanded to Luzon by 16 March 2020. On 17 March, the president announced a state of calamity and was under probation for 6 months. On 17 April, the Philippines was reported to have reduced the virus reproduction number from 1.5 to 0.65. In late April 2020, the local government units were not allowed to authorize quarantine measures without proper consent.

3.10.2 Forecasting of COVID-19 outbreak using the SIR model

Using the SIR model, the spread of the outbreak in the Philippines is forecasted. The SIR model-predicted profile is compared with the actual recorded cases, as shown in Fig. 15. The pandemic outbreak spread initially with a doubling time of 29.2 days. The estimated SIR model parameters are given in Table 3. With a growing number of cases, the predicted total epidemic duration may last for 666 days, in which the total growth phase duration is 157 days.

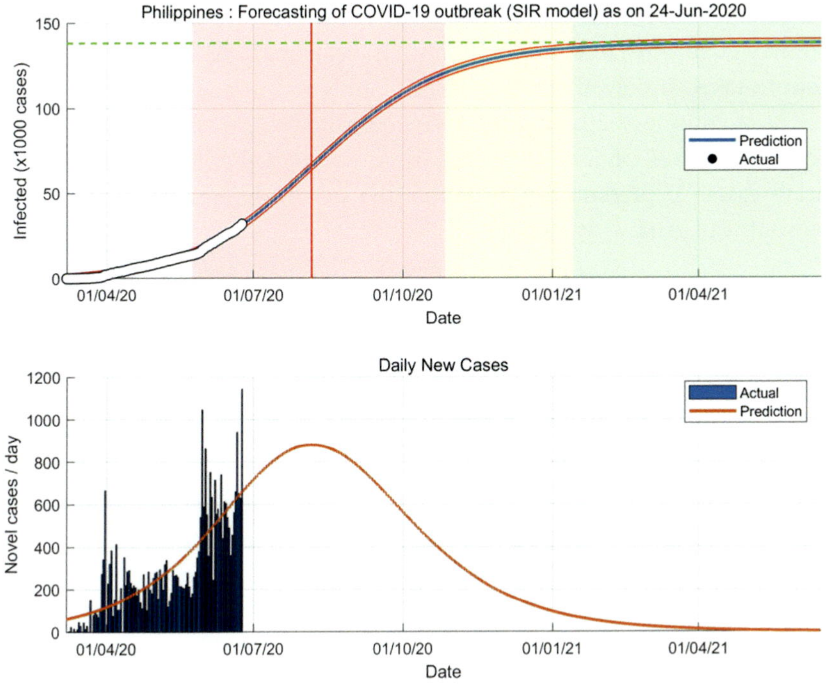

Fig. 15 Forecasting of COVID-19 outbreak using the SIR model for the Philippines. Based on the data available, so far, the SIR model predicts that the end of the epidemic (5 cases) is estimated to be 3 November 2021, and the end of the epidemic (1 case) is 11 January 2022. So far, the model predictions are perfect, resulting in an RMSE of 741.6 with R^2 of 0.993. Therefore the SIR model predictions are good enough, but with the government taking more preventive measures, the epidemic may end much earlier than the model predicted.

3.11 Analysis of COVID-19 pandemic in Singapore

3.11.1 The sequence of cases originated and government actions

On 23 January, Singapore became the second country, along with Vietnam, to confirm its first COVID-19 case in Southeast Asia. Singapore has experienced up to 4 waves of recurring outbreaks.[16] The first wave was described as early imported cases from China in January 2020, while the second wave was a growth of local clusters within Singapore from February 2020. The third wave came from Singapore citizens and permanent residents who had returned from abroad in March 2020, while the latest and fourth wave in Singapore was due to the spread of COVID-19 among migrant workers living in close quarters.

To control the spread, the Singapore government introduced the COVID-19 (Temporary Measures) Act 2020 and Control Order

Regulations 2020. Singapore restricted travel into the country as early as January 2020 and banned all short-term travel from 23 March 2020.[17] Other actions taken involved the closure of schools and nonessential workplaces.

As of 24 June 2020, Singapore has confirmed at least 42,623 COVID-19 confirmed cases, 36,299 recovered cases, conducted 684,359 tests, and 26 death cases. At present, Singapore has the second-highest number of cases in Southeast Asia.

3.11.2 Forecasting of COVID-19 outbreak using the SIR model

Using the SIR model, the outbreak's spread in Singapore is forecasted. The SIR model-predicted profile is compared with the actual recorded cases, as shown in Fig. 16. The pandemic outbreak spread initially with a doubling time of 7.2 days. The estimated SIR model parameters are given in Table 3. With a growing number of cases, the predicted total epidemic duration may last for 305 days, in which the total growth phase duration is 52 days. Based on the available data, the SIR model predicts that the end of the epidemic (5 cases) is estimated to be 8 October 2020, and the end of the epidemic (1 case)

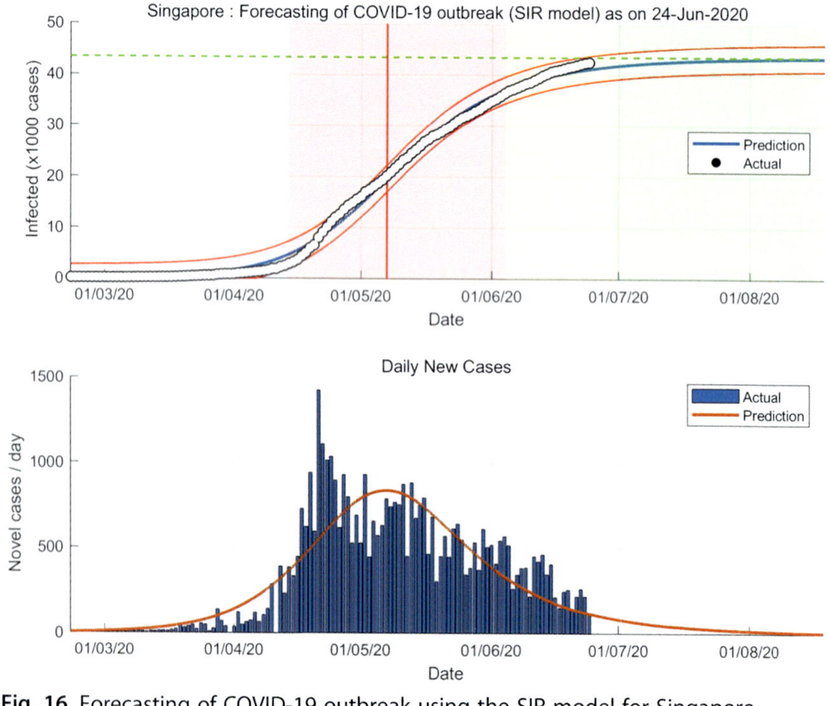

Fig. 16 Forecasting of COVID-19 outbreak using the SIR model for Singapore.

is 7 November 2020. So far, the model predictions are perfect, and it has resulted in RMSE of 861.6 with R^2 of 0.997. Therefore it indicates that the SIR model predictions are good enough, but with the government taking more preventive measures, the epidemic may end much earlier than the model predicted.

3.12 Analysis of COVID-19 pandemic in Thailand

3.12.1 The sequence of cases originated and government actions

In Thailand, the first case of COVID-19 cases was reported on 13 January 2020, with its first local transmission on 31 March 2020. One of its highest transmissions occurred in mid-March through a Muay Thai fight at the Boxing Stadium, and cases rose by over a hundred each day over the weeks. As of 24 June 2020, there have been a total of 3156 confirmed cases in Thailand, with 3023 recovered cases and 58 deaths. A total of 468,175 tests have been conducted.

Thailand's response to the pandemic included surveillance and contract tracing, screening at international airports and hospitals, as well as investigations in outbreak clusters with returningresidents to undergo self-quarantine. On 5 March 2020, travel restrictions were announced; by 19 March 2020, medical certificates were required for international arrivals to the country. A curfew was ordered, which took effect on 3 April from 10 pm to 4 am to curb the spread of the virus, combined with the travel ban preventing foreigners from entering the country. The transmission rate has fallen to near zero by mid-May, so there has been a gradual easing of restrictions in the country.

3.12.2 Forecasting of COVID-19 outbreak using the SIR model

Using the SIR model, the outbreak's spread in Thailand is forecasted. The SIR model-predicted profile is compared with the actual recorded cases, as shown in Fig. 17. The pandemic outbreak spread initially with a doubling time of 4 days. The estimated SIR model parameters are given in Table 3. The predicted total epidemic duration may last for 143 days, in which the total growth phase duration is 25 days. Based on the available data, the SIR model predicts that the end of the epidemic (5 cases) is estimated to be 11 June 2020, and the end of the epidemic (1 case) is 5 July 2020. So far, the model predictions are perfect, and it has resulted in RMSE of 56.6 with R^2 of 0.998. Therefore the SIR model predictions are good enough.

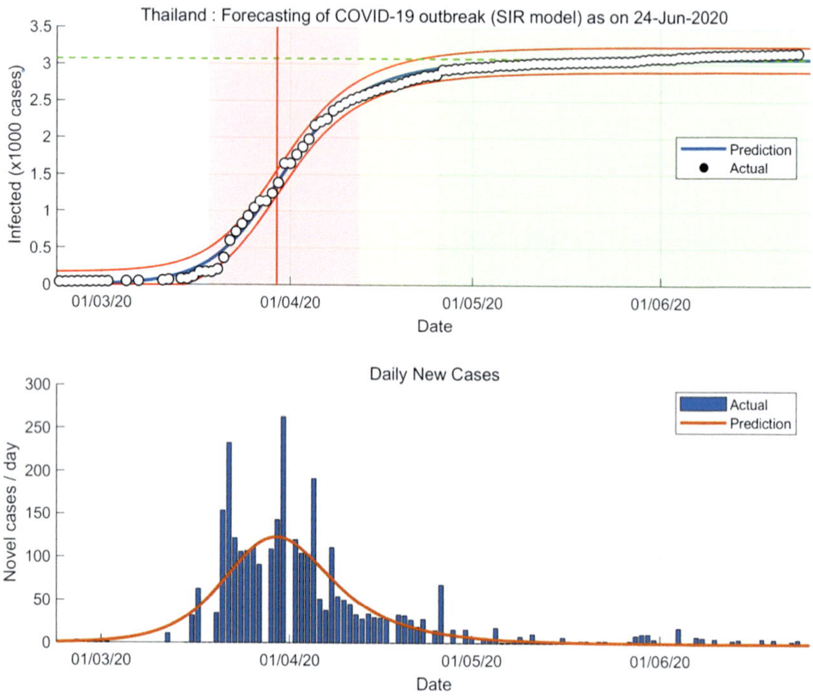

Fig. 17 Forecasting of COVID-19 outbreak using the SIR model for Thailand.

3.13 Analysis of COVID-19 pandemic in Vietnam

3.13.1 The sequence of cases originated and government actions

The first two COVID-19 cases in Vietnam were first reported on 23 January 2020, a father who had traveled from Wuhan, China, and supposedly infected his son whom he was visiting in Vietnam. As of 24 June 2020, there are 349 infected cases, 329 recovered cases, and 275,000 tests that have been conducted in the country. Vietnam is one of the few countries not to have any COVID-19 related deaths. The capital of Vietnam, Hanoi, is the worst affected area with 121 cases or 35% of total cases in the country.

Vietnam is recognized as having one of the best epidemic control programs in the world. On 22 March 2020, Vietnam took preventive measures to halt imported cases by suspending general flights into the country and only allowed controlled air travel subject to official approval. In contrast to its regional neighbors and other countries such as the United States, China, and the United Kingdom, the total number of cases in Vietnam is relatively low. Despite this, Vietnam is regarded to have experienced two waves of the COVID-19 spread in the country.

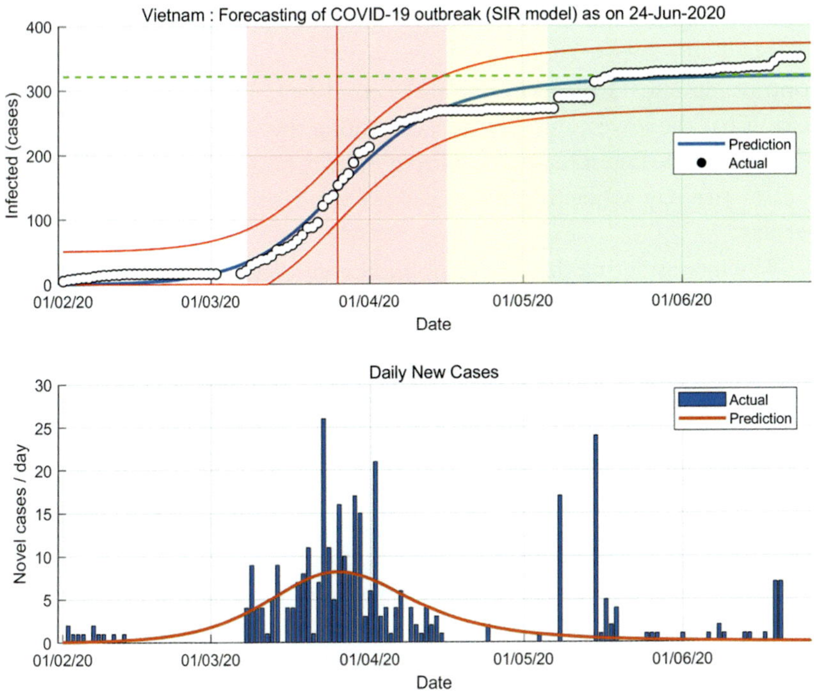

Fig. 18 Forecasting of COVID-19 outbreak using the SIR model for Vietnam.

3.13.2 Forecasting of COVID-19 outbreak using the SIR model

Using the SIR model, the outbreak's spread in Vietnam is forecasted. The SIR model-predicted profile is compared with the actual recorded cases, as shown in Fig. 18. The pandemic outbreak spread initially with a doubling time of 5.5 days. The estimated SIR model parameters are given in Table 3. The predicted total epidemic duration may last for 147 days, in which the total growth phase duration is 39 days.

Based on the data available so far, the SIR model predicts that the end of the epidemic (5 cases) is estimated to be 19 May 2020, and the end of the epidemic (1 case) is 19 June 2020. So far, the model predictions are perfect, and it has resulted in RMSE of 15.8 with R^2 of 0.985. Therefore the SIR model predictions are good enough.

4. Conclusions

The top 5 largest economies (Indonesia, Thailand, Singapore, Malaysia, and the Philippines) in Southeast Asia also represent the top 5 most significant number of COVID-19 cases in Southeast Asia. While Indonesia represents the largest economy, it also has the largest number of cases. In contrast, despite Thailand having the second-largest economy in Southeast Asia, it has the lowest number of cases among the top 5 largest economies. Also shown the fastest recovery, with most cases ranging between only 0 and 5 cases per day while Indonesia has averaged approximately 1000 cases per day.

When considering the economic and commercial features, Thailand has shown the best performance among all countries in controlling the pandemic. At the same time, Laos registered the lowest number of cases in Southeast Asia despite having a population of 7 million and the 9th largest economy in Southeast Asia. In this regard, Laos is arguably the safest country in Southeast Asia in terms of any potential future viral outbreaks.

As the collective economies of ASEAN are projected to grow to the top 5 economies of the world, this study will present the view of these ASEAN countries in terms of controlling pandemics.

Even though down the line, the policies of each country may change over the time and be in a better position, this study provides present insight into the strength and vulnerability of a country's infrastructure, policies, perople's preparedness and country's ability to respond to a crisis. The results presented in this study facilitate a benchmark for the governments, corporations, and individuals to understand the lacking infrastructure and medical facilities and develop better systems for potential future disease outbreaks.

Contribution

RRK (Conceptualization, modeling, editing, visual graphics); MZSAH (Data analysis, editing); YK (Data downloading, editing).

References

1. Routley N. *Visualizing the world's busiest ports*. Visual Capatalist; 2019.
2. Cook M. *US-Southeast Asia trade is increasing, but so are deficits*. Asia Pacific Bulletin; 2019.
3. Harding B, Tran KM. *US-Southeast Asia trade relations in an age of disruption*. Center for Strategic and International Studies; 2019.
4. Layos J, Pena PJ. *Can innovation save us? Understanding the role of innovation in mitigating the Covid-19 pandemic in ASEAN-5 economies*. vol. 8. De La Salle University Business Notes & Briefings; 2020.
5. Abuza Z. *Explaining successful (and unsuccessful) COVID-19 responses in Southeast Asia*. The Diplomat; 2020. p. 1–10.
6. Harko T, Lobo FSN, Mak MK. Exact analytical solutions of the Susceptible-Infected-Recovered (SIR) epidemic model and of the SIR model with equal death and birth rates. *Appl Math Comput* 2014;**236**:184–94.

7. Toda AA. *Susceptible-infected-recovered (SIR) dynamics of covid-19 and economic impact.* arXiv preprint; 2020, arXiv:2003.11221.
8. Wang W, Liu Q-H, Zhong L-F, Tang M, Gao H, Stanley HE. Predicting the epidemic threshold of the susceptible-infected-recovered model. *Sci Rep* 2016;**6**.
9. Shinde GR, Kalamkar AB, Mahalle PN, Dey N, Chaki J, Hassanien AE. Forecasting models for Coronavirus disease (COVID-19): a survey of the state-of-the-art. *SN Comput Sci* 2020;**1**:1–15.
10. Batista M. *Estimation of the final size of the coronavirus epidemic by the logistic model.* Cold Spring Harbor Laboratory; 2020.
11. Batista M. Estimation of the final size of the COVID-19 epidemic. *MedRxiv* 2020. https://doi.org/10.1101/2020.02.16.20023606.
12. Rahman MA. Data-driven dynamic clustering framework for mitigating the adverse economic impact of covid-19 lockdown practices. *Sustain Cities Soc* 2020;102372.
13. Worldometers. *Covid-19 Coronavirus pandemic.* Worldometers; 2020.
14. Hamid MZSA, Karri RR. Overview of preventive measures and good governance policies to mitigate the COVID-19 outbreak curve in Brunei. In: *COVID-19: systemic risk and resilience.* Cham: Springer; 2021. p. 115–40.
15. Hamid MZSA. An Analysis of the success of suppressing COVID-19 cases in Brunei Darussalam. *Int J Adv Res* 2020;**8**:718–25.
16. Pung R, Chiew CJ, Young BE, Chin S, Chen MI, Clapham HE, et al. Investigation of three clusters of COVID-19 in Singapore: implications for surveillance and response measures. *Lancet* 2020;**395**(10229):1039–46.
17. Ng Y, Li Z, Chua YX, Chaw WL, Zhao Z, Er B, et al. Evaluation of the effectiveness of surveillance and containment measures for the first 100 patients with COVID-19 in Singapore—January 2–February 29, 2020. *MMWR Morb Mortal Wkly Rep* 2020;**69**:307–11.

Index

Note: Page numbers followed by *f* indicate figures *t* indicate tables, and *b* indicate boxes.

S

Printed in the United States
by Baker & Taylor Publisher Services